PUBLIC RELATIONS

PUBLIC RELATIONS

NINTH EDITION

Strategies and Tactics

STUDY EDITION

Dennis L. Wilcox

School of Journalism & Mass Communications

San Jose State University

Glen T. Cameron

School of Journalism

University of Missouri

Allyn & Bacon

Boston   New York   San Francisco

Mexico City   Montreal   Toronto   London   Madrid   Munich   Paris

Hong Kong   Singapore   Tokyo   Cape Town   Sydney

Editor-in-Chief: Karon Bowers
Acquisitions Editor: Jeanne Zalesky
Series Editorial Assistant: Megan Lentz
Development Editor: Deb Hanlon
Production Editor: Claudine Bellanton
Editorial Production Service: TexTech International
Manufacturing Buyer: Debbie Rossi
Electronic Composition: TexTech International
Interior Design: Gina Hagen
Photo Researcher: Katharine S. Cebik
Cover Administrator: Kristina Mose-Libon

10 9 8 7 6 5 4 3 2 1   WEB   13   12   11   10   09

Allyn & Bacon
is an imprint of

PEARSON

www.pearsonhighered.com

ISBN-10: 0-205-62622-X
ISBN-13: 978-0-205-62622-9

WHY YOU NEED THIS NEW EDITION

The field of public relations is always changing. New forms of media and technologies have changed the shape of public relations in the last few years, causing corporations to expand their audiences and reach out to more people in more ways than they ever imagined before. Our goal with this revision is to provide the most up-to-date, engaging, and comprehensive resource for new students of public relations. This edition discusses reaching today's diverse and multicultural society on the local, national, and global level with new technologies, while hinting at where the public relations field is headed in the future.

Our knowledge of public relations grows regularly as new campaigns are launched, celebrities find themselves in need of media representation, and corporations move to improve their public reputations. This revision includes many new examples of today's public relations campaigns, real-life ethical situations, and other popular examples to illustrate public relations issues in a familiar and stimulating way.

A variety of both general and specific changes were made to this edition to ensure the text remained a current, engaging, and practical resource for today's public relations students. Pages xix–xxii of this preface present detailed information on what is new to the ninth edition. A brief overview of some of the most important changes follows:

- ◆ A completely revised Chapter 11, Reaching a Multicultural and Diverse Audience, now has a stronger focus on diverse and multicultural audiences and explores the characteristics of many special publics and how to effectively include them in various public relations programs. Such publics as Generation X, Baby Boomers, women, the gay community, the African-American community, the Hispanic community, and the physically disabled are all covered in this revised chapter.

- ◆ Chapter 13, New Technologies in Public Relations, includes the newest techniques of reaching audiences through "social media." We explore the phenomenon of YouTube, Facebook, and MySpace, as well as the use of blogs, podcasts, and electronic transmission of news in public relations campaigns.

- ◆ This edition incorporates the most current statistical and demographic data to accurately reflect current practice.

- ◆ Over 75 percent of the new PR Casebooks are new to this edition. These popular boxed features help generate interest and spark classroom discussion. PR Casebooks in each chapter illustrate the "nuts and bolts" of a real and contemporary public relations program or campaign to engage students and heighten their knowledge and enthusiasm for the field of public relations.

- ◆ We have also added new quotations from experienced professionals in each chapter. These concise, pointed statements provide the essence of professional insight and wisdom. These quotations not only highlight important themes from the text, but also pique student interest in the material.

BRIEF CONTENTS

CONTENTS

Part 1   Role

CHAPTER 1
What Is Public Relations?   1

CHAPTER 2
The Evolution of Public Relations   39

CHAPTER 3
Ethics and Professionalism   72

CHAPTER 4
Public Relations Departments and Firms   97

Part 2   Process

Part 3   Strategy

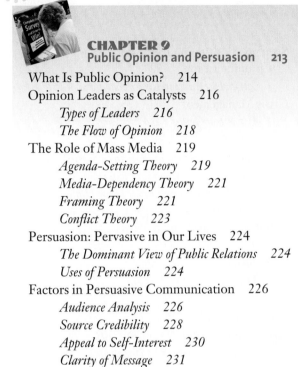

CHAPTER 12
Public Relations and the Law 299

CHAPTER 13
New Technologies in Public
Relations   335

Part 4   Tactics

CHAPTER 14
News Releases, Media Alerts, and Pitch
Letters   366

CHAPTER 15
Radio, Television, and the Web   389

CHAPTER 16
Media Interviews, News Conferences,
and Speeches   418

Part 5   Application

CHAPTER 17
Corporations   444

CHAPTER 18
Politics and Government   473

CHAPTER 19
Global Public Relations   503

CHAPTER 20
Nonprofit Organizations   528

The ninth edition of *Public Relations: Strategies and Tactics* continues its widely-acclaimed reputation for being the most comprehensive, up-to-date introductory text on the market. This edition, like others before it, also continues to successfully blend theory, concepts, and actual practice into a highly attractive format that is clear and easy for students to understand without being superficial or shallow.

The book's writing style and colorful design will engage the interest of students, and they will rapidly find that reading a textbook doesn't have to be boring. At the same time, the book will appeal to instructors who want their students to have an in-depth understanding of public relations as a problem-solving process involving ethical responsibility and the application of key principles.

Indeed, the continuing popularity of this book among both students and faculty relates to the consistent inclusion of new issues and case studies that students recognize from yesterday's headlines. This new edition is no exception. Every chapter has examples of award-winning campaigns and current issues that students will find relevant, informative, and interesting.

New in the Ninth Edition

We authors have revised and updated major portions of the book to reflect today's diverse and multicultural society on the local, national, and global level. The suggestions of adopters and reviewers regarding the eighth edition have been given serious consideration, and the result is a strong new edition that retains the best of past editions but also captures the essence of today's current practice and concerns. New content includes:

A stronger focus on diverse and multicultural audiences

A completely revised Chapter 11, Reaching a Multicultural and Diverse Audience, explores the characteristics of many special publics and how to effectively include them in various public relations programs. The fastest growing ethnic group in the United States, Hispanics, is thoroughly covered, as well as such publics as Generation X, Baby Boomers, women, the gay community, the African-American community, and the physically disabled. In addition, we discuss ethnic media and how to reach multicultural audiences on a global basis.

Updated and expanded content on new technologies and social media

Chapter 13, New Technologies in Public Relations, has been revised to include the new techniques of reaching audiences through what has been called "social media." The phenomenon of YouTube, Facebook, and MySpace is explored, as well as the use of blogs, podcasts, and electronic transmission of news in public relations campaigns. Attention also is given to satellite media tours, Webcasts, and online newsrooms in Chapter 13, as well as in the tactics section of the book, Chapters 14–16.

Examples of new technologies used in public relations campaigns are found throughout the book. Some examples include:

◆ Abundant Forests Alliance's extensive use of their website to inform the public about sustainable forest management (Chapter 1)

◆ Coca-Cola's "blog-fest," a strategy to get feedback about core values from employees around the world (Chapter 3)

◆ India's implementation of video mailers to encourage condom use (Chapter 6)

◆ Gillette's creation of a website (www.noscruf.org) to promote the clean-shaven look among young men (Chapter 7)

◆ Philips Norelco's online campaign (including YouTube) to promote its new "Bodygroom" shaver (Chapter 13)

◆ Purina's innovative use of podcasts about pet care (Chapter 15)

Expansion of concept on competition, conflict, and crisis

This book is unique among introductory texts in that it reflects groundbreaking research on the role of public relations in managing competition, conflict, and crisis. Students learn how organizations assess risks and threats, and decide on a course of action that ranges from advocacy (defense) to accommodation (apology for misdeeds). Various strategies for coping with a crisis are clearly explained in Chapter 10, Conflict Management: Dealing with Issues, Risks, and Crises. In this chapter, some new situations are explored:

◆ Wal-Mart's efforts in reputation management

◆ The Canadian fur industry's labors to overturn bans on seal products

◆ Kentucky Fried Chicken's response to pressure from the People for the Ethical Treatment of Animals (PETA)

◆ McDonalds's efforts to defuse a charge of racism

◆ The World Diamond Council's response to the movie *Blood Diamond*

◆ The handling of toy companies (like Mattel and RC2) of recent massive toy recalls

◆ Wendy's' program of restoring its reputation after being the victim of a hoax

◆ China's approach to counter global perceptions of inferior and unsafe products

◆ The way American companies and pension funds are dealing with pressure from the Darfur Coalition to disinvest in stocks that benefit the Sudanese government

Updated statistics about the public relations industry

The most current statistical and demographic data have been incorporated into this edition. Students and professors will find new data throughout the book that accurately reflects current practice. Some examples include:

◆ Salaries for entry-level work and income of experienced practitioners in various fields, including breakouts showing salaries for men and women (Chapter 1)

◆ The size and revenues of the public relations industry in the United States (Chapter 1)

◆ The number of female professionals in the field and their progress toward management titles (Chapter 2)

- Current membership totals for various organizations, such as PRSA (Chapter 3)
- Current staffing profiles and expenditures of public relations departments from the USC Strategic Public Relations Center (Chapter 4)
- Revenues of global communication conglomerates (Chapter 4)
- Census information about ethnic groups in the United States (Chapter 11)
- Current court rulings about employers monitoring of employee emails (Chapter 12)
- New regulations regarding lobbying activity (Chapter 18)
- Campaign spending for the 2008 Presidential election (Chapter 18)
- Updated charts from Giving USA about philanthropy (Chapter 20)

Updated "On the Job" boxed features in every chapter

A complete list of "On the Job" boxes can be found on the inside front cover.

On the Job: A Multicultural World

Each chapter highlights recent programs and campaigns that have reached diverse audiences in the United States and around the world. New examples in this edition include:

- Bank of America's SafeSend program for transferring money to family members in Mexico (Chapter 1)
- Company campaigns in other nations (Chapter 4)
- A campaign in Washington, D.C. to inform the poor and illiterate how to reduce their utility bills (Chapter 5)
- A USAID campaign in India to promote the use of condoms (Chapter 6)
- A program by Royal Caribbean Cruise to promote African-American art (Chapter 11)
- Paramount's outreach to the Hispanic community for its film, *Nacho Libre* (Chapter 11)
- The Darfur Coalition's activities pressuring American corporations to disinvest in Sudanese companies (Chapter 20)

On the Job: Ethics

A major strength of this book is the exploration of ethical issues relevant to the subject matter of the chapter. Particular attention is given to current situations and issues familiar to students. The objective is to encourage robust class discussion, so each box ends with several questions to help students understand the crux of moral dilemmas faced by practitioners in daily practice. New examples of moral dilemmas and questionably ethical situations that are posed in this edition include:

- How to make a hiring decision between a well qualified woman, male, and an African-American (Chapter 2)
- Edelman Worldwide's use of a fake blog on behalf of client Wal-Mart (Chapter 3)
- How to write a news release about a questionable online survey of women drinking and engaging in sex during college spring breaks (Chapter 5)

- How to conduct a word-of-mouth campaign without revealing the sponsor (Chapter 7)
- Home Depot's bussing of supporters to a city council meeting considering approval of a new store (Chapter 10)
- The firing of broadcaster Don Imus for making controversial remarks regarding race (Chapter 11)
- The ethics of Mattel's massive toy recall (Chapter 12)

New PR Casebooks to generate interest and discussion

Each chapter, as in past editions, has a PR Casebook that describes the "nuts and bolts" of a public relations program or campaign. A complete list of Casebooks appears on the inside front cover. In this edition, there are many new PR Casebooks that will engage the students and heighten their knowledge, as well as enthusiasm, for the field of public relations. They include:

- Fleishman-Hillard's E.R.A.S.E. program for inner-city New York City schools (Chapter 4)
- A cause-related program for charity by Sunkist Growers through the distribution of lemonade stands to kids (Chapter 6)
- The introduction of Apple's iPhone (Chapter 7)
- Kermit the Frog's 50th anniversary celebration in Kermit, Texas (Chapter 8)
- The Kansas City Health Department's campaign to the gay community about the dangers of syphilis (Chapter 9)
- China's attempt to restore its reputation after numerous product recalls (Chapter 10)
- Heinz's campaign promoting personalized Ketchup bottles (Chapter 14)
- Dell Computer's crisis in coping with exploding batteries (Chapter 17)
- Google's increased lobbying in Washington (Chapter 18)
- CALCUSA's Campaign to educate men about sexual violence (Chapter 20)
- The tragic shootings Virginia Tech (Chapter 21)
- The Duke University lacrosse team scandal (Chapter 21)
- Mel Gibson's efforts to restore of reputation after making anti-Semitic comments (Chapter 22)

Quotations from leading professionals

Selected quotations from experienced professionals are highlighted in each chapter. These short, pithy statements give the essence of a professional's insights and wisdom. We feel this approach provides practitioners' viewpoints for students in an accessible way.

Organization of the Book

The text is divided into five parts:

Part One: Role

Part Two: Process

Part Three: Strategy

Part Four: Tactics

Part Five: Application

Part One: Role

This section of the book gives students a thorough grounding in public relations as a pervasive, fully-developed field of activity in today's society and global economy. It properly defines the broad scope of public relations, its societal value, and the workplace settings where public relations is practiced. **Chapter 1** explains what public relations is and students learn an understanding of public relations as a systematic, problem-solving process. It discusses the differences and similarities between public relations, journalism, advertising, and marketing. **Chapter 2** discusses the history of public relations in terms of major eras of development and the individuals that made a significant contribution to the field. Emphasis is placed on the last half of the twentieth century, and how the role and function of public relations have evolved over the years. This chapter now also discusses the direction of trend lines in public relations and potential challenges PR professionals may face in the next 50 years. **Chapter 3** exposes students to the ethical and professional standards of today's practice with discussion on the codes of conduct for several professional organizations. **Chapter 4** covers the structure of public relations departments and their role in various organizational structures.

Part Two: Process

The four chapters in this part form a unified whole, taking students in sequence through the basic steps involved in a public relations program—research, planning, communication, and evaluation. In this way, students gain a deeper understanding and appreciation of public relations as a multiple-step process. To explain the process, the chapters follow the public relations programs of several organizations from conception to evaluation. **Chapter 5** discusses the essential first step: research. Students are exposed to different levels of qualitative and quantitative research and are taught how to construct a basic questionnaire and how to reach respondents. **Chapter 6** discusses program planning and the importance of setting goals and objectives for a public relations program. It also covers the eight essential parts of a public relations plan, including information on how to identify target audiences, create budgets, do timelines, and evaluate the effort. **Chapter 7** is an overview of major communication theories as they apply to various techniques for accomplishing everything from making individuals aware of a message to actually changing their behavior in terms of opinions or product purchase. **Chapter 8** discusses the pros and cons of various measurement methods and defines techniques for measuring message exposure, audience awareness, audience attitudes, and audience action.

Part Three: Strategy

This part discusses the fundamental concepts of strategy from the standpoint of acquainting student with broad-based concepts such as persuasion, audience characteristics, law, and new technologies. **Chapter 9** covers the influence of opinion leaders and explains source credibility, timing and context, and appeal to self-interest. **Chapter 10** provides students with an easy-to-understand theoretical framework so they can systematically respond to risks and crises. **Chapter 11** teaches students that the "general public" is really a group of "publics" with specific characteristics. This chapter has been considerably updated for this edition, with more emphasis on reaching audiences of various ethnic and multicultural backgrounds, as well as audiences of different age groups, and audiences with disabilities. **Chapter 12** explains libel, privacy, copyright, plagiarism, and trademarks. Rules and regulations of regulatory agencies, such as the FTC, SEC, FCC, and FDA that affect the content of public relations materials, are also outlined. With the rapid rise of the Internet, **Chapter 13** has been thoroughly updated to include reaching audiences through "social media," and now covers blogs, podcasts, webcasts, online newsrooms, and other online phenomena, such as YouTube, MySpace, and more.

Part Four: Tactics

This section focuses on "how-to" skills that the student needs to actually produce and write public relations materials. **Chapter 14** teaches students how to write news releases, media alerts, pitch letters, and media kits. There are numerous "how to" checklists, samples from various public relations campaigns, and even a section on what makes a good publicity photo. In **Chapter 15,** students are exposed to broadcast news writing, how to arrange guests on talk shows, satellite media tours, and the components of a video news release. **Chapter 16** shows students how to write a speech, give a speech, and use PowerPoint in presentations. The basics of preparing for a one-on-one media interview are covered, as well as how to organize a news conference and a media tour.

Part Five: Application

This section teaches students about the practical ways in which the process, strategies, and tactics are applied in major areas of practice. These chapters, which make the text comprehensive, build upon the basics that students have learned in the first 16 chapters. **Chapter 17** outlines the public relations challenges facing today's modern, global corporation. Such topics as media relations, consumer boycotts, multicultural marketing, investor relations, cause-related marketing, environmental activism, philanthropy, and corporate sponsorship of events are covered. **Chapter 18** discusses lobbying and the problems of influence peddling, as well as the nature of governmental public relations work at the federal, state, and city level. In **Chapter 19,** students gain an appreciation of global public relations and the challenges of cross-cultural communications. **Chapter 20** discusses the nature of public relations work in trade groups, labor unions, professional associations, charities, social agencies, and activist groups. Resource development and how to conduct a fund-raising campaign are also explored. **Chapter 21** highlights the public relations activities of universities, grade schools, and high schools. Students learn about how to reach special publics to accomplish goals and objectives. Finally, in **Chapter 22,** students learn about "celebrity" publicity and promotion, and the techniques of conducting "personality" campaigns for rock groups, professional athletes, and movie stars. Tourism, a large industry, is also highlighted as a career area.

Student Learning Tools

Each chapter of *Public Relations: Strategies and Tactics* includes several learning tools to help students better understand and remember the principles of public relations, and to give them the practice they need to apply those principles to real-life situations.

This edition continues its tradition of providing key student learning aids at the end of every chapter. In each chapter, you will find:

- **Chapter opening preview.** The preview shows students the major sections and structure of the chapter.
- **"On the Job" boxed features.** Each chapter includes updated "On the Job" boxes that highlight additional insights, multicultural programs, and ethical considerations. They challenge students to formulate their own solutions and opinions and supplement information in the regular text.
- **PR Casebook.** A real-life case study of a public relations program that summarizes and elaborates on the chapter topic. The objective is to show students how the concepts and principles are used in actual practice. Over 75% of the PR Casebooks are new to the ninth edition.
- **End-of-chapter summary.** The major themes and issues are summarized for the student at the end of each chapter.
- **End-of-chapter "Case Activity."** A public relations situation or dilemma, based on actual cases, is posed and students are asked to apply what they have just read to a real-life situation. These activities have been updated for the ninth edition.
- **Questions for review and discussion.** A list of questions at the end of each chapter helps students prepare for tests and also stimulates class discussion.
- **Suggested readings.** These updated lists of end-of-chapter readings give students additional references for exploring topics brought up in the chapter.
- **Useful Web sites and bibliography.** This updated collection of selected books, periodicals, and directories at the end of the book provides a more complete list of references for students wishing to conduct further research.

See also the next section on supplements for new online materials that are now available to students.

Supplements

Instructors and students have a variety of ancillary tools available to them that will help make teaching and learning with *Public Relations: Strategies and Tactics* easier.

- **Instructor's Manual and Test Bank, by Vince Benigni, College of Charleston.** The Instructor's Manual includes chapter outlines, lecture topics, sample syllabi, learning objectives, class activities, and discussion questions. The Test Bank includes over 700 multiple choice, true/false, and essay questions.
- **Computerized Test Bank.** The Test Bank is also available through Allyn & Bacon's computerized testing system. This fully networkable test generating software is available electronically through Pearson Education's Instructor's Resource Center (www.pearsonhighered.com/irc). The user-friendly interface allows you to view, edit, and add questions, transfer questions to tests, and print tests in a variety of fonts. Search and sort features allow you to locate questions quickly and to arrange them in whatever order you prefer. Available on request to adopters.
- **PowerPoint Presentation, by Tia Tyree, Howard University.** The PowerPoint slides provide main ideas and key examples from each chapter of the text.

Figures and graphs from the text can also be found in this presentation, which is available to adopters through Pearson Education's Instructor's Resource Center (www.pearsonhighered.com/irc).

mycommunicationlab

♦ **MyCommunicationLab for Public Relations (Access Code Required).** MyCommunicationLab for Public Relations is a state-of-the-art interactive and instructive solution for introductory public relations courses, designed to be used as a supplement to a traditional lecture course, or to completely administer an online course. The site www.mycommunicationlab.com gives you and your students access to a wealth of resources all geared to meet the individual teaching and learning needs of every instructor and every student. Combining an E-book, a portfolio builder, multimedia, video clips, activities, research support, practice tests, and exams, MyCommunicationLab for Public Relations engages students and prepares them to enter the world of public relations with confidence.

♦ **Public Relations Study Site**, by Holly Pieper, Mansfield University. This Web site features public relations study materials for students, including flashcards and a complete set of practice tests for all major topics. Students will also find web links to valuable sites for further exploration of major topics. The site can be accessed at www.pearsonpublicrel.com.

Acknowledgements

We would like to thank those who reviewed the previous edition and made many suggestions that we have incorporated into this revision: Josh Boyd, Purdue University; Karyn Brown, Mississippi State University; Robert A. Carroll, York College of Pennsylvania; Jennifer Chin, University of North Carolina Wilmington; Gregg Feistman, Temple University; Steve G. Mandel, Pennsylvania State University; Teresa Mastin, Michigan State University; Maureen Taylor, Rutgers University; Beth Wood, Indiana University; Brenda J. Wrigley, Syracuse University.

We express our deep appreciation to those who reviewed drafts of the manuscript for previous editions.

About the Authors

Dennis L. Wilcox, Ph.D.

Dr. Wilcox is professor emeritus of public relations at San Jose State University and former director of the School of Journalism & Mass Communications. He is an accredited (APR) member of the Public Relations Society of America (PRSA) and is also in the organization's College of Fellows recognizing his life-long contributions to the profession. Wilcox is a former chair of the PRSA Educator's Academy and the public relations division of the Association for Education in Journalism & Mass Communications (AEJMC). Among his many awards is PRSA's "Educator of the Year" and the Xifra-Heras Award from the University of Girona (Spain) for contributions to international public relations education.

Wilcox is currently active in the International Public Relations Association (IPRA) and is a member of the Arthur W. Page Society, an organization of senior public relations executives. Wilcox, author or co-author of seven books, including *Public Relations Writing & Media Techniques*, now travels extensively giving university lectures and professional workshops in such diverse nations as Chile, Argentina, Latvia, Romania, Spain, Ukraine, Serbia, South Africa, Australia, and Thailand. His philosophy, to quote St. Augustine, is "The world is a book, and those who do not travel read only a page."

Glen T. Cameron, Ph.D.

Dr. Cameron is the Maxine Wilson Gregory Chair in Journalism Research and the co-founder of the Health Communication Research Center in the Missouri School of Journalism. He is a prolific writer and researcher in organizational communications and public relations. A recent bibliometric analysis, for example, named Dr. Cameron as the most published scholar in public relations over the past eight years. He is the author of more than 300 chapters, articles, and convention papers. In addition, Cameron lectures frequently around the world to university and professional audiences about a number of topics, including his widely acclaimed Contingency Theory that offers a fresh and vigorous approach to conflict management in public setting.

His pioneering software development includes **Public PR Research Software™**, a widely used tool in marketing and public relations. Cameron has won numerous national awards for his public relations research, including the Public Relations Society of America's (PRSA) "pathfinder" award and is the three-time winner of the Institute for Public Relations SMART Grant for innovations in public relations research. Currently, he is on the editorial board of eight scholarly journals. He is a regular consultant for such diverse clients as Monsanto, Missouri Foundation for Health, CDC, NCI, USDA, and Pulitzer Technologies.

1

CHAPTER

What Is Public Relations?

The Challenge of Public Relations

It is 9 A.M. and Anne-Marie, a senior account executive in a San Francisco public relations firm, is at her desk reading the local dailies and also scanning online news sites to determine whether there are any stories about her clients or discussing an issue that may impact them.

She downloads a *Wall Street Journal* article about the increasing risk of tainted food from foreign suppliers and makes a note to have her student intern do some more research about this issue. One of Anne-Marie's clients is a restaurant chain, and she senses an opportunity for the client to capitalize on the media interest by informing the press and the public about what they are doing to ensure the quality and safety of their meals.

She then finishes a draft of a news release about a client's new software product and e-mails it to the client for approval. She also attaches a note that an electronic news service can deliver it to newspapers across the country later in the day. Anne-Marie's next activity is a brainstorming session with other staff members in the conference room to generate creative ideas about a special event to raise funds for the local AIDS foundation. When she gets back to her office, she finds a number of telephone messages. A reporter for a trade publication needs background information on a story he is writing; a graphic designer has finished a rough draft of a client's brochure; a catering manager has called about making final arrangements for a VIP reception at an art gallery; and a video producer asks whether she can attend the taping of a video news release next week.

Lunch is with a client who wants her counsel on how to position the company as environmentally conscious and dedicated to sustainable development. After lunch, Anne-Marie heads back to the office. She asks a junior account executive to check arrangements for a news conference next week in New York. She then telephones a key editor to "pitch" a story about a client's new product. Anne-Marie also touches base with other members of her team, who are working on a 12-city media tour by an Olympic champion representing an athletic-shoe manufacturer.

At 4 P.M., Anne-Marie checks several computer databases to gather information about the industry of a new client. She again checks online news updates to determine whether anything is occurring that involves or affects her firm's clients. At 5 P.M., as she winds down from the day's hectic activities, she reviews news stories from a electronic clipping service about another client, an association of strawberry producers. She is pleased to find that her feature story, which included recipes and color photos, appeared in 150 dailies.

But the day isn't quite done. Anne-Marie is on her way to attend a chapter meeting of the Public Relations Society of America (PRSA) where the speaker will discuss the impact of the new "Social Media" on public relations. It's her way of doing continuing education since her graduation from college four years ago with a public relations major.

As this scenario illustrates, the challenge of public relations is multifaceted. A public relations professional must have skills in written and interpersonal communication, research, negotiation, creativity, logistics, facilitation, and problem solving.

Indeed, those who want a challenging career with plenty of variety often choose the field of public relations. The U.S. Bureau of Labor Statistics estimates that the field already employs 350,000 nationwide and predicts a 39.8 percent increase in employment through 2014 for public relations specialists. In addition, *Money* magazine (May 2006) ranked the position of public relations specialist 20th on its list of "50 Best Jobs" for job opportunity and potential salary. The magazine also graded various occupations on several factors; public relations got a "D" for stress levels, but a "B" on creativity.

Global Scope

It's difficult to estimate worldwide figures, but the Global Alliance (www.globalpr.org), with about 60 national and regional public relations associations representing 160,000 members, estimates that some 3 million people worldwide practice public relations as their main professional activity. In the United Kingdom alone, for example, there are an estimated 50,000 public relations professionals.

Indeed, there are an estimated 200 national and regional public relations organizations around the world. A partial list that shows the geographic diversity includes the following: Public Relations Institute of Southern Africa (PRISA), the Spanish Association of Communicators (DIRCOM), the Public Relations Institute of Australia (PRIA), the Public Relations Society of Serbia, the Canadian Public Relations Society (CPRS), the Public Relations Society of Kenya (PRSK), the Institute of Public Relations (United Kingdom), the Romania Public Relations Association (RPRA), the Public Relations Agencies Association of Mexico (PRAA), Relaciones Publigas America Latina (ALARP), the Consejo Professional de Relaciones Publicas of Argentina, the Public Relations

on the job
INSIGHTS

100th Anniversary Kiss

Special event planning, promotion, and publicity are important activities in public relations work. A good example is how Hershey's celebrated the 100th anniversary of its popular Kisses Chocolate. Instead of baking the traditional birthday cake, the company constructed a 12-foot-high, 30,540-pound confection that also took 16,460 feet of foil wrapping. The unveiling and birthday party took place at Hershey's Chocolate World attraction in Hershey, Pennsylvania.

Here, Jane Boatfield from Guinness World Records stands at the podium to give Michelle Buck, Hershey's senior vice president, a warm welcome and to deliver a certificate from Guinness declaring the new record for "The World's Largest Piece of Chocolate." The anniversary story,

and a photo of the giant Kiss, received extensive media coverage throughout the country. In addition, a Web site (www.kisssomeone.com) was set up to give consumers the history of Kisses Brand Chocolate and a slide show showing the construction of the giant candy. Photo courtesy of Cheryl Georgas, The Hershey Company.

Society of India (PRSI), and the Middle East Public Relations Association (MEPRA). A new organization, the Public Relations Confederation of Islamic Countries (PRCIC), was founded in mid-2007 and is based in Tehran, Iran.

Large numbers of students around the world are studying public relations as a career field. In the United States, about 34,000 students in 2005–2006 were majoring in public relations, advertising/public relations, or strategic communications, according to the annual survey of 460 journalism and mass communications programs by the Association for Education in Journalism and Mass Communications (AEJMC). In addition, the Public Relations Student Society of America (PRSSA) now has chapters on 286 college campuses, with 9,600 members.

In Europe, an estimated 100 universities also offer studies in the subject. Public relations, for example, is becoming a popular course of study in the developing economies of Serbia, Romania, Latvia, Estonia, Ukraine, and the Russian Federation. Many Asian universities, particularly those in Thailand, Korea, Indonesia, India, and the Philippines, also offer major programs. China claims that more than 500,000 students are studying aspects of public relations in colleges and training institutions. Australia and New Zealand have a long history of public relations education. In South America, particularly in Argentina, Chile, and Brazil, public relations is a popular course of study at many universities. South African universities have the most developed public relations curriculum on the African continent, but programs of study can also be found in Nigeria, Ghana, and Kenya. The Middle East, particularly the United Arab Emirates, introduced public relations into university curriculums during the mid-1990s. In sum, public relations is a well-established academic subject that is taught and practiced throughout the world.

In terms of economics, the public relations field is most extensively developed in the United States. A 2007 survey of the industry by Research and Markets Ltd. in Ireland, for example, found almost 7,000 public relations firms in the U.S. with combined annual revenue of over $6 billion. This figure, however, doesn't include more billions spent by all kinds of organizations, including corporations, for public relations staffing and activities.

One difficulty with ascertaining exact numbers, of course, is how "public relations" is defined. Vernonis Suhler Stevenson, a specialty banker in the communications industry, also reports that a combined $141 billion annually is spent on public relations, in-store promotions, direct mail, and sponsorships. Another $176 billion is spent on advertising. Public relations, in essence, is still a cottage industry compared to advertising and its variations such as direct mail. There is considerable blurring of lines regarding whether corporate event sponsorships are public relations, advertising, or marketing.

Figures for the rest of the world are somewhat sketchy. It's estimated, for example, that European companies spend about $3 billion a year on public relations. European figures continue to increase because of the expansion of the European Union (EU) and the developing market economies of Russia and the other independent nations of the former Soviet Union.

Major growth is also occurring in Asia for several reasons. China is literally the "new frontier." Since opening its economy to market capitalism, China's economy is increasing at the rate of 10 percent annually, and the public relations industry is thriving. The China International Public Relations Association (CIPRA) reports there are now 20,000 practitioners in the country. In 2006, there were also 2,000 public relations firms, an increase of 500 from the previous year. The *Economist* reports that the public relations market in China will be $1.8 billion by 2010, second only to Japan in the region.

China's membership in the World Trade Organization (WTO) also has led to more public relations activity by international companies engaged in a fierce competition for the bonanza of Chinese customers, numbering in the millions. The biggest development, according to the *Economist*, is the soaring demand for public relations among Chinese companies as they actively seek local consumers, foreign investments, and international outlets for their goods. China will host the 2008 summer Olympics and the 2010 Shanghai World Expo. These events are expected to further fuel the dynamic growth of public relations in China.

Other nations, such as Malaysia, Korea, Thailand, Singapore, Indonesia, and India, are also rapidly expanding their free market economies, which creates a fertile environment for increased public relations activity. India has great economic and public relations potential because, like China, it has over one billion people and is moving toward a more robust market economy. Latin America and Africa also present growth opportunities. A more detailed discussion of international public relations is found in Chapter 19.

A Variety of Definitions

People often define public relations by some of its most visible techniques and tactics, such as publicity in a newspaper, a television interview with an organization's spokesperson, or the appearance of a celebrity at a special event.

What people fail to understand is that public relations is a process involving many subtle and far-reaching aspects. It includes research and analysis, policy formation, programming, communication, and feedback from numerous publics. Its practitioners operate on two distinct levels—as advisers to their clients or to an organization's top management and as technicians who produce and disseminate messages in multiple media channels.

A number of definitions have been formulated over the years. One early definition that gained wide acceptance was formulated by the newsletter *PR News*: "Public relations is the management function which evaluates public attitudes, identifies the policies and procedures of an individual or an organization with the public interest, and plans and executes a program of action to earn public understanding and patience."

Rex Harlow, a pioneer public relations educator who founded what eventually became the Public Relations Society of America (PRSA), once compiled more than 500 definitions from almost as many sources. After mulling them over and talking with leaders in the field, Harlow came up with this definition:

> Public relations is a distinctive management function which helps establish and maintain mutual lines of communication, understanding, acceptance, and cooperation between an organization and its publics; involves the management of problems or issues; helps management keep informed on and responsive to public opinion; defines and emphasizes the responsibility of management to serve the public interest; helps management keep abreast of and effectively utilize change, serving as an early warning system to help anticipate trends; and uses research and sound ethical communication techniques as its principal tools.

More succinct definitions are provided by theorists and textbook authors. Scott M. Cutlip, Allen H. Center, and Glen M. Broom state in *Effective Public Relations* that "public relations is the management function that identifies, establishes, and maintains mutually beneficial relationships between an organization and the various publics on whom its success or failure depends." The management function is also emphasized more than 20 years ago in *Managing Public Relations* by James E. Grunig and Todd Hunt. They state that public relations is "the management of communication between an organization and its publics."

A good definition for today's modern practice is offered by Professors Lawrence W. Long and Vincent Hazelton, who describe public relations as "a communication function of management through which organizations adapt to, alter, or maintain their environment for the purpose of achieving organizational goals." Their approach represents the widely accepted concept that public relations is more than persuasion. It should also foster open, two-way communication and mutual understanding with the idea that an organization also changes its attitudes and behaviors in the process—not just the target audience.

Inherent in this philosophy of public relations is the basic idea that the objective is to build mutually beneficial relationships between the organization and its various publics. In other words, organizational policies and actions should be a win-win situation for both the organization and the public.

A good example of a win-win situation was the decision by various apparel and footwear manufacturers (Nike, Reebok, GEAR for Sports, Tommy Hilfiger, etc.) to engage in a dialogue with labor and human rights groups about working conditions in their overseas factories after considerable negative publicity on their use of "sweatshop" labor. The result was the creation of the Fair Labor Association, which created a uniform code of conduct and a monitoring process to document whether member companies were in compliance.

In this instance, the companies improved their corporate reputations and avoided consumer boycotts by activist college groups, human rights groups, and labor unions. The workers in these factories got better working conditions in terms of wages, health, and safety. And consumers felt somewhat less guilty about wearing expensive sneakers and name-brand clothes made by exploited Third World labor.

National and international public relations organizations, including the PRSA, also have formulated definitions. Here is a sampling of definitions from around the world:

- "Public relations is influencing behaviour to achieve objectives through the effective management of relationships and communications." (British Institute of Public Relations (IPR), whose definition has also been adopted in a number of Commonwealth nations)

- "Public relations is the management, through communication, of perceptions and strategic relationships between an organization and its internal and external stakeholders." (Public Relations Institute of Southern Africa)

- "Public relations practice is the art and social science of analyzing trends, predicting their consequences, counseling organization leaders, and implementing planned programs of action which serve both the organization's and the public's interest." (A definition approved at the World Assembly of Public Relations in Mexico City in 1978 and endorsed by 34 national public relations organizations)

Although current definitions of public relations have long emphasized the building of mutually beneficial relationships between the organization and its various publics, a more assertive definition has emerged over the past decade. Glen Cameron, coauthor of this book and at the University of Missouri School of Journalism, defines public relations as the "strategic management of competition and conflict for the benefit of one's own organization—and when possible—also for the mutual benefit of the organization and its various stakeholders or publics."

This definition places the public relations professional first and foremost as an advocate for the employer or client, but acknowledges the importance of mutual benefit when circumstances allow. This definition should not imply that the public relations professional acts only in the self-interest of the employer without due regard for honesty, integrity, and organizational transparency. Indeed, there is an ethical framework that guides the professional in all his or her work, which is discussed further in Chapter 3.

It isn't necessary, however, to memorize any particular definition of public relations. It's more important to remember the key words that are used in most definitions that frame today's modern public relations. The key words are:

◆ **Deliberate.** Public relations activity is intentional. It is designed to influence, gain understanding, provide information, and obtain feedback (reaction from those affected by the activity).

◆ **Planned.** Public relations activity is organized. Solutions to problems are discovered and logistics are thought out, with the activity taking place over a period of time. It is systematic, requiring research and analysis.

◆ **Performance.** Effective public relations is based on actual policies and performance. No amount of public relations will generate goodwill and support if the organization is unresponsive to community concerns. A Pacific Northwest timber company, despite a campaign with the theme "For Us, Every Day Is Earth Day," became known as the villain of Washington State because of its insistence on logging old-growth forests and bulldozing a logging road into a prime elk habitat.

◆ **Public interest.** Public relations activity should be mutually beneficial to the organization and the public; it is the alignment of the organization's self-interests with the public's concerns and interests. For example, the ExxonMobil Corporation sponsors quality programming on public television because it enhances the company's image; by the same token, the public benefits from the availability of such programming.

◆ **Two-way communication.** Public relations is more than one-way dissemination of informational materials. It is equally important to solicit feedback. As Jim Osborne, former vice president of public affairs at Bell Canada, says, "The primary responsibility of the public relations counselor is to provide (management) a thorough grasp of public sentiment."

◆ **Management function.** Public relations is most effective when it is a strategic and integral part of decision making by top management. Public relations involves counseling and problem solving at high levels, not just the dissemination of information after a decision has been made.

To summarize, you can grasp the essential elements of effective public relations by remembering the following words and phrases: deliberate . . . planned . . . performance . . . public interest . . . two-way communication . . . strategic management function. The elements of public relations just described are part of an interactive process that makes up what is called public relations activity. In the following section, public relations as a process is discussed.

on the job

A MULTICULTURAL WORLD

Bank of America Reaches Out to the Hispanic Community

More than half of the Hispanics living in the United States regularly send money to loved ones in their home countries. At the same time, 70 percent of them use wire transfer services that charge relatively high fees.

The Bank of America (B of A) realizing the potential market of the 25 million Latin Americans living in the United States, had a better idea. The bank launched a program called SafeSend, which allowed Hispanics to send remittances free if they opened a BofA checking account.

Fleishman-Hillard public relations was engaged to generate awareness among the Hispanic community about the SafeSend program. The kickoff focused on Mexican Mother's Day because that traditionally was the time of year when remittances were the highest. A national news release, a radio news release, and a video news release (VNR) were distributed to major Spanish-language media outlets, as well as the general press.

In addition, the bank began hosting Fiesta Fridays in its various facili-

A 10-foot-high Mexican piggy bank symbolized the Bank of America's SafeSend program at an event in Los Angeles.

ties and provided materials in Spanish so potential customers could become better acquainted with its products and services. Other events also were used. At a Los Angeles event, for example, a 10-foot-high Mexican piggy bank was used to symbolize the savings that SafeSend could offer. Piggy banks were also used at regional Cinco de Mayo festivals in California and Texas.

As a result, the SafeSend program received considerable coverage in the Hispanic press. More important, BofA opened 3,295 new direct-deposit accounts with SafeSend in the initial weeks. Before this campaign, the bank had already been the first one to introduce Spanish-language ATMs, bilingual customer service, and a Spanish-language Web site.

Public Relations as a Process

Public relations is a process—that is, a series of actions, changes, or functions that bring about a result. One popular way to describe the process, and to remember its components, is to use the RACE acronym, first articulated by John Marston in his book *The Nature of Public Relations*. Essentially, RACE means that public relations activity consists of four key elements:

◆ **R**esearch. What is the problem or situation?

◆ **A**ction (program planning). What is going to be done about it?

+ **Communication (execution).** How will the public be told?
+ **Evaluation.** Was the audience reached and what was the effect?

Part Two of this text (Chapters 5–8) discusses this key four-step process.

Another approach is to think of the process as a never-ending cycle in which six components are links in a chain. Figure 1.1 shows the process.

1. **Step 1: *Research and Analysis.*** This consists of inputs that determine the nature and extent of the public relations problem or opportunity. These may include feedback from the public, media reporting and editorial comment, analysis of trend data, other forms of research, personal experience, and government pressures and regulations.

2. **Step 2: *Policy Formulation.*** Public relations personnel, as advisors to top management, make recommendations on policy and what actions should be taken by the organization.

3. **Step 3: *Programming.*** Once a policy or action is agreed on, public relations staff begin to plan a communications program that will further the organization's objectives. They will set objectives, define audiences, and decide on what strategies will be used on a specific timeline. Budget and staffing are also major considerations.

4. **Step 4: *Communication.*** Public relations personnel execute the program through such vehicles as news releases, media advisories, newsletters, Internet and Web postings, special events, speeches, and community relations programs.

5. **Step 5: *Feedback.*** The effect of these efforts is measured by feedback from the same components that made up the first step. Did the media mention the key messages?

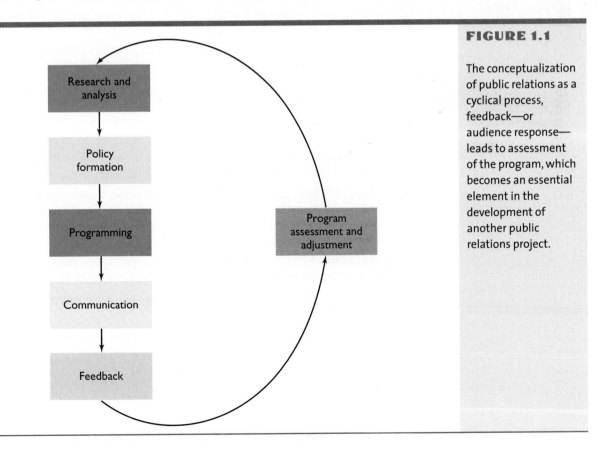

FIGURE 1.1

The conceptualization of public relations as a cyclical process, feedback—or audience response—leads to assessment of the program, which becomes an essential element in the development of another public relations project.

Did people change their attitudes or opinions? Did sales go up? Did the organization preserve or enhance its reputation?

6. **Step 6:** *Assessment.* The cycle is then repeated. The success or failure of the policy or program is assessed as a way of determining whether additional efforts are needed, or whether new issues or opportunities must be addressed. Thus, it is a continuing loop process.

Note that public relations plays two distinct roles in this process, thus serving as a "middle ground" or "linking agent." On one level, public relations interacts directly with external sources of information, including the public, media, and government, and relays these inputs to management along with recommendations. On a second level, public relations becomes the vehicle through which management reaches the public with assorted messages.

The Components of Public Relations

The basic components of public relations, according to a monograph issued by the PRSA Foundation, include:

- Counseling. Providing advice to management concerning policies, relationships, and communications.
- Research. Determining attitudes and behaviors of publics in order to plan public relations strategies. Such research can be used to (1) generate mutual understanding or (2) influence and persuade publics.
- Media relations. Working with mass media in seeking publicity or responding to their interests in the organization.
- Publicity. Disseminating planned messages through selected media to further the organization's interests.
- Employee/member relations. Responding to concerns, informing, and motivating an organization's employees or members.
- Community relations. Planned activity with a community to maintain an environment that benefits both the organization and the community.
- Public affairs. Developing effective involvement in public policy and helping an organization adapt to public expectations. The term is also used by government agencies to describe their public relations activities and by many corporations as an umbrella term to describe multiple public relations activities.
- Government affairs. Relating directly with legislatures and regulatory agencies on behalf of the organization. Lobbying can be part of a government affairs program.
- Issues management. Identifying and addressing issues of public concern that affect the organization.
- Financial relations. Creating and maintaining investor confidence and building good relationships with the financial community. Also known as investor relations or shareholder relations.
- Industry relations. Relating with other firms in the industry of an organization and with trade associations.
- Development/fund-raising. Demonstrating the need for and encouraging the public to support an organization, primarily through financial contributions.

on the job
INSIGHTS

Public Relations Society of America Official Statement on Public Relations

Public relations helps our complex, pluralistic society to reach decisions and function more effectively by contributing to mutual understanding among groups and institutions. It serves to bring private and public policies into harmony.

Public relations serves a variety of institutions in society such as businesses, trade unions, government agencies, voluntary associations, foundations, hospitals, and educational and religious institutions. To achieve their goals, these institutions must develop effective relationships with many different audiences or publics such as employees, members, customers, local communities, shareholders, and other institutions, and with society at large.

The managements of institutions need to understand the attitudes and values of their publics in order to achieve institutional goals. The goals themselves are shaped by the external environment. The public relations practitioner acts as a counselor to management, and as a mediator, helping to translate private aims into reasonable, publicly acceptable policy and action.

As a management function, public relations encompasses the following:

♦ Anticipating, analyzing, and interpreting public opinion, attitudes, and issues which might impact, for good or ill, the operations and plans of the organization.

♦ Counseling management at all levels in the organization with regard to policy decisions, courses of action and communication, and taking into account their public ramifications and the organization's social or citizenship responsibilities.

♦ Researching, conducting, and evaluating, on a continuing basis, programs of action and communication to achieve informed public understanding necessary to the success of an organization's aims. These may include marketing, financial, fundraising, employee, community or government relations, and other programs.

♦ Planning and implementing the organization's efforts to influence or change public policy.

♦ Setting objectives, planning, budgeting, recruiting and training staff, and developing facilities—in short, managing the resources needed to perform all of the above.

♦ Examples of the knowledge that may be required in the professional practice of public relations include communication arts, psychology, social psychology, sociology, political science, economics, and the principles of management and ethics. Technical knowledge and skills are required for opinion research, public issues analysis, media relations, direct mail, institutional advertising, publications, film/video productions, special events, speeches, and presentations.

In helping to define and implement policy, the public relations practitioner utilizes a variety of professional communication skills and plays an integrative role both within the organization and between the organization and the external environment.

♦ Multicultural relations/workplace diversity. Relating with individuals and groups in various cultural groups.

♦ Special events. Stimulating an interest in a person, product, or organization by means of a well-planned event also, activities designed to interact with publics and listen to them.

♦ Marketing communications. Combination of activities designed to sell a product, service, or idea, including advertising, collateral materials, publicity, promotion, direct mail, trade shows, and special events.

These components, and how they function, constitute the substance of this textbook.

Other Terms for Public Relations

Public relations is used as an umbrella term on a worldwide basis. Most national membership associations, from the Azerbaijan Public Relations Association to the Zimbabwe Institute of Public Relations, identify themselves with that term.

Some Positive Descriptive Terms

Individual companies and other groups, however, often use other terms to describe the public relations function. *O'Dwyer's PR Services Report* once surveyed *Fortune* magazine's list of the largest 500 corporations and found that the most common name is *corporate communications*. Other common names are *corporate affairs*, *corporate relations*, *external communications*, *public affairs*, and just plain *communication*. Some companies link public relations with marketing. Chase Manhattan, for example, has a corporate marketing and communications unit.

Jack O'Dwyer notes that the organization for high-level executives is still called the Public Relations Seminar (PRS) but that few of its members have public relations titles. Of the 33 senior executives who were inducted into PRS in 2007, for example, only Jane Garvey of Convergys had the title "vice president of corporate communications and public relations." Ben & Jerry's, the ice-cream maker, prides itself on being a bit wacky, so its public relations staff calls themselves "Public Elations Multi-Mediologists." The CEO is called the "Chief Euphoria Officer."

Public information is the term most widely used by social service agencies, universities, and government agencies. The implication is that only information is being disseminated, in contrast to persuasive communication, generally perceived as the purpose of public relations. Social services agencies often use the term *community relations*, and the military is fond of *public affairs*. Increasingly, many nonprofits are also using the term *marketing communications* as they reorient to the idea that they must sell their services and generate donations in a highly competitive environment.

In many cases, it is clear that companies and organizations use *public information*, *public affairs*, or *corporate communications* as euphemisms for *public relations*. This, in part, is a reaction to the misuse of the original term by the public and the media. On occasion, a reporter or government official will use the term *public relations gimmick* or *ploy* to imply that the activities or statements of an organization are without substance or sincerity.

The popularity of *corporate communications* is also based on the idea that the term is broader than *public relations*, which is often incorrectly perceived as only *media relations*. Corporate communications, many contend, encompasses all communications of the company, including advertising, marketing communications, public affairs, community relations, and employee communications.

Other organizations use a term that better describes the primary activity of the department. It is clear, for example, that a department of investor relations deals primarily with stockholders, institutional investors, and the financial press. Likewise, a department of environmental affairs, community relations, or employee communications is self-explanatory. A department of marketing communications primarily emphasizes product publicity and promotion. The organization and functions of communications departments are discussed in Chapter 4.

Like departments, individuals specialize in subcategories of public relations. A person who deals exclusively with placement of stories in the media is, to be precise, a *publicist*. A *press agent* is also a specialist, operating within the subcategory of public relations that concentrates on finding unusual news angles and planning events or "happenings" that attract media attention—a stunt by an aspiring Hollywood actress,

on the job INSIGHTS

The Wonderful World of Public Relations

Public relations is an exciting field that offers variety, creativity, and opportunity to work on any number of projects. Here's a sampling of outstanding campaigns that received PRSA's prestigious Silver Anvil award in 2007.

FedEx's Flight of the Penguins

When the New Orleans Audubon Aquarium reopened in the aftermath of Hurricane Katrina, FedEx volunteered to fly 19 penguins temporarily housed in California back to Louisiana. A well-organized homecoming celebration was planned. Media covered the penguins waddling on and off planes and onto red carpets. A jazz band and city officials met the plane in New Orleans and a FedEx motorcade (complete with police escort) delivered them to the aquarium. At the reopening ceremony, FedEx presented a $100,000 check for the ongoing care of the penguin habitat.

Macy's Sale of Baskets from Rwanda

The department store chain formed a partnership with Rwandan women called "Rwanda: Path to Peace." Its purpose was to help the women of Rwanda sell their one-of-a-kind baskets, profits from which would substantially improve their social and economic situations destroyed by the genocide of 1994. Macy's goal was to sell 20,000 baskets, and public relations specialists placed articles in print and broadcast media about the "baskets for peace." Several Rwandan women were also flown to the United States to talk with customers and do media interviews. Macy's sold out of the baskets in four months.

Virginia's "Smart Beginnings"

The Virginia Department of Social Services conducted a statewide campaign to promote the importance of investing in early childhood education after research found that children who enter kindergarten not ready to learn are at a higher risk of eventually dropping out of school. Public relations counsel helped the department launch a public education campaign with the support of the governor and create a bipartisan task force of political and business leaders to set up an Early Learning Council and foundation.

Dell's Battery Recall

The computer manufacturer and its global communications team had the challenge of recalling 4.2 million Dell-branded lithium-ion batteries, with cells manufactured by Sony. The global communications team concentrated its efforts on reaching media with information about the recall and how customers could get a replacement battery. In addition, a company blog about the recall was expanded, and there was constant e-mail communication to analysts and investors. Within a week of the announcement, Dell had received more than 50 million hits on its Web site, responded to 135,000 phone calls, and had requests for 150,000 battery replacements. Dell's communications staff was credited with ensuring that the media and the public knew that the company had voluntarily issued the recall, and that it was based on only six incidents (no injuries) among the almost 20 million batteries in the marketplace.

for example, or an attempt to be listed in the Guinness Book of Records by baking the world's largest apple pie. *Publicist* is an honorable term in the entertainment and celebrity business, but is somewhat frowned on by the mainstream public relations industry. Chapter 22 discusses the work of New York and Hollywood publicists.

Some Stereotypes and Less Flattering Terms

Unfortunately, the public and the media often have a much different image of public relations as a profession. A common stereotype is that public relations is a great field because you meet exciting and interesting people, go to parties, and generally spend the day doing a lot of schmoozing.

Entertainment programs often present a misleading image about the nature of public relations work. Samantha Jones (Kim Cattrall) portrays the owner of a public relations firm in the television series *Sex and the City*. Real public relations work, however, requires more than dressing up and going to dinner parties.

Many people gain these perceptions from television programs such as *Sex and the City*, which is now in reruns. Ellen Tashie Frisna, a professor at Hofstra University, writes in *Tactics*, "Samantha Jones (Kim Cattrall), the sexiest of the show's characters, owns a PR agency. And she is—shall we say—experienced. She talks about her career as a way to meet men. (Her conquests include clients and temps.) Sorry, kids—the real world of public relations isn't like that." And Diane Krider, a professor of public relations at Central Michigan University, adds, "the show doesn't seem to show Samantha actually working."

Of course, other television programs and movies also give somewhat negative stereotypes about public relations. ABC's *Spin City*, for example, featured Michael J. Fox as the deputy mayor of New York who protected his bumbling boss from the media and public. Public relations was even the focus of a television reality show called *PowerRGirls* on MTV. It featured a celebrity publicist in New York, Lizzie Grubman, who seemed to live quite the socialite life. The show, thankfully, died an early death.

The movies *Phone Booth*, *The Sweet Smell of Success*, and even *The Devil Wears Prada* also add to the portrayals of sleazy publicists who have virtually no personal or professional moral compass. Some films are satires, but still project a negative image of public relations. *Thank You for Smoking*, a movie adapted from the book by Christopher Buckley, is a particularly good satire about a public relations person defending the tobacco industry. *Wag the Dog*, starring Dustin Hoffman and Robert DeNiro, is also a satire focusing on how an embattled president creates a fake war with the help of public relation pros to improve his image.

Other negative stereotypes are perpetuated by journalists. Frank Rich, an influential columnist for the *New York Times*, has used a number of adjectives over the years to describe public relations. They include "marketing," "sales," "sloganeering," "propaganda," and "lacking in principles and substance." Gene Weingarten, a columnist for the *Washington Post*, seems to agree. In one column, he called public relations people "pathetic, desperate dillweeds." Joe Norcera, a business columnist for the *New York Times*, used less colorful language to describe his frustration with Apple public relations reps when the i-Phone was introduced. He tried to find out how Apple was going to deal with the situation when the nonremovable batteries needed replacement. All he got was a standard answer that the "i-Phone's battery life was longer than any other smartphone." Norcera wrote, "This is another Apple innovation: the robotic spokesman who says only what he's programmed to say."

In all these cases we cited, the journalists have expressed frustration when they feel that public relations personnel are stonewalling, providing misleading information, or not being readily accessible to fully answer questions. This is traditionally a problem of effective media relations and, quite frankly, incompetence occurs in all fields, including public relations. Chapters 14 and 15 discuss the responsibilities of public relations personnel to provide assistance to media personnel.

On occasion, public relations is referred to as *spin*. The term *spin doctor* is a more recent entry into the lexicon of public relations. It first appeared in 1984, according to *Safire's Political Dictionary* by William Safire, in a *New York Times* editorial about the activities of President Ronald Reagan's reelection campaign. In the beginning, the meaning of *spin* was restricted to what often were considered the unethical and misleading activities and tactics of political campaign consultants. By the mid-1990s, however, the media widely used the term to describe any effort by public relations personnel to put a positive slant on an event or issue.

Robert Dilenschneider, president of his own public relations firm in New York, once wrote in a *Wall Street Journal* article:

> I think the time has come for public relations professionals to condemn 'spin' and label 'spin doctors' for what they are: purveyors of deception, manipulation, and misinformation. Spin is antithetical to legitimate public relations, which aims to enhance the image of companies and individuals to generate public approval for the programs and policies they advance . . . Spin is to public relations what pornography is to art. . . .

Indeed, spin seems to have established itself as a popular slang term for any information with a point of view. It has even become popular as a title in books about public relations, as in *PR: A Social History of Spin*, by Stuart Ewan; *The Father of Spin: Edward L. Bernays and The Birth of Public Relations*, by Larry Tye; *Spin Man: The Topsy-Turvy World of Public Relations*, by Thomas Madden; *Spin Cycle: How the White House and the Media Manipulate the News*, by Howard Kurtz; and *Spin: How to Turn the Power of the Press to Your Advantage*, by Michael Sitrick. A more academic term for spin is the concept of *framing*. Multiple research studies show how media, as well as public relations personnel, "frame" issues. See Chapter 6 about the theory of framing.

Another derogatory term with a longer history is *flak* or *flack*. These words are derisive slang terms that journalists often use for a press agent or anyone else working in public relations. It's like calling a journalist a "hack." Although in recent years most publications, including the *Wall Street Journal*, have refrained from using the "F" word in print, trade publications such as *Editor & Publisher* still occasionally use it.

Public relations is often stereotyped as simply "image building" as expressed in this somewhat humorous *New Yorker* cartoon. The image of an organization, however, is made up of many factors and public relations is only one of them. (Copyright © The New Yorker Collection 2004. Mick Stevens from cartoonbank.com. All rights reserved.)

The term has a mixed history. According to Wes Pedersen, a former director of communications for the Public Affairs Council, the term *flack* originated in 1939 in *Variety*, the show business publication. It began using *flack* as a synonym for press agent, he says, "in tribute to the skills of Gene Flack in publicizing motion pictures." Others say the word *flak* was used during World War I to describe heavy ground fire aimed at aircraft. At times, journalists consider the barrage of daily news releases they receive a form of flak that interferes with their mission of informing the public.

Within the public relations community, feeling also exists that *PR* is a slang term that carries a somewhat denigrating connotation. The late Sam Black, a public relations consultant in the United Kingdom and author of several books on public relations, says, "The use of 'PR' was probably originated as a nickname for 'press relations,'" the primary activity of public relations in its early years (see Chapter 2).

Although PR is now more than press relations, the nickname is commonly used in daily conversation and is widely recognized around the world. A good compromise, which this book uses, is to adopt a style of spelling out "public relations" in the body of a text or article but to use the shorter term, "PR," if it is used in a direct quote.

How Public Relations Differs from Journalism

Writing is a common activity of both public relations professionals and journalists. Both also do their jobs in the same way. They interview people, gather and synthesize large amounts of information, write in a journalistic style, and are trained to produce good copy on deadline. In fact, many reporters eventually change careers and become public relations practitioners.

This has led many people, including journalists, to the incorrect conclusion that little difference exists between public relations and journalism. For many, public relations is simply being a "journalist-in-residence" for a nonmedia organization.

However, despite the sharing of many techniques, the two fields are fundamentally different in scope, objectives, audiences, and channels.

Scope

Public relations, as stated earlier, has many components, ranging from counseling to issues management and special events. Journalistic writing and media relations, although important, are only two of these elements. In addition, effective practice of public relations requires strategic thinking, problem-solving capability, and other management skills.

Objectives

Journalists gather and select information for the primary purpose of providing the public with news and information. As Professors David Dozier and William Ehling explain, ". . . communication activities are an end in themselves." Public relations personnel also gather facts and information for the purpose of informing the public, but the objective is different. Communication activity is only a means to the end. In other words, the objective is not only to inform but to change people's attitudes and behaviors in order to further an organization's goals and objectives.

Whereas journalists are objective observers, public relations personnel are advocates. Harold Burson, chairman of Burson-Marsteller, makes the point:

To be effective and credible, public relations messages must be based on facts. Nevertheless, we are advocates, and we need to remember that. We are advocates of a

on the job ETHICS

Whose Ethics? An Undercover Journalist Takes on Public Relation Firms

Both journalists and public relations professionals agree that ethical behavior is required, indeed expected, in their work. On occasion, however, there is considerable difference of opinion about who is being unethical.

Ken Silverstein, Washington editor of *Harper's* magazine, decided to do a story about public relations and lobbying firms in Washington, D.C. His premise was that these firms are simply "for hire" and have no ethical qualms about representing any client with enough cash.

To prove his point, Silverstein posed as a consultant with a fictional London investment firm that was acting on behalf of the Turkmenistan government. He then went to two firms, APCO Worldwide and Cassidy & Associates, to find out how they would improve the image of Turkmenistan, a Central Asian country rich in energy resources but

with a repressive government that is often cited by activists for its poor human rights record. Both firms presented ideas about a standard-type public relations program, such as arranging meetings with administration officials and members of Congress, plus the placement of favorable opinion articles.

Silverstein's article, "Their Men in Washington: Undercover with DC's Lobbyists for Hire," was published in the July 2007 issue of *Harper's*. He admitted in the article that he lied to the firms about his true identity but claimed it was a legitimate way to get the story. APCO Worldwide, however, expressed outrage about Silverstein's deception, calling it a "violation of recognized journalistic principles." And even media reporter Howard Kurtz in the *Washington Post* said that the deception wasn't worth it, serving only to further public distrust of the media's overall credibility.

Silverstein's article and method of getting it generated a lot of discussion in the blogosphere. Some called Silverstein unethical; others said the firms were. For others, it was not a big deal; lobbyist and Public Relation firms are just representatives, not arbiters of justice. One lobbyist told *PRWeek* that he would "represent the devil if the price was right." He added, "I wouldn't do anything illegal, but if a person or entity is looking for some help communicating with Congress, I will do it, and it doesn't really matter to me who it is."

What do you think? Was Silverstein unethical by lying about his identity to get a story? Or are the firms unethical if they work on behalf of a repressive government? As a reporter, would you lie to get a story? Or, as a public relations person, would you take Turkmenistan as a client? Why or why not? We'll return to this situation in later chapters.

particular point of view—our client's or our employer's point of view. And while we recognize that serving the public interest best serves our client's interest, we are not journalists. That's not our job.

Audiences

Journalists write primarily for a mass audience—readers, listeners, or viewers of the medium for which they work. By definition, mass audiences are not well defined, and a journalist on a daily newspaper, for example, writes for the general public. A public relations professional, in contrast, carefully segments audiences into various demographic and psychological characteristics. Such research allows messages to be tailored to audience needs, concerns, and interests for maximum effect.

Channels

Most journalists, by nature of their employment, reach audiences through one channel—the medium that publishes or broadcasts their work. Public relations professionals use a variety of channels to reach the audiences previously described. The channels employed may be a combination of mass media outlets—newspapers, magazines, radio, and television. Or they may include direct mail, brochures, posters, newsletters, trade journals, special events, podcasts, blogs, Web sites, and even posting a video on YouTube.

How Public Relations Differs from Advertising

Just as many people mistakenly equate publicity with public relations, there is also some confusion about the distinction between publicity (one area of public relations) and advertising.

Although publicity and advertising both utilize mass media for dissemination of messages, the format and context are different. Publicity—information about an event, an individual or group, or a product—appears as a news item or feature story in the mass media. Material is prepared by public relations personnel and submitted to the news department for consideration. Editors, known as gatekeepers, determine whether the material will be used or simply thrown away.

Advertising, in contrast, is paid space and broadcast time. Organizations and individuals typically contract with the advertising department of a mass media outlet for a full-page ad or a one-minute commercial. An organization writes the advertisement, decides the type and graphics, and controls where and when the advertisement will be run. In other words, advertising is simply renting space in a mass medium. The lion's share of revenue for all mass media comes from the selling of advertising space.

Other differences between public relations activities and advertising include:

◆ Advertising works almost exclusively through mass media outlets; public relations relies on a number of communication tools—brochures, slide presentations, special events, speeches, news releases, feature stories, and so forth.

◆ Advertising is addressed to external audiences—primarily consumers of goods and services; public relations presents its message to specialized external audiences (stockholders, vendors, community leaders, environmental groups, and so on) and internal publics (employees).

◆ Advertising is readily identified as a specialized communication function; public relations is broader in scope, dealing with the policies and performance of the entire organization, from the morale of employees to the way telephone operators respond to calls.

◆ Advertising is often used as a communication tool in public relations, and public relations activity often supports advertising campaigns. Advertising's primary function is to sell goods and services; the public relations function is to create an environment in which the organization can thrive. The latter calls for dealing with economic, social, and political factors that can affect the organization.

The major disadvantage of advertising, of course, is the cost. A full-page ad in the national edition of the *Wall Street Journal*, for example, is $164,000 for black and white and $220,000 for full color. Advertising campaigns on network television, of course, can run into the millions of dollars. For example, advertisers paid $2.6 million for a 30-second Super Bowl ad in 2007. Because of this, companies are increasingly using a tool of public relations—product publicity—that is more cost effective and often more credible because the message appears in a news context. One national study, for example, found that almost 70 percent of consumers place more weight on media coverage than advertising when determining their trust of companies and buying a product or service.

How Public Relations Differs from Marketing

Public relations is distinct from marketing in several ways, although their boundaries often overlap. In fact, a poll of 1,015 U.S. adults by Harris Interactive/PRSA in 2006 found that 83 percent of the respondents agreed with the statement that public relations is "just another tool that companies can use to market their products or state their positions on various issues."

The functions overlap, for example, because both deal with an organization's relationships and employ similar communication tools to reach the public. Both have the ultimate purpose of assuring an organization's success and economic survival. Public relations and marketing, however, approach this task from somewhat different perspectives or worldviews.

This difference is illustrated by the descriptions of each field that a distinguished panel of educators and practitioners in public relations and marketing developed during a colloquium at San Diego State University. After a day of debate, they formed this definition of public relations:

> Public relations is the management process whose goal is to attain and maintain accord and positive behaviors among social groupings on which an organization depends in order to achieve its mission. Its fundamental responsibility is to build and maintain a hospitable environment for an organization.

The group defined marketing's goal in different terms:

> Marketing is the management process whose goal is to attract and satisfy customers (or clients) on a long-term basis in order to achieve an organization's economic objectives. Its fundamental responsibility is to build and maintain markets for an organization's products or services.

In other words, public relations is concerned with building relationships and generating goodwill for the organization; marketing is concerned with customers and selling products and services.

James E. Grunig, editor of *Excellence in Public Relations and Communication Management*, put the differences between public relations and marketing in sharp contrast:

> . . . the marketing function should communicate with the markets for an organization's goods and services. Public relations should be concerned with all the publics of the organization. The major purpose of marketing is to make money for the organization by increasing the slope of the demand curve. The major purpose of public relations is to save money for the organization by building relationships with publics that constrain or enhance the ability of the organization to meet its mission.

In this passage, Grunig points out a fundamental difference between marketing and public relations in terms of how the public is described. Marketing and advertising professionals tend to speak of "target markets," "consumers," and "customers." Public relations professionals tend to talk of "publics," "audiences," and "stakeholders." These groups may be any publics that are affected by or can affect an organization. According to Grunig, "Publics can arise within stakeholder categories—such as employees, communities, stockholders, governments, members, students, suppliers, and donors, as well as consumers."

How Public Relations Supports Marketing

Philip Kotler, professor of marketing at Northwestern University and author of a leading marketing textbook, says public relations is the fifth "P" of marketing strategy, which includes four other Ps—Product, Price, Place, and Promotion. As he wrote in the *Harvard Business Review*, "Public relations takes longer to cultivate, but when energized, it can help pull the company into the market."

When public relations is used to support directly an organization's marketing objectives, it is called *marketing communications*. This was identified as a component of public relations earlier in the chapter. Another term, coined by Thomas Harris in his book *The Marketer's Guide to Public Relations*, is *marketing public relations*. He says:

> I make a clear distinction between those public relations functions which support marketing, which I call Marketing Public Relations (MPR) and the other public relations activities that define the corporation's relationships with its non-customer publics, which I label Corporate Public Relations (CPR).

Dennis L. Wilcox, in his text *Public Relations Writing and Media Techniques*, lists eight ways in which public relations activities contribute to fulfilling marketing objectives:

1. Developing new prospects for new markets, such as people who inquire after seeing or hearing a product release in the news media

2. Providing third-party endorsements—via newspapers, magazines, radio, and television—through news releases about a company's products or services, community involvement, inventions, and new plans

3. Generating sales leads, usually through articles in the trade press about new products and services

4. Paving the way for sales calls

5. Stretching the organization's advertising and promotional dollars through timely and supportive releases about it and its products

6. Providing inexpensive sales literature, because articles about the company and its products can be reprinted as informative pieces for prospective customers

7. Establishing the corporation as an authoritative source of information on a given product

8. Helping to sell minor products that don't have large advertising budgets

Harris summarizes:

> In its market-support function, public relations is used to achieve a number of objectives. The most important of these are to raise awareness, to inform and educate, to gain understanding, to build trust, to make friends, to give people reasons to buy and finally to create a climate of consumer acceptance.

Toward an Integrated Perspective

Although well-defined differences exist among the fields of advertising, marketing, and public relations, there is an increasing realization that an organization's goals and objectives can be best accomplished through an integrated approach.

This understanding gave rise in the 1990s to such terms as *integrated marketing communications*, *convergent communications*, and *integrated communications*. Don Schulz, Stanley Tannenbaum, and Robert Lauterborn, authors of *Integrated Marketing Communications*, explain the title of their book as follows:

> A concept of marketing communication planning that recognizes the added value of a comprehensive plan that evaluates the strategic roles of a variety of communication disciplines—e.g., General Advertising, Direct Response, Sales Promotion, and Public Relations—and combines these disciplines to provide clarity, consistency, and maximum communication impact.

Several factors have fueled the trend toward integration. First is the downsizing of organizations. Many of them have consolidated departments and have also reduced staff dedicated to various communication disciplines. As a result, one department, with fewer employees, is expected to do a greater variety of communication tasks.

Second, organizational marketing and communication departments are making do with tighter budgets. Many organizations, to avoid the high cost of advertising, look for alternative ways to deliver messages. These may include (1) building buzz via word of mouth, (2) targeting influentials, (3) Web marketing, (4) grassroots marketing, (5) media relations and product publicity, and (6) event sponsorship.

Third is the increasing realization that advertising, with its high costs, isn't the silver bullet that it used to be. Part of the problem is the increasing clutter of advertising (one estimate is that the American consumer is exposed to 237 ads a day, or about 86,000 annually) and its general lack of credibility among consumers.

The IMC model

FIGURE 1.2

This illustration shows the components of an integrated marketing communication's model.

Al and Laura Ries, authors of the popular book (at least among public relations people) *The Fall of Advertising and The Rise of PR*, write, "We're beginning to see research that supports the superiority of PR over advertising to launch a brand. A recent study of 91 new product launches shows highly successful products are more likely to use PR-related activities than less successful ones." They go on to say, ". . . PR creates the brand. Advertising defends the brand."

Fourth, it is now widely recognized that the marketing of products and services can be affected by public and social policy issues. Environmental legislation influences packaging and the content of products, a proposed luxury tax on expensive autos affects sales of those cars, and a company's support of Planned Parenthood or health benefits for same-sex partners may spur a product boycott.

The impact of such factors, not traditionally considered by marketing managers, has led many professionals to believe that organizations should do a better job of integrating public relations and public affairs into their overall marketing considerations. In fact, David Corona, writing in the *Public Relations Journal* some years ago, was the first one to advance the idea that marketing's sixth "P" should be public policy.

Jack Bergen, senior vice president of corporate affairs and marketing for Siemens Corporation, agrees. He told *PRWeek* that public relations is the best place for leading strategy in marketing. He continued,

> In developing strategy, you have multiple stakeholders. PR people understand the richness of the audience that have an interest in the company; advertising just focuses on customers. Strategy is the development of options to accomplish an objective. PR people can develop these as they have the multiplicity of audiences and channels to use to reach them.

The concept of integration, therefore, is the increasing sophistication of organizations to use a variety of strategies and tactics to convey a consistent message in a variety of forms. The metaphor might be the golfer with a variety of clubs in her bag. She may use one club (public relations) to launch a product, another club (advertising) to reinforce the message, and yet another club (Web marketing) to actually sell the product or service to a well-defined audience.

The golf metaphor also reflects a realization on the part of management and marketing executives that public relations is an effective strategy in several important areas. Marketing executives in a 2006 *PRWeek* survey, for example, ranked the effectiveness of public relations higher than advertising or marketing in nine areas:

- ◆ Brand reputation
- ◆ Corporate reputation
- ◆ Cultivating thought leaders
- ◆ Strategy development
- ◆ Launching a new product
- ◆ Building awareness
- ◆ Generating word of mouth
- ◆ Message development
- ◆ Overcoming a crisis

Careers in Public Relations

A person entering public relations may develop a career in numerous areas of this increasingly diverse field. Similarly, the variety of personal traits and skills that bring success is wide. Although certain abilities, such as writing well, are basic for all areas, experienced public relations practitioners may go on to develop increased skills in a particular practice area, such as investor relations, governmental affairs, or brand management, or even crisis communications and corporate social responsibility.

A Changing Focus in Public Relations

Traditionally, it was widely believed that public relations practitioners should begin their careers as newspaper reporters or wire service correspondents to polish their writing skills and to learn firsthand how the media function. In an earlier era (see Chapter 2), a large percentage of public relations people did indeed have newspaper or broadcast experience. In fact, many of the leading pioneers in public relations were originally journalists.

This, however, is no longer true for several reasons. First, the field of public relations has broadened far beyond the concept of "media relations" and placing publicity in the mass media. Today, much writing in public relations is done for controlled media such as company publications, direct mail campaigns to key audiences, speech writing, brochures, and material posted on the organization's Web site. No media savvy or contacts are necessary. Writing skill and knowledge of the media are still vital, but so is training in management, logistics, event management, coalition building, budgeting, and supervision of personnel. Consequently, a *PRWeek* survey found that less than a third of current practitioners are former journalists.

The growth of public relations as a career field distinctly separate from journalism has spawned any number of public relations courses, sequences, and majors. The Commission on Public Relations Education, which includes public relations educators and representatives from all of the major professional organizations, has set the standard by saying that the ideal curriculum should have seven basic courses: (1) introduction to public relations, (2) case studies in public relations, (3) public relations research, measurement, and evaluation, (4) public relations writing and production, (5) public relations planning and management, (6) public relations campaigns, and (7) supervised public relations internship. Increasingly, many universities are offering joint public relations/advertising programs, in part because of the growing trend in integrated marketing communications, which was discussed earlier in this chapter.

Public relations, at least in the United States, has traditionally been taught in departments and schools of journalism. But some professionals are even questioning whether this makes sense in the 21st century because public relations is no longer exclusively a journalistic-type activity that involves working with the media. James Lukaszewski, a well-known consultant and speaker in the public relations field, is quite blunt. He wrote in *The Strategist*, "At minimum, PR programs belong in marketing sequences rather than journalism sequences. The sooner we can reflect a more managementlike perspective, the more quickly we'll find ourselves called in for our advice and counsel."

Indeed, many European universities offer a public relations curriculum in other academic areas. At the University of Belgrade in Serbia, for example, public relations is located in the Faculty of Economics. And in Latvia, the strongest public relations program in the country is taught at the Turiba School of Business Administration.

on the job
INSIGHTS

Nine Ways Public Relations Contributes to the Bottom Line

I t is often said that public relations is a management process, not an event. Patrick Jackson, active in the top leadership of the PRSA for many years and one of the best-known public relations counselors in the United States, formulated the following chart showing how public relations can contribute to the success of any organization.

PROCESS	PRINCIPAL ACTIVITIES	OUTCOMES
1. Awareness and information	Publicity, promotion, audience targeting, publications	Pave the way for sales, fundraising, stock offerings, etc.
2. Organizational motivation	Internal relations and communications, OD interventions	Build morale, teamwork, productivity, corporate culture; work toward One Clear Voice Outreach
3. Issue anticipation	Research, liaison with all publics, issue anticipation teams	Early warning of issues, social/political change, constituency unrest
4. Opportunity identification	Interaction with internal and external audiences, "knowing the business"	Discover new markets, products, methods, allies, positive issues
5. Crisis management	Respond to or blanket issues, disasters, attacks; coalition building	Protect position, retain allies and constituents, keep normal operations going despite battles
6. Overcoming executive isolation	Counseling senior managers about what's really happening, research	Realistic, competitive, enlightened decisions
7. Change agentry	Corporate culture, similar techniques, research	Ease resistance to change, promote smooth transition, reassure affected constituencies
8. Social responsibility	Social accountancy, research, mount public interest projects and tie-ins, volunteerism, philanthropy	Create reputation, enhance economic success through "double bottom line," earn trust
9. Influencing public policy	Constituency relations, coalition building, lobbying, grassroots campaigns	Public consent to activities, products, policies; political barriers removed

The Range of Public Relations Work

Women and men entering public relations may work in company departments, public relations firms that serve clients, or a wide range of organizations that require public relations services. A 2006 national survey by PRSA and Bacon's Information, Inc. gives a snapshot of where public relations professionals are employed. The result:

Corporations (private and public)	34 percent
Nonprofits/Foundations	19 percent
Public relations firms	17 percent
Government (all levels)	10 percent
Educational institutions	8 percent
Independent consulting	8 percent
Health care	1 percent
Professional Associations	1 percent
Other	2 percent

Detailed discussion of these areas appears in later chapters.

Personal Qualifications and Attitudes

Any attempt to define a single public relations type of personality is pointless, because the field is so diverse that it needs people of differing personalities. Some practitioners deal with clients and the public in person on a frequent basis; others work primarily at desks, planning, writing, and researching. Many do both.

Five Essential Abilities

Those who plan careers in public relations should develop knowledge and ability in five basic areas, no matter what area of work they enter. These are (1) writing skill, (2) research ability, (3) planning expertise, (4) problem-solving ability, and (5) business/economics competence.

1. Writing skill. The ability to put information and ideas onto paper clearly and concisely is essential. Good grammar and good spelling are vital. Misspelled words and sloppy sentence structure look amateurish. The importance of writing skill is emphasized in a career advice column in *Working Woman*: "I changed careers, choosing public relations as having the best potential, but found it difficult to persuade employers that my writing and interpersonal skills were sufficient for an entry-level job in the profession."

2. Research ability. Arguments for causes must have factual support instead of generalities. A person must have the persistence and ability to gather information from a variety of sources, as well as to conduct original research by designing and implementing opinion polls or audits. Too many public relations programs fail because the organization does not assess audience needs and perceptions. Skillful use of the Internet and computer databases is an important element of research work. Reading current newspapers and magazines also is important. See Figure 1.1.

> " PR people are the story tellers. It's our job to help find the authenticity at the core of our companies and clients, and tell those stories to the world in real words that will really be heard. "
>
> ——— Fred Cook, president of Golin Harris public relations

3. Planning expertise. A public relations program involves a number of communication tools and activities that must be carefully planned and coordinated. A person needs to be a good planner to make certain that materials are distributed in a timely manner, events occur without problems, and budgets are not exceeded. Public relations people must be highly organized, detail-oriented, and able to see the big picture.

4. Problem-solving ability. Innovative ideas and fresh approaches are needed to solve complex problems or to make a public relations program unique and memorable. Increased salaries and promotions go to people who show top management how to solve problems creatively.

5. Business/economics competence. The increasing emphasis on public relations as a management function calls for public relations students to learn the "nuts and bolts" of business and economics. According to Joel Curren, senior vice president of CKPR in Chicago, "The greatest need PR people have is understanding how a business and, more importantly, how a public company operates." Rachel Beanland, a professional interviewed by *Public Relations Tactics*, noted that almost all of the recent Public Relations grads she talked to wished they had taken a marketing course. In sum, students preparing for careers in public relations should obtain a solid grounding by taking courses in economics, management, and marketing.

This Wal-Mart employment ad illustrates the variety of public relations jobs available in a large retail chain.

It should be noted, of course, that all jobs in public relations don't require all five essential abilities in equal proportion. It often depends on your specific job responsibilities and assignments. See the Insight box (What Employers Want: 10 Qualities) for more tips from employment specialists.

Systematic research has shown that there is a hierarchy of roles in public relations practice. Professors Glen Broom and David Dozier of San Diego State University were among the first researchers to identify organizational roles ranging from the communication technician to the communication manager.

Practitioners in the technician role, for example, are primarily responsible for producing communication products and implementing decisions made by others. They take photographs, write brochures, prepare news releases, and organize events. They function primarily at the "tactical" level of public relations work; they do not participate in policy decision making, nor are they responsible for outcomes. Many entry-level positions in public relations are at the technician level, but there are also many experienced practitioners whose specialty is "tactical" duties such as writing and editing newsletters, maintaining information on the company's intranet or Web site, or even working primarily with the media in the placement of publicity.

At the other end of the scale is the communication manager. Practitioners playing this role are perceived by others as the organization's public relations experts. They make communication policy decisions and are held accountable by others and themselves for the success or failure of communication programs. Managers counsel senior management, oversee multiple communication strategies, and supervise a number of employees who are responsible for "tactical" implementation.

Other studies conducted since Broom and Dozier's have indicated that the differences between managers and technicians aren't that clear-cut. In smaller operations, a public relations professional may perform daily activities at both the manager and the technician level. Another way of looking at job levels in public relations is given in the Insights box on page 30. In addition, the Wal-Mart ad gives a real-world example of the kinds of skills and experience that employers are seeking.

The Value of Internships

Internships are extremely popular in the communications industry, and a student whose résumé includes practical work experience along with a good academic record has an important advantage. The Commission on Public Relations Education believes the internship is so important that it is one of the seven basic courses it recommends for any quality college or university public relations curriculum.

An internship is a win-win situation for both the student and the organization. The student, in most cases, not only receives academic credit, but also gets firsthand knowledge of work in the professional world. This gives the student an advantage in getting that all-important first job after graduation. In many cases, recent graduates

on the job INSIGHTS

What Employers Want: 10 Qualities

*P*R *Tactics*, the monthly publication of the PRSA, asked job-placement experts what set of skills and experience was needed in today's employment market. Here are the top 10 suggestions:

Good Writing

Excellent writing skills are more necessary now than ever before.

Intelligence

Although the descriptions vary from "bright," "clever," and "quick-witted," all placement executives agree that modern public relations isn't a refuge for those with a mediocre mind and only a good personality.

Cultural Literacy

Employers want individuals who are well rounded and well educated about the arts, humanities, and current events. According to *PR Tactics*, "You can't expect management to take your advice if you have no shared frame of reference."

Know a Good Story When You See One

The ability to manage your organization's image—in both large and small ways—starts with the identification and management of good stories that give the organization visibility, build brand recognition, and enhance the organization's reputation.

Media Savvy

Media convergence means that there are now multiple platforms—print media, Webcasts, Internet news sites, radio and television, and so on. Each platform has different deadlines, formats, and needs. Understanding this and being able to work with editors in each area is essential.

Contacts

"Cordial relationships with people in media, government, industry groups, and nonprofits, as well as colleagues in other companies will serve you well. The ability to pick up the phone and get crucial information or make things happen is essential."

Good Business Sense

The best companies weave public relations into their overall business strategy. To work at that level, however, public relations practitioners need to have a firm understanding of how the business operates in general and an employer's industry in particular.

Broad Communications Experience

All midlevel and senior positions require the individual to have familiarity with all aspects of communications, from the in-house newsletter to media relations and investor relations.

Specialized Experience

After getting some general experience, the individual should consider developing a specialty. Health care, finance, and technology are some of the promising areas.

Avoid Career Clichés

If the only reason for getting into the business is because you "like people" and enjoy organizing events, you should think about another field. Employers are looking for broad-based individuals with multiple communication and problem-solving skills.

Source: Hulin, Belinda. "10 Things You Need to Succeed." *Public Relations Tactics*, April 2004, p. 11.

often are hired by their former internship employers because they have already proved themselves.

Indeed, *PRWeek* reporter Sara Calabro says:

Agencies and corporate communications departments are beginning to see interns as the future of their companies, not merely as gophers that they can pass the grunt work off to. While a few years ago, it was typical for an intern to work for nothing, it is almost unheard of for an internship to be unpaid these days. Examples of the essential work now entrusted to interns include tasks such as media monitoring, writing press releases, financial estimating, and compiling status reports. In many cases, interns are being included in all team and client meetings, as well as brainstorming sessions.

Many major public relations firms have formal internship programs. At Edelman Worldwide, for example, students enroll in "Edel-U," an internal training program that exposes them to all aspects of agency work. The summer internship program at Weber Shandick in Boston is called "Weber University." Calabro cites Jane Dolan, a senior account executive, who says that upper management is always incredibly impressed with the work that interns do for their final projects. "It is amazing to see them go from zero to 100 in a matter of months," says Dolan.

Hill & Knowlton also has an extensive internship training program in its New York office, taking about 40 interns a year from an applicant pool of about 600 to 700 students. In its view, the internship program is "the cheapest and most effective recruiting tool available." Ketchum also gets about 800 resumes each year for 12 to 14 summer positions, which pays a weekly stipend. According to Scott Proper, SVP at Ketchum, "You can walk the halls any day and find former interns in pretty senior positions."

It's not always possible, of course, for a student to do an internship in Chicago or New York. However, many opportunities are available at local public relations firms, businesses, and nonprofit agencies. It is important, however, that the organization have at least one experienced public relations professional who can mentor a student and

on the job
INSIGHTS

Public Relations Personality Checklist

This checklist, based on careful evaluation, can measure the effectiveness of your personality in terms of the public relations profession.

Rate each item "yes" or "no." Each "yes" counts for 4 points. A "no" doesn't count. Anything below 60 is a poor score. A score between 60 and 80 suggests you should analyze your weak areas and take steps to correct them. Scores above 80 indicate an effective public relations personality.

- Good sense of humor
- Positive and optimistic
- Friendly, meet people easily

- Can keep a conversation going with anybody
- Take frustration and rejection in stride
- Able to persuade others easily
- Well-groomed, businesslike appearance
- Flair for showmanship
- Strong creative urge
- Considerate and tactful
- Adept in use of words
- Able to gain management's confidence
- Enjoy being with people
- Enjoy listening

- Enjoy helping other people resolve problems
- Curious about many things
- Enjoy reading in diverse areas
- Determined to complete projects
- High energy level
- Can cope with sudden emergencies
- See mistakes as learning experiences
- Factual and objective
- Respect other people's viewpoints
- Perceptive and sensitive
- Quickly absorb and retain information

Source: PRSSA Forum.

ensure that he or she gets an opportunity to do a variety of tasks to maximize the learning experience. For More information on guidelines and programs, see the online Internship Guide posted by a Public Relations Society of America task force (www.prsa.org).

Although national and international firms routinely pay interns, this often is not the case at the local level. Many smaller companies claim that they cannot afford to pay, or that the opportunity to gain training and experience should be more than adequate compensation. Dave DeVries, a senior public relations manager for the PCS Division of Sprint, disagrees. He wrote in PRSA's *Tactics*, "Unpaid internships severely limit the field of potential candidates" because, as he points out, the best and brightest students will always gravitate to employers who pay.

Indeed, there seems to be a strong correlation between paid internships and starting salaries in the field. Most public relations firms and departments usually provide some level of paid internships, and entry-level salaries are comparatively high. On the other hand, television stations are notorious for not paying interns, and entry-level salaries are the lowest ($24,400) in the communications field. Salaries will be discussed shortly.

> "Internship programs can be much more than a means to get young, inexpensive talent. Designed properly, they can offer a significant return on investment for agencies."
> —— Mark Hand, reporter for *PRWeek*

Salaries in Public Relations

Public relations work pays relatively well compared to other communications professions. Many practitioners say they like the income and opportunities for steady advancement, and they also enjoy the variety and fast pace that the field provides.

Entry-Level Salaries

Several surveys have attempted to pinpoint the national average salary for recent graduates in their first full-time job in the public relations field. Probably the most definitive survey is the one conducted by Lee Becker and his associates at the University of Georgia. They work with journalism and mass communications programs throughout the nation to compile a list of recent graduates who are then surveyed (www.grady.uga.edu/annualsurveys/).

The latest data available, published in 2007, shows that the median entry-level salary for all recent graduates working in the communications field was $30,000. Public relations graduates, as the chart below indicates, made more than print and broadcast journalists but slightly less than those working on trade publications or the World Wide Web. The median annual salaries reported by recent graduates in the various fields are as follows:

Public relations	$30,000
Daily newspapers	$27,000
Weeklies	$24,700
Radio	$27,000
Television	$24,400
Cable television	$30,000
Advertising	$30,000
Consumer magazines	$28,000
Newsletters/trades	$31,000
World Wide Web	$31,500

Another survey, conducted by *PRWeek*, places a more optimistic figure on starting salaries in public relations. Its 2007 survey of salaries, for example, found that entry-level salaries—professionals with less than two years' experience—averaged $40,000. In its annual career guide, *PRWeek* estimates that entry-level jobs in corporations range from $32,000 to $48,000. In public relations firms, the range is $28,000 to $40,000 for 0–3 years of experience.

Salaries for Experienced Professionals

Key components of *PRWeek*'s 2007 salary survey are listed in the Insights box on page 32, which shows the national average for all practitioners is about $81,000. Salaries are somewhat higher for those with 21 or more years' experience: The median salary then jumps to $155,000. When salaries are compared by gender, however, there are some major differences, which will be discussed shortly.

Salaries, of course, depend on a number of factors, including geographic location, job title, the industry, and even the type of public relations specialty. Major metropolitan areas, for example, generally have higher salaries, but there are some regional differences, according to the *PRWeek* survey. Practitioners based in the Western United States, for example, have median incomes of $90,600, which is slightly above the $90,100 in the Northeastern states. Practitioners in the Midwest have a median income of $79,200, but those living in the Northwest earn about $74,000. The Southeast comes in at $68,800, about a $1,000 more than the lowest-paid area of the nation, the southern Central states ($67,700). Differences, to a degree, somewhat coincide with the cost of living in these areas.

Job title also means a lot. A senior vice president (SVP) receives a median salary of $192,650 whereas an account manager at a public relations firm gets $59,800. The lowly account coordinator, usually the entry-level position for recent graduates, gets a median salary of $30,300. In terms of work setting, corporate median salaries are $94,190 and nonprofits/charities are at the bottom of the list with $63,190. Surprisingly, self-employed consultants report good incomes in *PRWeek*'s survey of practitioners, with median incomes of $95,620. In terms of specialty areas, work in telecommunications tops the chart at $105,800. On the other hand, the area of travel/tourism pays the least with $56,600 as a median income.

In terms of specialty areas, practitioners specializing in reputation management report median incomes of $115,500, followed by crisis management ($95,830). Financial public

---

on the job
INSIGHTS

Job Levels in Public Relations

- **Entry-Level Technician**   Use of technical "craft" skills to disseminate information, persuade, gather data, or solicit feedback

- **Supervisor**   Supervises projects, including planning, scheduling, budgeting, organizing, leading, controlling, and problem solving

- **Manager**   Constituency and issue-trend analysis; departmental management, including organizing, budgeting, leading, controlling, evaluating, and problem solving

- **Director**   Constituency and issue-trend analysis; communication and operational planning at departmental level, including planning, organizing, leading, controlling, evaluating, and problem solving

- **Executive**   Organizational leadership and management skills, including developing the organizational vision, corporate mission, strategic objectives, annual goals, businesses, broad strategies, policies, and systems

Source: Adapted from the *Public Relations Professional Career Guide.* Public Relations Society of America, 33 Maiden Lane, New York, NY 10038.

relations is also a good specialty if you want to maximize income. Community relations, on the other hand, may be good for personal satisfaction but not financial reward ($54,170).

You should be aware that *PRWeek's* salary figures are based on responses from 1,500 practitioners, and the salaries reported may not be indicative of the entire field. For example, the median salary for executive vice presidents was based on only 25 responses. The average salary for a senior vice president was based on 42 responses. In the absence of more complete salary data, however, surveys by publications such as *PRWeek* have become a standard reference in the industry.

The Arthur W. Page Society, a group of senior communication executives representing many of America's Fortune 500 corporations, also conducts an annual survey of its members regarding budgets and executive compensation. In general, compensation for the top communications officer in the organization ranges from $269,000 to almost $500,000. In general, salaries increase with the size of the corporation. There are, of course, other forms of compensation. Former Edelman Worldwide vice chairman Leslie Dach received $3 million in Wal-Mart shares for taking the executive vice president post at the retail giant, according to *Jack O'Dwyer's Newsletter*. His annual salary was not disclosed.

A good source for checking current salaries for public relations in major cities throughout the United States and around the world is www.workinpr.com. It posts current openings and also provides the salary ranges for various job classifications.

Salaries for Women: The Gender Gap

National statistics, compiled by the U.S. Department of Labor, show that women in all occupations earn about 76 cents for every $1 earned by a man. Another study, by the American Association of University Women, says recent female college graduates earn only 80 percent of what male graduates earn. The public relations field is no exception. The *PRWeek* survey found the median salary for men was $105,450, whereas women made $70,800, or about a third less than their male peers.

Indeed, this discrepancy in salaries exists across several levels of experience. Men and women, with less than five years' experience, have median incomes of $48,000 and $43,810 respectively. The gap becomes larger after more than five years' experience: Men earn $124,222 compared to $85,470 for women.

A number of studies have probed the pay differential between men and women in public relations. The first studies, starting in the 1980s, simply noted the gap without taking into consideration the multiple factors that could lead to discrepancies. Some of these factors included (1) the number of years in the field, (2) technician duties versus managerial responsibilities, (3) the nature of the industry, (4) the size of the organization, and (5) women's attempts to balance work and family. The 2007 *PRWeek* survey, for example, notes that the average male respondent has worked in the field for 13.6 years as compared to the average female respondent with only 8.6 years in the field. One respondent (a male, of course) explained the salary difference by saying, ". . . women tend not to negotiate very well on their behalf."

Julie O'Neil, a professor at Texas Christian University, has another explanation. She says, "Women are segregated into the lower-level technician role, spending time on routine activities such as writing, editing, and handling media relations. Conversely, more men are promoted into the more powerful managerial role, engaging in such activities as counseling senior management, and making key policy decisions."

Others have tried to explain the salary differential in other ways. Women, for example, tend to take more time off than men to raise children or for other personal

on the job INSIGHTS

An Overview of Salaries in the Public Relations Field

P *RWeek* conducts an annual survey of salaries. The following tables are excerpted from the 2007 survey, which received responses from 1,500 practitioners in the field.

Respondents by Gender

Female	64 percent
Male	36 percent

Median Overall Salaries

All respondents	$ 80,930
Men	$105,450
Women	$ 70,800

Salary by Gender/Years of Experience

Less than 5 years

Men	$ 48,000
Women	$ 43,810

More than 5 years

Men	$124,222
Women	$ 85,470

Median Salary by Years of Experience

Less than 2 years	$ 40,380
3–4 years	$ 49,680
5–6 years	$ 61,790
7–10 years	$ 80,060
11–15 years	$101,190
16–20 years	$126,840
More than 21 years	$155,000

Median Salary by Work Setting

Self-Employed	$ 95,620
Corporation	$ 94,190
Public Relations Firm	$ 77,500
Trade Association	$ 75,000
Government	$ 73,610
Education	$ 65,790
Nonprofit	$ 63,190

Median Salary by Discipline

Reputation Mgt	$115,570
Crisis Mgt	$ 95,830
Financial PR	$ 95,310
Employee Comm	$ 87,500
Brand Mgt	$ 82,260
Government Relations	$ 76,960
Marketing Comm	$ 76,910
Community Relations	$ 54,170

Median Salary by Sector

Telecommunications	$105,800
Food & Beverage	$102,700
Arts/Entertainment	$ 72,600
Financial Services	$ 96,900
Health Care	$ 95,100
Manufacturing	$ 94,100
Tech/Internet	$ 89,200
Sports	$ 87,500
Government	$ 69,500
Education	$ 66,900
Trade Associations	$ 66,800
Nonprofit/Charity	$ 63,800
Retail	$ 60,000
Travel/Tourism	$ 56,600

Median Salary by Job Level

Executive VP	$192,650
Senior VP	$170,700
VP	$150,000
Account Supervisor	$ 71,100
PR Manager	$ 70,300
Account Manager	$ 59,800
Account Coordinator	$ 30,300

Source: "Salary Survey 2007." *PRWeek*, February 26, 2007, pp. 15–22. www.prweek.com

reasons. Others have pointed out that women have a tendency to work in areas of public relations that traditionally have low salaries, such as community relations, employee communications, or nonprofits. In contrast, a large percentage of practitioners in finance and investor relations—which pay well—are men.

Professors Linda Aldoory (University of Maryland) and Elizabeth Toth (formerly of Syracuse University and now at the University of Maryland) also explored discrepancies in salaries in an article for the *Journal of Public Relations Research* (2002). They explored a number of factors, but essentially concluded:

> The difference in the average salary of male respondents compared to female respondents was statistically significant. Regression analysis revealed that years of public relations experience accounted for much of the variance, but that gender and job interruptions also accounted for the salary difference. Age and education level were not found to be a significant influence on salary.

The role of women in public relations, and the increased feminization of the field (70 percent of the practitioners in the United States are women), will be discussed as a major trend line in the next chapter.

The Value of Public Relations

This chapter has outlined the size and global scope of public relations, provided some definitions, discussed the various activities of public relations, and explored how it differs from and is similar to journalism, advertising, and marketing. The case for an organization integrating all of its communications for maximum effectiveness has also been made. We've also discussed careers in public relations, the qualities needed in public relations professionals, and the salaries that can be earned in the field of public relations.

Today more than ever, the world needs not more information but sensitive communicators and facilitators who can explain the goals and aspirations of individuals, organizations, and governments to others in a socially responsive manner. Experts in communication and public opinion must provide their employers and clients with knowledge of what others are thinking to guide them in setting their policies for the common good.

Indeed, in this era of heightened environmental concern, accountability, and transparency, no organization exists solely for its own purposes; it must also serve society as a whole. Another way of expressing this point is the idea that no organization can exist without the express permission of the government and society at large.

> We provide a voice in the marketplace of ideas, facts, and viewpoints to aid informed public debate.
> ——Public Relations Society of America, defining the role of public relations in today's society

Tom Glover, writing in *Profile*, the magazine of the Institute of Public Relations in the United Kingdom, believes "[c]lear and consistent communication helps organizations achieve their goals, employees to work to their potential, customers to make informed choices, investors to make an accurate assessment of an organization, and society to form fair judgments of industries, organizations, and issues."

Public relations provides businesses and society with a vital service. On a practical level, Laurence Moskowitz, chairman and CEO of Medialink, says that public relations is ". . . informative. It's part of the news, the program, the article, the stuff readers and

PRCASEBOOK

Abundant Forests for All: An Integrated Public Affairs Campaign

Do you know that the United States is covered by 750 million acres of forestland, an amount that has remained essentially unchanged for the past century? Or that the annual net growth of U.S. forests is 36 percent higher than the volume of annual tree removals?

Probably not. And that's why the wood and paper products industry formed the Abundant Forests Alliance (AFA). The industry faced the challenge of correcting common misconceptions about forest management and also telling its story about sustainable forestry practices. Porter Novelli, a national public relations firm, was given the assignment of developing an integrated communications program that would reach consumers, customers, and opinion leaders.

The slogan of the AFA campaign was "Renew, Reuse, and Respect." Research indicated that the key target audience should be 35-to-54-year-old college-educated women with kids at home because they are networked in their communities and have some interest in the environment. They also place value on leaving a legacy of making the planet a better place for future generations. Porter Novelli dubbed them "legacy moms."

The AFA campaign was launched with the publication of a children's book, *The Tree Farmer*, written by Chuck Leavell, the keyboardist for the Rolling Stones who also happens to be a tree farmer. The book used the theme of "Renew, Reuse, Respect" and was positioned as an activity for legacy moms and their children to do together.

To support the launch, three basic public relations tactics were used: (1) the establishment of a Web site (www.thetreefarmer.org), (2) media outreach to publications such as *Real Simple* and *Ladies Home Journal*, and (3) a satellite media tour with Chuck Leavell, which included an interview on CNN. In addition, Leavell appeared on the *Today* show on behalf of AFA where he talked with Matt Lauer about the importance of trees, tree farms, and how wood contributes to our daily lives. At the end of the interview, Leavell made a donation of 200,000 books to *Today*'s Holiday Toy Drive which was met with cheers and applause from the crowd gathered on the plaza.

AFA also organized several other charitable and environmental education projects. In Gulfport, Mississippi, Leavell donated 10,000 books to local children living in the area destroyed by Hurricane Katrina. AFA also worked with Project Learning Tree (PLT), a nonprofit, to fund environmental outreach programs in Dallas and Los Angeles.

The second component of the AFA campaign focused on the use of wood and paper products. It commissioned lifestyle expert Katie Brown to develop gift ideas made of wood and paper that children could make for Mother's Day. Another tactic was in-store scrapbooking demonstrations at 500 Wal-Mart stores that attracted more than 60,000 participants. A series of podcasts, called "Scrapcasts," were developed by professional paper artist Lynette Young and made available on AFA's Web site. Each episode features tips and ideas on creating scrapbooks. The podcasts were publicized in lifestyle magazines and a radio media tour. The highlight was an interview with Young on *Live with Regis and Kelly*.

Paid advertising also was a part of the AFA campaign (see example on this page). A series of lifestyle-oriented ads featured special moments and occasions such as a

This is one of the appealing ads that the Abundant Forest Alliance placed in magazines such as *Family Circle* to publicize its Web site.

The true magic
of forests is that even when you leave them, you never really do.

From the wood in our homes to the paper at the office, it's amazing how often forests touch all of our lives. Maybe you're wondering, if we use so many of these products, will there be enough trees for future generations? Yes, if we balance the needs of nature with our needs. That's why the people of the wood and paper products industry plant more than 1.7 million new trees every day, work to protect wildlife habitats and encourage recycling. So while this day may not last forever, at least our forests can. Learn more at abundantforests.org.

Abundant Forests Alliance
Renew. Reuse. Respect.™

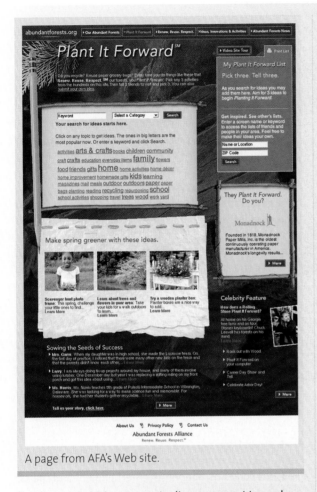

A page from AFA's Web site.

such publications as *Ladies Home Journal, Time, Newsweek,* and *Vanity Fair.* There was also online banner advertising.

Another form of integration was the development of an extensive Web site, www.abundantforests.org. It is a resource for legacy moms and is filled with tips and tools to help them stay engaged with environmental responsibility and to learn more about paper and wood as a renewable resource. In addition to the Scrapcast already mentioned, the site includes such items as a downloadable hiking journal, a "Know Your Trees" page that tell viewers what kind of trees are used for such items as baseball bats and pencils, and how to make your own gifts with paper and wood.

The most recent development on AFA's Web site is an interactive Plant It Forward program. Here, visitors can create a "playlist" of their favorite ideas, post their comments and ideas, and even find others who are registered on the site. The site was highlighted by *Parenting Magazine* as "A Site We Love."

AFA's campaign, which is ongoing, has been a success. In the first year, the campaign generated 234 million impressions (a number based on the circulation of publications and estimated size of broadcast audiences) and 118,000 unique Web visitors, spending an average of 4.38 minutes at the site. More important, survey research shows improved public perceptions about the state of forests in North America, the number of trees cut versus the number grown, and the commitment of the wood and paper products industry to preserving forests in North America.

The $10 million campaign was named the Public Affairs Campaign of the Year (2007) by *PRWeek*, and it also received several awards of excellence from the advertising industry for multimedia campaigns.

family camping trip, a mom stealing a moment to read a book, and a woman gift-wrapping an elegant present. The idea was to convey the beauty of wood and paper, but also include facts about the industry's efforts to properly manage the nation's forests. Ad placements were made in

viewers want. . . ." Indeed, the Harris Interactive/PRSA survey previously mentioned also found that 71 percent of its respondents agreed with the statement that public relations professionals can "help raise awareness about important issues that the public might not know about."

Patrick Jackson, a former president of the PRSA and publisher of *PR Reporter,* said it best:

As soon as there was Eve with Adam, there were relationships, and in every society, no matter how small or primitive, public communication needs and problems inevitably emerge and must be resolved. Public relations is devoted to the essential function of building and improving human relationships.

SUMMARY

Global Scope

Public relations is well established in the United States and throughout the world. Growth is strong in Europe and Asia, particularly China.

A Variety of Definitions

Common terms in most definitions of public relations are *deliberate, planned, performance, public interest, two-way communication*, and a *strategic management function*. Also popular is the concept of building and maintaining mutually beneficial relationships.

Public Relations as a Process

The public relations process can be described with the RACE acronym: **R**esearch, **A**ction, **C**ommunication, **E**valuation. The process is a constant cycle; feedback and program adjustment are integral components of the overall process.

The Components of Public Relations

Public relations work includes the following components: counseling, media relations, publicity, community relations, governmental affairs, employee relations, investor relations, development/fund-raising, special events, and marketing communications.

Other Terms for Public Relations

Public relations is an umbrella term; many large organizations prefer such terms as *corporate communications, corporate affairs, public affairs*, or even *global communications* to describe the public relations function. Less flattering terms include *flack* and *spin doctor*.

How Public Relations Differs from Journalism

Although writing is an important activity in both public relations and journalism, the scope, objectives, and channels are different for each field.

How Public Relations Differs from Advertising

Publicity, one area of public relations, uses mass media to disseminate messages, as does advertising. The format and context, however, differ. Publicity goes through media gatekeepers who make the ultimate decision whether to use the material as part of a news story. Advertising involves paid space and time and is easily identified as being separate from news/editorial content.

How Public Relations Differs from Marketing

The functions of public relations often overlap with marketing, but the primary purpose of public relations is to build relationships and generate goodwill with a variety of publics. Marketing focuses on customers and the selling of products/services. Public relations can be part of a marketing strategy; in such cases, it is often called marketing communications.

Toward an Integrated Perspective

An organization's goals and objectives are best achieved by integrating the activities of advertising, marketing, and public relations to create a consistent message. Integration requires teamwork and the recognition that each field has strengths that complement and reinforce one another.

The Changing Face of Public Relations

In the past, those entering public relations were often former journalists, but that is no longer the case because public relations has evolved beyond publicity and media relations. In addition, public relations is now widely recognized as its own distinct academic discipline in colleges and universities throughout the world.

The Range of Work

Public relations professionals are employed in a variety of fields: corporations, nonprofits, entertainment and sports, politics and government, education, and international organizations and businesses.

Five Essential Abilities

Those who plan careers in public relations should be competent in the following areas: writing, research, planning, problem-solving, and business/economics.

Internships Are Valuable

Students should participate in internships throughout college as part of their preprofessional training in public relations. Paid internships are the most desirable.

Salaries in Public Relations

Entry-level salaries are higher in public relations than in many other communications fields. An entry-level person can earn a salary in the $30,000 to $40,000 range, whereas a more experienced professional can earn into the six figures. Although the gender gap has somewhat narrowed, in general, women earn less than men.

The Value of Public Relations

The world today doesn't need more information; it needs sensitive, well-educated individuals who can interpret the information and determine why and how it is relevant to people's lives. Public relations people must explain the goals and objectives of their clients and employers to the public and, at the same time, provide them with guidance about their responsibility to the public interest.

CASE ACTIVITY What Would You Do?

Cold Stone Creamery is a relatively new ice-cream company that faces stiff competition in the marketplace from such established brands as Ben & Jerry's, Baskin-Robbins, and Häagen-Dazs.

The first store was established in Tempe, Arizona, in 1998. Since then, the company has expanded to more than 500 stores (franchises) nationwide. Its market niche is that customers can personalize their serving by choosing a base flavor and then mixing it with a number of toppings. Employees do the mixing by hand on a frozen granite stone (hence the company name).

The challenge, of course, is to generate more store revenue and to increase market share. Research shows that the typical Cold Stone customer is a woman between the ages of 24 and 35, but that she also brings her friends and other family members with her.

The company has decided to do an integrated communications program for the next year that would involve public relations, advertising, and in-store marketing promotions for some new products, such as ice-cream cakes and nonfat flavors. The focus would be on enhancing the visibility of its stores at the local level and making it a distinct brand among the clutter of other ice-cream franchises in the community. Do some brainstorming. What ideas and activities would you suggest? You have to be creative because you don't have a big budget.

QUESTIONS for Review and Discussion

1. How many people are estimated to work in public relations around the world? Is public relations growing as a field in terms of employees and revenues?
2. There are many definitions of public relations. Of those listed, which one do you prefer? Why?
3. What key words and phrases are found in most definitions of public relations?
4. What does the acronym RACE stand for?
5. Public relations is described as a loop process. What component makes it a loop rather than a linear process?
6. Review the official statement on public relations by the PRSA. In what way did it change your initial perception of public relations as a field?
7. What are the components of basic public relations practice? Which one sounds the most interesting to you as a possible career specialty?
8. What other terms are used by organizations to describe the public relations function? Do you have preference for any of them? Explain.
9. How do you think portrayals of various careers in films and television shows shape public perceptions? Do you think series such as *Sex and the City* paint a negative or positive image of public relations as a career? Or do such portrayals make public relations appear to be more glamorous than it actually is?
10. What is spin? To some, it has negative connotations that conjure up images of manipulation and dishonesty. To others, it's simply a slang word for telling the organization's perspective on an issue or product. What do you think? Would you like to be called a "spin doctor"?
11. Do you consider *PR* to be a slang term that should be avoided? Why or why not?
12. How does public relations differ from the fields of journalism, advertising, and marketing?
13. How does public relations support marketing? Some experts say that public relations can launch a new product or service better than advertising. Do you

agree or disagree? It's also asserted that public relations creates brands, and that advertising can only reinforce and defend a brand. What are your thoughts?

14. What is the concept of integrated communications, which some people also call integrated marketing communications (IMC)? What four factors have led to the growth of integrated campaigns?

15. Public relations people work for a variety of organizations. What type of organization would you prefer if you wanted to work in public relations?

16. The text mentions five essential qualities for working in public relations. On a scale of 1 to 10, how would you rate yourself on each ability?

17. Why is it important for a student to complete an internship in college? Do you think interns should be paid?

18. Job placement directors say that employers are looking for 10 qualities in applicants. Can you name at least 5 of the 10 qualities?

19. Discuss entry-level salaries in public relations. Do you think they are too low, or are they about what you expected? What about the salaries for experienced professionals?

20. Is there still a gender gap in salaries? If so, do you think that it is caused by overt discrimination or do other factors explain the salary gap?

21. The PR Casebook on the Abundant Forests Alliance outlines an integrated campaign. What tactics were used? Do you think this campaign was well done? Why or why not?

SUGGESTED READINGS

Bowen, Shannon A. "I Thought It Would Be More Glamorous: Perceptions and Misconceptions Among Students in the Public Relations Principles Course." *Public Relations Review*, Vol. 29, No. 2, 2003, pp. 199–214.

Bureau of Labor Statistics. "Occupational Outlook Handbook: Public Relations Specialists." www.bisgov/oco/ocoso86htm. Excellent overview with facts and figures.

Bush, Michael. "The PR Industry from the Outside: PR Pros Rightfully Tout the Discipline's Role in the Marketing Mix." *PRWeek*, September 11, 2006, p. 15.

Capozzi, Louis. "Moving Forward: A Blueprint for Ensuring the PR Industry's Future Success." *The Strategist*, Winter 2006, pp. 37–39.

Gordon, Andrew. "Winning Teams: Integrated Marketing Is More than a Vague Concept or a Buzzword." *PRWeek*, March 29, 2004, p. 17.

Grunig, James E. "Furnishing the Edifice: Ongoing Research on Public Relations as a Strategic Management Function." *Journal of Public Relations Research*, Vol. 18, No. 2, 2006, pp. 151–176.

Guiniven, John. "Majoring in Public Relations: The Pros and Cons." *Public Relations Tactics*, July 2006, p. 6.

Hand, Mark. "Making Internships Beneficial for Both Students and Agencies." *PRWeek*, August 1, 2005, p. 10.

Lukaszewski, James E. "What's Next? The Relationship of Public Relations to Management, Journalism, and Society." *The Strategist*, Winter 2007, pp. 21–23.

Noble, Stacy. "TV portrayals of women in PR are bad for our industry." *PRWeek*, August 1, 2005, p. 3.

Paluszek, John. "Looking Forward: A Global Leadership Opportunity for Public Relations in the 21st Century." *The Strategist*, Fall 2006, pp. 29–31.

"Salary Survey 2007." *PRWeek*, February 26, 2007, pp. 16–22.

Seitel, Fraser. "What Is the Difference Between Marketing, Advertising and PR? *O'Dwyer's PR Report*, May 2006, pp. 39, 42.

Statesman, Alison. "From Columns to Clients: As More Print Journalists Turn to Public Relations, What Will It Mean for the Profession?" *The Strategist*, Winter 2006, pp. 6–8.

Trickett, Eleanor. "Outside Look Shows PR's Role in Marketing Gaining Respect." *PRWeek*, September 11, 2006, p. 9.

CHAPTER 2

The Evolution of Public Relations

A Short History of Public Relations

The practice of public relations is probably as old as human communication itself. In many ancient civilizations, such as those of Babylonia, Greece, and Rome, people were persuaded to accept the authority of government and religion through common public relations techniques: interpersonal communication, speeches, art, literature, staged events, publicity, and other such devices. None of these endeavors were called public relations, of course, but the purpose and effect were often the same as today's modern practice.

Ancient Beginnings

A news release carved in stone. The Rosetta Stone was found by Napoleon's army and dates to 196 B.C. It contains a decree acknowledging the first anniversary of the coronation of Ptolemy V.

It has often been said that the Rosetta Stone, which provided the key to modern understanding of ancient Egyptian hieroglyphics, was basically a publicity release touting the pharaoh's accomplishments. Similarly, the ancient Olympic Games used promotional techniques to enhance the aura of athletes as heroes in much the same way as the 2008 Beijing summer games. Even speech writing in Plato's time was similar to speech writing today. The speechwriter must know the composition of the audience, never talk down to it, and impart information that is credible and persuasive.

Julius Caesar was probably the first politician to publish a book, *Commentaries*, which he used to further his ambitions to become emperor of the Roman Empire. He also organized elaborate parades whenever he returned from a successful battle to burnish his image as an outstanding commander and leader. After Caesar became a consul of Rome in 59 B.C., he had clerks make a record of senatorial and other public proceedings and post them on walls throughout the city. These *Acta Diurna*, or "Daily Doings," were probably one of the world's first newspapers. Of course, Caesar's activities got more space than his rivals.

Saint Paul, the New Testament's most prolific author, also qualifies for the public relations hall of fame. In fact, R. E. Brown of Salem State College says, "Historians of early Christianity actually regard Paul, author and organizer, rather than Jesus himself, as the founder of Christianity." He goes on to quote James Grunig and Todd Hunt, who wrote in *Managing Public Relations*:

> It's not stretching history too much to claim the success of the apostles in spreading Christianity through the known world in the first century A.D. as one of the great public relations accomplishments of history. The apostles Paul and Peter used speeches, letters, staged events, and similar public relations activities to attract attention, gain followers, and establish new churches. Similarly, the four gospels in the New Testament, which were written at least 40 years after the death of Jesus, were public relations documents, written more to propagate the faith than to provide a historical account of Jesus' life.

The Middle Ages

The Roman Catholic Church was a major practitioner of public relations throughout the Middle Ages. Pope Urban II persuaded thousands of followers to serve God and gain forgiveness of their sins by engaging in the Holy Crusades against the Muslims. Six centuries later, the church was among the first to use the word *propaganda*, with the establishment by Pope Gregory XV of the College of Propaganda to supervise foreign missions and train priests to propagate the faith.

Meanwhile, in Venice, bankers in the 15th and 16th centuries practiced the fine art of investor relations and were probably the first, along with local Catholic bishops, to adopt the concept of corporate philanthropy by sponsoring such artists as Michelangelo.

Early Beginnings in America

The United States was first settled by immigrants, primarily those from England. Various land companies with a license from the Crown actively promoted colonization to generate revenues from what the colonists were able to manufacture or grow. In other words, colonization in many cases was strictly a commercial proposition. The Virginia Company in 1620, for example, distributed flyers and brochures throughout Europe offering 50 acres of free land to anyone willing to migrate.

An early example of promotion in the New World was Sir Walter Raleigh's attempts to convince settlers to move to Virginia. In 1584, Raleigh sent back glowing accounts to England of what was actually a swamp-filled Roanoke Island. Eric the Red did the same thing back in 1000 A.D. when he discovered a land of ice and rock and named it Greenland. The Spanish explorers publicized the never-discovered Seven Cities of Gold and even the fabled Fountain of Youth to attract willing participants for further exploration and colonization.

After the American colonies were well established, publicity and public relations techniques were used to promote various institutions. In 1641, Harvard College published a fund-raising brochure. King's College (now Columbia University) issued its first news release in 1758, which announced its commencement exercises.

Public relations also played an active role in American independence. The Boston Tea Party, which *PRWeek* has called the "... the greatest and best-known publicity stunt of all time . . . ," was the inspiration of Samuel Adams, a man with a refined sense of how symbolism can sway public opinion. The colonists threw crates of tea leaves from a British trade ship into Boston Harbor to protest excessive British taxation, and the rest is history. Adams and his colleagues also labeled the killing of several colonists by British troops at a demonstration as the "Boston Massacre" and further persuaded the American colonists to revolt against Great Britain.

Also instrumental in bringing lukewarm citizens around to the cause of American independence was Tom Paine's *Common Sense*. More than 120,000 copies of the pamphlet were sold in three months, an early example of political communication to a national audience. Influencing the makeup of the new political system were the *Federalist Papers*, which comprised 85 letters written by Alexander Hamilton, James Madison, and John Jay under a single pen name. The effort laid the foundation for distributing syndicated opinion pieces via the mass media, a concept that is still being used today in public relations.

The 1800s was the golden age of the press agent. John Burke was the promotional genius behind Buffalo Bill's Wild West Show, which drew record crowds thoughout the United States and Europe. Buffalo Bill and Annie Oakley were the rock stars of their age.

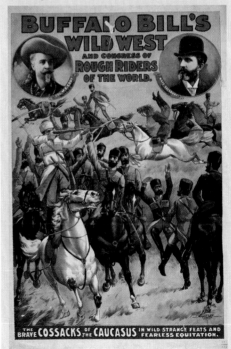

Phineas T. Barnum, a master of "hype" and promotion, made Tom Thumb a show business personality and an international celebrity.

American Development in the 19th Century

The 1800s was a period of growth and expansion in the United States. It also was the golden age of the press agent, which Webster's *New World Dictionary* defines as "a person whose work is to get publicity for an individual, organization, etc." The period was also the age of hype, which is the shrewd use of the media and other devices to promote an individual, a cause, or even a product or service, such as a circus.

Press agents were able to glorify Davy Crockett as a frontier hero to draw political support away from Andrew Jackson, attract thousands to the touring shows of Buffalo Bill and sharpshooter Annie Oakley, make a legend of frontiersman Daniel Boone, and promote hundreds of other personalities.

These old-time press agents and the show people they most often represented played on the credulity of the public in its longing to be entertained. Advertisements and press releases were exaggerated to the point of being outright lies. Doing advance work for an attraction, the press agent dropped tickets on the desk of a newspaper editor, along with the announcements. Voluminous publicity generally followed, and the journalists and their families flocked to their free entertainment with scant regard for the ethical constraints that largely prohibits such practices today. Small wonder then that today's public relations practitioner, exercising the highly sophisticated skills of evaluation, counseling, communications, and influencing management policies, shudders at the suggestion that public relations grew out of press agentry. And yet some aspects of modern public relations have their roots in the practice.

The Ultimate Showman   Phineas T. Barnum, the great American showman of the 19th century, was the master of what historian Daniel Boorstin calls the pseudoevent, which is a planned happening that occurs primarily for the purpose of being reported. Barnum, who was born in 1810, used flowery language and exaggeration to promote his various attractions in an age when the public was hungry for any form of entertainment.

Thanks to Barnum, Tom Thumb became one of the sensations of the century. He was a midget, standing just over two feet and weighing 15 pounds, but he was exceptional at singing, dancing, and performing comedy monologues. Barnum made a public relations event of the marriage of General Tom Thumb to another midget. He even got extensive European booking for Thumb by introducing him first to society leaders in London, who were enchanted by him. An invitation to the palace followed, and from then on Thumb played to packed houses every night. Barnum, even in his day, knew the value of third-party endorsement.

Another Barnum success was the promotion of Jenny Lind, the "Swedish Nightingale." Lind was famous in Europe, but no one in America knew about her beautiful voice until Barnum took her on a national tour and made her a pop icon even before the Civil War. He obtained full houses on opening nights in each community by donating part of the proceeds to charity. As a civic activity, the event attracted many of the town's opinion leaders, whereupon the general public flocked to attend succeeding performances—a device still employed today by entertainment publicists.

on the job
A MULTICULTURAL WORLD

The Beginnings of Public Relations in Other Nations

The British scholar J. A. R. Pimlott once wrote, "Public relations is not a peculiarly American phenomenon, but it has nowhere flourished as in the United States. Nowhere else is it so widely practiced, so lucrative, so pretentious, so respectable and disreputable, so widely suspected, and so extravagantly extolled."

It's important to realize, however, that other nations have their own histories. The following is a representative sample.

Germany

Railroads and other large business enterprises began publicity efforts as far back as the mid-19th century. Alfred Krupp, who founded the Krupp Company, the premier industrial firm in Germany and eventually the base of the Nazi war power, wrote in 1866, "We think . . . it is time that authoritative reports concerning factory matters, in accordance with the facts should be propagated on a regular basis through newspaper reports which serve an enlightened public."

Great Britain

The Marconi Company, a world leader in wireless telegraphy, established a department in 1910 to distribute news releases about its achievements and operations. In 1911, the first government public relations campaign was launched by the Insurance Commission to explain the benefits of the National Insurance Act, an unpopular measure that had attracted much adverse publicity.

The Air Ministry appointed the first government press officer in 1919, and a year later the Ministry of Health selected Sir Basil Clarke, a former Reuters correspondent, as director of information. By 1922, the government launched the British Broadcasting Service (BBC) as a way to communicate British values and viewpoints to its colonies and other nations.

Professional public relations counseling for business was introduced in the country in 1924, when Sir Basil Clarke, a former government press officer, established a firm in London. For his first client, a dairy group, he promoted the idea of milk pasteurization, an innovation that had met with some resistance from the public. A year later, Sir John Elliott was appointed a public relations officer of the Southern Railway Company.

Australia

Public relations in Australia largely consisted of publicity efforts until after World War II. When U.S. General Douglas MacArthur arrived after his escape from Corregidor in 1942, he introduced the term *public relations* and, with a highly skilled staff, demonstrated numerous ways of promoting his image and the war effort.

The industry grew steadily and, in 1960, the Public Relations Institute of Australia (PRIA) was formed. Notable practitioners have included George Fitzpatrick, credited with being the first Australian to conduct public relations, and Eric White who, according to one source, "virtually created the public relations industry" in Australia. As early as the 1960s, White oversaw extensions of his firm to six Pacific Rim countries.

Taiwan

In Taiwan, as in many nations, the government was the first entity to utilize public relations tactics. In the 1950s, the Taiwanese government used public relations to conduct "nation building." Several government information offices were formed to release government news to the public. The Public Relations Foundation, a professional body of practitioners, was established in 1956. In 1958, the group announced a policy for government agencies and private organizations to promote public relations. One of the organization's vehicles is *Public Relations Magazine*, which is used to promote professionalism in the field.

Philippines

The public relations industry in the Philippines was transplanted from the West in the 1940s. In fact, the country is considered the "Pacific birthplace of public relations." U.S. Army public information officers regularly issued news releases to the Philippine press during World War II.

(CONTINUED)

After the war, the concept spread to local businesses, and the Business Writers Association of the Philippines was organized to promote the idea of corporate social responsibility.

Notable of the early Filipino pioneers is Pete Teodoro. He was public relations director of Elizalde & Company, a paint manufacturer, and is credited with undertaking the first organized public relations campaign to generate goodwill and business from local contractors and architects. In 1966, the San Miguel Corporation, one of the country's largest and most famous companies, known worldwide for its San Miguel beer, established the first public relations department.

Spain

The growth of public relations in Spain started in the 1950s and paralleled political, economic, and media developments in Spain. An advertising agency, Danis Advertising of Barcelona, launched a public relations campaign in 1955 to build community goodwill for a corporate client and its product. One of the directors of that campaign, Joaquin Maestre, started his own public relations firm in 1960. According to one historian, the advent of public relations consultancies, "marked the beginning of a 'dynamic consumer market' for public relations services, which led to setting up the first public relations agencies as a direct response to the 'market demand for services.'"

The Russian Federation

The collapse of the Soviet Union in 1991 ushered in a free-market economy and democratic reforms that caused the rapid growth of the public relations field in government and private business. With the new openness, global companies began selling products and services in the new Russia with the assistance of Western-style advertising, public relations, and promotion.

In addition, Russian companies began to understand the importance of publicizing their products and services. Before that time, most "public relations" was conducted by the government. In the mid-1990s, a Russian association of public relations professionals was organized to promote standards and provide continuing education. Most observers think the public relations industry will continue to expand as the economy grows.

Thailand

Public relations in Thailand, as in many nations, dates back to the 1950s. Esko Pajasalmi from Finland is credited with starting the first public relations firm. He started his firm, Presko, after serving more than a decade as a Christian missionary in northern Thailand. Presko eventually became that nation's largest public relations firm and set the standard for other firms that followed.

One early Presko campaign was for Colgate-Palmolive, after its tooth-paste was falsely accused of containing pork fat. The Muslim community was horrified, and Colgate immediately lost 100 percent of the market in southern Thailand. Pajasalmi contacted Muslim leaders and took them to inspect the factories, managing to convince them that the rumors were unfounded. Business boomed again.

United Arab Emirates

Rapid business and economic development in the past two decades, particularly in Dubai, has encouraged the growth of public relations. By the mid-1980s, the majority of government departments and other major institutions had created a public relations department. In addition, a number of international public relations firms arrived in the mid-1980s to service the operations of multinational companies with operations in the Middle East. Today, about 40 public relations firms are based in the UAE and have about 60 percent of the business in the Middle East. Sadri Barrage, president of the Middle East Public Relations Association (MEPRA), which was formed in 2001, wrote, "The widespread use of public relations agencies in the UAE and the region is a normal phenomenon because of the huge economic activity in the country that requires . . . the tasks of media liaison, promotion, advertising, product launch, and the like."

Westward Expansion Throughout the 19th century, publicity and promotion helped to populate the western United States. Land speculators distributed pamphlets and publicity that described almost every community as "the garden spot of the West," which one critic of the time called "downright puffery, full of exaggerated statements, and high-wrought and false-colored descriptions." One brochure about Nebraska, for example, described the territory as the "Gulf stream of migration . . . bounded on the north by the 'Aurora Borealis' and on the south by the Day of Judgment." Other brochures were more down-to-earth, describing the fertile land, the abundant water, and the opportunity to build a fortune.

American railroads, in particular, used extensive public relations and press agentry to attract settlers and expand operations. As Andy Piasecki, lecturer at Queen Margaret University College in Edinburgh, Scotland, describes it:

> The expansion of the railroads was dependent on publicity and promotion. This is hardly surprising that any investment in western expansion was dependent on finding a population. Many railroad companies were colonization agencies as much as they were transport companies. Without people, no railroads could be sustained and because there were, at this time, few people out West, they had to be brought in. . . .

Consequently, such companies as the Burlington and Missouri Railroad took it upon themselves to promote Western settlement from England and other places. The Burlington and Missouri Railroad set up an information office in Liverpool that distributed fact sheets and maps and placed stories in the local press. In addition, the railroad promoted lectures about migrating to the American West. According to Piasecki, "The pièce de resistance for the Burlington was a kind of early road show . . . an elaborately illustrated lecture with 85 painted views, each covering 250 square feet."

In addition, the railroad solicited the services of "independent" observers who wrote and spoke about the glories of the American West as the land of opportunity. Bernhard Warkentin was one such spokesperson. He "traveled widely with railroad officials," according to historian David A. Haury. Warkentin arrived from Russia in 1872 to survey the U.S. political and economic situation on behalf of the members of his Mennonite religious sect. His task was embraced by the rail companies and he was taken by train to several locales. He wrote home about what he saw. Haury wrote: "Railroad representatives met the Mennonite delegates, financed tours, promised freedom of conscience, and offered land at bargain prices." Between 1874 and 1884, 15,000 Mennonites settled in the Plains states.

The publicity and promotion paid off. Piasecki notes, "During the 1870s and the 1880s, the railroads attracted something like 4.5 million people to the Midwestern states, and they were responsible for the establishment there of almost 2 million farms. None of this could have been achieved without complex communication strategies closely linked to business objectives. . . ."

Near the end of the 19th century, the Santa Fe Railway launched a campaign to lure tourists to the Southwest. It commissioned dozens of painters and photographers to depict the dramatic landscape and show romanticized American Indians weaving, grinding corn, and dancing.

Politics and Activism   The early 19th century also saw the development of public relations tactics on the political and activist front. Amos Kendall, a former Kentucky newspaper editor, became an intimate member of President Andrew Jackson's "kitchen cabinet" and probably was the first presidential press secretary.

Kendall sampled public opinion on issues, advised Jackson, and skillfully interpreted his rough ideas, putting them into presentable form as speeches and news releases. He also served as Jackson's advance agent on trips, wrote glowing articles that he sent to supportive newspapers, and probably was the first to use newspaper reprints in public relations; almost every complimentary story or editorial about Jackson was reprinted and widely circulated. Article reprints are still a standard tactic in today's modern practice.

Supporters and leaders of such causes as abolition, suffrage, and prohibition employed publicity to maximum effect throughout the century. One of the most

Groups advocating the right of women to vote in the United States used a variety of public relations tactics to press their cause. Here, a group of suffragists participate in a 1914 parade in Washington, D.C. Through such parades and demonstrations, they received media coverage and informed the public about their cause. Today, other groups representing various causes still continue to hold demonstrations, parades, and rallies.

influential publicity ventures for the abolition movement was the publication of Harriet Beecher Stowe's *Uncle Tom's Cabin*. Sarah J. Hale, editor of *Godey's Ladies Book*, a best-selling magazine, ardently promoted women's rights. Amelia Bloomer, a women's rights advocate, got plenty of media publicity by wearing loose-fitting trousers in protest of the corset. Noted temperance crusader Carrie Nation became nationally known by invading saloons with an axe. Her name lives on—a bar in California is named Carrie Nation's.

Professor Carolyn M. Byerly of Ithaca College says that these activist campaigns for social reform qualify as public relations operations and deserve a place in the history of the field. She cites Genevieve Gardner McBride, who points out that, in Wisconsin, support for a constitutional amendment giving women the right to vote was carried out through a carefully managed information campaign that included "publicity, press agentry, publications, petition drives, advertising, merchandising, lobbying, membership recruitment and training, special events, fund-raising, issues management, and crisis PR."

Activists for social movements and causes have been using public relations tactics throughout history. In the 1860s, naturalist John Muir wrote in the *New York Times* and other publications about the importance of protecting the Yosemite Valley in California. In 1889 he worked with the editor of *Century Magazine*, Robert Underwood Johnson, to promote a campaign requesting congressional support for Yosemite National Park. The activist public relations campaign succeeded and generations have enjoyed the benefits of a protected Yosemite. Teddy Roosevelt also visited Yosemite for publicity purposes, which will be discussed shortly.

Professors Michael Smith of La Salle University and Denise Ferguson of the University of Indianapolis write that the primary purpose of activist organizations "is to influence public policy, organizational action, or social norms and values." They also note that activist organizations face the same challenges of other organizations and, therefore, use the same strategic communication tactics to achieve their goals. For example, activists often embrace conflict as a means of gaining news coverage and stirring up support from their grassroots base.

Corporate Development   A wave of industrialization and urbanization swept the nation after the Civil War. Concentrations of wealth developed throughout manufacturing and trade. Amid the questioning of business practices, which intensified in the early 20th century, in 1888 the Mutual Life Insurance Company hired a journalist to write news releases designed to improve its image. In 1889, Westinghouse Corporation established what is thought to be the first in-house publicity department to promote the concept of alternating current (AC) versus Thomas Edison's direct current (DC) system. George Westinghouse eventually won a bruising public relations battle with Edison, and AC became the standard in the United States. In 1897, the term *public relations* was first used by the Association of American Railroads in a company listing.

1900 to 1950: The Age of Pioneers

As the use of publicity gained increased acceptance, the first publicity agency, known as the Publicity Bureau, was established in Boston in 1900. Harvard College was its most prestigious client. George F. Parker and Ivy Ledbetter Lee opened a publicity office in New York City in 1905. Parker continued to work in political public relations, but Lee went on to become an advisor and counselor to prominent individuals and major industrial enterprises. He and other public relations pioneers are discussed shortly, but first some mention should be made of several business and political leaders who thoroughly understood the power of effective public relatons.

Samuel Insull   At the corporate level, the Chicago Edison Company broke new ground in public relations techniques under the skillful leadership of its president, Samuel Insull. Well aware of the special need for a public utility to maintain a sound relationship with its customers, Insull created a monthly customer magazine, issued a constant stream of news releases, and even used films for public relations purposes. In 1912, he started the "bill stuffer" by inserting company information into customer bills—a technique used by many utilities today. By the 1920s, Insull was one of the country's foremost power brokers, controlling utilities in 5,000 towns and 32 states. He did much to expand the market for electricity by promoting electrical appliances with the theme that it liberated women from household drudgery.

Henry Ford   Henry Ford was America's first major industrialist, and he was among the first to use two basic public relations concepts. The first was the notion of positioning, the idea that credit and publicity always go to those who do something first. The second idea was being accessible to the press. Joseph Epstein, author of *Ambition*, says, "He may have been an even greater publicist than mechanic."

In 1900, Ford obtained coverage of the prototype Model T by demonstrating it to a reporter from the *Detroit Tribune*. By 1903, Ford achieved widespread publicity by racing his cars—a practice still used by today's automakers. Ford also positioned himself as the champion of the common man and was the first automaker to envision that a car should be affordable to everyone. He garnered further publicity and became the hero of working men and women by being the first automaker to double his worker's wages to $5 per day.

Ford became a household name because he was willing to be interviewed by the press on almost any subject. A populist by nature, he once said, "Business is a service, not a bonanza," an idea reiterated by many of today's top corporate executives who believe in what is now called corporate social responsibility (CSR).

His reputation, toward the end of his life, was somewhat tarnished when he strongly opposed unionization of his plants and employed toughs to break up attempts to organize workers.

Teddy Roosevelt   President Theodore Roosevelt (1901–1909) was a master at promoting and publicizing his pet projects. He was the first president to make extensive use of news conferences and press interviews to drum up public support when Congress was often critical or nonsupportive. He was an ardent conservationist and knew the publicity value of the presidential tour. For example, he took a large group of reporters and photographers to see the wonders of Yosemite National Park as a way of generating favorable press coverage and public support for the creation of additional national forests and national parks. While president, Roosevelt set aside 150 million acres for public recreational use and essentially became the "father" of the American conservation movement.

Roosevelt's nickname was "Teddy," which he didn't particularly like, but it did endear him to the public. Part of Roosevelt's legacy was that the Teddy Bear was named after him because he enjoyed bear hunting. On one such trip, accompanied by reporters, he spared a small bear and the reporters wrote about it. A toymaker saw the story and began to make and market "Teddy" bears in recognition of the president's humane gesture. Another story, perhaps more accurate, is that the *New York Times* used his nickkname in a humorous poem about two bears named Teddy B and Teddy G, which then became the names of two bears in the Bronx Zoo. Their popularity with the public caused toy manufacturers to market toy bears as teddy bears, which also increased Roosevelt's popularity; he's probably the only U.S. president to have a stuffed animal named after him, which survives to this day.

President Franklin D. Roosevelt apparently took notes from Teddy. His supporters organized nationwide birthday balls in 1934 to celebrate his birthday and raise funds for infantile paralysis research. This led to the creation of the March of Dimes. The campaign by Carl Byoir & Associates, a leading public relations firm at the time, orchestrated 6,000 events in 3,600 communities and raised more than $1 million.

Ivy Lee: The First Public Relations Counsel   The combination of stubborn management attitudes and improper actions, labor strife, and widespread public criticism produced the first public relations counselor, Ivy Ledbetter Lee. Although, as previously noted, the Princeton graduate and former business journalist for the *New York Times*, *New York World*, and the *New York American* began as a publicist, he shortly expanded that role to become the first public relations counsel.

When Lee opened his public relations firm, Parker and Lee, in 1905, he issued a declaration of principles that signaled a new model of public relations practice: public information. Lee's emphasis was on the dissemination of truthful, accurate information rather than the distortions, hype, and exaggerations of press agentry.

One of Lee's first clients was the Anthracite Coal Roads and Mines Company. He was retained to help articulate the owner's position during a strike by its workers. Also, in 1906, Lee was retained by the Pennsylvania Railroad as a "publicity counselor" to handle media relations. His first task was to convince management that the policy of operating in secret and refusing to talk with the press, typical of many large corporations at the time, was a poor strategy for fostering goodwill and public understanding. When the next rail accident occurred, Lee provided press facilities, issued what is claimed to be the first news release of the modern age, and took reporters to the accident site. Although such action appeared to the conservative railroad directors to be reckless indiscretion, they were pleasantly surprised that the company received fairer press comment than on any previous occasion.

It wasn't long before other railroads also adopted a more open information policy. By 1912, Lee had become the executive assistant to the president of the Pennsylvania Railroad, which Scott Cutlip, in his comprehensive history of public relations, called, "the first known instance of a public relations person being placed at the management level."

One of Lee's major accomplishments was the 1913–1914 railroad freight hike campaign. The Pennsylvania Railroad, after years of rising expenses, needed a five percent railroad freight rate hike to remain in business but there was considerable public opposition and also a skeptical Interstate Commerce Commission (ICC). Lee believed the public and the ICC could be persuaded to accept higher rates if they were given the facts and made aware of the situation. The central message was that the railroads provided an essential service to the nation and the government was not allowing them to charge a fair rate for this service.

Burton St. John III, in a *Public Relations Review* article, recounts how Lee conducted his campaign. He not only widely distributed the railroad industry's case to the press, but he also broke with past publicity practices by clearly identifying the source of the information. Lee also gave the ICC the information before distributing it to the press. After each ICC hearing, he distributed the railroad's testimony to the press, railroad employees, railway riders, congressmen, state legislators, college presidents, and other opinion leaders such as clergy. Other techniques were leaflets and bulletins for railway riders and community opinion leaders, a speaker's bureau, and reprints of speeches.

All these efforts paid off. Public opposition declined, and chambers of commerces around the country bombarded the ICC with resolutions supporting the railroad. The ICC approved the five percent rate hike. Burton concludes, "Lee's propaganda campaign for the Pennsylvania Railroad is a landmark in the history of public relations."

Lee counseled a number of companies and charitable organizations during his lifetime, but he is best known for his work with the Rockefeller family. In 1914, John D. Rockefeller Jr. hired Lee in the wake of the vicious strike-breaking activities known as the Ludlow Massacre at the Rockefeller family's Colorado Fuel and Iron Company (CF&I) plant. Lee went to Colorado to do some fact-finding (research) and talked to both sides. He found that labor leaders were effectively getting their views out by talking freely to the media, but that the company's executives were tight-lipped and inaccessible. The result, of course, was a barrage of negative publicity and public criticism directed at CF&I and the Rockefeller family.

Public relations counselor Ivy Lee convinced John D. Rockefeller that he should visit miners at the family's Colorado Fuel & Iron Company, the site of considerable labor unrest and union organizing activity that led to the "Ludlow Massacre." Here, Rockefeller watches children of miners marching into school.

Lee, drawing on his rate hike experience, proposed a series of informational bulletins by management that would be distributed to opinion leaders in Colorado and around the nation. The leaflets were designed to be thought pieces about various issues concerning mining, manufacturing, and labor. In all, 19 bulletins were produced over a period of several months and sent to a mailing list of 19,000. Even at this early time, Lee recognized the value of directly reaching opinion leaders who, in turn, were highly influential in shaping public discussion and opinion.

Lee organized a number of other public relations activities on behalf of CF&I during 1914 and 1915, including convincing the governor of Colorado to write an article supporting the position taken by the company. Lee also convinced Rockefeller to visit the plant and talk with miners and their families. Lee made sure the press was there to record Rockefeller eating in the workers' hall, swinging a pickax in the mine, and having a beer with the workers after hours. The press loved it. Rockefeller was portrayed as being seriously concerned about the plight of the workers, and the visit led to policy changes and more worker benefits.

All of these activities, of course, also prevented the United Mine Workers from gaining a foothold. George McGovern, a former Democratic Party candidate for president, wrote his doctoral dissertation on the Ludlow Massacre and commented, "It was the first time in any American labor struggle where you had an organized effort to use what has become modern public relations to sell one side of a strike to the American people."

Lee continued as a counselor to the Rockefeller family and its various companies, but he also counseled a number of other clients, too. For example, he advised the American Tobacco Company to initiate a profit-sharing plan, the Pennsylvania Railroad to beautify its stations, and the movie industry to stop inflated advertising and form a voluntary code of censorship. See the PR Casebook box on page 51 for his work with New York's first subway.

He is remembered today for his four important contributions to public relations: (1) advancing the concept that business and industry should align themselves with the public interest, (2) dealing with top executives and carrying out no program unless it had the active support of management, (3) maintaining open communication with the news media, and (4) emphasizing the necessity of humanizing business and bringing its public relations down to the community level of employees, customers, and neighbors.

George Creel   The public information model that Lee enunciated in his counseling was also used by George Creel, who was also a former newspaper reporter. He was asked by President Woodrow Wilson to organize a massive public relations effort to unite the nation and to influence world opinion during World War I.

In their book *Words That Won the War*, James O. Mock and Cedric Larson write: "Mr. Creel assembled a brilliant and talented group of journalists, scholars, press agents, editors, artists, and other manipulators of the symbols of public opinion as America had ever seen united for a single purpose." Among its numerous activities, the Creel Committee persuaded newspapers and magazines to contribute volumes of news and advertising space to encourage Americans to save food and to invest heavily in Liberty Bonds, which were purchased by more than 10 million people. Thousands of businesses set up their own groups of publicity people to expand the effort.

President Wilson accepted Creel's advice that hatred of the Germans should be played down and that loyalty and confidence in the government should be emphasized. The committee also publicized the war aims and ideals of Woodrow Wilson—to make the world safe for democracy and to make World War I the war to end all wars. The

PR CASEBOOK

Constructive Public Relations for the New York Subway

Ivy Lee, known as the first public relations counselor, was retained by the New York Subway system in 1916 to foster public understanding and support.

The Interborough Rapid Transit Company (IRT) faced many new challenges as it began its second decade of service. It was completing construction and expanding service, but it also faced competition from a rival system, the Brooklyn Rapid Transit Company (later known as BMT).

Under Lee's direction, the IRT took an innovative approach, communicating directly with its passengers through pamphlets, brochures, and posters "to establish a close understanding of its work and policies." The most

famous and influential products of Lee's campaign were two concurrently appearing poster series: The Subway Sun and The Elevated Express.

Between 1918, when the first posters appeared, and 1932, when the series ended, these posters became New York institutions. They entertained and informed millions of subway commuters during the First World War and through the Great Depression.

Posters, for example, were used to announce the introduction of coin-operated turnstiles, which Lee called "a change which revolutionized the daily habits of millions of people." They were also used to explain the need for fare increases in the 1920s and to extol fast and direct train service to baseball games at Yankee Stadium and the Polo Grounds. Posters also offered riders information on how to get to other city institutions. The poster shown promotes the Museum of Natural History and provides directions.

Designed to resemble the front page of a newspaper, The Subway Sun and The Elevated Express announced the opening of the 42nd Street shuttle between Grand Central Station and Times Square; asked riders to not block the doors; and urged them to visit the city's free swimming pools. As the subways became more crowded, the IRT used these posters to promote its "open air" elevated lines as a more comfortable alternative.

Today, more than 90 years later, Lee's idea of communicating directly to passengers through posters, pamphlets, and brochures is still being used by public transit systems around the world. And many of the themes are the same as in Lee's day—public safety, system improvements, travel advisories, subway etiquette, and public service announcements.

American Red Cross, operating in cooperation with the Creel Committee, enrolled more than 19 million new members and received more than $400 million in contributions during the period.

This massive publicity effort had a profound effect on the development of public relations by demonstrating the success of these techniques. It also awakened an awareness in Americans of the power of mediated information in changing public attitudes and behavior. This, coupled with postwar analysis of British propaganda devices, resulted in a number of scholarly books and college courses on the subject, including a recent re-assessment of propaganda by international public relations scholars Patricia A. Curtin and T. Kenn Gaither.

Edward L. Bernays: Father of Modern Public Relations   The Creel Committee was the training ground of many individuals who went on to become successful and widely known public relations executives and counselors. One such person was Edward B. Bernays who, through brilliant campaigns and extensive self-promotion, became known as the "father of modern public relations" by the time of his death in 1995 at the age of 103.

Edward L. Bernays, a legendary figure in public relations with a career spanning about three-quarters of a century, died at the age of 103 in 1995. He became known as the "father of modern public relations."

Bernays, who was the nephew of Sigmund Freud, conceptualized a new model of public relations that emphasized the application of social science research and behavioral psychology to formulate campaigns and messages that could change people's perceptions and encourage certain behaviors. Unlike Lee's public information model that emphasized the accurate distribution of news, Bernays's model was essentially one of advocacy and scientific persuasion. It included listening to the audience, but the purpose of feedback was to formulate a more persuasive message. Professor emeritus James Grunig of the University of Maryland, a major theorist in public relations, has labeled this the two-way asymmetric model, one of four classic models that are outlined on page 53.

Bernays became a major spokesperson for the "new" public relations through his book *Crystallizing Public Opinion*, which was published in 1923. His first sentence announced: "In writing this book I have tried to set down the broad principles that govern the new profession of public relations counsel." In the following pages, Bernays outlined the scope, function, methods, techniques, and social responsibilities of a public relations counsel—a term that was to become the core of public relations practice.

The book, published a year after Walter Lippmann's insightful treatise on public opinion, attracted much attention, and Bernays was even invited by New York University to offer the first public relations course in the nation. However, not everyone was happy with Bernays or his book. The editor of the *New York Herald Tribune* wrote,

> Bernays has taken the sideshow barker and given him a philosophy and a new and awesome language. He is no primitive drum-beater . . . He is devoid of swank and does not visit newspaper offices (as did the circus press agents); and yet, the more thoughtful newspaper editors . . . should regard Bernays as a menace, and warn their colleagues of his machinations.

Clients, however, did not seem to share such concerns and Bernays, over the course of his long career, had many successful campaigns that have become classics. Here is a sampling:

◆ **Ivory Soap.** Procter & Gamble sold its Ivory Soap by the millions after Bernays came up with the idea of sponsoring soap sculpture contests for school-aged children. In the first year alone, 22 million schoolchildren participated in the contest, which eventually ran for 35 years. Bernays's brochure with soap sculpture tips, which millions of children received in their schools, advised them to "use discarded models for face, hands, and bath," adding, "You will love the feeling of cleanliness that comes from Ivory soap bath once a day." Thomas Harris, a Chicago counselor, quotes Bernays; "Soap

on the job INSIGHTS

Four Classic Models of Public Relations

A four-model typology of public relations practice was formulated by Professors James Grunig of the University of Maryland and Todd Hunt of Rutgers University in their 1984 book *Managing Public Relations*. The models, which have been used widely in public relations theory, help to explain how public relations has evolved over the years from the press agentry of the 19th century to an emphasis on scientific persuasion and building relationships in the late 20th century.

Press Agentry/Publicity

This is one-way communication, primarily through the mass media, to distribute information that may be exaggerated, distorted, or even incomplete to "hype" a cause, product, or service. Its purpose is advocacy, and little or no research is required. P. T. Barnum was the leading historical figure during this model's heyday from 1850 to 1900. Sports, theater, music, film, and the classic Hollywood publicist are the main fields of practice today.

Public Information

One-way distribution of information, not necessarily with a persuasive intent, is the purpose. It is based on the journalistic ideal of accuracy and completeness, and the mass media is the primary channel. There is fact-finding for content, but little audience research regarding attitudes and dispositions. Ivy Lee, a former journalist, is the leading historical figure during this model's development from about 1910 into the 1920s. Government, nonprofit groups, and other public institutions are primary fields of practice today.

Two-Way Asymmetric

Scientific persuasion is the purpose, and communication is two-way, with imbalanced effects. The model has a feedback loop, but the primary purpose of the model is to help the communicator better understand the audience and how to persuade it. Research is used to plan the activity and establish objectives as well as to learn whether an objective has been met. Edward Bernays is the leading historical figure during the model's beginning in the 1920s. Marketing and advertising departments in competitive businesses and public relations firms are the primary places of practice today.

Two-Way Symmetric

Gaining mutual understanding is the purpose, and communication is two-way with balanced effects. Formative research is used mainly to learn how the public perceives the organization and to determine what consequences organizational actions/policy might have on the public. The result may be counseling management to take certain actions or change policies. Evaluative research is used to measure whether a public relations effort has improved public understanding. This idea, also expressed as "relationship building" is to have policies and actions that are mutually beneficial to both parties. Edward B. Bernays, later in his life, supported this model and is considered a leading advocate of this approach. Educators and professional leaders are the main proponents of this model, which has been used by many professionals since the 1980s. The fields of practice today include organizations that engage in issue identification, crisis and risk management, and long-range strategic planning.

---

sculpture became a national outlet for children's creative instincts and helped a generation that enjoyed cleanliness."

◆ **Ballet Russe.** The challenge was to build a following for a Russian dance troupe in the middle of World War I, when ballet was considered a scandalous form of entertainment. According to *PRWeek*, "Bernays used magazine placements, created a publicity guide, and used overseas reviews to make men in tights respectable and put ballerina dreams into the heads of little girls." A more detailed overview of this campaign can be found at the Museum of Public Relations (www.prmuseum.com).

♦ **Light's Golden Jubilee.** To celebrate the 50th anniversary of Thomas Edison's invention of the electric light bulb, Bernays arranged the worldwide attention-getting Light's Golden Jubilee in 1929. It was his idea, for example, that the world's utilities would shut off their power all at one time, for one minute, to honor Edison. President Herbert Hoover and many dignitaries were on hand, and the U.S. Post Office issued a commemorative two-cent postage stamp. Bill Moyers, in an interview with Bernays in 1984, asked, "You know, you got Thomas Edison, Henry Ford, Herbert Hoover, and masses of Americans to do what you wanted them to do. You got the whole world to turn off its lights at the same time. That's not influence, that's power." Bernays responded, "But you see, I never thought of it as power. I never treated it as power. People want to go where they want to be led."

Journalist Larry Tye has outlined a number of campaigns conducted by Bernays in his book *The Father of Spin: Edward B. Bernays and the Birth of Public Relations.* Tye credits Bernays with having a unique approach to solving problems. Instead of thinking first about tactics, Bernays would always think about the "big idea" on how to motivate people. The bacon industry, for example, wanted to promote its product, so Bernays came up with the idea of doctors across the land endorsing a hearty breakfast. No mention was made of bacon, but sales soared anyway as people took the advice and started eating the traditional breakfast of bacon and eggs.

Bernays, as previously mentioned, is widely acknowledged as the founder of modern public relations. One historian even described him as "the first and doubtless the leading ideologist of public relations." Bernays constantly wrote about the profession of public relations and its ethical responsibilities—even to the point of advocating the licensing of public relations counselors. He also eventually advocated that public relations should be a two-way street of mutual understanding and interaction with the public rather than just scientific persuasion.

Although he was named by *Life* magazine in 1990 as one of the 100 most important Americans of the 20th century, it should be noted that Bernays had a powerful partner in his wife, Doris E. Fleischman, who was a talented writer, ardent feminist, and former Sunday editor of the *New York Tribune*. Fleischman was an equal partner in the work of Bernays's firm, interviewing clients, writing news releases, editing the company's newsletter, and writing and editing books and magazine articles. Bernays called Fleischman "the brightest woman I've ever met in my life" and the "balance wheel of our operation."

Other Pioneers   A number of individuals, either through the force of their personality, their expertise, or their professional success, also have contributed to the history and lore of public relations.

> " . . . all business in a democratic country begins with public permission and exists by public approval. "
>
> ——Arthur W. Page

♦ **Arthur W. Page.** Page became vice president of the American Telephone & Telegraph (AT&T) Company in 1927 and is credited with establishing the concept that public relations should have an active voice in higher management. Page also expressed the belief that a company's performance, not press agentry, comprises its basis for public approval. More than any other individual, Page is credited with laying the foundation for the field of corporate public relations. He served on the boards of numerous corporations, charitable groups, and universities.

After his death in 1960, a group of AT&T associates established a society of senior communication executives in his name. The Arthur W. Page Society, comprising about 300 senior-level public relations executives, has several meetings a year and publishes various monographs on communications management. The society posts on its Web site (www.awpagesociety.com) the six principles of public relations management developed by the society's namesake:

1. Tell the truth. Let the public know what's happening and provide an accurate picture of the company's character, ideals, and practices.

2. Prove it with action. Public perception of an organization is determined 90 percent by doing and 10 percent by talking.

3. Listen to the customer. To serve the company well, understand what the public wants and needs. Keep top decision makers and other employees informed about public reaction to company products, policies, and practices.

4. Manage for tomorrow. Anticipate public reaction and eliminate practices that create difficulties. Generate goodwill.

5. Conduct public relations as though the whole company depends on it. Corporate relations is a management function. No corporate strategy should be implemented without considering its impact on the public. The public relations professional is a policy maker capable of handling a wide range of corporate communications activities.

6. Remain calm, patient, and good-humored. Lay the groundwork for public relations miracles with consistent, calm, and reasoned attention to information and contacts. When a crisis arises, remember that cool heads communicate best.

Page recognized an additional truth: A company's true character is expressed by its people. This makes every active and retired employee a part of the public relations organization. So it is the responsibility of the public relations function to support each employee's capacity to be an honest, knowledgeable ambassador to customers, friends, and public officials.

♦ **Benjamin Sonnenberg.** It was Sonnenberg who suggested that Texaco sponsor performances of the Metropolitan Opera on national radio. Sponsorship of the Saturday afternoon series, which began in 1940, continued for a half-century. He believed that a brief mention of the client in the right context is better than a long-winded piece of flattery. He proposed Texaco's sponsorship as a way to reach opinion leaders and position the company as a patron of the arts. Biographer Isadore Barmash described Sonnenberg as "the most influential publicist of the mid-twentieth century." He had an opulent townhouse in New York and entertained many of America's most powerful men and women. Asked what the secret of his success was, he quipped, "I build large pedestals for small people."

♦ **Jim Moran.** Moran was a publicist and press agent who became famous for his media-grabbing stunts. He publicized the book *The Egg and I* by sitting on an ostrich egg for 19 days until it hatched. On another occasion, he walked a bull though an exclusive New York china shop.

♦ **Rex Harlow.** Considered by many to be the "father of public relations research," Harlow was probably the first full-time public relations educator. As a professor at Stanford University's School of Education, he taught public relations courses on a regular basis and also conducted multiple workshops around the nation. Harlow also founded the American Council on Public Relations, which later became the

Public Relations Society of America (PRSA). In 1952, he founded *Social Science Reporter*, one of the first newsletters in the field.

◆ **Leone Baxter.** Baxter and her partner, Clem Whitaker, are credited with founding the first political campaign management firm in the United States. The firm handled several California governor and U.S. Senate campaigns, advised General Dwight Eisenhower when he ran for president in 1952, and counseled Richard Nixon on the famous "Checkers" speech that saved his career as vice president.

◆ **Henry Rogers.** In the mid-1930s, Rogers, with Warren Cowan, established a highly successful public relations firm in Hollywood to serve the movie industry. One of his early clients was an unknown starlet named Rita Hayworth who needed some publicity. Rogers, in the true tradition of the press agent, convinced *Look* magazine to do a feature with the news angle that Hayworth spent every cent she earned on clothes. He even produced a telegram from the Fashion Couturiers Association of America (a fictitious organization) that declared Hayworth the best-dressed offscreen actress. *Look* assigned the photographer, Rogers convinced the clothiers to provide the wardrobe, Hayworth struck a seductive pose that made the cover, and her career was on its way. Rogers later became a corporate counsel. Of his image-building years, he said, "Dog food and movie stars are much alike because they are both products in need of exposure."

◆ **Eleanor Lambert.** The "grande dame" of fashion public relations, Lambert is credited with putting American designers such as Bill Blass and Calvin Klein on the map when European brands dominated the industry. She also compiled the "Best-Dressed" list for 62 years, which always received extensive media publicity. Lambert was active in New York fashion and the arts. She, for example, was the public relations counsel for the introduction of the Whitney Museum in 1930.

◆ **Elmer Davis.** President Franklin D. Roosevelt appointed Davis head of the Office of War Information (OWI) during World War II. Using the Creel Committee as a model, Davis mounted an even larger public relations effort to promote the sale of war bonds, obtain press support for wartime rationing, encourage the planting of "victory gardens," and spur higher productivity among American workers to win the war. The Voice of America (VOA) was established to carry news of the war to all parts of the world, and the movie industry made a number of feature films in support of the war. The OWI was the forerunner of the U.S. Information Agency (USIA), which was established in 1953.

◆ **Moss Kendrix.** "What the public thinks counts!" was the mantra of Kendrix, an African American, who founded the Moss Kendrix Organization in 1944 offering advertising and public relations services. He is credited with being the first African American to acquire a major corporate account, the Coca Cola Company. During his lifetime, he designed countless public relations and advertising campaigns for such organizations as Carnation, the National Dental Association, the National Educational Association, and Ford Motor Company. The Museum of Public Relations (www.prmuseum.com) succinctly summarizes his contribution: "He educated his corporate clients about the buying power of the African-American consumer, and helped to make America realize that African-Americans were more complex than the derogatory images depicted in the advertising of the past."

1950 to 2000: Public Relations Comes of Age

During the second half of the 20th century, the practice of public relations became firmly established as an indispensable part of America's economic, political, and social development.

The booming economy after World War II produced rapid growth in all areas of public relations. Companies opened public relations departments or expanded existing ones. Government staffs increased in size, as did those of nonprofits, such as educational institutions and health and welfare agencies. Television emerged in the early 1950s as a national medium and as a new challenge for public relations expertise. New counseling firms sprang up nationwide.

The growth of the economy was one reason for the expansion of public relations, but there were other factors, too:

◆ major increases in urban and suburban populations;

◆ the growth of a more impersonalized society represented by big business, big labor, and big government;

◆ scientific and technological advances, including automation and computerization;

◆ the communications revolution in terms of mass media;

◆ bottomline financial considerations often replacing the more personalized decision making of a previous, more genteel, society.

Many citizens felt alienated and bewildered by such rapid change, cut off from the sense of community that characterized the lives of previous generations. They sought power through innumerable pressure groups, focusing on causes such as environmentalism, working conditions, and civil rights. Public opinion, registered through new, more sophisticated methods of polling, became increasingly powerful in opposing or effecting change.

Both physically and psychologically separated from their publics, American business and industry turned increasingly to public relations specialists for audience analysis, strategic planning, issues management, and even the creation of supportive environments for the selling of products and services. Mass media also became more complex and sophisticated, so specialists in media relations who understood how the media worked were also in demand.

By 1950, an estimated 17,000 men and 2,000 women were employed as practitioners in public relations and publicity. Typical of the public relations programs of large corporations at midcentury was that of the Aluminum Company of America (ALCOA). Heading the operation was a vice president for public relations-advertising, who was aided by an assistant public relations director and advertising manager. Departments included community relations, product publicity, motion pictures and exhibits, employee publications, the news bureau, and speech writing. The *Alcoa News* magazine was published for all employees, and separate publications were published for each of the 20 plants throughout the United States. The company's main broadcast effort was sponsorship of Edward R. Murrow's *See It Now* television program.

By 1960, the U.S. Census counted 23,870 men and 7,271 women in public relations, although some observers put the figure at approximately 35,000. Today, the number of public relations practitioners has increased dramatically to about 350,000 nationwide, according to the U.S. Census Bureau. The latest estimate from the U.S. Department of Labor predicts that public relations will be one of the fastest-growing fields, with 39.8 percent growth for public relations specialists and 36.6 percent for public relations managers from 2004 to 2014.

Evolving Practice and Philosophy   The period from 1950 to 2000 marked distinct changes in the practice and philosophy of public relations. To place these changes in context, it's probably prudent to review some of what has been presented so far. First, the 1800s were marked by the press agentry model, which was best represented by the hype and exaggerations of P. T. Barnum and various land developers. By the early 20th century, however, public relations began to reinvent itself along journalistic lines, mainly because former newspaper reporters such as Ivy Lee started to do public relations work and counseling. Cynthia Clark of Boston University picked up the evolution in a succinct review that appeared in the *Public Relations Review*.

Clark says that before the 1920s, public relations was simply an extension of the journalistic function and was focused on "the dissemination of information or one-way communication models in which the quality of information was important but audience feedback had yet to be fully considered." James Grunig, in his interpretation of the evolutionary models of public relations, called this the *public information* model of public relations.

In the 1920s, thanks to breakthroughs in social science research, the focus of public relations shifted to the psychological and sociological effects of persuasive communication on target audiences. Both Rex Harlow and Edward Bernays, among others, believed that any campaign should be based on feedback and an analysis of an audience's dispositions and value system so messages could be structured for maximum effect. Grunig labeled this the *two-way asymmetric* model because it involved scientific persuasion based on the research of the target audience.

The 1960s saw Vietnam War protests, the civil rights movement, the environmental movement, interest in women's rights, and a host of other issues. Antibusiness sentiment was high, and corporations adjusted their policies to generate public goodwill and understanding. Thus, the idea of issues management was added to the job description of the public relations manager. This was the first expression of the idea that public relations should be more than simply persuading people that corporate policy was correct. During this period, the idea emerged that perhaps it would be beneficial to have a dialogue with various publics and adapt corporate policy to their particular concerns. Grunig labeled this approach *two-way symmetrical communication* because there's balance between the organization and its various publics; the organization and the public can influence each other.

The 1970s was an era of reform in the stock market and investor relations. The Texas Gulf Sulfur case changed investor relations forever by establishing the idea that a company must immediately disclose any information that may affect the value of its stock. The field of investor relations boomed.

By the 1980s, the concept that public relations was a management function was in full bloom. The term *strategic* became a buzzword, and the concept of management by objective (MBO) was heavily endorsed by public relations practitioners as they sought to prove to higher management that public relations did indeed contribute to the bottom line. Many definitions from this time emphasized public relations as a management function. As Derina Holtzhausen of the University of Florida notes, "Public relations management highlights organizational effectiveness, the strategic management of the function through strategic identification of publics, and issues management to prevent crisis."

Reputation, or *perception*, management was the buzzword of the 1990s. Burson-Marsteller, one of the largest public relations firms, decided that its business was not public relations but, rather, "perception management." Other firms declared that their business was "reputation management." However, there was some debate as to whether reputations can be managed, because reputation is the cumulative effect of numerous actions and activities.

The basic idea, however, was that public relations people worked to maintain credibility, to build solid internal and external relationships, and to manage issues. Inherent in this was the idea that public relations personnel should use research to do (1) environmental monitoring, (2) public relations audits, (3) communication audits, and (4) social audits. By doing these things, it would be possible to enhance corporate social responsibility (CSR).

By 2000, a number of scholars and practitioners began to conceptualize the practice of public relations as "relationship management," the basic idea being that public relations practitioners are in the business of building and fostering relationships with an organization's various publics. The idea has also caught on in marketing; *relationship marketing* is an effort to form a solid, ongoing relationship with the purchaser of a product or service.

Relationship management builds on Grunig's idea of two-way symmetrical communication, but goes beyond this by recognizing that an organization's publics are, as Stephen Bruning of Capital University notes, "active, interactive, and equal participants of an ongoing communication process." Bruning continues, "Typically, organizations are fairly effective at fulfilling content communication needs (communicating to key public members what is happening), but often fall short of fulfilling key public member relational communication needs (making the key public member feel they are valued in the relationship)."

An extension of relationship management is the *dialogic* (dialogue) model of public relations that has emerged since 2000. Michael Kent of Montclair University and Maureen Taylor of Rutgers University wrote in a *Public Relations Review* article that "A theoretical shift, from public relations reflecting an emphasis on managing communication, to an emphasis on communication as a tool of negotiating relationships, has been taking place for some time." Kent and Taylor say that good dialogic communication requires skills such as the following:

> . . . listening, empathy, being able to contextualize issues within local, national and international frameworks, being able to identify common ground between parties, thinking about long-term rather than short-term objectives, seeking out groups and individuals with opposing viewpoints, and soliciting a variety of internal and external opinions on policy issues.

The concept of dialogue places less emphasis on mass media distribution of messages and more on interpersonal channels. Kent and Taylor, for example, say that the Internet and World Wide Web are excellent vehicles for dialogue if the sites are interactive. They write, "The Web can be used to communicate directly with publics by offering real-time discussions, feedback loops, places to post comments, sources for organizational information, and postings of organizational member biographies and contact information."

Although there has been a somewhat linear progression in public relations practice and philosophy as the field has expanded, today's practice represents a mixture of public relations models. The Hollywood publicist/press agent and the public information officer for the government agency are still with us. We also still have marketing communications, which almost exclusively uses the concept of scientific persuasion and two-way asymmetric communication. However, when it comes to issues management and relationship building, the two-way symmetric and dialogue models seem to be the most appropriate.

Another model that is gaining acceptance goes back to the idea that public relations should do more than build relationships. Professor Glen Cameron of the University of Missouri, and coauthor of this book, says public relations should be more assertive and is best defined as the strategic management of competition and conflict in the best interests of the organization and, when possible, also in the interest of key publics. This concept is discussed further in Chapter 10.

on the job INSIGHTS

Classic Campaigns Show the Power of Public Relations

During the last half of the 20th century, a number of organizations and causes have used effective public relations to accomplish highly visible results. *PRWeek* convened a panel of public relations experts and came up with some of the "greatest campaigns ever" during this time period.

♦ **The Civil Rights Campaign.** Martin Luther King Jr. was an outstanding civil rights advocate and a great communicator. He organized the 1963 civil rights campaign and used such techniques as well-written, well-delivered speeches; letter writing; lobbying; and staged events (nonviolent protests) to turn a powerful idea into reality.

♦ **NASA.** From the very beginning NASA fostered media accessibility at Houston's Johnson Space Center. For example, NASA director Chris Kraft insisted that television cameras be placed on the lunar lander in 1969, and in later years reporters were invited inside mission control during the Apollo 13 mission. According to *PRWeek*, "Those historic moments have helped the public overlook the huge taxpayer expense and numerous technical debacles that could otherwise have jeopardized the future of the organization."

♦ **Cabbage Patch Kids.** Public relations launched the craze for the adoptable dolls and created a "must have" toy. The campaign set the standard for the introduction of a

new product and showed what a strong media relations program can do for a product.

♦ **Seat Belt Campaign.** In the 1980s, the U.S. automotive industry got the nation to "buckle up" through a public relations campaign. Tactics included winning the support of news media across the country, interactive displays, celebrity endorsements, letter-writing campaigns, and several publicity events, such as buckling a 600-foot-wide safety belt around a Hollywood sign. Notes *PRWeek*, "The results of one of the biggest public relations campaigns of all time were phenomenal, with the number of people 'buckling up' rising from 12 to 50 percent—it is now even higher."

♦ **Hands Across America.** The largest human gathering in history was a public relations stunt in 1986 that saw 7 million people across 16 states join hands to form a human chain to raise money for the hungry and the homeless. Even President Ronald Reagan participated.

♦ **StarKist Tuna.** When negative media coverage threatened the tuna industry because dolphins were getting caught in fishermen's nets, StarKist led the industry in changing fishing practices with conferences, videos, and an Earth Day coalition. About 90 percent of the public heard about the company's efforts, and StarKist was praised as an environmental leader.

The power of public relations was used in the civil rights movement to create public awareness and support. Here, Martin Luther King Jr. addresses a massive rally in Washington, D.C., and delivers his "I have a dream" speech.

♦ **Tylenol Crisis.** This has become the classic model for a product recall. When Johnson & Johnson found out that several people had died from cyanide-laced Tylenol capsules, a national panic erupted. Many thought the company would never recover from the damage caused by the tampering. However, the company issued a complete recall, redesigned the packaging so that it was tamper-proof, and launched a media campaign to keep the public fully informed. The result was that Tylenol survived the crisis and again became a best-seller.

♦ **Windows 95 Launch.** This campaign is easily in the product launch hall of fame. Microsoft, through media relations and publicity, achieved a unprecedented 99 percent awareness level among consumers before the product even hit the shelves.

♦ **Understanding AIDS.** This successful health education campaign changed the way that AIDS was perceived by Americans. In addition to a national mailing of a brochure titled "Understanding AIDS," there were grassroots activities that specifically targeted African Americans and Hispanics.

Source: "The Greatest Campaigns Ever." *PRWeek*, July 15, 2002, pp. 14–15.

Trend Lines in Today's Practice

Technological and social changes continue to transform aspects of public relations practice during the first decade of the 21st century. The following sections discuss the feminization of the field, the search for more ethnic and cultural diversity, and other trends that will shape the field's practice in the years to come.

Feminization of the Field

In terms of personnel, the most dramatic change has been the transformation of public relations from a male-dominated field to one in which women now constitute about 70 percent of practitioners.

The shift has been going on for several decades. In 1979, women made up 41 percent of the public relations field. By 1983, they became the majority (50.1 percent) of the public relations workforce. A decade later, the figure stood at 66.3 percent. By 2000, the percentage had leveled off at about 70 percent, where it remains today.

In contrast, the total number of women in the U.S. workforce is about 60 percent, according to the U.S. Bureau of Labor Statistics. The national organizations also reflect the trend. About 75 percent of the membership in the International Association of Business Communicators (IABC) are now women, and the PRSA says that more than 60 percent of its members are now women. As a comparison, the Radio & TV Directors Association reports that women now constitute 57 percent of televison anchors, 58 percent of television reporters, and 66 percent of the news producers in the United States.

About 65 percent of all majors in journalism and mass communications programs are now women, and it's estimated that 70 percent of public relations majors are female. It's worth noting that women also constitute the majority of students in law school, medical school, veterinary programs, and a number of other academic disciplines. A major reason for this is that more women are in the educational pipeline. For every 58 women, only 42 men enroll in college. And, four years later, studies show that for every 50 women who graduate, only 37 men do.

A number of reasons are given for the major influx of women into the field of public relations. Some of these reasons include the following:

1. women find a more welcoming environment in public relations and see more opportunities for advancement than in other communications fields, such as newspaper work;

2. women still make more money in public relations than comparable female-dominated fields, such as teaching and social work;
3. a woman can start a public relations firm without a lot of capital;
4. women tend to have better listening and communication skills than men; and
5. women are more sensitive than men in facilitating two-way communication.

> Women thrive in this industry because we're good at it—it taps into our natural abilities. We're highly intuitive, detail-oriented, and have a strong service mentality. We're good at finding the common ground and creating emotional bonds, which is the essence of a brand-target relationships.
>
> ——Marina Maher, founder and president of her own public relations firm, expressed these ideas in a *PRWeek* article

At the same time, a number of studies show that the majority of women in public relations earn less money than their male counterparts (see the salary survey information in Chapter 1) and are usually found at the tactical level of public relations practice rather than the management/counseling role.

The optimists say that women are still relatively new to the field and, with time, will eventually rise to their fair share of top posts. Feminist scholars refer to this assimilation model as liberal feminism. Radical feminists, however, disagree with this reasoning. They say that increasing the number of women in management is not enough, and that nothing less than a complete restructuring of society and its institutions will end gender discrimination and bias.

University of Maryland professors Linda Aldoory and Elizabeth Toth, writing in the *Journal of Public Relations Research*, say, "Surveys and focus groups continue to offer valid and reliable statistics and experiences attesting to the fact that, although the public relations profession is almost 70 percent women today, men are often favored for hiring, higher salaries, and promotions to management positions."

Indeed, women in higher levels of management are still unusual in business and industry. A study by D. Meyerson and J. Fletcher that was published in the *Harvard Business Review* found that women constituted only 10 percent of the senior managers in Fortune 500 companies and less than 4 percent of the uppermost ranks of CEOs, presidents, and executive vice presidents. It should also be noted, however, that women still comprise only 25 to 35 percent of the students in MBA programs—the traditional academic path to management positions.

The executive ranks in the public relations field also are predominantly male, but the number of females has increased dramatically in the past several years. The Arthur W. Page Society, which is composed of senior-level communication executives, is now about 35 percent female. The Public Relations Seminar (PRS), consisting of the top communications executives from the nation's 200 largest corporations, also remains predominantly male, but there is increasingly more female representation. More than half of the 33 new members in 2007 were female. Until the 1970s, both the Page Society and PRS were more than 90 percent male. Several women who have achieved senior status in public relations are featured in a gallery of photos on page 63.

A number of feminist scholars have explored the dimensions and impact of women in public relations, and some of their works are listed in the Suggested Readings at the end of the chapter.

As early as the 1970s, there was passionate debate about the large influx of women into the field. Many public relations leaders (men, of course) expressed a deep concern that feminization of the field would lower the status of public relations as a management

This group of high-ranking executives exemplifies the rise of women to senior positions in large corporations and public relations firms. From left to right, *top row:* Mary Lynn Cusick, SVP of Marketing and Communications, Bob Evans Farms, Inc.; Lisa R. Davis, VP of corporate communications, AstraZeneca Corporation; Aedhmar Hynes, CEO of Text 100 Public Relations. *Second row:* Denise Kaigler, Head of Global Corporate Communications, Reebok and US Adidas Group; Mary Ellen Keating, SVP of Corporate Communications and Public Affairs, Barnes & Noble, Inc.; Jill Nash, SVP of Communications, Yahoo. *Third row:* Shirley Powell, SVP of Corporate Communications, Turner Broadcasting System; Joan H. Walker, SVP of Corporate Relations, Allstate Insurance Company; C. Perry Yeatman, SVP of International Corporate Affairs and Global Issues Management, Kraft Foods.

function and that salaries in the field would drop given the history of other female-dominated fields, such as nursing, education, and social work.

Some alleged that business and industry were simply hiring women in public relations to show a commitment to affirmative action. Indeed, the Velvet Ghetto study of 1978 by the International Association of Business Communicators (IABC) found that companies did tend to load up their public relations departments with women to compensate for their scarcity in other professional and managerial capacities that lead to top management. The idea was that a company could have a woman vice president of public relations as "window dressing" without giving her any real management authority.

These arguments and fears have somewhat dissipated over the years. Public relations as a high-status occupation still has mixed reviews, but the power and influence of women in the management suite is stronger today than it has ever been. Also, salaries remain fairly high compared to other female-dominated fields. As for the Velvet Ghetto, most women who now occupy top positions reject the idea that they were hired as "window dressing." Aedhmar Hynes, CEO of Text 100, told *PRWeek*, "I have worked damned hard to get to where I am, but so have all the men who are in senior management positions."

Statistics and surveys still show, however, that there continues to be a gender gap in salaries as well as fewer women than men in senior management. A number of reasons have been offered, but the most recent research seems to indicate that the biggest factor is years of experience in the field. Youjin Choi and Linda Childers Hon of the University of Florida found that "[t]he number of years of respondents' professional experience was the single significant predictor of income." Aldodry and Toth also found years of experience to be a significant factor in income inequity, but they cited additional evidence that gender and interrupting a career affected salaries and job advancement as well.

The organizational environment also may affect a female's rise to top management. This theory is called the *structionalist perspective*. Toth argues that more women than men fulfill the technician role—a less powerful role than the managerial role—because of different experiences received on the job. Choi and Hon also say organizational structure is a problem because women in many organizations are excluded from influential networks, have a paucity of role models, and must work in male-dominated environments.

Choi and Hon, however, did find that organizations (such as many public relations firms) where women occupied 40 to 60 percent of the managerial positions were "gender integrated" and more friendly environments for the advancement of women than male-dominated organizational structures. In other words, organizations committed to gender equity were those organizations that practiced the most excellent public relations.

Recruitment of Minorities

According to the U.S. Census Bureau, minorities now constitute almost 33 percent of the 300 million people in the United States. The fastest-growing, and now largest group, is Hispanics. Hispanics are now 14 percent of the population, compared with 12.8 percent for Blacks/African Americans—a statistical difference of about 500,000 people. Asian/Pacific Islanders make up 4 percent, and Native Americans comprise 1 percent of the population.

The number of minorities in public relations falls considerably short of equaling the population at large, and a major concern of the profession is to make the field of public relations more representative of the population as a whole. Traditionally, the fields of journalism, advertising, and public relations have been white, upper-middle-class occupations. Unfortunately, despite the increase of minorities in the general population, not much has changed. Whites still comprise nearly 90 percent of public relations specialists in the United States, according to the U.S. Bureau of Labor Statistics.

Some industry surveys report a somewhat brighter diversity picture. In 2006, a *PRWeek* survey of 146 corporations found that communication staffs were 76.4 percent Caucasian, 7.4 percent African American, 4.0 percent Asian or Pacific Islander, 4.2 percent Hispanic, 0.3 percent Native American, and 2.9 percent Other. A survey of

179 public relations firms reported about the same percentages, but there was a slightly higher percentage of Hispanics and a slightly lower percentage of African Americans employed at public relations firms.

Many public relations employers express the desire to hire more minority candidates, but they have difficulty doing so because they receive so few applications. One problem is the education pipeline. About 200,000 undergraduates were studying journalism and mass communications (including public relations) across the country in 2005–2006, according to an annual study by the Association for Education and in Journalism and Mass Communications (AEJMC). Of that number, slightly less than 30 percent were what is described as minorities. Hispanics, which are the largest minority in the general population, constituted only 10 percent of journalism and mass communications enrollments in about 460 programs. This, however, is a signficant increase from recent years. The number of African Americans has remained somewhat stable at about 10 percent of total enrollments, Asian Americans are 3 percent, and Native Americans comprise 2 percent.

There is now a concentrated effort to attract more minorities. PRSA (www.diversity.prsa.org) and other major public relations organizations are increasing minority scholarships, organizing career fairs, and giving awards to local chapters that institute diversity programs. In a more recent development, Tyco Corporation funded a $300,000 three-year program with the Lagrant Foundation in Los Angeles to set up an internship program for minorities in public relations and advertising. Tyco, however, got a black eye when it tried to cancel the grant because of poor corporate earnings. As a result of the negative publicity, the company decided to honor its original commitment.

In addition, groups such as the National Black Public Relations Society (BPRS), the Hispanic Public Relations Association (HPRA), and the Asian American Advertising and Public Relations Association (AAAPRA) are being asked to help public relations firms and companies identify aspiring job applicants. Leaders of these minority associations, however, say that employers must make a more concerted effort to recruit minorities to public relations by going to traditionally black colleges, participating in more college career fairs, enlisting the aid of college professors to identify good candidates, and even placing job ads in publications that reach a variety of ethnic groups.

The globalization of public relations has also created a strong need for diversified ethnic staffs. Staff members are needed with language skills, personal knowledge of other nations, and sensitivity to the customs and attitudes of others. Knowledge of Spanish and Asian languages, such as Chinese, will be especially valuable.

on the job ETHICS

Making a Hiring Decision

There's a shortage of men and minorities in the public relations field, and your public relations firm is no exception. About 80 percent of the professional staff are women, including one woman who is Hispanic. As the owner of the firm, you believe in diversity and have a job opening for an assistant account executive. Seven of the applicants are women (White), and three applicants are men, including an African American. One of the female applicants is really outstanding, but the White male and the African American also have good credentials and could do the job. What should you do? Given the high percentage of women already in your firm, and the need for some gender balance in the workplace, would you hire one of the two men instead? And, if so, which one? Or would you go with the top candidate, who is another female?

> "The public relations industry, long an enclave of well-paid, college-educated, white professionals, is finally waking up to the reality that it needs to do better PR to attract people of color."
>
> ——Tannette Johnson-Elie, columnist, *Milwaukee Journal-Sentinel*

Transformation of the Field: The Next 50 Years

Feminization of the field and the recruitment of a more diverse workforce are already established trends, but other issues and trends will also transform the practice of public relations in the coming years. The following are some of the major trend lines.

A Multicultural World   The necessity for diversity in public relations staffs has just been discussed, but of equal importance is the recognition that we now live in a multicultural world that requires sensitivity and knowledge of multiple audiences. Minorities, for example, will comprise one-third of the U.S. population by 2016. In terms of projected global economic growth to 2020, China and India will account for about 40 percent, as compared to the United States at 15 percent and Europe at less than 10 percent. Corporations, such as Dow Chemical, already have 80 percent of its employees located at 156 manufacturing plants outside the United States; and Starbucks plans 30,000 stores worldwide in the coming years.

At the same time, by 2020, there will be an estimated 700 million individuals in the world over 65 years of age. By 2050, 42 percent of Japan's population will be over 60. There is great potential for increased cultural clashes; 25 percent of France's population, for example, will be Muslim by 2030. The world is getting connected; by 2010, two billion people will be on the Internet and another two billion will have cell phones. Fred Cook, president of Golin Harris, says, "The seismic shift to globalization and multiculturalism will transform communication. It will not be enough to address emerging cultures by simply creating separate practices to focus on individual ethnic groups. In the coming decades, the current ethnocentric approach to public relations will be replaced by a more holistic perspective." See Chapter 11, Reaching a Multicultural Audience.

The Public Demand for Transparency   Instant global communications, corporate finance scandals, government regulation, and the increased public demand for accountability have made it necessary for all society's institutions, including business and industry, to be more transparent in their operations.

A position paper by Vocus, a communications software firm, says it best: "An organization's every action is subject to public scrutiny. Everything—from the compensation provided to a departing CEO to the country from which a manufacturing plant orders its materials—is considered open to public discourse."

The Institute of Public Relations (IPR) in the United Kingdom says that the role of public relations has changed considerably over the last decade: "Instead of being used primarily as a way to influence and secure media coverage, organizations are using public relations to communicate with their stakeholders as society demands more transparency."

> " The PR industry must continue to evolve beyond traditional media relations or it will end like buggy whip manufacturers—experts at placing stories with media that no longer exist. "
>
> ———Fred Cook, president and CEO, Golin Harris public relations

Expanding the Role of Public Relations   Professionals have already repositioned public relations as being more than media relations and publicity, but those hard-fought gains will need to be reinforced in the coming years as marketing and management consultants enter the field offering the ability to also build relationships with various publics. Tom Gable, a public relations counselor in San Diego, says, "Our challenge and opportunity will be to own the areas of positioning, branding, reputation management, and building relationships for the long term with multiple constituencies." Increasingly, public relations personnel will play an even greater role in planning and executing integrated communications campaigns.

The New Imperative: Corporate Social Responsibility (CSR)   Global warming, environmental integrity, sustainable development, fair treatment of employees on a global basis, product quality and safety, and ethical supply chains are now on the agenda of all organizations. All elements of the organization are involved in the creation of the socially responsible corporation, but public relations plays an essential central role. James Murphy, global managing director of communications for Accenture, expresses it well: "PR staffs are in the forefront of building trust and credibility—and coordinating corporate social responsibility efforts. These are the people who deal with trust issues all the time; therefore, we're in a good position to address them." CSR is further discussed in Chapter 17.

Increased Emphasis on Measurement and Evaluation   Public relations professionals will continue to improve measurement techniques for showing management how their activities actually contribute to the bottom line.

One dimension is the return on investment (ROI). According to Kathy Cripps, chair of the Council of Public Relations Firms, two other important dimensions of measurement are (1) measuring outcomes—the long-term effectiveness of a public relations program and (2) measuring outputs—how well a program was executed and how effective its tactics were.

Management increasingly demands better measurement, and Ed Nicholson, director of media relations at Tyson Foods, says, "We're compelled to create measurable objectives and evaluation that goes beyond clip counts and impressions and demonstrate delivered value to the organization." Measurement and evaluation are further discussed in Chapter 8.

Managing the 24/7 News Cycle   The flow of news and information is now a global activity that occurs 24 hours day, 7 days a week. This means that public relations personnel must constantly update information, answer journalists' inquiries at all hours of the day, and be aware that any and all information is readily available to a worldwide audience.

New media and technology make it possible to disseminate news and information 24 hours a day, but the effect is often information overload. In addition to the proliferation of traditional media outlets, there are virtually millions of Web sites. A major challenge to today's practitioners is how to cope with the cascade of information and how to give it shape and purpose so that it's relevant to multiple audiences.

The Fragmentation of Mass Media   Traditional media isn't what it used to be. Circulation of English-language dailies in the United States has dropped 11 percent since 1990. Network evening news ratings have fallen 34 percent since 1998. Local news share is down 16 percent since 1997. Even cable news ratings have been flat since 2001. "Mass media," according to Fred Cook of Golin Harris, "is rapidly being atomized— moving from mainstream to multistream."

In other words, public relations personnel are now expanding their communication tools to account for the fact that no single mass media, or combination of them, will be a good vehicle for reaching key publics. See Chapter 13 for more information.

One new avenue is the ethnic press, whose growth has been particularly dramatic. Over the past 13 years, Spanish-language newspaper circulation has nearly quadrupled to 1.7 million. In addition, there are more than 600 Asian media outlets in the United States and the number increases almost daily. Another avenue is the Internet, which has seen its audience dramatically increase in just a few years. More than 55 percent of Internet users aged 18 to 34 obtain news online in a typical week, according to a UCLA Internet study.

Another trend line is the electronic preparation of media materials. The printed news release and media kit are rapidly becoming artifacts of the past. An IABC study found that electronic newsletters, e-mail notices, Web sites, and even CDs or DVDs are rapidly replacing print materials. See Chapters 14 and 15.

The Rise of Social Media   Mass media may be declining in power and influence, but a new category of "mass" communication has rapidly developed in the past several years as the Internet continues to reinvent itself on practically a daily basis. Today, public relations professionals reach and interact with audiences via RSS feeds, blogs, vlogs, podcasts, Webcasts, MySpace, YouTube, and even Second Life. In early 2007, for example, YouTube (owned by Google) was already streaming 200 million videos a day and MySpace (owned by News Corp.) claimed a global membership of 180 million. FaceBook had 6 million members and was growing by 1 million every few days. All these technologies are collectively called "social media" and offer public relations practitioners unparalleled opportunities for communicating, listening, and interacting with large numbers of individuals on a global basis. See Chapter 13, New Technologies and Social Media.

Outsourcing to Public Relations Firms   The outsourcing trend developed some years ago, but now it's almost universal. A survey by Ian Mitroff, Gerald Swerling, and Jennifer Floto published in *The Strategist* notes, "The use of agencies is now the norm in American business across all revenue categories and industries in this study: 85 percent of respondents (corporate executives) work with outside PR firms." This is not to say that corporate public relations departments are disappearing, but, increasingly, such tactics as media relations, annual reports, and sponsored events are being outsourced to public relations firms. In addition, it's entirely possible that even writing news releases and making media calls will be outsourced to places such as India. In fact, Indian companies already make about $280 million annually from outsourced advertising production. See Chapter 4, Firms and Departments.

The Need for Lifelong Learning   Public relations personnel, given the rapid additions to knowledge in today's society, will need to continually update their knowledge base just to stay current. New findings in a variety of fields are emerging that can be applied to public relations practice. Some of these fields are behavioral genetics, evolutionary social psychology, economics, the physics of information, social network analysis, semiotic game theory, and the use of technology to create relationships and dialogue with various publics.

In addition, the need to specialize in a particular field or area of public relations will increase because it's becoming almost impossible for a generalist to master the detailed knowledge required for such areas as health care and financial relations. One growing specialty area is environmental communication. In general, as mentioned in Chapter 1, tomorrow's practitioners will need more business knowledge and management skills as the field moves away from a purely journalistic orientation.

SUMMARY

The Roots of Public Relations

Although public relations is a 20th-century term, the roots of the practice go back to ancient Egyptian, Greek, and Roman times.

Early Beginnings in America

Private companies attracted immigrants to the New World through promotion and glowing accounts of fertile land. The American Revolution, in part, was the result of such staged events as the Boston Tea Party and the writing of the *Federalist Papers*.

The Age of Press Agentry and Hype

The 1800s were the golden age of the press agent. P. T. Barnum pioneered many techniques that are still used today. In addition, the settlement of the West was due in large part to promotions by land developers and American railroads. Toward the end of the 19th century, corporations began to use public relations as a response to public criticism of their policies and actions.

The Age of Public Relations Pioneers

From 1900 to 1950, the practice of public relations was transformed by individuals such as Henry Ford, Ivy Lee, George Creel, Edward B. Bernays, and Arthur Page. The concept moved from press agentry to the more journalistic approach of distributing accurate public information.

Public Relations Comes of Age

The period from 1950 to 2000 saw the consolidation of public relations as a major established force in American society. As the U.S. population grew, the economy expanded, and big business became the norm, organizations found it necessary to employ public relations specialists to effectively communicate with the mass media and a variety of publics. This was the age of scientific persuasion, management by objective, and strategic thinking.

Evolving Practice and Philosophy

At the turn of the century, public relations was widely considered to be a management function. Its purpose was to engage in "reputation management" and to build mutually beneficial relationships with various constituencies. Public relations also took an increased role in launching new products, building brands, and positioning the organization in the marketplace.

Females Become the Majority

A major trend in public relations has been the influx of women into the field. Women now comprise 70 percent of public relations practitioners in America. This has raised questions about gender discrimination, why women hold more tactical than managerial positions, and whether there is still a "glass ceiling."

Recruitment of Minorities

The public relations workforce is still overwhelmingly white. Efforts are being made to diversify the workforce to better represent ethnic/minority groups. Hispanics now constitute the largest minority in the United States, but are poorly represented in public relations practice.

Other Trends: The Next 50 Years

Public relations professionals will face a host of challenges during the first decade of the 21st century, including communicating in a multicultural world, facilitating organizational transparency, managing corporate social responsibility (CSR) programs, doing a better job of measurement and evaluation, managing the 24/7 news cycle, utilizing multiple communication channels, mastering the new technologies of communication, and engaging in lifelong learning.

CASE ACTIVITY What Would You Do?

A major trend in public relations has been the feminization of the field, with current estimates placing the percentage of women professionals at 70 percent. Working in class in small groups of 2 to 5 students, discuss what you think the implications of this trend are for the profession. Select a spokesperson for your group and work together to prepare a five-minute briefing for the class on the role of women in public relations. Some starting points might be:

- salary differentials
- the supposed unique skills and strengths that women and men bring to public relations
- the historical role of women in public relations
- go in your own direction as a group!

QUESTIONS for Review and Discussion

1. The roots of public relations extend deep into history. What were some of the early antecedents to today's public relations practice?

2. The Boston Tea Party has been described as the "greatest and best-known publicity stunt of all time." Would you agree? Do you feel that staged events are a legitimate way to publicize a cause and motivate people?

3. Which concepts of publicity and public relations practiced by P. T. Barnum should modern practitioners use? Which should they reject?

4. Describe briefly the publicity strategies employed by Henry Ford and Theodore Roosevelt.

5. What are the four important contributions Ivy Lee made to public relations?

6. Arthur W. Page enunciated six principles of public relations management. Do you think these "principles" are as relevant today as they were in the 1930s?

7. What's your assessment of Ivy Lee's work for the Rockefeller family in the Colorado Fuel & Iron Company labor strife? Do you think his approach was sound? What would you have done differently?

8. What effect did the Creel Committee have on the development of public relations?

9. Edward B. Bernays, who has been called the "father of modern public relations," had many innovative, successful campaigns. Of those listed in the book, which one is your favorite? Why?

10. Benjamin Sonnenberg once said, "I build large pedestals for small people" as an explanation of what he did in public relations. Would you agree that this is the essence of public relations? Why or why not?

11. Name at least three individuals who made major contributions to the development of public relations in the United States.

12. Summarize the major developments in the philosophy and practice of public relations from the 1920s to 2000.

13. James Grunig outlined four models of public relations practice. Name and describe each one. Do the models help explain the evolution of public relations theory?

14. Public relations is now described as "relationship management." How would you describe this concept to a friend? A newer concept is the idea that the purpose of public relations is to establish a "dialogue" with individuals and various publics. Is this a worthy concept?

15. Females now constitute the majority of public relations personnel. How do you personally feel about this? Does it make the field of public relations more attractive or less attractive to you?

16. Public relations is still considered a "lily white" profession. How do you think more minorities can be attracted to the field?

17. Identify and describe at least three major trends that will affect public relations practice in the future.

SUGGESTED READINGS

Aldoory, Linda, and Toth, Elizabeth. "Leadership and Gender in Public Relations: Perceived Effectiveness of Transformational and Transactional Leadership Styles." *Journal of Public Relations Research*, Vol. 16, No. 2, 2004, pp. 157–183.

Aldoory, Linda, and Toth, Elizabeth. "Gender Discrepancies in a Gendered Profession: A Developing Theory for Public Relations." *Journal of Public Relations Research*, Vol. 14, No. 2, 2002, pp. 103–126.

Anderson, William B. "We Can Do It: A Study of the Women's Field Army Public Relations Efforts." *Public Relations Review*, Vol. 30, No. 2, 2004, pp. 187–196.

Brody, E. W. "Have You Made the Transition? Are You Practicing Public Relations in the 21st Century Rather Than the 20th?" *Public Relations Quarterly*, Spring 2004, pp. 7–8.

Choi, Youjin, and Hon, Linda Childers. "The Influence of Gender Composition in Powerful Positions on Public Relations Practitioners' Gender-Related Perceptions." *Journal of Public Relations Research*, Vol. 14, No. 3, 2002, pp. 229–263.

Cook, Fred. "It's a Small World After All: Multiculturalism, Authenticity, Connectedness Among Trends to Watch in Next 50 Years." *The Strategist*, Winter 2007, pp. 30–33.

Curtin, Patricia A., and Gaither, T. Kenn. *International Public Relations: Negotiating Culture Identity and Power*. Thousand Oaks, CA: Sage, 2007.

Cutlip, Scott M. *The Unseen Power: A History of Public Relations*. Mahwah, NJ: Lawrence Erlbaum, 1994.

"Diversity Survey 2006." *PRWeek*, December 11, 2006, pp. 14–16, 19–20.

Grunig, Larissa, Toth, Elizabeth, and Hon, Linda Childers. *Women in Public Relations: How Gender Influences Practice.* New York: Guilford Press, 2001.

Harrison, Shirley, and Moloney, Kevin. "Comparing Two Public Relations Pioneers: American Ivy Lee and British John Elliott." *Public Relations Review*, Vol. 30, No. 2, 2004, pp. 205–214.

Martinelli, Diana K., and Mucciarone, Jeff. "New Deal Public Relations: A Glimpse into FDR Press Secretary Stephen Early's Work." *Public Relations Review*, Vol. 33, No. 1, March 2007, pp. 49–57.

O'Neil, Julie. "An Analysis of the Relationship Among Structure, Influence, and Gender: Helping to Build a Feminist Theory of Public Relations." *Journal of Public Relations Research*, Vol. 15, No. 2, 2003, pp. 151–179.

Pompper, Donnalyn. "Linking Ethnic Diversity and Two-Way Symmetry: Modeling Female African American Practitioner Roles." *Journal of Public Relations Research*, Vol. 16, No. 3, 2004, pp. 269–299.

Procter-Rogers, Cheryl. "Celebrating Women's Role in PR," *PRWeek*, March 27, 2006, p. 3.

Stole, Inger L. *Advertising on Trial: Consumer Activism and Corporate Public Relations in the 1930's.* Champaign: University of Illinois Press, 2006.

Shortman, Melanie, and Bloom, Jonah. "The Greatest Campaigns Ever?" *PRWeek*, July 15, 2002, pp. 14–15.

St. John, Burton. "The Case for Ethical Propaganda within a Democracy? Ivy Lee's Successful 1913–1914 Railroad Rate Campaign." *Public Relations Review*, Vol. 32, 2006, pp. 221–228.

Van Ruler, Betteke. "The Communication Grid: An Introduction of a Model of Four Communication Strategies." *Public Relations Review*, Vol. 30, No. 2, 2004, pp. 123–143.

What Is Ethics?

J. A. Jaksa and M. S. Pritchard provide a good definition of ethics in their book *Methods of Analysis*. "Ethics," they say, "is concerned with how we should live our lives. It focuses on questions about what is right or wrong, fair or unfair, caring or uncaring, good or bad, responsible or irresponsible, and the like."

A person's conduct is measured not only against his or her conscience, but also against some norm of acceptability that has been determined by society, professional groups, and a person's employer. The difficulty in ascertaining whether an act is ethical lies in the fact that individuals have different standards and perceptions of what is "right" or "wrong." Most ethical conflicts are not black or white, but fall into a gray area.

A person's belief system can also determine how that person acts in a specific situation. Philosophers say that the three basic value orientations are

1. *Absolute*. The absolutist believes that every decision is either "right" or "wrong," regardless of the consequences. It is based on the philosophy of Immanuel Kant that the end cannot justify the means.

2. *Existential*. The existentialist, whose choices are not made in a prescribed value system, decides on the basis of immediate practical choice. This approach is somewhat grounded in Artistotle's idea that individuals should seek a balance, or midpoint, between two extremes. In other words, Artistotle would disagree with Kant by saying, "never say never."

3. *Situational*. The situationalist believes that each decision is based on what would cause the least harm or the most good. This often is called the utilitarian approach. This concept was advanced by John Stuart Mill, who believed the end could justify the means as long as the result benefited the greatest number of people.

Another approach, which has been handed down through the centuries, is simply the Golden Rule—love your neighbor as yourself. Another way of putting it is "treat others as you would like to be treated." This approach assumes that individuals will achieve their highest potential if they practice such virtues as honesty, courage, compassion, generosity, fidelity, integrity, fairness, self-control, prudence, and love of God.

Various organizations have interpreted the writings of various philosophers, often arcane and complex, to come up with more simplified rules for ethical behavior. Rotary International, for example, has the Four-Way Test for ethical decision making: (1) Is it the truth? (2) Is it fair to all concerned? (3) Will it build goodwill and better friendships? and (4) Will it be beneficial to all concerned?

Public relations professionals, of course have the burden of making ethical decisions that take into consideration (1) the public interest, (2) the employer's self-interests, (3) the standards of the public relations profession, and (4) their personal values. In an ideal world, these four spheres would not conflict and clear-cut guidelines make ethical decisions easy. In reality, however, making the right ethical decision is often a complex process involving many considerations.

Mark Weiner, senior vice president of Cison US, Inc., says it best in an article that appeared in PRSA's *The Strategist*. He wrote, "How many PR people have been asked to over-represent a product? How many agencies have been asked to take sides on issues that conflict with a healthy environment? The answer is that many of us participate in areas where ethical standards are vague at best." In other words, the response to these thorny issues usually depend on the individual's interpretation of truth-telling, promise-keeping, loyalty, and what is morally right.

The Ethical Advocate

Another issue of concern to students, as well as public relations critics, is whether a public relations practitioner can ethically communicate at the same time he or she is serving as an advocate for a particular client or organization. To some, traditional ethics prohibits a person from taking an advocacy role because that person is "biased" and trying to "manipulate" people.

David L. Martinson of Florida International University makes the point, however, that the concept of role differentiation is important. This means that society, in general, expects public relations people to be advocates, just as they expect advertising copywriters to make a product sound attractive, journalists to be objective, and attorneys to defend someone in court. Because of this concept, Martinson believes that "Public relations practitioners are justified in disseminating persuasive information so long as objective and reasonable persons would view those persuasive efforts as truthful." He continues, in a monograph published by the public relations division of the Association for Education in Journalism and Mass Communications:

> " We are advocates of what we believe to be the truth and not merely blind advocates for our organizations. We need to take all of this very seriously and on a very personal level. "
>
> ————W. D. (Bill) Nielsen, former VP of public affairs for Johnson & Johnson, speaking at the 44th annual lecture of the Institute for Public Relations

Reasonable persons recognize that public relations practitioners can serve important societal goals in an advocacy (role defined) capacity. What reasonable persons require, however, is that such advocacy efforts be directed toward genuinely informing impacted publics. Communication efforts . . . will not attempt, for example, to present false/deceptive/misleading information under the guise of literal truth no matter how strongly the practitioner wants to convince others of the merits of a particular client/organization's position/cause. . . . Role differentiation is not a license to "lie, cheat, and/or steal" on behalf of clients whether one is an attorney, physician, or public relations practitioner.

"Hold everything! The P.R. department just sent over _this_ chart."

This *New Yorker* cartoon, although humorous, gives the impression that the purpose of public relations is to twist the facts. In reality, the moral imperative for a public relations professional is to tell the truth.

The Role of Professional Organizations

Professional organizations such as the Public Relations Society of America (PRSA) and the International Association of Business Communicators (IABC) have done much to develop the standards of ethical, professional public relations practice and to help society understand the role of public relations. Although such organizations represent only a small percentage of the total number of individuals working in public relations, they set the ethical standards for, and foster professionalism among, public relations practitioners. The following section gives a thumbnail sketch of the largest professional groups serving the public relations profession.

The Public Relations Society of America

The largest national public relations organization in the world is the Public Relations Society of America (PRSA); the group's Web site can be found at www.prsa.org. PRSA is headquartered in New York City. It has almost 22,000 members organized into 110 chapters nationwide. It also has 19 professional interest sections that represent such areas as employee communications, counseling firms, entertainment and sports, food and beverage, multicultural communications, public affairs and government, nonprofit organizations, travel and tourism, and even public relations educators. About a third of the PRSA membership work in a corporate environment; another 20 percent work for a public relations firm.

The Strategist and *Tactics* magazines are published by the Public Relations Society of America (PRSA) as one way of providing professional development for its members.

PRSA has an extensive professional development program that offers short courses, seminars, teleconferences, and Webcasts throughout the year. Some typical topics from a recent listing of events included seminars on strategic management planning, media relations building, crisis communication strategy, employee communication programs, and emerging trends in reputation management. Topical workshops have included "The Impact and Implications of Immigration Reform," "Buzz PR and Experiential Marketing," and "Social Media Update: Legal Implications."

In addition to workshops and seminars, PRSA holds an annual meeting and publishes two major periodicals. *Tactics* is a monthly tabloid of current news and professional tips. *The Strategist* is a quarterly magazine that contains in-depth articles about the profession and issues touching on contemporary public relations practice. The organization also sponsors the Silver Anvil and Bronze Anvil awards that recognize outstanding public relations campaigns. The Silver Anvil awards, started in 1946, have honored more than 1,000 organizations in 54 categories for excellence in planning and implementation. The Bronze Anvils recognize outstanding examples of tactical communication vehicles such as media kits, newsletters, video news releases, and satellite media tours. A number of these award-winning campaigns and materials are included in this book.

PRSA is also the parent organization of the Public Relations Student Society of America (PRSSA), whose Web site can be found at www.prssa.org. This group

PRSSA Public Relations Student Society of America

celebrated its 40th anniversary in 2007 and is the world's largest preprofessional public relations organization, having 287 campus chapters with almost 10,000 student members.

The student group, which has its own national officers, serves its members at the local chapter level through a variety of campus programs and maintains a close working relationship with the local sponsoring PRSA chapter. It has a national publication, *Forum*, and sponsors a national case study competition so that students have the opportunity to exercise the analytical skills and mature judgment required for public relations problem solving. The organization awards a number of scholarships, holds regional and national conventions, and actively promotes mentoring between students and professionals in the field. PRSSA members, after graduation, are eligible to become associate members of PRSA.

The International Association of Business Communicators

The second-largest organization is the International Association of Business Communicators (IABC). The group's Web site can be accessed at www.iabc.com. It has almost 15,000 members in 70 nations. About 90 percent of the membership, however, is from the United States and Canada. The Toronto Chapter is the largest chapter with 1,400 members. Other large chapters outside North America are the United Kingdom with 227 members and the New South Wales (Sydney, Australia, area) chapter with 211. According to an IABC profile of members, almost half of its membership works in a corporate environment.

IABC, headquartered in San Francisco, has similar objectives as the PRSA. Its mission is to "provide lifelong learning opportunities that give IABC members the tools and information to be the best in their chosen disciplines." It does this through year-round seminars and workshops and an annual meeting. The organization also has an awards program, the Gold Quill, that honors excellence in business communication. Of the 1,170 entries received in 2007 from 22 nations, 102 entries were selected to receive top awards for excellence. The IABC publication is *Communication World*; it features professional tips and in-depth articles on current issues. It also has *CW Bulletin*, which is e-mailed to members. IABC also sponsors about 25 student chapters on various campuses with a total membership of about 750.

The International Public Relations Association

A third organization, thoroughly global in scope, is the International Public Relations Association (IPRA), which is based in London. The group's Web site is available at www.ipra.org. IPRA has about 1,000 members in almost 100 nations. Its membership is primarily senior international public relations executives, and its mission is "to provide intellectual leadership in the practice of international public relations by making available to our members the services and information that will help them to meet their professional responsibilities and to succeed in their careers."

The international orientation of IPRA makes it somewhat different from national groups. It bases its code of ethics on the charter of the United Nations. The first point of its 13-point code states that members shall endeavor "to contribute to the achievement of the moral and cultural conditions enabling human beings to reach their full stature and enjoy the rights to each they are entitled under the 'Universal Declaration of Human Rights.'" In terms of dealing with misinformaton, IPRA states that members shall refrain from "Circulating information which is not based on established and ascertainable facts."

IPRA organizes regional and international conferences to discuss issues in global public relations, but it also reaches its widespread membership through its Web site and *Frontline*, its major online publication. It also issues Gold Papers on public relations practice, conducts an annual awards competition (Golden World Awards), and is currently conducting a media transparency campaign to encourage media in various nations not to accept bribes in exchange for news coverage. See the Insights box on page 90.

Other Groups

The PRSA, IABC, and IPRA are the largest broad-based organizations for communicators and public relations professionals. In addition, there are smaller, more specialized organizations. Three of the better-known ones in the United States include the Council for the Advancement and Support of Education (CASE), the National Investor Relations Institute (NIRI), and the National School Public Relations Association (NSPRA). There also are a number of statewide groups, such as the Florida Public Relations Association, the Maine Public Relations Council, the Texas Public Relations Association, and the Puerto Rico Public Relations Association (Asociacion de Relacionistas Profesionales de Puerto Rico).

Professional Codes of Conduct

Practically every national public relations organization has a code of ethics, and the codes of such organizations as the Canadian Public Relations Society (CPRS), the Public Relations Institute of Southern Africa (PRISA), and the Public Relations Institute of Australia (PRIA) are very similar to the PRSA code (see the Insights box on page 78).

Most national organizations place heavy emphasis on educating their members about professional standards rather than having a highly structured grievance process in place. They do reserve the right, however, to censure or expel members who violate the organization's code or who are convicted of a crime in a court of law. PRSA, at one time, did have an elaborate judicial process, but in 33 years, only about 10 members were ever disciplined by the organization.

The IABC's code is based on the principle that professional communication is not only legal and ethical, but also in good taste and sensitive to cultural values and beliefs. Members are encouraged to be truthful, accurate, and fair in all of their communications.

According to IABC, the organization "fosters compliance with its code by engaging in global communication campaigns rather than through negative sanctions." The code is published in several languages, and IABC bylaws require that articles on ethics and professional conduct be published in the organization's monthly publication, *Communication World*. In addition, the organization includes sessions on ethics at its annual meeting, conducts workshops on ethics, and encourages chapters to include discussions of ethics in their local programs. PRSA and other organizations have similar programs.

> " Three principles are essential:
> - Professional communication is legal
> - Professional communication is ethical
> - Professional communication is in good taste "
> ——IABC Code of Ethics

Critics often complain that such codes of ethics "have no teeth" because there's really no punishment for being unethical and unprofessional. About the only penalty

on the job
INSIGHTS

PRSA's Code of Ethics

The Public Relations Society of America (PRSA) has a fairly comprehensive code of ethics for its members. The group believes that "professional values are vital to the integrity of the profession as a whole."

Its six core values are as follows:

- Advocacy: Serving the public interest by acting as responsible advocates for clients or employers.
- Honesty: Adhering to the highest standards of accuracy and truth in advancing the interests of clients and employers.
- Expertise: Advancing the profession through continued professional development, research, and education.
- Independence: Providing objective counsel and being accountable for individual actions.
- Loyalty: Being faithful to clients and employers, but also honoring an obligation to serve the public interest.
- Fairness: Respecting all opinions and supporting the right of free expression.

The following is a summary of the major provisions and the kinds of activities that would constitute improper conduct.

Free Flow of Information

The free flow of accurate and truthful information is essential to serving the public interest in a democratic society. You should not give an expensive gift to a journalist as a bribe so that he or she will write favorable stories about the organization or its products/services. Lavish entertainment and travel junkets for government officials, beyond the limits set by law, also are improper.

Competition

Healthy and fair competition among professionals should take place within an ethical framework. An employee of an organization should not share information with a public relations firm that is in competition with other firms for the organization's business. You should not disparage your competition or spread malicious rumors about them to recruit business or to hire their employees.

Disclosure of Information

Open communication is essential to informed decision making in a democratic society. You should not conduct grassroots and letter-writing campaigns on behalf of undisclosed interest groups. In addition, you should not deceive the public by employing people to pose as "volunteers" at a public meeting. This also applies to booking "spokespersons" on talk shows without disclosing that they are being paid by an organization or special interest for their appearance. Intentionally leaving out essential information or giving a false impression of a company's financial performance is considered "lying by omission." If you do discover that inaccurate information has been given out, you have a responsibility to correct it immediately.

Safeguarding Confidences

Client trust requires appropriate protection of confidential and private information. You should not leak proprietary information that could adversely affect some other party. If you change jobs, you should not use confidential information from your previous employer to benefit the competitive advantage of your new employer.

Conflicts of Interest

Avoid real, potential, or perceived conflicts of interest among clients, employers, and the public. A public relations firm should inform a prospective client that it already represents a competitor or has a conflicting interest. A firm, for example, should not be doing public relations for two competing fast-food restaurant chains.

Enhancing the Profession

Public relations professionals should work constantly to strengthen the public's trust in the profession. You should not say a product is safe when it isn't. If it's unsafe under certain usage or conditions, you have an obligation to disclose this information.

For the complete code, please consult PRSA's Web site at www.prsa.org.

that an organization can impose is to expel a person from the organization; however, that person can continue to work in public relations.

Problems with code enforcement, however, are not unique to public relations groups. Professional organizations, including the Society for Professional Journalists, are voluntary organizations, and they don't have the legal authority to ban members from the field because no licensing is required to practice, which will be discussed shortly. Such organizations run a high risk of being sued for defamation or restricting the First Amendment guarantee of free speech if they try to expel a member or restrict his or her occupation.

Consequently, most professional groups believe that the primary purpose of establishing codes of ethics is not enforcement, but rather education and information. The Global Alliance, consisting of about 60 national and regional public relations groups, strongly endorses professional development and states that members should "actively pursue personal professional development." Thus, all groups seek to enunciate standards of conduct that will guide members in their professional lives. It seems to work. Several studies have shown that the members of PRSA and other organizations have a much higher awareness of ethics and professional standards than nonmembers.

Codes for Specific Situations

Various organizations, as noted, have established codes for the general practice of public relations, but various groups have also endorsed codes of conduct for specific situations and issues, such as the distribution of financial information, video news releases, the use of the Internet, environmental sensitivity, and even corporate practice.

Financial Information   The National Investors Relations Institute (NIRI), for example, adopted a new 12-point code of ethics in the wake of corporate financial scandals such as Enron, WorldCom, and Tyco. NIRI (www.niri.org) requires all its members to affirm the code in writing. The code holds members responsible for such things as (1) exercising independent professional judgment, (2) keeping track of company affairs and all investor laws and regulations, and (3) ensuring full and fair disclosure. Members sanctioned for violating laws or SEC regulations are expelled from the organization.

Video News Releases   Controversy about the use of video news releases (VNRs) by television stations and whether the viewing public has been informed about the source of information also has prompted greater attention to ethical behavior by the stations and the public relations industry that produces VNRs for any number of clients. On one hand, the Television stations are being faulted for not telling viewers the source of video footage that is often used in newscasts. In fact, the Center for Media and Democracy found that 77 stations had aired VNRs without disclosing the source. An earlier survey by *TV Guide* found that almost half of Television station news directors failed to identify the source of VNRs on their news programs. *TV Guide*, as well as activist groups, have labeled VNRs "fake news."

On the other hand, producers of VNRs have been criticized for not properly identifying the sponsor (or client) of the material. One technique, for example, was having an actor pose as a newsperson on the VNR and simply saying, "This is Jane Doe, reporting from Washington." VNR producers, however, say VNRs are clearly identified in the packaging and in advisories to television news editors. "Don't blame the makers of VNRs," said Bob Kimmel, senior vice president of the News/Broadcast

The controversy over the use of video news releases by television stations, and not disclosing the source of them, is captured by this cartoon. Copyright: *O'Dwyer's PR Report*, 2007. Artist: Bill Kress.

Network, a producer and distributor of such releases. Kimmel continued, "We are doing everything we can by putting the source of the material on the VNR. We can't control what happens at the news level, however." Many stations apparently don't like to admit that they use video material that is not produced by their own staffs.

The VNR controversy got the attention of the Federal Communications Commission (FCC), which began to investigate whether Television stations had violated its guidelines about disclosure of third-party information and sponsorship of material used in newscasts. This, in turn, prompted 14 producers of VNRs to organize a National Association of Broadcast Communicators (NABC) (www.broadcastcommunicators.org) to assure the public and television industry critics (as well as the FCC) that all VNRs produced by them contained accurate information and were clearly labeled as coming from a corporate sponsor. Ethical guidelines endorsed by the NABC include:

- Information contained in a VNR must be accurate and reliable. Intentionally false and misleading information must be avoided.
- A video news release must be identified as such, both on the video's opening slate and on any advisory material and scripts.
- The sponsor of the release must be clearly identified on the tape. The name and phone number of the sponsor must be provided on the video for journalists to contact for further information.
- Persons interviewed on the VNR must be accurately identified by name, title, and affiliation in the video.

The Radio-Television News Directors Association (RTNDA) also has a voluntary ethics code that tells members to disclose the source of third-party content whenever possible. Both NABC and RTNDA believe voluntary compliance is preferable to "government regulatory intrusion into newsroom operations." Also at issue is the constitutional issue of free speech. See Chapter 15 for more information on VNRs.

Internet Public Relations   Should public relations personnel covertly build a buzz for their client or employer's products in online chat rooms without revealing that they are being paid for praising the product?

This question was raised by Richard Edelman, president and CEO of Edelman Worldwide, when he found out some of his staff were doing just that. "They were going in on an unattributed basis and saying, 'Well, the Game Cube—or whatever—is the world's greatest thing,' and, meanwhile, not revealing that 'Hi, I work for Nintendo,' "Edelman told *PRWeek*. His conclusion, "No, we can't do that. It's wrong, and it ruins our credibility."

Because of such practices, the Arthur W. Page Society, an organization of senior-level communication executives, and 10 other major public relations organizations decided it was time to establish a set of principles for public relations on the Web. In addition to calling for truth and accuracy in all Web content, the organizations also endorsed adherence to the following guidelines:

- Disclose any affiliations in chatroom postings
- Offer opportunities for dialogue and interaction with experts
- Reveal the background of experts, disclosing any potential conflicts of interest or anonymous economic support of content
- Practice principled leadership in the digital world, adhering to the highest standards.

Such guidelines are good for public relations professionals, but they can also apply to top corporate management. The president of Whole Foods, John Mackey, got considerable negative publicity in mid-2007 when it was revealed that he anonymously posted favorable comments about Whole Foods on a Yahoo stock forum and bashed his competitor, Wild Oats Markets, over an eight-year period. The revelation damaged the reputation of Whole Foods as a wholesome organization, so to speak, but it also prompted an investigation by the Securities and Exchange Commission (SEC) to determine whether Mackey violated the agency's disclosure guidelines.

Ethical standards for the Internet seem to be evolving case by case. See the ethics box on page 82 about "fake" blogs organized by Edelman Worldwide for its client, Wal-Mart.

Corporate Practice   Many public relations firms and companies also have established codes of conduct and regularly schedule training sessions for their employees. CarryOn Communications in Los Angeles, for example, uses case studies that ask staff to evaluate ethically compromising situations and practice resolving the situation.

Ketchum tells its employees, as do many other firms, "We will deal with clients in a fair and businesslike fashion, providing unbiased, professional recommendations to move their business ahead." Ketchum's code deals with (1) truth and accuracy in communications, (2) how to handle confidential information, (3) what gifts and entertainment are acceptable and not acceptable, (4) fair dealings with suppliers and vendors, (5) safeguarding of client proprietary information, and (6) abuse of "inside" information.

Of course, it is one thing to have a code of conduct in the employee handbook and another to actually practice what is being preached. Public relations executives have the responsibility to ensure that ethics becomes an integral part of the "corporate culture"

> " Staffers who feel their ethics aren't compromised by clients or colleagues will more likely succeed and do their best work. "
>
> ——Ted McKenna, reporter for *PRWeek* in an article on ethics training in PR firms

on the job
ETHICS

Fake Blogs: New Marketing Channel or Really Bad Idea?

Edelman Worldwide had a great idea for its client, Wal-Mart, which was concerned about its image and reputation. Why not send a couple on a RV trip around the United Sates and have them write a daily blog about their experiences as they stopped off at various Wal-Mart stores and talked to happy employees and satisfied customers. They would be an ordinary, retired couple who were loyal Wal-Mart customers on their first maiden trip in an RV to see the United States.

Several aspects of this trip and proposed blog were not disclosed. First, the cost of the RV and the travel costs were paid by Working Families for Wal-Mart, a "grassroots" organization organized and staffed by Edelman employees on behalf of the giant retailer. Second, Jim and Laura was not exactly an ordinary couple, nor were they even married to each other. "Jim" was James Thresher, a photographer for the *Washington Post*. "Laura" was a freelance writer. Both were on the Edelman payroll.

Business Week, several weeks into the RV excursion, outed Edelman and its client, Wal-Mart, by disclosing the actual identities of the couple and the financial arrangements. The magazine, along with a host of bloggers and other commentators, chastised Edelman for misleading the public and setting up a fake blog, which is now called a "flog." Even *Fortune* magazine commented, "Not cool."

Others were not so definite. One public relations practitioner didn't think it was a big deal because it was common for public relations firms to set up fake grassroots groups anyway. One blogger thought the idea of having a couple (even a fake one) was just a storytelling device. Others commented that blogs probably should not be held to the same standards of truth and accuracy that are expected in journalism.

What do you think? Were Edelman and its client, Wal-Mart, unethical by setting up a "fake" blog? Or is it just smart marketing in a new channel of communication?

and also set an example for staff when it comes to ethical behavior. Campaigns making ethics a core value at General Dynamics and Coca-Cola are discussed in the PR Casebook on page 94.

Professionalism, Licensing, and Accreditation

Is public relations a profession? Should its practitioners be licensed? Does the accreditation of practitioners constitute a sufficient guarantee of their talents and integrity? These and other such questions are addressed in this section.

Professionalism

Among public relations practitioners, there are considerable differences of opinion about whether public relations is a craft, a skill, or a developing profession. Certainly, at its present level, public relations does not qualify as a profession in the same sense that medicine and law do. Public relations does not have prescribed standards of educational preparation, a mandatory period of apprenticeship, or state laws that govern admission to the profession.

There are, however, divergent views among public relations practitioners about what constitutes professionalism. Frank Ovaitt, president of the Institute for Public

Relations, summarizes a paper by Betteke van Ruler at the University of Amsterdam, who explored concepts of professionalism. Ovaitt says academics tend to think in terms of a *knowledge model*. "When practitioners show little interest in theory, and formal public relations education is not a requirement for employment," he says, "academics conclude that public relations is far from being a profession." Oviatt continues:

> Practitioners, on the other hand, may instinctively prefer more client-oriented models: the *competition model* that defines a profession based on permanent competition to provide expert services; and the *personality model*, in which commitment, creativity, and enthusiasm are hallmarks of a professional. Adding to the confusion, van Ruler believes that public relations associations lean toward the *status model*, which defines a profession as an elite group using specialized knowledge to gain status, power, and autonomy. The emphasis on accreditation is one indication of status model orientation.

Adding to the confusion about professionalism is the difficulty of ascertaining what constitutes public relations practice. John F. Budd Jr. a veteran counselor, wrote in *Public Relations Quarterly*: "We act as publicists, yet we talk of counseling. We perform as technologists in communication, but we aspire to be decision-makers dealing in policy." The debate whether public relations is a profession no doubt will continue for some time. But, for many, the most important principle is for the individual to act like a professional. This means that a practitioner should have:

- A sense of independence.
- A sense of responsibility to society and the public interest.
- Manifest concern for the competence and honor of the profession as a whole.
- A higher loyalty to the standards of the profession and fellow professionals than to the employer of the moment. The reference point in all public relations activity must be the standards of the profession and not those of the client or the employer.

Unfortunately, a major barrier to professionalism is the attitude that many practitioners themselves have toward their work. As James Grunig and Todd Hunt state in their text *Managing Public Relations*, practitioners tend to hold more "careerist" values than professional values. In other words, they place higher importance on job security, prestige in the organization, salary level, and recognition from superiors than on the values just listed. For example, 47 percent of the respondents in a survey of IABC members gave a neutral or highly negative answer when asked whether they would quit their jobs rather than act against their ethical values. And 55 percent considered it "somewhat ethical" to present oneself misleadingly as the only means of achieving an objective. Almost all agreed, however, that ethics is an important matter, worthy of further study.

On another level, many practitioners are limited in their professionalism by what might be termed a "technician mentality." These people narrowly define professionalism as the ability to do a competent job of executing the mechanics of communicating (preparing news releases, brochures, newsletters, etc.) even if the information provided by management or a client is in bad taste, is misleading, lacks documentation, or is just plain wrong.

Another aspect of the technician mentality is the willingness to represent issues or products that go against your own beliefs and moral code. One survey on ethical awareness, conducted by professors Lee Wilkins at the University of Missouri and Renita Coleman at the University of Texas, asked advertising personnel whether they would take a multimillion dollar beer account even though they were against alcohol consumption. Most of respondents answered yes to this and similar questions, causing advertising to be ranked somewhat near the bottom on the list of occupations in terms of ethical awareness. Public relations personnel, given the same questions, did somewhat better; they ranked sixth on the list of occupations for ethical awareness.

Some practitioners defend the technician mentality, however, arguing that public relations people are like lawyers in the court of public opinion. Everyone is entitled to his or her viewpoint and, whether the public relations person agrees or not, the client or employer has a right to be heard. Thus, a public relations representative is a paid advocate, just as a lawyer is. The only flaw in this argument is that public relations people are not lawyers, nor are they in a court of law where judicial concepts determine the roles of defendant and plaintiff. In addition, lawyers have been known to turn down clients or resign from a case because they doubted the client's story.

In Chapter 12, which concerns legal aspects of public relations, it is pointed out that courts are increasingly holding public relations firms accountable for information disseminated on behalf of a client. Thus, it is no longer acceptable to say, "The client told me to do it."

Licensing

Proposals that public relations practitioners be licensed were discussed before PRSA was founded. One proponent, Edward L. Bernays, who was instrumental in formulating the modern concept of public relations (see Chapter 2), believed that licensing would protect the profession and the public from incompetent, shoddy opportunists who do not have the knowledge, talent, or ethics required of public relations professionals.

The problem is stated by PRSA's task force on demonstrating professionalism:

> Pick up any metropolitan newspaper and scan the employment ads. Under the "public relations" classification, you are likely to find opportunities for door-to-door salespersons, receptionists, used-car salesmen, singles bar hostesses and others of less savory reputation. The front pages of the newspapers are full of stories about former government employees peddling influence and calling it public relations.

Thus, under the licensing approach, only those individuals who pass rigid examinations and tests of personal integrity could call themselves "public relations" counselors. Those not licensed would have to call themselves "publicists" or adopt some other designation.

Several arguments for licensing and registration have been advanced. Advocates say that it would help (1) define the practice of public relations, (2) establish uniform educational criteria, (3) set uniform professional standards, (4) protect clients and employers from imposters and charlatans, (5) protect qualified practitioners from unfair competition from the unethical and unqualified, and (6) raise the overall credibility of public relations practitioners. One survey, for example, found that a company public relations representative was next to the bottom as a credible spokesperson, ranking slightly above athletes and entertainers.

Opponents of licensing say that it won't work and that it is unfeasible for the following reasons: (1) any licensing in the communications field would violate the First Amendment guarantee of freedom of speech; (2) civil and criminal laws already exist to deal with malpractice; (3) licensing is a function of state governments, and public relations people often work on a national and international level; (4) licensing ensures only minimum competence and professional standards, it doesn't necessarily ensure high ethical behavior; (5) the credibility and status of an occupation are not necessarily ensured through licensing (attorneys, for example, don't enjoy particularly high status and prestige because they are licensed, nor do licensed practical nurses); and (6) setting up the machinery for licensing and policing would be very costly to the American taxpayer.

The opponents seem to have won the day. Today, there is no particular interest on the part of the public relations industry, the consumer movement, or even state governments to initiate any form of legislated licensing. An alternative to licensing is accreditation, which many public relations groups do actively endorse and promote.

Accreditation

The major effort to improve standards and professionalism in public relations around the world has been the establishment of accreditation programs. This means that practitioners voluntarily go through a process in which they are "certified" by a national organization that they are competent, qualified professionals.

PRSA, for example, began its accreditation program more than 40 years ago. Other national groups, including the IABC, the Canadian Public Relations Society (CPRS), the British Institute of Public Relations (BIPR), the Public Relations Institute of Australia (PRIA), and the Public Relations Institute of Southern Africa (PRISA), to name just a few, also have established accreditation programs.

The approach used by most national groups is to have written and oral exams and to have candidates submit a portfolio of work samples to a committee of professional peers. IABC, for example, places a major emphasis on the individual's portfolio of accomplishments as part of its ABC (Accredited Business Communicator) certification. The candidate also must outline the objectives of a campaign, present the overall communications strategy, and provide evaluation of the results. About 5 percent of IABC's 14,700 members have earned ABC designation. In 2007, IABC signed an agreement with the Shanghai Public Relations Association (SPRA) to offer the IABC accreditation program to its members.

Most groups also have guidelines as to how many years of experience are required before a person can apply for accredited or membership status. IABC, for example, requires a minimum of five years' experience and a bachelor's degree. South Africa's PRISA, on the other hand, ensures some knowledge of the field by requiring that each candidate first complete a Certificate in Public Relations Management before taking the exam.

Some groups are beginning to require continuing education as a prerequisite for professional certification. The PRIA, for example, requires members to earn Certified Practitioner (CP) status by completing 40 hours of continuing education each year. But most national groups—including PRSA—have no continuing education requirements for its accredited members, let alone the rank and file.

The PRSA Approach   PRSA was one of the first in the world to establish an accreditation program, and so it's worth examining in some detail how it works. For many years, the accreditation process included both an oral and a written exam, but not a portfolio of professional work. In 2003, however, the entire accreditation process was completely restructured to better reflect the growing body of knowledge and diversity in the field. Candidates are now required to take a preview course (available online), complete a "readiness" questionnaire, and show a portfolio of work to a panel of professional peers before taking the written exam, which is available at test centers throughout the United States. The requirement for a minimum of five years' experience was dropped in 2004.

The 2.5-hour exam tests knowledge of the field and gives proportional weight to various core topics: research, planning, execution, and evaluation of programs (30 percent); ethics and law (15 percent); communication models and theories (15 percent); business literacy (10 percent); management skills (10 percent); crisis communication management (10 percent); media relations (5 percent); information technology (2 percent); history and current issues in public relations (2 percent); and advanced communication skills (1 percent).

Candidates who pass earn the credential "APR" (Accredited in Public Relations). To date, about 4,000 practitioners have earned APR status, or about 20 percent of the PRSA's membership. A continuing controversy within PRSA is the policy that only members with APR status can run for national office. Impassioned debate about this subject has dominated the PRSA governing assembly for several years. Advocates of the policy say APR should be a minimal requirement for national office in a professional organization. Opponents say the policy disenfranchises the overwhelming majority of members from fully participating in the affairs of the society.

Administration of the APR exam falls under the auspices of the Universal Accreditation Board (UAB), which was created by PRSA in 1998 (www.praccreditation.org) It allows non-PRSA members from other professional groups who have joined the UAB to take the accreditation exam. The consortium of groups, however, is not exactly "universal." It mainly consists of various state organizations, such as the Florida Public Relations Association, and specialized groups, such as the National School Public Relations Association, that don't have their own accreditation programs.

Other Steps Toward Professionalism

PRSA, IABC, and other national groups have various programs designed to advance the profession of public relations. They include (1) working with universities to standardize curricula, (2) implementing research projects, and (3) recognizing outstanding practitioners who mentor and serve as role models.

Education   PRSA, IABC, and other organizations, such as the National Communication Association (NCA), have worked with the public relations division of the Association for Education in Journalism and Mass Communications (AEJMC) to improve and standardize the curricula of public relations at the undergraduate and master's degree levels.

One result of this cooperation was the Commission on Public Relations Education (www.commpred.org), which consists of leading educators and practitioners representing a number of professional communication groups. The commission's latest report (2006) "Public Relations Education for the 21st Century: The Professional Bond," called for more involvement of the professional community in the educational process. The report noted, "While the record of broad support for public relations education by professional groups is growing, there is a critical need for similar action by individual practitioners and the firms, companies and organizations with which they are associated and in which they are influential."

The commission, as in past reports, recommended that coursework in public relations should comprise 25 to 40 percent of all undergraduate credit hours. Of those, at least half should be clearly identified as public relations courses covering such topics as (1) principles, (2) case studies, (3) research and evaluation, (4) writing and production, (5) planning and management, (6) campaigns, and (7) supervised internships. The commission also recommended that students complete a minor or a double major in another discipline, such as business, economics, or the behavioral sciences.

Research   Various groups have added to the body of knowledge of public relations through the commissioning of research studies, monographs, books, and reports. IPRA, for example, has issued a number of "gold papers" over the years on such topics as environmental communications and sustainability, consumerism, and corporate social responsibility. IABC has published a number of books and monographs on such topics as intranets, communication management, and face-to-face communications.

The best-known think tank for public relations research is the Institute for Public Relations (IPR), which celebrated its 50th anniversary in 2006. Headquartered at the University of Florida, IPR is an independent nonprofit organization of educators and practitioners "that builds and documents research-based knowledge in public relations, and makes this knowledge available and useful to practitioners, educators, and their clients." Research papers and other information are available for free on its Web site (www.instituteforpr.org). In recent years, it has commissioned a number of studies regarding measurement and evaluation in public relations practice. The IPR motto says a lot: "Dedicated to the science beneath the art."

Another research center, of more recent vintage, is the Strategic Public Relations Center at the University of Southern California (USC) Annenberg School for Communication. It conducts an annual survey, among other research, that primarily documents public relations as a management function. Statistics on public relations evaluation methods, departmental budgets, level of staffing, and management reporting relationships are compiled. The center has an online database, PR Management Database (PRMD), that is available free of charge at www.annenberg.usc.edu/sprc.

The two major academic journals in public relations are the *Public Relations Review* and the *Journal of Public Relations Research*. Both publications publish a variety of scholarly articles about public relations and communications theory, in-depth analyses of public relations issues and campaigns, and survey research.

Recognition of Senior Professionals   Several national groups, such as PRSA and IABC, have established "Fellow" programs that recognize career achievement and contributions to the profession. PRSA, for example, has a College of Fellows that has grown to about 500 members. In addition, annual awards by PRSA, IABC, and other professional groups honor educators and practitioners who are leaders in the field.

Ethics in Individual Practice

Despite codes of professional practice and formalized accreditation, ethics in public relations boils down to deeply troubling questions for the individual practitioner: Will I lie for my employer? Will I deceive to gain information about another agency's clients? Will I cover up a hazardous condition? Will I issue a news release presenting only half the truth? Will I use the Internet to post messages anonymously promoting a client's product? Will I quit my job rather than cooperate in a questionable activity? In other words, to what extent, if any, will I compromise my personal beliefs?

These and similar questions plague the lives of public relations personnel, although surveys do show that a high number hold such strong personal beliefs and/or work for such highly principled employers that they seldom need to compromise their personal values. If employers make a suggestion that involves questionable ethics, the

on the job INSIGHTS

Use of "Front Groups" Poses Ethical Concerns

The proliferation of so-called front groups waging purported grassroots campaigns to achieve public relations goals has created much debate in the field in recent years.

The establishment of dozens of such groups evoked a strongly worded statement from the board of directors of the PRSA.

PRSA specifically condemns the efforts of those organizations, sometimes known as "front groups," that seek to influence the public policy process by disguising or obscuring the true identity of their members or by implying representation of a much more broadly based group than exists.

Almost every "save the environment" organization has spawned a counter group. For example, the Forest Alliance of British Columbia posed as a grassroots movement opposing the International Coali- tion to Save British Columbia's Rain- forests, composed of 25 "green" groups. It was later revealed that the Canadian timber industry paid Burson-Marsteller $1 million to cre- ate the alliance, whose aim was to convince the public that environ- mental destruction has been exag- gerated and to persuade lawmakers to abolish unprofitable environ- mental regulations.

Names given to many of the orga- nizations are confusing, if not down- right deceptive. Northwesterners for More Fish was the name chosen for a "grassroots" coalition of utilities and other companies in the Northwest under attack by environmental groups for depleting the fish popu- lation. In California's Riverside County, a public relations firm organized Friends of Eagle Mountain on behalf of a mining company that wanted to create the world's largest landfill in an abandoned iron ore pit. A prohunt- ing group that works to convince people that wildlife is so plentiful that there is no reason not to kill some of it is known as the Abundant Wildlife Society of North America.

A Gallup Poll once showed that the majority of Americans consid- ered themselves environmentalists. In the face of such findings, "People sometimes create groups that try to fudge a little bit about what their goals are," said Hal Dash, president of Cerrell Associates, a Los Angeles public relations firm that has repre- sented clients with environmental problems.

Questioned about the tactics used in so-called grassroots cam- paigns, more than half of profes- sionals surveyed by *PRNews* said that it is unethical for parties to fail to mention that their impetus for contacting a government official or other organization is due to a vested interest or membership in another organization sponsoring the campaign.

public relations person often can talk them out of the idea by citing the possible conse- quences of such an action—adverse media publicity, for example.

"To thine own self be true," advised New York public relations executive Chester Burger at an IABC conference. A fellow panelist, Canadian politician and radio com- mentator Stephen Lewis, observed: "There is a tremendous jaundice on the part of the public about the way things are communicated. People have elevated superficiality to an art form. Look at the substance of what you have to convey, and the honesty used in conveying it." With the audience contributing suggestions, the panelists formulated the following list of commendable practices:

◆ Be honest at all times.

◆ Convey a sense of business ethics based on your own standards and those of society.

◆ Respect the integrity and position of your opponents and audiences.

◆ Develop trust by emphasizing substance over triviality.

- Present all sides of an issue.
- Strive for a balance between loyalty to the organization and duty to the public.
- Don't sacrifice long-term objectives for short-term gains.

Adherence to professional standards of conduct—being truly independent—is the chief measure of a public relations person. Faced with such personal problems as a mortgage to pay and children to educate, practitioners may be strongly tempted to become yes men (or yes women) and decline to express their views forcefully to an employer, or to resign. Yet, Norman Mineta, former Secretary of Transportation and now vice chairman of Hill & Knowlton, is quite blunt: "Yes-people need not apply. As professionals, we must encourage a culture of honesty, integrity, and intellectual curiosity among our peers and employees."

Thus, it can be readily seen that ethics in public relations really begins with the individual—and is directly related to his or her own value system as well as to the good of society. Although it is important to show loyalty to an employer, practitioners must never allow a client or an employer to rob them of their self-esteem.

Ethical Dealings with News Media

The most practical consideration facing a public relations specialist is his or her dealings with the news media. The standard rubric is that you must be totally honest to maintain your credibility and gain the trust of journalists and editors. Allthough this is true, the axiom "The devil is in the details" also applies. Honesty, for example, doesn't automatically mean that you need to answer every question that a reporter might ask. You often have to use discretion because you also have an obligation to represent the best interests of your client or employer. There may be proprietary information or detailed information about organizational plans that cannot be released for public consumption. There also may be personal information about executives or employees that are protected by privacy laws.

Consequently, it is also "honest" to tell a reporter that you cannot provide information or make a comment on an issue because of mitigating circumstances. Trust can be maintained even when practitioners say "no comment" and refuse to answer questions that go beyond information reported in the news releases, according to a study by Professors Michael Ryan and David L. Hartinson, published in *Journalism Quarterly*. Practitioners and journalists tend to agree on how they define lying. Both, for example, believe that giving evasive answers to reporters' questions constitutes lying. The practitioner is much better off (and honest) by simply telling the reporter that he or she can't or won't answer the question.

Gifts

Achieving trust is the aim of all practitioners, and it can only be achieved through highly professional and ethical behavior. It is for this reason that public relations practitioners should not undermine the trust of the media by providing junkets of doubtful news value, extravagant parties, expensive gifts, and personal favors for media representatives. Journalists, for the most part, will think you are trying to bribe them to get favorable coverage.

Gifts of any kind, according to PRSA, can contaminate the free flow of accurate and truthful information to the public. See the insert box on the PRSA code of ethics on page 78. Although the exact words, "corrupting the channels of communication,"

on the job
A MULTICULTURAL WORLD

Cash for News Coverage Raises Ethical Concerns

In Russia and Eastern Europe, it's not uncommon for companies and public relations practitioners to pay journalists to get a news release or a product photo published in the news columns of a newspaper or mentioned on a television news program. The Russians call this practice "zakazukha." In the Ukraine, they call it "black propaganda."

A survey by the IPRA also found that "pay-for-play" was practiced extensively in Africa, the Middle East, and Southern Europe. To a much lesser extent, it occurs in Asia, Western Europe, Australia, and the United States.

IPRA and five other global organizations have joined forces to support a set of principles designed to foster greater transparency between public relations professionals and the media in an attempt to end bribery for media coverage throughout the world. The other organizations are the International Press Institute, the International Federation of Journal-

ists, Transparency International, the Global Alliance for Public Relations and Communications Management, and the Institute for Public Relations Research and Education.

The guidelines call for the following:

- News material should appear as a result of the news judgment of journalists and editors, not as a result of any payment in cash or in kind or any other inducements.

- Material involving payment should be clearly identified as advertising, sponsorship, or promotion.

- No journalist or media representative should ever suggest that news coverage will appear for any reason other than its merit.

- When samples or loans of products or services are necessary for a journalist to render an objective opinion, the length of time

should be agreed in advance and loaned products should be returned.

- The media should institute written policies regarding the receipt of gifts or discounted products and services, and journalists should be required to sign the policy.

"In too many countries, bribery of the news media robs citizens of truthful information that they need to make individual and community decisions," said Don Wright, then president of IPRA. He continues, "We started this campaign with the goal of creating greater transparency and eliminating unethical practices in dealings between news sources and the media." IPRA and the Institute for Public Relations Research and Education (IPR) have also started a biennial international index of bribery and the media to monitor progress in the reduction of media corruption around the world.

---

are no longer used in the PRSA code, there are still the same strictures about gifts of products, travel, and services to reporters. There is some blurring of lines, however, when it comes to such items as coffee mugs, T-shirts, or even a bottle of Ketchup that are enclosed in media kits as a promotional gimmick. In most cases, such items are of little value and not considered a "gift." Some dailies, however, have a policy of not accepting even such minor items.

More expensive product samples, however, generate more scrutiny. A good example is Microsoft and its public relations firm, Edelman Worldwide, during the launch of the Vista operating system. Edelman chose 90 influential bloggers, asking them whether they wanted to receive an Acer Ferrari laptop loaded with the new Vista software to review. The bloggers were also told that they could return the laptop, donate it, or keep it. Controversy arose when some bloggers mentioned their new laptops without disclosing that they were gifts from Microsoft. Other bloggers, not getting a computer, criticized Microsoft and Edelman for trying to buy favorable reviews of Vista with such an expensive gift. As far as Edelman was concerned, there was no attempt to bribe the recipients; it was simply providing a product for review. What raised eyebrows, however, was that the product in question (the Vista software) came encased in an expensive computer.

DeVries public relations, on behalf of client Pantene, also was heavily criticized by bloggers and the media for sending out a survey to journalists asking them which types of gifts they would prefer to receive, among other questions. Reporters could choose from a gift certificate at an upscale retailer, a certificate for a car service or cleaning service, fashion supplies, and electronics such as an iPod. Stephanie Smirnov, managing director of the beauty practice at DeVries, defended the survey. She told *Jack O'Dwyer's Newsletter*, "We would never put together a program that would ask any of our editor colleagues to compromise their own ethics. We knew that by giving the option, as opposed to just showing up on their doorstep with a gift, that they would self-select appropriately." Thus, the blurring of lines. Is it ethical to offer a gift and then leave it to the journalist to either accept or reject it?

Although gift giving is ethically suspect in the United States, other nations have different standards. A survey conducted by Insight and MediaSource, for example, found that 41 percent of Arabic-language journalists in the Middle East might be more inclined to use a news release if it came with a gift. Another area of ethical concern is paying a reporter's expenses for covering an event or news conference. Although the practice is not done in the United States, it's not uncommon in other nations. In one survey, almost a third of European journalists expected public relations people to pay their expenses. The percentage rises to almost 60 percent in Asian nations. Another issue, called "pay for play," is discussed in the box on page 92.

Blurring Lines in the News Business

Although it may be assumed that public relations representatives would benefit from being able to influence journalists with gifts or offers of paid advertising in exchange for news coverage, this is not the case. A major selling point of public relations work is the third-party credibility of reporters and editors. The public trusts journalists to be objective and to be somewhat impartial in the dissemination of information. If the public loses that trust because they feel the media can be "bought," the information provided by public relations sources also becomes less trusted.

"I don't think it's as blatant as putting cash in an editor's hand," says Mark Hass, chief executive of Manning, Selvage, and Lee, in a *New York Times* interview. Often, it is only the agreement that the organization will buy advertising in the publication with the understanding that an article or a favorable product review will be part of the package. Or, in some cases such as the auto industry, some editors and journalists are paid consultants to the auto companies. As a *Wall Street Journal* article commented, "Welcome to the world of automotive enthusiast journalism where the barriers that separate advertisers from journalists are porous enough for paychecks to pass through." There's also considerable suspicion that the the Car of the Year on the cover of an auto magazine is the

> **"** Our messages are credible only if the media that carry them are credible. If we hurt media credibility, we hurt our own. **"**
>
> ——— Tim Yost, communications director for ASC, a Detroit automotive manufacturer, in *Public Relations Tactics*

on the job
INSIGHTS

PRSA Addresses Ethics of Paying for News Placement in Iraq

In late 2005, when accusations were made that the U.S. military was paying Iraqi journalists for a positive spin on the U.S. operations in Iraq, the Public Relations Society of America saw a need and an opportunity to address the ethical relationships between Public Relations practitioners and journalists.

Judith T. Phair, president and CEO of PRSA, released a statement regarding the "pay for play" articles. She noted in her prepared statement that "leaders of the Public Relations Society of America overwhelmingly adopted a resolution that condemns in the strongest possible terms, any lack of transparency in communications with the media that hides the origin of the communications."

Phair's statement continued:

PRSA has consistently voiced concerns about the blurring of lines between tactical disinformation campaigns and straightforward communications from military spokespersons in time of war. PRSA advocates complete disclosure of sources and sponsorship of all information provided to the media.

PRSA takes very seriously its responsibility to provide leadership and guidance on matters that affect the flow of information in a free society. It is clearly a violation of the PRSA code and contrary to the basic principles of the ethical practice of our profession for a public relations professional to pay a news outlet to run stories that are presented as editorial content produced by that news organization.

PRSA acknowledged in its statement that an entity as large as the U.S. government may have a hard time maintaining control over its activities and messaging strategies. It also noted that there is a very real temptation to do whatever it takes to get a positive message out about your organization, especially in times of crisis and conflict. However, Phair wrote:

There are no shortcuts in those endeavors. Open, two-

Judith T. Phair, 2005 president and CEO of PRSA.

way communications remains paramount—even in the face of frustration and failure . . .

PRSA's leaders are calling for communications based upon openness, honesty and candor as the best, most effective way to demonstrate the principles of freedom for which the United States stands.

result of an automaker's extensive purchase of advertising space in the magazine. Is this just coincidence, or part of an "understanding"?

Magazines serving a particular industry or a specific area, such as home decorating or bridal fashions, are increasingly blurring the line between news features and advertisements. Tony Silber, who writes about the magazine industry, told *PRWeek*, "If you look at shelter magazines, they are going to have advertisers' products in their decorated spreads of homes." Product placements are discussed in detail in Chapters 11 and 15.

Transparency and disclosure is another problem. Is it ethical for a public relations firm, for example, to hire a freelance writer to write favorable stories about the client? The Lewis Group, according to *PRWeek*, paid more than $10,000 to a freelancer to write flattering stories in the local newspaper about its client, Health South's Richard

Scrushy, who was on trial for fraud. Again, there is some blurring of lines here. Whose responsibility is it to inform the public that the freelancer was being paid? Is this the obligation of the public relations firm, or is it the responsibility of the writer to inform the newspaper's editors or acknowledge payment in her article? The same question came up in 2005 when Ketchum paid columnist and broadcast commentator Armstrong Williams $240,000 to say nice things about the U.S. Department of Education's No Child Left Behind program. The incident was labeled by some critics as the "No Journalist Left Unpaid Program." See more about the Ketchum/Armstrong controversy in Chapter 12, page 323.

The situations just described are referred to as "pay for play." In another situation, Peter Ferrara wrote op-ed articles advocating Social Security privatization for various newspapers without disclosing that he paid by a major Washington lobbyist, Jack Abramoff. According to the *AARP Bulletin*, he didn't think there was anything wrong with taking money from third parties for writing the articles under his own name. Newspapers, however, took a different view. The *Manchester (NH) Union-Leader* announced it would no longer run Ferrara's columns, commenting "When a columnist is a paid shill—a trust is broken. A journalist's stock in trade is trust, and our op-ed pages are no place for columnists who have proven untrustworthy." See the Multicultural box on page 90 about the issue of "pay for play" in other nations. Also, see the box about PRSA's statement on the American military paying Iraq journalists for favorable coverage on page 92.

The need for transparency and disclosure also are issues in the broadcast industry. Should a spokesperson on a television talk show reveal his or her employer? This question came to the forefront when it was revealed in the press that the Toy Guy (Christopher Byrne), who appears on scores of local and national television shows with his selections of the best and hottest toys for the Christmas season, is actually paid hundreds of thousands of dollars by various toy companies to promote their products. A *New York Daily News* reporter asked Shannon Eis, spokeswomen for the Toy Industry Association, whether television viewers should be informed that Byrne is paid. She responded, "I don't know if it's right. I can't say yes or no." Representatives of several toy companies were more definitive. They said that there was nothing wrong with what Byrne was doing and that it was a long-established industry practice.

Paul Holmes, a columnist for *PRWeek*, took a different view. He wrote, "It's hard to read this kind of thing and not conclude that the entire toy industry is corrupt, united in its shared contempt for consumers and by its denial that this kind of sleazy practice is acceptable."

Celebrities appearing on talk shows such as NBC's *Today* show also raise the issue of transparency. Actress Kathleen Turner, for example, told Diane Sawyer on ABC's *Good Morning America* about her battle with rheumatoid arthritis and mentioned that a drug, Enbrel, helped ease the pain. What Turner didn't reveal, and Sawyer didn't tell the audience, was that she was being paid to appear by the company that manufactured the drug. After the *New York Times* broke the story, the embarrassed networks said they would initiate a policy that viewers will be told of a celebrity's ties to corporations.

The blurring of lines in today's media continues to be a major concern for both public relations professionals and journalists. Indeed, a PRSA/Bacon's Inc. survey found that the greatest single challenge facing practitioners was "upholding credibility within an environment where the lines between PR, advertising, and journalism are growing increasingly vague."

PRCASEBOOK

Instilling Values and Ethics: A Tale of Two Companies

A number of organizations have ongoing ethics program in order to establish a corporate culture that emphasizes core values and ethical behavior in the workplace. Two corporations, General Dynamics and Coca-Cola, received PRSA Silver Anvil awards in 2007 for their programs involving employees in the process.

General Dynamics Armament and Technical Products

In the wake of various corporate scandals such as Enron, the president of General Dynamics set a goal of creating a world-class ethics program. He appointed a director of ethics and set three objectives for the company's communication's department: (1) increase employee awareness of company ethical standards, (2) increase employee involvement in the ethics process, and (3) establish the company as an ethics leader.

Internal tactics included the Ethics and Basic Beliefs Film Festival, an Ethics Awareness Day, an ethics Web site, brochures, posters, and newsletters. External tactics included award entries in state and national ethics award competitions, keynote speeches on ethics by the company president, and selected interviews with media to highlight the company's ethics progam.

The program, after a year, was considered a success. Employee awareness of the ethics program rose from 75 percent to 90 percent. Employee involvement in the ethics process increased 104 percent, and the company received the North Carolina Business Hall of Fame Excellence in Ethics Award.

Coca-Cola Company

The company, with employees in 45 nations, decided to have an online conversation with all of its employees about its values and culture. The program, dubbed "Blog Blast '06," challenged employees to define what it means to "live the values" and describe how specific behaviors could drive better business results.

Burson-Marsteller public relations was engaged to promote and publicize the Blog Fest around the world. An important component included educating employees on how to use the technology and overcoming the cultural values of employees in many nations who are not comfortable giving feedback to management. Pre-event publicity included the creation of both digital ad print pieces that were used in Coca-Cola's offices around the world. In addition, a global activation team of internal communications professionals was established to build regional interest and translate informational materials for local employees. As the Blog Fest approached, e-mail invitations for employees to participate were sent, and a video blog tutorial was posted on the company's intranet.

The Blog Fest, which lasted seven days, generated 2,409 employee posts from around the world. In addition, employees viewed 136,862 pages. According to management, "Employee feedback about the discussion was overwhelmingly positive, and the conversation unleashed a tremendous amount of passion, energy, and excitement about the company's future." The global blog discussion also got rank-and-file employees more involved and aware of the company's core values and aspirations for long-term sustainable growth.

SUMMARY

What Is Ethics?

Ethics refers to a person's value system and how he or she determines right or wrong. The three basic value orientations are (1) absolutist, (2) existentialist, and (3) situationalist. Another concept is simply the Golden Rule.

The Ethical Advocate

Even if one is an advocate for a particular organization or cause, one can behave in an ethical manner. Because of the concept of role differentiation, society understands that the advocate is operating within an assigned role, much like a defense lawyer or prosecuting attorney in court.

Professional Organizations

Groups such as PRSA, IABC, and IPRA provide an important role in setting the standards and ethical behavior of the profession. Most professional organizations have published codes of conduct and educational programs.

Front Groups Are Unethical

It is the responsibility of public relations professionals to disclose the funding and identity of individuals who claim to be "citizen groups" but actually represent the disguised interests of their actual sponsors.

Professionalism

True public relations professionals have a loyalty to a higher standard and to the public interest. They are more than "careerists" and practice public relations with more than a "technician mentality." They are not hired guns who simply parrot whatever the client or organization wants them to say.

Licensing and Accreditation

Freedom of speech concerns severely limit the concept of licensing in the communication fields, including public relations. Accreditation programs for practitioners, plus continuing education, is an attractive alternative.

Gifts for Journalists

Professional groups in both public relations and journalism condemn the giving of expensive gifts or services to journalists because the practice undermines the media's credibility and the public trust.

The Blurring of Ethical Lines

In today's media environment, there is a blurring of lines between public relations, advertising, and journalism in terms of content. The importance of transparency and disclosure is highly relevant when journalists/commentators accept payment from third parties, or when a celebrity spokesperson appears on a talk show without mentioning who is paying for their appearance. Economic pressures are forcing many publications, particularly specialty magazines, to connect paid advertising with editorial content. Such blurring of lines are of concern to both public relations personnel and journalists.

CASE ACTIVITY What Would You Do?

A number of situations can raise ethical questions in the public relations business. Resolving them is often the process of sifting through a number of factors including your philosophical orientation, your personal belief system, and your understanding of professional standards. The following are some situations that may arise in your work.

◆ Your employer wants you to write a news release about a new energy drink that is being launched. He asks you to mention that the U.S. Olympic Committee likes the product so much that it is planning to provide the drink to all U.S. Olympic athletes. In reality, there has been some contact with U.S. Olympic officials, and one official agreed that the product could be useful to athletes.

◆ You make a pitch to a trade editor that your company would make a good feature in her magazine because it leads the industry in adopting "green"

technology in its plants. The editor agrees that this is a good story, but then mentions that this feature has a better chance of being published if your company could also buy a full-page ad.

◆ Your resort hotel has just completed a major renovation and you invite several travel writers to spend the weekend as the hotel's guest. Ideally, they will like what they see and will write an article about the hotel's improved facilities. One travel writer calls you and asks whether it's all right to bring his wife and two children with him.

What ethical concerns are raised by these situations? What would you do in each situation? You might review the PRSA code and review the ethical and professional concepts discussed in this chapter.

QUESTIONS for Review and Discussion

1. What is ethics? How can individuals disagree about what constitutes an ethical dilemma or concern?
2. Describe the three basic philosophic positions— Absolute, Existential, and Situational. Which one best fits your approach to ethics?
3. Can a public relations person be an advocate for a cause and still be ethical? What is the concept of role differentiation?
4. What role do professional organizations play in setting the standards of public relations practice?

5. Describe, in general, the activities of PRSA, IABC, and IPRA.
6. A number of professional groups have codes of ethics. What are some common characteristics of these codes? What differences are there, if any?
7. What is the controversy about television stations using video news releases (VNRs) provided by public relations sources?
8. What ethical rules apply to Internet public relations and participation in chat groups?
9. Is public relations a profession? Why, or why not?
10. Name the four ways that an individual can act like a professional.
11. In what ways does the concept of "careerism" and "technician mentality" undermine the establishment of public relations as a profession.
12. What are the pros and cons of licensing in public relations? Would you support licensing? Why or why not?
13. What is the accreditation process in public relations? What is involved? Would you aspire to be accredited? Why or why not?
14. What are the two major think tanks in the public relations field? What do they do?
15. What is a "front" group? Do you think they are unethical? Why or why not?
16. The Pentagon had a program that gave Iraqi journalists cash for running favorable stories about the U.S. occupation. Do you think such a practice is ethical? Why or why not?
17. Should public relations personnel give gifts to journalists? Why or why not?
18. What is the concept of "pay for play"? Who's more unethical: the public relations person who offers the cash, or the journalist who accepts it?
19. Celebrities often appear on television programs such as the *Today* show. Should they also disclose what company or organization is paying them to appear? Why or why not?
20. When companies operate in other nations, should they adhere to the standards of their home country or adapt to the ethical standards of the host nation? For example, should American companies pay bribes to journalists in Russia if that is the standard operating practice?

SUGGESTED READINGS

Baker, S., and Martinson, D. "Out of the Red Light District: Five Principles for Ethically Proactive Public Relations." *Public Relations Quarterly*, Fall 2002, pp. 15–20.

Bowen, Shannon A. "Expansion of Ethics as the Tenth Generic Principle of Public Relations Excellence: A Kantian Theory and Model for Managing Ethical Issues." *Journal of Public Relations Research*, Vol. 16, No. 1, 2004, pp. 65–92.

David, Prabu. "Extending Symmetry: Toward a Convergence of Professionalism, Practice, and Pragmatics in Public Relations." *Journal of Public Relations Research*, Vol. 16, No. 2, 2004, pp. 185–211.

Holmes, Paul. "In Paying for Its Television Experts, the Toy Industry Is Playing U.S. Consumers for Fools." *PRWeek*, January 5, 2004, p. 8.

Kim, Yungwook, and Choi, Youjin. "Ethical Standards Appear to Change with Age and Ideology: A Survey of Practitioners." *Public Relations Review*, Vol. 29, No. 1, 2003, pp. 79–89.

Martinson, David L. "Ethical Decision Making in Public Relations: What Would Aristotle Say?" *Public Relations Quarterly*, Fall 2000, pp. 18–21.

Mercer, Laura. "For Those Entering Public Relations: How to Be Recognized as a True Professional." *Public Relations Tactics*, April 2004, p. 24.

Nolan, Hamilton. "Edelman Acknowledges Mistakes in Blog Matter." *PRWeek*, October 23, 2006, p. 3.

O'Brien, Keith. "Edelman Defends Ethics of Vista PC Gifting Tactic." *PRWeek*, January 8, 2007, p. 5.

Schmelzer, Randi. "Accreditation Receives High Marks From Most Firms." *PRWeek*, May 28, 2007, p. 7.

Seitel, Fraser. "Public Relations Ethics." *O'Dwyer's PR Report*, April 2007, p. 36.

Sowa, Brian C. "Ethical Simulations and Ethics Minutes." *Public Relations Quarterly*, Spring 2006, pp. 22–28.

"Topic: Is Licensing PR Practitioners a Practical Solution?" *Public Relations Tactics*, September 2006, pp. 18–20.

Weidlich, Thom. "The Ethics of Entertaining Journalists: In Building Media Relationships, Knowing Each Outlet's Rules as to What They Accept and Expect Is Key, But the Gift They Still Prefer Most Is a Solid Story." *PRWeek*, August 23, 2004, p. 20.

Weiner, Mark. "A Trio of Tests: Proving Value, Credibility, and Maintaining Ethical Standards." *The Strategist*, Spring 2007, pp. 36–37.

Public Relations Departments and Firms

TOPICS COVERED IN THIS CHAPTER INCLUDE:

Public Relations Departments

Public relations departments serve various roles and functions within companies and organizations. The following sections discuss the public relations function in organizational structures, names of departments, line and staff functions, sources of friction with other departments, and the pros and cons of working in a department.

Role in Various Organizational Structures

For more than a century, public relations departments have served companies and organizations. George Westinghouse reportedly created the first corporate public relations department in 1889 when he hired two men to publicize his pet project, alternating current (AC) electricity. Their work was relatively simple compared to the mélange of physical, sociological, and psychological elements that contemporary departments employ. Eventually, Westinghouse won out over Thomas A. Edison's direct current (DC) system, and his method became the standard in the United States. Westinghouse's public relations department concept has also grown into a basic part of today's electronic world.

Today, public relations is expanding from its traditional functions to exercise its influence in the highest levels of management.

Importance in Today's World   In a changing environment, and faced with the variety of pressures previously described, executives increasingly see public relations not as publicity and one-way communication, but as a complex and dynamic process of negotiation and compromise with a number of key publics. James Grunig, now professor emeritus of public relations at the University of Maryland, calls the new approach "building good relationships with strategic publics," which will require public relations executives to be "strategic communication managers rather than communication technicians."

Grunig, head of a six-year IABC Foundation research study on *Excellence in Public Relations and Communications Management*, continues:

> When public relations helps that organization build relationships, it saves the organization money by reducing the costs of litigation, regulation, legislation, pressure campaign boycotts, or lost revenue that result from bad relationships with publics—publics that become activist groups when relationships are bad. It also helps the organization make money by cultivating relationships with donors, customers, shareholders and legislators.

The results of a IABC study seem to indicate that chief executive officers (CEOs) consider public relations to be a good investment. A survey of 200 organizations showed that CEOs gave public relations operations a 184 percent return on investment (ROI), a figure just below that of customer service and sales/marketing.

Ideally, professional public relations people assist top management in developing policy and communicating with various groups. Indeed, the IABC study emphasizes that CEOs want communication that is strategic, based on research, and involves two-way communication with key publics. See the Insights box on page 99 about the attributes that a CEO wants in a chief communications officer.

Dudley H. Hafner, executive vice president of the American Heart Association (AHA), echoed these thoughts:

on the job INSIGHTS

So You Want to Make a Six-Figure Salary?

CEOs of major corporations have high expectations for their chief communications officers, who are commonly called vice president (VP) or even senior vice president (SVP) of corporate communications. The Arthur W. Page Society, an elite group of senior communications executives, surveyed CEOs to find out what key attributes they were looking for in a communications head.

Detailed knowledge of the business. Be an expert in communications, but you should also have a knowledge of business in general and the details of the company in particular.

Extensive communications background. Experience and extensive relationships are assumed, but you need expertise in what the company needs. A company in a highly regulated industry, for example, puts a premium on government and political experience.

A crystal ball. You need to anticipate how different audiences will react to different events, messages, and channels.

C-suite credibility. It's crucial to be accepted in what is called the "C-Suite." Experience in actually running a business or a division is one form of earning one's "credentials."

Extensive internal relationships. You need to have your finger on the pulse of the company and know employees at every level of the operation.

Team player. Decisions are made on a collaborative basis. You need to have strong relationships with colleagues and the respect of the CEO's inner circle.

Educator. CEOs want you to educate them and the rest of the company on communications skills in general, and how to develop strategies for communicating the company's values.

In the non-profit business sector, as well as in the for-profit business of America, leadership needs to pay close attention to what our audiences (supporters or customers as well as the general public) want, what they need, what their attitudes are, and what is happening in organizations similar to ours. Seeking, interpreting, and communicating this type of critical information is the role of the communications professional.

Importance of Organizational Structure   Research indicates, however, that the role of public relations in an organization often depends on the type of organization, the perceptions of top management, and even the capabilities of the public relations executive.

Research studies by Professors Larissa Grunig at the University of Maryland and Mark McElreath at Towson State University, among others, show that large, complex organizations have a greater tendency than do smaller firms to include public relations in the policy-making process. Companies such as IBM and General Motors, which operate in a highly competitive environment, are more sensitive than many others to policy issues and public attitudes and to establishing a solid corporate identity. Consequently, they place more emphasis on news conferences, formal contact with the media, writing executive speeches, and counseling management about issues that could potentially affect the corporate bottom line. See the Insights box on page 100 for a typical employment ad posted by Amazon.com.

In such organizations, which are classified as *mixed organic/mechanical* by management theorists, the authority and power of the public relations department are quite high. Public relations is part of what is called the "dominant coalition" and has a great deal of autonomy.

In contrast, a small-scale organization of low complexity that offers a standardized product or service feels few public pressures and little governmental regulatory interest. It has scant public relations activity, and staff members perform such technician roles as producing the company newsletter and issuing routine news releases. Public relations in such traditional organizations has little or no input into management decisions and policy formation.

Research also indicates that the type of organization involved may be less significant in predicting the role of its public relations department than are the perceptions and expectations of its top management. In many organizations, top-level management perceives public relations as primarily a journalistic and technical function—media relations and publicity. In large-scale mechanical organizations of low complexity, there is also a tendency to think of public relations as only a support function of the marketing department.

Such perceptions by top management severely limit the role of the public relations department as well as its power to take part in management decision making. Instead, public relations is relegated to being a tactical function, simply preparing messages without input on what should be communicated. In many cases, however, public relations personnel self-select technician roles because they lack a knowledge base in research, environmental scanning, problem solving, and managing total communications strategies. Research by Professors Elizabeth Toth, Linda Hon, Linda Aldoory, and Larissa Grunig also suggests that many practitioners prefer and choose the technician roles because they are more personally fulfilled by working with tactics than with strategy.

The most admired *Fortune* 500 corporations, in terms of reputation, tend to think of public relations as more of a strategic management tool. A study by the University of Southern California (USC) Annenberg Strategic Public Relations Center (www.annenberg.usc.edu/sprc) and the Council of Public Relations Firms found that these companies dedicated a larger percentage of their gross revenues to public relations activities, extensively used outside public relations firms to supplement their own large staffs, and didn't have public relations reporting to the marketing department.

> A significant part of our function has to do with strategic communications—altogether too much crisis communications.
>
> — John Buckley, EVP of corporate communications for AOL.

PRWeek, summarizing the survey, said, "PR Departments that closely align their own goals with their companies' strategic business goals receive greater executive support, have larger budgets, and have a higher perceived contribution to their organizations' success."

The primary indicator of a department's influence and power, however, is whether the top communications officer has a seat at the management table. To gain and maintain a seat at the management table should be an ongoing goal of public relations practitioners. Experts indicate that it is increasingly common for the top public relations practitioner in an organization to report to the CEO. In its 2006 survey of 500 senior-level practitioners, the Annenberg Strategic Public Relations Center found that 64 percent of all respondents and 77 percent of *Fortune* 500 respondents reported to the "C-Suite" (CEO, COO, or chairman). The report adds, "They were much more likely to indicate that their CEOs believe PR contributes to market share, financial success, and sales, than those reporting to other parts of the organization."

Jerry Swerling, director of the Annenberg survey, summarizes:

C-Suite reporting leads to many other pluses for PR. Statistical correlations revealed that respondents reporting to the C-Suite were significantly more likely to report that PR is taken seriously within the organization, gets a higher level of support from senior management, and participates in organizational strategic planning; that their CEOs believe reputation contributes to organizational success; that the various communications functions within the organization are bettter integrated and coordinated; and that their organizations are flexible, people first, and proactive.

Julie O'Neil of Texas Christian University researched the sources of influence for corporate public relations practitioners. She reported in a *Public Relations Review* article that having influence in the company was based on four factors: (1) perception of

> They need to be able to antici-pate the reactions of govern-ments, private interest groups, shareholders, factions, and so forth, in real time.
>
> —— CEO of a large corporation on what he expects in a chief communications officer, in a survey by the Arthur W. Page Society Survey.

value by top management, (2) practitioners taking on the managerial role, (3) reporting to the CEO, and (4) years of professional experience. In another study, Bruce Berger of the University of Alabama and Bryan Reber of the University of Georgia interviewed 162 public relations professionals and found that the top sources of influence among those practitioners were (1) relationships with others, (2) professional experience, (3) performance record, (4) persuasive skills with top executives, and (5) professional expertise.

Names of Departments

A public relations department in an organization goes by many names. And, most often, it is not "public relations."

In the largest corporations (the *Fortune* 500), the terms *corporate communications* or *communications* outnumber *public relations* by almost four to one. *O'Dwyer's PR Services Report*, in a survey of the *Fortune* 500 companies, found 200 such departments and only 48 public relations departments. Among those switching from "public relations" to "corporate communications" in recent years are Procter & Gamble and Hershey Candies. In both cases, the companies say that the switch occurred because the department had expanded beyond traditional "public relations" activities such as media relations to include such areas as employee communications, shareholder communications, annual reports, consumer relations, branding, reputation management, and corporate philanthropy.

Such activities, however, are considered subcategories of modern public relations, so consultant Alfred Geduldig has offered another reason. He told *O'Dwyer's PR Services Report* that the term *public relations* had suffered from repeated derogatory usage, causing companies to move away from the term. He also thought that the term *corporate communications* was a sign that public relations people were doing many more things in a company than in the past, reflecting an integration of communications services.

Other names used for public relations departments in the corporate world include *corporate relations*, *marketing and corporate affairs*, *investor relations*, *public affairs*, *marketing communications*, *community relations*, and *external affairs*. Government agencies, educational institutions, and charitable organizations use such terms as *public affairs*, *community relations*, *public information*, and even *marketing services*.

Organization of Departments

The head executive of a public relations or similarly named department usually has one of three titles: manager, director, or vice president. A vice president of corporate communications may have direct responsibility for the additional activities of advertising and marketing communications.

A department usually is divided into specialized sections that have a coordinator or manager. Common sections found in a large corporation are media relations, investor relations, consumer affairs, governmental relations, community relations, marketing communications, and employee communications. The Insights box on page 104 identifies the expertise needed by public relations departments.

Large, global corporations such as IBM and General Motors have several hundred employees in various areas of corporate and marketing communications, and the IBM organizational chart on page 103 (see Figure 4.1), is a good example of how a large

IBM's Corporate Communications
(July 2007)

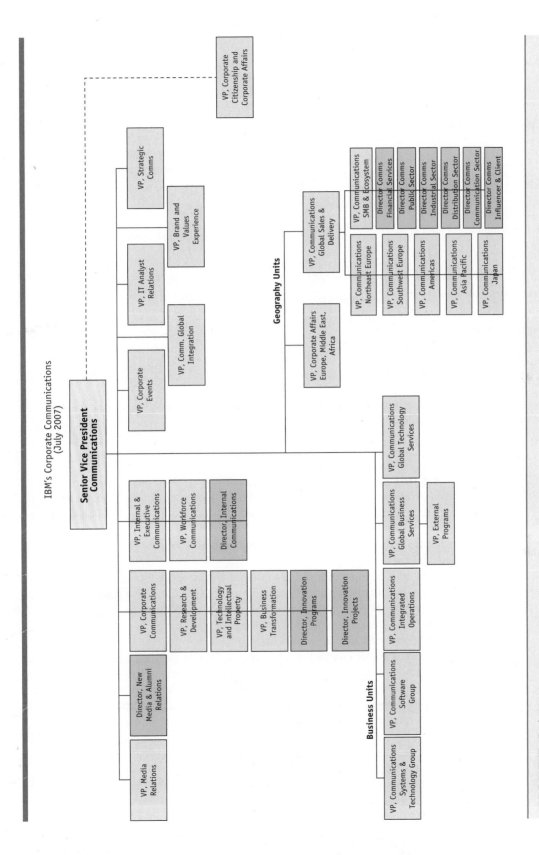

FIGURE 4.1

This chart shows the overall organization of IBM's global communications team. It shows delegation of responsibilities by function, business unit, and geography under a senior vice president of communications. Courtesy of Jon Iwata, SVP of communications, IBM Corporation.

on the job
INSIGHTS

Expertise Required in a Department

The Excellence in Public Relations and Communication Management study, funded by IABC, identified 15 areas of specialized expertise that should be present in a public relations department:

Strategic and Operational Management Knowledge

- Develop strategies for solving problems
- Manage organizational response to issues
- Develop goals and objectives for department

- Prepare budgets
- Manage people

Research Knowledge

- Perform environmental scanning
- Determine public reactions to your organization
- Use research to segment publics
- Conduct evaluation research

Negotiation Knowledge

- Negotiate with activist publics

- Help management understand opinions of publics
- Use conflict resolution theories with publics

Persuasion Knowledge

- Persuade a public that your organization is right
- Use attitude theory in a campaign
- Get publics to behave as your organization wants

Source: Dozier, David, with Grunig, James, and Grunig, Larissa. *The Manager's Guide to Excellence in Public Relations and Communication Management.* Mahwah, NJ: Lawrence Erlbaum, 1995, p. 64.

operation is structured. Corporate communications, under a senior vice president of communications, has almost 30 vice presidents (VPs) and almost a dozen directors, each with their own staffs. IBM staff are aligned in various divisions, which are organized by both function and product area. There are VPs of media relations and internal communications, but there are also VPs of communications for the technology group and global business services.

This example, however, should not mislead you about the size and budget of public relations departments. The USC Annenberg study found that *Fortune* 500 companies typically have 24 professionals in the corporate communications/public relations department. The average annual budget was $8.5 million for *Fortune* 500 companies and $2.2 million for *Fortune* 501–1000 firms.

The vast majority of companies, of course, are much smaller in size and have fewer staff in the public relations area. One study by the Conference Board of medium-sized U.S. corporations found that the typical public relations department had nine professionals. Another survey by PRSA and Bacon's Information, Inc. found that only 13 percent of the respondents worked for an organization that had more than 10 employees working in public relations. Another 45 percent worked in a department with two to five employees. Almost a third of the respondents reported that they were the only public relations employee in their organization.

Public relations personnel may also be dispersed throughout an organization in such a manner that an observer has difficulty in ascertaining the extent of public relations activity. Some may be housed under marketing communications in the marketing department. Others may be assigned to human resources as communication specialists producing newsletters and brochures. Still others may be in marketing, working exclusively on product publicity. Decentralization of the public relations function, and the frictions it causes, will be discussed later in this chapter.

Line and Staff Functions

Traditional management theory divides an organization into line and staff functions. A line manager, such as a vice president of manufacturing, can delegate authority, set production goals, hire employees, and directly influence the work of others. Staff people, in contrast, have little or no direct authority. Instead, they indirectly influence the work of others through suggestions, recommendations, and advice.

According to accepted management theory, public relations is a staff function. Public relations people are experts in communication; line managers, including the chief executive officer, rely on them to use their skills in preparing and processing data, making recommendations, and executing communication programs to meet organizational objectives.

Public relations staff members, for example, may find through a community survey that people have only a vague understanding of what the company manufactures. To improve community comprehension and create greater rapport, the public relations department may recommend to top management that a community open house be held at which product demonstrations, tours, and entertainment would be featured.

Notice that the department recommends this action. It would have no direct authority to decide on its own to hold an open house or to order various departments within the company to cooperate. If top management approves the proposal, the department may take responsibility for organizing the event. Top management, as line managers, have the authority to direct all departments to cooperate in the activity. See the Insights box on this page about activities performed by a corporate department.

Although public relations departments can function only with the approval of top management, there are varying levels of influence that departments may exert. These levels will be discussed shortly.

Access to Management   The power and influence of a public relations department usually result from access to top management, which uses advice and recommendations to formulate policy. That is why public relations, as well as other staff functions, is located high in the organizational chart and is called on by top management

---

on the job INSIGHTS

The Functions of a Corporate PR/Communications Department

A 2006 survey of corporations by *PRWeek* asked respondents what activities their departments performed. Listed below is the percentage of in-house departments responsible for the following public relations functions.

Media Relations	79.5%
Crisis Management	62.6%
Employee Communications	59.4%
Online Communications	58.0%
Special Events	56.6%
Community Relations	55.7%
Reputation Management	54.8%
Product/Brand Communication	51.1%
Marketing	45.7%
Public Affairs/Governmental Relations	35.2%
Annual/Quarterly Reports	34.7%
Product/Brand Advertising	34.2%
Issues Advertising	31.1%
Cause-related Marketing	27.9%
Financial/Investor Relations	21.5%
Monitoring Blogs	20.5%
Writing Blogs	12.3%
Blog Relations	11.9%

Source: "Corporate Survey 2006." *PRWeek*, October 9, 2006, p. 21.

to make reports and recommendations on issues affecting the entire company. In today's environment, public acceptance or nonacceptance of a proposed policy is an important factor in decision making—as important as costing and technological ability. This is why the former president of RJR Nabisco, F. Ross Johnson, told the *Wall Street Journal* in an interview that his senior public relations aide was "Numero Uno" and quipped, "He is the only one who has an unlimited budget and exceeds it every year." A good example of how the corporate communications team at American Standard Companies contributed to the bottom line is shown in the PR Casebook on page 107.

Levels of Influence   Management experts state that staff functions in an organization operate at various levels of influence and authority. On the lowest level, the staff function may be only *advisory*: Line management has no obligation to take recommendations or even request them.

When public relations is purely advisory, it is often not effective. A good example is the Enron scandal. The energy company generated a great deal of public, legislative and media criticism because public relations was relegated to a low level and was, for all practical purposes, nonexistent.

Johnson & Johnson, on the other hand, gives its public relations staff function higher status. The Tylenol crisis, in which seven persons died after taking capsules containing cyanide, clearly showed that the company based much of its reaction and quick recall of the product on the advice of public relations staff. In this case, public relations was in a *compulsory-advisory* position.

Under the compulsory-advisory concept, organization policy requires that line managers (top management) at least listen to the appropriate staff experts before deciding on a strategy. Don Hellriegel and John Slocum, authors of the textbook *Management*, state: "Although such a procedure does not limit the manager's decision-making discretion, it ensures that the manager has made use of the specialized talents of the appropriate staff agency."

Another level of advisory relationship within an organization is called *concurring authority*. For instance, an operating division wishing to publish a brochure cannot do so unless the public relations department approves the copy and layout. If differences arise, the parties must agree before work can proceed. Many firms use this mode to prevent departments and divisions from disseminating materials that do not conform with company standards. In addition, the company must ascertain that its trademarks are used correctly to ensure continued protection.

Concurring authority, however, may also limit the freedom of the public relations department. Some companies have a policy that all employee magazine articles and external news releases must be reviewed by the legal staff before publication. The material cannot be disseminated until legal and public relations personnel have agreed on what will be said. The situation is even more limiting on public relations when the legal department has *command authority* to change a news release with or without the consent of public relations. This is one reason that newspaper editors find some news releases so filled with "legalese" as to be almost unreadable.

There are times when legal counsel and public relations practitioners work collaboratively. When Norfolk Southern Railroad embarked on a bid to buy Conrail, Norfolk Southern's public relations executive Robert Fort recalled that in-house representatives of public relations and law met daily. "We had to be very careful what we said and how we said it and also to get it reported to the Securities and Exchange Commission on a daily basis," said one of Norfolk Southern's in-house lawyers. Fort said that legal and public relations personnel were on equal footing.

PRCASEBOOK

The Challenge of Corporate Public Relations

American Standard Companies, a global manufacturer with 60,000 employees in 50 countries, had virtually no communications department until several years ago. Then, at that time, it hired Shelly London as VP of communications to build a program from scratch to support the company's three major businesses.

Her first challenge was to gain national visibility for the company's new whole-house air-filtration system in the national media. She organized health influencers to provide third–party credibility, and also enlisted the company's employees to spread the word. Her efforts pushed the product 16 percent ahead of its competitor.

Another challenge of the communications team was working with HR to solve the problem of low productivity in an Asian ceramics plant making toilets, bathtubs and sinks. A Productivity Partnership was launched that communicated with employees about the value of increased productivity, which also received support from the union. The result was that productivity improved by 55 percent and manufacturing costs dropped 40 percent.

A third aspect of London's job was to manage the announcement that one of the company's ceramic operations would be closed. The communications team kept management visible and accessible throughout the process to address staff questions and concerns.

PRWeek named London and her staff the "Corporate Communications Team of the Year 2007." The judges noted, "Overall, the company's communications team proved its business value several times over."

"In the past . . . eventually, if there is a point of contention between PR and law, law usually wins," he explained. "In this case, the law department was actually asking us, and not only asking us for our advice, but then used it when we gave it to them. I think they recognized that this was an historic event about to take place here and that as it unfolded it was going to have to be won on the basis of public opinion."

Sources of Friction

Ideally, public relations is part of the managerial subsystem and contributing to organizational strategy. Public relations is, say professors James and Larissa Grunig, "the management of communication between an organization and its publics." However, other staff functions also are involved in the communication process with internal and external publics. And, almost invariably, friction occurs. The four areas of possible friction are legal, human resources, advertising, and marketing.

Legal   The legal staff is concerned about the possible effect of any public statement on current or potential litigation. Consequently, lawyers often frustrate public relations personnel by taking the attitude that any public statement can potentially be used against the organization in a lawsuit. Conflicts over what to release, and when, often have a paralyzing effect on decision making, causing the organization to seem unresponsive to public concerns. This is particularly true in a crisis, when the public demands information immediately. Public relations practitioners who are members of the management team often combat this reality, when appropriate, by taking a tough stance and aggressively making a case to the CEO that public opinion and erosion of brand or market share may be more expensive than the outcome of potential litigation.

Human Resources   The traditional personnel department has now evolved into the expanded role of "human resources," and there are often turf battles over who is responsible for employee communications. Human resources personnel believe they should control the flow of information. Public relations administrators counter that satisfactory external communications cannot be achieved unless effective employee relations are conducted simultaneously. Layoffs, for example, affect not only employees, but also the community and investors.

Advertising   Advertising and public relations departments often collide because they compete for funds to communicate with external audiences. Philosophical differences also arise. Advertising's approach to communications is, "Will it increase sales?" Public relations asks, "Will it make friends?" These differing orientations frequently cause breakdowns in coordination of overall strategy.

Marketing   Marketing, like advertising, tends to think only of customers or potential buyers as key publics. Public relations, on the other hand, defines publics in a broader way—any group that can have an impact on the operations of the organization. These publics include governmental agencies, environmental groups, neighborhood groups, and a host of other publics that marketing would not consider customers.

> *We're no longer in silos where marketing does its own thing, and PR does its own thing.*
>
> — Kim Plaskett, director of corporate communications for Greyhound

This led James Grunig, editor of the IABC study, to conclude, "We believe, then, that public relations must emerge as a discipline distinct from marketing and that it must be practiced separately from marketing in the organization." Logic dictates, however, that an organization needs a coordinated and integrated approach to communications strategy. Indeed, one survey found that 65 percent of corporate managers were now spending more time on developing integrated communications programs.

The following suggestions may help achieve this goal:

- Representatives of departments should serve together on key committees to exchange information on how various programs can complement each other to achieve overall organizational objectives. If representatives from human resources, public relations, legal, and investor relations would present a united front to senior managers, their influence would likely be increased exponentially.
- Collaboration or coalition-building among departments with shared interests in communication issues can also help achieve organization-wide business goals.
- Heads of departments should be equals in job title. In this way, the autonomy of one department is not subverted by another.
- All department heads should report to the same superior, so that all viewpoints can be considered before an appropriate strategy is formulated.
- Informal, regular contacts with representatives of other departments help dispel mind-sets and create understanding and respect for each other's viewpoint.
- Written policies should be established to spell out the responsibilities of each department. Such policies are helpful in settling disputes over which department has authority to communicate with employees or alter a news release.

Some organizational charts for public relations and other departments are shown in Figure 4.2.

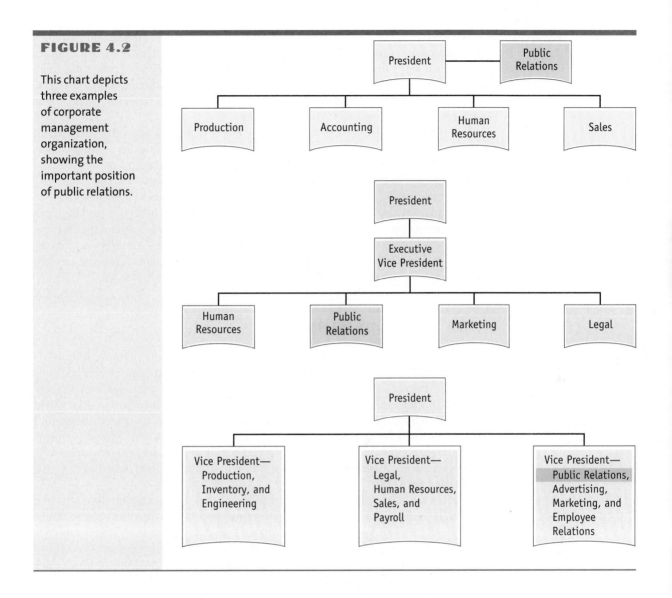

FIGURE 4.2

This chart depicts three examples of corporate management organization, showing the important position of public relations.

The Trend Toward Outsourcing

A major trend for American corporations has been the outsourcing of services, whether telecommunications, accounting, customer service, software engineering, or even legal services. The trend line also is for more organizations to outsource their communication activities to public relations firms and outside contractors. Indeed, the USC and Council of Public Relations Firms study found that *Fortune* 500 companies now spend 25 percent of their public relations budgets on outside firms. Almost 90 percent of the companies use outside public relations counsel to varying degrees.

A national survey by *PRWeek* found that companies of all sizes spent an average of more than 40 percent of their public relations budget on the services of outside firms. In high technology, the percentage was even higher—a whopping 66 percent of the corporate budget. In contrast, nonprofits allocated an average of 38 percent of their budgets for external public relations services.

The most frequent reason given for outsourcing is to bring expertise and resources to the organization that can't be found internally. A second reason is the need to supplement internal staffs during peak periods of activity. The most frequently outsourced activities, according to a study by Bisbee & Co. and Leone Marketing Research, were, in descending order, (1) writing and communications, (2) media relations, (3) publicity, (4) strategy and planning, and (5) event planning.

The trend toward outsourcing, say many experts, follows what has occurred in advertising. Today, about 90 percent of corporate and institutional advertising is handled by agencies rather than by in-house departments. It currently appears that the major beneficiary of this trend will be public relations firms.

The traditional "agency of record" (AOR) concept, however, seems to be in decline. Today's major corporations, instead of using just one firm, now use multiple firms for various projects. The 2006 Annenberg study, for example, found that *Fortune* 500 companies now work with three or four different agencies in order to "cherry-pick" the best agency for a particular situation. Public relations firms, and the services they offer, are discussed next.

Public Relations Firms

Public relations firms (often called *agencies* in the trade) are found in every industrialized nation and most of the developing world. With regard to size, public relations firms range from one- or two-person operations to global giants such as Weber-Shandwick, which employs almost 3,000 professionals in 81 offices around the world (www.webershandwick.com). The scope of services provided to clients varies, but there are common denominators. Big or small, each firm gives counsel and performs tactical services required to carry out an agreed-on program. The firm may operate as an adjunct to an organization's public relations department or, if no department exists, conduct the entire effort.

The United States, because of its large population and economic base, has the world's most public relations firms with an estimated 7,000 companies that no doubt include many one- or two-person operations. The *2007 O'Dwyer's Directory of U.S. Firms* has a more formal listing of about 2,000 firms, representing more than 8,500 client organizations. U.S. firms also generate the most fee income. In fact, the international committee of the Public Relations Consultancies Association reported in a worldwide study that the fee income of American firms "plainly dwarfs those in all other regions." Research and Markets, Ltd., in its 2007 survey, estimates U.S. revenues at more than $6 billion.

Several organizations report continued growth of U.S. revenues and increased staffing. *PRWeek*'s Agency Business Report 2007 reported that revenues were up 17 percent in 2005 and another 15 percent in 2006. In the same period, there has been a 12 percent increase in employees; Edelman Worldwide, the largest independently owned firm with about $325 million in annual revenues, added 354 people in 2006.

The Council of Public Relations Firms (www.prfirms.org) reported its members' revenues increased 13.9 percent in 2006 and estimated another 12 percent growth in 2007. More than half of the firms' revenues were generated in marketing communications (51 percent), followed by corporate communications (26 percent), and public affairs (11 percent). Another report by financial investment company Veronis Suhler Stephenson, a specialist in the communications industries, forecasts that the public relations industry will grow 11.1 percent through 2010. Fueling all this growth, as already mentioned, is the increased outsourcing of work by corporations.

A Golden Opportunity at Edelman, San Francisco

Edelman is seeking qualified candidates for several career opportunities in its San Francisco office, ranging from Senior Account Executive to Vice President. The ideal candidates will thrive in a creative environment that rewards pioneer thinking and entrepreneurial success and have three to ten years of professional public relations experience in one or more of the following fields:

- **Consumer Brands**
- **Financial Services**
- **Corporate Communications**
- **Healthcare**

About Edelman
Edelman is the world's largest independent public relations firm, with over 2,000 employees and 46 offices worldwide. The firm was named PRWeek's Large Agency of the Year for 2006 and AdvertisingAge named Edelman the best PR firm in 2005. Our mission: to provide public relations counsel and strategic communications services that enable our clients to build strong relationships and to influence attitudes and behaviors in a complex world.

Employee Benefits
Edelman offers a comprehensive benefits package and a variety of opportunities for training and professional development.

To Apply
For a complete list and detailed descriptions of the career opportunities we have available, please visit the Careers section of our website at www.edelman.com and search by office to apply online for the position that best suits your interests and experience.

Edelman

Edelman is an equal opportunity employer, committed to a diverse workforce.

This employment ad in *PRWeek* for Edelman Worldwide shows the type of career opportunities available in a public relations firm.

American public relations firms have proliferated in proportion to the growth of the global economy. As American companies expanded after World War II into booming domestic and worldwide markets, many corporations felt a need for public relations firms that could provide them with professional expertise in communications.

Also stimulating the growth of public relations firms were increased urbanization, expansion of government bureaucracy and regulation, more sophisticated mass media systems, the rise of consumerism, international trade, and the demand for more information. Executives of public relations firms predict future growth as more countries adopt free market economies and there is greater proliferation of independent media. In addition, the skyrocketing use of the Internet has fueled the global reach of public relations firms.

on the job
ETHICS

When It's Time to Resign an Account

Credibility and a reputation for integrity are important assets to a public relations firm in terms of keeping clients and adding new ones. Because of this, a firm will sometimes resign an account for ethical reasons.

Patrice Tanaka, CEO of PT & Co., resigned her agency's biggest account after the client adopted an antigay position. She told *PRWeek*, "We tried to explain that it wasn't smart business practice, and we didn't think it was ethical to not welcome any segment of the population."

Fleishman-Hillard resigned from the Firestone tire account after deciding the firm could not ethically

> **" Things are not remediable when there's deception or dishonesty. "**
> ———— Jim Allman, CEO
> of DeVries public relations

defend Firestone's position regarding the safety of its tires during a tire-recall controversy and allegations that Firestone failed to act on infor-

mation that defective tires were causing a number of injuries and deaths.

In Washington, D.C., three executives of Qorvis Communications left the firm because, according to press reports, they felt uneasy defending the government of Saudi Arabia against accusations that Saudi leaders had turned a blind eye to terrorism. Following 9/11, the firm had a $200,000 monthly retainer with Saudi Arabia to help to improve that country's image with the American public. According to the *New York Times*, friends said that the three executives were concerned that the firm's reputation was being tarnished by its work for the Saudi government.

On occasion, a public relations firm finds it necessary to resign an account because of client behavior. A Michigan firm, for example, decided to terminate a contract with a resort client because the point of contact was rude and abusive to agency staff and even to their own employees. In

such a situation, the firm didn't feel it could service the client in an effective manner. In another situation, Edelman Worldwide resigned an account after staff changes at a longstanding client resulted in abuse of agency employees.

Many public relations firms, before taking on a possibly controversial client, will discuss the situation with their employees to determine whether any staff would feel uncomfortable working with the client. Hill & Knowlton, some years ago, made the mistake of signing on the Catholic Bishops for an antiabortion campaign. Several employees quit, and others said they would refuse to work on the account.

Public relations firms may also resign from accounts if the client asks them to distribute misleading or incorrect information. The code of ethics for the Council of Public Relations Firms notes, "In communicating with the public and media, member firms will maintain total accuracy and truthfulness. To preserve both the reality and perception of professional integrity, information that is found to be misleading or erroneous will be promptly corrected . . . ."

Services They Provide

Today, public relations firms provide a variety of services:

- ◆ **Marketing communications**. This involves promotion of products and services through such tools as news releases, feature stories, special events, brochures, and media tours.

- **Executive speech training**. Top executives are coached on public affairs activities, including personal appearances.
- **Research and evaluation**. Scientific surveys are conducted to measure public attitudes and perceptions.
- **Crisis communication**. Management is counseled on what to say and do in an emergency such as an oil spill or a recall of an unsafe product.
- **Media analysis**. Appropriate media are examined for targeting specific messages to key audiences.
- **Community relations**. Management is counseled on ways to achieve official and public support for such projects as building or expanding a factory.
- **Events management**. News conferences, anniversary celebrations, rallies, symposiums, and national conferences are planned and conducted.
- **Public affairs**. Materials and testimony are prepared for government hearings and regulatory bodies, and background briefings are prepared.
- **Branding and corporate reputation**. Advice is given on programs that establish a company brand and its reputation for quality.
- **Financial relations**. Management is counseled on ways to avoid takeover by another firm and effectively communicate with stockholders, security analysts, and institutional investors.

A public relations firm was retained to publicize and organize the grand opening of the Smithsonian's National Museum of the American Indian. The ceremonies, which generated extensive media coverage, featured representatives from various tribes in full regalia.

Public relations firms also offer specialty areas of service as trend lines are identified. Burson-Marsteller now has a practice specialty in labor to help corporations deal with unions. Earlier, the firm set up a specialty area in environmental communications. After September 11, 2001, Fleishman-Hillard set up a practice in homeland security. Other firms offer specialty services in such areas as litigation public relations, crisis management, technology, and health care. Fleishman-Hillard has even formed an animal care practice group to serve the growing interest in the health of the country's pets.

Many major public relations firms, as the reader should have already noticed, have discarded the term *public relations* from their official names. Thus, it's just Burson-Marsteller, Ketchum, Hill & Knowlton, and Porter Novelli or Edelman Worldwide. One exception is Ogilvy Public Relations Worldwide, whose institutional ad is shown on page 114. Other firms use the term *communications*. For example, Fenton Communications describes itself as a "public interest communications firm" because it specializes in various causes. One client was "Win Without War," an umbrella group of advocacy groups opposed to U.S. policy in Iraq.

Increasingly, public relations firms emphasize the counseling aspect of their services, although most of their revenues come from implementing tactical aspects, such as writing news releases and organizing special events or media tours. The transition to counseling is best expressed by Harold Burson, chairman of Burson-Marsteller, who once told an audience, "In the beginning, top management used to say to us, 'Here's the message, deliver it.' Then it became, 'What should we say?' Now, in smart organizations, it's 'What should we do?' "

Public relations firms with global reach offer prospective clients a variety of services. This advertisement for Ogilvy Public Relations Worldwide has a lot to do with listening instead of just talking in the new age of digital communications

Because of the counseling function, we use the phrase *public relations firm* instead of *agency* throughout this book. Advertising firms, in contrast, are properly called *agencies* because they serve as agents, buying time or space on behalf of a client.

A good source of information about public relations counseling is the Council of Public Relations Firms, which has about 75 member firms. The group provides information on its Web site (www.prfirms.org) about trends in the industry and how to select a public relations firm as well as a variety of other materials. It also offers the popular publication, *Careers in Public Relations: Opportunities in a Dynamic Industry*. The group also operates a career center and posts résumés on its Web site of individuals looking for employment with a public relations firm.

Global Reach

Public relations firms, large and small, usually are found in metropolitan areas. On an international level, firms and their offices or affiliates are situated in most of the

on the job

A MULTICULTURAL WORLD

Campaigns in Other Nations Make a Difference

Public relations firms around the world handle a variety of assignments. Here are some that have recently received a Golden World award from the International Public Relations Association (IPRA):

◆ **Zarakoi Iletisim agency** (Turkey). Conducted a "No to Domestic Violence" campaign with *Hurriyet* newspaper to educate Turkish citizens about the serious social problem of domestic abuse. The campaign, which also worked with various social agencies, trained 9,000 women and men in the Istanbul metro area on conflict resolution and legal rights. A conference on domestic abuse generated widespread media coverage.

◆ **Ogilvy Public Relations** (China). Worked with IBM's China Group to educate more than 8,000 employees about the core values of the corporation by producing a booklet, "Savor the Blue." It was a compilation of stories from rank-and-file employees

about how they went through changes at different stages of IBM's history and how the changes contributed to their careers. According to Ogilvy, "It assisted IBM employees to clearly internalize IBM's redefined core values, boosted morale, and resonated with a diverse audience externally."

◆ **Gitam Porter Novelli** (Israel). Conducted a campaign on behalf of the Israel Cancer Association to bring attention to breast cancer, the most prevalent form of cancer in Israel. To this end, the firm organized a fashion show where top designers created outfits utilizing the color of pink, the universal color of breast cancer awareness and femininity. The clothes were modeled by prominent female public figures and victims of breast cancer. The show was broadcast on national television, generated extensive media coverage, and increased the number of women getting screened.

◆ **Ruder Finn Asia** (Singapore). Organized a series of events celebrating Citigroup's 100 years of business in Asia. One event was sponsorship of 21 concerts by the New York Philharmonic in 14 Asian cities. As a result, Citigroup gained new business.

◆ **Weber-Shandwick** (Germany). Coordinated a campaign by McDonald's in Germany to celebrate World Children's Day by having children use tray liners to pen their wishes for the future. The top two wishes: peace/no war and better schools and playgrounds.

◆ **United Partners Ltd**. (Bulgaria). The firm, on behalf of Procter & Gamble, organized and publicized a "Teen Information Center" Web site. Experts in psychology, sex education, drug abuse, and personal relationships were trained to answer inquiries from teenagers via the Web site. Procter & Gamble's objective was corporate citizenship.

world's major cities and capitals. Fleishman-Hillard, for example, has more than 2,000 employees in 83 offices across six continents. Edelman Worldwide, the world's largest independently owned firm, has almost 1,500 employees in the United States and another 2,000 employees in 48 offices worldwide. For examples of award-winning work by firms in other nations, see the Multicultural World box on this page.

The importance of international operations is reflected in the fact that most of the major public relations firms generate substantial revenues from international operations. Edelman, for example, had $325 million in revenues in 2006, but it's estimated that more than a third of this revenue came from its international offices. Burson-Marsteller, with 57 offices abroad and 45 affiliate offices, generates an estimated 40 percent of its revenues from international operations. London-based Incepta/Citigate generates almost 70 percent of its income from international operations.

International work isn't only for large firms. Small- and medium-sized firms around the world have formed working partnerships with each other to serve client needs. The largest such group is Worldcom, with 86 firms in 39 nations. Other major groups include Pinnacle, with 60 firms in 30 nations, PROI with 41 firms in 26 nations, Euro-com Worldwide with 29 firms in 39 nations, and Iprex with 58 firms in 25 nations.

Essentially, firms in an affiliation cooperate with each other to service clients with international needs. A firm in India, for example, may call its affiliate in Los Angeles to handle the details of news coverage for a visiting trade delegation from India. One of Worldcom's accounts is Bausch & Lomb, which involves 17 affiliates in 20 separate markets. Bob Oltmanns, then head of Iprex, told *PRWeek*, "One of the reasons we started in the first place was to provide clients with a need for reach beyond their own markets with a viable alternative to the large multinational agencies."

International public relations is an area of growth that will be discussed in detail in Chapter 19.

The Rise of Communication Conglomerates

Until the 1970s, the largest public relations firms were independently owned by their founders or, in some cases, by employee stockholders. A significant change began in 1973 when Carl Byoir & Associates, then the largest U.S. public relations firm, was purchased by the advertising firm of Foote, Cone, & Belding. In short order, other large public relations firms were purchased by major advertising agencies.

Today, both public relations firms and advertising agencies have become part of large, diversified holding companies with global reach (see the Insights box on page 117). Omnicom, based in New York, is the largest, reporting 2006 worldwide revenues of $11.38 billion. It owns, for example, three major public relations firms—Fleishman-Hillard, Ketchum, and Porter Novelli. All three have international offices and Ketchum even did work for President Putin of the Russian Federation when he was chair of the G8 Summit conference.

WPP, based in London, is second in worldwide revenues, with $10.9 billion. It has a stable of major public relations firms, including Hill & Knowlton, which was one of the first firms to gain national visibility more than 50 years ago when it defended the tobacco industry against allegations that smoking caused cancer. It gained even further notoriety when it represented the "Citizens for a Free Kuwait" in 1991, which was a front group for the Kuwaiti government. WPP also owns Burson-Marsteller, also considered one of the leaders in the industry.

Interpublic Group (IPG) is third with $6.2 billion in worldwide revenues and not only owns Foote, Cone & Belding (now called DraftFCB) and other advertising agencies, but also six major public relations firms. They include Weber-Shandwick, claimed to be the world's largest firm, as well as Golin/Harris International, Carmichael Lynch Spong, DeVries PR, MWW Group, and Tierney Communications.

Large conglomerates acquire public relations firms for several reasons. One is the natural evolutionary step of integrating various communication disciplines into "total communication networks." Supporters of integration say that no single-function agency or firm is equipped with the personnel or resources to handle complex, often global, integrated marketing functions efficiently for a client. In addition, joint efforts by public relations and advertising professionals can offer prospective clients greater communications impact, generate more business, and expand the number of geographical locations around the world.

A second reason is pure business. Holding companies find public relations firms to be attractive investments. According to *PRWeek*, revenues from advertising clients

on the job INSIGHTS

Large Public Relations Firms Part of Conglomerates

An estimated 60 percent of the global business in public relations is conducted by firms that are owned by holding companies that also own advertising agencies, marketing firms, billboard companies, direct mail firms, and special event specialty shops. The following are the three major holding companies by 2006 total worldwide revenues and what percentage came from their public relations operations.

Omnicom

Total revenue: $11.38 billion

Percentage of revenue from PR: 10.1% ($1.1 billion)

Major public relations firms owned: Fleishman-Hillard, Ketchum, Porter Novelli, Brodeur Worldwide, Clark & Weinstock, Gavin Anderson & Co., Cone, and Mercury Public Affairs

WPP

Total revenue: $10.9 billion

Percentage of revenue from PR: 10.1% ($1.07 billion)

Major public relations firms owned: Burson-Marsteller, Cohn & Wolfe, GCI Group, Hill & Knowlton, Ogilvy PR Worldwide, Public Strategies, and Robinson Lerer Montgomery

Interpublic Group

Total revenue: $6.19 billion

Percentage of revenue from PR: 15.5% ($928 million)

Revenues based on three major firms: MWW Group, Weber-Shandick, and Golin/Harris International. Other firms are DeVries PR, Carmichael Lynch Spong, Rogers & Cowan, and Tierney Communications.

Source: "Agency Business Report 2007." *PRWeek*, April 23, 2007, Supplement, pp. 1–54.

have remained somewhat static over the years, whereas public relations firms have experienced double-digit growth in the same time frame.

Toward More Integration   Although earlier efforts to create "total communication networks" for clients often met with limited success, there is now increasing evidence that the strategy may be working. Considerable new business is also generated when units of the same conglomerate refer customers to each other. As communication campaigns become more integrated, even more synergy has become commonplace.

Holding companies originally started out primarily as a stable of advertising agencies under one umbrella, but they have evolved considerably beyond that with the acquisition of public relations firms and other specialty communication companies. London-based WPP, for example, now employs 69,000 people in more than 100 nations.

Sir Martin Sorrell, chairman of WPP (London), told a *Wall Street Journal* interviewer:

If you want to upset me, call me an advertising agency. The strategic objective is for two-thirds of our revenue to come from nontraditional advertising in 5 to 10 years. Because of fragmentation, TiVo, and Sky Plus, clients and ourselves have to look at everything. Instead of focusing on network television, we have to look at public relations and radio and outdoor and mobile messaging and satellite. Media planning becomes more important.

Sir Martin also makes the point that one size doesn't fit all when it comes to global communications strategies and campaigns. Campaigns still have to be tailored to local customs, ethnic groups, and religious preferences. Muslims now constitute 26 percent of the world's population and, by 2014, they will be 30 percent. By the same year, two-thirds of the world's population will be Asian.

Structure of a Counseling Firm

A small public relations firm may consist only of the owner (president) and an assistant (vice president), who are supported by an administrative assistant. Larger firms have a more extended hierarchy.

The organization of Ketchum in San Francisco is fairly typical. The president is based in Ketchum's New York office, so the executive vice president is the on-site director in San Francisco. A senior vice president is associate director of operations. Next in line are several vice presidents who primarily do account supervision or special projects.

An account supervisor is in charge of one major account or several smaller ones. An account executive, who reports to the supervisor, is in direct contact with the client and handles most of the day-to-day activity. At the bottom of the list is the assistant account executive, who does routine maintenance work compiling media lists, gathering information, and writing rough drafts of news releases.

Recent college graduates usually start as assistant account executives. Once they learn the firm's procedures and show ability, promotion to account executive may occur within 6 to 18 months. After two or three years, it is not uncommon for an account executive to become an account supervisor.

Executives at or above the vice-presidential level usually are heavily involved in selling their firm's services. In order to prosper, a firm must continually seek new business and sell additional services to current clients. Consequently, the upper management of the firm calls on prospective clients, prepares proposals, and makes new business presentations. In this very competitive field, a firm not adept at selling itself frequently fails.

Firms frequently organize account teams, especially to serve a client whose program is multifaceted. One member of the team, for example, may set up a nationwide media tour in which an organization representative is booked on television talk shows. Another may supervise all materials going to the print media, including news stories, feature articles, background kits, and artwork. A third may concentrate on the trade press or perhaps arrange special events. See the Insights box on page 119 for a first-person account of what it's like to work in a public relations firm and then a corporation. The Insights box on page 121 gives the pros and cons of working in both settings.

How Public Relations Firms Get Business

Organizations, even if they have internal public relations staff, often use the services of public relations to supplement staffing, do a special project, or because they need specific expertise in a particular situation. In fact, the Strategic Public Relations Center at the University of Southern California (USC) reports that public and private companies spend about 25 percent of their total public relations budget on the services of public relations firms.

A common approach to engaging the services of a public relations firm is to issue what is called a "Request for Proposal," known as a RFP. Firms are invited to make a presentation regarding their capabilities and express their ideas about what program they would create to address the potential client's particular needs. This is a highly competitive situation and firms use their most skilled presenters to "sell" their services and ideas.

on the job
INSIGHTS

Comparing Work in a PR Firm and a Corporation

Stacy Nobles, like many professionals, has worked in a public relations firm and also on the corporate side. She was formerly with Peppercom public relations and is now senior manager of corporate communications for Wolters Kluwer company in New York. Below is her first-person account:

What's it like working in an agency versus working as an in-house corporate communications professional? In my experience, starting my career in the agency world has been invaluable. It's helped me gain the experiences needed to run my own corporate communications program. So, let me start by describing agency life.

While at a Manhattan agency, some of my clients were major *Fortune* 500 companies. My day included working with my colleagues to craft the right messaging for a company and conversations with the media about my clients' businesses and what differentiates them. It also included phone calls with top communications executives to discuss pending media interviews (based on actually reading what a reporter had written). Sometimes, my job included crisis communications, or counseling a client on how to best to communicate with its audiences during an unexpected event. Other times, my job was to work with my client contacts—marketing and communications executives—to help them communicate to their bosses why their jobs are critical

and why they should be involved in key company decisions.

And then I became one of those marketing and communications executives. As the senior manager of corporate communications for Wolters Kluwer Corporate Legal Services, I now know what my clients went through every day. Now I'm the person who's responsible for managing my company's internal and external perceptions. I handle all aspects of media relations (e.g., pitch development, press release writing, media list building, interview prep, etc.), and all other external communications initiatives, which sometimes includes the occasional crisis. I work with executives to ensure they're media trained and on-message, develop a subject-matter-expert program to increase our thought-leadership through speaking and media opportunities, and manage all of the content offered at our own events and conferences.

On top of that, I also oversee the internal communications function. I helped create and staff the position, which is tasked with creating an internal newsletter, developing a quarterly executive video, executing four town hall meetings per year and managing all internal messaging to ensure the sales teams have the right information to communicate with customers.

When I moved in-house, I thought my days of juggling multiple clients with different projects and needs were over. But I was wrong. I oversee and manage corporate communications plans for six different business

Stacy Nobles speaks from experience.

units. With those six business units come six marketing managers, six executive-level managers, and six different sets of customers. On top of that, my company is a division under a bigger company, Wolters Kluwer (based in Amsterdam, the Netherlands). So, not only is my immediate boss a "client" with demands and expectations to meet, but it's also as if each of the six business units and the vice president of corporate communications for Wolters Kluwer are also clients. And then there's the ultimate client, the CEO.

Working in-house means I actually have to juggle even more than when I was at an agency—without a team! At an agency, most of the praise I received came from the agency executives. When I made a mistake, I had a team and supervisors to

(CONTINUED)

A good example of a RFP situation is the Ministry of Tourism for the Cayman Islands government that sought a public relations firm to promote the island nation in the U.S. market. The RFP specified that the winning public relations firm would (1) develop and implement a public affairs/media action plan, (2) maintain an international news bureau, (3) provide spokesperson training as needed, (4) provide consultation on reactive media issues, and (5) devise an appropriate measurement strategy.

The RFP also listed the criteria for evaluating proposals. It stated that public relations firms should be well established with a proven track record and preference would be given to firms with Caribbean experience. The RFP also specified that a decision would be made on the basis of such criteria as: (1) quality of the proposal, (2) strategic and practical approach, (3) proven expertise of personnel assigned to the account, (4) effective use of resources, and (5) a proven track record of working with similar clients.

RFPs can be a single page or, in the case of governmental agencies, run 20 or 30 pages. Public relations firms, after analyzing what is requested and the budget allocated, then decide whether to make a presentation or to pass up the opportunity.

Pros and Cons of Using a Public Relations Firm

Because public relations is a service industry, a firm's major asset is the quality of its people. Potential clients thinking about hiring a public relations firm usually base their decisions on that fact, according to a survey of *Fortune* 500 corporate vice presidents.

Basic attributes that an organization wants from a firm, according to another survey of 600 clients, was (1) understands your business and the industry, (2) responds to all your needs and requests in a timely manner, and (3) works within your budget. Clients also give high priority to (1) accurate work, (2) high-quality staff, (3) consistent delivery of key messages to target audiences, (4) outstanding client service, (5) a measurable return on investment, and (6) creative programs that meet business objectives. Both firms and potential clients also consider possible conflicts of interest. A firm, for example, cannot ethically represent two clients that are directly competing with each other. Other concerns can also come up. See the Ethics box on page 112 for some insights on why a public relations firm will resign an account.

> We use agencies almost as extensions of our internal staff. We work as partners.
> —— Paul James, communications manager of Harley-Davidson

Advantages   Public relations firms offer several advantages:

♦ *Objectivity*. The firm can analyze a client's needs or problems from a new perspective and offer fresh insights.

A Job at a Corporation or a PR Firm?

Recent college graduates often ponder the pros and cons of joining a corporate department or going to work for a PR firm. The following summarizes some of the pluses and minuses:

PR FIRM: BREADTH OF EXPERIENCE	CORPORATE PR: DEPTH OF EXPERIENCE
See "On the Job: Insights Comparing Work in a PR Firm and a Corporation."	Jobs more difficult to find without experience; duties more narrowly focused.
Variety. Usually work on several clients and projects at same time. Possibility of rapid advancement.	Sometimes little variety at entry level.
Fast-paced, exciting.	Growth sometimes limited unless you are willing to switch employers.
Seldom see the impact of your work for a client; removed from "action."	Can be slower paced.
Abilities get honed and polished. (This is where a mentor really helps.)	Heavy involvement with executive staff; see impact almost instantly. You are an important component in the "big picture."
Networking with other professionals leads to better job opportunities.	Strength in all areas expected. Not a lot of time for coaching by peers.
Learn other skills, such as how to do presentations and budgets and establish deadlines.	Sometimes so involved in your work, you don't have time for networking.
Intense daily pressure on billable hours, high productivity. Some firms are real "sweat shops."	Same "client" all the time. Advantage: Get to know organization really well. Disadvantage: Can become boring.
Somewhat high employment turnover.	Less intense daily pressure; more emphasis on accomplishing longer-term results.
Budgets and resources can be limited.	Less turnover.
Salary traditionally low at entry level.	More resources usually available.
Insurance, medical benefits can be minimal.	Salaries tend to be higher.
Little opportunity for profit-sharing, stock options.	Benefits usually good, sometimes excellent.
High emphasis on tactical skills, production of materials.	More opportunities available.

◆ *A variety of skills and expertise.* The firm has specialists, whether in speech-writing, trade magazine placement, or helping with investor relations.

◆ *Extensive resources.* The firm has abundant media contacts and works regularly with numerous suppliers of products and services. It has research materials, including data information banks, and experience in similar fields.

◆ *International jobs*, like handling the corporate sponsorship issues with an Olympics, benefits from the extensive resources of a firm.

◆ *Offices throughout the country.* A national public relations program requires coordination in major cities. Large firms have on-site staffs or affiliate firms in many cities and even around the world.

◆ *Special problem-solving skills.* A firm may have extensive experience and a solid reputation in desired areas. For example, Burson-Marsteller is well known for expertise in crisis communications, health and medical issues, and international coordination of special projects. Hill & Knowlton is known for expertise in public affairs, and Ketchum is the expert in consumer marketing.

◆ *Credibility*. A successful public relations firm has a solid reputation for professional, ethical work. If represented by such a firm, a client is likely to get more attention among opinion leaders in mass media, government, and the financial community.

Disadvantages   There are also drawbacks to using public relations firms:

◆ *Superficial grasp of a client's unique problems*. Although objectivity is gained from an outsider's perspective, there is often a disadvantage in the public relations firm's not thoroughly understanding the client's business or needs.

◆ *Lack of full-time commitment*. A public relations firm has many clients to service. Therefore, no single client can monopolize its personnel and other resources.

◆ *Need for prolonged briefing period*. Some companies become frustrated because time and money are needed for a public relations firm to research the organization and make recommendations. Consequently, the actual start of a public relations program may take weeks or months.

◆ *Resentment by internal staff*. The public relations staff members of a client organization may resent the use of outside counsel because they think it implies that they lack the ability to do the job.

◆ *Need for strong direction by top management*. High-level executives must take the time to brief outside counsel on specific objectives sought.

◆ *Need for full information and confidence*. A client must be willing to share its information, including the skeletons in the closet, with outside counsel. See the Ethics box on page 112 for an illustration of why cooperation between the firm and client is essential.

◆ *Costs*. Outside counsel is expensive. In many situations, routine public relations work can be handled at lower cost by internal staff.

Fees and Charges

A public relations firm charges for its services in several ways. The three most common methods are:

1. *Basic hourly fee, plus out-of-pocket expenses*. This method is commonly used by attorneys, accounting firms, and management consultants. The number of hours spent on a client's account is tabulated each month and billed to the client. Work by personnel is billed at various hourly rates. Out-of-pocket expenses, such as cab fares, car rentals, airline tickets, and meals, are also billed to the client. In a typical $100,000 public relations campaign, about 70 percent of the budget is spent on staff salaries.

2. *Retainer fee*. A basic monthly charge billed to the client covers ordinary administrative and overhead expenses for maintaining the account and being "on call" for advice and strategic counseling. Many clients have in-house capabilities for executing communication campaigns but often need the advice of experts during the planning phase. Many retainer fees also specify the number of hours the firm will spend on an account each month. Any additional work is billed at normal hourly rates. Out-of-pocket expenses are usually billed separately.

3. *Fixed project fee.* The public relations firm agrees to do a specific project, such as an annual report, a newsletter, or a special event, for a fixed fee. For example, a counseling firm may write and produce a quarterly newsletter for $30,000 annually. The fixed fee is the least popular among public relations firms because it is difficult to predict all work and expenses in advance. Many clients, however, like fixed fees for a specific project because it is easier to budget and there are no "surprises."

A fourth method, not widely used, is the concept of *pay-for-placement.* Clients don't pay for hours worked but for actual placements of articles in the print media and broadcast mentions. Fees for a major story can range anywhere from $1,500 to $15,000 depending on the prestige, circulation, or audience size of the media outlet that uses a story proposed by a pay-for-placement firm. PayPerClip, for example, charges $5,000 for a feature in a national woman's magazine.

The vast majority of public relations firms don't use this business model for several reasons. First, it reduces public relations to simply media relations and media placement, when it is a much broader field. Second, it presents cash-flow problems because payment isn't made until a placement is made. Third, media gatekeepers ultimately decide what to use and what not to use; placement is never guaranteed despite countless hours spent by a staff person "pitching" the story.

The primary basis of the most common methods—the basic hourly fee, the retainer fee, and the fixed project fee—is to estimate the number of hours that a particular project will take to plan, execute, and evaluate. The first method—the basic hourly fee—is the most flexible and most widely used among large firms. It is preferred by public relations people because they are paid for the exact number of hours spent on a project and because it is the only sound way that a fee can be determined intelligently. The retainer fee and the fixed project fee are based on an estimate of how many hours it will take to service a client.

A number of variables are considered when a public relations firm estimates the cost of a program. These may include the size and duration of the project, geographical locations involved, the number of personnel assigned to the project, and the type of client. A major variable, of course, is billing the use of the firm's personnel to a client at the proper hourly rate.

A senior account executive, for example, may earn $60,000 annually and receive benefits (health insurance, pension plan, etc.) that cost the firm an additional $13,000. Thus, the annual cost of the employee to the firm totals $73,000. Using 1,600 billable hours in a year (after deducting vacation time and holidays), the account executive makes about $46 per hour.

The standard industry practice, however, is to bill clients at least three times a person's salary. This multiple allows the firm to pay for office space, equipment, insurance, supplies, and try to operate at a profit level of about 10 to 20 percent before taxes. Thus, the billing rate of the account executive is about $140 per hour. The principals of a counseling firm, because of their much higher salaries, often command $200 to $500 per hour, depending on the size and capabilities of the firm. On the other hand, an assistant account executive may be billed out at only $85 per hour. One nationwide survey conducted by an executive search firm found that the average hourly rate, across all public relations firm sizes and billable titles, was $213.

The primary income of a public relations firm comes from the selling of staff time, but some additional income results from markups on photocopying, telephone, fax, and artwork the firm supervises. The standard markup in the trade is between 15 and 20 percent. Firms occasionally do pro bono work for charitable causes. (See the PR Casebook on page 124 about a program for inner-city schools in New York City.)

PRCASEBOOK
Fleishman-Hillard Reaches Out to Inner-City Children

Asthma is the leading cause of school absenteeism and hospitalization for children nationwide, and New York City's inner-city children have an asthma rate four times the national level.

Such a statistic prompted Fleishman-Hillard's (F-H) New York office to do something about it as part of its own community relations program. The firm, with the voluntary efforts of senior management and staff, researched the problem of how to reach disadvantaged children with information and even medical advice. The solution, it believed, was to reach children in the schools, but that required permission and cooperation from school administrators. The F-H team, however, got the support of N.Y.C. schools chancellor Joel Klein, and Project E.R.A.S.E (Eradicating Respiratory Asthma in Schools to help children Excel) was born. The project, at no cost to the families or the schools, had three components. The first one was building support and cooperation with school principals and parent coordinators. Medical specialists went to parent meetings to talk about asthma and Project E.R.A.S.E. to garner support for the program. Second was the development of brochures and posters that would inform parents and children about the symptoms of asthma. All materials were translated into appropriate languages. The third component was having medical specialists actually visit the schools and provide diagnosis, advice on treatment, and management of asthma.

F-H also assembled partners from both the public and private sectors. Several broadcast stations signed on, a fund-raising firm volunteered its services, and a law firm provided free legal advice. Steiner Sports, an agent for professional athletes, arranged for a celebrity athlete, Richard Jefferson, to be a role model for the kids because he also suffered from a severe asthma condition.

A pilot program was successful in two needy N.Y.C. schools and the program is continuing in other inner-city schools. Some results after the first year: School absences because of asthma dropped 50 percent, hospitalizations dropped 75 percent, and ER visits declined 25 percent. The drop in ER and hospitalizations saved low-income parents and health agencies about $140,000.

Fleishman-Hillard printed its materials in English and Spanish to reach inner-city children in New York City. This brochure, for Spanish-speaking parents, gave them tips about the symptoms of asthma in their children.

Fleishman-Hillard's E.R.A.S.E program, done as a voluntary effort, received PRSA's 2007 Silver Anvil award in multicultural public relations and also the Best of Silver Anvil Award. In addition, it received *PRWeek*'s Community Relations Campaign of the Year. Julia Hood, editor of *PRWeek*, editorialized ". . . What transported this program to Campaign of the Year status was its integrity and authenticity, its focus on a community issue that was relevant for its staff, and for the greater population."

SUMMARY

Public Relations Departments

Most organizations have public relations departments. Such departments may also be called by other names, such as *corporate communications*. Organizations, depending on their culture and the wishes of top management, structure the public relations function in various ways. Public relations professionals often serve at the tactical and technician level, but others are counselors to the top executive and have a role in policy making. In management theory, public relations is a staff function rather than a line function.

Public Relations Firms

Public relations firms come in all sizes and are found worldwide, providing a variety of services. In recent decades, many public relations firms have either merged with advertising agencies or become subsidiaries of diversified holding companies. Advantages of using outside firms include versatility and extensive resources, among other considerations; but they can also lack the full-time commitment of an in-house department, need a lot of direction, and are often more expensive. Revenues primarily come from charging a basic hourly fee, plus out-of-pocket expenses.

CASE ACTIVITY What Would You Do?

You will graduate from college in several months and plan on pursuing a career in public relations. After several interviews, you receive two job offers.

One is with a high-technology company that makes inkjet printers and scanners for the consumer market. The corporate communications department has about 20 professionals, and it is customary for beginners to start in employee publications or product publicity. Later, with more experience, you might be assigned to do marketing communications for a product group or work in a specialized area such as investor relations, governmental affairs, or even community relations.

The second job offer is from a local office of a large, national public relations firm. You would begin as an assistant account executive and work on several accounts, including a chain of fast-food restaurants and an insurance company. The jobs pay about the same, but the corporation offers better insurance and medical plans. Taking into consideration the pros and cons of working for public relations firms versus corporations, what job would best fit your abilities and preferences? Explain your reasons.

QUESTIONS for Review and Study

1. How have the role and function of public relations departments changed in recent years?
2. In what ways do the structure and culture of an organization affect the role and influence of the public relations department?
3. What kinds of knowledge does a manager of a public relations department need today?
4. Many departments are now called *corporate communications* instead of *public relations*. Do you think the first term is more appropriate? Why or why not?
5. What is the difference between a line and a staff function? To which function does public relations belong, and why?
6. Why is a compulsory-advisory role within an organization a good one for a public relations department to have?
7. What four areas of the organization cause the most potential for friction with public relations? Explain.
8. In your opinion, should public relations or human resources be responsible for employee communications? Why?
9. Public relations people express a fear that they will lose influence and be relegated to purely technical functions if they are controlled by the marketing department. Do you think their fears are justified? Why or why not?
10. Name at least seven services that a public relations firm offers clients.
11. What are the three largest communications conglomerates in the world?
12. How important is international business to American public relations firms?

13. Why do large holding companies find the acquisition of public relations firms so attractive?

14. What are the pros and cons of using a public relations firm?

15. What are the standard methods used by a public relations firm to charge for its services?

16. Under what circumstances should a public relations firm resign from an account?

17. What is an AOR and a RFP?

SUGGESTED READINGS

Auletta, Ken. "Annals of Communications. The Fixer: Why New Yorkers Call Howard Rubenstein When They've Got a Problem." *New Yorker*, February 12, 2007. Profile of legendary public relations practitioner.

Berger, B. K. "Power Over, Power With, and Power to Relations: Critical Reflections on Public Relations, the Dominant Coalition, and Activism." *Journal of Public Relations Research*, Vol. 17, No. 1, 2005, pp. 5–28.

Bush, Michael. "The PR Industry From the Outside." *PRWeek*, September 11, 2006, p. 15.

Chabria, Anita. "Billing Models that Pay Off for Both Sides." *PRWeek*, July 18, 2005, p. 28.

Cody, Steve. "Taking the Lead: Communicators as Innovation Catalysts." *The Strategist*, Spring 2006, pp. 8–11.

Heyman, W. C. "Study Shows Mix of Personal, Professional Patterns Combine to Signal Likely Success in PR Profession." *Public Relations Quarterly*, Vol. 49, No. 3, 2004, pp. 7–10.

Lewis, Tanya. "Relationships That Deliver Results." *PRWeek*, May 14, 2007, pp. 18–27. Annual agency excellence survey.

Lewis, Tanya. "Networks Foster a Collaborative Spirit." *PRWeek*, April 16, 2007, p. 13. Global networks of public relations firms.

Lewis, Tanya. "When a Relationship Nears Its Endgame: Most Agency–Client Relationships Have Rough Patches, But Some Can't be Saved." *PRWeek*, February 20, 2006, p. 26.

Moss, Danny, Newman, Andrew, and DeSanto, Barbara. "What Do Communication Managers Do? Defining and Refining the Core Elements of Management in a Public Relations/Corporate Communications Context." *Journalism and Mass Communications Quarterly*, Vol. 82, No. 4, 2005, pp. 873–890.

O'Brien, Keith. "On the Right Track: Corporate Survey 2006." *PRWeek*, October 9, 2006, pp. 18–22.

O'Neil, Julie. "An Investigation of the Sources of Influence of Corporate Public Relations Practitioners." *Public Relations Review*, Vol. 29, No. 2, 2003, pp. 159–169.

Plowman, K. D. "Conflict, Strategic Management, and Public Relations." *Public Relations Review*, Vol. 31, No. 1, 2005, pp. 131–138.

Rayburn, J., and Hazelton, V. "Survey Provides Profile of Independent Practitioner: Examines Practice Areas, Income and Profit." *Public Relations Tactics*, March 2005, pp. 15–16.

Trickett, Eleanor. "Outside Look Shows PR's Role in Marketing Gaining Respect." *PRWeek*, September 11, 2006, p. 9.

CHAPTER

5

Research

TOPICS COVERED IN THIS CHAPTER INCLUDE:

The Importance of Research
Defining the Research Role
Using Research
Research Techniques

Secondary Research
Archival Research
Library and Online Databases
The Internet and World Wide Web

Qualitative Research
Content Analysis
Interviews

Focus Groups
Copy Testing
Ethnographic Techniques

Quantitative Research
Random Sampling
Sample Size

Questionnaire Construction
Carefully Consider Wording
Avoid Loaded Questions
Consider Timing and Context

Avoid the Politically Correct Answer
Give a Range of Possible Answers
Questionnaire Guidelines

How to Reach Respondents
Mail Questionnaires
Telephone Surveys
Personal Interviews
Omnibus Surveys
Web and E-Mail Surveys

The Importance of Research

Effective public relations is a process, and the essential first step in the process is research. Today, research is widely accepted by public relations professionals as an integral part of the planning, program development, and evaluation process.

Defining the Research Role

In basic terms, research is a form of listening. Broom and Dozier, in their book *Using Research in Public Relations*, say, "Research is the controlled, objective, and systematic gathering of information for the purpose of describing and understanding."

Before any public relations program can be undertaken, information must be gathered and data must be collected and interpreted. Only by performing this first step can an organization begin to make policy decisions and map out strategies for effective communication programs. This research often becomes the basis for evaluating the program once it has been completed. The results of an evaluation can lead to greater accountability and credibility with upper management. (See Chapter 8 for details.)

Various types of research can be used to accomplish an organization's objectives and meet its need for information. The choice of what type of research to use really depends on the particular subject and situation. As always, time and budget are major considerations, as is the perceived importance of the situation. Consequently, many questions should be asked before formulating a research design:

- What is the problem?
- What kind of information is needed?
- How will the results of the research be used?
- What specific public (or publics) should be researched?
- Should the organization do the research in-house or hire an outside consultant?
- How will the research data be analyzed, reported, or applied?
- How soon will the results be needed?
- How much will the research cost?

These questions will help the public relations person determine the extent and nature of the research needed. In some cases, only informal research may be required, because of its low cost or the need for immediate information. In other cases, a random scientific survey may be selected, despite its costs and time requirement, because a large retailer such as Wal-Mart or Home Depot wants to know how a community might vote on a referendum to approve the construction of a "big-box" store. The pros and cons of each research method will be discussed later in the chapter.

Using Research

Research is a multipronged tool that is involved in virtually every phase of a communications program. In general, studies show that public relations departments spend about 3 to 5 percent of their budget on research. Some experts contend that it should be 10 percent. Public relations professionals use research in the following ways:

- **To achieve credibility with management.** Executives want facts, not guesses and hunches. The inclusion of public relations personnel in an organization's policy and decision making, according to the findings of IABC's research on excellence in communication management, is strongly correlated with their ability to do research and relate their findings to the organization's objectives.

◆ **To define audiences and segment publics.** Detailed information about the demographics, lifestyles, characteristics, and consumption patterns of audiences helps to ensure that messages reach the proper audiences. A successful children's immunization information campaign in California was based on State Health Department statistics that showed that past immunization programs had not reached rural children and that Hispanic and Vietnamese children were not being immunized in the same proportion as other ethnic groups.

◆ **To formulate strategy.** Much money can be spent pursuing the wrong strategies. Officials of the New Hampshire paper industry, given the bad press about logging and waterway pollution, thought a campaign was needed to tell the public what it was doing to reduce pollution. An opinion survey of 800 state residents by a public relations firm, however, indicated that the public was already generally satisfied with the industry's efforts. Consequently, the new strategy focused on reinforcing positive themes such as worker safety, employment, and environmental responsibility.

◆ **To test messages.** Research is often used to determine what particular message is most salient with the target audience. According to one focus group study for a campaign to encourage carpooling, the message that resonated the most with commuters was saving time and money, not air quality or environmental concerns. Consequently, the campaign emphasized how many minutes could be cut from an average commute by using carpool lanes and the annual savings in gasoline, insurance, and car maintenance.

◆ **To help management keep in touch.** In a mass society, top management is increasingly isolated from the concerns of employees, customers, and other important publics. Research helps bridge the gap by periodically surveying key publics about problems and concerns. This feedback is a "reality check" for top executives and often leads to better policies and communication strategies.

◆ **To prevent crises.** An estimated 90 percent of organizational crises are caused by internal operational problems rather than by unexpected natural disasters. Research can often uncover trouble spots and public concerns before they become page-one news. (See the section on issues management in Chapter 10.) Analyzing complaints made to a toll-free number or monitoring Internet chat rooms and blogs can often tip off an organization that it should act before a problem attracts widespread media attention.

◆ **To monitor the competition.** Savvy organizations keep track of what the competition is doing. This is done through surveys that ask consumers to comment on competing products, content analysis of the competition's media coverage, and reviews of industry reports in trade journals. Such research often helps an organization shape its marketing and communication strategies to position a product and capitalize on a competitor's weaknesses.

◆ **To sway public opinion.** Facts and figures, compiled from a variety of primary and secondary sources, can change public opinion. Shortly before an election in Ohio, 90 percent of the voters supported a state ballot measure that would require cancer warnings on thousands of products from plywood to peanut butter. A coalition called Ohioans for Responsible Health Information, which opposed the bill, commissioned universities and other credible outside sources to research the economic impact of such legislation on consumers and major industries. The research, which was used as the basis of the grassroots campaign, caused the defeat of the ballot measure, with 78 percent of the voters voting "no."

◆ **To generate publicity.** Polls and surveys can generate publicity for an organization. Indeed, many surveys seem to be designed with publicity in mind. Simmons Mattress once polled people to find out how many people slept in the nude. Norelco Phillips, which introduced a new shaver for men called Bodygroom, got publicity for the new product by citing a telephone survey that more than half of the male respondents preferred a hairless back to any other body part. Another 72 percent said they used a razor blade to remove hair in even the most sensitive places. See the news release regarding the survey on page 131. A case study about Bodygroom is in Chapter 13.

> " Research gives a context in which to talk about the product. "
>
> ———Lisa Eggerton, SVP and head of consumer practice, RSCG Magnet

There are, however, some general rules about how to write news releases about the results of polls and surveys. (See the Insights box on page 131.)

◆ **To measure success.** The bottom line of any public relations program is whether the time and money spent accomplished the stated objective. As one of its many programs to boost brand awareness, Miller Genuine Draft sponsored a "reunion ride" on Harley-Davidson Corporation's 90th anniversary. Ketchum generated extensive media publicity about the "ride" and Miller's sponsorship that was 98 percent positive. Perhaps more important, sales increased in all but two of the cities included in the event. Evaluation, the last step of the public relations process, is discussed in Chapter 8. The following sections will discuss ways of doing research.

Research Techniques

When the term *research* is used, people tend to think only of scientific surveys and complex statistical tabulations. In public relations, however, research techniques can be as simple as gathering data and information.

In fact, a survey of practitioners by Walter K. Lindenmann, former senior vice president and director of research for Ketchum, found that three-fourths of the respondents described their research techniques as casual and informal rather than scientific and precise. The research technique cited most often by the respondents was literature searches/database information retrieval.

This technique is called *secondary research*, because it uses existing information in books, magazine articles, electronic databases, and so on. In contrast, with primary research, new and original information is generated through a research design that is directed to answer a specific question. Some examples of primary research are in-depth interviews, focus groups, surveys, and polls.

Another way of categorizing research is by distinguishing between qualitative and quantitative research. Lindenmann contrasts the basic differences between qualitative and quantitative research in Table 5.1. In general, qualitative research affords the researcher rich insights and understanding of a situation or a target public. It also provides "red flags" or warnings when strong or adverse responses occur. These responses may not be generalizable, but they provide the practitioner with an early warning. Quantitative research is often more expensive and complicated, but it enables a greater ability to generalize to large populations. If enormous amounts of money are to be spent on a national campaign, an investment in quantitative research may be necessary.

on the job
INSIGHTS

Rules for Publicizing Surveys and Polls

The Council of American Survey Research Organizations (CASRO), a nonprofit national trade organization of more than 150 survey research companies, states that survey findings released to the public should contain the following information:

- The sponsor of the study
- The name of the research company conducting the study

- A description of the study's objectives
- A description of the sample, including the size of the sample and the population to which the results are intended to be generalized
- The dates of data collection
- The exact wording of the questions asked
- Any information that the researcher believes is relevant to

help the public make a fair assessment of the results

In addition, CASRO recommends that other information should be readily available in case anyone asks for it. This information includes the following: (1) the type of survey conducted, (2) the methods used to select the survey sample, (3) how respondents were screened, and (4) the procedure for data coding and analysis.

PHILIPS

Press Information

July 12, 2006

Hair today, gone tomorrow! Philips Norelco offers guys a more convenient way to trim and shave unwanted body hair

STAMFORD, CONN. - - For some guys, shedding the winter coat means more than finding extra space in the closet. A recent survey commissioned by Philips Norelco and conducted by Opinion Dynamic Corporation revealed that more than 64% of men[1] are more likely to trim and groom their body hair during the warmer spring and summer months. Hearing the call of the wild, Philips Norelco recently introduced Bodygroom, a simple, easy-to-use full-body groomer that is designed to shave everywhere below the chin.

"Men are becoming increasingly conscious of their body hair and especially with the warmer summer months upon us, they're looking for easier ways to trim and shave the hair below their chin," said Arjen Linders, VP Marketing, Philips Norelco. "Until now, there have only been few options for the hairy, but we're hoping to change that by offering a simpler solution in the Philips Norelco Bodygroom."

Among men who already groom their body hair, there is clearly a need for better – and safer options. In fact, more than 72% of the men surveyed indicated that they use a razor blade to remove hair in even the most sensitive places –ouch! To help educate guys and provide useful information on an otherwise taboo topic, Philips Norelco Bodygroom launched www.shaveeverywhere.com – a fun Web site that features an unforgettable character who's not afraid to talk about the perks of a well-groomed body. Proof that men are looking for advice on a better way to groom, the site has drawn more than one million unique visitors in the first month.

---

[1] National telephone survey of 500 men ages 24-54 conducted by Opinion Dynamics Corporation in April 2006.

This is the first page of the Philips Norelco news release about the results of a telephone survey about how men felt about body hair. The survey was a news "hook" to get media attention for its new product BodyGroom, but the news release followed proper research protocols by providing information about the survey and how it was conducted. See the footnote at the bottom of the page. Also, on the second page (not shown) the company provided a seven-line description of the research methodology and also a five-line profile of the survey organization, Opinion Dynamics Corporation..

Table 5.1

Qualitative versus Quantitative Research

QUALITATIVE RESEARCH	QUANTITATIVE RESEARCH
"Soft" data	"Hard" data
Usually uses open-ended questions, unstructured	Usually uses close-ended questions, requires forced choices, highly structured
Exploratory in nature; probing, fishing-expedition type of research	Descriptive or explanatory type of research
Usually valid, but not reliable	Usually valid and reliable
Rarely projectable to larger audiences	Usually projectable to larger audiences
Generally uses nonrandom samples	Generally uses random samples
Examples: Focus groups; one-on-one, in-depth interviews; observation; participation; role-playing studies; convenience polling	Examples: Telephone polls, mail surveys, mall intercept studies, face-to-face interviews, shared cost, or omnibus studies; panel studies

The following sections briefly describe the three broad, and somewhat overlapping approaches to research. They are (1) secondary research, (2) qualitative research, and (3) quantitative research based on scientific sampling.

Secondary Research

This broad area may include a variety of techniques ranging from archival research in an organization's files to reference books, computer databases, and online searches. Some public relations professionals refer to some of these techniques as "qualitative" research, which is more thoroughly discussed shortly.

Archival Research

Many public relations campaign begins with an inventory of organizational materials that can shed light on such things as (1) the success of the product or service in the past, (2) analysis of what geographical areas provide the most sales, and (3) a profile of the typical customer who buys the product or uses the service. The marketing department often provides the most detailed information about the demographics of who buys a product or service. A common source of this information is the warranty or product registration cards that consumers fill out, which essentially is a marketing survey.

A good example is a public relations campaign for Rosetta Stone, a CD-ROM and online language learning software program, to increase brand awareness and sales. Rosetta Stone customer research showed that over 70 percent of the purchasers were men with an average age of 38, who were already highly educated and affluent

> " Archives provide the resources for background research, which is the essential first step in most other research techniques. "
>
> —Robert Kendall, author of *Public Relations Campaign Strategies*

($60,000+ in annual income). Sales figures also indicated that purchase was highest in the fourth quarter (just before Christmas) and many customers had received the product as a gift. Given this baseline data, the public relations firm of Carmichael Lynch Spong was able to figure out new strategies to reach out to new customers and core customers in other months of the year.

Library and Online Databases

College students are already familiar with the multiple reference books, academic journals, and trade publications found in every library. In many cases, these materials also are on CD-ROM or online through library access or, in the real world, a subscription basis. Four major sources for conducting what also is known as a literature review are:

- Academic Search Premier, which offers full text for almost 5,000 publications, including more than 3,600 peer-reviewed journals.
- Expanded Academic Index (InfoTrac), which indexes about 1,500 general magazines (including the *New York Times*) and selected scholarly journals in the field.
- LexisNexis, which is a full-text database of newspapers, magazines, newswires, transcripts of TV and radio news, and trade publications.
- Factiva (formerly Dow Jones Interactive), which includes full text of about 6,000 magazines and newspapers.

Some common reference sources used by public relations professionals include the *Statistical Abstract of the United States*, which summarizes census information; the Gallup Poll and the Gallup Index, which provide an index of public opinion on a variety of issues; *American Demographics*, which reports on population shifts and lifestyle trends; and *Simmons' Media and Markets*, an extensive annual survey of households on product usage by brand and exposure to various media.

Literature searches, the most often used informal research method in public relations, can tap an estimated 1,500 electronic databases that store an enormous amount of current and historical information. Public relations departments and firms use online databases in a number of ways:

- To research facts and figures to support a proposed project or campaign that requires top management approval
- To keep up-to-date with news about clients and their competitors
- To track an organization's media campaigns and a competitor's press announcements
- To locate a special quote or impressive statistic for a speech or report
- To track the press and business reaction to an organization's latest actions
- To locate an expert who can provide advice on an issue or a possible strategy
- To keep top management apprised of current business trends and issues
- To learn the demographics and attitudes of target publics

An example of how a literature review is helpful in formulating a campaign is the case of Lay's Potato Chips. The company made the decision to use sunflower oil (good "fats") while reducing "bad" fats (saturated oil) in its products, but it had to convince health/nutrition influentials that the product dubbed "junk food" could have heart-health benefits.

Ketchum, Frito-Lay's public relations firm, based its campaign on a thorough review of science and medical literature for the strongest research demonstrating the heart-health benefits of consuming a diet rich in such things as sunflower oil. Ketchum also searched the literature to find out how healthy-oils research is positioned in other products. Armed with this research, Ketchum was able to plan a campaign that convinced health professionals such as dietitians to give their seal of approval, so to speak, on Frito-Lay's "oil change."

The Internet and World Wide Web

The Internet is a powerful research tool for the public relations practitioner. Any number of corporations, nonprofits, trade groups, special interest groups, foundations, universities, think tanks, and government agencies post reams of data on the Internet, usually in the form of home pages on the World Wide Web.

Online search engines, such as Google, MSN, and Yahoo, make a universe of information available on a multilane information highway readily accessible to everyone. With literally millions of possible Web sites, search engines make it possible for a researcher to simply type in a keyword or two, click "Go," and in a few seconds receive all of the links that the search engine has found that relate to a given topic. In addition, there is a Google Groups section of the Google Web site (groups-beta.google.com), where helpful information can be found on everything from recreation to business to the arts. Another feature, popular with public relations professionals, is Google Trends, a tool from Google Labs. It gives a quick overview of how often a particular topic has been researched in a certain time frame. (See the Insights box below for more Web-based databases).

on the job
INSIGHTS

Doing Research on the Internet

Public relations planning often begins with a literature search on the Internet, which is also called *secondary research.* Here's a sample of sites that public relations professionals find particularly useful:

United States Census Bureau: www.census.gov

National Opinion Research Center: www.norc.uchicago.edu

Pew Research Center for the People & The Press: www.people-press.org

Roper Center for Public Opinion Research: www.ropercenter.uconn.edu

Survey Research Center: www.srl.uic.edu

Bureau of Labor Statistics: www.bis.gov

Statistical Abstract of the United States: www.census.gov/stat_abstract

Vanderbilt Television News Archive: tvnews.vanderbilt.edu/

Institute for Public Relations: www.instituteforpr.org

O'Dwyer's Newsletter: www.odwyerpr.com

Public Relations Society of America: www.prsa.org

International Association of Business Communicators: www.iabc.com

Council of Public Relations Firms: www.prfirms.org

International Public Relations Association: www.ipra.org

Mattel Toys, for example, saw a rapid increase in searches about toy safety in 2007 after announcing a major recall of toys made in China. Such an increase told Mattel's public relations staff that toy safety was high on the public agenda and the company must be aggressive in communicating its commitment to fix the problem. The diamond industry no doubt used Google Trends and other monitoring software to track searches about the source of diamonds after the movie *Blood Diamond* arrived in theaters. Again, it was an indication that the issue was creating buzz among the public and that the industry should proactively communicate its side of the story. More information about the Internet is in Chapter 13.

Qualitative Research

A great deal of public relations research is qualitative; such research is good for probing attitudes and perceptions, assessing penetration of messages, and testing messages. This section explores (1) content analysis, (2) interviews, (3) focus groups, and (4) copy testing, and (5) ethnographic techniques.

Content Analysis

Content analysis is the systematic and objective counting or categorizing of information. In public relations, content analysis is often used to measure the amount of media coverage and the content of that coverage. This research method can be relatively informal or quite scientific in terms of random sampling and establishing specific subject categories. It is often applied to news stories about an organization or issues that affect the organization. See Chapter 10 for a discussion of issues management.

At a basic level, a researcher can assemble news clips and count the number of column inches or minutes of broadcast time. A more sophisticated and meaningful content analysis, however, is when the media coverage is analyzed from the standpoint of such factors as (1) the percentage of favorable, neutral, and negative mentions about the company or its product or service, (2) the overall tone of the article or broadcast mention, and (3) the percentage of articles that contained key message points that the organization wanted to communicate.

Professor Robert Kendall, now retired from the University of Florida, adds that content analysis involves

> . . . systematic analysis of any of several aspects of what a communication contains, from key words or concept references, such as company name or product; to topics, such as issues confronting the organization; to reading ease of company publications; or to all elements of a company video production.

A good example of content analysis is how one public relations firm evaluated press coverage of a campaign to celebrate the 100th anniversary of a client.

> A low-budget content analysis was carried out on 427 newspaper, magazine, radio, and television placements referring both to the client and its product. The research found that the client's principal themes and copy points were referred to in most of the media coverage the company had received.

Another example is the Campaign to End Black AIDS, which was conducted by Fleishman-Hillard public relations on behalf of the Abbott Magic Johnson Foundation. A content analysis of media coverage found that 45 percent of the media placements contained the campaign's core message of encouraging "at-risk" African Americans in Los Angeles to get tested. Chapter 8 will discuss measurement and evaluation techniques in greater detail.

Another use of content analysis is to determine whether a need exists for additional public relations efforts. Faneuil Hall Marketplace in Boston stepped up its public relations activities after it discovered that the number of travel articles about it had decreased. An anniversary celebration of the Marketplace helped to generate increased coverage. In other situations, an organization will commission a content analysis of media coverage given to its competitors. Insights can be gained about the competition's marketing strategies, strengths, and weaknesses. The results often help shape an organization's marketing, advertising, and public relations programs to gain a bigger share of media attention.

Content analysis also can be applied to Internet chat groups and blogs, as well as letters and phone calls. They provide good feedback about problems with the organization's policies and services. A pattern of blog postings, letters, and phone calls pointing out a problem is often evidence that the organization needs to address the situation. A number of companies, such as Carma International, Cymfony, and VMS, can slice and dice media data in any number of ways for its clients.

Surveys of public opinion, often taken by researchers on the street or in shopping malls, help public relations practitioners target audiences they wish to reach and to shape their messages.

Interviews

As with content analysis, interviews can be conducted in several different ways. Almost everyone talks to colleagues on a daily basis and calls other organizations to gather information. In fact, public relations personnel faced with solving a particular problem often "interview" other public relations professionals for ideas and suggestions.

If information is needed on public opinion and attitudes, many public relations firms will conduct short interviews with people in a shopping mall or at a meeting. This kind of interview is called an *intercept interview*, because people are literally intercepted in public places and asked their opinions. They are also called *convenience polls* because it's relatively easy to stand in a mall and talk to people.

The intercept interview is considered by researchers to be highly unscientific and unreliable, but it does give an organization some sense of current thinking or exposure to certain key messages. For example, a health group wanted to find out whether the public was actually receiving and retaining crucial aspects of its message. To gather such information, intercept interviews were conducted with 300 adults at six malls. Both unaided and aided recall questions were asked, to assess the overall impact of the publicity.

on the job
A MULTICULTURAL WORLD

Reaching a Diverse Audience About Electric Rates

How do you reach an audience when almost 40 percent of your audience is illiterate, 20 percent live below the poverty line, and many speak a language other than English? That's exactly what Dittus Communications faced—not in a developing nation, but Washington, D.C.

The challenge was legislation passed by the city council that deregulated electricity so that residents could choose service from several competing suppliers instead of just one company having a monopoly. A Customer Education Advisory Board—a partnership of government, local utility, and consumer advocacy groups—was formed and given the assignment of implementing a two-year public education campaign to inform D.C. residents about their electricity supply choices.

The problem was how to effectively communicate with D.C.'s diverse population, many of them illiterate, poor, and having limited English skills. Dittus Communications started with a literature search to gain information about the demographic profile of D.C. residents. Personal interviews were then conducted with city officials and leaders of local nonprofit and faith-based organizations to gain insight into the best way to reach the population. One key finding was that messages had to be simple, direct, and feature one single fact at a time. It was also necessary to have multiple communication tools that could be customized for hard-to-reach audiences. To reach the illiterate audience, for example, radio announcements and talks at community and faith-based organizations were used.

Ongoing research tracking the residents' awareness of electricity choices found that women were more interested in the topic than men, so additional female models were used in the campaign's advertising. Ultimately, the campaign helped increase resident confidence about making electricity choices. Almost 45 percent of the population felt more capable of decision making than when the effort began.

The campaign received *PRWeek*'s 2007 award for Best Use of Research/Measurement. The judges were impressed by the campaign's "straightforward" qualities that made it an "ideal case study for research."

Intercept interviews last only two to five minutes. At other times, the best approach is to do in-depth interviews to get more comprehensive information. Major fund-raising projects by charitable groups, for example, often require in-depth interviews of community and business opinion leaders. The success of any major fund drive, those seeking $500,000 or more, depends on the support of key leaders and wealthy individuals.

This more in-depth approach is called *purposive interviewing*, because the interviewees are carefully selected based on their expertise, influence, or leadership in the community. For example, the Greater Durham, North Carolina, Chamber of Commerce interviewed 50 "movers and shakers" to determine support for an extensive image-building and economic development program. See the Multicultural box above about how interviews with community leaders in Washington, D.C., helped plan an information campaign.

Focus Groups

A good alternative to individual interviews is the *focus group*. The focus group technique is widely used in advertising, marketing, and public relations to help identify attitudes and motivations of important publics. Another purpose of focus groups is to formulate or pretest message themes and communication strategies before launching a full campaign.

Longwood University in Virginia and its public relations firm, CRT/Tanka, is a good example of using focus groups to figure out how to rebrand the university as more than just an institution that trained teachers and served as a "second choice" for college-bound students. More than 20 focus groups with students, faculty, and alumni generated a lot of ideas and suggestions. This, along with extensive one-on-one interviews with business and community leaders, led to a successful marketing campaign that led to a 200 percent increase in Web site visits and a 237 percent increase in the number of prospective students who toured the campus.

Focus groups usually consist of 8 to 12 people who represent the characteristics of the target audience, such as employees, consumers, or community residents. During the interview, a trained facilitator uses nondirective interviewing techniques that encourage group members to talk freely about a topic or give candid reactions to suggested message themes. The setting is usually a conference room, and the discussion is informal. A focus group may last one or two hours, depending on the subject matter.

A focus group, by definition, is an informal research procedure that develops qualitative information rather than hard data. Results cannot be summarized by percentages or even projected onto an entire population. Nevertheless, focus groups are useful in identifying the range of attitudes and opinions among the participants. Such insights can help an organization structure its messages or, on another level, formulate hypotheses and questions for a quantitative research survey.

Increasingly, focus groups are being conducted online. The online technique can be as simple as posing a question to a chat or interest group online. Researchers also are using more formal selection processes to invite far-flung participants to meet in a prearranged virtual space. In the coming years, techniques and services will be well developed for cost-effective, online focus group research.

In another adaptation of new media, engineering management professor Hal Nystrom recently conducted focus groups for a Monsanto subsidiary that were then Webcast to the client. The focus group files remained available for review via password on the Web. Time and location are becoming less relevant to conducting focus groups, increasing the potential of this research method.

Copy Testing

All too often, organizations fail to communicate effectively because they produce and distribute materials that the target audience can't understand. In many cases, the material is written above the educational level of the audience. Consequently, representatives of the target audience should be asked to read or view the material in draft form before it is mass-produced and distributed. This can be done one-on-one or in a small group setting.

A brochure about employee medical benefits or pension plans, for example, should be pretested with rank-and-file employees for readability and comprehension. Executives and lawyers who must approve the copy may understand the material, but a worker with a high school education might find the material difficult to follow.

Another approach to determine the degree of difficulty of the material is to apply a readability formula to the draft copy. Fog, Flesch, and similar techniques relate the number of words and syllables per sentence or passage with reading level. Highly complex sentences and multisyllabic words require an audience with a college education.

Ethnographic Techniques

Public relations often take a page from anthropology to conduct research. One technique is observation of individual or group behavior. One director of public relations, for example, wanted to know how effective bulletin boards were in terms of informing employees in an industrial plant, so he stationed staff near bulletin boards to record how many employees actually stopped and read something off the board. In another situation, a public relations representative sat in a coffee house for most of one day to gain insights about the type of customer that came in, how much they spent, and how long they stayed.

On occasion, role-playing can be helpful for gaining insights into the strengths and weaknesses of an organization. One public relations professional with a college as a client had his daughter apply to the university and several others in the area just to see how the college compared with others in terms of handling prospective students. He also got feedback from his daughter about how well she was treated in the process.

Quantitative Research

The research techniques discussed thus far can provide good insights to public relations personnel and help them formulate effective programs. Increasingly, however, public relations professionals need to conduct polls and surveys using highly precise scientific sampling methods. Such sampling is based on two important factors: randomness and a large number of respondents. See the PR Casebook at the end of the chapter about a campaign based on a random survey.

Random Sampling

Effective polls and surveys require a *random sample*. In statistics, this means that everyone in the targeted audience (as defined by the researcher) has an equal or known chance of being selected for the survey. This is also called a *probability sample*.

In contrast, a *nonprobability survey* is not random at all. Mall-intercept interviews, for example, are usually restricted only to shoppers in the mall at the time the interviewers are working. A number of factors affect exactly who is interviewed, including the time of day and the location of the intercept interviews. Researchers doing interviews in the morning may have a disproportionate number of homemakers, whereas interviews after 5 P.M. may include more high school students and office workers. Also, if the researcher stands outside a record store or athletic shoe outlet, the average age of those interviewed may be much younger than that of the general population.

A random sample could be accomplished if researchers were present at all hours and conducted interviews throughout the mall. This would ensure a more representative sampling of mall shoppers, particularly if a large number of shoppers were interviewed. Researchers must be careful, however, about projecting results to represent an entire city's population. Market surveys show that the demographic characteristics of shoppers vary from mall to mall. In other words, the selection of malls for random intercept interviewing often depends on how the researcher defines the target audience.

A survey sponsored by the International Franchise Association shows how sample selection can distort results. The organization touted its findings that "92 percent of franchise owners were successful." The survey, however, involved only franchises still operating, not those that had failed.

The most precise random sample is one generated from lists that have the name of every person in the target audience. This is relatively simple when conducting a random survey of an organization's employees or members, because the researcher can randomly select, for example, every 25th name on a list. However, care must be taken to avoid patterns in the lists based on rank or employee category. It is always advisable to choose large intervals between selected names so that the researcher makes numerous passes through the list. In addition, computerized lists may enable random selection of a specified number of names.

Another common method to ensure representation is to draw a random sample that matches the characteristics of the audience. This is called *quota sampling*. Human resource departments usually have breakdowns of employees by job classification, and it is relatively easy to proportion a sample accordingly. For example, if 42 percent of the employees work on the assembly line, then 42 percent of the sample should be assembly-line workers. A quota sample can be drawn on any number of demographic factors—age, sex, religion, race, income—depending on the purpose of the survey.

Random sampling becomes more difficult when comprehensive lists are not available. In those cases, researchers surveying the general population often use telephone directories or customer lists to select respondents at random. A more rigorous technique employs random generation of telephone numbers, assuring that new and unlisted numbers are included in the sample.

A travel company used this *random digit dialing* (RDD) method for a nationwide telephone survey of 1,000 adult Americans to determine whether the hurricane that devastated the island of Kauai affected vacation plans to visit the other Hawaiian islands not struck by the hurricane. On the basis of the results, the travel company restructured its advertising and public relations messages to emphasize that resorts on the other islands were open for business as usual.

Sample Size

In any probability study, sample size is always a big question. National polling firms usually sample 1,000 to 1,500 people and get a highly accurate idea of what the U.S. adult population is thinking. The average national poll samples 1,500 people, and the margin of error is within 3 percentage points 95 percent of the time. In other words, 19 out of 20 times that the same questionnaire is administered, the results should be within the same 3 percentage points and reflect the whole population accurately.

In public relations, the primary purpose of poll data is to get indications of attitudes and opinions, not to predict elections. Therefore, it is not usually necessary or practical to do a scientific sampling of 1,500 people. A sample of 250 to 500 will give relatively accurate data—with a 5 or 6 percent variance—that will help determine general public attitudes and opinions. A sample of about 100 people, accurately drawn according to probability guidelines, will include about a 10 percent margin of error.

This percentage of error would be acceptable if a public relations person, for example, asked employees what they want to read in the company magazine. Sixty percent may indicate that they would like to see more news about opportunities for promotion. If only 100 employees were properly surveyed, it really doesn't matter whether the actual percentage is 50 or 70 percent. The larger percentage, in either case, would be sufficient to justify an increase in news stories about advancement opportunities.

This is also true in ascertaining community attitudes. If a survey of 100 or fewer citizens indicates that only 25 percent believe that an organization is a good community

on the job
ETHICS

Sex and Alcohol: The AMA's News Release

The American Medical Association (AMA) wanted to call public attention to the issue of "risky" behavior by college students during spring break. AMA's strategy was to commission a survey of female college students so it would have some "facts" to demonstrate the seriousness of the issue.

The resulting news release stated that its survey of 644 college women and graduates aged 17 to 35 showed troubling findings about drinking habits on spring-break trips. For instance, 92 percent of respondents said it was easy to get alcohol on these trips. The news release also stated, "one in five respondents regretted the sexual activity they

engaged in during spring break, and 12 percent felt forced or pressured into sex." Because of the topic, which included sex, the Associated Press moved the story and many media outlets reported the survey results.

What the news release didn't say was that the survey was less than scientific. It was an online survey in which respondents self-selected themselves to participate. In other words, the survey was not a random or representative sample of female college students. The news release also didn't mention that a quarter of the respondents had never gone on a spring-break trip, so their opinions were actually secondhand impres-

sions or perceptions of what occurs at spring break.

Carl Bialik, who writes a column for the *Wall Street Journal* titled "The Numbers Guy," called the AMA about the validity of the survey. He was told by an AMA spokesperson, "We used the poll mostly to bring national attention to the issue." What do you think of this answer? Was the news release misleading? Do you think sending out news releases reporting survey results based on nonscientific research methods is ethical? The news release did accomplish the objective of getting "national attention," so does the end justify the means?

citizen, it really doesn't matter whether the result is 15 or 35 percent. The main point is that the organization must take immediate steps to improve its performance.

One problem with Web surveys, which will be discussed shortly, is that the sample size can't be determined in advance. Such surveys also lack random selection. Reporting the results of such surveys often raises some ethical issues. See the Ethics box above.

> For public relations research to provide support and assistance to the strategic planning and program development process, a mix of both qualitative and quantitative research is preferable.
>
> ——Walter K. Lindenmann, specialist in public relations research and measurement

Questionnaire Construction

Although correct sampling is important in gaining accurate results, pollsters generally acknowledge that sampling error may be far less important than the errors that result from the wording and order of questions in a survey and even the timing of a survey.

Carefully Consider Wording

Wording the questions on a questionnaire is a time-consuming process, and it is not unusual for a questionnaire to go through multiple drafts to achieve maximum clarity.

The question "Is it a good idea to limit handguns?" differs from "Do you think registration of handguns will curtail crime?" On first glance, the two questions seem to be asking the same thing. On closer examination, however, one can realize that a respondent could easily answer "yes" to the first question and "no" to the second.

The first question asks whether limiting handguns is a good idea. The second asks whether people think it will curtail crime. A third question that might elicit a different response would be, "Do you think that laws curtailing the use of handguns would work?" Thus, the questions emphasize three different aspects of the problem. The first stresses the value of an idea, the second explores a possible effect, and the third examines the practicality of a proposed solution. Research shows that people often think something is a good idea, but do not think it would work. Another related problem is how respondents might interpret the words *limit* and *curtail*. To some, these words may refer to a total ban on handguns, whereas others may think they suggest that guns should be kept away from people with criminal records. It's simply a matter of semantics, which is a good area of study for aspiring public relations professionals.

Avoid Loaded Questions

Some organizations engage in what is called *advocacy research*. They send out surveys with questions that use highly charged words that elicit an emotional reaction from the respondent. Such questions are considered "loaded" because they are intentionally skewed to generate a predictable response. Such surveys often are done in the arena of politics and public policy debate.

Republican Party pollsters, for example, asked respondents whether they agreed or disagreed with the statement, "We should stop excessive legal claims, frivolous lawsuits, and overzealous lawyers." Not surprisingly, an overwhelming majority of the respondents agreed. Another example of a loaded question is one created by the American Civil Liberties Union (ACLU), which asked respondents whether they agreed with the statement, "I believe that the President does not need to use unauthorized and illegal powers to keep us safe, that warrantless spying on Americans is unnecessary, and illegal and that, in America, no one—including the President—is above the law."

Public relations practitioners have a professional obligation to avoid using the rubric of "surveys" if the objective is really advocacy research. Such "surveys" are misleading and tarnish the reputation of legitimate survey research.

Consider Timing and Context

Responses to survey questions are influenced by events, and this should be taken into consideration when reviewing the results of a survey. The public's esteem for an airline, for example, will be lower if a survey is conducted just after a plane crash. Mattel's corporate reputation also dipped when it recalled millions of toys in for safety reasons. On the positive side, surveys by AT&T about its reputation and brand recognition soared after the announcement that it would be the sole carrier for Apple's new iPhone.

Consequently, polls and surveys should be conducted when the organization isn't in the news or connected to a significant event that may influence public opinion. In neutral context, a more valid survey can be conducted about an organization's reputation, products, or services.

Large organizations, such as Exxon/Mobil, General Electric, and Microsoft, counterbalance the effects of one-time events through regular monitoring of such items as media coverage, Internet discussion groups, blogs, and measurements of brand awareness. This technique, called *benchmarking*, is done by a number of companies who use software programs to track and monitor a client's reputation almost on a daily basis. See Chapter 8 on evaluation for more details.

Avoid the Politically Correct Answer

Another problem with questionnaire design involves questions that tend to elicit the "correct" response. This is also called a *courtesy bias*. In such a situation, respondents often choose answers that they think are the "politically correct" answer that the sponsor of the survey wants to hear or reflects favorably on them as a good worker or citizen. For example, surveys show that more than 80 percent of Americans consider themselves "environmentalists." As skeptics point out, however, would anyone admit that he or she was not concerned about the environment?

Surveys of public relations practitioners about the value of research also show a degree of courtesy bias in choosing the politically correct answer. Almost 90 percent of public relations practitioners agree that research is a necessary and integral part of public relations work. Almost the same percentage, however, agree that research is talked about more often than it is done.

Those conducting employee surveys also fall into the "courtesy" trap by posing such questions as "How much of each newsletter do you read?" or "How well do you like the column by the president?" Employees may never read the newsletter or think that the president's column is ridiculous, but they know the "correct" answer should be that they read the "entire issue" and that the president's column is "excellent."

Researchers try to avoid politically correct answers by making questionnaires confidential and by promising anonymity to the people who are surveyed. Because employees often perceive the public relations department to be part of management, it is often best to employ an outside research firm to conduct employee surveys to ensure more honest answers.

Give a Range of Possible Answers

Answer categories also can skew a questionnaire. It is important that answer choices are provided that cover a range of opinions. Several years ago, a national polling organization asked the question, "How much confidence do you have in business corporations?" but provided only the following answer categories: (a) a great deal, (b) only some, and (c) none at all. A large gap exists between "a great deal" and the next category, "only some."

Such categories invariably skew the results to show very little confidence in business. A better list of answers might have been (a) a great deal, (b) quite a lot, (c) some, (d) very little, and (e) none. Another approach is to use such categories as (a) above average, (b) average, and (c) below average. The psychological distance between the three choices is equal, and there is less room for the respondent's interpretation of what "quite a lot" means.

In general, "yes or no" questions are not very good for examining respondents' perceptions and attitudes. An answer of "yes" or "no" provides little feedback on the strength or weakness of a respondent's opinion. A question such as "Do you agree with the company's policy of requiring drug testing for all new employees?" can be answered by "yes" or "no," but more useful information would be obtained by setting up a Likert-type scale—(a) strongly agree, (b) agree, (c) undecided, (d) disagree, and (e) strongly disagree. These types of answers enable the surveyor to probe the depth of feeling among respondents and may serve as guidelines for management in making major changes or just fine-tuning the existing policy.

Another way of designing a numeric scale to pinpoint a respondent's beliefs or attitudes is to use a 5-point scale. Such a question might say, "How would you evaluate the company's efforts to keep you informed about job benefits?" Please circle one of the following numbers ("1" being a low rating and "5" being a high rating).

The advantage of numeric scales is that medians and means can be calculated. In the previous example, the average from all respondents might be 4.25, which indicates that employees think the company does keep them informed about job benefits, but that there is still room for communication improvement.

Questionnaire Guidelines

The following are some general guidelines for the construction of questionnaires:

- Determine the type of information that is needed and in what detail.
- State the objectives of the survey in writing.
- Decide which group(s) will receive the questionnaire.
- Decide on the size of the sample.
- State the purpose of the survey and guarantee anonymity.
- Use closed-end (multiple-choice) answers as often as possible. Respondents find it easier and less time-consuming to select answers than to compose their own.
- Design the questionnaire in such a way that answers can be easily coded for statistical analysis.
- Strive to make the questionnaire no more than 25 questions. Long questionnaires put people off and reduce the number of responses, particularly in print questionnaires, because it is easy to see how long the survey will take to complete.
- Use categories when asking questions about education, age, and income. People are more willing to answer when a range is used. For example, what best describes your age? (a) Under 25, (b) 26 to 40, and so on.
- Use simple, familiar words. Readability should be appropriate for the group being sampled.
- Avoid ambiguous words and phrases that may confuse the respondents.
- Remember to consider the context and placement of questions. A question placed before another can influence response to the later question.
- Provide space at the end of the questionnaire for respondents' comments. This allows them to provide additional information that may not have been covered in the main body of the questionnaire.
- Pretest the questions with representatives of the target audience for understanding and possible bias. Their feedback will help improve the final draft.

How to Reach Respondents

A questionnaire is only as good as the delivery system that gets it to respondents. This section presents the pros and cons of (1) mail questionnaires, (2) telephone surveys, (3) personal interviews, (4) omnibus surveys, and (5) Web and e-mail surveys.

Mail Questionnaires

Questionnaires may be used in a variety of settings. They may be handed out at a manufacturing plant, at a county fair, or even in a bank lobby. However, for several different reasons, most survey questionnaires are mailed to respondents for four primary reasons: (1) researchers have better control as to who actually receives the questionnaire, (2) large geographic areas can be covered economically, (3) it is less expensive to use a paper-based questionnaire than to hire interviewers, and (4) large numbers of people can be reached at minimal cost.

However, mail questionnaires do have some disadvantages. The biggest is the low response rate. A mail questionnaire by a commercial firm sent to the general public usually produces a response rate of 1 to 2 percent. If the survey concerns issues considered highly relevant to the general public, the response rate might increase to 5 to 20 percent. A much better response rate would be generated, however, if a questionnaire were mailed by an organization to its members. In this case, the response rate may be 30 to 80 percent. The more closely people identify with the organization and the questions, the better the response.

The response rate to a mail questionnaire can be increased, say the experts, if all the guidelines of questionnaire construction are followed. In addition, researchers should keep the following suggestions in mind:

◆ Include a stamped, self-addressed return envelope and a personally signed letter explaining the importance of participating in the survey.

◆ Provide an incentive. Commercial firms often encourage people to fill out questionnaires by including a token amount of money or a discount coupon. Other researchers promise to share the results of the survey with the respondents.

◆ Mail questionnaires by first-class mail. Some research shows that placing special-issue stamps on the envelope attracts greater interest than simply using a postage meter.

◆ Mail a reminder postcard three or four days after the questionnaire has been sent.

◆ Do a second mailing (either to nonrespondents or to the entire sample) two or three weeks after the first mailing. Again, enclose a stamped, self-addressed return envelope and a cover letter explaining the crucial need for the recipient's participation.

Telephone Surveys

Surveys by telephone, particularly those that are locally based, are used extensively by research firms. The telephone survey has four major advantages: (1) The feedback is immediate, (2) the telephone is a more personal form of communication, (3) it's less intrusive than interviewers going door to door, and (4) the response rate, if the survey is short and handled by skilled phone interviewers, can reach 80 to 90 percent.

The major disadvantage of telephone surveys is the difficulty in getting access to telephone numbers. In many urban areas, as many as one-third to one-half of all numbers are unlisted. Although researchers can let a computer program pick numbers through random dialing, this method is not as effective as actually knowing who is being called. Another barrier is convincing respondents that a legitimate poll or survey is being taken. Far too many salespeople, and even charitable organizations, attempt to sell goods or get donations by posing as researchers.

Personal Interviews

The personal interview is the most expensive form of research because it requires trained staff and travel. If travel within a city is involved, a trained interviewer may only be able to interview 8 or 10 people a day, and salaries and transportation costs make it expensive. Considerable advance work is required to arrange interviews and appointments. Such interviews, taking 20 minutes to an hour, are much more intensive than the mall-intercept interviews discussed on page 136.

In some instances, however, personal interviews can be cost-effective. They can generate a wealth of information if the setting is controlled. Many research firms conduct personal interviews at national conventions or trade shows, where there is a concentration of people with similar interests. An equipment company, for example, may hire a research firm to interview potential customers at a national trade show about its products or services.

Omnibus Surveys

The word *omnibus* means something that serves several purposes. In survey research, it means that an organization "buys" one or two questions in a national survey conducted by a national polling firm such as Gallup or Harris. For example, General Mills may place one or two questions in a national poll that ask respondents what professional athlete they most admire as a way to find new endorsers for its breakfast foods. In the same survey, the American Cancer Society may place a question to find out what percentage of women know the common symptoms of ovarian cancer. If awareness is low, such a finding shows that a public information campaign is needed.

One reason for using what is also called a *piggyback survey* is cost. An organization pays much less to participate in a such a poll than to conduct its own survey. A second reason is expertise. Firms such as Gallup or Harris have the skill and organization to do a survey properly and efficiently. Piggyback surveys, however, do have limitations. An organization can get only a small snapshot of public opinion with one or two questions, and such surveys only work well if the objective is to get feedback from a broad population.

Web and E-Mail Surveys

> Online surveys are easier and less intrusive than a phone call.
>
> ———Giselle Lederman, survey methodologist for Zoomerang

The newest way to reach respondents is through the Internet. One such method is to post a questionnaire on an organization's Web site and then ask visitors to complete it online. The advantage of this is that once the visitor completes the survey, his or her response is immediately available and the results can be added to a running tabulation of results.

A good example of an online research survey is one that Church & Dwight, the maker of Trojan Condoms, conducted before it launched its new Elexa line of condoms and sexual health products, including a vibrating ring targeting women. The online survey, aimed at women ages 18 to 59, was to understand "women's sexual journeys." The responses enabled the company to position the new product line through a research report called the "Elexa Study of Women and Desire" that, of course, generated a great deal of media coverage.

PRCASEBOOK

Research Drives Ovarian Cancer Campaign

Ovarian cancer is known as the "silent killer" because its vague symptoms often are not diagnosed until the disease has started to spread. The good news is that women have a 90 percent chance of survival if they are diagnosed at an early stage.

The challenge, however, was increasing awareness of ovarian cancer in an environment where other forms of cancer had received the bulk of media coverage. The Ovarian Cancer National Alliance (Washington, D.C.) and the National Ovarian Cancer Association (Toronto) decided that it was vitally important to "turn up the volume" when an independent study confirmed that 96 percent of women could not identify the most common symptoms of ovarian cancer, 12 percent had not even heard of the disease, and 33 percent wrongly believed that a Pap test could screen for it.

These alarming statistics were the catalyst for a concentrated media campaign by Female Engineered Marketing (Buffalo, N.Y.), which decided to donate its services to making women more aware of this disease. "Our poll was really startling and the media got the link; it brought a lot of attention to the cause," says Annie Atkinson, communication consultant for the National Ovarian Cancer Association.

Female Engineered Marketing (FEM) produced public service announcements (PSAs) for print, radio, and television, which became the backbone of the campaign. The PSAs had bold and dynamic graphics and were designed to appeal to men and women alike. Messages and creativity were similar in both the United States and Canada. The poll results about the low awareness of ovarian cancer prompted media outlets in the United States and Canada to run the PSAs. In Canada alone, the radio PSAs were run more than 450 times.

The media efforts coincided with September's Ovarian Cancer Month and the annual "Walk of Hope," which attracted almost twice as many participants as the previous year. In addition, there was a twofold increase in donations ($600,000) for ovarian cancer research. In the United States, President Bush issued a proclamation acknowledging the seriousness of the disease and declared September Ovarian Cancer Awareness Month.

Beth Herskovits, writing for *PRWeek*, commented:

> The strength of this campaign grew from its ability to provide hard metrics to draw attention to an under-recognized problem. The importance of the poll was evident. With the numbers in front of them, the media did one better than running the PSAs—many outlets produced news and features stories, as well.

As *PRWeek* pointed out, "What lifestyle reporter doesn't want to know that 'American women want great sex.'" The survey found, for example, that "84% of women agree that a good sex life is part of a healthy life," and "76% say that, at the request of a partner, they have tried something new sexually that they have enjoyed." Cassandra Johnson, a product manager for Elexa, told *PRWeek*, "We were expecting that the research would help refine the voice of the campaign and key messages, and give us something thought-provoking to say to the media and to women about female sexuality."

Researchers use several methods to attract respondents to a Web site, including (1) banner ads announcing the survey on other Web sites or online networks, (2) sending e-mail invitations to members of the target audience, (3) telephoning individuals with an invitation to participate, (4) sending a postcard, and (5) offering incentives such as gift coupons. In general, online surveys should take no more than 20 minutes to answer and should include a mix of closed questions, such as multiple-choice, and a few open-ended questions. Good graphics, audio, and video also encourage participation.

If reaching the exact audience is important, another approach is an e-mail survey that is sent to a list of known respondents. Organizations can compile e-mail lists of clients or customers, but it's also now possible to purchase e-mail address lists from a variety of sources. Full-service Web survey companies can target populations, collect responses, and deliver data to the client. Some well-known companies are zoomerang, Biz360, Question Pro, and Qualtrics.

As in all research methods, there are advantages and disadvantages of using Web and e-mail surveys. The three major advantages are that (1) large samples are generated in a short amount of time, (2) they are more economical than even mail questionnaires or phone interviews, (3) and data can be analyzed continually. The three major disadvantages are (1) respondents are usually self-selected, (2) there is no control over the size of the sample or selection of respondents, and (3) probability sampling is not achievable.

Such surveys, however, often provide what is needed for the particular situation and the information gives planners sufficient information to make educated guesses about an appropriate marketing or public relations strategy. And of course, if the survey involves sex or another provocative topic, any survey—scientific or not—generates media coverage.

SUMMARY

The Importance of Research

Research is the basic groundwork of any public relations program. It involves the gathering and interpretation of information. Research is used in every phase of a communications program.

Secondary Research

Secondary research often begins by doing archival research, which reviews the organization's data on sales, profile of customers, and so on. Another source is information from library and online databases. Search engines such as Google, MSN, and Yahoo allow practically everyone to find information and statistics on the Internet and the World Wide Web. Thus, the expression often heard, "Let's Google it."

Qualitative Research

The value of this technique is to gain insights into how individuals behave, think, and make decisions. It's also used to ascertain whether key messages were communicated by the media. The primary techniques are (1) content analysis, (2) interviews, (3) focus groups, (4) copy testing, and (5) ethnographic observation and role playing.

Quantitative Research

This kind of research demands scientific rigor and proper sampling procedures so that information can be representative of the general population. Random sampling allows everyone in the target audience the chance to be in the sample. Sample size determines the margin of error in the statistical findings.

Questionnaire Construction

There are many factors to consider when designing a questionnaire, including wording, biased questions, politically correct answers, and answer categories. There are a number of guidelines, such as deciding what you want to find out, keeping the questionnaire relatively short, defining the target audience, and selecting the appropriate sample size.

Reaching Respondents

Survey respondents may be reached by mail, telephone, personal interviews, and omnibus surveys. Increasingly, surveys are being done via the Web and e-mail, but these digital methods have drawbacks because the respondents are self-selected and may not be representative of the population as a whole.

CASE ACTIVITY What Would You Do?

Universal Manufacturing Corporation is located in a Midwestern city of 500,000 people. At 6,000 employees, it is one of the largest employers in the county, and the company has been at its present location for the past 50 years. Despite this record, management believes that the company doesn't have a strong identity and lacks visibility in the community.

The director of public relations has been asked to prepare a new public relations plan for the coming fiscal year.

She recommends that the company first conduct research to determine exactly what its image is in the community.

If you were the public relations director, what kind of secondary research would you do? What qualitative and quantitative research would you recommend? The idea is to get some hard data on which to base a community relations campaign with the appropriate core messages directed to various segments of the community.

QUESTIONS for Review and Discussion

1. Why is research important to public relations work?
2. What questions should a person ask before formulating a research design?
3. Identify at least five ways that research is used in public relations.
4. How can survey research be used as a publicity tool?
5. List at least five informal research methods.
6. What are online databases? How are they used by public relations professionals?
7. How can the Internet and World Wide Web be used as research tools?
8. What is the procedure for organizing and conducting a focus group? What are the pros and cons of using focus groups?
9. What is an intercept interview?
10. What is the difference between probability (random) and nonprobability samples?
11. What guidelines should be followed when releasing the results of a survey to the media and the public?
12. What percentage margin of error is associated with various sample sizes? What size samples are usually adequate for public relations work?
13. Identify at least five guidelines that should be followed when preparing a questionnaire.
14. What are the pros and cons of each of the following: mail questionnaires, telephone surveys, personal interviews, and piggyback surveys?

SUGGESTED READINGS

Bialik, Carl. "Watching the Pollsters." *Wall Street Journal* Online, June 1, 2006.

Charland, Bernie. "The Mantra of Metrics: A Realistic and Relevant Approach to Measuring the Impact of Employee Communications." *The Strategist*, Fall 2004, pp. 30–32.

Creamer, Matthew. "Sharing Intelligence: PR People Should Be Pushing for More Access to Better Research." *PRWeek*, February 9, 2004, p. 17.

Dysart, Joe. "Building Web Traffic With On-Site Polls." *Public Relations Tactics*, April 2003, p. 6.

Lacono, Erica. "Getting Straight to the Point." *PRWeek*, July 24, 2006, p. 29. Research shapes messages in campaigns.

Lacono, Erica. "Leading the Brand: Solid Research Can Take a Brand to a Whole New Level." *PRWeek*, July 18, 2005, p. 27.

Lindenmann, Walter K. "Public Relations Research for Planning and Evaluation." May, 2006. A monograph available from the Institute for Public Relations (www.ipr.org).

McQuire, Craig. "When Research Made a Difference." *PRWeek*, February 6, 2006, p. 17.

Stacks, Don W. *Primer of Public Relations Research*. New York: Guilford Press, 2002.

Ward, David. "Master of All Whom You Survey." *PRWeek*, September 26, 2006, p. 22.

Program Planning

The Value of Planning

The second step of the public relations process, following research, is program planning. In the RACE acronym mentioned in Chapter 1, this step was labeled "Action" because the organization starts making plans to do something about an issue or situation. Before any public relations activity can be implemented, it is essential that considerable thought be given to what should be done and in what sequence to accomplish an organization's objectives.

A good public relations program should be an effective strategy to support an organization's business, marketing, and communications objectives. Jim Lukaszewski, a veteran public relations counselor, adds, "Strategy is a unique mixture of mental energy, injected into an organization though communication, which results in behavior that achieves organizational objectives."

In other words, public relations planning should be strategic. As Glen Broom and David Dozier say in their text *Using Public Relations Research*, "Strategic planning is deciding where you want to be in the future (the goal) and how to get there (the strategies). It sets the organization's direction proactively, avoiding 'drift' and routine repetition of activities." A practitioner must think about a situation, analyze what can be done about it, creatively conceptualize the appropriate strategies and tactics, and determine how the results will be measured. Planning also involves the coordination of multiple methods—news releases, special events, Web pages, press kits, CD-ROM distribution, news conferences, media interviews, brochures, newsletters, speeches, and so on—to achieve specific results.

Planning a public relations program requires brainstorming sessions like this one, at which participants discuss the characteristics of the target audience and work to come up with innovative and creative tactics that will accomplish the organization's objectives.

Systematic and strategic planning prevents haphazard, ineffective communication. Having a blueprint of what is to be done and how it will be executed makes programs more effective and public relations more valuable to the organization.

Approaches to Planning

Planning is like putting together a jigsaw puzzle. Research, which was discussed in Chapter 5, provides the various pieces. Next, it is necessary to arrange the pieces so that a coherent design, or picture, emerges. The best planning is systematic, that is, gathering information, analyzing it, and creatively applying it for the specific purpose of attaining an objective.

This section presents two approaches to planning. In both cases, the emphasis is on asking and answering questions to generate a roadmap for success.

Management by Objective

One popular approach to planning is a process called *management by objective* (MBO). MBO provides focus and direction for formulating strategy to achieve specific organizational objectives. According to Robert E. Simmons, author of *Communication Campaign Management*, the use of MBO in planning ensures the "production of relevant messages and establishes criteria against which campaign results can be measured."

In their book *Public Relations Management by Objectives*, Norman R. Nager and T. Harrell Allen discuss nine basic MBO steps that can help a practitioner conceptualize everything from a simple news release to a multifaceted communications program. The steps can serve as a planning checklist that provides the basis for strategic planning.

1. **Client/employer objectives.** What is the purpose of the communication, and how does it promote or achieve the objectives of the organization? Specific objectives such as "to make consumers aware of the product's high quality" are more meaningful than "to make people aware of the product."

2. **Audience/publics.** Who exactly should be reached with the message, and how can that audience help achieve the organization's objectives? What are the characteristics of the audience, and how can demographic information be used to structure the message? The primary audience for a campaign to encourage carpooling consists of people who regularly drive to work, not the general public.

3. **Audience objectives.** What is it that the audience wants to know, and how can the message be tailored to audience self-interest? Consumers are more interested in how a new computer will increase their productivity than in how it works.

4. **Media channels.** What is the appropriate channel for reaching the audience, and how can multiple channels (news media, brochures, special events, and direct mail) reinforce the message among key publics? An ad may be good for making consumers aware of a new product, but a news release may be better for conveying more credible consumer information about the product.

5. **Media channel objectives.** What is the media gatekeeper looking for in a news angle, and why would a particular publication be interested in the information? A community newspaper is primarily interested in a story with a local angle. A television station is interested in stories that have good visuals.

6. **Sources and questions.** What primary and secondary sources of information are required to provide a factual base for the message? What experts should be

interviewed? What archival, secondary, and primary research should be conducted? A quote from a project engineer about a new technology is better than a quote from the marketing vice president. A survey, properly conducted, might be best for media interest if there's an interesting statistic or finding.

7. **Communication strategies.** What environmental factors will affect the dissemination and acceptance of the message? Are the target publics hostile or favorably disposed to the message? What other events or pieces of information negate or reinforce the message? A campaign to conserve water is more salient if there has been a recent drought.

8. **Essence of the message.** What is the planned communication impact on the audience? Is the message designed merely to inform, or is it designed to change attitudes and behavior? Telling people about the dangers of global warming is different than telling people what they can do about it.

9. **Nonverbal support.** How can photographs, graphs, films, and artwork clarify and visually enhance the written message? Bar graphs or pie charts are easier to understand than columns of numbers.

A Strategic Planning Model

By working through the checklist adapted from Nager and Allen's book, a practitioner has in place the general building blocks for planning. These building blocks serve as background to create a specific plan. Ketchum offers more specific questions in its "Strategic Planning Model for Public Relations." Its organizational model makes sense to professionals and clients alike, moving both parties toward a clear situation analysis needed to make planning relevant to the client's overall objectives. As Larry Werner, executive vice president of Ketchum, points out, "No longer are we simply in the business of putting press releases out; we're in the business of solving business problems through communications."

Facts

- **Category facts.** What are recent industry trends?
- **Product/service issues.** What are the significant characteristics of the product, service, or issue?
- **Competitive facts.** Who are the competitors, and what are their competitive strengths, similarities, and differences?
- **Customer facts.** Who uses the product and why?

Goals

- **Business objectives.** What are the company's business objectives? What is the time frame?
- **Role of public relations.** How does public relations fit into the marketing mix?
- **Sources of new business.** What sectors will produce growth?

Audience

- **Target audiences.** What are the target audiences? What are their "hot" buttons?
- **Current mind-set.** How do audiences feel about the product, service, or issue?
- **Desired mind-set.** How do we want them to feel?

on the job INSIGHTS

Amazon PR Thought-Process Model

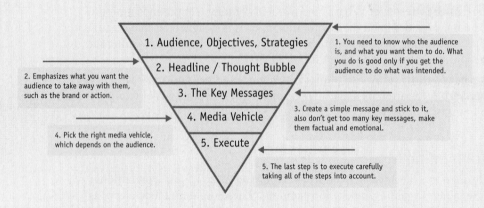

Research

1. Audience, Objectives, Strategies

1. You need to know who the audience is, and what you want them to do. What you do is good only if you get the audience to do what was intended.

2. Headline / Thought Bubble

2. Emphasizes what you want the audience to take away with them, such as the brand or action.

3. The Key Messages

3. Create a simple message and stick to it, also don't get too many key messages, make them factual and emotional.

4. Media Vehicle

4. Pick the right media vehicle, which depends on the audience.

5. Execute

5. The last step is to execute carefully taking all of the steps into account.

Results

Amazon.com successfully employs a public relations model to focus its communication planning process. Planning progresses toward the point of the triangle, and results are measured after execution. Amazon.com's director of public relations, Bill Curry, emphasizes that the objective of the public relations efforts is to drive sales, but the model works equally well to focus any public relations planning process on the essentials that need to be determined to ensure success.

Source: pr reporter, April 1, 2002.

Key Message

◆ **Main point**. What one key message must be conveyed to change or reinforce mind-sets?

Another interesting planning model is one used by Amazon.com, which is shown in the Insights box above. These various approaches to planning lead to the next important step—the writing of a strategic public relations plan. The next section explains the elements of such a plan.

Elements of a Program Plan

A public relations program plan identifies what is to be done, why, and how to accomplish it. By preparing such a plan, either as a brief outline or as an extensive document, the practitioner can make certain that all the elements have been properly considered and that everyone involved understands the "big picture."

It is common practice for public relations firms to prepare a program plan for client approval and possible modification before implementing a public relations campaign. At that time, both the public relations firm and the client reach a mutual understanding of the campaign's objectives and how to accomplish them. Public relations departments of organizations also map out a particular campaign or show the department's plans for the coming year.

Although there can be some variation, public relations plans include eight basic elements:

> " A program plan is the formal, written presentation of your research findings and program recommendations for strategy, tactics, and evaluation. "
>
> ——Ronald Smith, author of *Strategic Planning for Public Relations*

1. Situation
2. Objectives
3. Audience
4. Strategy
5. Tactics
6. Calendar/timetable
7. Budget
8. Evaluation

This section will elaborate on these elements and give examples from campaigns that received PRSA Silver Anvil Awards for excellence.

Situation

Valid objectives cannot be set without a clear understanding of the situation that led to the conclusion that a public relations program was needed. Three traditional situations often prompt a public relations program: (1) The organization must conduct a remedial program to overcome a problem or negative situation; (2) the organization needs to conduct a specific one-time project to launch a new product or service; or (3) the organization wants to reinforce an ongoing effort to preserve its reputation and public support.

Loss of market share and declining sales often require a remedial program. The Pokemon brand, for example, was highly popular a decade ago but had lost consumer loyalty and toy store shelf space in recent years because of competition and newer game videos. Thus, a public relations plan was implemented on the 10th anniversary of the game to revitalize consumer interest in the brand. This campaign will be discussed in subsequent sections. Another example is Sunkist Growers, which is highlighted in the PR Casebook on page 156. One impetus for its program was a decline in the purchase of Sunkist lemons as competition increased from foreign imports.

One-time, specific events often lead to public relations programs. One such campaign was for the grand opening of San Antonio's new public library. It was important to plan a celebration that showcased the facility as an educational, cultural, and entertainment resource for everyone. Another event was the annual San Diego Boat Show, which increased attendance by positioning the show for the entire family instead of just boating enthusiasts. A product is only new once, so Kodak introduced the world's first dual-lens digital camera around the 78th annual Academy Awards ceremonies.

In the third situation, program plans are initiated to reinforce corporate reputation or to preserve customer loyalty or public support. Department 56, a leading

PR CASEBOOK

Sunkist Turns Lemons Into Lemonade For a Cause

A public relations plan contains eight basic elements. The following is an outline of a plan that marketing cooperative Sunkist Growers and its public relations firm, Manning Selvage & Lee (MS&L), developed for a campaign that has raised $800,000 for charitable organizations in the past several years. The campaign also received *PRWeek*'s 2007 Cause-Related Campaign of the Year.

Situation

Sunkist, for many years, provided American households with 80 percent of its lemons. In recent years, however, foreign competition has somewhat soured the market. Sunkist wanted to revitalize its brand identity and decided to expand an already-established program in cause marketing. The program was "Take a Stand," which provided lemonade stands and Sunkist juicers to 7- to 12-year-olds who pledged to sell lemonade and then contribute their proceeds to a charity of their choice.

Objectives

- Extend reach of "Take a Stand" program from 2,000 pledges in the previous two years to 10,000.
- Increase lemon sales by 10 percent in key markets to strengthen the relationships with major retailers.
- Leverage media to tell the Sunkist story on a national scale and reach 10 million consumer impressions (combined circulation and broadcast audience exposed to stories).
- Increase www.sunkist.com page views by 50 percent.

Target Audience

Women ages 25 to 35 with families. Previous research indicated that 65 percent of Sunkist purchasers were married, educated, employed, and have annual household incomes of $50,000+. Moms were also targeted because research showed they make about 80 percent of household purchasing decisions. In addition, other research studies found that 82 percent of women said they considered an organization's support of charities and the community in forming brand decisions.

Strategies

- Leverage Sunkist "Take a Stand" spokesperson and Grammy-winning country artist Billy Dean to generate awareness about the program with moms in target markets.
- Build relationships with key retailers.
- Leverage key partners to bring additional visibility to the program as well as reach target audience of parents in general.
- Develop a strategic media outreach campaign that uses the national spokesperson and also focuses on stories about why kids set up lemonade stands in their local communities.

Tactics

- Kickoff concert in Nashville featuring spokesperson Billy Dean. Partners in the concert were community groups working with kids: Big Brothers/Big Sisters, Nashville Humane Society, and National Kidney Foundation.
- Placement of heartwarming stories in the local media about kids and their lemonade stands raising money for charity. Feature stories in such periodicals as

Singer Billy Dean, celebrity spokesperson for Sunkist, poses for a photo op at a child's lemonade stand.

Parenting Magazine, predominantly aimed at moms, offering Sunkist lemonade stands for their kids.

♦ Distribution of an attractive media kit to food editors that included news releases and background on the "Take a Stand" program. See a sample news release on page 385 in Chapter 14.

♦ Distribution of a matte feature story to media about the "Take a Stand" program and tips on how kids should set up their stand and promote it in the neighborhood. See page 381 in Chapter 14 for a text of this feature.

♦ Coordination of a Billy Dean concert, barbecue, and sales of lemonade during the Little League Baseball (LLB) World Series. Billy Dean also sang the national anthem to begin the series and the concert raised money to benefit the Little League charity that builds ballparks in disadvantaged urban areas.

♦ Partnered with Harris Teeter, with 150 stories in the southeast United States, to do a four-week "Take a Stand" promotion in all of its stores.

Calendar

The program was researched and planned during the first four months of the year. The kickoff (concert by Billy Dean) was in early May and the promotion/publicity aspects of the program continued through the summer months.

Budget

$200,000 for staffing and collateral materials

Evaluation

All objectives were met or exceeded:

♦ Instead of 10,000 stands produced and distributed, the total reached 11,000.

♦ Lemon sales increased in key markets. In the promotion with Harris Teeter stores, there was a 38 percent increase in lemon sales. A side effect was that other store chains not carrying Sunkist lemons asked to be part of the program.

♦ Media coverage was extensive. Coverage in national outlets included *Parenting Magazine,* Fox News Channel, and Radio Disney. Local print and broadcast coverage covered local success stories by interviewing kids about why they took Sunkist up on the offer to take a stand for charity. More than 17 million media impressions were tabulated.

♦ Sunkist.com page views increased 200 percent over the previous year.

designer and manufacturer of miniature lighted village collectibles, already had a successful business, but it wanted new customers. Its public relations program to accomplish this included distribution of brochures on home decoration for the Christmas holidays and participation by its dealers in local efforts to decorate Ronald McDonald houses. Clorox has been around for about a century, so it faced the problem of preserving its reputation and customer loyalty as other "new and improved" products from competitors appeared on the market. It built a public relations program around its product, Clorox. Anywhere, to reinforce the concept that the company was still America's oldest, most trusted cleaner.

In a program plan, relevant research often is included as part of the situation. In the case of Pokemon, a media audit showed that media coverage of the product had declined substantially in a five-year period. In the Sunkist situation, it was documented that the brand was losing market share to less expensive lemon imports. The key to increasing attendance at the San Diego Boat Show was research that showed that families wanted to vacation close to home and were looking for more affordable ways to have family-oriented recreational activities. Also, research by the National Marine Manufacturers Association (NMMA) showed that starter-level boat purchases were on the upswing.

For Clorox, a series of interviews indicated that mothers with small children were most concerned about a bacteria-free home, and that their most trusted source of information on new products came from friends and family. This led Clorox to invest in a word-of-mouth campaign. Kodak's research led to a tie-in with the Academy Awards. Research showed that the Academy Awards are the equivalent of the Super Bowl for women, and that women aged 25–54 are heavily influenced by products that are associated with celebrity and glamour. In the case of Department 56, consumer market analysis revealed a strong link between consumers interested in home decorating and those involved in collecting.

Objectives

Once the situation or problem is understood, the next step is to establish objectives for the program. A stated objective should be evaluated by asking: (1) Does it really address the situation? (2) Is it realistic and achievable? (3) Can success be measured in meaningful terms?

> " Before goals and tactics are drafted, PR directors must thoroughly understand their organization's business plan. "
>
> ———David B. Oates, a principal in Stalwart Communications, San Diego

An objective is usually stated in terms of program outcomes rather than inputs. Or, put another way, objectives should not be the "means" but the "end." A poor objective, for example, is to "generate publicity for a new product." Publicity is not an "end" in itself. The actual objective is to "create consumer awareness about a new product." This is accomplished by such tactics as news releases, special events, and brochures.

It is particularly important that public relations objectives complement and reinforce the organization's objectives. Professor David Dozier of San Diego State University expressed the point well in a *Public Relations Review* article: "The prudent and strategic selection of public relations goals and objectives linked to organizational survival and growth serves to justify the public relations program as a viable management activity."

Basically, objectives are either informational or motivational.

Informational Objectives   Many public relations plans are designed primarily to expose audiences to information and to increase awareness of an issue, an event, or a product. The five objectives of public relations activity will be discussed in Chapter 7. The first two of these—message exposure and accurate dissemination of messages—are the most common. Many communication and marketing professionals believe that the major criteria for public relations effectiveness are (1) an increase in public awareness and (2) delivery of key messages.

The following are some examples of informational objectives:

- **Pokemon**: "Engage core consumers in a celebration of the brand, and drive them to www.pokemon.com."
- **Clorox**: "Generate widespread awareness of the gentle benefits of Clorox Anywhere."
- **National Association of Manufacturers** (NAM): "Educate target audiences on the fundamental importance of manufacturing to our nation's current competiveness and future prosperity."
- **Blockbuster**: "Create awareness and trial among movie lovers for new service called Blockbuster Total Access."
- **Cathay Pacific Airways**: "Educate consumers about its promotions, rewards, and mileage program."

One difficulty with informational objectives is measuring how well a particular objective has been achieved. Public awareness and the extent of education that takes place are somewhat abstract and difficult to quantify. Some novices try to quantify informational objectives by stating something like "Increase awareness 30 percent." That's very difficult to prove unless an organization has solid baseline research determining the awareness level of the target audience before the campaign was launched—and then does another scientific sample after the campaign to measure any differences in the audience's knowledge or perceptions.

Another approach that many organizations and public relations firms take is to infer that "awareness" or "education" occurred because there were a large number of media placements. For example, Clorox somewhat quantified its informational objective above by stating that it would improve awareness by ". . . generating more than 50 million media impressions." In reality, message exposure doesn't necessarily mean increased public awareness.

Motivational Objectives   Although changing attitudes and influencing behavior are difficult to accomplish in a public relations campaign, motivational objectives are much easier to measure than informational ones. That's because they are bottom-line oriented and are based on clearly measurable results that can be quantified. This is true whether the objective is an increase in product sales, a sellout crowd for a theatrical performance, expanded donations to a charitable agency, or a target number of media placements regarding the product, service, or issue.

The following are some examples of motivational objectives:

- **San Diego Boat Show**: "Increase the show's attendance by 30 percent from 20,076 to 26,098."
- **Kodak**: "Garner more than 30 million media impressions of the V570 in top-tier celebrity and entertainment media."
- **Clorox**: "Stimulate awareness and word-of-mouth by reaching at least 3,000 key target audience members with information about Clorox."
- **Pokemon**: "Secure 500 stories in mainstream and trade outlets."
- **Longwood University**: "Increase visitor traffic to Longwood's admissions Web site by 30 percent over previous year."

Although many public relations programs will specify an increased number or percentage as a target, others don't. Novartis Animal Health US and its public relations firm, Exponent, merely established the goal of increasing sales over the previous year. That increase, of course, could be minimal and still meet the objective of the campaign. Objective setting is the joint responsibility of the public relations firm and the client. Both sides have to keep in mind that objectives, as already mentioned, must be realistic, achievable, and measurable in some way. Chapter 8 further discusses measurement and evaluation.

It should also be noted that a public relations program will often have a mix of informational and motivational objectives. The Magic Johnson Foundation in Los Angeles, for example, established the following informational objectives for its Campaign to End Black AIDS: (1) build national visibility and increase national attention on the importance of HIV prevention, and (2) direct the community to credible information resources and mobilize them to change the course of HIV. The motivational objective was "Increase HIV testing among African Americans in Los Angeles."

Audience

Public relations programs should be directed toward specific and defined audiences or publics. Although some campaigns are directed to a general public, such instances are the exception. Even the word-of-mouth campaign for Clorox Anywhere, a household item, was specifically targeted to moms with children under six and also active in the community.

In other words, public relations practitioners target specific publics within the general public. This is done through market research that can identify key publics by such demographics as age, income, social strata, education, existing ownership or consumption of specific products, and where people live. For example, market research told Pokemon that its primary audience were kid gamers, aged 6 to 20, and their parents who already own Pokemon products. A second audience was Pokemon bloggers who run popular fan sites that serve the Pokemon community online. The third audience was retailers licensed to sell the game.

In many cases, the product or service often self-defines a specific audience. Take, for example, Novartis Animal Health US, which launched a campaign to promote its new drug for older dogs with arthritis. The target audience was not the general public, but simply dog owners (skewed toward women 18 to 54 with household income of $40,000+) who regularly provide health care for their pets. A second primary audience were veterinarians who would be prescribing the drug. The audience for a condom campaign in India was also somewhat self-defined (see the Multicultural box on page 161).

The following are examples of how others organizations have defined target audiences.

◆ **Potato Board**: "Women, ages 25–64, particularly those with children living at home, and food and nutrition media."

◆ **Frito-Lay**: "The potato chip consumer, which represents 83 percent of all households according to Simmons Market Research Bureau."

◆ **Cranberry Marketing Committee**: "Nurse practitioners, dietitians, and physician assistants."

◆ **Tyson Foods**: "Business customers (grocery stores) and general consumers of Tyson products."

Many campaigns have multiple audiences, depending on the objectives of the campaign. Tyson Foods, mentioned above, used public relations to promote its "Powering the Fight Against Hunger," which donated its products through local charitable agencies to fight hunger. Its target publics were (1) grocery retailers, (2) general consumers of Tyson products, (3) key business and civic leaders in local communities, (4) Tyson team members in markets throughout the country, and (5) hunger relief and other direct service agencies.

Some organizations and public relations firms identify the media as a "public." On occasion, in programs that seek media endorsements or that try to change how the media report on an organization or an issue, editors and reporters can become a legitimate "public." In general, however, mass media outlets fall in the category of a means to an end. They are channels to reach defined audiences that need to be informed, persuaded, and motivated.

A better approach, if the campaign is primarily designed to generate media coverage, is to have two categories. Rosetta Stone, the language software company, listed "target publics" as consumers segmented by various demographics. It also listed "target media" as national daily newspapers, travel-leisure and in-flight magazines,

on the job

A MULTICULTURAL WORLD

India Changes Attitudes About Condom Use

Men in India seem to have a hang-up about buying and using condoms, which concened the Ministry of Health and Family Welfare. There actually had been a decline in condom sales and usage over the years, so a campaign was planned to reverse the trend. USAID provided project funding and Weber Shandwick/India was selected to execute a plan that would increase greater acceptance of condoms among sexually active single and married men, aged 20 to 29 years.

Research showed that men had several perceptions about condoms that had to be addressed. One was embarrassment about talking about condoms. Another was that shopkeepers and chemists were also embarrassed about selling condoms. A third issue was the perception by men that condoms were only needed by "high-risk" groups, not themselves. Consequently, a campaign titled *Condom Bindaas Bol!* (Say Condom Freely) was launched with two key messages: (1) Condom is not a bad word and should be discussed freely, and (2) condoms are for everyone, not just high-risk groups.

The public relations campaign focused on three aspects. First was partnerships and endorsements. Famous television celebrities were recruited to record brief public service announcements to communicate the message. In addition, Weber Shandwick forged alliances with regional print and broadcast media to develop stories about the campaign to raise public awareness.

The second aspect was meetings with editorial boards of major publications to garner editorial support and to highlight the results of the research study about men's perceptions of condoms. In addition, a retailer contest encouraged shopkeepers to increase sales by overcoming their embarrassment about selling the product to customers. The third element was the use of new media. A video mailer was prepared that provided one scenario of how a shy customer is encouraged by a retailer to ask for a condom. Another approach was a podcast using Youtube (www.youtube.com) with links mailed to media, corporations, and the general public.

As a result of the *Condom Bindaas Bol!* campaign, there was a 22 percent increase in the condom market. Research also indicated a 16 percent increase (54 to 70 percent) among the target audience, who now believe condoms are not only for high-risk behavior. The campaign received a Golden Award from the International Public Relations Association (IPRA).

---

national syndicated writers and columnists, and online media. The demographics of the "target audience" basically determines the characteristics of the "target media."

Strategy

A strategy is a somewhat broad statement describing how an objective is to be achieved. A strategy provides guidelines and key message themes for the overall program, and also offers a rationale for the actions and program components that are planned. A single strategy may be outlined or a program may have several strategies, depending on the objectives and the designated audiences.

The Pokemon campaign to build renewed awareness about its brand and products, for example, had four strategies that set the direction of the campaign. They were:

1. Build brand-success awareness among media and licensees—communicate Pokemon's leadership and staying power.

2. Include consumers in the 10th anniversary celebration activities—reward and excite Pokemon fans by providing experimental opportunities to celebrate the brand's 10th anniversary.

3. Announce new licensing partnerships—surprise the licensing and retailer community with exciting new partnerships.

4. Convert awareness, fan involvement, and partnerships into media coverage through major events.

Key Messages   Public relations plans, as part of the strategy, often contain a listing of key messages that the campaign wants to get across to the target audiences and the media. In the case of Pokemon, the three key messages were:

1. At 10 years, Pokemon is a global cultural phenomenon that has touched the lives of millions of children worldwide.

2. Pokemon appeals to kids and parents.

3. The future of Pokemon is unlimited as it continues to grow and innovate.

> " A tactic is a public relations action designed to have a particular effect on an organization's relationship with a particular public. "
>
> ———David Guth and Charles Marsh, authors of *Public Relations: A Values-Driven Approach*

Tactics

Tactics, in contrast to strategies, are the nuts-and-bolts or tactical part of the plan. They describe the specific activities that put each strategy into operation and help to achieve the stated objectives. In the public relations field, the implementation of various tactics is actually doing the plan and, in many ways, is the most visible part of any plan. Tactics involves using various methods to reach target audiences with key messages. Chapters 14 through 16 discuss tactical communication tools in greater detail. To help the reader better understand the difference between strategies and tactics, the tactics of the Pokemon campaign plan are listed below under each of the four strategies.

♦ **Strategy 1: Build brand success awareness**

Tactics: (1) Secure a four-page cover story in *License*, the top trade publication, about Pokemon's 10th anniversary and staying power; (2) secure other features in major trade publications such as *Toy & Family Entertainment, Licensing Book*, and *Toy Fair Times*; (3) establish an interactive booth at Toy Fair trade show, using a giant 10th anniversary time line to bring the brand's history to life and showcase new products; (4) distribute media kit about the brand's history and 10th anniversary celebration activities to media attending the Toy Fair and Pokemon's fans via the company's news center; and (5) distribute B-roll video news release to New York-based broadcast media and the major news distribution centers (news feeds).

♦ **Strategy 2: Include core consumers in the 10th anniversary activities**

Tactics: (1) Organize a 10th anniversary mall tour to stop in 24 major cities and include such activities as a video-game competition leading to a national championship later in the year; and (2) partner with Kids WB! to do a 10th anniversary television special that will feature a never-seen-before Mirage Pokemon.

♦ **Strategy 3: Announce new licensing partnerships**

Tactics: (1) Announce major licensing partnerships at major trade show; (2) announce that Cartoon Network will be the new home for the top-rated Pokemon Television series, which is now in its ninth season.

♦ **Strategy 4: Convert awareness, fan involvement to media coverage**

Tactics: (1) Organize giant anniversary party in New York City's Bryant Park and invite Pokemon fans and media to attend; (2) arrange for Mayor Michael Bloomberg to declare "Pokemon Day" in New York; (3) arrange for a live stage show and give fans opportunity to play yet-to-be-released Pokemon video games at the party; (4) stream the party live at www.pokemon.com to reach kids and parents online; (5) host Pokemon fansite bloggers as media VIPs; (6) distribute media kits and event photos to media; (7) distribute a B-roll video news release of the event broadcast stations nationally via satellite; and (8) partner with Teen Kids News to produce a kid-focused segment that will run in 200 markets.

Coming up with tactics for a campaign requires a lot of creativity on the part of a public relations firm. One approach is a brainstorming session that can generate any number of ideas from the practical to the impractical. The goal is to come up with ideas that are innovative and unusual, but still are grounded in accomplishing the objectives of the program. Judith Rich, a creativity expert with her own firm in Chicago, says, "It's important that creativity is not seen as a chore but rather as a challenge. Encourage spontaneity and playfulnesss, and let people dream big." Product launches, in particular, require major creativity in terms of designing eye-catching media kits and planning events that attract people. As Kathy Carliner, SVP of Golin Harris, says, "You need something that is fun and irresistible to get people's attention." See the Ethics box on page 164 about how two high-class Vodkas were launched.

Calendar/Timetable

The next step is to determine a timetable for the campaign or program. Depending on the objectives and complexity of the program plan, a campaign may last less than three months. Other programs may take more than a year to implement all the strategies and tactics required to accomplish program objectives. The following are three aspects of establishing a calendar and timetable for a progam.

The Timing of a Campaign   Program planning should take into account the environmental context of the situation and the time when key messages are most meaningful to the intended audience. A campaign to encourage carpooling, for example, might be more successful if it follows a major price increase in gasoline or a government report that traffic congestion has reached gridlock proportions. Continuing news coverage and public concern about an issue or event also triggers public relations campaigns. The toy industry, for example, launched campaigns to emphasize what they were doing to ensure the safety of its products after the industry was rocked with massive recalls in 2007.

Some subjects are seasonal. Department 56, the designer and manufacturer of miniature lighted village collectibles and other holiday giftware, timed the major bulk of its campaign for November to take advantage of the Christmas holidays, when there was major interest in its product lines. Charitable agencies, such as Second Harvest, also gear their campaigns around Thanksgiving and Christmas, when there is increased interest in helping the unfortunate.

on the job
ETHICS

Promoting High-Class Vodka

The market for luxury liquors is very competitive and it's difficult to introduce new brands into such a highly saturated market. This was the challenge faced by two competing vodka brands, Stolichnaya and Grey Goose, and each engaged in some creative program planning.

Stoli decided to position its new Elit vodka as a brand of luxury, celebrity, and opulence by partnering with an exclusive diamond retailer, Penny Preville, to associate the clarity of the vodka (a four-step distilling process) with the clarity of fine diamonds. The jewelry firm developed a new line

of Elit diamond products, and it was introduced to the press on a cross-country flight on an Elit-branded private jet. The flight featured a fashion show, a meal by a celebrity chef, and a well-known mixologist who made customized Stoli Elit cocktails.

The planning for the new brand of Grey Goose, La Poire pear-vodka, was more localized to New York City. The company and its public relations firm, Harrison & Shriftman, first sent key magazine editors four days of pear-inspired mailings with small gifts from such companies as Red Door Candles and Harry & David

that would capture "all of the sensory elements of the vodka" without actually telling the editors about the vodka itself. On the fifth day, the firm revealed the brand and invited editors to a private tasting with La Poire cocktails in an orchardlike setting.

What do you think of these two approaches to promote and publicize new luxury vodkas? Both involved "wining and dining" journalists and editors to generate media coverage, so was this a good plan? Why or why not? Would you feel comfortable doing these particular campaigns?

By the same token, strawberry producers increase public relations efforts in May and June, when a crop comes to market and stores have large supplies of the fruit. Similarly, a software program on income-tax preparation attracts the most audience interest in February and March, just before the April 15 filing deadline. In another situation, a vendor of a software program designed to handle personal finances launched a public relations/marketing program in January. The timing was based on research indicating that people put "getting control of personal finances" high on their list of New Year's resolutions.

Sometimes, as in the case of Kodak's new camera, campaign timing is dictated by the date of the Academy Awards, which was the centerpiece of the campaign. Rosetta Stone, the CD and online language-learning software, chose various holidays as message themes for a continuing public relations campaign. On New Year's, Rosetta Stone was pitched as a solution for those who made a resolution to learn a new language. On Valentine's Day, the company released a survey of top European cities for romance, and suggested learning a romantic language. Christmas, of course, was holiday season and the product was pitched as a perfect gift for the holidays.

Other kinds of campaigns depend less on environmental or seasonal context. Frito-Lay's campaign announcing its use of sunflower oil instead of cottonseed oil could be done almost any time; so could the Clorox Anywhere program to reinforce brand identity.

Scheduling of Tactics   The second aspect of timing is the scheduling and sequencing of various tactics or activities. A typical pattern is to concentrate the most effort at the beginning of a campaign, when a number of tactics are implemented. The launch phase of a campaign, much like that of a rocket, requires a burst of activity just to break the awareness barrier. After the campaign has achieved orbit, however, less energy and fewer activities are required to maintain momentum.

To further the rocket analogy, public relations campaigns often are the first stage of an integrated marketing communications program. Once public relations has created awareness and customer anticipation of a new product, the second stage may be a marketing and advertising campaign. A good example is the iPhone, which generated thousands of news stories before it was available for purchase. Ads for iPhone didn't appear until several months after the launch of the new product.

Compiling a Calendar   An integral part of timing is advance planning. A video news release, a press kit, or a brochure often takes weeks or months to prepare. Arrangements for special events also take considerable time. Practitioners must take into account the deadlines of publications. Monthly periodicals, for example, frequently need information several months before publication. A popular talk show may book guests three or four months in advance.

In other words, the public relations professional must think ahead to make things happen in the right sequence, at the right time. One way to achieve this goal is to compile timelines and charts that list the necessary steps and their required completion dates.

Calendars and timelines take various forms. One simple method is to post activities for each day on a large monthly calendar and who's assigned responsibility for the particular project. Gantt charts are popular for scheduling purposes and can be formatted easily using such programs as Microsoft's Excel. Essentially, a Gantt chart is a column matrix that has two sides. The left side has a vertical list of activities that must be accomplished, and the top has a horizontal line of days, weeks, or months. Such charts can also track, for example, when a media kit must be written, designed, turned over to a printer, and the date of final delivery. See below for a simplified example of a Gantt chart.

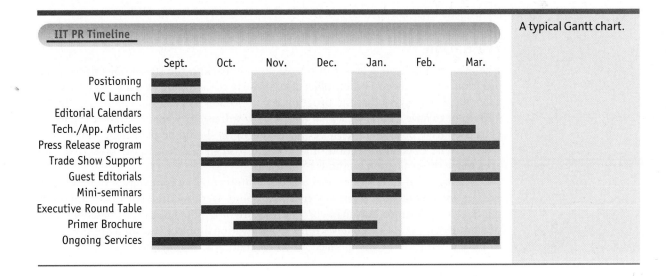

A typical Gantt chart.

Budget

No program plan is complete without a budget. Both clients and employers ask, "How much will this program cost?" In many cases, the reverse approach is taken. Organizations establish an amount they can afford and then ask the public relations staff or firm to write a program plan that reflects the amount allocated. Some public relations budgets of campaigns already discussed were as follows:

- **Frito-Lay's Change the Oil**: $1.7 million to cover a three-phase campaign
- **Kodak**: $160,000
- **Longwood University**: $900,000
- **Cranberry Marketing Board**: $450,000
- **Blockbuster Total Access**: $300,000, exclusive of the celebrity appearance fee
- **Tyson's Fight Against Hunger**: $110,000. Another $300,000 was financial support to charitable agencies, and another $2.3 milion worth of products were donated.

A budget is often divided into two categories: (1) staff time and (2) out-of-pocket expenses. The latter often goes by the acronym *OOP* and includes such collateral material as news releases, media kits, brochures, video news releases (VNRs), transportation, and even photocopying. In the Kodak campaign, for example, its $160,000 budget was divided into $70,000 for the public relations firm and $90,000 for OOP. As a general rule, however, staff and administrative time usually takes the lion's share of any public relations budget. In a $100,000 campaign done by a public relations firm, for example, it is not unusual for 70 percent to be salaries and administrative fees. Information about how public relations firms charge fees was presented in Chapter 4.

One method of budgeting is to use two columns. The left column will list the staff cost for writing a pamphlet or compiling a press kit. The right column will list the actual OOP expense for having the pamphlet or press kit designed, printed, and delivered. Internal public relations staffs, whose members are on the payroll, often complete only the OOP expenses. It is good practice to allocate about 10 percent of the budget for contingencies or unexpected costs.

Evaluation

The evaluation element of a plan relates directly back to the stated objectives of the program. As discussed earlier, objectives must be measurable in some way to show clients and employers that the program accomplished its purpose. Consequently, it's important to have a good idea what metrics you will use to evaluate whether the plan's objectives have been met. Again, evaluation criteria should be realistic, credible, and specific. The evaluation section of a program plan should restate the objectives and then name the evaluation methods to be used.

Evaluation of an informational objective often entails a compilation of news clips and an analysis of how often key message points were mentioned. Other methods might be to determine how many brochures were distributed or the estimated number of viewers who saw a video news release. Motivational objectives often are measured and evaluated by increases in sales or market share, the number of people who called an 800 number for more information, or by benchmark surveys that measure people's perceptions before and after a campaign.

Evaluation and measurement techniques are thoroughly discussed in Chapter 8, and reference will be made to many of the campaigns mentioned in this chapter. To give the reader some idea of how campaign success is evaluated, however, the Pokemon campaign evaluation is summarized below by highlighting how each campaign objective was met. The campaign, conducted by Ketchum public relations, received a 2007 Silver Anvil award from PRSA in the category of reputation/brand management.

- ◆ **Objective 1: Communicate the popularity and staying power of Pokemon by securing 500 stories in media outlets**
  - ◆ More than 550 print, broadcast, radio and Internet placements (not including blogs) around the country reached an estimated audience of 60 million.
  - ◆ Over 90 percent of the coverage mentioned Pokemon's 10th anniversary and its popularity across multiple product lines.
  - ◆ National coverage ranged from *Live with Regis & Kelly* to *U.S. News & World Report* to *Brandweek* and *Licensing*.
  - ◆ Coverage was gained in all 50 states and all top 25 media markets, including stories in major dailies.

- ◆ **Objective 2: Engage core customers in celebration of the brand and drive them to the Web site**
  - ◆ The Pokemon Journey Across America mall tour and the Pokemon Party of the Decade attracted more than 150,000 kids and parents.
  - ◆ Built relationships with the online fan community by ensuring press materials were posted to www.pokemon.com before they were distributed to the press, providing a live Webcast of the Party of the Decade, and hosting fansite bloggers as media VIPs at the party.
  - ◆ Yearlong activities moved consumer traffic to the brand site from a rank of 43rd most visited children's Web sites to 28th in rank of most popular sites within a nine-month period.

- ◆ **Objective 3: Reinforce the brand's leadership position among licensees through trade media coverage**
  - ◆ More than 10 feature stories in key toy/licensing trade publications in an eight-month period.
  - ◆ A new toy licensee partnership with a major distributor that increased the number of Pokemon products on store shelves.

The next chapter discusses the third element of the public relations process, communication. This basically deals with the implementation and execution of a program plan.

SUMMARY

The Value of Planning

After research is done, the next step in the public relations process is planning a program or campaign to accomplish organizational objectives. Such planning must be strategic, creative, and pay close attention to reaching key audiences. A program's objectives can be purely informational to create awareness, or more motivational to actually increase participation or sales.

Approaches to Planning

One classic approach is the management by objective (MBO) model that systematically categorizes objectives, communication strategies, audiences, and the essence of the message. Public relations firms often have their own planning model, which often includes market research, demographic segmentation of target audiences, and establishment of key messages.

Elements of a Program Plan

A program plan is either a brief outline or an extensive document identifying what is to be done and how. Public relations firms prepare these for client approval and there is joint consultation about budgets, strategies, and tactical communication tools. A public relations plan, at minimum, should contain eight elements: situation/opportunity, objectives, audience, strategy, tactics, calendar or timeline, budget, and evaluation.

CASE ACTIVITY What Would You Do?

Longview State University is located in a small, Midwestern town where one of the major student activities on the weekend is numerous parties involving alcohol consumption. One popular game among the students, for example, is Beer Pong, which often leads to binge drinking. Campus and city police report a major rise in "disturbance" complaints, and arrests for public drunkenness are up 150 percent.

Something must be done, so the college president asks your senior-level campaigns class to come up with a public relations program that would (1) inform and educate students about the dangers of binge drinking,

(2) convince students to drink more responsibly, and (3) actually lower the number of arrests for public drunkeness. Do some research on binge drinking among college students and what other campuses have done about the problem. Then, based on this research, write a program plan for Longview State using the eight-point planning outline described in this chapter. You should be creative and use a variety of tactics to accomplish your objectives. Your class is volunteering to do the plan, and the budget for collateral materials is less than $5,000.

QUESTIONS for Review and Discussion

1. Why is planning so important in the public relations process?
2. What is MBO, and how can it be applied to public relations planning?
3. Name the eight elements of a program plan.
4. Identify the three situations that often require a public relations campaign.
5. Explain the difference between an informational objective and a motivational objective.
6. Should a practitioner define an audience as the "general public?" Why or why not?
7. What is the difference between a strategy and a tactic?
8. Review the Sunkist Growers Casebook on page 156. Do you think it was a well-designed campaign?
9. Why are timing and scheduling so important in a public relations campaign?
10. What is the largest expense in a campaign conducted by a public relations firm?
11. Why is evaluation of a campaign linked to the program's objectives?

SUGGESTED READINGS

Ahles, Catherine B. "Campaign Excellence: A Survey of Silver Anvil Award Winners Compares Current PR Practice With Planning Campaign Theory." *The Strategist*, Summer 2003, pp. 46–53.

Austin, Cathy. "Embracing Your Firm's Right Brain: Wake Up Your Inner Creativity." *Public Relations Tactics*, August 2007, p. 16.

Austin, Erica, and Pinkleton, Bruce. *Strategic Communication Management: Planning and Managing Effective Communication Programs*. Mahwah, NJ: Lawrence Erlbaum, 2001.

Daughtery, Emma. "Strategic Planning in Public Relations: A Matrix That Ensures Tactical Soundness." *Public Relations Quarterly*, Spring 2003, pp. 21–26.

LaMotta, Lisa. "Launches Must be Products of Creativity." *PRWeek*, May 22, 2006, p. 30.

Oates, David B. "Measuring the Value of Public Relations: Tying Efforts to Business Goals." *Public Relations Tactics*, October 2006, p. 12.

Rich, Judith. "Want to Lead Creativity? Why Not Try Something New?" *The Strategist*, Spring 2006, pp. 12–13.

Samansky, Arthur W. "Successful Strategic Communications Plans Are Realistic, Achievable, and Flexible." *Public Relations Quarterly*, Summer 2003, pp. 24–26.

Silver Anvil Award summaries for 2007. www.prsa.org.

Smith, Ronald D. *Strategic Planning for Public Relations*, 2nd ed. Mahwah, NJ: Lawrence Erlbaum, 2005.

Temple, K. B. "Setting Clear Goals: The Key Ingredient to Effective Communication Planning." *Public Relations Quarterly*, Summer 2003, pp. 32–35.

Ward, David. "When a Stunt's Only a Starting Point." *PRWeek*, July 31, 2006, p. 18.

Wilson, Laurie J. *Strategic Program Planning for Effective Public Relations Campaigns*. Dubuque, IA: Kendall-Hunt, 2004.

CHAPTER 7

Communication

The Goals of Communication

The third step in the public relations process, after research and planning, is *communication*. This step, also called *execution*, is the most visible part of public relations work.

Implementing the Plan

In a public relations program, as pointed out in Chapter 6, communication is the implementation of a decision, the process and the means by which objectives are achieved. A program's strategies and tactics may take the form of news releases, news conferences, special events, brochures, speeches, newsletters, Webcasts, rallies, posters, and even word of mouth.

The goals of the communication process are to inform, persuade, motivate, or achieve mutual understanding. To be an effective communicator, a person must have basic knowledge of (1) what constitutes communication and how people receive messages, (2) how people process information and change their perceptions, and (3) what kinds of media and communication tools are most appropriate for a particular message.

Concerning the last point, Kirk Hallahan of Colorado State University makes the point that today's communication revolution has given public relations professionals a full range of communication tools and media, and the traditional approach of simply obtaining publicity in the mass media—newspapers, magazines, radio, and television—is no longer sufficient, if it ever was. He writes:

> PR program planners need to reexamine their traditional approaches to the practice and think about media broadly and strategically. PR media planners must now address some of the same questions that confront advisers. What media best meet a program's objectives? How can media be combined to enhance program effectiveness? What media are most efficient to reach key audience?

Hallahan's concept of an integrated public relations media model, which outlines five categories of media, is shown in Table 7.1. Another model worth noting is one used by computer manufacturer HP. Its model, shown in Figure 7.1, shows a message-based communications spectrum that includes programs, audiences, and various communication vehicles. Many of these media are discussed in Part 4, Tactics.

A Public Relations Perspective

A number of variables must be considered when planning a message on behalf of an employer or client. Patrick Jackson, who was editor of *pr reporter* and a senior counselor, believed that the communicator should ask whether the proposed message is (1) appropriate, (2) meaningful, (3) memorable, (4) understandable, and (5) believable to the prospective recipient. According to Jackson, "Many a wrongly directed or unnecessary communication has been corrected or dropped by using a screen like this."

In addition to examining the proposed content, a communicator should determine exactly what objective is being sought through the communication. James Grunig, professor emeritus of public relations at the University of Maryland, lists five possible objectives for a communicator:

1. **Message exposure.** Public relations personnel provide materials to the mass media and disseminate other messages through controlled media such as newsletters and brochures. Intended audiences are exposed to the message in various forms.

Table 7.1

An Integrated Public Relations Media Model. The Variety and Scope of Media and Communication Tools Available to Public Relations Professionals Runs the Spectrum from Mass Media (Public Media) to One-On-One Communication (Interpersonal Communication). Here, in Chart Form, is a Concept Developed by Professor Kirk Hallahan at Colorado State University.

CHARACTERISTIC	PUBLIC MEDIA	INTERACTIVE MEDIA	CONTROLLED MEDIA	EVENTS/ GROUPS	ONE-ON-ONE
Key use	Build awareness	Respond to queries; exchange information	Promotion; provide detailed information	Motivate attendees; reinforce attitudes	Obtain commitments; resolve problems
Examples	Newspapers, magazines, radio, television	Computer based: World Wide Web, databases, e-mail listservs, news-groups, chat rooms, bulletin boards	Brochures, news-letters, sponsored magazines, annual reports, books, direct mail, point-of-purchase displays, video-brochures	Speeches, trade shows, exhibits, meetings/ conferences, demonstrations, rallies, sponsor-ships, anniversaires	Personal visits, lobbying, personal letters, telephone calls, telemarketing
Nature of communication	Nonpersonal	Nonpersonal	Nonpersonal	Quasi-personal	Personal
Direction of communication	One-way	Quasi-two-way	One-way	Quasi-two-way	Two-way
Technological sophistication	High	High	Moderate	Moderate	Low
Channel ownership	Media organizations	Common carrier or institution	Sponsor	Sponsor or other organization	None
Messages chosen by	Third parties and producers	Receiver	Sponsor	Sponsor or joint organization	None
Audience involvement	Low	High	Moderate	Moderate	High
Reach	High	Moderate-low	Moderate-low	Low	Low
Cost per impression	Extremely low	Low	Moderate	Moderate	High
Key challenges to effectiveness	Competition, media clutter	Availability, accessibility	Design, distribution	Attendance, atmosphere	Empowerment, personal dynamics

2. **Accurate dissemination of the message.** The basic information, often filtered by media gatekeepers, remains intact as it is transmitted through various media.

3. **Acceptance of the message.** Based on its view of reality, the audience not only retains the message, but accepts it as valid.

4. **Attitude change.** The audience not only believes the message, but makes a verbal or mental commitment to change behavior as a result of the message.

5. **Change in overt behavior.** Members of the audience actually change their current behavior or purchase the product and use it.

Grunig says that most public relations experts usually aim at the first two objectives: exposure to the message and accurate dissemination. The last three objectives depend in large part on a mix of variables—predisposition to the message, peer reinforcement, feasibility of the suggested action, and environmental context, to name a few. The first two objectives are easier to accomplish than attitude change (see Chapter 9).

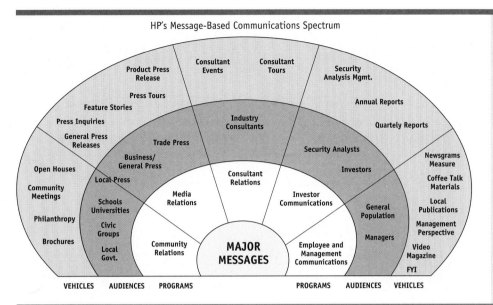

HP's Message-Based Communications Spectrum

FIGURE 7.1

A variety of communication vehicles, audiences, and programs must be considered when an organization wants to communicate key messages. This chart, developed by Roy Verley when he was VP of corporate communications at Hewlett-Packard (HP), shows the multiple aspects.

Although the communicator cannot always control the outcome of a message, researchers recognize that effective dissemination is the beginning of the process that leads to opinion change and adoption of products or services. Therefore, it is important to review all components of the communication process.

David Therkelsen, a veteran public relations counselor and former CEO of the American Red Cross in St. Paul, Minnesota, succinctly outlines the process:

> To be successful, a message must be received by the intended individual or audience. It must get the audience's attention. It must be understood. It must be believed. It must be remembered. And ultimately, in some fashion, it must be acted upon. Failure to accomplish any of these tasks means the entire message fails.

Therkelsen appropriately places the emphasis on the audience and what it does with the message. The following sections elaborate on the six elements he enumerates: (1) receiving the message, (2) paying attention to the message, (3) understanding the message, (4) believing the message, (5) remembering the message, and (6) acting on the message.

Receiving the Message

Several communication models explain how a message moves from the sender to the recipient. Some are quite complex, attempting to incorporate an almost infinite number of events, ideas, objects, and people that interact among the message, channel, and receiver.

Five Communication Elements

Most communication models, however, incorporate four basic elements. David K. Berlo's model is an example. It has a sender/source (encoder), a message, a channel, and a receiver (decoder). A fifth element, feedback from the receiver to the sender, is now incorporated in modern models of communication.

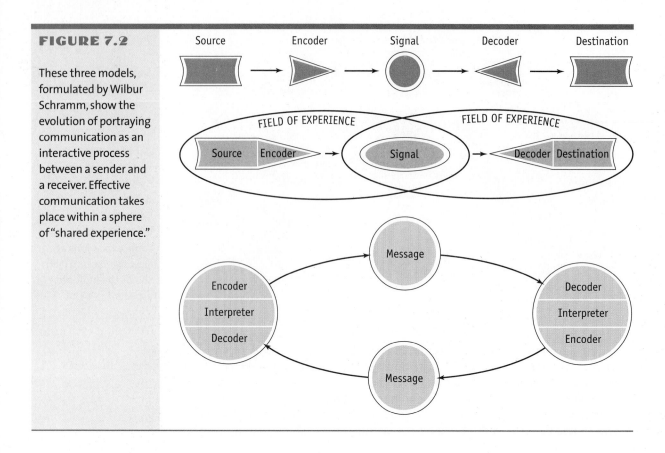

These three models, formulated by Wilbur Schramm, show the evolution of portraying communication as an interactive process between a sender and a receiver. Effective communication takes place within a sphere of "shared experience."

Mass media researcher Wilbur Schramm's early models (see Figure 7.2) started with a simple communication model (top diagram), but he later expanded the process to include the concept of "shared experience" (middle diagram). In other words, little or no communication is achieved unless the sender and the receiver share a common language and even an overlapping cultural or educational background. The importance of this "shared experience" becomes apparent when a highly technical news release about a new computer system causes a local business editor to shake his or her head in bewilderment.

Schramm's third model (bottom diagram) incorporates the idea of continuous feedback. Both the sender and the receiver continually encode, interpret, decode, transmit, and receive information. The loop process also is integral to models that show the public relations process of research, planning, communication, and evaluation. This concept was illustrated in Chapter 1, which showed public relations as a cyclical process. Communication to internal and external audiences produces feedback that is taken into consideration during research, the first step, and evaluation, the fourth step. In this way, the structure and dissemination of messages are continuously refined for maximum effectiveness.

The Importance of Two-Way Communication

Another way to think of feedback is two-way communication. One-way communication, from sender to receiver, only disseminates information. Such a monologue is less effective than two-way communication, which establishes a dialogue between the sender and receiver.

Grunig goes even further to postulate that the ideal public relations model should be *two-way symmetrical* communication, that is, communication is balanced between the sender and the receiver. He says: "In the symmetric model, understanding is the principal objective of public relations, rather than persuasion."

In reality, research shows that most organizations have mixed motives when they engage in two-way communication with targeted audiences. Although they may employ dialogue to obtain a better sense of how they can adjust to the needs of an audience, their motive often is asymmetrical—to convince the audience of their point of view through dialogue.

The most effective two-way communication, of course, is two people having a face-to-face conversation. Small-group discussion also is effective. In both forms, the message is fortified by gestures, facial expressions, intimacy, tone of voice, and the opportunity for instant feedback. If the listener asks a question or appears puzzled, the speaker has an instant cue and can rephrase the information or amplify a point.

Barriers to communication tend to mount as one advances to large-group meetings and, ultimately, to the mass media. Organizational materials can reach thousands and, through the mass media, even millions of people at the same time, but the psychological and physical distance between sender and receiver is considerably lengthened. Communication is less effective because the audience no longer is involved with the source. No immediate feedback is possible, and the message may undergo distortion as it passes through mass media gatekeepers.

Models of communication emphasize the importance of feedback as an integral component of the process. As they implement communication strategies, public relations personnel need to give it careful attention.

Paying Attention to the Message

Sociologist Harold Lasswell has defined the act of communication as "Who says what, in which channel, to whom, with what effect?"

Although in public relations much emphasis is given to the formation and dissemination of messages, this effort is wasted if the audience pays no attention. It is therefore important to remember the axiom of Walt Seifert, who taught public relations at Ohio State University for many years. He says: "Dissemination does not equal publication, and publication does not equal absorption and action." In other words, "All who receive it won't publish it, and all who read or hear it won't understand or act upon it."

> Who says what, in which channel, to whom, with what effect?
> —— Sociologist *Harold Lasswell*

Some Theoretical Perspectives

Seifert and social psychologists recognize that the majority of an audience at any given time are not particularly interested in a message or in adopting an idea. This doesn't mean, however, that audiences are merely passive receivers of information. Werner Severin and James Tankard, in their text *Communication Theories*, quote one researcher as saying:

> The communicator's audience is not a passive recipient—it cannot be regarded as a lump of clay to be molded by the master propagandist. Rather, the audience is made up

of individuals who demand something from the communication to which they are exposed, and who select those that are likely to be useful to them.

This is called the *media uses and gratification theory* of communication. Its basic premise is that the communication process is interactive. The communicator wants to inform and even persuade; the recipient wants to be entertained, informed, or alerted to opportunities that can fulfill individual needs.

In other words, audiences come to messages for very different reasons. People use mass media for such purposes as (1) surveillance of the environment to find out what is happening, locally or even globally, that has some impact on them; (2) entertainment and diversion; (3) reinforcement of their opinions and predispositions; and (4) decision making about buying a product or service.

The media uses and gratification theory assumes that people make highly intelligent choices about which messages require their attention and fulfill their needs. If this is true, as research indicates it is, the public relations communicator must tailor messages that focus on getting the audience's attention.

One approach is to understand the mental state of the intended audience. Grunig and Hunt, in *Managing Public Relations*, suggest that communication strategies be designed to attract the attention of two kinds of audiences: those who passively process information and those who actively seek information.

Passive Audiences   Individuals in this category pay attention to a message only because it is entertaining and offers a diversion. They can be made aware of the message through brief encounters: a billboard glimpsed on the way to work, a radio announcement heard in the car, a television advertisement broadcast before a show begins, and information available in a doctor's waiting room. In other words, passive audiences use communication channels that can be utilized while they are doing little else.

For this reason, passive audiences need messages that have style and creativity. The person must be lured by photos, illustrations, and catchy slogans into processing information. Press agentry, the dramatic picture, the use of celebrities, radio and television announcements, and events featuring entertainment can make passive audiences aware of a message. The objectives of a communication, therefore, are simply exposure to and accurate dissemination of a message. In most public relations campaigns, communications are designed to reach primarily passive audiences. See the Insights box on page 177 about Gillette's effort to convince young men to shave more often.

Active Audiences   A communicator's approach to audiences that actively seek information is different. These people are already at the interest stage of the adoption process (discussed later) and seek more sophisticated supplemental information. An example is the person who has already determined that a particular car model is attractive and is predisposed to buy one. He or she, at this point, actively seeks more detailed information. This may include a brochure from the dealership or downloading detailed information from the automaker's Web site. The person will also read in-depth newspaper and magazine articles and reviews about the vehicle, and perhaps even attend an auto show to talk with sales representatives. In the case of an issue, a person actively seeking information may attend a talk or sign up for a symposium or a conference on the subject.

At any given time, of course, the intended audience has both passive and active information seekers in it. It is important, therefore, that multiple messages and a variety of communication tools be used in a full-fledged information campaign so that both passive and active audiences can be effectively reached.

on the job
INSIGHTS

Women Mobilize Against Scruffy-Faced Men

The unshaven look seems to be in fashion these days for men, ranging from male fashion models to celebrities and even the average guy who wants to look "cool." So what is a razor manufacturer committed to the clean-shaven look to do?

Gillette and its public relations firm, Porter Novelli, decided that something must be done after research indicated that shaving frequency was declining among younger men. The research also indicated, however, that only 3 percent of the women surveyed preferred scruffy men. That piece of information became the centerpiece of a campaign to leverage the influence that women exert in their partner's grooming decisions to create greater support for the clean-shaven look.

The challenge, however, was how to do a creative campaign that would make men pay attention to the message. The creative solution was a somewhat edgy promotional event primarily designed to generate widespread media coverage. The company created a tongue-in-cheek protest group called the National Organization of Social Crusaders Repulsed by Unshaven Faces (NoScruf) whose "members" were women who vowed to stop shaving until their men started doing so. The ultimatum given to guys was, "Lose the scruff or lose the girl."

The "movement" began online at NoScruf.org, which featured deliberately amateurish graphics and humorous streaming videos that reinforced the idea of a grassroots

Gillette's staged rally for clean-shaven men was a highly visual event that attracted media attention.

campaign. The Web site featured news reports and video clips. In one video titled, "In Your Dreams, Stubble Boy," a scruffy young man gets a glimpse of what the world would be like if women stopped shaving.

The site also featured two female celebrities as "founders" of the NoScruf movement. They were Kelly Monaco, first winner of *Dancing With the Stars* and now a television actor, and Brooke Burke, widely known as a swimsuit model and ranked in men's magazines as one of the sexiest women in the world. According to one news release, Monaco said, "We at NoScruf have a message for scruffy guys out there who want to get close to us: 'In your dreams, stubble-boy!'"

The two female celebrities were also on hand at a protest rally staged in New York's Herald Square. They led a group of 50 attractive young women in NoScruf-branded T-shirts, proudly

sporting fake unshaven underarm hair and placards reading, "We Won't Shave Until You Do." The protest rally seemed so real that even a CNN producer on his way to work called in a news crew to cover it. The rally was also featured on *Today* and generated coverage in other major cities. According to Porter Novelli, "The humor, incongruous make-up and celebrity presence collectively translated into uniformly favorable coverage. The core message that women are hugely dissatisfied with their scruffy boyfriends was reinforced repeatedly."

As a result of media covering the protest rally, the NoScruf Web site received more than two million hits, with 65,000 unique visitors in 24 hours. The short video, "In Your Dreams, Stubble Boy," was viewed more than seven million times. The campaign received *PRWeek*'s 2007 Promotional Event of the Year.

The Concept of Triggering Events   Some years ago, Patrick Jackson who was then the editor of *pr reporter*, suggested that public relations practitioners should spend more time thinking about what behaviors they were trying to motivate in target publics, rather than on what information is being communicated. His behaviorial communication model had four components, but the major concept was the idea that public relations practitioners should build triggering events into their planning that causes people to act on their latent willingness to behave in a certain way.

A triggering event, for example, might be a natural disaster such as Hurricane Katrina, which devastated New Orleans. Although this was not planned, it was the catalyst for thousands of people to act on their latent readiness to help their fellow citizens, which also gave charitable organizations such as the Red Cross the ability to dramatize their work and successfully capitalize on the event to raise millions of dollars. A triggering event doesn't have to be a hurricane; it can also be the launch of a new product such as the iPhone or even the publication of the latest *Harry Potter* book. In either case, the "event" was the catalyst for people to actually go out and buy the item.

Other Attention-Getting Concepts

Communicators should think in terms of the five senses: sight, hearing, smell, touch, and taste. Television and film or videotape are the most effective methods of communication because they engage an audience's senses of sight and hearing. They also offer attractions of color and movement. Radio, on the other hand, relies on only the sense of hearing. Print media, although capable of communicating a large amount of information in great detail, rely only on sight.

Individuals learn through all five senses, but psychologists estimate that 83 percent of learning is accomplished through sight. Hearing accounts for 11 percent. Fifty percent of what individuals retain consists of what they see and hear. For this reason, speakers often use visual aids.

These figures have obvious implications for the public relations practitioner. Any communication strategy should, if possible, include vehicles of communication designed to tap the senses of sight or hearing or a combination of the two. In other words, a variety of communication tools is needed, including news releases, publicity photos, special events, videotapes, billboards, newsletters, radio announcements, video news releases, media interviews, and news conferences. This multiple approach not only assists learning and retention, it also provides repetition of a message in a variety of forms that accommodate audience needs.

Other research suggests that audience attention can be generated if the communicator raises a "need" level first. The idea is to "hook" an audience's attention by beginning the message with something that will make its members' lives easier or benefit them in some way. An example is a message from the Internal Revenue Service. It could begin with a reminder about the necessity of filing tax returns on time, but it would get far more audience attention if it opened by urging people to take all the exemptions for which they were eligible. The prospect of paying less taxes would be alluring to most people.

Public relations writers also should be aware that audience attention is highest at the beginning of a message. Thus, it is wise to state the major point at the beginning, give details in the middle, and end with a summary of the message.

Another technique to garner audience attention is to begin a message with a statement that reflects audience values and predispositions. This is called channeling (see Chapter 9). According to social science research, people pay attention to messages that reinforce their predispositions.

on the job
A MULTICULTURAL WORLD

Microsoft Promotes Child Safety in the Ukraine

Microsoft, as a global company, operates in many nations and the Ukraine is no exception. The company, however, was primarily associated with the protection of intellectual property rights in Ukraine, and it wanted to increase its community relations outreach.

The company and its public relations firm, Public Relations & Promotion Group (PRP) in Kiev, decided that an appropriate cause would be the increasing problem of child safety on the Internet. Ukraine was already rated among the top sources of cyber crime and child pornography, and local law enforcement agencies had limited resource to fight cyber crime.

PRP recommended that Microsoft initiate a Children Safety online project using the following stages: (1) Launch a Children Safety online page on the Microsoft Ukraine corporate Web site; (2) organize a seminar with academics, leaders of nongovernmental organizations, and editors of major Ukrainian media to discuss legislative issues related to cyber crime and child pornography; and (3) organize a second seminar with members of parliament and the heads of enforcement agencies to discuss how to best enforce the law.

The results were impressive. Over 50 journalists (inlcuding nine TV channels) attended the press conference announcing the Web site launch resulting in multiple stories on all the major channels and in 60 Ukrainian publications. The first seminar was attended by 22 high-level representatives from the academic, NGO sector, and leading information technology companies. The second seminar also attracted 22 representatives from government, plus 22 journalists who covered the seminar.

Microsoft was lauded as a socially responsible industry leader, and the campaign made citizens aware of the Web site, plus the problem of cyber crime and child pornography. The seminars helped foster greater governmental efforts to deal with the problem, and schools throughout the Ukraine now include the Children Safety Online links in the curriculum discussing "Life Safety." Microsoft and its public relations firm, PRP, received a national award from the Ukrainian Association of Public Relations for their efforts.

Prior knowledge and interest also make people pay more attention to messages. If a message taps current events or issues of public concern already in the news, there is an increased chance that the audience will pay attention. See the Multicultural box above about Microsoft's community relations program in the Ukraine.

Understanding the Message

Communication is the act of transmitting information, ideas, and attitudes from one person to another. Communication can take place, however, only if the sender and receiver have a common understanding of the symbols being used.

Effective Use of Language

Words are the most common symbols. The degree to which two people understand each other is heavily dependent on their common knowledge of word symbols. Anyone who has traveled abroad can readily attest that very little communication occurs between two people who speak different languages. Even signs translated into English for tourists often lead to some confusing and amusing messages. A brochure for a Japanese hotel, for example, said, "In our hotel, you will be well fed and agreeably drunk. In every room there is a large window offering delightful prospects."

Even if the sender and receiver speak the same language and live in the same country, the effectiveness of their communication depends on such factors as education, social class, regional differences, nationality, and cultural background.

Employee communication specialists are particularly aware of such differences as a multicultural workforce becomes the norm for most organizations. One major factor is the impact of a global economy in which organizations have operations and employees in many countries. A second factor is the increasingly multicultural composition of the American workforce. One study says that 85 percent of new entrants in the workforce are now white women, immigrants, African Americans, Hispanics, and Asians. For many of these workers, English will be a second language.

These statistical trends will require communicators to be better informed about cultural differences and conflicting values in order to find common ground and build bridges between various groups. At the same time, a major task will be to communicate in clear and simple terms. A national survey by the Educational Testing Service found that 42 million American adults fall within the lowest category of literacy. Other studies show that one in eight employees reads at no better than a fourth-grade level. Chapter 11 more thoroughly explores diverse and multicultural audiences and how to reach them.

Writing for Clarity

The nature of the audience and its literacy level are important considerations for any communicator. The key is to produce messages that match, in content and structure, the characteristics of the audience.

The Illinois Public Health Department had the right idea when it commissioned a song in rap-music style as one way to inform low-income, poorly educated groups about the dangers of AIDS. The words and music of the "Condom Rag," however, were offensive to elected officials, who cancelled the song.

This example poses the classic dilemma for the expert communicator. Should the message be produced for supervisors, who may be totally different in background and education from the intended audience, or should it be produced with the audience in mind? The obvious answer is the latter, but it is often difficult to convince management of this. One solution is to copy-test all public relations materials on a target audience. This helps convince management—and communicators—that what they like isn't necessarily what the audience wants, needs, or understands.

Another approach is to apply readability and comprehension formulas to materials before they are produced and disseminated. Learning theory makes the case: The simpler the piece of writing, the easier it will be for audiences to understand.

The most widely known readability formula is by Rudolph Flesch. Another is by Barr, Jenkins, and Peterson. Both are based on average sentence length and the number of one-syllable words per 100 words. If a randomly selected sample of 100 words contains 4.2 sentences and 142 syllables, it is ranked at about the ninth-grade level. This is the level for which most news releases and daily newspapers strive. In other words, long, complex sentences (more than 19 words) and multisyllabic words ("compensation" instead of "pay") reduce comprehension for the average reader.

The Cloze procedure, developed by William Taylor, also tests comprehension. The concept comes from the idea of closure, the human tendency to complete a familiar but incomplete pattern. In the Cloze procedure, copy is tested for comprehension and redundancy by having test subjects read passages in which every fifth or ninth word is removed. Their ability to fill in the missing words determines whether the pattern of words is familiar and people can understand the message.

Audience understanding and comprehension also can be increased by applying some of the following concepts.

Use Symbols, Acronyms, and Slogans   Clarity and simplicity of message are enhanced by the use of symbols, acronyms, and slogans. Each is a form of shorthand that quickly conceptualizes an idea and travels through extended lines of communication.

The world is full of symbols, such as the Christian cross, the Jewish Star of David, and the crusading sword of the American Cancer Society. Corporate symbols such as the Mercedes Benz star, the Nike swoosh, and the multicolored, now holographic, apple of Apple Computer are known throughout the world. The concept is called *branding*, and corporations invest considerable time and money to make their names and logos a symbol for quality and service.

A symbol should be unique, memorable, widely recognized, and appropriate. Organizations spend considerable time and energy searching for unique symbols that convey the essence of what they are or what they hope to be. Considerable amounts of money are then spent on publicizing the symbols and creating meanings for them.

Acronyms are another shorthand for conveying information. An acronym is a word formed from the initial letters of other words. The Group Against Smokers' Pollution goes by the acronym GASP; Juvenile Opportunities in Business becomes JOB. And the National Organization for Women has the acronym NOW, which says a great deal about its political priorities.

In many cases, the acronym—because it is short and simple—becomes the common name. The mass media continually use the term *AIDS* instead of *Acquired Immune Deficiency Syndrome*. And *UNESCO* is easier to write and say than *United Nations Educational, Scientific, and Cultural Organization*.

Slogans help condense a concept. Massive advertising and promotion have made "Don't Leave Home without It" readily identified with American Express. "The Ultimate Driving Machine" is strongly identified with BMW, which is an acronym for Bavarian Motor Works. MasterCard has effectively used the "Priceless" theme in its marketing for the past several years.

Avoid Jargon   One source of blocked communication is technical and bureaucratic jargon. Social scientists call it *semantic noise* when such language is delivered to a general audience. Jargon interferes with the message and impedes the receiver's ability to understand it. An example of a jargonized news release is one from a high-tech company that started with this lead sentence:

> American Portwell Technologies, Inc., a wholly owned subsidiary of Portwell, Inc., a world-leading innovator in the Industrial PC (IPC) market and a member of the Intel Communications Alliance, announces its new AREMO-4196, a 19' 4U industrial rack-mount chassis that includes a flexible 14-slot backplane.

This news release may be OK for a trade publication serving the particular industry, but it would be totally inappropriate for a business editor, or even the high-tech editor, on a daily newspaper. A failure to understand the audience means a failure in communication.

Avoid Clichés and Hype Words   Highly charged words with connotative meanings can pose problems, and overuse of clichés and hype words can seriously undermine the credibility of the message.

The *Wall Street Journal*, for example, mocked the business of high-technology public relations with a story titled, "High-Tech Hype Reaches New Heights." A reporter analyzed 201 news releases and compiled a "Hype Hit Parade" that included the 11 most overused and ineffective words. They were *leading, enhanced, unique, significant, solution, integrated, powerful, innovative, advanced, high performance*, and *sophisticated*.

Similar surveys have uncovered overused words in business and public relations. Factiva, a media monitoring and measurement company, analyzed about 14,000 articles in business publications to compile a chart of frequently used business adjectives. Leading the list was the term *next generation*. Other most frequently used words, in descending order, were *robust, flexible, world class, easy to use*, and *cutting edge*.

Avoid Euphemisms   According to Frank Grazian, founding editor of *Communication Briefings*, a *euphemism* is "an inoffensive word or phrase that is less direct and less distasteful than the one that represents reality."

Public relations personnel should use positive, favorable words to convey a message, but they have an ethical responsibility not to use words that hide information, mislead, or offend. Probably little danger exists in saying a person is *hearing impaired* instead of *deaf*. Some euphemisms can even cause amusement, such as when car mechanics become *automotive internists*, and luxury cars are called *preowned* on the used-car lot.

More dangerous are euphemisms that actually alter the meaning or impact of a word or concept. Writers call this *doublespeak*—words that pretend to communicate but really do not. Governments are famous for doublespeak. In Afghanistan and Iraq, the U.S. military often describe civilian casualties and destruction as "collateral damage." And the the term *ethnic cleansing* was used in the Balkans to sanitize the murder of thousands in Kosovo. A government economist once called a recession "a meaningful downturn in aggregate output."

Corporations also use euphemisms and doublespeak to hide unfavorable news. Reducing the number of employees, for example, is often called *right-sizing, skill-mix adjustment*, or *career assignment and relocation*. An airline once called the crash of a plane "the involuntary conversion of a 727."

Use of euphemisms to hide or mislead obviously is contrary to professional public relations standards and the public interest. As William Lutz writes in *Public Relations Quarterly*, "Such language breeds suspicion, cynicism, distrust, and, ultimately, hostility."

Avoid Discriminatory Language   In today's world, effective communication also means nondiscriminatory communication. Public relations personnel should double-check every message to eliminate undesirable gender, racial, and ethnic connotations.

With regard to gender, it is unnecessary to write about something as being *man-made* when a word such as *synthetic* or *artificial* is just as good. Companies no longer have *manpower*, but rather *employees, personnel*, and *workers*. Most civic organizations have *chairpersons* now, and cities have *firefighters* instead of *firemen* and *police officers* instead of *policemen*. Airlines, of course, have *flight attendants*, not *stewardesses*. It also is considered sexist to write about a woman's physical characteristics or dress, particularly if such comments would not be made about a man.

Messages should not identify any individual by ethnic designation, but it may be necessary in some situations to designate a particular ethnic or racial group. Although fashions and preferences change, today's writers use *Asian American* instead of the now-pejorative *Oriental*. And the term *Hispanic* is now more acceptable than the politically charged *Spanish-speaking*. The term *Latino*, however, raises some controversy; some women say that it is sexist because the "o" in Spanish is male.

The term *black* seems to be making a comeback, according to the U.S. Department of Labor, which surveyed 60,000 households several years ago about the names of race and ethnic categories to use in job statistics. Forty-four percent of the blacks preferred this designation, whereas another 28 percent preferred *African American* and 12 percent chose *Afro-American*. As a matter of policy, many newspapers use *African American* on first reference and *black* on second reference. Headlines almost always use *black* because it is short.

Believing the Message

One key variable in the communication process, discussed further in Chapter 9, is *source credibility*. Do members of the audience perceive the source as knowledgeable and expert on the subject? Do they perceive the source as honest and objective or as representing a special interest? Audiences, for example, ascribe lower credibility to statements in an advertisement than to the same information contained in a news article, because news articles are selected by media gatekeepers.

Source credibility is a problem for any organizational spokesperson because the public already has a bias. In one study conducted for the GCI Group, Opinion Research Corporation found that more than half of Americans surveyed are likely to believe that a large company is probably guilty of some wrongdoing if it is being investigated by a government agency or if a major lawsuit is filed against the company. At the same time, only one-third would trust the statements of a large company.

The problem of source credibility is the main reason that organizations, whenever possible, use respected outside experts or celebrities as representatives to convey their messages.

The *sleeper effect* also influences source credibility. This concept was developed by Carl Hovland, who stated: "There is decreased tendency over time to reject the material presented by an untrustworthy source." In other words, even if organizations are perceived initially as not being very credible sources, people may retain the information and eventually separate the source from the opinion. On the other hand, studies show that audiences register more constant opinion change if they perceive the source to be highly credible in the first place.

A second variable in believability is the *context* of the message. Action (performance) speaks louder than a stack of news releases. A bank may spend thousands of dollars on a promotion campaign with the slogan, "Your Friendly Bank—Where Service Counts," but the effort is wasted if employees are not trained to be friendly and courteous.

Incompatible rhetoric and actions can be somewhat amusing at times. At a press briefing about the importance of "buying American," the U.S. Chamber of Commerce passed out commemorative coffee mugs marked in small print on the bottom, "Made in China."

Another barrier to the believability of messages is the audience's *predispositions*. This problem brings to mind the old saying, "Don't confuse me with the facts, my mind is already made up." In this case, Leon Festinger's theory of *cognitive dissonance* should be understood. In essence, it says that people will not believe a message contrary to their predispositions unless the communicator can introduce information that causes them to question their beliefs.

Dissonance can be created in at least three ways. First, make the public aware that circumstances have changed. Oil companies, for example, say the era of cheap gasoline is over because a rising middle class in such nations as India and China also have cars and are now competing with U.S. drivers for the available supply. Second, give information about new developments. Public perceptions about China making unsafe toys somewhat changed when Mattel finally admitted that 18 million of the toys it recalled were because of design flaws instead of manufacturing problems. A third approach is to use an unexpected spokesperson. Chevron, for example, sought to overcome opposition to its oil exploration policies by getting endorsements from several respected leaders in the conservation movement.

Involvement is another important predisposition that impacts how messages are processed by audience members. Involvement can be described in simple terms as interest or concern for an issue or a product. Those with higher involvement often process persuasive messages with greater attention to detail and to logical argument (central processing), whereas those with low involvement for the topic are impressed more by incidental cues, such as an attractive spokesperson, humor, or the number of arguments given. The public relations professional can use the involvement concept to devise messages that focus more on "what is said" for high-involvement audiences and more attention to "who says it" for low-involvement audiences.

Remembering the Message

For several reasons, many messages prepared by public relations personnel are repeated extensively:

- ◆ Repetition is necessary because all members of a target audience don't see or hear the message at the same time. Not everyone reads the newspaper on a particular day or watches the same television news program.

- ◆ Repetition reminds the audience, so there is less chance of a failure to remember the message. If a source has high credibility, repetition prevents erosion of opinion change.

- ◆ Repetition helps the audience remember the message itself. Studies have shown that advertising is quickly forgotten if not repeated constantly.

- ◆ Repetition can lead to improved learning and increase the chance of penetrating audience indifference or resistance.

Researchers say that repetition, or *redundancy*, also is necessary to offset the "noise" surrounding a message. People often hear or see messages in an environment filled with distractions—a baby crying, the conversations of family members or office staff, a barking dog—or even while daydreaming or thinking of other things.

Consequently, communicators often build repetition into a message. Key points may be mentioned at the beginning and then summarized at the end. If the source is asking the receiver to call for more information or write for a brochure, the telephone number or address is repeated several times. Such precautions also fight *entropy*, which means that messages continually lose information as media channels and people process the information and pass it on to others. In one study about employee communications, for example, it was found that rank-and-file workers got only 20 percent of a message that had passed through four levels of managers.

The key to effective communication and retention of the message is to convey information in a variety of ways, using multiple communication channels. This helps people remember the message as they receive it through different media and extends the message to both passive and active audiences.

A good example of using multiple communication tools is a campaign to get a bond issue passed for Macomb Community College in Michigan. The message was quite simple: Vote "Yes." A nonprofit citizens group used 13 communication tools to put the message across: news releases, media interviews, news conferences, rallies, debates, campaign buttons, speaker's bureau, posters, direct mail, flyers, newsletters, phone calls to registered voters, and an essay contest. The bond issue passed.

> " Communicators must have a thorough understanding of their audiences, and they must stay very current with the media being used by those audiences. "
> ——— *Jerry Swerling,* director of the Strategic Public Relations Center at USC Annenberg

Acting on the Message

The ultimate purpose of any message is to have an effect on the recipient. Public relations personnel communicate messages on behalf of organizations to change perceptions, attitudes, opinions, or behavior in some way. Marketing communications, in particular, has the objective of convincing people to buy goods and services.

The Five-Stage Adoption Process

Getting people to act on a message is not a simple process. In fact, research shows that it can be a somewhat lengthy and complex procedure that depends on a number of intervening influences. One key to understanding how people accept new ideas or products is to analyze the adoption process. The five stages, shown in Figure 7.3, are summarized as follows:

1. **Awareness.** A person becomes aware of an idea or a new product, often by means of an advertisement or a news story.
2. **Interest.** The individual seeks more information about the idea or the product, perhaps by ordering a brochure, picking up a pamphlet, or reading an in-depth article in a newspaper or magazine.
3. **Evaluation.** The person evaluates the idea or the product on the basis of how it meets specific needs and wants. Feedback from friends and family is part of this process.
4. **Trial.** Next, the person tries the product or the idea on an experimental basis, by using a sample, witnessing a demonstration, or making qualifying statements such as, "I read. . . ."
5. **Adoption.** The individual begins to use the product on a regular basis or integrates the idea into his or her belief system. The "I read . . ." becomes "I think . . ." if peers provide support and reinforcement of the idea.

It is important to realize that a person does not necessarily go through all five stages with any given idea or product. The process may be terminated after any step. In fact, the process is like a large funnel. Although many are made aware of an idea or a product, only a few will ultimately adopt it.

FIGURE 7.3

This graph shows the steps through which an individual or other decision-making unit goes in the innovation-decision process from first knowledge of an innovation to the decision to adopt it, followed by implementation of the new idea and confirmation of the new decision.

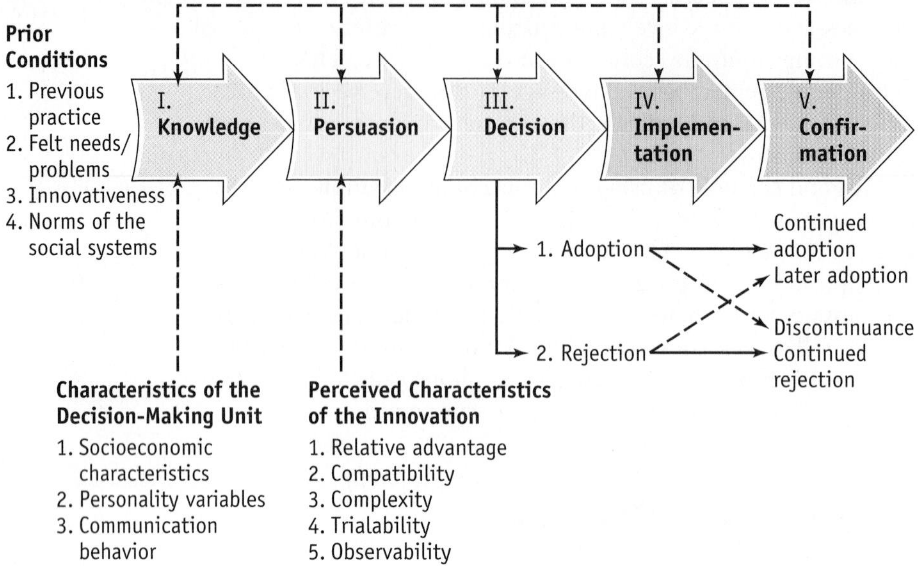

Prior Conditions
1. Previous practice
2. Felt needs/ problems
3. Innovativeness
4. Norms of the social systems

I. **Knowledge** → II. **Persuasion** → III. **Decision** → IV. **Implementation** → V. **Confirmation**

1. Adoption → Continued adoption / Later adoption
2. Rejection → Discontinuance / Continued rejection

Characteristics of the Decision-Making Unit
1. Socioeconomic characteristics
2. Personality variables
3. Communication behavior

Perceived Characteristics of the Innovation
1. Relative advantage
2. Compatibility
3. Complexity
4. Trialability
5. Observability

A number of factors affect the adoption process. Everett Rogers, author of *Diffusion of Innovation*, lists at least five:

1. **Relative advantage**. The degree to which an innovation is perceived as better than the idea it replaces.

2. **Compatibility**. The degree to which an innovation is perceived as being consistent with the existing values, experiences, and needs of potential adopters.

3. **Complexity**. The degree to which an innovation is perceived as difficult to understand and use.

4. **Trialability**. The degree to which an innovation may be experienced on a limited basis.

5. **Observability**. The degree to which the results of an innovation are visible to others.

The communicator should be aware of these factors and attempt to implement communication strategies that will overcome as many of them as possible. Repeating a message in various ways, reducing its complexity, taking into account competing messages, and structuring the message to meet the needs of the audience are ways to do this.

The Time Factor

Another aspect that confuses people is the amount of time needed to adopt a new idea or product. Depending on the individual and situation, the entire adoption process can take place almost instantly if the result is of minor consequence or requires low-level commitment. Buying a new brand of soft drink or a bar of soap is relatively inexpensive and often done on impulse. On the other hand, deciding to buy a new car or vote for a particular candidate may involve an adoption process that takes several weeks or months.

Rogers's research shows that people approach innovation in different ways, depending on their personality traits and the risk involved. There are five levels:

- ◆ **Innovators**: Individuals who are venturesome and eager to try new ideas.
- ◆ **Early Adopters**: Savvy individuals who keep up with new ideas and new products, often the opinion leader for their friends and colleagues.
- ◆ **Early Majority**: Individuals who take a deliberate, pragmatic approach to adopting ideas.
- ◆ **Late Majority**: Individuals who are often skeptical and somewhat resistant but bow to peer pressure.
- ◆ **Laggards**: Individuals who are very traditional and the last group to adopt a new idea or product.

Psychographics, discussed in Chapter 9, can often help communicators segment audiences that have "Innovator" or "Early Adopter" characteristics and would be predisposed to adopting new ideas. See the PR Casebook on page 188 about the early adopters of Apple's new iPhone.

How Decisions are Influenced

Of particular interest to public relations people is the primary source of information at each step in the adoption process.

Awareness Stage   Mass media vehicles such as advertising, short news articles, feature stories, and radio and television news announcements are the most influential. A news article or a television announcement makes people aware of an idea, event, or new product. They also are made aware through such vehicles as direct mail, office memos, simple brochures, and online news sites.

Interest Stage   There is reliance on mass media vehicles, but individuals actively seek information and pay attention to longer, in-depth articles. They rely more on detailed brochures, specialized publications, small-group seminars, web sites, and meetings to provide details.

Evaluation, Trial, and Adoption Stages   Personal experience, group norms, and opinions of family and friends become more influential than mass media. Also influential is personal contact and conversation with individuals who are perceived as credible sources and experts. Feedback, negative or positive, may determine adoption. For this reason, word-of-mouth public relations and marketing campaigns have become popular in recent years. The section below outlines the basic concept.

Word-of-Mouth Campaigns

The influence of peers and colleagues in the adoption process has been known for years, probably since Eve said to Adam, "Try this apple." Now, word of mouth (WOM) has been institutionalized by a number of organizations to reach consumers and other audiences through their friends and colleagues. Procter & Gamble (P&G) was an early pioneer in the field. Its Tremor Division, for example, enlisted 225,000 teenagers to tell their friends about brands such as Herbal Essences and Old Spice. P&G has also signed up about 500,000 mothers to receive coupons and sample products in the hope that these women will tell their friends and colleagues about the products.

PR CASEBOOK

Early Adopters Ring Up iPhone Sales

David Flashner, 25, stood in line for 21 hours. D. J. Ostrowski, 20, stood in line for nine hours. And Brandon Saunders, 16, waited in line with his 70-year-old grandmother for eight hours. "If Apple made sliced bread, yeah, I'd buy it," said Andrew Kaputsa, standing outside an Apple store in Chicago.

> **If Apple made sliced bread, yeah, I'd buy it.**
> —— *Andrew Kaputsa,* standing in line to buy an iPhone

These individuals, referred to as *icultists* by the media, are also known as the *innovators* and *early adopters* in the diffusion of innovation theory. In many cases, they are the technophiles who habitually rush out to buy first-generation electronics. As Ross Rubin, a wireless expert at a research firm, told a newspaper reporter, "It's an 'early-adopter' product for those who really care about getting the latest, snazziest technology product and those who care about brands."

Innovators or early adopters are particularly important publics for public relations and marketing experts because they are the vanguard who help form public opinion about an issue or a new product. They are considered the "experts" among their friends and peers on a particular product and, through word of mouth, a product can soar in

A happy customer shows off his new iPhone to the crowd still waiting in line to buy the new cellphone.

sales or take a nosedive. These individuals also are known as *influencers* or *catalysts.*

Although the technophiles are the most influential in terms of a product such as the iPhone, there's also the *iconverts*, who play an important role in influencing their peers. They are described by Jeremy Peters in the *New York Times* as "not-so-savvy customers who did not know much about the iPhone other than that they had to have it." Having an iPhone, for example, gives these individuals status among their peers even though they aren't in the category of being icultists.

Skilled marketing, promotion, and public relations also drive buzz about a new product. According to *Advertising Age*, "The iPhone may have been one of the most well-orchestrated launches in history, selling a record of 270,000 phones in its first two days." And David Pogue, the technology columnist for the *New York Times*, wrote,

> Talk about hype. In the last six months, Apple's iPhone has been the subject of 11,000 print articles, and turns up about 69 million hits on Google. Cultists are camping out in front of Apple stores; bloggers call it the 'Jesus phone.' All this before a single consumer has even touched the thing.

Apple kept consumer, media, and blogger interest at high levels in the six months before the launch with the strategy of being somewhat secretive about the new phone. This, in turn, fueled intense speculation and "buzz" about its exact features, its cost, and even how many would be available on the first day of sales. In addition, Apple kept the wraps on the whole project by allowing only four select reviewers, including Walter S. Mossberg of the *Wall Street Journal* and David Pogue of the *New York Times*, to take iPhone test-drives before the launch date. The reviews, by agreement, were not published until the day that all those early adopters standing in line could actually enter an Apple or AT&T store at 6 P.M. and buy the new cellphone.

The 6 P.M. time on a Friday chosen for the launch was not a coincidence. Apple and AT&T public relations staff anticipated that the icultists would compete to be the first in line, and that they would be willing to camp out overnight or spend all day in a line if necessary. This, of course, generated considerable media coverage across the nation as TV news crews and daily newspapers spent the day covering the crowds gathering around Apple and AT&T stores. In addition to video and photos, news reporters conducted interviews and got such quotes as "It's like Christmas in June." Because of the 6 P.M. timing, local television stations also had time to get new visuals and soundbites for the 11 P.M. news. These news reports showed happy customers coming out of the stores saying, "It's the best new thing that's come along in a long time; it's beautiful."

Not a bad beginning for a cellphone selling for $500 to $600 with a minimum $60 monthly service plan. Only time will tell whether the iPhone eventually attracts others in the diffusion of innovation process—the early majority, the late majority, and eventually the laggards, who are the last to adopt anything. One strategy for reaching the majority, however, was a $200 reduction in the price of the phone barely two months after it was introduced. The price cut didn't please many icultists who had paid a premium for bragging rights, but it no doubt sped up adoptions by the early majority.

The popularity of WOM is based on recent research that reinforces the classic theory of adoption articulated by Everett Rogers and others many years ago. One recent study, for example, found that 72 percent of consumers are influenced by their own experience, and another 56 percent by friends and family. In contrast, only 10 percent say they are influenced to buy a product from seeing an ad on television or in the newspaper. In another study, it was found that 75 percent of word-of-mouth communication occurs offline and in person.

> **Word of mouth will only work if it's based on a platform of ethics.**
> —*Andy Sernovitz,* CEO of the Word of Mouth Marketing Association (WOMMA)

Other studies have found that a key factor in WOM is to identify and reach *opinion leaders*, who are also known as *influentials* or *catalysts*. Opinion leaders and their characteristics are discussed more thoroughly in Chapter 9, but a study by the Keller Fay Group and Manning Selvage & Lee found that conversation catalysts (either online or in person) average about 200 weekly word-of-mouth conversations, and a large percentage of these conversations mention various products and brands.

An example of a successful WOM marketing campaign is one by U.K. petfood maker Masterfoods. The company identified 10,000 consumers likely to generate positive word-of-mouth reports to others if they liked the product, Whiskas Oh So. These "influencers" were then mailed free samples and coupons to pass on to family and friends. Sales of the product among those who received WOM recommendations and coupons from their friends were 11 times higher than consumers who didn't receive any information or coupons from a family member or friend.

In the case of the Clorox Anywhere campaign mentioned in the previous chapter, one key element of the public relations program was to send a mailing to 2,000 moms, allowing them to sample the product and, ideally, refer it to their friends. The mailing also offered these women the opportunity to get more involved by signing up to be Clorox At-Home Advisors and give feedback about various company products. Follow-up research showed that 50 percent of the moms made a referral to a friend after receiving the mailing and, within a month of the mailing, more than 160 moms registered as Clorox At-Home Advisors. In other situations, WOM campaigns have raised some ethical concerns. See the Insights box on page 190.

The success of word-of-mouth strategies shows that public relations communicators need to think about the entire communication process—from the formulation of the message to the ways in which receivers ultimately process the information and make decisions. By doing so, communicators can form more effective message strategies and use a wider variety of communication vehicles to effectively reach audiences and motivate them in some way.

on the job
ETHICS

Word-of-Mouth Campaigns: Crossing the Line?

Word-of-mouth (WOM) tactics are now a major communications tool in the marketing industry and increasingly used in public relations campaigns. The basic principle is that friends and peers are more influential than traditional tactics in terms of changing opinions and motivating people to try new products.

An example of a WOM campaign is how Sony Ericsson introduced a new camera phone. It hired 600 actors in various cities to ask people on the street to take pictures with the new camera, while the actors also praised the device. In another situation, Eastman Kodak hired peope to walk around fairs and amusement parks with a new camera around their necks as part of the introduction process. Some book publishers have also hired people to read certain books in coffee shops and on mass transit as a way of creating "buzz" about a title. Of course, movie studios have been known to hire people to stand outside a multiplex and rave about a particular film.

Such campaigns, however, have generated some controversy. Some say it's a form of "stealth" communications because the public isn't told that the hired actor or "peer" is being paid. Procter & Gamble was even criticized because teenagers and housewives touting its products to friends and relatives received a steady supply of free samples from the company. At the same time, there was no requirement that these "advocates" had to disclose their relationship to P&G, although they were free to do so.

Another form of WOM is profiled in the Insights box on page 177. In this situation, Gillette created a fake organization and demonstration to promote clean-shaving among men. The campaign, however, didn't mention that Gillette was behind it so, in *PRWeek*'s words, "making it appear to be a true grassroots effort."

What do you think? Do word-of-mouth campaigns, such as those just described, cross the ethical line? The Word of Mouth Marketing Association (www.womma.org), for example, has a code of ethics requiring transparency and full disclosure. Online standards call for transparency regarding the sponsor of a communication, accuracy of information, and protection of confidential information. (See also the ethics box in Chapter 1 about a blog organized by Edelman Public Relations on behalf of Wal-Mart.) The PRSA code mentions that public relations firms should disclose "any existing or potential conflicts of interest," but that primarily applies to clients—not WOM campaigns.

If you decided to use WOM strategies in a public relations program, what ethical guidelines would you adopt?

SUMMARY

The Goals of Communication
Communication, also called *execution*, is the third step in the public relations process. Five possible objectives at this stage are message exposure, accurate dissemination of the message, acceptance of the message, attitude change, and change in overt behavior.

Receiving the Message
Successful communication involves interaction, or shared experience, because the message must be not only sent but received. The larger the audience, the greater the number of barriers to communication.

Paying Attention to the Message
Because audiences have different approaches to receiving messages, communicators must tailor the message to get the recipient's attention. They need to understand the audience's mental state. Messages for passive audiences must have style and creativity, whereas messages for an audience actively seeking information must have

more sophisticated content. In either case, the effective message will raise the audience's "need" level by providing some obvious benefit.

Understanding the Message

The most basic element of understanding between communicator and audience is a common language. This is becoming a greater issue with the emphasis on multiculturalism. Public relations practitioners must consider their audiences and style their language appropriately, taking into consideration literacy levels, clarity and simplicity of language, and avoidance of discriminatory or offensive language.

Believing the Message

Key variables in believability include source credibility, context, and the audience's predispositions, especially their level of involvement.

Remembering the Message

Messages are often repeated extensively to reach all members of the target audience and to help them remember and enhance their learning. One way to do this is to convey information in several ways, through a variety of channels.

Acting on the Message

The success of a message is in its effect on the recipient. Five steps in acceptance of new ideas or products are awareness, interest, evaluation, trial, and adoption. The adoption process is affected by relative advantage, compatibility, complexity, trialability, and observability. The time needed to adopt a new idea or product can be affected by the importance of the decision as well as the personality of the person receiving the message. The primary source of information varies at each step of the adoption process. Word-of-mouth (WOM) campaigns are increasingly being used to take advantage of peer influence in the persuasion process.

CASE ACTIVITY What Would You Do?

Extensive information campaigns are being mounted throughout the world to inform people of the dangers of Acquired Immune Deficiency Syndrome (AIDS). Information specialists must utilize a variety of communication strategies and tactics to create public awareness and change individual behavior patterns.

At the same time, the communication process is very complex because a number of variables must be considered. Using this chapter as a guide, how would you apply the various communication concepts and theories to the task of informing people about AIDS?

QUESTIONS for Review and Discussion

1. Kirk Hallahan lists five categories of media and communication tools. What are they, and what are some of the pros and cons of each?
2. James Grunig says that there are at least five possible objectives for a communicator. What are they? What two objectives do most public relations campaigns try to achieve?
3. What are the five basic elements of a communication model?
4. Why is two-way communication (feedback) an important aspect of effective communication?
5. What are the advantages and disadvantages, from a communication standpoint, of reaching the audience through mass media channels?

6. Explain the behavioral communication model. What is the importance of the "triggering event?"
7. What is the premise of the media uses and gratification theory?
8. What kinds of messages and communication channels would you use for a passive audience? An active information-seeking audience?
9. Why is it necessary to use a variety of messages and communication channels in a public relations program?
10. Why is it important to write with clarity and simplicity? How can symbols, acronyms, and slogans help?
11. Explain the concept behind readability formulas.
12. Why is it important to build repetition into a message?

13. Explain the five steps of the adoption process. What are some of the factors that affect the adoption of an idea or product?
14. What is WOM, and why are many organizations now using it as a major strategy for marketing and public relations campaigns?
15. What is your opinion of the Apple launch of iPhone? Would you agree that this was a "well-orchestrated" product launch? Why or why not?

SUGGESTED READINGS

Beardsley, John. "Get Smart: Using the Right Word at the Right Time." *The Strategist*, Spring 2006, pp. 29–31.

DeVito, Joseph. *Essentials of Human Communication*, 6th ed. Boston: Allyn & Bacon, 2007.

Hallahan, Kirk. "Strategic Media Planning: Toward an Integrated Public Relations Media Model." In *Handbook of Public Relations*, ed. Robert Heath. Thousand Oaks, CA: Sage, 2000.

Kiviat, Barbara. "Word on the Street." *Time*, April 23, 2007, p. 64.

Matthews, Robert. "How to Work a Rumour Mill." *Financial Times*, June 28, 2007, p. 10. Word-of-mouth marketing.

O'Dwyer, Jack. "Word-of-Mouth PR Crosses Ethical Lines." *O'Dwyer's PR Services Report*, January 2005, p. 11.

Perloff, Richard M. *The Dynamics of Persuasion*, 2nd ed. Mahwah, NJ: Lawrence Erlbaum, 2003.

Vranica, Suzanne. "Laughing All the Way to the Bank: Viral Marketers Count on Consumers to Pass the Word." *Wall Street Journal*, July 10, 2007, p. R4.

Wylie, Ann. "Make Your Copy Clear and Concise: The Easier Your Story Is to Read, the More People Will Read It." *Public Relations Tactics*, June 2006, p. 15.

Evaluation

TOPICS COVERED IN THIS CHAPTER INCLUDE:

The Purpose of Evaluation

The fourth step of the public relations process is evaluation. It is the measurement of results against established objectives set during the planning process discussed in Chapter 6.

Evaluation is well described by Professor James Bissland formerly of Bowling Green State University. He defines it as "the systematic assessment of a program and its results. It is a means for practitioners to offer accountability to clients—and to themselves."

Results and accountability also are themes of Professors Glen Broom and David Dozier of San Diego State University. In their text *Using Research in Public Relations*, they state, "Your program is intended to cause observable impact—to change or maintain something about a situation. So, after the program, you use research to measure and document program effects."

Frank Wylie, emeritus professor at California State University in Long Beach, summarizes:

> We are talking about an orderly evaluation of our progress in attaining the specific objectives of our public relations plan. We are learning what we did right, what we did wrong, how much progress we've made and, most importantly, how we can do it better next time.

The desire to do a better job next time is a major reason for evaluating public relations efforts, but another equally important reason is the widespread adoption of the management-by-objectives system by clients and employers of public relations personnel. They want to know whether the money, time, and effort expended on public relations are well spent and contribute to the realization of an organizational objective, such as attendance at an open house, product sales, or increased awareness of ways to prevent obesity in children.

Objectives: A Prerequisite for Evaluation

Before any public relations program can be properly evaluated, it is important to have a clearly established set of measurable objectives. These should be part of the program plan (discussed in Chapter 6), but first some points need to be reviewed.

First, public relations personnel and management should agree on the criteria that will be used to evaluate success in attaining objectives. A Ketchum monograph simply states, "Write the most precise, most results-oriented objectives you can that are realistic, credible, measurable, and compatible with the client's demands on public relations."

Second, don't wait until the end of the public relations program to determine how it will be evaluated. Albert L. Schweitzer at Fleishman-Hillard public relations in St. Louis makes the point: "Evaluating impact/results starts in the planning stage. You break down the problem into measurable goals and objectives, then after implementing the program, you measure the results against goals."

If an objective is informational, measurement techniques must show how successfully information was communicated to target audiences. Such techniques fall under the rubrics of "message dissemination" and "audience exposure," but they do not measure the effect on attitudes or overt behavior and action.

Motivational objectives are more difficult to accomplish. If the objective is to increase sales or market share, it is important to show that public relations efforts caused the increase rather than advertising or other marketing strategies. Or, if the objective is to change attitudes or opinions, research should be done before and after the public relations activity to measure the percentage of change.

Although objectives may vary, the following checklist contains the basic evaluation questions that any practitioner should ask:

+ Was the activity or program adequately planned?
+ Did the recipients of the message understand it?
+ How could the program strategy have been more effective?
+ Were all primary and secondary audiences reached?
+ Was the desired organizational objective achieved?
+ What unforeseen circumstances affected the success of the program or activity?
+ Did the program or activity fall within the budget set for it?
+ What steps can be taken to improve the success of similar future activities?

Current Status of Measurement and Evaluation

Public relations professionals have made considerable progress in evaluation measurement and the ability to tell clients and employers exactly what has been accomplished. Sophisticated software programs and techniques are being used, including computerized news clip analysis, survey sampling, quasi-experimental designs in which the audience is divided into groups that see different aspects of a public relations campaign, and attempts to correlate efforts directly with sales.

Today, the trend toward more systematic evaluation is well established. Katherine Paine, founder of her own public relations measurement firm, says that the percentage of a public relations budget devoted to measurement and evaluation was about 1 percent in the 1990s, but is now closer to 5 percent. A recent study by the USC Annenberg Strategic Public Relations Center found about the same percentage; the average corporation devoted 4 percent of its total public relations budget to evaluation and measurement. By 2010, some optimists project that the amount will increase to 10 percent because there is constant pressure on all parts of the organization—including public relations—to justify budgets and prove their value to the bottom line.

> If you have not carved off at least 10 percent of your budget to measure your impact, you're flying blind, and you have no way of proving your value.
>
> —— *Mark Stouse*, director of worldwide communications for BMC

There are, however, still those who say that public relations is more art than science and is extremely difficult to measure. Walter K. Lindenmann, a former senior vice president and director of research at Ketchum, takes a more optimistic view. He wrote in *Public Relations Quarterly*: "Let's get something straight right off the bat. First, it is possible to measure public relations effectiveness. . . . Second, measuring public relations effectiveness does not have to be either unbelievably expensive or laboriously time-consuming."

Lindenmann suggests that public relations personnel use a mix of evaluation techniques, many borrowed from advertising and marketing, to provide more complete evaluation. In addition, he notes that there are at least three levels of measurement and evaluation (see Figure 8.1).

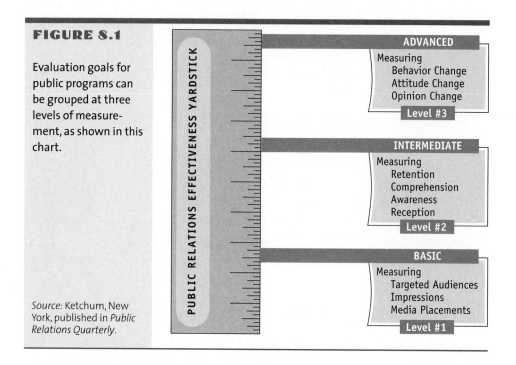

FIGURE 8.1

Evaluation goals for public programs can be grouped at three levels of measurement, as shown in this chart.

Source: Ketchum, New York, published in *Public Relations Quarterly*.

On the most basic level are compilations of message distribution and media placement. The second level, which requires more sophisticated techniques, deals with the measurement of audience awareness, comprehension, and retention of the message. The most advanced level is the measurement of changes in attitudes, opinions, and behavior.

The following sections outline the most widely used methods for evaluating public relations efforts. These include (1) measurement of production, (2) message exposure, (3) audience awareness, (4) audience attitudes, and (5) audience action. Supplemental activities such as communication audits, readability tests, event evaluation, and split messages also are discussed. In most cases, a skilled practitioner will use a combination of methods to evaluate the effectiveness of a program.

Measurement of Production

One elementary form of evaluation is simply to count how many news releases, feature stories, photos, letters, and the like are produced in a given period of time. This kind of evaluation is supposed to give management an idea of a staff's productivity and output. Public relations professionals, however, do not believe that this evaluation is very meaningful, because it emphasizes quantity instead of quality. It may be more cost-effective to write fewer news releases and spend more time on the few that really are newsworthy. It may, for example, be more important for a staff person to spend five weeks working on an article for the *Wall Street Journal* or *Fortune* than to write 29 routine personnel releases.

Another side of the production approach is to specify what the public relations person should accomplish in obtaining media coverage. One state trade association evaluated its director of media relations on the expectation that (1) four feature stories would be run in any of the 11 largest newspapers in the state and (2) news releases would be used by at least 20 newspapers, including 5 or more among the 50 largest.

Such evaluation criteria is somewhat unrealistic and almost impossible to guarantee, because media gatekeepers—not the public relations person—make such decisions. Management may argue, however, that such placement goals provide incentive to the public relations staff and are tangible criteria in employee performance evaluation.

Closely allied to the production of publicity materials is their distribution. Thus, a public relations department might report, for instance, that a total of 756 news releases were sent to 819 daily newspapers, 250 weeklies, and 137 trade magazines within one year or that 110,000 copies of the annual report were distributed to stockholders, security analysts, and business editors. A Centers for Disease Control and Prevention campaign to inform parents about the early symptoms of autism in children, for example, reported that 21,000 resource kits were distributed to health professionals and another 60,000 were distributed to parents.

Measurement of Message Exposure

The most widely practiced form of evaluating public relations programs is the compilation of print and broadcast mentions. Public relations firms and company departments working primarily on a local basis, for example, often have a staff member scan area newspapers for client or product mentions. Large companies with regional, national, or even international outreach usually retain monitoring services to scan large numbers of publications. It's possible to have such services monitor television newscasts in major markets, local and national talk shows, Internet chat groups, podcasts, and even blogs.

Burrelles/Luce, for example, claims it can monitor 40 million blogs and Internet forums, 16,054 Web news sources, 10,355 daily and nondaily newspapers, 7,893 magazines and trade journals, and 926 TV and cable stations. Another monitoring service, National Aircheck, is able to search almost 8,000 hours of news talk radio each week. Robb Wexler, president of the firm, told *O'Dwyer's PR Report*, "We should be able to tell someone within 10 to 15 minutes where and when they're being talked about."

The result of all this electronic research is the ability for the organization or its public relations firm to do a fairly accurate count of how many media stories are generated by the program or campaign. The Tyson Foods Fight Against Hunger campaign, for example, generated 260 stories in print, broadcast, and online placements. The Cranberry Marketing Committee, in its campaign to educate the public and health professionals about the benefits of cranberries, was able to generate 184 stories in the media. The number of media placements, however, is just the first level of assessing the exposure of the message to potential audiences.

Media Impressions

In addition to the number of media placements, public relations departments and firms report how many people may have been exposed to the message. These numbers are described as *media impressions*, the potential audience reached by a periodical, a broadcast program, or an Internet Web site.

If, for example, a story about an organization appears in a local daily that has a circulation of 130,000, the media impressions are 130,000. If another story is published the next day, this counts for 130,000 more impressions. Estimated audiences for radio and television programs, certified by auditing organizations, also are used to compile media impressions. Thus, if there's even a brief mention of a new product or service on *Today*, this might constitute 20 million impressions if that is the audited size of the audience that regularly watches the program.

Some firms inflate the number of "impressions" by also estimating the number of people who are not actual subscribers, but may read a newspaper because it's delivered to the office or home. So instead of 130,000 impressions, it would be 520,000 impressions if it was estimated that four additional individuals had access to the newspaper. The Cranberry Marketing Committee, for example, claimed that its 184 stories generated more than 382 million impressions, but this figure seems to indicate a large inflation factor.

A regional or national news story can generate millions of impressions by simple multiplication of each placement by the circulation or audience of each medium. Frito-Lay's announcement that it was swapping cottonseed oil for sunflower oil in the making of its potato chips, for example, generated more than 175 million impressions. The breakdown, in part, included (1) 13 million impressions for a televison news release, (2) 93 million impressions from print and Internet mentions, (3) 11 million impressions for an audio news release, and (4) 13 million impressions from a mat feature release distributed to print media. (See the Casebook on page 199 about Kermit the Frog's special day in Texas.)

Media impressions are commonly used in advertising to document the breadth of penetration of a particular message. Such figures give a rough estimate of how many people are potentially exposed to a message. They don't, however, document how many people actually read or heard the stories and, more important, how many absorbed or acted on the information. Other techniques needed for this kind of evaluation are discussed later in this chapter.

Hits on the Internet

A cyberspace version of media impressions is the number of people reached via an organization's World Wide Web site or home page. Each instance of a person accessing a site is called a *hit* or a *visit*.

A good example is Purple Moon, a software developer of girls' interactive entertainment. It used a Web site to promote its CD-ROM product, "Friendship Adventures." According to the company and its public relations firm, Ketchum,

> Media relations and grassroots online programs helped drive traffic resulting in 700,000 visitors in the first six months and an average of 6 million impressions per month, equaling or surpassing those of top kids' sites including Disney.com and Sports Illustrated for Kids.

In the national campaign to increase awareness of autism, the Centers for Disease Control and Prevention reported 540,000 unique visitors and more than 50,000 materials downloaded from its Web site. Even Mr. Potato Head did pretty well. The U.S. Potato Board, with the assistance of Fleishman-Hillard, reported that the "Potato HeadQuarters.com site attracted 7,000+ unique visitors who spent an average of 5.5 minutes at the site, reviewing an average of 6.6 pages" about the health benefits of potatoes. Often, a comparison is offered. Longwood University, for example, reported a 185 percent increase in unique visitors to its Web site from the previous year after a campaign to recruit more students.

PRCASEBOOK

A Texas Town Honors Kermit the Frog

Many public relations programs have the primary objective of exposing the public to a message by using events and other activities to generate media coverage. Kermit the Frog's 50th anniversary became such an event and the setting was, appropriately, Kermit, Texas.

The Muppets Holding Company (MHC), now a subsidiary of Walt Disney Company, wanted to revitalize Kermit the Frog's popularity so it retained Porter Novelli (PN) public relations to put together a 50th anniversary celebration that would honor Kermit's "meteoric rise from swamp to international icon." The perfect place to kick off such a celebration, of course, was Kermit, Texas, a town of 5,700. The objective was quite simple: (1) generate national media coverage of Kermit the Frog's 50th anniversary, and (2) garner more than 20 million media impressions.

The frog's wholesome appeal, coupled with parents having a strong nostalgic connection with the Muppets, appealed to Kermit city leaders. The MHC/PN team worked with them over a period of several months to ensure that Kermit's engaging, irreverent personality would be a key part of the city's official celebration. The town council declared October 14 "Kermit the Frog Day" and on that day, the mayor presented Kermit the Frog with the key to the city at a news conference. Other tributes to the famous frog included

- A park dedication
- Renaming a street "Kermit the Frog Avenue"

- Repainting the town's water tower with his image
- Arrangements for a one-day Kermit the Frog cancellation stamp to postmark all mail leaving the post office
- Naming him high school Homecoming Queen and also honorary Homecoming King
- Having him serve as Grand Marshal of the annual Homecoming Parade, which included dozens of Kermit-themed parade floats
- A gathering of hundreds of townspeople on the school's football field who stood in formation to create a "50," as well as an outline of Kermit's head for an aerial photo.

Kermit also appeared in-studio at the local CBS and NBC affiliates in Midland one day prior to the event to spark local awareness of the celebration. After the big day, Kermit conducted one-on-one interviews with the local television stations, the Associated Press, and several major dailies. For national exposure, the MHC/PN team distributed a B-roll video news release via satellite, which was used by more than 400 TV stations.

The MHC/PN team met its objectives. Evaluation of national media coverage showed placements on ABC's *Good Morning America,* NBC's *Early Today,* CNN's "Headline News," MSNBC's "Entertainment Hot List," Fox News Channel's "Weekend Live" and "Fox & Friends," and the Weather Channel. More than 150 newspapers and Web sites nationwide picked up the Associated Press article, and more than 90 percent of the news coverage included at least three key messages.

The second objective was to generate more than 20 million media impressions. This objective was more than doubled with more than 700 media placements, generating 48 million media impressions. Porter Novelli noted, "The studio was able to reach a large national audience (47.5 million impressions) for a cost of $0.002 per impression." In addition, Kermit the Frog's 50th anniversary had the effect of generating increased interest in the Muppets and "helped to create traction for the brand within television projects, retail channels, and home video."

Scenes from a celebration: The citizens of Kermit, Texas, went all out to celebrate Kermit the Frog's 50th birthday.

Advertising Equivalency (AVE)

Another standard approach is to calculate the value of message exposure. This is done by converting stories in the regular news columns or on the air into equivalent advertising costs. In other words, a 5-inch article in a trade magazine that charges $100 per column inch for advertising would be worth $500 in publicity value.

Some practitioners even take the approach of calculating the cost of advertising for the same amount of space and then multiplying that total three to six times to reflect the common belief that a news story has greater credibility than an advertisement. A good example, again, is the Cranberry Marketing Committee. It and its public relation firm, Publicis Consultants, no doubt used a multiplier to estimate that the total publicity value of its 184 stories was more than $17 million.

There is no empirical evidence, however, to support any multiple factor. Professor Don Stacks at the University of Miami has conducted several research studies about AVE, and concluded, "We failed to find the existence of a multiplier." Other professionals, not using systematic research, have come to the same conclusion. Ron Levy, now former president of North American Precis Syndicate, told *Jack O'Dwyer's Newsletter*, that the technique was "blatantly ridiculous."

> Once you start comparing a PR placement to an ad, that raises a whole spectrum of issues.
>
> —— *Don Bartholomew,* director of research at MWW Group

Other professionals say it's like comparing apples and oranges. One reason why the two can't be compared is the fundamental difference between advertising and publicity. Advertising copy is directly controlled by the organization and can be oriented to specific objectives. The organization also controls the size and placement of the message. News mentions, on the other hand, are determined by media gatekeepers and can be negative, neutral, or positive. In addition, a news release can be edited to the point that key corporate messages are deleted. In other words, the organization can't control size, placement, or content.

It thus becomes a question of what is being measured. Should an article be counted as equivalent advertising space if it is negative? It also is questionable whether a 15-inch article that mentions the organization only once among six other organizations is comparable to the same amount of advertising space. And the numbers game doesn't take into account that a 4-inch article in the *Wall Street Journal* may be more valuable in reaching key publics than a 20-inch article in the *Cedar Rapids* (IA) *Gazette*.

There are, however, defenders of the AVE approach to evaluation. Some argue that such metrics help corporate management put a value on public relations. Others say it helps marketing executives decide on how to split resources between public relations and marketing. Even Mark Weiner, president of measuring firm Delahaye, says, "So what's bad about ad values? If works for some people, who's to say that they're unequivocally wrong or unprofessional even if we believe that better methods exist." See the Ethics box on page 201 for an ethical dilemma regarding AVEs.

In summary, the dollar-value approach to measuring publicity effectiveness is somewhat suspect, and there has been little use of such metrics in PRSA Silver Anvil award entries. About the closest one gets is a dollar evaluation of public service announcements (PSAs) on radio or television. Johnson & Johnson, for example, conducted a Safe Pools for Safe Kids campaign and reported "There was more than $2 million worth of free advertising including more than 1,000 TV spots from Turner Broadcasting's efforts."

Another concern is that AVEs concentrate on outputs, not outcomes, and relegates public relations to a media relations function. At the same time, the equating of publicity with advertising rates for comparable space does not engender good media relations.

The technique reinforces the opinion of many media gatekeepers that all news releases are just attempts to get free advertising.

Systematic Tracking

As noted earlier, message exposure traditionally has been measured by sheer bulk. New advances in computer software and databases, however, now make it possible to track media placements in a more sophisticated way.

Computer software and databases can now be used to analyze the content of media placements by such variables as market penetration, type of publication, tone of coverage, sources quoted, and mention of key copy points. Ketchum, for example, can build up to 40 variables into its computer program, including the tracking of reporter bylines to determine whether a journalist is predisposed negatively or positively to the client's key messages.

Specialty measurement firms such as Vocus, Cymfony, VMS, and Factiva do extensive analysis for a variety of clients on a number of metrics such as (1) analysis of coverage telling how a company's news coverage compares with the competition, (2) share of voice in terms of how much a company's coverage comprises the amount of coverage about the industry or subject, (3) tone showing whether the slant of coverage is positive or negative, (4) percentage of time that stories mention key messages, and (5) analysis of what third-party experts, consumers, and bloggers say about the organization. See the two charts (Figures 8.2 and 8.3) on page 202 for some sample pie charts compiled by a measurement firm.

The Tyson Foods' Fight Against Hunger campaign is an example of systematic analysis. The 260 stories, previously mentioned, were analyzed for content. It was found that 98 percent of the stories had a positive tone and included the charitable-giving message. In addition, 85 percent of the stories mentioned Tyson in the top third of the story and 41 percent included key messaging regarding Tyson's commitment to fighting hunger. In the Kodak campaign to introduce a new camera tied to the Academy Awards event, analysis showed that a photo of the new camera was included in 72 percent of the stories, and that the camera's dual-lens feature was in 61 percent of the stories.

Systematic monitoring can also benchmark coverage before and after a campaign to determine whether an organization's publicity efforts paid off in terms of placements and mention of key messages.

An example of benchmarking is the campaign that Capitoline/MS&L public relations conducted on behalf of the Turkish government to make Americans more aware of Turkey as a travel destination. By comparing the number of stories before and after the campaign was launched, Carma International found that articles with Turkey as the primary destination increased 400 percent. Favorable articles on Turkey increased 90 percent from the previous year.

FIGURE 8.2

Media analysis by Factiva Insight from Dow Jones uses text mining and visualization technologies to present a graphical view of third-party data in the Factiva database and on the Web. The chart shows the amount of coverage various pharmaceutical companies received in a one-month period.

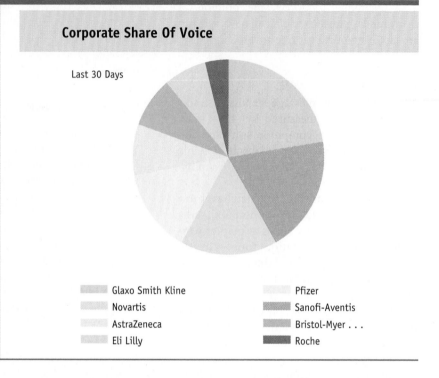

Corporate Share Of Voice

Last 30 Days

Glaxo Smith Kline		Pfizer	
Novartis		Sanofi-Aventis	
AstraZeneca		Bristol-Myer . . .	
Eli Lilly		Roche	

FIGURE 8.3

The chart shows an analysis of media coverage for a company in terms of what percentage of stories were neutral, favorable, and unfavorable. Such data helps organizations assess the effectiveness of their media relations efforts.

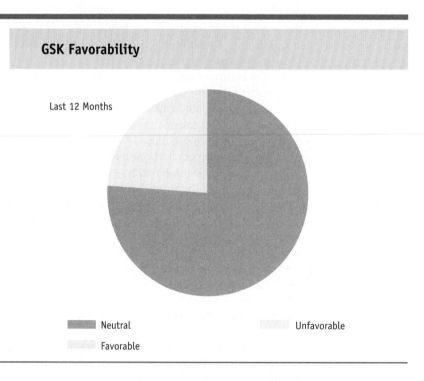

GSK Favorability

Last 12 Months

Neutral		Unfavorable
Favorable		

Another example is the Johnson & Johnson public service campaign to increase parental awareness about dangers to children in swimming pools. A benchmark survey by Harris Interactive before and after the campaign found that awareness of pool-drain hazards increased from 26 percent to 32 percent. In the autism campaign, benchmark analysis showed that significantly fewer pediatricians advocated a "wait and see" approach when parents share a concern about their child's development (30 percent versus 14 percent in the previous year).

Another form of analysis is comparing the number of news releases sent with the number actually published and in what kinds of periodicals. Such analysis often helps a public relations department determine what kinds of publicity are most effective and earn the most return on investment (ROI). As Katharine Paine, president of KD Paine & Partners, says, "The world doesn't need more data. What it needs is analyzed data."

Requests and 800 Numbers

Another measure of media exposure is to compile the number of requests for more information. A story in a newspaper or an appearance of a company spokesperson on a broadcast often provides information as to where people can get more information about a subject.

In many cases, a toll-free 800 number is provided. Dayton Hudson Corporation, owner of several department-store chains, used a toll-free hotline number as part of its "Child Care Aware" program to help educate parents about quality child care and how to get it. In a six-month period, 19,000 calls were received from people seeking advice and copies of a brochure.

Requests for materials also can show the effectiveness of a public relations program. An information program by the U.S. Centers for Disease Control on AIDS prevention, for example, received nearly 2,000 phone calls on its information hotline after its "Safe Sex" program on the Public Broadcasting Service (PBS). In addition, the program and resulting publicity generated 260 requests for videotapes and 400 requests for "Smart Sex" organization kits. Novartis Animal Health US, as part of its introduction of a new drug for arthritic dogs, had over 100,000 requests for its Step Up & Play kits.

Return on Investment (ROI)

Another way to evaluate exposure to the message is to determine the cost of reaching each member of the audience. The technique is commonly used in advertising to place costs in perspective. Although a 30-second commercial during the 2007 Super Bowl telecast cost $2.6 million, advertisers believed it was well worth the price because an audience of more than 150 million would be reached for less than a half-cent each. This was a relatively good bargain, even if three or four million viewers probably visited the refrigerator or the bathroom while the commercial played.

Cost-effectiveness, as this technique is known, also is used in public relations. *Costper-thousand* (CPM) is calculated by taking the cost of the publicity program and dividing it by the total media impressions (discussed earlier). SkyTel, for example, spent $400,000 to publicize its new two-way paging and messaging system and obtained 52 million impressions, about seven-tenths of a cent per impression. In another example, a campaign by the Virginia Department of Tourism to attract Canadian visitors cost $5,500, but generated 90,000 consumer inquiries. This made the cost per inquiry only six cents. The same approach can be done with events, brochures, and newsletters.

> "It was clear to us that you can't go and ask for money . . . unless you can show a return. You can't show a return unless you have measurement."
>
> —— *Valerie M. Cunningham,* VP of corporate marketing for Xerox

Nike produced a sports video for $50,000, but reached 150,000 high school students, for a per-person cost of 33 cents.

Many professionals also call this *ROI*, or *return on investment*. In other words, if an organization spends $500,000 on a campaign that results in a $20 million increase in sales, the ROI is 40 times the cost. Increasingly, public relations professionals are measuring public relations in terms of (1) what sales or revenues are generated, and (2) how much they have saved the company in terms of avoiding a crisis or litigation. One measuring firm, CCW, gave an example in an advertisement for its services. If public relations contributed just 3.5 percent to a major airline's stock price in terms of reputation management, the impact on the company's market value would be $400 million. The Blockbuster Total Access campaign, for example, had a good ROI because it helped generate 700,000 new subscribers to the service.

Audience Attendance

Counting attendance at events is a relatively simple way of evaluating the effectiveness of pre-event publicity. The New York Public Library centennial day celebration, for example, attracted a crowd of 10,000 for a sound-and-laser show and speeches. In addition, 20,000 visitors came to the library on the designated centennial day and more than 200,000 people from around the world visited the library's exhibitions during the year.

Attendance at trade shows also is done. The Cranberrry Marketing Committee, for example, counted 4,500 total visitors to its booth at three major trade shows. In addition, a seminar sponsored by the trade group was attended by 100 dietitians. The public relations firm for the San Diego Boat Show, c3 Communications, also counted attendees at the event as part of its evaluation metric.

Poor attendance at a meeting or event can indicate inadequate publicity and promotion. Another major cause is lack of public interest, even when people are aware that a meeting or event is taking place. Low attendance usually results in considerable finger-pointing; thus, an objective evaluation of exactly what happened—or didn't happen—is a good policy.

Measurement of Audience Awareness

Thus far, techniques of measuring audience exposure and accurate dissemination have been discussed. A higher level of evaluation is to determine whether the audience actually became aware of the message and understood it.

Walter Lindenmann calls this the second level of public relations evaluation. He notes:

> At this level, public relations practitioners measure whether target audience groups actually received the messages directed at them: whether they paid attention to those messages, whether they understood the messages, and whether they have retained those messages in any shape or form.

The tools of survey research are needed to answer such questions. Members of the target audience must be asked about the message and what they remember about it. Public awareness of what organization sponsors an event also is important. BayBank found that only 59 percent of the spectators recognized the bank as sponsor of the Head of the Charles Regatta. Through various innovations, increased publicity efforts, and more signage at the following year's regatta, BayBank raised public awareness to 90 percent. (The bank has since been absorbed by another banking firm.) See how British Airways measured employee awareness on this page.

Another way of measuring audience awareness and comprehension is *day-after recall*. Under this method, participants are asked to view a specific television program or read a particular news story. The next day, they are then interviewed to learn which messages they remembered.

Ketchum, on behalf of the California Prune Board, used this technique to determine whether a 15-city media tour was conveying the key message that prunes are a high-fiber food source. Forty women in Detroit considered likely to watch daytime television shows were asked to view a program on which a Prune Board spokesperson would appear. The day after the program, Ketchum asked the women questions about the show, including their knowledge of the fiber content of prunes. Ninety-three percent remembered the Prune Board spokesperson, and 65 percent, on an unaided basis, named prunes as a high-fiber food source.

AT&T also used unaided recall to determine public awareness of the company's "new" branding after its merger with SBC. It found (1) unaided brand awareness of the new AT&T more than tripled in a six-month period, and (2) nationally, 68 percent of consumers were aware of the message that AT&T delivers technology relevant to their needs.

on the job
A MULTICULTURAL WORLD

How to Reach Employees in 63 Nations

A decade after it was privatized, British Airways (BA) was one of the world's leading airlines. However, it decided to reinforce its mission "To Be the Undisputed Leader in World Travel" by launching a new corporate identity program on a worldwide basis.

The objective was to reach 70 percent of the 55,000 staff members worldwide prior to the public launch of the new corporate identity program. It was reasoned that if the employees were aware of the key messages behind the campaign, they could also convey the key messages to various publics, including customers. British Airways used 13 satellites to link 30,000 guests and employees at 126 locations in 63 countries for a simultaneous, all-time-zone launch.

This is how the airline evaluated the results:

An average of 89 percent of overseas employees, ahead of the 70 percent target, saw the new BA prior to June 10. Almost 80 percent of 444 articles from 49 countries were positive, and 48 percent used visuals. Key messages were conveyed in 78 percent of the articles.

Measurement of Audience Attitudes

Closely related to audience awareness and understanding of a message are changes in an audience's perceptions and attitudes. A major technique to determine such changes is the *baseline study*. Basically, a baseline study is a measurement of audience attitudes and opinions before, during, and after a public relations campaign. Baseline studies, also called *benchmark studies*, graphically show the percentage difference in attitudes and opinions as a result of increased information and publicity. A number of intervening variables may account for changes in attitude, of course, but statistical analysis of variance can help pinpoint how much the change is attributable to public relations efforts.

> " You want to gauge audience or customer response. "
> —— *Katie Paine,* president of KD Paine & Partners

The insurance company Prudential Financial regularly conducts baseline studies. One survey found that the company scored high in respondent familiarity, but achieved only a 29 percent favorable rating in fulfilling its corporate social responsibilities.

As a result, the company launched "The Prudential Helping Hearts Program." This effort provided $2 million in matching grants to volunteer emergency medical squads

(EMS) to help purchase portable cardiac arrest equipment used to treat heart attack victims before they reach the hospital. After a year of publicizing the program and making grants, Prudential found that its overall corporate image had risen to 29 percent.

The American Iron and Steel Institute did a baseline study to determine the effectiveness of its campaign to inform the public about the industry's recycling efforts. Before the program, only 52 percent of the respondents in Columbus, Ohio, were aware that steel cans are recyclable. After the campaign, the percentage had risen to 64 percent.

The value of the baseline survey is underscored by Frank R. Stansberry, former manager of guest affairs for Coca-Cola. He said, "The only way to determine if communications are making an impact is by pre- and posttest research. The first survey measures the status quo. The second one will demonstrate any change and the direction of that change."

Measurement of Audience Action

The ultimate objective of any public relations effort, as has been pointed out, is to accomplish organizational objectives. As David Dozier of San Diego State University aptly points out, "The outcome of a successful public relations program is not a hefty stack of news stories. . . . Communication is important only in the effects it achieves among publics."

The objective of an amateur theater group is not to get media publicity; the objective is to sell tickets. The objective of an environmental organization such as Greenpeace is not to get publicity on behalf of whales, but to motivate the public (1) to write elected officials, (2) to send donations for its preservation efforts, and (3) to get protective legislation passed.

The ultimate objective of a company is to sell its products and services, not get 200 million media impressions. A good example is in the Insights box on page 207. Although the objective of many public relations campaigns are to simply raise awareness in which the number of media placements and impressions plays a large role in evaluation, such campaigns should be seen in the context of the adoption theory that was described at the end of Chapter 7. In other words, raising awareness and interest are the first two stages of the five-step process to ultimately motivate people to adopt an idea, vote for a candidate, use a service, or buy a product.

Thus, public relations efforts ultimately are evaluated on how they help an organization achieve its objectives. Cingular Wireless (before it merged with AT&T) and its public relations firm, Ketchum, employed a variety of primary and secondary research methods, including data analysis of highway traffic safety statistics that showed that teens are four times more likely to be in distraction-related accidents, and focus groups with educators to better understand how to communicate with teens. In their winning PRSA Silver Anvil award application, Ketchum recounted how the measurable objectives that were developed for the "Be Sensible! Cingular Wireless Helps Teens Manage Driving Distractions" were addressed. The evaluation recap illustrates rigorous measurement of both awareness and audience actions:

Objective One: Create awareness of the dangers of distracted driving among 3 million teens over a three-year period:

- ◆ More than 10,000 high schools and 4,200 private driving schools have requested and received the teen-driving program.
- ◆ We have reached 5.6 million teens to date, significantly surpassing our three-year goal with 11 months still to go!

on the job INSIGHTS

Sales: For Many Companies, This is the Ultimate Evaluation

In the corporate world, one behavioral outcome of company performance is almost always measured daily and with great precision. It is sales of products and services. Sabrina Horn calls for a shift in thinking about the role of public relations in driving sales figures: "To those outside marketing, public relations is frequently misunderstood as nothing more than a tactical press release machine. Unfortunately, PR is often an afterthought to strategic planning."

By being involved in the strategic plan, the role of public relations can be broader, and objectives can be set that are clearly linked to sales, for example, "increase sales leads by 50 percent in financial services through precision public relations efforts targeted at the new customer base." It is essential to then plan strategies that can help achieve this objective and, finally, to devise measures that evaluate impact on sales performance.

BUSINESS GOAL	PR STRATEGY	MEASUREMENT TOOLS
Increase sales leads by 50 percent in financial services for new customers.	Product launches, including tours, press releases, a customer testimonial program, direct mail of CD-ROM presenting services, and repeated urging of new prospective customers to call the toll-free number and ask for Operator 39 to receive special discounts.	1. Telemarketing staff maps source of incoming calls back to articles published as the result of press releases.
		2. Sales lead tracking system is programmed to track callers' requests for Operator 39—the marker for the public relations effort.

With early participation in the planning process and some clever techniques, it is possible for public relations to contribute to the sales figures that are already being captured by your company.

Sources: O'Dwyer's PR Services Report, March 2002.

- From the 1,000 educator surveys received to date:
- 93 percent of teachers strongly agree/agree that this program gives students a new perspective on the role of driver distraction in vehicle collisions.
- 92 percent strongly agree/agree that the program generated student interest in the topic of driver distraction.
- 99 percent of instructors said they would use the program again.

Objective Two: Integrate Be Sensible: Don't Drive Yourself to Distraction video into five state driver education programs :

- Maryland, Virginia, Maine, Ohio, Georgia, New Jersey, New York, Indiana, Kansas, Alabama, and Florida state driver education administrators have embraced the Be Sensible teen program by distributing the program to all driver education teachers statewide.
- Cingular's Be Sensible: Don't Drive Yourself to Distraction program has been the recipient of several education awards, including the CINE Golden Eagle and U.S. International Film and Video Festival Silver Screen.

Measurement of Supplemental Activities

Other forms of measurement can be used in public relations activities. This section discusses (1) communication audits, (2) pilot tests and split messages, (3) meeting and event attendance, and (4) newsletter readership.

Communication Audits

The entire communication activity of an organization should be evaluated at least once a year to make sure that every primary and secondary public is receiving appropriate messages. David Hilton-Barber, a past president of the Public Relations Institute of South Africa (PRISA), once wrote: "The most important reasons for an audit are to help establish communication goals and objectives, to evaluate long-term programs, to identify strengths and weaknesses, and to point up any areas which require increased activity."

A communication audit, as an assessment of an organization's entire communication program, could include the following:

- ◆ Analysis of all communication activities—newsletters, memos, policy statements, brochures, annual reports, position papers, mailing lists, media contacts, personnel forms, graphics, logos, advertising, receptionist contacts, waiting lounges for visitors, and so on.
- ◆ Informal interviews with rank-and-file employees and middle management and top executives.
- ◆ Informal interviews with community leaders, media gatekeepers, consumers, distributors, and other influential persons in the industry.

A number of research techniques, as outlined in Chapter 5, can be used during a communication audit, including mail and telephone surveys, focus groups, and so forth. The important point is that the communications of an organization should be analyzed from every possible angle, with the input of as many publics as possible. Security analysts may have something to say about the quality of the company's financial information; municipal leaders are best qualified to evaluate the company's efforts in community relations. Consumers, if given a chance, will make suggestions about quality of sales personnel and product instruction booklets.

Pilot Tests and Split Messages

Evaluation is important even before a public relations effort is launched. If exposure to a message is to be maximized, it is wise to pretest it with a sample group from the targeted audience. Do its members easily understand the message? Do they accept the message? Does the message motivate them to adopt a new idea or product?

A variation of pretesting is the *pilot test*. Before going national with a public relations message, companies often test the message and key copy points in selected cities to learn how the media accept the message and how the public reacts. This approach is quite common in product marketing because it limits costs and enables the company to revamp or fine-tune the message for maximum exposure. It also allows the company to switch channels of dissemination if the original media channels are not exposing the message to the proper audiences.

The *split-message* approach is common in direct mail campaigns. Two or three different appeals may be prepared by a charitable organization and sent to different audiences.

The response rate is then monitored (perhaps the amount of donations is totaled) to learn what message and graphics seemed to be the most effective.

Other Web-based techniques are outlined in Chapter 13, New Technologies in Public Relations.

Meeting and Event Attendance

It has already been pointed out that meetings can be evaluated to some degree by the level of attendance. Such data provide information about the number of people exposed to a message, but it doesn't answer the more crucial question of what they thought about the meeting.

Public relations people often get an informal sense of an audience's attitudes by its behavior. A standing ovation, spontaneous applause, complimentary remarks as people leave, and even the expressions on people's faces provide clues as to how a meeting was received. On the other hand, if people are not responsive, if they ask questions about subjects supposedly explained, if they express doubts or antagonism, the meeting can be considered only partly successful.

Public relations practitioners use a number of information methods to evaluate the success of a meeting, but they also employ more systematic methods. The most common technique is an evaluation sheet that participants fill out at the end of the meeting.

A simple form asking people to rate such items as location, costs, facilities, and program on a 1-to-5 scale (1 being the best) can be used. Other forms may ask people to rate aspects of a conference or meeting as (1) excellent, (2) good, (3) average, (4) poor, or (5) very poor.

Evaluation forms also can ask how people heard about the program and what suggestions they have for future meetings. Another approach is to ask attendees whether they heard or believed the key messages of a spokeperson's presentation and whether they would like to receive any follow-up information from the organization.

Newsletter Readership

Editors of newsletters should evaluate readership annually. Such an evaluation can help ascertain (1) reader perceptions, (2) the degree to which stories are balanced, (3) the kinds of stories that have high reader interest, (4) additional topics that should be covered, (5) the credibility of the publication, and (6) the extent to which the newsletter is meeting organizational objectives.

Note that systematic evaluation is not based on whether all the copies of a newsletter have been distributed or picked up. This information doesn't tell the editor what the audience actually read, retained, or acted upon.

A newsletter, newspaper, or even a brochure can be evaluated in a number of ways. The methods include (1) content analysis, (2) readership interest surveys, (3) readership recall of articles actually read, (4) application of readability formulas, and (5) the use of advisory boards.

Content Analysis   Based on a representative sample of past issues, stories may be categorized under general headings such as (1) management announcements, (2) new product developments, (3) new personnel and retirements, (4) features about employees, (5) corporate finances, (6) news of departments and divisions, and (7) job-related information.

Such a systematic analysis will show what percentage of the publication is devoted to each category. It may be found that one division rarely is covered in the employee newsletter or that management pronouncements tend to dominate the entire publication. Given the content-analysis findings, editors may decide to shift the content.

Readership Interest Surveys   The purpose of these surveys is to get feedback about the types of stories employees are most interested in reading. The most common survey method is simply to provide a long list of generic story topics and have employees rate each as (1) important, (2) somewhat important, or (3) not important. The International Association of Business Communicators (IABC) conducted such a survey on behalf of several dozen companies and found that readers were not very interested in "personals" about other employees (birthdays, anniversaries, and the like).

A readership interest survey becomes even more valuable when it is compared with the content analysis of a publication. Substantial differences signal a possible need for changes in the editorial content.

Article Recall   The best kind of readership survey occurs when trained interviewers ask a sampling of employees what they have read in the latest issue of the publication. Employees are shown the publication page by page and asked to indicate which articles they have read. As a check on the tendency of employees to report that they have read everything, interviewers also ask them (1) how much of each article they have read and (2) what the articles were about. The results are then content-analyzed to determine which kinds of articles have the most readership.

A variation of the readership-recall technique involves individual evaluation of selected articles for accuracy and clarity. For example, an article about a new production process may be sent before or after publication to the head of production for evaluation. On a form with a rating scale of excellent, good, fair, and deficient, the person may be asked to evaluate the article on the basis of such factors as (1) technical data provided, (2) organization, (3) length, (4) clarity of technical points, and (5) quality of illustrations.

Advisory Boards   Periodic feedback and evaluation can be provided by organizing an employee advisory board that meets several times a year to discuss the direction and content of the publication. This is a useful technique because it expands the editor's feedback network and elicits comments that employees might be hesitant to tell the editor face-to-face.

A variation of the advisory board method is to occasionally invite a sampling of employees to meet and discuss the publication. This approach is more systematic than just soliciting comments from employees in the hallway or cafeteria.

SUMMARY

The Purpose of Evaluation
Evaluation is the measurement of results against objectives. This can enhance future performance and also establish whether the goals of management by objective have been met.

Objectives: A Prerequisite for Evaluation
Objectives should be part of any program plan. There must be agreed-upon criteria used to evaluate success in obtaining these objectives.

Current Status of Measurement and Evaluation
Studies indicate that about 4 or 5 percent of a typical public relations budget is allocated to evaluations and measurement. On the most basic level, practitioners can measure message distribution and media placements. The second level would be measurement of audience awareness, comprehension, and retention. The most advanced level is the measurement of changes in attitudes, opinions, and behaviors.

Measurement of Production

The most elementary form of measurement is a tabulation of how many news releases, brochures, annual reports, and so on are distributed in a single year. Measurement of production gives management an idea of a staff's productivity and output.

Measurement of Message Exposure

Several criteria can be used to measure message exposure, including the compilation of media placements in print, broadcast, and Internet media. One common method is calculating media impressions, which is the potential audience reached with a message. Advertising equivalency, commonly called AVE, is calculated by converting news stories to the cost of a comparable amount of paid space. More sophisticated methods include systematic tracking using software and databases to find out such information as tone of coverage, percentage of key messages used, and percentage of coverage related to the competition. Sometimes, exposure is evaluated by determining how much it cost to reach each member of the target audience.

Measurement of Audience Awareness

The next level of evaluation is whether the audience became aware of and understood the message. Audience awareness can be measured through survey research that often uses unaided recall to determine whether the audience understood and remembers the message.

Measurement of Audience Attitudes

Changes in audience attitudes can be evaluated through a baseline or benchmark study, measuring awareness and opinions before, during, and after a public relations campaign.

Measurement of Audience Action

Ultimately, public relations campaigns are evaluated based on how they help an organization achieve its objectives through changing audience behavior, whether it involves sales, fund-raising, or the election of a candidate.

Measurement of Supplemental Activities

A yearly communication audit helps ensure that all publics are receiving appropriate messages. Several techniques can be used to pretest a public relations effort, such as pilot tests and split messages. Meeting and event attendance can be measured both by the number of attendees and by their behavior, which is an indicator of their acceptance of a message. Newsletter readership can be evaluated by content analysis, interest surveys, and article recall.

CASE ACTIVITY What Would You Do?

The Ohio Department of Transportation, with 17 rideshare groups, is planning a Rideshare Week. The objective is to increase participation in carpooling and use of mass transit during this special week. A long-term objective, of course, is to increase the number of people who use carpools or mass transit on a regular basis.

Your public relations firm has been retained to promote Ohio Rideshare Week. Your campaign will include a news conference with the governor encouraging participation, press kits, news releases, interviews on broadcast talk shows, special events, and distribution of Rideshare information booklets at major businesses.

What methods would you use to evaluate the effectiveness of your public relations efforts on behalf of Ohio Rideshare Week?

QUESTIONS for Review and Discussion

1. What is the role of stated objectives in evaluating public relations programs?
2. What primary method of evaluation do public relations people use? Is there any evidence that other methods increasingly are being used?
3. What are some general types of evaluation questions that a person should ask about a program?
4. List four ways that publicity activity is evaluated. What, if any, are the drawbacks of each one?

5. Do you think news stories about a product or service should be evaluated in terms of comparable advertising costs? Why or why not?

6. What are the advantages of systematic tracking and content analysis of news clippings?

7. How are pilot tests and split messages used to determine the suitability of a message?

8. How does measurement of message exposure differ from measurement of audience comprehension of the message?

9. How are benchmark studies used in the evaluation of public relations programs?

10. What is a communication audit?

11. What methods can be used to evaluate a company newsletter or magazine?

SUGGESTED READINGS

Austin, Erica, and Pinkleton, Bruce. *Strategic Communication Management: Planning and Managing Effective Communication Programs.* Mahwah, NJ: Lawrence Erlbaum, 2001.

Bush, Michael. "How P&G Measures Up." *PRWeek,* March 27, 2006, pp. 14–15.

Cameron, Glen T. "Does Publicity Outperform Advertising? An Experimental Test of the Third-Party Endorsement." *Journal of Public Relations Research,* Vol. 6, No. 3, 1994, pp. 185–207.

Hazley, Greg. "Blog Tracking Advances; Whether PR is Ready or Not." *O'Dwyer's PR Report,* June 2006, pp. 25, 33.

Iacona, Erica. "A Measuring the Value of AVEs." *PRWeek,* March 19, 2007, p. 13.

Iacona, Erica. "A Measured Response." *PRWeek,* November 13, 2006, pp. 12–13. How companies measure public relations.

Iacona, Erica. "Measurement That Adds Up." *PRWeek,* March 13, 2006, p. 15. Comparing evaluation techniques in public relations and marketing.

Iacona, Erica. "Revolutionizing the Clip Book: The Clip Book Has Become Digitalized and Includes Complex Measurement." *PRWeek,* November 14, 2005, pp. 12–13.

Iacono, Erica. "The Quest for ROI: The Value and Proof of ROI Differs from Company to Company." *PRWeek,* March 14, 2005, p. 15.

Lindenmann, Walter K. "Guidelines and Standards for Measuring and Evaluating PR Effectiveness." Institute for Public Relations (www.instituteforpr.com).

Nail, Jim. "Media Measurement and Analysis in the Consumer-Generated Media Age." *Public Relations Tactics,* August 2006, p. 14.

Puckett, Joanne, and Rockland, David. "Don't Be Scared: Having a ROI Conversation With Clients." *Public Relations Tactics,* July 2006, p. 14.

Stacks, Don. "Multiplier or Not: PR On Par With Ads." *PRWeek,* April 23, 2007, p. 8.

Weiner, Mark. "Dispelling the Myth of PR Multipliers and Other Inflationary Audience Measures." Institute for Public Relations, August 2006. www.instituteforpr.org

Weiner, Mark. "Proving, Improving ROI of PR." *O'Dwyer's Public Services Report,* June 2005, pp. 10, 12–13.

Complete this Survey and Enter to Win!

Two VIP Tickets
Jimmy Buffett Concert
Saturday, February 26th

9

CHAPTER

Public Opinion and Persuasion

What Is Public Opinion?

Americans talk about public opinion as if it were a monolithic entity overshadowing the entire landscape. Editorial cartoonists humanize it in the form of John or Jane Q. Public, characters who symbolize what people think about any given issue. The reality is that public opinion is somewhat elusive and extremely difficult to measure at any given moment.

In fact, to continue the metaphor, public opinion is a number of monoliths perceived by John and Jane Q. Public, all existing at the same time. Few issues create unanimity of thought among the population, and public opinion on any issue is split in several directions. It also may come as a surprise to note that only a small number of people at any given time take part in public opinion formation on a specific issue. But once people and the press begin to speak of public opinion for an issue as an accomplished fact, it can take on its own momentum. According to Elisabeth Noelle-Neumann's spiral-of-silence theory, public opinion can be an almost tangible force on people's thinking. Noelle-Neumann defines *public opinion* as opinions on controversial issues that one can express in public without isolating oneself. This implies the element of conformity that public opinion can impose on individuals who want to avoid alienation.

There are two reasons for the profound influence of vocal segments of society and public-opinion momentum. First, psychologists have found that the public tends to be passive. It is often assumed that a small, vocal group represents the attitude of the public when, in reality, it is more accurate to say that the majority of the people are apathetic because an issue doesn't interest or affect them. Thus, "public" opposition to such issues as nuclear power, gay marriage, abortion, and gun control may really be the view of a small but significant number of concerned people.

Second, one issue may engage the attention of one part of the population, whereas another arouses the interest of another segment. Parents, for example, may form public opinion on the need for improved secondary education, whereas senior citizens constitute the bulk of public opinion on the need for increased Social Security benefits.

These two examples illustrate the most common definition of *public opinion*: "Public opinion is the sum of individual opinions on an issue affecting those individuals." Another popular definition states: "Public opinion is a collection of views held by persons interested in the subject." Thus, a person unaffected by or uninterested in (and perhaps unaware of) an issue does not contribute to public opinion on the subject.

Inherent in these definitions is the concept of *self-interest*. The following statements appear in public opinion research:

◆ Public opinion is the collective expression of opinion of many individuals bound into a group by common aims, aspirations, needs, and ideals.

◆ People who are interested or who have a vested or self-interest in an issue—or who can be affected by the outcome of the issue—form public opinion on that particular item.

◆ Psychologically, opinion basically is determined by self-interest. Events, words, or other stimuli affect opinion only insofar as their relationship to self-interest or a general concern is apparent.

♦ Opinion does not remain aroused for a long period of time unless people feel their self-interest is acutely involved or unless opinion—aroused by words—is sustained by events.

♦ Once self-interest is involved, opinion is not easily changed.

Research studies also emphasize the importance of *events* in the formation of public opinion. Social scientists, for example, have made the following generalizations:

♦ Opinion is highly sensitive to events that have an impact on the public at large or a particular segment of the public.

♦ By and large, public opinion does not anticipate events. It only reacts to them.

♦ Events trigger formation of public opinion. Unless people are aware of an issue, they are not likely to be concerned or have an opinion. Awareness and discussion lead to crystallizing of opinions and often a consensus among the public.

♦ Events of unusual magnitude are likely to swing public opinion temporarily from one extreme to another. Opinion does not stabilize until the implication of the event is seen with some perspective. The terrorist attacks on the World Trade Center and the Pentagon on 9/11 are perhaps the most galvanizing events as far in the new century to swing public opinion regarding external threats to safety and security. The groundswell of militant public opinion probably served as the driving force for the U.S. invasion of Afghanistan and then Iraq.

People also have more opinions, and are able to form them more easily, with respect to goals than with the methods necessary to reach those goals. For example,

Demonstrations and rallies play a major role in creating public awareness and persuading individuals that their cause is valid. Here, advocates of immigration reform allowing Hispanics already in the United States to achieve legal status participate in a rally.

according to polls, there is fairly strong public opinion for improving the quality of the nation's schools. However, there is little agreement on how to do this. One group advocates higher salaries for "master" teachers, another endorses substantial tax increases for school operations. A third group urges more rigorous standards, such as the No Child Left Behind Act. All three groups, plus others with still more solutions, make up public opinion on the subject.

Opinion Leaders as Catalysts

Public opinion on an issue may have its roots in self-interest or in events, but the primary catalyst is public discussion. Only in this way does opinion begin to crystallize, and pollsters can measure it.

Serving as catalysts for the formation of public opinion are people who are knowledgeable and articulate about specific issues. They are called *opinion leaders*. Sociologists describe them as:

1. highly interested in a subject or issue,
2. better informed on an issue than the average person,
3. avid consumers of mass media,
4. early adopters of new ideas, and
5. good organizers who can get other people to take action.

Types of Leaders

Sociologists traditionally have defined two types of leaders. First are the *formal opinion leaders*, so called because of their positions as elected officials, presidents of companies, or heads of membership groups. News reporters often ask them for statements when a specific issue relates to their areas of responsibility or concern. People in formal leadership positions also are called *power leaders*.

Second are the *informal opinion leaders*, those who have clout with peers because of some special characteristic. They may be role models who are admired and emulated or opinion leaders who can exert peer pressure on others to go along with something. In general, informal opinion leaders exert considerable influence on their peer groups by being highly informed, articulate, and credible on particular issues. The Irish singer Bono is a current example of an informal leader who has had a great impact on public opinion regarding issues such as world hunger and poverty. The actor George Clooney has emerged as another opinion leader on a wide range of social issues. Although many Americans find his ideas about the political process controversial, Clooney's advocacy to end genocide in the Darfur region of the Sudan in Africa is generally accepted.

People seldom make a decision on their own but are influenced by their friends, parents, educators, supervisors, church leaders, physicians, public officials, movie stars or singers, and the media in general when deciding to vote for a president or city mayor, or to purchase a car or even toothpaste. Public relations professionals attempt to influence these leaders just as they seek to influence the public at large. For example, those seeking stronger laws requiring helmets for motorcyclists are making use of statistics about increased motorcycle fatalities, but are likely holding sway in shifting public opinion by pointing to the highly publicized motorcycle accident of NFL star Ben Roethlisberger. According to *USA Today*, proponents of motorcycle helmets were

on the job INSIGHTS

The Life Cycle of Public Opinion

Public opinion and persuasion are important catalysts in the formation of a public issue and its ultimate resolution. The natural evolution of an issue involves five stages:

1. **Definition of the issue.** Activist and special interest groups raise an issue, perhaps a protest against scenic areas being threatened by logging or strip mining. These groups have no formal power but serve as "agenda stimuli" for the media that cover controversy and conflict. Visual opportunities for television coverage occur when activists hold rallies and demonstrations.

2. **Involvement of opinion leaders.** Through media coverage, the issue is put on the public agenda and people become aware of it. Opinion leaders begin to discuss the issue and perhaps see it as being symbolic of broader environmental issues. According to research in *Roper Reports*, 10 to 12 percent of the population that the magazine calls "The Influentials" drive public opinion and consumer trends.

3. **Public awareness.** As public awareness grows, the issue becomes a matter of public discussion and debate, garnering extensive media coverage. The issue is simplified by the media into "them versus us." Suggested solutions tend to be at either end of the spectrum.

4. **Government/regulatory involvement.** Public consensus begins to build for a resolution as government/regulatory involvement occurs. Large groups identify with some side of the issue. Demand grows for government to act.

5. **Resolution.** The resolution stage begins as people with authority (elected officials) draft legislation or interpret existing rules and regulations to make a statement. A decision is made to protect the scenic areas or to reach a compromise with advocates of development. If some groups remain unhappy, however, the cycle may repeat itself.

galvanized to speak out when the Pittsburgh Steelers quarterback broke facial bones in a collision with a car in which Roethlisberger wasn't wearing a helmet.

A survey of 20,000 Americans by the Roper Organization found that only 10 to 12 percent of the general public are opinion leaders. These "influentials," those whom other people seek out for advice, fit the profile of:

1. being active in the community,
2. having a college degree,
3. earning relatively high incomes,
4. regularly reading newspapers and magazines,
5. actively participating in recreational activities, and
6. showing environmental concern by recycling.

Regis McKenna, a marketing communications expert responsible for the original launch of the Apple Macintosh, likes to think of opinion leaders as luminaries because "There are about 20 to 30 key people in every industry who have major influence on trends, standards, and an organization's reputation." He also knows that journalists seek quotes from key opinion leaders in an industry whenever a new product is introduced.

The Flow of Opinion

Many public relations campaigns, particularly those in the public affairs area, concentrate on identifying and reaching key opinion leaders who are pivotal to the success or failure of an idea or project. In the 1940s, sociologists Elihu Katz and Paul Lazarsfeld discovered the importance of opinion leaders during a study of how people chose candidates in an election. They found that the mass media had minimal influence on electoral choices, but voters did rely on person-to-person communication with formal and informal opinion leaders.

These findings became known as the *two-step flow theory* of communication. Although later research confirmed that it really was a multiple-step flow, the basic idea remained intact. Public opinion is really formed by the views of people who have taken the time to sift information, evaluate it, and form an opinion that is expressed to others.

The *multiple-step flow model* is graphically illustrated in Figure 9.1 by a series of concentric circles. In the epicenter of action are opinion makers. They derive large amounts of information from the mass media and other sources and then share that information with people in the adjoining concentric circle, who are labeled the "attentive public." The latter are interested in the issue but rely on opinion leaders to

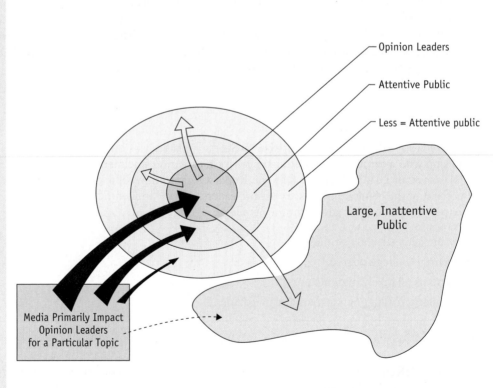

FIGURE 9.1

Media are a major influence on the knowledge and attitudes of opinion leaders for topics of interest to them. Similarly, the less important a topic is to people, the less attentive they are to the media coverage. Less attentive publics are more likely to be influenced by opinion leaders, with some prior conditioning of their knowledge and attitudes by casual monitoring of news. Inattentive publics are only incidentally affected by news coverage, if at all. Inattentives rely heavily on opinion leaders.

Opinion Leaders

Attentive Public

Less = Attentive public

Large, Inattentive Public

Media Primarily Impact Opinion Leaders for a Particular Topic provide synthesized information and interpretation. The outer ring consists of the "inattentive public." They are unaware of or uninterested in the issue and remain outside the opinion-formation process. The multiple-step flow theory, however, means that some eventually will become interested in, or at least aware of, the issue.

Another variation of the two-step model is *N-step theory*. Individuals are seldom influenced by one opinion leader but interact with different leaders around one issue. For example, patients can seek information from their primary-care physician but may also turn to any individual in a close relationship, such as parents or children, when forming a significant opinion or making a decision about health concerns.

Mass media effects are limited by personal influences. Diffusion of innovation theory, discussed in Chapter 7, explains that individuals adopt new ideas or products through the five stages: awareness, interest, trial, evaluation, and adoption. According to Everett Rogers, author of *Diffusion of Innovations*, individuals are often influenced by media in the first two steps, but by friends and family members in the third and fourth steps. And each individual is the decision maker who will adopt a new idea or product and reach the final step.

The Role of Mass Media

One traditional way that public relations personnel reach opinion leaders and other key publics is via the mass media—radio, television, newspapers, and magazines. *Mass media*, as the term implies, means that information from a public relations source can be efficiently and rapidly disseminated to literally millions of people.

Although journalists often argue that they rarely use public relations materials, one has only to look at the daily newspaper to see the quote from the press officer at the sheriff's department, the article on a new computer product, the statistics from the local real estate board, or even the after-game interview with the winning quarterback. In almost all cases, a public relations source at the organization provided the information or arranged the interview. Indeed, Oscar H. Gandy Jr. of the University of Pennsylvania says that up to 50 percent of what the media carry comes from public relations sources in the form of "information subsidies."

Gandy and other theorists have concluded that public relations people—via the mass media—are major players in forming public opinion because they often provide the mass media with the information in the first place. This opinion also is echoed by Elizabeth L. Toth and Robert L. Heath, authors of *Rhetorical and Critical Approaches to Public Relations*. They say, "Few professions have so many skilled and talented individuals contributing to the thoughts, actions, and policies of our nation."

To better understand how public relations people inform the public and shape public opinion via the mass media, it is necessary to review briefly several theories about mass media effects.

Agenda-Setting Theory

One of the early theories, pioneered by Max McCombs and Don Shaw, contends that media content sets the agenda for public discussion. People tend to talk about what they see or hear on the 6 o'clock news or read on the front page of the newspaper. Media, through the selection of stories and headlines, tell the public what to think about, but not necessarily what to think. See Figure 9.2 that shows how the media set the agenda for public relations discussions of Dubai buying U.S. port facilities.

FIGURE 9.2

Over a brief time, media coverage builds awareness of an issue—which in turn can increase activist, public discussion of the issue. Compelling issues then garner further media coverage, leading to greater salience (i.e., top-of-mind status) for the issue among a broader segment of the population. New stories may then follow about the prevailing direction of public opinion, based either on reporter perceptions or polling data. Treating public opinion as firmly set then leads to the spiral-of-silence in which less engaged individuals conform to the general direction of public opinion.

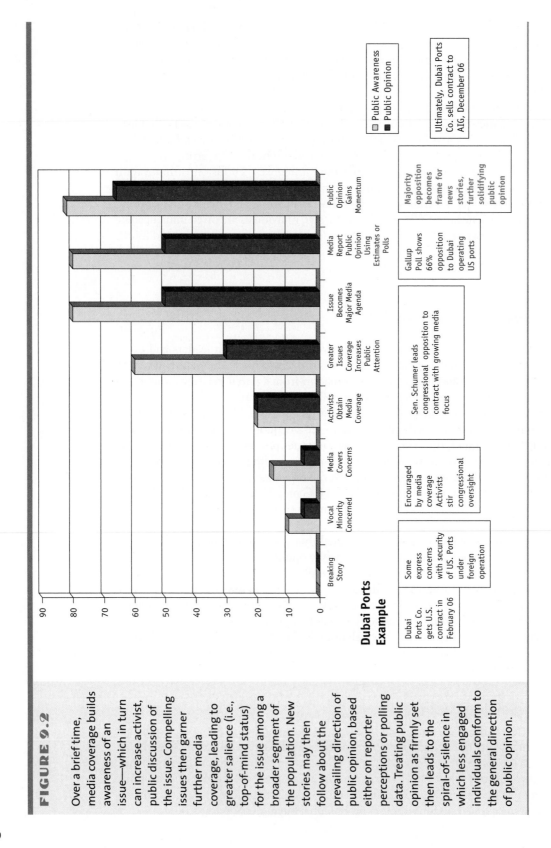

Dubai Ports Example

□ Public Awareness
■ Public Opinion

Dubai Ports Co. gets U.S. contract in February 06

Some express concerns with security of US. Ports under foreign operation

Encouraged by media coverage Activists stir congressional oversight

Sen. Schumer leads congressional opposition to contract with growing media focus

Gallup Poll shows 66% opposition to Dubai operating US ports

Majority opposition becomes frame for news stories, further solidifying public opinion

Ultimately, Dubai Ports Co. sells contract to AIG, December 06

Breaking Story · Vocal Minority Concerned · Media Covers Concerns · Activists Obtain Media Coverage · Greater Issues Coverage Increases Public Attention · Issue Becomes Major Media Agenda · Media Report Public Opinion Using Estimates or Polls · Public Opinion Gains Momentum

Social scientist Joseph Klapper calls this the *limited-effects model* of mass media. He postulates, "Mass media ordinarily does not serve as a necessary and sufficient cause for audience effects, but rather functions among and through a nexus of mediating factors and influence." Such factors may include the way that opinion leaders analyze and interpret the information provided by the mass media. More recently, Wayne Wanta and others have explored second-level agenda-setting effects, finding evidence that the media not only set an agenda, but also convey a set of attributes about the subject of the news. These positive or negative attributes are remembered and color public opinion. For example, a number of news stories regarding the disappearance of Alabama high school student Natalee Holloway have focused on the potential danger for tourists in Aruba, when indeed the island has a relatively low rate of crime compared to other countries in the region. This may lead to the public perception in the United States that travel to Aruba is ill-advised.

From a public relations standpoint, even getting a subject on the media agenda is an accomplishment that advances organizational goals. Sales of Apple's iPod rose as the media reported its success and the public became aware of this "hot" item. Research is under way to document how public relations efforts can build the media agenda, and thus affect public opinion. Research evidence from scholars such as Patricia Curtin, Qi Qiu, and Spiro Khiousis suggests that public relations effort does contribute to the creation of news media agendas. Agenda building research will continue to explore and empirically document how public relations sets the agenda that the media then adopts, ultimately impacting what audiences think about, if not what they think.

Media-Dependency Theory

Although the agenda-setting function of the media is generally valid, other research indicates that mass media can have a "moderate" or even "powerful" effect on the formation of opinions and attitudes. When people have no prior information or attitude disposition regarding a subject, the mass media play a role in telling people what to think.

Mass media effects also are increased when people cannot verify information through personal experience or knowledge. They are highly dependent on the media for information. This tendency is particularly evident in crisis situations, which also often leave reporter and editor dependent on official spokespersons for information as the story breaks. Researchers Debbie Steele and Kirk Hallahan found: "Official sources enjoy an advantage in the early phases of a crisis or issue, particularly when media and others are still in the discovery phase of coverage and the primary emphasis is merely to identify the extent of the problem." Therefore, if much of this crucial initial information comes from official spokespersons of organizations, it's an opportunity for public relations to shape the tone and content of a story, to put a particular emphasis on the story. In sum, media dependency often occurs when the media are, in turn, quite dependent on public relations sources.

Framing Theory

The term *framing* has a long history in mass media research. Traditionally, framing was related to journalists and how they selected certain facts, themes, treatments, and even words to "frame" a story. According to researchers Julie L. Andsager at University of Iowa and Angela Powers at Northern Illinois University, "Mass media scholars have long argued that it is important to understand the ways in which journalistic framing of issues occurs because such framing impacts public understanding and, consequently, policy formation." For example, how media frame the debate over

on the job
ETHICS

Bottled Water: The Framing of an Issue

Americans drank more than 8 billion gallons (31 billion liters) of bottled water in 2006, and the consumption is going up about 10 percent a year. At the same time, the United States has plenty of safe, clean tap water—as opposed to the United Nations estimate that 1.1 billion people around the globe lack safe drinking water.

The producers of bottled water are quite pleased with the expanding

> " An entire generation is growing up thinking they have to get their water out of a bottle. "
> ———— *Gigi Kellett*, director of the "Think Outside the Bottle" campaign

$11 billion American market for bottled water, but various environmental groups are starting to frame drinking bottled water as ecologically incorrect. The Natural Resources

Defense Council (NRDC) is one group and another group, Corporate Advocacy International, has even launched a Think Outside the Bottle campaign to persuade people that drinking bottled water is an act of environmental irresponsibility in an era of global warming.

They argue that all those plastic bottles are made with oil, and fewer than a quarter of them are ever recycled. The result is about a billion pounds (900 million kilograms) clogging landfills. There's also the creation of greenhouse gasses (the major source of global warming) produced by the transport of bottled water from such exotic places as Fiji, the Alps, and even Iceland. *Time* magazine, for example, calculated that a case of Fiji water produces nearly seven pounds of greenhouses gasses on its 5,500 mile

trip from the South Pacific to Los Angeles.

The American Beverage Association (ABA) is concerned that its sales will be threatened if activists are successful in positioning (framing) bottled water as a symbol comparable to driving a gas-guzzling SUV. Several cities, including San Francisco and New York, have already barred municipal departments from buying bottled water and some prestige restaurants have officially announced that they will no longer sell bottled water.

Both water producers and the consumer advocacy groups have launched campaigns to influence public opinion and to frame the issue to their advantage. What do you think? Is it ethical to market bottled water in a country that has clean, safe tap water? Is it ethical for consumer advocacy groups to make bottled water a symbol of environmental irresponsibility? Does drinking bottled water pose an ethical concern for you? Why or why not?

---

health care and the role of HMOs often plays a major role in public perceptions of the problem. See the Insights box on this page about the ethics of framing bottled water as an environmental problem.

Increasingly, however, scholars are applying framing theory to public relations efforts. One research paper by James Tankard and Bill Israel of the University of Texas was titled, "PR Goes to War: The Effects of Public Relations Campaigns on Media Framing of the Kuwait and Bosnian Crises." Their basic contention was that the governments involved in the conflicts used public relations professionals to help frame the issues involved. The issues, once framed, were then picked up by the press.

Tankard and Israel point out that the media dependency of most Americans—who often have little direct knowledge of these places or the complex issues involved—means that they accept the media's version of reality, which originally came from what the two researchers describe as "special interest groups or other groups with particular causes."

Political science professors Shanto Iyengar and Donald Kinder focus on the media's power to prime people in a more subtle but significant form of persuasive effect. From their point of view, public relations professionals working for political campaigns seek to emphasize considerations that will help voters decide in their favor, often enlisting the expertise of a popular leader, and to downplay those that will hurt their cause. The goal is ultimately to encourage voters to change the basis on which they make decisions about voting rather than simply change their choices about a given candidate or issue. Using this approach in early 2007, Senator Hillary Clinton sought to frame her nomination as the Democratic candidate for president as inevitable. However, huge fund-raising gains by Senator Barak Obama destroyed that frame as news media focused on both candidates as serious front runners for the Democratic nomination.

Conflict Theory

According to conflict resolution scholars Morton Deutsch and Peter Colman, conflict in the public arena can be a constructive process that builds toward consensus. Often, controversies serve to shape public opinion, with public relations professionals taking on the challenge to minimize or resolve controversy in conflict situations. For example, the three major search engines—Microsoft, Yahoo, and Google—have stepped up their public relations efforts to neutralize opposition from human rights groups who have criticized them for "kowtowing" to the Chinese government.

As often as public relations practitioners mitigate conflict, they generate or promote conflict or controversy to gain positive position in the marketplace of ideas. This *escalation strategy* is made easier by the tendency for mass media to play a key role in the coverage of conflict, with a predisposition to define news as conflictual. On the other hand, not only does media coverage sometimes put an issue on the public's agenda to the advantage of a public relations practitioner, but it may also serve as the honest broker between parties contending with each other. For example, mediated communication as part of international diplomacy can be an effective means of resolving conflict, particularly at the early stages of the dispute. In the case of the capture of 15 British sailors and Marines in Iranian waters, the British government carried out its arguments for their release exclusively in the media, refusing to meet face-to-face with Iranian officials. Ultimately, the dispute was resolved with the release of the 15 captives.

Because the media are so crucial in presenting and explaining conflicts, but also in keeping them from escalating, it is necessary for parties involved in public relations to know how to work with the media effectively to settle conflicts. Similarly, the media play a central role when public relations professionals want a conflict to escalate somewhat, to bring the issue to the fore for strategic purposes. Unfortunately, all too often, conflict is regarded as more newsworthy than resolution. Details about a culpable politician or corporate malfeasance are far more interesting to the public than the reporting of an amicable settlement or an acquittal. Public relations professionals must take this media tendency into account.

Persuasion: Pervasive in Our Lives

Persuasion has been around since the dawn of human history. It was formalized as a concept more than 2,000 years ago by the Greeks, who made *rhetoric*, the art of using language effectively and persuasively, part of their educational system. Aristotle was the first to set down the ideas of *ethos*, *logos*, and *pathos*, which roughly translate as "source credibility," "logical argument," and "emotional appeal."

More recent scholars, such as Richard Perloff, author of *The Dynamics of Persuasion*, say, "Persuasion is an activity or process in which a communicator attempts to induce a change in the belief, attitude, or behavior of another person or group of persons through the transmission of a message in a context in which the persuadee has some degree of free choice."

Such a definition is consistent with the role of public relations professionals in today's society. Indeed, Professor Robert Heath of the University of Houston says:

> . . . public relations professionals are influential rhetors. They design, place, and repeat messages on behalf of sponsors on an array of topics that shape views of government, charitable organizations, institutions of public education, products and consumerism, capitalism, labor, health, and leisure. These professionals speak, write, and use visual images to discuss topics and take stances on public policies at the local, state, and federal levels.

The Dominant View of Public Relations

The dominant view of public relations, in fact, is one of persuasive communication actions performed on behalf of clients, according to Professors Dean Kruckeberg at the University of Northern Iowa and Ken Starck at the University of Iowa. Oscar Gandy Jr. adds that ". . . the primary role of public relations is one of purposeful, self-interested communications." And Edward Bernays even called public relations the "engineering" of consent to create "a favorable and positive climate of opinion toward the individual, product, institution or idea which is represented." See Chapter 2 for definitions by Edward L. Bernays.

To accomplish this goal, public relations personnel use a variety of techniques to reach and influence their audiences. At the same time, persuasion or rhetoric should be considered more than a one-way flow of information, argument, and influence. In the best sense, Toth and Heath say that persuasion should be a dialogue between points of view in the marketplace of public opinion, where any number of persuaders are hawking their wares.

Indeed, persuasion is an integral part of democratic society. It is the freedom of speech used by every individual and organization to influence opinion, understanding, judgment, and action.

Uses of Persuasion

Persuasion is used to (1) change or neutralize hostile opinions, (2) crystallize latent opinions and positive attitudes, and (3) conserve favorable opinions.

The most difficult persuasive task is to turn hostile opinions into favorable ones. There is much truth to the adage, "Don't confuse me with the facts; my mind is made up." Once people have decided, for instance, that HMOs are making excessive profits or that a nonprofit agency is wasting public donations, they tend to ignore or disbelieve any contradictory information. Everyone, as Walter Lippmann has described, has

on the job
A MULTICULTURAL WORLD

Persuasion in the Marketplace: A New Pickup Truck in Thailand

Thailand is the world's second-largest pickup market after the United States. In fact, almost two-thirds of the vehicles on the road in Thailand are pickup trucks, which makes it a very competitive market. General Motors had been manufacturing the Chevrolet sedan in the country since 2000, but the decision was made in 2004 to launch the Colorado, its first pickup truck in Thailand.

The automotive giant faced several challenges. The market for pickup trucks was already saturated, and there were other, less expensive brands on the market. The opportunity, however, was the projection that sales of pickup trucks would increase by 15 percent and the lifecycle of vehicles in Thailand was about five years, compared to 7 to 10 years in Western markets. Focus groups also indicated that Thai drivers were getting bored with mainstream Japanese vehicles and were looking for something "new" in terms of a "rough and rugged" vehicle that

would make them feel more safe and secure.

Although GM's primary audience was consumers, the major vehicle for reaching them was the automotive/lifestyle media. Several key messages were selected. One was Chevrolet's global "Like a Rock" theme and the other was a more localized theme, "True Truck Spirit," that combined the idea of the "true" heritage of an American-style truck, with the "free spirit" of driving that appealed to Thai consumers. GM's public relations and marketing staff also capitalized on the Colorado name to project an image of the American West. Seventy journalists, for example, were invited to test-drive the new truck involving on-and off-road driving at a specially constructed "wild west" fort in a disused quarry. According to Weber Shandwick Thailand, GM's public relations firm, "From the log-fashioned fort gate and manned watchtower to the two-sleeper canvass tents, the reporters were given a feel of what life in the American

wild west was like." Another press event where journalists could test drive a second, more powerful model was held several months later at an airport, renamed "Colorado Airport" for the event.

Other events were also held that emphasized the truck's connection to the American West. At its launch at a large concert venue in Bangkok, for example, a canyon wall split open and the Colorado was driven onto the stage. In addition, there was a "Buy Colorado, Visit Colorado" competition. Everyone who purchased a Colorado had the chance to win a trip to the state of Colorado, and the five winners were publicized in the media.

The result was impressive. Chevrolet achieved a 220 percent sales growth, helping it move from 14th place in the Thai market to 7th place. Also, the Colorado became the fifth-best-selling pickup in Thailand in less than a year. The campaign received a Golden Award from the International Public Relations Association (IPRA) for the marketing of a new product.

pictures in his or her head based on an individual perception of reality. People generalize from personal experience and what peers tell them. For example, if a person has an encounter with a rude clerk, the inclination is to generalize that the entire department store chain is not very good.

Persuasion is much easier if the message is compatible with a person's general disposition toward a subject. If a person tends to identify Toyota as a company with a good reputation, he or she may express this feeling by purchasing one of its cars. See the Insights box on this page about how General Motors tailored messages for Thai consumers. Nonprofit agencies usually crystallize the public's latent inclination to aid the less fortunate by asking for a donation. Both examples illustrate the reason that organizations strive to have a good reputation—it is translated into sales and donations. The concept of *message channeling* will be discussed in more detail later in the chapter.

The easiest form of persuasion is communication that reinforces favorable opinions. Public relations people, by providing a steady stream of reinforcing messages, keep the reservoir of goodwill in sound condition. More than one organization has survived a major problem because public esteem for it tended to minimize current difficulties. Continual efforts to maintain the reservoir of goodwill is called *preventive public relations*, and it is the most effective type of public relations.

Factors in Persuasive Communication

A number of factors are involved in persuasive communication, and the public relations practitioner should be knowledgeable about each one. The following is a brief discussion of (1) audience analysis, (2) source credibility, (3) appeal to self-interest, (4) clarity of message, (5) timing and context, (6) audience participation, (7) suggestions for action, (8) content and structure of messages, and (9) persuasive speaking. In addition, see the Insights box on page 227 that gives an inventory of techniques for persuading and motivating people.

Audience Analysis

Knowledge of audience characteristics such as beliefs, attitudes, concerns, and lifestyles is an essential part of persuasion. It helps the communicator tailor messages that are salient, answer a felt need, and provide a logical course of action.

Basic demographic information, readily available through census data, can help determine an audience's gender, income level, education, ethnic background, and age groupings. Other data, often prepared by marketing departments, give information on a group's buying habits, disposable income, and ways of spending leisure time. In many cases, the nature of the product or service easily defines the audience along the lines of age, gender, and income.

Another audience-analysis tool is *psychographics*. This method attempts to classify people by lifestyle, attitudes, and beliefs. The Values and Lifestyle Program, popularly known as VALS, was developed by SRI International, a research organization in Menlo Park, California. VALS is routinely used in public relations to help communicators structure persuasive messages to different elements of the population. A good illustration is the way Burson-Marsteller used VALS for its client, the National Turkey Foundation. The problem was simple: how to encourage turkey consumption throughout the year, not just at Thanksgiving and Christmas.

One element of the public was called "Sustainers and Survivors"; VALS identified them as low-income, poorly educated, often elderly people who ate at erratic hours, consumed inexpensive foods, and seldom ate out. Another element was the "Belongers," who were highly family oriented and served foods in traditional ways. The "Achievers" were those who were more innovative and willing to try new foods.

Burson-Marsteller tailored a strategy for each group. For Survivors and Sustainers, the message stressed bargain cuts of turkey that could be stretched into a full meal. The message for Belongers focused on cuts that signaled turkey, such as drumsticks. Achievers, who were better educated and had higher income levels, received the message about gourmet cuts and new, innovative recipes.

on the job INSIGHTS

Motivation—Ability—Opportunity Model for Enhancing Message Processing

The following chart summarizes the various communication strategies that can be used to reach publics who have little knowledge or interest in a particular issue, product, or service. The object, of course, is to structure persuasive messages that attract their attention.

ENHANCE MOTIVATION	ENHANCE ABILITY	ENHANCE OPPORTUNITY
Attract and encourage audiences to commence, continue processing	***Make it easier to process the message by tapping cognitive resources***	***Structure messages to optimize processing***
Create attractive, likable messages (create affect)	Include background, definitions, explanations	Expend sufficient effort to provide information
Appeal to hedonistic needs (sex, appetite, safety)	Be simple, clear	Repeat messages frequently
Use novel stimuli:	Use advance organizers (e.g., headlines)	Repeat key points within text—in headlines, text, captions, illustrations, etc.
◆ Photos	Include synopses	Use longer messages
◆ Typography	Combine graphics, text, and narration (dual coding of memory traces)	Include multiple arguments
◆ Oversized formats	Use congruent memory cues (same format as original)	Feature "interactive" illustrations, photos
◆ Large number of scenes, elements	Label graphics (helps identify which attributes to focus on)	Avoid distractions:
◆ Changes in voice, silence, movement	Use specific, concrete (versus abstract) words and images	◆ Annoying music
Make the most of formal features:	Include exemplars, models	◆ Excessively attractive spokespersons
◆ Format size	Make comparison with analogies	◆ Complex arguments
◆ Music	Show actions, train audience skills through demonstrations	◆ Disorganized layouts
◆ Color	Include marks (logos, logotypes, trademarks), slogans, and symbols as continuity devices	Allow audiences to control pace of processing
◆ Include key points in headlines	Appeal to self-schemas (roles, what's important to audience's identity)	Provide sufficient time
Use moderately complex messages	Enhance perceptions of self-efficacy to perform tasks	Keep pace lively and avoid audience boredom
Use sources who are credible, attractive, or similar to audience	Place messages in conducive environment (priming effects)	
Involve celebrities	Frame stories using culturally resonating themes, catchphrases	
Enhance relevance to audience—ask them to think about a question		
Use stories, anecdotes, or drama to draw into action		
Stimulate curiosity: Use humor, metaphors, questions		
Vary language, format, source		
Use multiple, ostensibly independent sources		

Source: Kirk Hallahan, "Enhancing Motivation, Ability, and Opportunity to Process Public Relations Messages." *Public Relations Review*, Vol. 26, No. 4, pp. 463–480.

on the job INSIGHTS

Appeals That Move People to Act

Persuasive messages often include information that appeals to an audience's self-interest. Here is a list of persuasive message themes:

- Make money
- Save money
- Save time
- Avoid effort
- More comfort
- Better health
- Cleaner
- Escape pain
- Gain praise
- Be popular
- Be loved/accepted
- Keep possessions
- More enjoyment

- Satisfy curiosity
- Protect family
- Be stylish
- Have beautiful things
- Satisfy appetite
- Be like others
- Avoid trouble
- Avoid criticism
- Be an individual
- Protect reputation
- Be safe
- Make work easier
- Be secure

Source: Charles Marsh. "Fly Too Close to the Sun." *Communication World,* September 1992, p. 24.

This segmentation of the consumer public into various VALS lifestyles enabled Burson-Marsteller to select appropriate media for specific story ideas. An article placed in *True Experience*, a publication reaching the demographic characteristics of Survivors and Sustainers, was headlined "A Terrific Budget-Stretching Meal." Articles in *Better Homes and Gardens* with such titles as "Streamlined Summer Classics" and stories about barbecued turkey on the Fourth of July were used to reach Belongers. Articles for Achievers in *Food and Wine* magazine and *Gourmet* included recipes for turkey salad and turkey tetrazzini.

Such audience analysis, coupled with suitably tailored messages in the appropriate media outlets, is the technique of *channeling.* Persuasive messages are more effective when they take into account the audience's lifestyles, beliefs, and concerns.

Source Credibility

A message is more believable to the intended audience if the source has *credibility.* This was Aristotle's concept of *ethos,* mentioned earlier, and it explains why organizations use a variety of spokespeople, depending on the message and the audience.

The California Strawberry Advisory Board, for example, arranged for a home economist to appear on television talk shows to discuss nutrition and to demonstrate easy-to-follow strawberry recipes. The viewers, primarily homemakers, identified with the representative and found her highly credible. By the same token, a manufacturer of sunscreen lotion uses a professor of pharmacology and a past president of the State Pharmacy Board to discuss the scientific merits of sunscreen versus suntan lotions.

The Three Factors   Source credibility is based on three factors. One is *expertise.* Does the audience perceive the person as an expert on the subject? Companies, for example, use engineers and scientists to answer news conference questions about how an engineering process works or whether an ingredient in the manufacturing process of a product presents a potential hazard.

The second component is *sincerity.* Does the person come across as believing what he or she is saying? Bono, leader of the Irish rock group U2, may not be considered an expert on all the products or causes he endorses, but he does get high ratings for sincerity.

The third component, which is even more elusive, is *charisma.* Is the individual attractive, self-assured, and articulate, projecting an image of competence and leadership? President Bill Clinton is an excellent example. His commanding presence and polished public speaking made him a charismatic figure. Clinton's approval rating remained high even in the midst of several scandals, including the threat of impeachment over the Monica Lewinsky affair. Throughout his presidency, Clinton projected an aura of authenticity.

Expertise is less important than sincerity and charisma if celebrities are used as spokespersons. Their primary purpose is to call attention to the product or service. Another purpose is to associate the celebrity's popularity with the product. This technique is called *transfer*; it is discussed later in this chapter as a propaganda device.

Problems with Celebrities   Using celebrities, however, has several possible downsides. One is the increasing number of celebrity endorsements to the point that the public sometimes can't remember who endorses what. A second problem can be overexposure of a celebrity, such as Tiger Woods, who earns millions of dollars annually from multiple products.

A third problem occurs when an endorser's actions undercut the product or service. When basketball star Kobe Bryant for example, was charged with sexual assault in 2003. Even though the case against him eventually was dismissed by the judge, the subsequent negative publicity led McDonald's to drop him as a spokesperson for the company. Bryant had also signed a $40 million contract to promote Nike athletic wear shortly before he was accused of sexual assault, but it was more than two years before the first ad featuring Bryant appeared for the shoe company. In a more mundane situation, Svedka Vodka announced that it would sponsor the 21st birthday bash of Lindsay Lohan in Las Vegas, but immediately dropped the sponsorship when she was arrested for underage drinking and suspicion of DUI before the party could even take place.

Sometimes, celebrities weather controversy relatively unscathed. For example, Martha Stewart's reputation as a domestic diva has remained intact despite a five-month prison stay and a $195,000 fine to settle insider-trading charges (see the PR Casebook in Chapter 12). Although sales of her magazine and products bearing her name suffered during her trial and imprisonment, they have since rebounded. Michael Jordan continues to endorse products even after being accused of adultery, illegal gambling, and a disastrous turn as a major league baseball player.

A fourth problem is when a celebrity decides to speak out on controversial public issues and even endorses political candidates. Such actions tend to reduce the celebrity's effectiveness as an endorser of products or services because they tend to alienate segments of the consumer public that disagree with their views. One survey, for example, found that a third of the respondents said they would avoid buying products endorsed by celebrities who express political views that they disagree with. The Dixie Chicks is an example of consumer backlash. After members of the group criticized President Bush for invading Iraq, sales of their albums took a nosedive among country music fans who supported the president and the war. Customers of Slim-Fast food company also complained about Whoopi Goldberg as a celebrity endorser of its products after she made fairly blunt criticisms of President Bush and his policies.

In summary, the use of various sources for credibility depends, in large part, on the type of audience being reached. That is why audience analysis is the first step in formulating persuasive messages.

> " Anytime an advertiser pins its image to a star, whether an athlete or an actor, it takes a chance that reality won't live up to the storyboard. "
> —— *Christina White,* reporter for the *Wall Street Journal*

Celebrities can add credibility and visibility to a host of products, issues, or social movements. Vice president Al Gore has become a recognizable spokesperson for the critical mass of unknown atmospheric research specialists in the scientific community who believe that global warming is escalating—and that the escalation is due in large part to human activity. In the case of the vice president, his celebrity was important in obtaining a platform to present inconvenient truths; at the same time, Gore's own celebrity has skyrocketed through speaking worldwide about the threat to the globe. His notoriety perhaps reached its zenith in his receiving an Oscar for his movie, *An Inconvenient Truth*.

Appeal to Self-Interest

Self-interest was described during an earlier discussion about the formation of public opinion. Publics become involved in issues or pay attention to messages that appeal to their psychological or economic needs.

Charitable organizations don't sell products, but they do need volunteers and donations. This is accomplished by careful structuring of messages that appeal to self-interest. This is not to say that altruism is dead. Thousands of people give freely of their time and money to charitable organizations, but they do receive something in return, or they would not do it. The "something in return" may be (1) self-esteem, (2) the opportunity to make a contribution to society, (3) recognition from peers and the community, (4) a sense of belonging, (5) ego gratification, or even (6) a tax deduction. Public relations people understand psychological needs and rewards, and that is why there is constant recognition of volunteers in newsletters and at award banquets. (Further discussion of volunteerism appears in Chapter 20.)

Sociologist Harold Lasswell says that people are motivated by eight basic appeals. They are:

- power
- respect
- well-being
- affection
- wealth
- skill
- enlightenment
- physical and mental vitality

Psychologist Abraham Maslow, in turn, says that any appeal to self-interest must be based on a hierarchy of needs. The first and lowest level involves basic needs such as food, water, shelter, and even transportation to and from work. The second level consists of security needs. People need to feel secure in their jobs, safe in their homes, and confident about their retirement. At the third level are "belonging" needs—people seek association with others. This is why individuals join organizations.

"Love" needs comprise the fourth level in the hierarchy. Humans have a need to be wanted and loved—fulfilling the desire for self-esteem. At the fifth and highest level in Maslow's hierarchy are self-actualization needs. Once the first four needs have been met, Maslow says that people are free to achieve maximum personal potential, for example, through traveling extensively or perhaps becoming experts on orchids.

Maslow's hierarchy helps to explain why some public information campaigns have difficulty getting the message across to people classified in the VALS lifestyle categories as "Survivors" and "Sustainers." Efforts to inform minorities and low-income groups about AIDS provide an example of this problem. For these groups, the potential danger of AIDS is less compelling than the day-to-day problems of poverty and satisfying the basic needs of food and shelter. To compound the challenge, health workers in Africa concede that one of the few affordable pleasures in life for the rural poor is sexual activity.

The challenge for public relations personnel, as creators of persuasive messages, is to tailor information to fill or reduce a need. Social scientists have said that success in persuasion largely depends on accurate assessment of audience needs and self-interests.

Clarity of Message

Many messages fail because the audience finds the message unnecessarily complex in content or language. The most persuasive messages are direct, simply expressed, and contain only one primary idea. The management expert Peter Drucker once said, "An innovation, to be effective, has to be simple and it has to be focused. It should do only one thing, otherwise it confuses." The same can be said for the content of any message.

Public relations personnel should always ask two questions: "What do I want the audience to do with the message?" and "Will the audience understand the message?" Although persuasion theory says that people retain information better and form stronger opinions when they are asked to draw their own conclusions, this doesn't negate the importance of explicitly stating what action an audience should take. Is it to buy the product, visit a showroom, write a member of Congress, make a $10 donation, or what?

If an explicit request for action is not part of the message, members of the audience may not understand what is expected of them. Public relations firms, when making a presentation to a potential client, always ask for the account at the end of the presentation.

Timing and Context

A message is more persuasive if environmental factors support the message or if the message is received within the context of other messages and situations with which the individual is familiar. These factors are called *timing* and *context*.

Information from a utility on how to conserve energy is more salient if the consumer has just received the January heating bill. A pamphlet on a new stock offering is more effective if it accompanies an investor's dividend check. A citizens' group lobbying for a stoplight gets more attention if a major accident has just occurred at the intersection.

Political candidates are aware of public concerns and avidly read polls to learn what issues are most important to voters. If the polls indicate that crime and unemployment are key issues, the candidate begins to use these issues—and to offer his or her proposals—in the campaign.

Timing and context also play an important role in achieving publicity in the mass media. Public relations personnel, as pointed out earlier in the text, should read newspapers and watch television news programs to find out what media gatekeepers consider newsworthy. A manufacturer of a locking device for computer files got extensive media coverage about its product simply because its release followed a rash of news stories about thieves' gaining access to bank accounts through computers. Media gatekeepers found the product newsworthy within the context of actual news events.

The value of information and its newsworthiness are based on timing and context. Public relations professionals disseminate information at the time it is most highly valued.

Audience Participation

A change in attitude or reinforcement of beliefs is enhanced by audience involvement and participation.

An organization, for example, may have employees discuss productivity in a quality-control circle. Management may already have figured out what is needed, but if workers are involved in the problem solving, they often come up with the same solution or even a better one. And, from a persuasion standpoint, the employees are more committed to making the solution work because it came from them—not as a policy or order handed down by higher management.

Participation also can take the form of samples. Many companies distribute product samples so consumers can conveniently try them without expense. A consumer who samples the product and makes a judgment about its quality is more likely to purchase it.

Activist groups use participation as a way of helping people actualize their beliefs. Not only do rallies and demonstrations give people a sense of belonging, but the act of participation reinforces their beliefs. The Million Man March held in Washington, D.C., is an excellent example of grassroots participation. The event, modeled after Martin Luther King's rallies in the nation's capital a generation earlier, mobilized African American men around a variety of social justice issues. Asking people to do something—conserve energy, collect donations, or picket—activates a form of self-persuasion and commitment.

Suggestions for Action

A principle of persuasion is that people endorse ideas only if they are accompanied by a proposed action from the sponsor. Recommendations for action must be clear. Public relations practitioners must not only ask people to conserve energy, for instance, but also furnish detailed data and ideas on how to do it.

A campaign conducted by Pacific Gas & Electric Company provides an example. The utility inaugurated a Zero Interest Program (ZIP) to offer customers a way to implement energy-saving ideas. The program involved several components:

- **Energy kit**. A telephone hotline was established and widely publicized so interested customers could order an energy kit detailing what the average homeowner could do to reduce energy use.
- **Service bureau**. The company, at no charge, sent representatives to homes to check the efficiency of water heaters and furnaces, measure the amount of insulation, and check doors and windows for drafts.
- **ZIP**. The cost of making a home more energy efficient was funded by zero-interest loans to any qualified customer.

Another good example is highlighted in the PR Casebook on page 233 here, the suggestion for action is providing a telephone number to get tested for syphilis.

Content and Structure of Messages

A number of techniques can make a message more persuasive. Writers throughout history have emphasized some information while downplaying or omitting other pieces of information. Thus, they addressed both the content and structure of messages.

PRCASEBOOK

Syphilis: Successfully Reaching a High-Risk Audience

The Kansas City (Missouri) Health Department had a problem. In just one year, there was a 300 percent rise in syphilis cases. Swift action was needed to control the outbreak, but the department also knew that an information campaign would not be effective using only strong fear and threat appeals. In addition, it would be necessary to reach high-risk audiences on a personal level and in their own environment.

With these thoughts in mind, the Kansas City (Missouri) Health Department partnered with Fleishman-Hillard (FH) public relations to do a two-month campaign to raise awareness about syphilis and promote testing among three primary audiences who were identified to be most at risk for contracting syphilis: (1) openly gay men, (2) men who have sex with other men but don't consider themselves homosexuals, and (3) sex workers.

FH took several approaches. First, the firm prepared several collateral pieces to support distribution of messages. They included: (1) "trick cards," business cards that included key messages and a telephone number for confidential testing, (2) glow-in-the-dark bracelets that displayed the message "Syphilis—It's treatable, Get Tested" with phone numbers, and (3) posters with such messages as "Did You Take Phil Home Last Night?" (see insert). Next, volunteer teams were recruited from local organizations and universities to distribute the materials to bars, night clubs, and adult book stores. The concept was to use peers of the men to deliver the messages.

Another approach was using a credible spokesperson among this special audience. Flo, a local drag queen, was widely accepted in the gay and straight communities and a credible source of information about how to avoid syphilis or get treated for the disease. She recorded a public service announcement (PSA), conducted media interviews, and made on-site presentations in nightclubs while in costume.

The campaign also drew the attention of the local media and even reached a national audience. The *Kansas City Star* ran a story on the front page of the metro section with a picture of Flo and volunteers. Several alternative publications, reaching the gay community, also ran stories. The Associated Press syndicated the story nationally.

The result was successful. More than 8 million media impressions were generated through various print and broadcast outlets, and 2,400 bracelets and 8,000 "trick" cards were distributed. The most important aspect was that the Kansas City Health Department was able to test 9,840 people, a 17 percent increase from the previous year. The campaign also received *PRWeek*'s 2007 award for public sector campaign of the year.

A poster with a relevant question made an impact on the gay community.

DID YOU TAKE PHIL HOME LAST NIGHT?

Syphilis is on the rise in Kansas City. Could you be at risk? Be smart and take control. For free, confidential testing, call
816-513-6152

SY PHIL IS
IT'S TREATABLE. GET TESTED.

Expert communicators continue to use a number of devices, including (1) drama, (2) statistics, (3) surveys and polls, (4) examples, (5) testimonials, (6) mass media endorsements, and (7) emotional appeals.

Drama   Because everyone likes a good story, the first task of a communicator is to get the audience's attention. This is often accomplished by graphically illustrating an event or situation. Newspapers often dramatize a story to get readers interested in an issue. Thus, we read about the family evicted from its home in a story on the increase in bankruptcies; the old man who is starving because of welfare red tape; or the worker disabled because of toxic waste. In newsrooms, this is called *humanizing an issue*.

Drama also is used in public relations. Relief organizations, in particular, attempt to galvanize public concern and donations through stark black-and-white photographs and emotionally charged descriptions of suffering and disease.

A more mundane use of drama is the so-called *application story*, sent to the trade press. This is sometimes called the *case study technique*, in which a manufacturer prepares an article on how an individual or a company is using the product. IBM, for example, provides a number of application stories about the unique ways in which its products are being used.

Statistics   People are impressed by statistics. Use of numbers can convey objectivity, size, and importance in a credible way that can influence public opinion. Caterpillar, for example, got considerable media publicity for its new 797 mining dump truck by combining statistics and some humor. In the news release for the largest truck in the world, it announced that the bed of the truck was so large that it could haul the following payloads: 4 blue whales, 217 taxicabs, 1,200 grand pianos, and 23,490 Barbie dolls.

Surveys and Polls   Airlines and auto manufacturers, in particular, use the results of surveys and polls to show that they are first in "customer satisfaction," "service," and even "leg room" or "cargo space." The most credible surveys are those conducted by independent research organizations, but readers still should read the fine print to see what is being compared and rated. Is an American-made auto, for example, being compared only with other U.S. cars or with foreign cars as well?

Examples   A statement of opinion can be more persuasive if some examples are given. A school board can often get support for a bond issue by citing examples of how the present facilities are inadequate for student needs. Environmental groups tell how other communities have successfully established greenbelts when requesting a city council to do the same. Automakers promote the durability of their vehicles by citing their performance on a test track or in a road race.

Testimonials   A form of source credibility, testimonials can be either *explicit* or *implied*. A campaign to curtail alcohol and drug abuse may feature a pop singer as a spokesperson or have a young woman talk about being paralyzed and disfigured as the victim of a drunk driver. Implied testimonials also can be effective. Proclamations by mayors and governors establishing Red Cross Day or Library Week are implied testimonials. The testimonial as a propaganda device is discussed later in the chapter.

> **Popularization happens when you get credible third parties to speak for your brand, and that is something PR can do extremely well.**
>
> ———*Scott Keogh,* chief marketing officer of Audi

Endorsements   In addition to endorsements by paid celebrities, products and services benefit from favorable statements by experts in what is called a *third-party endorsement*. A well-known medical specialist may publicly state that a particular brand of exercise equipment is best for general conditioning. Organizations such as the American Dental Association and the National Safety Council also endorse products and services.

Media endorsements, usually unpaid, can come through editorials, reviews, surveys, and news stories. A daily newspaper may endorse a political candidate, review restaurants and entertainment events, and even compile a survey ranking the best coffeehouses. The media also produce news stories about new products and services that, because of the media's perceived objectivity, are considered a form of third-party endorsement. The idea is that media coverage bestows legitimacy and newsworthiness on a product or service.

Emotional Appeals   Fund-raising letters from nonprofit groups, in particular, use this persuasive device. See the sample letter from the Defenders of Wildlife on page 236. Amnesty International, an organization dedicated to human rights and fighting state terrorism, began one direct-mail letter with the following message in large red type:

> "We Are God in Here . . ."
> . . . That's what the guards taunted the prisoner with as they applied electrical shocks to her body while she lay handcuffed to the springs of a metal bed. Her cries were echoed by the screams of other victims and the laughter of their torturers.

Such emotional appeals can do much to galvanize the public into action, but they also can backfire. Such appeals raise *ego defenses*, and people don't like to be told that in some way they are responsible. A description of suffering makes many people uncomfortable, and, rather than take action, they may tune out the message. A relief organization once ran full-page advertisements in magazines with the headline "You Can Help Maria Get Enough to Eat . . . Or You Can Turn the Page." Researchers say that most people, their ego defenses raised, turn the page and mentally refuse to acknowledge that they even saw the ad. In sum, emotional appeals that attempt to lay a guilt trip on the audience are not very successful.

Strong fear arousals also can cause people to tune out, especially if they feel that they can't do anything about the problem anyway. Research indicates, however, that a moderate fear arousal, accompanied by a relatively easy solution, is effective. A moderate fear arousal is: "What would happen if your child were thrown through the windshield in an accident?" The message concludes with the suggestion that a baby, for protection and safety, should be placed in a secured infant seat.

Psychologists say the most effective emotional appeal is one coupled with facts and figures. The emotional appeal attracts audience interest, but logical arguments also are needed.

Persuasive Speaking

Psychologists have found that successful speakers (and salespeople) use several persuasion techniques:

- ◆ **Yes–yes**. Start with points with which the audience agrees to develop a pattern of "yes" answers. Getting agreement to a basic premise often means that the receiver will agree to the logically developed conclusion.

- ◆ **Offer structured choice**. Give choices that force the audience to choose between A and B. College officials may ask audiences, "Do you want to raise taxes or raise tuition?" Political candidates ask, "Do you want more free enterprise or government telling you what to do?"

Snowflake

© 1998 Tom Soucek

Dear Friend,

For polar bear cubs like Snowflake, life starts out as a nearly impossible challenge.

Born with her sister Aurora in the frigid darkness of the Arctic winter, Snowflake weighed only about a pound at birth, the size of a cell phone. For months, she and her sister didn't leave the den where they were born, a small cave that their mother had dug in a snow bank. Helpless, they depended on their mother for the essentials of life — her body warmth and her nutrient-rich milk.

Snowflake and her sister will stay with their mother for more than two years. She will feed them, teach them to hunt, and protect them from predators.

With the fierce maternal protection of her mother, cuddly little Snowflake will grow up to become one of the most awesome animals on Earth.

But now, a looming new threat could cut short the lives of precious little polar bear cubs like Snowflake.

You see, the powerful oil lobby and its political allies in Congress are pushing to open Snowflake's home — the Arctic National Wildlife Refuge — to environmentally destructive oil and gas drilling. The Refuge's coastal plain is America's most important on-shore polar bear nursery, and scientist warn that the habitat destruction, pollution and other impacts of the plan could be deadly to the bears.

That's why I'm asking you to please "adopt" a polar bear cub like Snowflake by joining Defenders of Wildlife today with a contribution of $15 or more.

Defenders of Wildlife is helping lead the fight to save America's greatest wildlife sanctuary for Snowflake and the other wild animals that call it home. But to succeed, we urgently need the help of concerned individuals like you to overcome the enormous money and political clout of the oil lobby.

And we must act now — because politicians are already moving to hand over this unique natural treasure to Big Oil. Congressman Don Young (R-Alaska) — who decorates his office with animal skins — has already introduced legislation to allow drilling. The pristine 19 million-acre Arctic Refuge is the last place in North America where Arctic wildlife is fully protected. And the Refuge's coastal plain, often referred to as "America's Serengeti," is the biological heart of this

(over, please)

Defenders of Wildlife • 1101 Fourteenth Street, N.W. • Room 1400 • Washington, D.C. 20005
www.defenders.org • www.kidsplanet.org

Your continued activism is important. Please call your representatives in Washington to let them know you support the preservation of wildlife and its habitat. You can contact them at 202-224-3121. Thank you.

Successful persuasion by direct mail depends heavily on an eye-catching opening that persuades the recipient to read on rather than toss the letter aside. Letters such as this have a strong emotional appeal and often stir a reader's high concern for a particular situation. The plight of the polar bear has become a potent symbol of the effects of global warming.

◆ **Seek partial commitment**. Get a commitment for some action on the part of the receiver. This leaves the door open for commitment to other parts of the proposal at a later date. "You don't need to decide on the new insurance plan now, but please attend the employee orientation program on Thursday."

◆ **Ask for more, settle for less**. Submit a complete public relations program to management, but be prepared to compromise by dropping certain parts of the program. It has become almost a cliché that a department asks for a larger budget than it expects to receive.

A persuasive speech can either be one-sided or offer several sides of an issue, depending on the audience. A series of 1950s studies by Carl Hovland and his associates at Yale determined that one-sided speeches were most effective with persons favorable to the message, whereas two-sided speeches were most effective with audiences that might be opposed to the message.

By mentioning all sides of the argument, the speaker accomplishes three objectives. First, the speaker is perceived as having objectivity. This translates into increased credibility and makes the audience less suspicious of the speaker's motives. Second, the speaker is treating the audience as mature, intelligent adults. Third, including counterarguments allows the speaker to control how those arguments are structured. It also deflates opponents who might challenge the speaker by saying, "But you didn't consider . . ."

Panel discussions and debates present other problems. Psychologists say the last person on a panel to talk will probably be most effective in changing audience attitudes— or at least be remembered longer by the audience. But it has also been shown that the first speaker sets the standard and tone for the remainder of the discussion. Being first or last is better positioning than being between two presentations.

Useful Findings from Research on Persuasion

Many of the precepts offered in this chapter come from experience and from some level of common sense. Starting with the Office of War Information (see Chapter 2), researchers have also systematically studied persuasion processes. A number of research studies have contributed to a basic understanding of persuasion concepts. Here are some basic ideas from the text *Public Communication Campaigns*, edited by Ronald E. Rice and William J. Paisley, that can be used in public relations practice:

◆ Positive appeals are generally more effective than negative appeals for retention of the message and actual compliance.

◆ Radio and television messages tend to be more persuasive than print, but if the message is complex, better comprehension is achieved through print media.

◆ Strong emotional appeals and fear arousal are most effective when the audience has minimal concern about or interest in the topic.

◆ High fear appeals are effective only when a readily available action can be taken to eliminate the threat.

◆ Logical appeals, using facts and figures, are better for highly educated, sophisticated audiences than strong emotional appeals.

◆ Altruistic need, like self-interest, can be a strong motivator. Men are more willing to get a physical checkup to protect their families than to protect themselves.

◆ A celebrity or an attractive model is most effective when the audience has low involvement, the theme is simple, and broadcast channels are used. An exciting spokesperson attracts attention to a message that would otherwise be ignored.

Propaganda

No discussion of persuasion would be complete without mentioning propaganda and the techniques associated with it.

Garth S. Jowett and Victoria O'Donnell, in their book *Propaganda and Persuasion*, say, "Propaganda is the deliberate and systematic attempt to shape perceptions, manipulate cognitions, and direct behavior to achieve a response that furthers the desired intent of the propagandist." Its roots go back to the 17th century, when the Roman Catholic Church set up the *congregatio de propaganda* ("congregation for propagating the faith"). The word took on extremely negative connotations in the 20th century.

In World Wars I and II, propaganda was associated with the information activities of the enemy. Germany and Japan were sending out "propaganda," whereas the United States and its allies were disseminating "truth." Today, propaganda connotes falsehood, lies, deceit, disinformation, and duplicity—practices that opposing groups and governments accuse each other of employing.

Some have even argued that propaganda, in the broadest sense of the word, also includes the advertising and public relations activity of such diverse entities as Exxon and the Sierra Club. Social scientists, however, say that the word *propaganda* should be used only to denote activity that sells a belief system or constitutes political or ideological dogma.

Advertising and public relations messages for commercial purposes, however, do use several techniques commonly associated with propaganda. The most common are the following:

- **Plain folks**. An approach often used by individuals to show humble beginnings and empathy with the average citizen. Political candidates, in particular, are quite fond of telling about their "humble" beginnings.

- **Testimonial**. A frequently used device to achieve credibility, as discussed earlier. A well-known expert, popular celebrity, or average citizen gives testimony about the value of a product or the wisdom of a decision.

- **Bandwagon**. The implication or direct statement that everyone wants the product or that the idea has overwhelming support; for example, "Millions of Americans support a ban on abortion" or "Every leading expert believes . . ."

- **Card stacking**. The selection of facts and data to build an overwhelming case on one side of the issue, while concealing the other side. The advertising industry says a ban on beer advertising would lead to enormous reductions in network sports programming and a ban on cigarette advertising would kill many magazines.

- **Transfer**. The technique of associating the person, product, or organization with something that has high status, visibility, or credibility. Many corporations, for example, have paid millions to be official sponsors of the 2008 Olympic Games, hoping that the public would associate their products with excellence.

- **Glittering generalities**. The technique of associating a cause, product, or idea with favorable abstractions such as freedom, justice, democracy, and the American way. The White House named its military action in Afghanistan "Enduring Freedom" whereas the Iraqi campaign is called "Operation Iraqi Freedom." And, of course, American oil companies lobby for offshore drilling to keep "America energy independent."

A student of public relations should be aware of these techniques to make certain that he or she doesn't intentionally use them to deceive and mislead the public. Ethical responsibilities exist in every form of persuasive communication; guidelines are discussed at the end of the chapter.

Persuasion and Manipulation

The discussion on previous pages examined ways in which an individual can formulate persuasive messages. The ability to use these techniques often leads to charges that public relations practitioners have great power to influence and manipulate people.

In reality, the effectiveness of persuasive techniques is greatly exaggerated. Persuasion is not an exact science, and no surefire way exists to predict that people or media gatekeepers will be persuaded to believe a message or act on it. If persuasive techniques were as refined as the critics say, all people might be driving the same make of automobile, using the same soap, and voting for the same political candidate.

This doesn't happen because several variables intervene in the flow of persuasive messages. Elihu Katz says the two major intervening variables are selectivity and interpersonal relations; these are consistent with the limited-effects model of mass communication.

For purposes of discussion, the limitations on effective persuasive messages can be listed as (1) lack of message penetration, (2) competing messages, (3) self-selection, and (4) self-perception.

Lack of Message Penetration

The diffusion of messages, despite modern communication technologies, is not pervasive. Not everyone, of course, watches the same television programs or reads the same newspapers and magazines. Not everyone receives the same mail or attends the same meetings. Not everyone the communicator wants to reach will be in the audience eventually reached, despite advances in audience-segmentation techniques. There is also the problem of messages being distorted as they pass through media gatekeepers such as reporters and editors. Key message points often are left out or the context of the message is changed.

Competing Messages

In the 1930s, before much was known about the complex process of communication, it was believed that people received information directly, without any intervening variable. This was called the *bullet theory* or the *hypodermic-needle theory* of communication.

Today, communication experts realize that no message is received in a vacuum. Messages are filtered through a receiver's entire social structure and belief system including often profound influences of opinion leaders and even inexpert acquaintances. Nationality, race, religion, gender, cultural patterns, family, and friends are among the variables that filter and dilute persuasive messages. People receive countless competing and conflicting messages daily. Social scientists say a person usually conforms to the standards of his or her family and friends. Consequently, most people do not believe or act on messages that are contrary to group norms. Figure 9.3 depicts a technique for thinking about all of these influences by grouping them into three layers of knowledge that persuasive messages must penetrate to succeed.

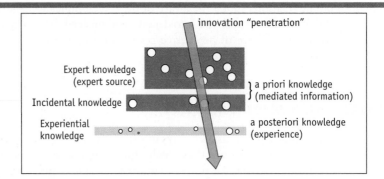

FIGURE 9.3

Penetration of Innovation Model. Professor Mugur Geana at the University of Kansas has developed a model that categorizes competing messages about a topic into three categories: (1) knowledge from experts and opinion leaders, either directly or through mass media; (2) incidental knowledge from media and conversations not considered to be expert opinion; and (3) knowledge from personal experience. The diagram shows how messages can build up until the individual arrives at a decision to change behavior.

Different accumulations of knowledge exist for different layers and their porosity (favorable persuasive effect toward adoption) changes as information from competing messages is accumulated. Adoption, such as trying a new product or deciding to quit smoking, is possible when porosity reaches a critical point.

Source: Glen Cameron.

Self-Selection

The people most wanted in an audience are often the least likely to be there. Vehement supporters or loyalists frequently ignore information and even facts from the other side. They do so by being selective in the messages that they want to hear. They read books, newspaper editorials, and magazine articles and view television programs that support their predispositions. This is why social scientists say that the media are more effective in reinforcing existing attitudes than in changing them.

> What people in PR have to understand is not only do you have the facts on your side, you have to know how to communicate them.
>
> ———*Peter Pitts,* senior vice president of Manning, Selvage & Lee

Self-Perception

Self-perception is the context through which messages are interpreted. People will perceive the same information differently, depending on predispositions and already formulated opinions. A good example is the controversy that erupted in 2006 when a Dubai corporation tried to purchase six U.S. port facilities. Given the "War on Terrorism" and many Americans having a high suspicion of any Arab nation, there was widespread opposition to the sale. It didn't really matter that Dubai was an ally of the United States and that the U.S. Coast Guard, plus other law enforcement agencies, would continue to control security at the ports. In other words, public relations personnel understand that perceptions can matter as much as any facts. See Figure 9.1.

The Ethics of Persuasion

Public relations people, by definition, are advocates of clients and employers. The emphasis is on persuasive communication to influence a particular public in some way. At the same time, as Chapter 3 points out, public relations practitioners must conduct their activities in an ethical manner.

The use of persuasive techniques, therefore, calls for some additional guidelines. Professor Richard L. Johannesen of Northern Illinois University, writing in *Persuasion, Reception and Responsibility*, a text by Charles Larson, lists the following ethical criteria for using persuasive devices that should be kept in mind by every public relations professional:

- Do not use false, fabricated, misrepresented, distorted, or irrelevant evidence to support arguments or claims.

- Do not intentionally use specious, unsupported, or illogical reasoning.

- Do not represent yourself as informed or as an "expert" on a subject when you are not.

- Do not use irrelevant appeals to divert attention or scrutiny from the issue at hand. Among the appeals that commonly serve such a purpose are smear attacks on an opponent's character, appeals to hatred and bigotry, innuendo, and "God" or "devil" terms that cause intense but unreflective positive or negative reactions.

- Do not ask your audience to link your idea or proposal to emotion-laden values, motives, or goals to which it actually is not related.

- Do not deceive your audience by concealing your real purpose, your self-interest, the group you represent, or your position as an advocate of a viewpoint.

- Do not distort, hide, or misrepresent the number, scope, intensity, or undesirable features of consequences.

- Do not use emotional appeals that lack a supporting basis of evidence or reasoning or that would not be accepted if the audience had time and opportunity to examine the subject itself.

- Do not oversimplify complex situations into simplistic, two-valued, either/or, polar views or choices.

- Do not pretend certainty when tentativeness and degrees of probability would be more accurate.

- Do not advocate something in which you do not believe yourself.

It is clear from the preceding list that a public relations professional should be more than a technician or a "hired gun." This raises the issue that public relations personnel often lack the technical and legal expertise to know whether information provided to them by the client or employer is accurate.

Robert Heath makes it clear that this doesn't excuse public relations professionals from ethical responsibility. He writes:

> The problem of reporting information that they cannot personally verify does not excuse them from being responsible communicators. Their responsibility is to demand that the most accurate information be provided and the evaluation be the best available.

Persuasive messages require truth, honesty, and candor for two practical reasons. First, Heath says that a message is already suspect because it is advanced on behalf of a client or organization. Second, half-truths and misleading information do not serve the best interests of the public or the organization.

SUMMARY

What Is Public Opinion?

Public opinion can be difficult to measure; there are few if any issues on which the public (which is in fact many publics) can be said to have a unanimous opinion. In fact, only a small number of people will have opinions on any given issue. Engaging the interest of a public will involve affecting its self-interest. Publics also react strongly to events.

Opinion Leaders as Catalysts

The primary catalyst in the formation of public opinion is public discussion. People who are knowledgeable and articulate on specific issues can be either formal opinion leaders (power leaders) or informal opinion leaders (role models). Opinion "flows" from these leaders to the public, often through the mass media.

Persuasion: Pervasive in Our Lives

The concept of persuasion has been around at least since the time of the ancient Greeks. The dominant view of public relations is of persuasive communications on behalf of clients. Persuasion can be used to change or neutralize hostile opinions, crystallize latent opinions and positive attitudes, and conserve favorable opinions.

Factors in Persuasive Communication

Factors involved in persuasion include audience analysis, source credibility, appeal to self-interest, message clarity, timing and context, audience participation, suggestions for action, content and structure of messages, and persuasive speaking.

Propaganda

Although the roots of the word *propaganda* go back to the 17th century, during the 20th century the word took on extremely negative connotations. During the World Wars, it was associated with the enemies' information activities. It is now used to refer to political or ideological persuasion, with emphasis on deceit and duplicity. Propaganda techniques can be the same as those used in advertising and other public relations messages.

Persuasion and Manipulation

Limitations on effective persuasion include lack of message penetration, competing messages, self-selection, and self-perception.

The Ethics of Persuasion

There are two practical reasons for an ethical approach to persuasive messages. First, publics will automatically have a level of suspicion because they know the communicator is promoting a client or organization. Second, the interests of that client or organization will not be well served by false or misleading communications.

CASE ACTIVITY What Would You Do?

The school system of a major city wants to draw attention to the need for more volunteer adult tutors in the city's 200 public schools. Budget cutbacks in teaching staff and other resources have made it a vital necessity to recruit volunteers who will work with students on an individual basis to improve reading and math skills.

Your public relations firm has volunteered to organize a public information campaign as part of the agency's pro bono services to the community. Drawing on what you have learned about public opinion, as well as both the art and science of persuasion, develop a one-to-two page miniproposal to present to the school system. Focus on how you would propose to put the needs of the school system on the news agenda for your community and how you would develop public relations strategies to shift public opinion toward greater volunteerism.

QUESTIONS for Review and Discussion

1. Public opinion is highly influenced by self-interest and events. What are these concepts?

2. What is the importance of opinion leaders in the formation of public opinion?

3. What theories about mass media effects have relevance for public relations?

4. What are the stages of public opinion in the life cycle of an issue?

5. Name the three objectives of persuasion in public relations work. What objective is the most difficult to accomplish?

6. Can you name and describe the nine factors involved in persuasive communication?

7. What are three factors involved in source credibility?

8. What are the pros and cons of using celebrities for product endorsements?

9. What are the levels of Maslow's hierarchy of needs? Why is it important for public relations people to understand people's basic needs?

10. Why is audience involvement and participation important in persuasion?

11. What techniques can be used to write persuasive messages?

12. Name several propaganda techniques. Should they be used by public relations people?

13. What are some ethical responsibilities of a person who uses persuasion techniques to influence others?

SUGGESTED READINGS

Berger, Bruce K., and Reber, Bryan H. *Gaining Influence in Public Relations: The Role of Resistance in Practice.* Mahwah, NJ: Erlbaum Associates, 2006.

Bush, Michael. "Influencers Drive Audi's U.S. Brand Strategy." *PRWeek,* May 20, 2007, p. 7.

De Burton, Simon. "Fancy a Touch of Star Status: The Relationship Between Brands and Celebrities." *Financial Times,* November 14, 2004, p. 5.

Hallahan, Kirk. "Enhancing Motivation, Ability, and Opportunity to Process Public Relations Messages." *Public Relations Review,* Vol. 26, No. 4, 2000, pp. 463–480.

Hansen-Horn, Tricia, and Neff, Bonita Dostal, *Public Relations: From Theory to Practice.* Boston: Allyn & Bacon, 2007.

Hiebert, Ray E. "Public Relations and Propaganda Framing the Iraq War: A Preliminary Review." *Public Relations Review,* Vol. 29, No. 4, 2003, pp. 243–255.

Kent, Michael L., and Taylor, Maureen, "Beyond Excellent: Extending the Generic Approach to International Public Relations: The Case

of Bosnia." *Public Relations Review,* Vol. 33, No. 1, March 2007, pp. 10–20.

Keller, Ed, and Berry, Jon. *The Influentials: One American in Ten Tells the Other Nine How to Vote, Where to Eat, and What to Buy.* New York: Free Press, 2003.

L'Etang, Jacquie, and Pieczka, Magda. *Public Relations: Critical Debates and Contemporary Practice.* Mahwah, NJ: Erlbaum Associates, 2006.

O'Brien, Keith. "The Court of Public Opinion." *PRWeek,* May 15, 2006, p. 13.

Perloff, Richard M. *The Dynamics of Persuasion,* 2nd ed. Mahwah, NJ: Lawrence Erlbaum, 2003.

Zhang, Juyan, and Cameron, Glen T. "The Structural Transformation of China's Propaganda: An Ellulian Perspective." *Journal of Communication Management,* Vol. 8, No. 3, 2004, pp. 307–321.

CHAPTER 10

Conflict Management: Dealing with Issues, Risks, and Crises

Strategic Conflict Management

Conflict takes many forms, from warfare between nations to spats between teenagers and their parents. Often, conflicts take place in the marketplace of public opinion as opposing groups clash over issues such as gun control, abortion, and immigration reform, or even where Home Depot or Wal-Mart will build a "big-box" store.

Many of these conflicts fall under the purview of public relations. This means that a public relations professional must develop communication strategies and processes *to influence the course of conflicts to the benefit of the organization and, when possible, to the benefit of the organization's many constituents.* Such use of public relations to influence the course of a conflict, and ultimately a crisis, is called *strategic conflict management.* Its key components are:

- Strategic—for the purpose of achieving particular objectives
- Management—planned, deliberate action
- Competition—striving for the same object, position, prize, as others
- Conflict—sharp disagreements or opposition resulting in a direct, overt threat of attack from another entity.

This approach to public relations is more assertive than most definitions, which place an emphasis on building mutually beneficial relationships between the organization and its various stakeholders. Indeed, building relationships is a key objective, but it is part of the larger role for public relations in helping an organization succeed. Professor Glen T. Cameron at the University of Missouri and coauthor of this book, says the management of competition and conflict is indeed more "muscular" public relations. He uses Olympic swimmer Natalie Coughlin (see Photo 10.1) to make his point. She embodies, Cameron says, the preparation, strength, and fair play required to compete against others.

The point is that public relations plays a key role in enabling both profit and nonprofit organizations to compete for limited resources (customers, volunteers, employees, donations, grants, etc.) and to engage in healthy, honest conflict with others who hold different views of what is best and right for society. Achieving these sorts of objectives increases the value of public relations to the organization. It is how public relations professionals earn influence, which leads to greater recognition by top management, increased respect in the field, and, ultimately, a better-paying, more secure position for public relations professionals.

Although competition and conflict are closely related to each other, this book makes a distinction between the two terms. *Competition,* a pervasive condition in life, occurs when two or more groups or organizations vie for the same resources. In business, these "resources" could be sales, share of market, contracts,

Natalie Coughlin embodies the view of public relations as strong and competitive in spirit, yet not macho or underhanded.

employees, and, ultimately, profits. In the nonprofit sector, the competition might be donations, grants, clients, volunteers, and even political influence.

Conflict, on the other hand, occurs when two groups direct their efforts against each other, devising actions and communication that directly or verbally attack the other group. Conflict arises, for example, when labor unions pressure Wal-Mart to unionize, or when the Sierra Club lobbies Home Depot to stop advertising on Fox News because its various commentators dismiss global warming, which is inconsistent with Home Depot's green initiatives. It also occurs when government regulators investigate Steve Jobs, CEO of Apple, for backdating stock options.

Experienced Public Relation experts, however, are quick to point out that many public relations practitioners will spend most of their professional life with fairly moderate levels of competition (such as marketing communications) and perhaps have few, if any, situations that involve conflict. For example, the development director for the Audubon Society may be competing to get donations for a new program from the same donors who are being approached for donations by the Sierra Club. The two professionals may be friends and perhaps one was actually the mentor of the other. On the other hand, a more heightened level of competition might exist between public relations professionals at Wal-Mart, Target, and Costco who compete with each other to increase consumer visibility and retail sales.

Most public relations activity and programs, as already noted, deal with competition between organizations for sales and customers. Conflict, in contrast, deals with attacks and confrontations between organizations and various stakeholders or publics. An example of a conflict, was when Target decided to ban the Salvation Army from collecting donations at its store entrances during the holiday season. The store immediately found itself in conflict with various community groups that charged the store with being a "grinch" and not supporting the needs of the poor and the homeless. Target then had to manage the attacks on the company's charitable spirit, as well as threats to its revenues and a possible consumer boycott.

Admittedly, the distinction between competition and conflict is partly a matter of degree, but also a matter of focus. In competition, the eye is on the prize—such as sales or political support, for example. For conflict, the eye is on the opposition, on dealing with or initiating threats of some sort or another. In either case, professional practice by this definition is vitally important to organizations. It requires a sense of mission and conviction that:

- ◆ Your organization's behavior is honorable and defensible
- ◆ Your organization is ethical
- ◆ Your organization's mission is worthy
- ◆ Your advocacy of the organization has integrity
- ◆ Your organization works at creating mutual benefit whenever possible.

The last point, striving for mutual benefit, is extremely important. It involves balancing the interests of an employer or client against a number of stakeholders. Often, professionals are able to accommodate both the interests of the organization and its various publics. By the same token, organizations may not be able to please all of its publics because there are differences in worldview. Wal-Mart may please labor unions by paying more employee benefits, but consumers who like low prices may object. Environmentalists may want to close a steel plant, but the employees and the local community may be the most avid supporters for keeping the plant open despite its pollution problems. Given competing agendas and issues, the public relations professional will need to look first to the needs of the organization and manage the inevitable conflicts that arise.

The Role of Public Relations in Managing Conflict

The influence of public relations on the course of a conflict can involve reducing conflict, as is often the case in crisis management. At other times, conflict is escalated for activist purposes, such as when antiabortion advocates not only picket health clinics but also assault clients, doctors, and nurses. Other strategies are less dramatic, such as oil industry advocates lobbying to open parts of the Alaskan wilderness to exploration, striving to win approval over time from the public—and, ultimately, Congress.

Indeed, conflict management often occurs when a business or industry contends with government regulators or activist groups that seem determined to curtail operations through what the industry considers excessive safety or environmental standards. At the same time, both the regulatory body and the activists engage in their own public relations efforts to make their case against the company.

A good example is the Canadian fur industry, which lobbied the European Union to defeat a seal-product ban because seal was the "ultimate eco-fabric." The Fur Council of Canada says seal hunting has been part of the country's historic heritage and, despite claims by activist groups, that the seals are killed in a humane way. Opposing groups such as the International Fund for Welfare and the Humane Society of the United States violently oppose seal hunting and are also using public relations tactics to convince legislators and consumers that the practice is cruel and inhumane. An earlier campaign showing photos of baby seals being clubbed to death, with plenty of red blood visible on white ice, convinced the U.S. Congress to ban all seal products more than 30 years ago. (See also the Multicultural box about Wal-Mart and Thai shrimp farmers.)

Professor Jae-Hwa Shin, now a professor at the University of Southern Mississippi, describes this dialogue between multiple parties as the "wrangle in the marketplace of ideas." And much like Olympic swimmers striving in the pool to represent their own interests, this wrangle is inevitable and perfectly acceptable, according to Shin. In fairness, sometimes the event resembles aggressive water polo more than a 100-meter butterfly.

Sometimes, an organization is able to catch a conflict at an early stage and reduce damage to the organization. However, in other cases, an issue may smolder and finally become a major fire. The prison-abuse scandal at Abu Ghraib prison in Iraq is a good example. The Pentagon ignored adverse reports about humiliation of prisoners until the problem eventually became front-page news. Dealing with problems early on is not only more efficient, it is usually the morally right thing to do. The basic concepts of issue and risk management will be discussed shortly.

Unfortunately, most conflict situations are not clear-cut in terms of an ideal solution. In many cases, public relations professionals will not be able to accommodate the concerns of an activist group or a particular public because of many other factors, including the survivability of the organization. KFC, for example, is not going out of the fried-chicken business just because People for the Ethical Treatment of Animals (PETA) is picketing stores because of the inhumane slaughter of chickens. In such cases, public relations professionals have to make tough calls and advocate strictly on

on the job
A MULTICULTURAL WORLD

Managing Conflict: Wal-Mart Wades Into Shrimp Farming

The giant retailer, Wal-Mart, is committed to environmental sustainability, but is finding that even this admirable goal presents problems in competition and conflict. A good example is how Wal-Mart's sustainable policies is in conflict with about 80 percent of the shrimp farms in Thailand, which are small family-owned operations.

The conflict started when the retailer decided, as the largest importer of shrimp in the United States, that only shrimp from Wal-Mart-certified Thai farms would be imported. Certification was given for the farmers who did such things as plant trees, remove contaminants in shrimp ponds with filters before discharging the water, and not use antibiotics in the ponds that would endanger other wildlife.

There's only one problem. The vast majority of Thai farmers cannot afford to upgrade their farms and complete the certification process. As a result, Rubicon Resources, a Los Angeles–based supplier of farmed shrimp to Wal-Mart, has stepped in to buy about 150 Thai farms and upgrade them. The effect is that it has widened the gap between the haves and have-nots in Thai shrimp farming. Thus, the Wal-Mart push for sustainability, although much more environmentally friendly, also favors U.S. corporate-style farming in Thailand at the expense of the family-owned farm.

Adding to the conflict are various environmental groups. Although they say Wal-Mart and the Global Aquaculture Alliance are on the right track, they argue that the standards are too weak and stop short of significant environmental safeguards because the rules for producers are too low.

This case illustrates the point that an organization, even with good intentions, makes policies and decisions that often bring it into conflict with some segment of the population or opposing groups. This is why public relations professionals must be well versed in strategic conflict management and how to deal with multiple publics that are affected in different ways by corporate actions.

behalf of their organization. How they decide what stand to take is the subject of the next section.

It Depends—A System for Managing Conflict

A public relations professional or team must determine the stance its organization will take toward each public or stakeholder involved in the conflict situation. Stance then determines strategy—what will be done and why. The stance-driven approach to public relations began with the discovery that virtually all practitioners share an unstated, informal approach to managing conflict and competition: "It depends."

In other words, the stance taken toward publics "depends" on many factors, which cause the stance to change in response to changing circumstances. Simply put, the outstanding practitioner monitors for threats, assesses them, arrives at a stance for the organization, and then begins communication efforts from that stance.

Practitioners face a complex set of forces that must be monitored and taken into consideration. One approach is the "threat appraisal" model, which is shown in Figure 10.1. Essentially, a threat to an organization requires an assessment of the demands that threat makes on the organization, as well as what resources are available to deal with the threat. An identified threat, for example, forces the public relations

FIGURE 10.1

Threat appraisal model.

Source: Yan Jin and Glen T. Cameron. "The Effects of Threat Type and Duration on Public Relations Practitioner's Cognitive, Affective and Conative Responses to Crisis Situations." *Journal of Public Relations Research,* Vol. 19, No. 3, 2007, p. 256.

professional to consider two major factors. One is *organizational*. Do you have the knowledge, time, finances, and management commitment to combat the threat? The second is *situational*. How do you assess the severity of the danger to the organization? What effort is required by you? Is it a difficult situation with potential for long duration, or is it a relatively simple matter that can be solved fairly quickly? How much is uncertain about the facts or actual situation? Oftentimes, the public relations professional must base decisions on past experience and instinct.

An example of how the threat appraisal model is used in the real world, is how McDonald's reacted when the mayor of Bogota, New Jersey, accused the restaurant chain of racism because it posted a billboard in Spanish to advertise its new iced coffee. He said the company was assuming local Latinos didn't speak English. McDonald's and its public relations firm, MWW Group, had to assess the threat to the company's reputation and how the media and the public (particularly the Hispanic public) would react to the charge of racism.

The appraisal indicated that a response was required, but at a localized level. It based its decision, in part, on researching the background and popularity of the mayor among Hispanics. It found that the mayor himself had distributed Spanish-language campaign materials in the past and he was not particularly popular in the generally Democratic Hispanic community because he was a Republican.

McDonald's then prepared its store managers in the tristate area to handle local media inquiries and also immediately sent backgrounders to editors and reporters about its long history of multicultural programs, including extensive annual scholarship grants to Hispanic students. Many media outlets referenced this information in stories about the controversial billboard, and McDonald's received generally positive coverage. Thus, the issue was short-lived and didn't snowball into a national controversy. Sales of iced coffee even increased 22 percent in the New York metro area.

A more complex threat appraisal involves the $11 billion bottled-water industry, which was also discussed in Chapter 9. The industry is under siege from environmental and consumer advocacy groups who say all those plastic bottles of water are generating greenhouse gases and contributing to global warming. The threat also is increased because water-filter companies such as Brita are capitalizing on the issue by marketing the idea of filtering tap water (with their products, of course) and using reusable bottles. According to Josh Dorfman, an author of environmental books, "Refilling your own personal water bottle with filtered water from the tap requires far less energy and wastes almost no resources relative to bottled water." How the bottled-water companies are managing this issue will be discussed shortly.

It is important to note that organizations assess threat in different ways. Films about industries are an example. In the case of Leonardo DiCaprio's film, *Blood Diamond*, the World Diamond Council spent about $25 million to inform jewelers and consumers that 99 percent of the diamonds on the market were certified as "conflict-free" and the movie didn't reflect the current situation in Africa. Michael Moore's new film *Sicko*, prompted health-care organizations and the pharmaceutical industry to mount a major defense about the misrepresentations in the film. On the other hand, the food industry decided that such films as *Fast-Food Nation* were simply movies and didn't need any proactive public relations initiatives.

It Depends: Two Basic Principles

The threat appraisal model, assessing the seriousness of the threat and the resources needed to combat it, is common in the practice of strategic public relations. The model illustrates the "it depends" approach, but there are two other principles that are important.

The first principle is that many factors determine the stance or position of an organization when it comes to dealing with conflict and perceived threats against one's organization. The second principle is that the public relations stance for dealing with a particular audience or public is dynamic, that is, it changes as events unfold. This is represented by a continuum of stances from pure advocacy to pure accommodation (see Figure 10.2). These two principles, which form the basis of what is called *contingency theory*, are discussed further in the next sections.

A Matrix of Contingency Factors

The public relations approach chosen is contingent on the many factors that professionals must take into account when assessing a threat. Glen Cameron and his colleagues have identified at least 86 contingent variables divided into 11 groups that caused organizations to adopt a particular stance on a conflict. The five external variables were identified as (1) external threats, (2) industry-specific environment, (3) general political/social environment, (4) external public characteristics, and (5) the issue under consideration. The six internal variables were (1) general corporate/organizational characteristics, (2) characteristics of the Public Relation department, (3) top management characteristics, (4) internal threats, (5) personality characteristics of internal, involved persons, and (6) relationship characteristics.

Glen Cameron, Jae-Hwa Shin, and Fritz Cropp at the University of Missouri then conducted a survey of 1,000 members of the Public Relations Society of America (PRSA) to explore what variables affect the stance that public relations professionals take, ranging from more advocacy to more accommodation, with a public regarding an issue in order to accomplish organizational goals.

The survey found that most practitioners reported the major influence of individual-level variables on public relations practice and adopting an organizational stance. This included such contingency variables as (1) individual communication competency, (2) personal ethical values, (3) ability to handle complex problems, (4) ability to recognize potential or existing problems, (5) familiarity with external publics or its representatives.

FIGURE 10.2

Contingency Continuum

This continuum from pure advocacy to pure accommodation forms the foundation for identifying the stance of an organization toward a given public at a given time. The diagram also illustrates how fast-moving public relations can be by showing how some organizations shift positions along the continuum as a conflict evolves.

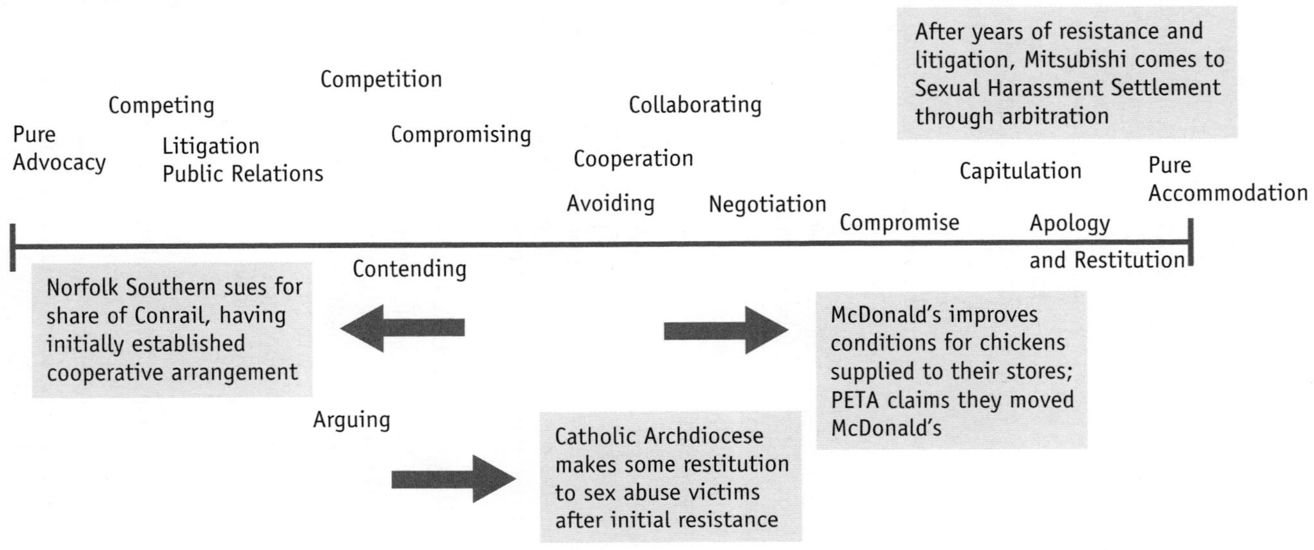

Pure
Advocacy

Competing
Litigation
Public Relations

Competition

Compromising

Collaborating

Cooperation

Avoiding   Negotiation

Compromise

Capitulation

Apology
and Restitution

Pure
Accommodation

Contending

Arguing

Norfolk Southern sues for share of Conrail, having initially established cooperative arrangement

Catholic Archdiocese makes some restitution to sex abuse victims after initial resistance

McDonald's improves conditions for chickens supplied to their stores; PETA claims they moved McDonald's

After years of resistance and litigation, Mitsubishi comes to Sexual Harassment Settlement through arbitration

Note: PR professionals will change stance as events and factors emerge as is indicated in the real life examples.

251

> ❝ Public relations practitioners should understand the…challenges of public relations practice by identifying what constraints they have in their activities and recognizing that their professional qualifications are important assets. ❞
>
> ——— *Jae-Hwa Shin,* University of Southern Mississippi

In other words, the expertise and experience of the public relations professional play a major role in formulating the proper strategy for dealing with a conflict or issue.

Organizational-level variables, however, are also important. Factors affecting the stance of an organization included (1) top management support of public relations, (2) public relations department communication competency, (3) public relations representation in top management, (4) top management's frequency of external contact, (5) the public relations department's perception of the external environment, (6) department funding, and (7) the organization's experience with the public. In other words, the values and attitudes of top management (known as the *dominant coalition*) also has a great influence on how the organization responds to conflict and threats.

In fact, Astrid Kersten of LaRoche College in Pittsburgh wrote in a *Public Relations Review* article that the organization's everyday culture and operations highly influences how organizations respond to conflict. She observes, however, that organizations often aren't very realistic in analyzing situations.

> What appears to us as rational and real is determined by the organizational culture we exist within and the economic and political reality that structures that culture. Conflict and crisis often reinforces organizational dysfunction. In times of uncertainty and danger, the organization reverts to denial, ritual, and rigidity and invokes its own version of reality as a basic defense against external evidence or attack.

The Contingency Continuum

The matrix, or list of possible variables, that influence an organization's response is helpful in understanding inputs into the complex decision-making process. Depending on circumstances, the attitudes of top management, and the judgment of public relations professionals, such factors may move the organization toward or away from accommodation of a public.

The range of response can be shown on a continuum from pure advocacy to pure accommodation (see Figure 10.2). Pure advocacy might be described as a hard-nosed stance of completely disagreeing or refuting the arguments, claims, or threats of a competitor or a group concerned about an issue. Later in the chapter, for example, the conflict management of Pepsi is examined when it was claimed that used syringes were found in cans of its product. In this case, Pepsi took the stance that such claims were a hoax and stood 100 percent behind its product, resisting suggestions that a product recall was needed.

The other extreme of the continuum is pure accommodation. In this case, the organization agrees with its critics, changes its policies, makes restitution, and even makes a full public apology for its actions. The example given in the chart is Mitsubishi. After years of resistance and litigation, it capitulated and settled a class-action suit regarding sexual harassment. Another good example of pure accommodation is Odwalla, which is also discussed later in the chapter. In this case, after it was found that a problem in production caused food poisoning of customers, it immediately issued a product recall, offered to pay all medical expenses of the victims, and made a full apology to the public.

There are other stances along the continuum that an organization can take. Norfolk Southern railroad, for example, used litigation public relations to shift stockholder opinion concerning an offer to take over Conrail. The Catholic Church is in the middle of the continuum as it copes with ongoing accusations of sexual misconduct by its priests. Various archdioceses finally moved from pure advocacy (denial of a problem) to cooperation and negotiation by making restitution to sex abuse victims after their initial resistance. Another part of the continuum is compromise; KFC improved condition for chickens supplied to their stores as a result of complaints by the animal rights group, PETA.

The key point about the continuum is that it identifies the stance of an organization toward a given public at a given time. It also shows the dynamism of strategic conflict management. In many cases, an organization will initially adopt a pure advocacy stance but, as the situation changes, new information comes to light, and public opinion shifts, the stance will change toward more accommodation. A variation of this continuum is also used to portray how organizations respond to a crisis situation, which is discussed on pages 263–264.

The Conflict Management Life Cycle

Much of what has been presented so far involves functions and processes for managing competition and conflict for one's organization. The concept of assessing the degree of threat, and its potential harm to the organization, has been discussed. Threat appraisal requires extensive knowledge, experience, and expertise on the part of a public relations professional in order to make correct assessments that will help the organization correctly manage the situation. And finally, a chart was presented showing how an organization's stance can be placed on a continuum from pure advocacy to pure accommodation.

Another way of understanding the entire conflict management process is to depict it as a life cycle for a problem or issue that professionals must track. Figure 10.3 shows the *Conflict Management Life Cycle* and includes numerous techniques that public relations people use to deal with conflict. Typically, events move in time from left to right though the four phases of the life cycle. At the end of the cycle, persistent issues will require that the process begins all over again on the left side of the cycle.

The conflict management life cycle shows the "big picture" of how to manage a conflict. Strategic conflict management can be divided into four general phases, but bear in mind that the lines between the phases are not absolute and that some techniques overlap in actual practice. Furthermore, in the exciting world of public relations, busy practitioners may be actively managing different competitive situations as well as conflicts in each of the four phases simultaneously. To better understand the conflict management life cycle, each phase will be briefly explained.

Proactive Phase

The proactive phase includes activities and thought processes that can prevent a conflict from arising or from getting out of hand. The first step in the phase is *environmental scanning*—the constant reading, listening, and watching of current affairs with an eye to the organization's interests. As issues emerge, *issues tracking* becomes more focused and systematic through processes such as the daily clipping of news stories. *Issues management* occurs when the organization makes behavioral changes or creates strategic plans in ways that address the emerging issue. In the proactive phase, well-run organizations will also develop a general *crisis plan* as a first step in preparing for the worst—an issue or an event that has escalated to crisis proportions.

FIGURE 10.3

The cycle of conflict depicts the four phases in conflict management experienced by public relations professionals. The cycle also includes a few examples of actual situations and how they arrayed on the contingency continuum.

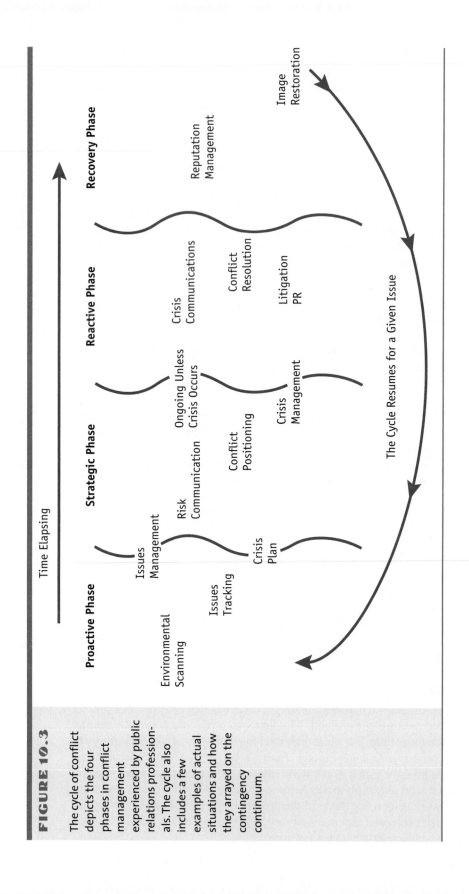

Strategic Phase

In the strategic phase, an issue that has become an emerging conflict is identified as needing concerted action by the public relations professional.

Three broad strategies take place in this phase. Through *risk communication*, dangers or threats to people or organizations are conveyed to forestall personal injury, health problems, and environmental damage. This risk communication continues so long as the risk exists or until the risk escalates into a crisis. *Conflict-positioning* strategies enable the organization to position itself favorably in anticipation of actions such as litigation, boycott, adverse legislation, elections, or similar events that will play out in "the court of public opinion." To be prepared for the worst outcome—that is, an issue that resists risk communication efforts and becomes a conflict of crisis proportions—a specific *crisis management plan* is developed for that particular issue.

Reactive Phase

Once the issue or imminent conflict reaches a critical level of impact on the organization, the public relations professional must react to events in the external communication environment as they unfold.

Crisis communications include the implementation of the crisis management plan as well as the hectic 24/7 efforts to meet the needs of publics such as disaster victims, employees, government officials, and the media. When conflict has emerged but is not careening out of control, conflict resolution techniques are used to bring a heated conflict, such as collapsed salary negotiations, to a favorable resolution. The public relations practitioner may employ strategies to assist negotiation or arbitration efforts to resolve conflict.

Often, the most intractable conflicts end up in the courts. Litigation public relations employs communication strategies and publicity efforts in support of legal actions or trials (see Chapter 12 for details on legal obligations in public relations).

Recovery Phase

In the aftermath of a crisis or a high-profile, heated conflict with a public, the organization should employ strategies either to bolster or repair its reputation in the eyes of key publics.

Reputation management includes systematic research to learn the state of the organization's reputation and then taking steps to improve it. As events and conflicts occur, the company responds with actions and communication about those actions. Poorly managed issues, excessive risk imposed on others, and callous responses to a crisis damage an organization's reputation. When this damage is extreme, *image restoration* strategies can help, provided they include genuine change by the organization.

Processes for Managing the Life Cycle

Not only do public relations practitioners face the challenge of addressing different conflicts in different phases of the life cycle, but no sooner do they deal with a conflict than the cyclical process starts over again for that very same issue. Environmental scanning is resumed to ensure that the conflict does not reemerge as an issue. Although challenging, conflict management is not impossible. Systematic processes described in the next sections of this chapter provide guidance and structure for this highly rewarding role played by public relations professionals in managing competition and conflict.

Those processes include (1) issues management, (2) risk communications, (3) crisis management, (4) and reputation management.

Issues Management

Essentially, *issues management* is a proactive and systematic approach to (1) predict problems, (2) anticipate threats, (3) minimize surprises, (4) resolve issues, and (5) prevent crises. Martha Lauzen, a professor at San Diego State University, says that effective issues management requires two-way communications, formal environmental scanning, and active sense-making strategies.

Another definition of issues management has been formulated by Coates, Coates, Jarratt, and Heinz in their book *Issues Management: How You Can Plan, Organize, and Manage for the Future.* They say, "Issues management is the organized activity of identifying emerging trends, concerns, or issues likely to affect an organization in the next few years and developing a wider and more positive range of organizational responses toward the future."

The basic idea behind issues management is *proactive planning*. Philip Gaunt and Jeff Ollenburger, writing in *Public Relations Review*, say, "Issues management is proactive in that it tries to identify issues and influence decisions regarding them before they have a detrimental effect on a corporation." See the Insights box on page 257 for a matrix on how to evaluate an issue's importance.

Gaunt and Ollenburger contrast this approach with crisis management, which is essentially reactive in nature. They note, "Crisis management tends to be more reactive, dealing with an issue after it becomes public knowledge and affects the company." In other words, active planning and prevention through issues management can often mean the difference between a noncrisis and a crisis, or, as one practitioner put it, the difference between little or no news coverage and a page-one headline. This point is particularly relevant because studies have shown that the majority of organizational crises are self-inflicted, because management ignored early warning signs.

The issue of the exploitation of women and children in Third World factories by American companies, for example, simmered for several years before it finally broke into the headlines after a worker activist group publicly accused Nike of using "sweatshop" labor to make its expensive and profitable athletic shoes and apparel.

Such revelations put the entire U.S. garment industry on the defensive. David Birenbaum, a consultant to the garment industry, wrote in the *Wall Street Journal* that the issue of using cheap Third World labor was not really new, but the public reaction to such practices was different. He wrote in an op-ed article:

> What's changed is that for the first time human rights concerns could become a major marketing issue. . . . More and more importers are now considering safety and other conditions in Asian factories. Few can afford not to, because all it takes is one disaster to damage a label's reputation.

All of the publicity and public outrage, however, might have been avoided if the various clothing and athletic shoe manufacturers had paid attention to the concept of issues management.

Public relations counselors W. Howard Chase and Barrie L. Jones were among the first practitioners to specialize in issues management. They defined the process as consisting of five basic steps: (1) issue identification, (2) issue analysis, (3) strategy options, (4) an action plan, and (5) the evaluation of results. The following is an illustration of how these steps could have been used by the garment industry.

on the job INSIGHTS

An Issues Management Matrix

Issues management involves assessing an issue and determining its importance to the organization. The Milwaukee-based firm of Bader Rutter & Associates uses the following matrix to rate issues on their potential to affect a client's business. For example, if an issue gets a 10 on its potential impact on the business and an 8 on the client's ability to influence the outcome, it will fall into the upper-right-hand quadrant of the matrix, meaning it should be a high priority.

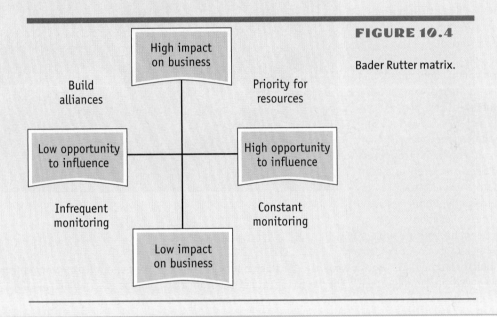

FIGURE 10.4

Bader Rutter matrix.

High impact on business

Build alliances

Priority for resources

Low opportunity to influence

High opportunity to influence

Infrequent monitoring

Constant monitoring

Low impact on business

Issue Identification

Organizations should track the alternative press, mainstream media, online chat groups, blogs, and the newsletters of activist groups to learn what issues and concerns are being discussed. Of particular importance is establishing a trend line of coverage. Concern about the working conditions of women and children in the garment industry began showing up as an emerging issue several years before the Kathie Lee Gifford exposé.

Issue Analysis

Once an emerging issue has been identified, the next step is to assess its potential threat to the organization. Another consideration is to determine whether the organization is vulnerable on the issue. Are its policies exploitative? Is the company being ethical and socially responsible by turning a blind eye to violations of human rights in the interest of high profit margins? Can revelations about sweatshop conditions affect sales or damage a label's reputation? Another ethical dilemma is posed by Home Depot in the Insights box on page 258.

on the job ETHICS

Issue Management: Home Depot Tries to Build a Store

The building and opening of "big-box" stores increasingly is a controversial issue in many local communities. Local store owners fear lower prices at such stores will kill their business, but other issues also emerge such as charges of racism.

Home Depot, for example, met opposition when it announced that it planned to build a store in Sunland, a suburb of Los Angeles. The company also decided, after conducting some issue analysis, that elements of community opposed the store because there was a fear that the store would attract scores of predominantly immigrant day laborers. These allegations of racism by Home Depot became the subject of a Los Angeles City Council meeting that quickly erupted into arguments over race and immigration as the council met to consider revoking the building permit or requiring the company to submit an environmental impact study before proceeding.

Local opponents denied Home Depot's racism argument and said it was simply a matter of preferring another large-scale retailer such as Macy's that, reported the *Los Angeles Times*, sells "socks instead of sockets." Joe Barrett, a prop designer for feature films, was quoted in the newspaper saying, "They (Home Depot) manufacture support, and

Supporters of a Home Depot proposal to open a Sunland store wore T-Shirts provided by the company at Los Angeles.

they manufactured this racism thing. They're trying to detract from the real story, and that is traffic and all their trucks."

What Barrett was referring to were allegations by local opponents that Home Depot bused in Latinos to create the illusion of community support. A Home Depot spokesperson said the company did not pay supporters to attend the council meeting, but did acknowledge that it took them to and from the meeting and furnished them with Home Depot T-shirts saying "Thank You Home Depot." However, the *Los Angeles Daily News* posted on its

Web site a leaked memo from the company's public relations firm that detailed how more than $24,000 was spent recruiting, feeding, clothing, and busing crowds from Sunland and adjacent communities to City Hall to express their support for the store.

What do you think about Home Depot's approach to this issue? Was it ethical to frame the conflict as a racist issue in the community? What about recruiting and paying individuals to attend the City Council meeting to support the building of the store? Do you think this is ethical? Why or why not?

Strategy Options

If the company decides that the emerging issue is potentially damaging, the next step is to consider what to do about it. One option might be to set higher standards for foreign contractors seeking the company's business. Another option: Work with human rights groups to monitor possible violations in foreign factories that produce the company's products. A third option might be to establish a new policy that would ensure that Third World workers receive decent pay and health benefits. The pros and cons of each option are weighed against what is most practical and economical for the company.

Action Plan

Once a specific policy has been decided on, the fourth step is to communicate it to all interested publics. These may include consumers, the U.S. Department of Labor, labor unions and worker activist groups, company employees, and the financial community. The action may be an opportunity to use the new policy as a marketing tool among consumers who make buying decisions based on a company's level of social responsibility.

Evaluation

With the new policy in place and communicated, the final step is to evaluate the results. Has news coverage been positive? Have activist groups called off product boycotts? Have the working conditions for women and children in the factories improved? Is the company being positioned as an industry leader? Have public perceptions of the company and the industry improved? If the company has acted soon enough, perhaps the greatest measurement of success is avoiding the media coverage that occurs if the problem becomes a crisis.

Issues Management and the Bottled-Water Industry

Issues and situations can be managed or even forestalled by public relations professionals before they become crises or before their conflictual nature leads to significant losses for the organization.

In the case of the bottled-water industry previously mentioned, the issue of being ecologically responsible has already hit the mainstream press so the industry has started to consider strategy options and formulate an action plan. In terms of strategy, Nestlé, which owns such brands as Arrowhead, has rolled out a lightweight bottle that uses 30 percent less plastic and a paper-saving label that is 30 percent smaller. Coca-Cola has redesigned bottles for its Dasani brand to reduce the use of raw materials by 30 percent.

Pepsi's Aquafina began to acknowledge that its water inside originates from the tap, and has also reduced the weight of its bottles by 40 percent. All these innovations are communicated to the public via public relations, advertising, and marketing in the hope that consumers will give the industry credit for being "green" and also continue to drink bottled water.

Strategic Positioning and Risk Communication

Following upon issues management is strategic positioning. Any verbal or written exchange that attempts to communicate information that positions the organization favorably regarding competition or an anticipated conflict is called *strategic positioning*. Ideally, the public relations professional is not only communicating in a way that positions the organization favorably in the face of competition and imminent conflict, but is also influencing the actual behavior of the organization favorably. For example, facing enormous financial losses and the need to lay off thousands of employees, General Motors announced that it was freezing executive salaries. Doing so reduced the level of criticism for layoffs of employees that followed.

Often, a public relations professional can engage in communication that may reduce risk for affected publics and for his or her employer. Communication regarding risk to public health and safety and the environment are particularly important roles for public relations professionals. (See Chapter 20, Nonprofit Organizations, for more on health communication as an important risk communication field in public relations.) The risk may be naturally occurring, such as undertows and riptides on beaches that require warning signs and flyers in hotel rooms. Or the risk may be associated with a product, such as over-the-counter drugs or a lawn mower.

Organizations, including large corporations, increasingly engage in risk communication to inform the public of risks, such as those surrounding food products, chemical spills, radioactive waste disposal, or the placement of drug-abuse treatment centers or halfway houses in neighborhoods. These issues deserve public notice in fairness to the general populace. Such risks may also result in expensive lawsuits, restrictive legislation, consumer boycotts, and public debate if organizations fail to disclose potential hazards. As is often the case, doing the right thing in conflict management is also the least disruptive in the long run.

> " You need to be upfront, direct and very proactive. The louder they send out this message, the better it is for the brand. "
>
> —— *Allen Adamson,* managing director of Landor Associates, a brand consultancy firm, commenting on Mattel's toy recall

Product recalls, in particular, require doing the "right thing." Toy-making giant Mattel, Inc. had two recalls practically back-to-back. In July 2007, it recalled one million Fisher-Price toys after it found excessive levels of lead paint in such dolls as Dora, Big Bird, and Elmo. A week later, Mattel recalled about nine million Chinese-made toys that contained magnets that could be swallowed by children or could have lead paint. In general, experts gave Mattel high marks for providing full information about the recall and the possible dangers to children. (Also, see the Ethics box in Chapter 12 about Mattel.)

In contrast, RC2, the manufacturer of Thomas trains, recalled 1.5 million of its Chinese-made toys with a single announcement and no follow-up. Company executives didn't answer media inquiries, and crisis experts criticized the company for not assuring customers that they were aggressively addressing the problem. The company also received additional unfavorable international publicity when a *New York Times* reporter wrote several stories about being detained and harassed at RC2's Chinese factory for nine hours when he tried to interview its management. One story was titled, "My Time as a Hostage, And I'm a Business Reporter." China, the source of all these recalled toys, also has what is called a "PR problem." See the PR Casebook box on page 270 about China's efforts to restore its reputation.

Other risk communication efforts have mixed success. A somewhat unsuccessful risk communication was the 2003 "mad cow scare" in Canada. Despite assurances by Canadian health officials and the beef industry that the fatal cow disease posed an "extremely small" risk to consumers, many countries stopped buying Canadian beef, severely damaging the Canadian cattle industry and driving up beef prices worldwide.

In contrast, Jeff Zucker of Burson-Marsteller points out that U.S. cattlemen have worked for years to get the message out that U.S. beef is the safest in the world. Thus, the discovery of a possibly infected cow in Washington State did not result in dire consequences for U.S. producers. Risk communication can minimize adverse effects on publics, but it also often reduces risk—of lawsuits, of damaged morale in the organization, and of diminished reputation—to the organization itself. When risk communication fails, however, the organization often faces a crisis.

Variables Affecting Risk Perceptions

Risk communication researchers have identified several variables that affect public perceptions:

◆ Risks voluntarily taken tend to be accepted. Smokers have more control over their health situation, for example, than airline passengers do over their safety.

◆ The more complex a situation, the higher the perception of risk. Disposal of radioactive wastes is more difficult to understand than the dangers of cigarette smoking.

◆ Familiarity breeds confidence. If the public understands the problem and its factors, it perceives less risk.

◆ Perception of risk increases when the messages of experts conflict.

◆ The severity of consequences affects risk perceptions. There is a difference between having a stomachache and getting cancer.

Suzanne Zoda, writing on risk communication in *Communication World*, gives some suggestions to communicators:

◆ Begin early and initiate a dialogue with publics that might be affected. Do not wait until the opposition marshals its forces. Vital to establishing trust is early contact with anyone who may be concerned or affected.

◆ Actively solicit and identify people's concerns. Informal discussions, surveys, interviews, and focus groups are effective in evaluating issues and identifying outrage factors.

◆ Recognize the public as a legitimate partner in the process. Engage interested groups in two-way communication and involve key opinion leaders.

◆ Address issues of concern, even if they do not directly pertain to the project.

◆ Anticipate and prepare for hostility. To defuse a situation, use a conflict-resolution approach. Identify areas of agreement and work toward common ground.

◆ Understand the needs of the news media. Provide accurate, timely information and respond promptly to requests.

◆ Always be honest, even when it hurts.

Crisis Management

In public relations, high-profile events such as accidents, terrorist attacks, disease pandemics, and natural disasters can dwarf even the best strategic positioning and risk management strategies. This is when crisis management takes over. The conflict management process, which includes ongoing issues management and risk communication efforts, is severely tested in crisis situations in which a high degree of uncertainty exists.

Unfortunately, even the most thoughtfully designed conflict management process cannot have a plan in place for every situation. Sometimes, in spite of risk communication to prevent an issue from becoming a major problem, that issue will grow into a crisis right before the professional's eyes. At such times, verifiable information about what is happening or has happened may be lacking. This causes people to become more active seekers of information and, as research suggests, more dependent on the media for information to satisfy the human desire for closure.

A crisis situation, in other words, puts a great deal of pressure on organizations to respond with accurate, complete information as quickly as possible. How an organization responds in the first 24 hours, experts say, often determines whether the situation remains an "incident" or whether it becomes a full-blown crisis.

What Is a Crisis?

Kathleen Fearn-Banks, in her book *Crisis Communications: A Casebook Approach*, writes, "A crisis is a major occurrence with a potentially negative outcome affecting the organization, company, or industry, as well as its publics, products, services, or good name."

In other words, an organizational crisis can constitute any number of situations. A *PRWeek* article makes the point:

> Imagine one of these scenarios happening to your company: a product recall; a plane crash; a very public sexual harassment suit; a gunman holding hostages in your office; an E. coli bacteria contamination scare; a market crash, along with the worth of your company stock; a labor union strike; a hospital malpractice suit . . .

Often, management tends to minimize or deny there's a crisis. However, there is a crisis if the organization's stakeholders—customers, vendors, employees, or even local community leaders—perceive the situation to be a crisis. JetBlue's management, for example, didn't particularly think it was a crisis when it cancelled hundreds of flights in the wake of 2007's Valentine's Day snowstorm that left thousands of passengers stranded for days and even kept passengers sitting on a runway in one plane for 10 hours. The airline failed to keep passengers (let alone employees) informed and didn't even bother to post updates on its Web site. The result was thousands of irate passengers and a deluge of 5,000 media inquiries, for which the airline was totally unprepared. In terms of agenda-setting and framing theory, as discussed in Chapter 9, the media often frame a situation as a crisis for the organization. And, as more than one pundit has stated, "Perception is reality."

Nor are crises always unexpected. One study by the Institute for Crisis Management (www.crisisexperts.com) found that only 14 percent of business crises were unexpected. The remaining 86 percent were what the Institute called "smoldering" crises in which an organization was aware of a potential business disruption long before the public found out about it. The study also found that management—or in some cases, mismanagement—caused 78 percent of the crises. In fact, a study by Weber Shandwick public relations with KRC Research found that the top three triggers for a crisis was (1) financial irregularites, (2) unethical behavior, and (3) executive misconduct.

"Most organizations have a crisis plan to deal with sudden crises, like accidents," says Robert B. Irvine, president of the institute. "However, our data indicates many businesses are denying or ducking serious problems that eventually will ignite and cost them millions of dollars and lost management time." With proper issues management and conflict planning, perhaps many of the smoldering crises could be prevented from bursting into flames.

A Lack of Crisis Planning

Echoing Irvine's thought, another study by Steven Fink found that 89 percent of the chief executive officers of *Fortune* 500 companies reported that a business crisis was almost inevitable; however, 50 percent admitted that they did not have a crisis management plan.

This situation has caused Kenneth Myers, a crisis consultant, to write, "If economics is the dismal science, then contingency planning is the abysmal science." As academics Donald Chisholm and Martin Landry have noted, "When people believe that because nothing has gone wrong, nothing will go wrong, they court disaster. There is noise in every system and every design. If this fact is ignored, nature soon reminds us of our folly."

Many "smoldering" crises can be prevented if professionals use more environmental scanning and issues management, leading to the development of a strategic management plan. A common crisis planning technique is rating both the "probability" of a particular crisis and its "impact" on the organization. A fire at a Mattel toy factory, for example, would probably receive a "2" rating for probability, and a similar score for impact because the company has multiple suppliers. On the other hand, the probability of unsafe products might be a "3" but rank as a "5" in terms of impact on the company because public trust would be eroded and sales would drop.

How to Communicate During a Crisis

Many professionals and books offer good checklists on what to do during a crisis. Here's a compilation of good suggestions:

- Put the public first.
- Take responsibility. An organization should take responsibility for solving the problem.
- Be honest. Don't obscure facts and try to mislead the public.
- Never say, "No comment." A Porter Novelli survey found that nearly two-thirds of the public feel that "no comment" almost always means that the organization is guilty of wrongdoing.
- Designate a single spokesperson.
- Set up a central information center.
- Provide a constant flow of information. When information is withheld, the cover-up becomes the story.
- Be familiar with media needs and deadlines.
- Be accessible.
- Monitor news coverage and telephone inquiries.
- Communicate with key publics.

Strategies for Responding to Crises

The list just presented offers sound, practical advice, but recent research has shown that organizations don't all respond to a crisis in the same way. Indeed, W. Timothy Coombs postulates that an organization's response may vary on a continuum from defensive to accommodative, which is similar to the contingency continuum explained on page 251. Coombs' list of crisis communication strategies that an organization may use:

- **Attack the accuser**. The party that claims a crisis exists is confronted and its logic and facts are faulted. Sometimes a lawsuit is threatened.
- **Denial**. The organization explains that there is no crisis.
- **Excuse**. The organization minimizes its responsibility for the crisis. Any intention to do harm is denied, and the organization says that it had no control over the events that led to the crisis. This strategy is often used when there is a natural disaster or product tampering.
- **Justification**. Crisis is minimized with a statement that no serious damage or injuries resulted. Sometimes, the blame is shifted to the victims, as in the case of the Firestone tire recall. This is often done when a consumer misuses a product or when there is an industrial accident.
- **Ingratiation**. Actions are taken to appease the publics involved. Consumers who complain are given coupons or the organization makes a donation to a charitable organization. Burlington Industries, for example, gave a large donation to the Humane Society after the discovery that it had imported coats from China with fur collars containing dog fur instead of coyote fur.
- **Corrective action**. Steps are taken to repair the damage from the crisis and to prevent it from happening again.
- **Full apology**. Organization takes responsibility and asks forgiveness. Some compensation of money or aid is often included.

The Coombs typology gives options for crisis communication management depending on the situation and the stance taken by the organization. He notes that organizations do have to consider more accommodative strategies (ingratiation, corrective action, full apology) if defensive strategies (attack accuser, denial, excuse) are not effective. The more accomodative strategies not only meet immediate crisis communication demands but can help subsequently in repairing an organization's reputation or restoring previous sales levels. He says, "Accommodative strategies emphasize image repair, which is what is needed as image damage worsens. Defensive strategies, such as denial or minimizing, logically become less effective as organizations are viewed as more responsible for the crisis."

> **When a public relations practitioner is involved in a crisis situation, external and long-term threats lead to the most severe consequences.**
>
> ——— *Yan Jin*, Virginia Commonwealth University

Often, however, an organization doesn't adopt an accommodative strategy because of corporate culture and other constraints included in the contingency theory of conflict management matrix. Organizations do not, and sometimes cannot, engage in two-way communication and accommodative strategies when confronted with a crisis or conflict with a given public. Some variables proscribing accommodation, according to Cameron, include: (1) management's moral conviction that the public is wrong; (2) moral neutrality when two contending publics want the organization to take sides on a policy issue; (3) legal constraints; (4) regulatory constraints such as the FTC or SEC; (5) prohibition by senior management against an accommodative stance; and (6) possible conflict between departments of the organization on what strategies to adopt.

In some cases, the contingency theory contends that the ideal of mutual understanding and accommodation doesn't occur because both sides have staked out highly rigid positions and are not willing to compromise their strong moral positions. For example, it is unlikely that the pro-life and pro-choice forces will ever achieve mutual understanding and accommodation. At other times, conflict is a natural state between competing interests, such as oil interests seeking oil exploration in Alaskan wildlife refuges and environmental groups seeking to block that exploration. Frequently, one's stance and strategies for conflict management entail assessment and balancing of many factors.

How Some Organizations Have Handled Crises

The crisis communication strategies outlined by Coombs are useful in evaluating how an organization handles a crisis. Intel, for example, first denied that there was a problem with its Pentium chip after some users reported the chip was not performing mathematical calculation, correctly. As the crisis deepened and was covered in the mainstream press, Intel tried the strategy of justification by saying that the problem wasn't serious enough to warrant replacing the chips. It minimized the concerns of end users such as engineers and computer programmers. Only after considerable damage had been done to Intel's reputation and IBM had suspended orders for the chip did Intel take corrective action to replace the chips, and Andy Grove, Intel's president, issued a full apology.

Exxon, still highly identified with the major oil spill in Prince William Sound, Alaska, also chose a defensive strategy when one of its ships, the *Exxon Valdez*, hit a reef in 1989 and spilled nearly 240,000 barrels of oil into a pristine environment. The disaster, one of history's worst environmental accidents, was badly mismanaged from the beginning.

Exxon management started its crisis communication strategy by making excuses. Management claimed that Exxon, as a corporation, wasn't at fault because (1) the weather wasn't ideal, (2) the charts provided by the U.S. Coast Guard were out of date, and (3) the captain of the ship was derelict in his duties by drinking while on duty. As clean-up efforts began, Exxon also tried to shift the blame by maintaining that government bureaucracy and prohibitions against the use of certain chemicals hampered the company's efforts.

Exxon also used the strategy of justification to minimize the damage, saying that environmentalists in the government were exaggerating the ill effects of the spill on bird and animal life. Meanwhile, negative press coverage was intense, and public outrage continued to rise. William J. Small of Fordham University, who researched the press coverage, wrote, "Probably no other company ever got a more damaging portrayal in the mass media." More than 18,000 customers tore up their Exxon credit cards, late-night talk show hosts ridiculed the company, and congressional committees started hearings. Exxon dropped from eighth to 110th on *Fortune*'s list of most-admired companies.

Exxon's response to all of these developments was somewhat ineffective. It did try the strategy of ingratiation by running full-page advertisements stating that the company was sorry for the oil spill—but did not take responsibility for it. Instead of calming the storm, that approach only further enraged the public. Exxon also took corrective action and cleaned up the oil spill, spending about $3 billion in its efforts. The company received little credit for this action, however, because most of the public believed it was done only under government pressure. And by the time the cleanup was finished, public attitudes about Exxon had already been formed.

It is important to note, however, that not all successful crisis communication strategies need to be accommodative. Pepsi-Cola was able to mount an effective defensive crisis communication strategy and avoid a recall when a hoax of nationwide proportions created an intense but short-lived crisis for the soft-drink company. (Also, see the

on the job INSIGHTS

Wendy's and the Fickle Finger of Fate

Restaurants and other food suppliers are particularly vulnerable to a crisis of major proportions when their products cause sickness and even death. In addition, reputation and sales can be seriously affected when the crisis is triggered by a hoax.

Wendy's restaurants was the victim of such a hoax in 2005 when Anna Ayala found a human finger (about 1.5 inches long with a nicely manicured nail) in her bowl of beef chili at a Wendy's in San Jose, California. She hired a lawyer and sued. The situation was so bizarre that the incident generated front-page news in the San Francisco Bay Area and then went national. As more than one observer noted, it was a perfect media story because of the high "gross-out" factor.

Wendy's, in the glare of extensive media coverage, had to act swiftly.

Its strategy was to (1) conduct due diligence to establish that the brand was not at fault, (2) ensure Wendy's core values drove all decisions and response, (3) brief and mobilize employees as the crisis developed, and finally, (4) build a postincident strategy to enhance Wendy's brand.

Due diligence required the restaurant chain to determine how a finger could get in a bowl of chili. The chain checked its local employees, and all of them had ten fingers. Its food vendors were also checked, and it was established that the meat in the chili came to the restaurants in only ground-up form. Once this was established, Wendy's offered a $100,000 reward for positive identification of the finger and opened a hotline to receive tips. Police also started to investigate. If there was a finger, was there a body somewhere?

The mystery of the finger and how it got into the chili could not be answered immediately, which is often the case in a crisis situation. In the meantime, Wendy's restaurants in the San Francisco area lost 20 to 50 percent of their business in the first month after the incident. The chain's other 6,600 restaurants nationally also experienced a decline in sales as a result of the continuing media coverage and even the comments of late-night talk show hosts. Jay Leno, for example, opened one monologue with, "I didn't know Wendy's sold finger food."

The alleged victim, Anna Ayala, was also on the media circuit. She even appeared on ABC's *Good Morning America* to tell her story. Wendy's public relations staff tried to dissuade ABC from doing the interview and, when that failed, the public relations staff prepared a company statement read on the air saying that the finger did not enter the food chain in its ingredients. They decided that a statement would be better than a Wendy's representative appearing on air with the woman because it would position the company as a big corporation picking on a poor victim.

Two months after the incident, which was still getting media coverage because of the police investigation, the case began to break. First, it was found that the alleged victim had also filed at least six lawsuits against other companies claiming unsafe products. Second, police found the owner of the missing finger, a coworker of Ayala's husband, who lost the finger in an industrial accident. He sold the finger to the husband for $loo. It didn't take long to figure out who put the finger in the chili.

Police arrested Ayala for her hoax and charged her with attempted grand theft stemming from the fact that Wendy's had lost millions because of her actions. The husband was also arrested for conspiracy to file a false insurance claim and attempted grand theft. Both pleaded guilty; Anna Ayala received 9 years in

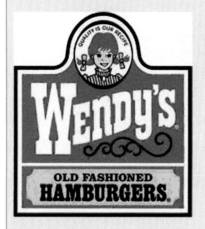

prison and her husband received 12 years. In addition, both were ordered to pay $170,000 for the lost wages of Wendy's employees and another $21.3 million to Wendy's. The chances of collecting such a large amount were about zero, so the company agreed to not collect if the couple never benefited from the situation through a book or movie deal.

Wendy's, being vindicated, began its fourth strategy of rebuilding its reputation and customer loyalty. It offered free Frosties and coupons to customers, and gave away almost 18 million of them in one weekend to thank customers for their loyalty.

Source: Adapted from Kathleen Fearn-Banks Crisis Communications: A Casebook Approach, 3rd ed., Mahweh, NJ: Lawrence Erlbaum Associates, 2007.

Insights on page 266 about Wendy's finger-in-the-chili hoax.) The crisis began when the media reported that a man in Tacoma, Washington, claimed that he had found a syringe inside a can of Diet Pepsi. As the news spread, men and women across the country made similar claims of finding a broken sewing needle, a screw, a bullet, and even a narcotics vial in their Pepsi cans. As a consequence, demands for a recall of all Pepsi products arose, an action that would have had major economic consequences for the company.

Company officials were confident that insertion of foreign objects into cans on the high-speed, closely controlled bottling lines was virtually impossible, so they chose to defend their product. The urgent problem, then, was to convince the public that the product was safe, and that any foreign objects found had been inserted after the cans had been opened.

Company officials and their public relations staff employed several strategies. One approach was to attack the accuser. Pepsi officials said the foreign objects probably got into the cans after they were opened, and even explained that many people make such claims just to collect compensation from the company. The company also announced that it would pursue legal action against anyone making false claims about the integrity of the company's products.

Pepsi also adopted the strategy of denial, saying that there was no crisis. Pepsi president Craig E. Weatherup immediately made appearances on national television programs and gave newspaper interviews to state the company's case that its bottling lines were secure. Helping to convince the public was U.S. Food and Drug Administration commissioner David Kessler, who said that a recall was not necessary.

These quick actions deflated the public's concern, and polls showed considerable acceptance of Pepsi's contention that the problem was a hoax. A week after the scare began, Pepsi ran full-page advertisements with the headline, "Pepsi is pleased to announce . . . Nothing." It stated, "As America now knows, those stories about Diet Pepsi were a hoax. . . . "

These varied cases illustrate one emphasis of contingency theory: No single crisis communication strategy is appropriate for all situations. Therefore, as Coombs indicates, "It is only by understanding the crisis situation that the crisis manager can select the appropriate response for the crisis."

Reputation Management

Reputation is defined as the collective representation of an organization's past performance that describes the firm's ability to deliver valued outcomes to multiple stakeholders. Put in plain terms, reputation is the track record of an organization in the public's mind.

Public relations scholar Lisa Lyon makes the point that reputation, unlike corporate image, is owned by the public. Reputation isn't formed by packaging or slogans. A good reputation is created and destroyed by everything an organization does, from the way it manages employees to the way it handles conflicts with outside constituents.

The Three Foundations of Reputation

Reputation scholars offer three foundations of reputation: (1) economic performance, (2) social responsiveness, and (3) the ability to deliver valuable outcomes to stakeholders. Public relations plays a role in all three foundations, but professionals who manage conflict effectively will especially enhance the latter two foundations of reputation. The social responsiveness of an organization results from careful issue tracking and effective positioning of the organization. It is further enhanced when risk communication is compelling and persuasive. The ability to make valuable contributions to stakeholders who depend on the organization results in part from fending off threats to the organization that would impair its mission.

Research techniques called *reputation audits* can be used to assess and monitor an organization's reputation. These can be as basic as *Fortune* magazine's list of "Most Admired Companies" (www.fortune.com/fortune/mostadmired) to rigorous global reputation measures, such as the Reputation Quotient offered by the Reputation Institute (www.reputationinstitute.com) in conjunction with Harris Interactive. Of particular interest to public relations professionals is the Media Reputation Index (MRI), which measures the effects of media coverage on corporate reputations. Working with Delahaye Medialink, the project documents the important role of media in reputation management. This relationship is depicted in Figure 10.5.

In addition to tracking and dealing proactively with issues, conveying risks to publics, and managing crises as they arise, public relations practitioners also will be

FIGURE 10.5

This diagram shows many of the forces affecting corporate reputation, most notably, how media coverage and performance of an organization impact reputation and, in return, how reputation influences the health of the organization.

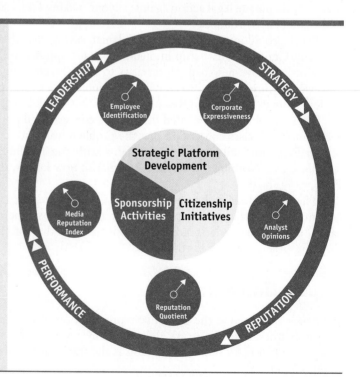

faced with the need to apologize when all efforts to manage conflict have fallen short. The future trust and credibility of the organization are at stake in how well this recovery phase of conflict management is handled.

The frequent platitude in postcrisis communication is that practitioners should acknowledge failings, apologize, and then put the events in the past as quickly as possible. However, Lyon has found that apology is not always effective because of the hypocrisy factor. When an organization has a questionable track record (i.e., a bad reputation), the apology may be viewed as being insincere and hypocritical. Coombs suggests a relational approach, which assumes that crises are episodes within a larger stakeholder–organizational relationship. Applying the contingency theory, considering how stakeholders perceive the situation can help communicators determine which strategy is best to rebuild the stakeholder–organization relationship and restore the organization's reputation.

Image Restoration

Reputation repair and recovery is a long-term process, and the fourth phase in the conflict management life cycle called the recovery phase. Research by Burson-Marsteller public relations, for example, found that it takes about three years for an organization to recover from a crisis that damages their reputation. The survey of 685 business influentials also found that quickly disclosing the details of a scandal or corporate misstep should be management's number-one strategy as it begins the process of restoring reputation.

Other strategies used by executives to recover reputation were, in descending order, (1) make progress/recovery visible, (2) analyze what went wrong, (3) improve governance structure, (4) make CEO and leadership accessible to the media, (5) fire employees involved in the problem, (6) committ to high corporate citizenship standards, (7) carefully review ethics policies, (8) hire outside auditors for internal audits, and (9) issue an apology from the CEO.

Professor William Benoit of the University of Missouri offers a more academic model, listing five general strategies for image restoration and a number of substrategies, adding to the options available to the public relations professional that can be used when the worst of a crisis has passed:

1. Denial
   - Simple denial—Your organization did not do what it is accused of.
   - Shift the blame—Someone else did it.
2. Evade responsibility
   - Provocation—Your organization was provoked.
   - Defeasibility—Your organization was unable to avoid its actions.
   - Accident—The bad events were an accident.
   - Good intentions—Good intentions went awry.
3. Reduce offensiveness
   - Bolstering—Refer to the organization's clean record and good reputation.
   - Minimization—Reduce the magnitude of negative feelings.
   - Differentiation—Distinguish the act from other similar, but more offensive, acts.
   - Transcendence—Justify the act by placing it in a more favorable context.

PRCASEBOOK

China Moves to Renovate Its Reputation

Nations, as well as corporations, often find themselves doing a crash course in reputation management. China, as a result of mounting criticism by Western nations about fake goods and the safety of its exports, took steps to bolster its image in mid-2007 after an unusual number of Chinese-made goods were recalled in Europe and the United States for safety reasons.

The products were everything from poisonous chemicals in pet food to faulty tires and millions of toys painted with toxic lead paint. The federal Consumer Products Safety Commission (CPSC; www.cpsc.gov) reported that the number of recalls for Chinese products had doubled in the past five years to 467 in 2006, an annual record. The CPSC also reported that China was responsible for about 60 percent of all recalls compared to 36 percent in 2000. Part of this is explained by the fact that China is also responsible for making about 70 to 80 percent of the toys sold in the United States.

The various recalls received considerable media coverage and also the concern of the European Union (EU) and the U.S. Congress. Legislators held hearings on food safety and some members even called for legislation to curtail Chinese imports. Chinese officials were concerned that, unless something was done to reassure Western governments and consumers, the mounting criticism

A toy factory in China.

could lead to sanctions and embargoes on Chinese goods around the world. Such situation would directly affect China's booming economy.

High-ranking Chinese officials decided that the best way to restore its reputation was to announce a series of bold moves to (1) improve food safety standards, (2) tighten controls on chemicals used by seafood and meat producers, and (3) create a system holding producers more accountable for selling unsafe goods. In a more dramatic move that underscored the seriousness of its commitment, the government executed the former head of the State Food and Drug agency for accepting bribes and failing to police the marketplace.

The government also sought the advice of several U.S.-based public relations firms that specialized in crisis management. One firm was Ogilvy PR/China, which advised officials to abandon China's traditional secrecy and be more upfront about any product deficiencies in order to restore confidence in its products. Scott Kronick, president of Ogilvy PR/China, told the *New York Times*, "What we do ... is help officials understand the global climate within which they are communicating and then share with them best practices on how to address the situation."

The advice seemed to work. Chinese officials became less adversarial and actually moved on the contingency continuum (page 251) from an advocacy and defensive position to the middle in terms of compromise and cooperation. Chinese officials began to give more news conferences and updates about efforts to improve product safety. They even admitted that 20 percent of its consumer goods and 14 percent of its tires for export failed safety inspections. Officials also are giving quarterly reports on product reforms to the European Union and posting updates on the Web sites of its embassies.

Some critics, however, remain skeptical. They doubt China has the capability to improve standards and police itself. Such pledges in the past have not been fulfilled. In fact, one concern of reputation experts is that China might make a big show of reform, but then go back to old practices once international pressure subsides.

In such a case, the country's reputation would become even more tarnished.

Reputation management also will be needed for the 2008 Beijing Olympics. The Chinese know the world spotlight is on them and they will be under intense international scrutiny. At the same time, the Chinese government traditionally has been intolerant of any political demonstrations, which often occur at such events. But heavy-handed policing will draw negative press and unnerve the International Olympic Committee and corporate sponsors. Ogilvy's Kronick told Chinese officials that the public understands that disaffected groups will demonstrate at public events. Therefore, he advised Chinese officials, "What you need to worry about is what your response is going to be and how you will act."

- ◆ Attack the accuser—Reduce the credibility of the accusations.
- ◆ Compensation—Reduce the perceived severity of the injury.
4. Corrective action—Ensure the prevention or correction of the action.
5. Mortification—Offer a profuse apology.

Benoit's typology for image restoration is somewhat similar to the Coombs list on page 264 about how organizations should respond to a crisis. Both scholars outline a response continuum from defensive (denial and evasion) to accommodation (corrective action and apology).

The image restoration strategy that an organization chooses depends a great deal on the situation, or what has already been described as the "it depends" concept. If an organization is truly innocent, a simple denial and presentation of the facts is a good strategy. However, not many situations are that clear-cut. Consequently, a more common strategy is acknowledging the issue, but making it clear that the situation was an accident or the result of a decision with unintended consequences. Benoit calls this the *strategy of evading responsibility*. Benoit lists six response strategies—all the way from bolstering by telling the public about the organization's good record to compensation for the victims. Ultimately, the most accommodative response is a profuse apology by the organization to the public and its various stakeholders.

The Benoit and Coombs continuums give a tool chest of possible strategies for dealing with a crisis or beginning image restoration, but it should be noted that a strategy or a combination of strategies may not necessarily restore reputation. A great deal depends on the perceptions of the public and other stakeholders. Do they find the explanation credible? Do they believe the organization is telling the truth? Do they think the organization is acting in the public interest? In many cases, an organization may start out with a defensive strategy only to find that the situation ultimately demands corrective action or an apology in order to restore its reputation.

Déjà vu—All Over Again

Empirical evidence from Benoit's work is ongoing, but it appears that image restoration can be an effective final stage in the conflict management process. But to paraphrase Yogi Berra, conflict management is like déjà vu all over again. The best organizations, led by the best public relations professionals, will strive to improve performance by starting once again along the left side of the conflict management life cycle on page 254 with tasks such as environmental scanning and issues tracking. Issues that are deemed important receive attention for crisis planning and risk communication. When preventive measures fail, the crisis must be handled with the best interests of all parties held in a delicate balance. Reputation then must be given due attention. At all times, the goal is to change organizational behavior in ways that minimize damaging conflict, not only for the sake of the organization, but also for its many stakeholders.

Indeed, the true value and the highest professionalism requires that students today also embrace their roles as managers of competition and conflict. Outstanding and successful public relations professionals must serve as more than communication technicians carrying out the tactics of organizing events, writing news releases, handling news conferences, and pitching stories to journalists. They also must take on the responsibility of managing conflict and weathering the inevitable crises that all organizations face at one time or another.

SUMMARY

A New Way of Thinking

By defining public relations as strategic management of competition and conflict, a fresh and vigorous approach to public relations is envisioned. Public relations is positioned to earn influence within organizations by focusing on achieving objectives.

Contingency Theory of Conflict Management

Some of the most crucial roles played by public relations professionals involve the strategic management of conflict. The contingency theory argues for a dynamic and multifaceted approach to dealing with conflict in the field.

Life Cycle of Conflict Management

Strategic conflict management can be broadly divided into four phases with specific techniques and functions falling into each phase. The life cycle emphasizes that conflict management is ongoing and cyclical in nature.

Issues Management

Issues management is a proactive and systematic approach to predict problems, anticipate threats, minimize surprises, resolve issues, and prevent crises. The five steps in the issues management process are issue identification, issue analysis, strategy options, an action plan, and the evaluation of results.

Risk Communication

Risk communication attempts to convey information regarding risk to public health and safety and the environment. It involves more than the dissemination of accurate information. The communicator must begin early, identify and address the public's concerns, recognize the public as a legitimate partner, anticipate hostility, respond to the needs of the news media, and always be honest.

Crisis Communication

The communications process is severely tested in crisis situations, which can take many forms. A common problem is the lack of crisis management plans even when a "smoldering" crisis is building. Organizations' responses may vary from defensive to accommodative. Corporate culture and other constraints may prevent adoption of an appropriate strategy.

Reputation Management

One of an organization's most valuable assets is its reputation. This asset is impacted by how the organization deals with conflict, particularly those crises that generate significant media attention. Using research to monitor reputation and making realistic responses after crises have passed can minimize damage to an organization's reputation. More important, returning to the proactive phase of conflict management to improve organizational performance will ultimately improve reputation.

CASE ACTIVITY   What Would You Do?

"Save Darfur" is the rallying cry of many human rights groups who say the government of Sudan is supporting a brutal guerrilla campaign against villagers of the Darfur region, where an estimated 200,000 have already died in the violence. Even the U.S. government has labeled the civil violence genocide.

One tactic that groups are using to put pressure on the Sudan regime to stop the violence is a campaign to have universities and state-employee pension funds divest of any holdings in companies that do business with Sudan. To date, six states have passed legislation to do just that and another 12 states are considering divestment legislation.

American corporations have already been barred from operating in Sudan since 1997, but dozens of multinational corporations market products or services in Sudan. You're the director of public relations for a state pension system and human rights groups are now pressuring your employer to divest from any companies doing business with Sudan. The director of the pension fund tells you that adopting such a policy would "severely hamper our ability to construct an effective, adequately diversified international equity portfolio if we had to divest from such companies as Alcatel and Siemens."

This is a classic case of conflict management and how to assess the strategies outlined on the contingency continuum on page 251. Would you recommend that the pension fund take an advocacy stance and defend the right to invest funds for the maximum benefit of its retirees? Or do you think that the pension fund should move to more accommodative strategies such as negotiation and compromise? Or, given the situation in Darfur, recommend that the pension fund capitulate to the demands of the human rights groups and voluntarily divest? Or would you recommend simply waiting to determine what the legislature might do in this situation? Explain your reasoning.

QUESTIONS for Review and Discussion

1. Do you accept the proposition that conflict management is one of the most important functions of public relations? Why or why not?

2. Why is it important to understand the concept of doing a threat appraisal? How would you go about doing one?

3. What are the five steps in the issues management process?

4. How can effective issues management prevent organizational crises?

5. Both Exxon and Pepsi used defensive crisis communication strategies. However, one succeeded and the other failed. What factors do you think made the difference?

6. What is risk communication?

7. Mattel, Inc. had to recall millions of toys made in China because they were unsafe. Why do you think this is a form of risk communication? Or should it be considered more of a crisis for the company?

8. What is the bottled-water industry doing about criticism that it's not "green" enough? Do you think the bottled-water industry is responding to criticism in a positive way?

9. A number of strategies have been outlined for responding to a crisis. Can you give a summary of the major strategies and in what kinds of situations they would be used?

10. How would you use the contingency theory of conflict management (the continuum from accommodation to advocacy) in advising management on a rising conflict situation?

11. Do you think that image restoration is merely a superficial fix or a substantive solution to adverse events? Support your view with some examples from current news stories.

12. The PR Casebook on page 270 discusses China's effort to improve its reputation after numerous product recalls. How do you assess its efforts?

13. What is your opinion of how China is handling being host to the Olympics? Do you think they followed the concepts of effective conflict management and reputation management? Why or why not?

SUGGESTED READINGS

Barboza, David. "China Moves to Refurbish a Damaged Global Image." *New York Times*, July 29, 2007, p. A9.

Barboza, David, and Story, Louise. "Train Wreck: The Company That Recalled Thomas Learns about Crisis Management." *New York Times*, June 19, 2007, pp. C1, 4.

Benoit, William L. "Image Repair in President Bush's April 2004 News Conference." *Public Relations Review*, Vol. 32, 2006, pp. 137–143.

Cho, Sooyoung, and Cameron, Glen T. "Public Nudity on Cell Phones: Managing Conflict in Crisis Situations." *Public Relations Review*, Vol. 32, 2006, pp. 199–201.

DeVries, David S., and Fitzpatrick, Kathy R. "Defining the Characteristics of a Lingering Crisis: Lessons from the National Zoo." *Public Relations Review*, Vol. 32, 2006, pp. 160–167.

Fearn-Banks, Kathleen. *Crisis Communications: A Casebook Approach.* Mahwah, NJ: Lawrence Erlbaum, 3rd ed., 2007.

Fombrun, Charles J., and van Riel, Cees. *Fame and Fortune: How Successful Companies Build Winning Reputations.* Upper Saddle River, NJ: Financial Times Prentice Hall, 2003.

Jin, Yan, and Cameron, Glen T. "The Effects of Threat Type and Duration on Public Relations Practitioner's Cognitive, Affective, and Conative Responses in Crisis Situations." *Journal of Public Relations Research*, Vol. 19, No. 3, 2007, pp. 255–281.

Kersten, Astrid. "Crisis as Usual: Organizational Dysfunction and Public Relations." Public Relations Review, Vol. 31, 2006, pp. 544–549.

King, Granville. "Image Restoration: An Examination of the Response Strategies Used by Brown and Williamson After Allegations of Wrongdoing." *Public Relations Review*, Vol. 32, 2006, pp. 131–136.

Martin, Ryan M., and Boynton, Lois A. "From Liftoff to Landing: NASA's Crisis Communications and Resulting Media Coverage Following the *Challenger* and *Columbia* Tragedies." *Public Relations Review*, Vol. 31, 2005, pp. 253–261.

McGuire, Craig. "Assembling a Crisis Management Toolkit." *PRWeek*, July 25, 2005, p. 18.

Nolan, Hamilton. "The New Crisis Landscape: When Crisis Hits, People Expect Answers Before all the Facts Are Known." *PRWeek*, February 19, 2007, p. 12.

Lukaszewski, James E. "Crisis Communications Models: Smooth Crisis Situations With Systematic Response Mechanisms." *Public Relations Tactics*, July 2006, p. 10.

Pang, A., Jin, Y., and Cameron, G. T. "Do We Stand on Common Ground? A Threat Appraisal Model for Terror Alerts Issued by the Department of Homeland Security." *Journal of Contingencies and Crisis Management*, Vol. 14, No. 2, 2006, pp. 82–96.

Shin, Jae-Hwa, and Cameron, Glen T. "Different Sides of the Same Coin: Mixed Views of Public Relations Practitioners and Journalists for Strategic Conflict Management." *Journalism and Mass Communications Quarterly*, Vol. 82, No. 2, 2005, pp. 318–338.

Shin, Jae-Hwa, Cameron, Glen T., and Cropp, Fritz. "Occam's Razor in the Contingency Theory: A National Survey on 86 Contingent Variables." *Public Relations Review*, Vol. 32, 2006, pp. 282–286.

Reaching a Multicultural and Diverse Audience

Diverse and Multicultural Nature of the Public Relations Audience

If the audience on which public relations practitioners focus their messages were a monolithic whole, their work would be far easier—and far less stimulating. The audience, in fact, is just the opposite: It is a complex intermingling of groups with diverse cultural, ethnic, religious, and economic attributes whose interests coincide at times and conflict at others.

> " All marketing efforts are wasted if they aren't culturally competent. "
>
> —— *Michael Soon Lee*, president of EthnoConnect

For example, many readers of this text would generalize that chronic disease such as arthritis and diabetes are facts of life for the baby boomer generation, born between 1946 and 1964 and now reaching their retirement years. Further, this large block of the population who are over 50 would be considered quite homogenous in terms of health and activity levels. But in conducting strategic research for the Missouri Department of Health and Senior Services, one of the coauthors determined distinct patterns of difference between those over and under age 65. Both subtargets reported in a random survey that they felt very healthy, with a positive outlook. Counterintuitively, the over-65 group lived a healthier lifestyle in many ways—more attention to regular medical checks, preventive screenings, and to daily activity such as walks. Readily available free time and more universal health coverage for the older subgroup make these healthful habits possible. The example points out that monolithic groups probably do not exist and that research on target audiences is crucial for understanding and reaching audiences effectively for any public relations goal.

For the public relations professional, knowledge of these shifting audience dynamics is an essential part of lifelong learning in the field. A successful campaign must be aimed at those segments of the mass audience that are most desirable for its particular purpose, and it must employ those media most effective in reaching them. Some of these segments are more easily identifiable and reachable as "prepackaged publics" because they present themselves as well-organized groups whose members have banded together in a common interest; they constitute ready-made targets for practitioners who have projects of concern to them. Examples of such prepackaged publics are members of civic, educational, and charitable organizations.

For audience segments that do not present themselves as an organized group with a membership list and a clear position on an issue, some generalizations can be made about audiences today:

◆ Diversity is the most significant aspect of the mass audience in the United States. Differences in geography, history, and economy among regions of the sprawling country are striking; ranchers in Montana have different attitudes than residents in the heavily populated Eastern seaboard cities. Yet people in the two areas do have national interests in common. Ethnicity, generational differences, and socioeconomic status also shape the audience segments that public relations practitioners address. For example, the American Heart Association (AHA) provides resources aimed at African American and Latino populations, reflecting differences in culture for each that impact compliance with diet and lifestyle to assure a healthy heart. The Power to End Stroke movement targets African Americans with a strategy to increase a sense of self-efficacy or personal empowerment over one's own health outcomes. Soul Food

Recipes, an AHA-supported publication, facilitates healthy eating habits to reduce the risk of stroke.

◆ The international audience for public relations has expanded swiftly. Growth of global corporations and expanded foreign marketing by smaller firms opens new public relations situations, as does increased foreign ownership of U.S. companies. International audiences are a diverse and significant target for public relations campaigns. For example, Xerox has a Worldwide Strategic PR division that serves markets in countries ranging from Afghanistan to Zimbabwe. Each nation has separate, culturally sensitive public relations initiatives including customer support, crisis management, media relations, and other forms of publicity.

◆ Technology can be used to segment the mass audience and compile related valuable information. Computer and other related technologies can be used to conduct both primary and secondary research to identify target audiences. Geographic and social statistics found in Census Bureau reports provides a rich foundation. Much of this data can be broken down by census tract and ZIP code. Data on automobile registrations, voter registrations, sales figures, mailing lists, and church and organization membership also can be merged into computer databases. One marketing research organization, Claritas Inc., has divided the Chicago metropolitan area into 62 lifestyle clusters. It has assigned a name to each cluster; for example, "Boomers & Babies," whose buying habits, Claritas says, include "rent more than five videos a month, buy children frozen dinners, read parenting magazines." The Internet and other related technogies also enables public relations efforts to be more efficient and effective to reach the audience beyond geographical bounds, but it requires quicker public relations responses to a swiftly changing audience.

◆ The public is increasingly visually oriented and seems to have a shorter attention span. They are often exposed to the dynamic impact of multimedia messages, including Web sites with streaming videos, regularly updated blogs, instant messaging, and Web forums. The enormous impact of television on daily life has increased visual orientation, with many people obtaining virtually all of their news from the television screen. Television news and entertainment programs are presented primarily in pictures at a swiftly changing pace. Such exposure may lead to a shortened attention span for current-events coverage and increased interest in new products. Political leaders' policies reach the public largely in 10-second "sound bites." Television also serves as a potent communicator of manners, mores, and aspirations. *American Idol* and reality shows, for example, have made the dream of becoming famous tangible, if only, as artist Andy Warhol predicted in 1968, for a figurative fifteen minutes.

◆ Audiences are increasingly taking control of information streams. They determine what content will be delivered to them as well as when and where. For example, sports fanatics can have real-time updates of box scores delivered to cell phone screens. Households time-shift evening newscasts using digital recording devices such as TIVO or computers running Windows XP Media Center Edition to watch the "six o'clock news" whenever it is convenient. News and current affairs consumption is increasingly on the go through wireless Web browsing on handheld devices as well as podcast and vodcast at broadband speed to wireless devices. See Chapter 13 for more details on the technology that drives strategy in this chapter for reaching audiences who control and shape media messages to an unprecedented degree.

◆ Fervent support is generated for single issues. Many individuals become so zealously involved in promoting or opposing a single issue that they lose the social and political balance so needed in a country. Such vehement behavior may create severe public relations problems for the objects of their attacks. Animal rights or right-to-life activists frequently have been accused of going too far. For example, in 2004, the New Jersey Grand Jury indicted a militant animal rights group, Stop Huntingdon Animal Cruelty, for demonstrating against the biological research company Huntingdon Life Sciences. Their tactics included physically assaulting workers, firebombing cars, harassing communications, and bomb threats.

   ◆ Heavy emphasis is placed on personality and celebrity. Sports stars, television and movie actors, and rock music performers are virtually worshipped by some fans. When stars embrace causes, some people follow them reflexively. More and more, celebrities are used as spokespersons and fund-raisers, even though their expertise as performers does not necessarily qualify them as experts or opinion leaders for complex issues, such as the environment or world trade. For example, actors such as Richard Gere, George Clooney, and Susan Sarandon are outspoken advocates of political positions, whereas other film stars such as Paul Newman and Robert Redford prefer to work for causes behind the scenes. Actors Ronald Reagan and Arnold Schwarzenegger, and professional wrestler Jesse Ventura, each capitalized on their fame to rise to political office with varying degrees of success.

   ◆ Strong distrust of authority and suspicion of conspiracy can arise from sensationalistic investigative reporting. Especially after Richard Nixon resigned the presidency in the wake of the Watergate scandal, journalists and American news consumers are quick to suspect their leaders of wrongdoing. The unethical business practices of executives at Enron, Tyco, WorldCom, Arthur Andersen, and other large corporations have led to a general distrust of large businesses. With the enormous demands on television news to fill a 24-hour newshole with content, viewers are so inundated with exaggerated political promises, see so much financial chicanery, and are exposed to so much misleading or even contradictory information that many of them distrust what they read and hear. They suspect evil motives, and tend to enjoy gossips and believe rumors. The need for public relations programs to develop an atmosphere of justifiable, rational trust is obvious.

Many of these trends will continue throughout the new century, creating an ongoing need for flexibility and growth among public relations practitioners. The variety and number of employment opportunities in public relations will be fueled in part by these changes in audience characteristics. Professionals who supplement media tactics with strategies to communicate directly with targeted, key constituents will be in high demand. By combining these general principles with the many data sources available from commercial services as well as open source databases provided by government and nonprofit groups, public relations professionals can zero in on key audiences for a communication program.

Public relations has become more research-driven and strategic in practice; audiences are targeted precisely and, in some instances, messages are customized at the individual level. For example, in health-care settings, e-mail messages can be tailored to the individual patient based on his or her most recent examination. Not only can the practitioner target a precise public, but in many cases the professional can actually bypass the media and communicate directly with the target audience. The use of communication channels that reach directly to the audience is called *controlled media*. Using a database, an organization can send letters directly to key decision makers, such as stockholders, for example. The same technique can be used by directing e-mail or broadcast faxes to key constituents in political, environmental, and social action arenas.

Publications directed at employees and customers serve as examples of controlled media. Two of the most effective and popular controlled media are sponsored video and online media.

Reaching Diverse Age Groups

As the demographic makeup of the United States continues to change, three major age groups deserve special attention. They are youth and young adults, baby boomers, and seniors. The following is a brief snapshot of each group.

Youth and Young Adults

Public relations professionals recognize the importance of the youth market. Children and teenagers represent an important demographic to marketers because they influence their parents' buying decisions, have their own purchasing power, and will mature into adult consumers. According to the consumer market research company Packaged Facts, today's youth market (15- to 24-year olds) has over $350 billion of purchasing power.

In a *pr reporter* article, Marianne Friese of Ketchum succinctly stated the importance of the youth audience: "They rival the baby boom in sheer size and their global purchasing power is enormous." Smaller families, dual incomes, and postponing having children until later in life lead to greater disposable income. Likewise, greater attention to the importance of child rearing, advocated on television talk shows, Web sites targeted to parents, self-help books, and magazine articles, combined with advertising messages associating brand loyalty with good parenting have led to increased spending. Guilt can play a role as well. Parents pressed for time may substitute material goods for time spent with children and teenagers.

Today's children have greater autonomy and decision-making power within the family than in previous generations. Children often pester or nag their parents into purchasing items they may not otherwise buy. *Kidfluence*, a 2001 marketing publication, notes how pestering can be divided into two categories—"persistence" and "importance." *Persistence nagging* (a plea that is repeated over and over again) is less sophisticated than *importance nagging*, which appeals to parents' desire to provide the best for their children. Like every new generation before them, these children cause adults to fret about their character but show signs that they, too, will rise to the challenges that come with maturity.

The youth market has often been identified as *Generation Y* (GY), a term used to describe people born after 1980. They succeed *Generation X* (GX) born between 1965 and 1980.

Because they are such voracious consumers of electronic media, some pundits have labeled today's youth and young adult audiences as the *E-Generation*. Both the X and Y generations share this propensity for online pastimes. Their world will be diverse and global in perspective, and, like no previous generation, they will understand world cultures and markets. The Fortino Group (Pittsburgh) projects that the Y generation will spend 23 years online. Spending one-third of their lives online will have interesting impacts:

- They will spend equal time interacting with friends online and in person.
- Initial interaction online will precede most dating and marriages.

- They will spend more time online than in interaction with parents by tenfold.
- They will be more reserved in social skills.
- They will be savvy and skeptical about online identities such as chat participants.
- They will not tolerate print forms, slow application processes, and archaic systems.

Generation Y values relationships and trust. In a survey of 1,200 teens worldwide, Ketchum's Global Brand Marketing Practice found:

- Parents still rule when it comes to advice about careers and drugs, and even for product decisions.
- Trust in information is derived from relationships.
- The top five sources of advice are parents, doctors, clergy, friends, and teachers.
- As avid and skilled Internet users, GY remains savvy about unfiltered and unpoliced content.
- Teens also recognize the credibility of editorial content compared to ads and even public service announcements, with television being the most trusted medium for them.
- Garnering publicity for products and issues will impact GY, whether directed at them or at those to whom they look for advice.

> " Those wishing to be successful in the market can't ignore the boomer numbers, the wealth, and the spending power they have. "
>
> ——— *Pat Conroy,* vice chairman of consumer business practices for Deloitte & Touche accounting firm

Baby Boomers

This age group, born between 1946 and 1964, represents the tidal wave of Americans born after World War II, when thousands of GIs returned home and started raising families. Today, as a large percentage of these men and women begin to add a "6" to their birthdays, they comprise a market of 76 million people, or about 28 percent of the U.S. population. Of this number, 60 million are over age 55.

Baby boomers, unlike their parents' generation, have grown up in an age of prosperity and continue to have few qualms about spending on consumer goods instead of saving for retirement. Because of their wealth and numbers, many corporations and nonprofit groups have taken a keen interest in reaching this market. Toyota, for example, has promoted its Highlander by tailoring communications to baby boomers who now have "empty nests" because their children are in college or have already established their own careers. One ad, for example, emphasizes the message, "For your newfound freedom."

Boomers, now 42 to 60, are maturing and starting to share many of the same concerns as their immediate elders, the seniors, who will be discussed next. In other words, they are naturally concerned about health care, insurance, retirement planning, personal investing, and other issues. Companies such as Procter & Gamble and L'Oreal Paris are also seeing the demand for new beauty products that cater to mature adults who lead active lifestyles and want to look vibrant and healthy, not necessarily younger.

Even the Centers for Disease Control and Prevention (CDC) is tailoring its public service announcements to boomers. One public service announcement (PSA) about colorectal cancer, the second-leading cancer killer in the United States, targeted the 50+ age group with a tailored message about being around for your children and grandchildren. Patricia Cook, vice president of Ogilvy Public Relations Worldwide, who produced the PSA for CDC, told *PRWeek*, "The idea of being there for your children and grandchildren is powerful. Messages about how to stay healthy and enjoy life as long as possible were found to be important to the over 50 age group."

Baby boomers, as a result of growing up in the 1960s and 1970s, also tend to be what is described by one writer as a "rather active, socially conscious bunch." Catherine Welker of Strauss Radio Strategies told *PRWeek*, "Many are parents, voters, retirees, and potentially have disposable income. This is a generation most likely to get involved in a cause." According to the U.S. Census Bureau, about 60 million baby boomers have already reached the age of 55; they are rapidly becoming the new Seniors, which is discussed next.

Seniors

This group frequently is defined as men and women 65 years or older, although some sociologists and marketing experts, including the American Association of Retired Persons (AARP), include everyone over age 50. A typical 50-year-old, in good health and working full-time, usually doesn't quite see himself or herself as a "senior."

Medical advances have improved life expectancy to the point that today almost 36.3 million Americans are age 65 or older (12% of the population), according to the U.S. Census Bureau. A heavy upsurge in the senior population will peak at 50 million (21%) by 2010, when the post–World War II baby boomers begin to reach age 65. These older citizens form an important opinion group and a consumer market with special interests.

When appealing to seniors, public relations people should try to ignore the stereotypes of "old folks" so often depicted in the movies and television. Some 80-year-old women sit in rocking chairs, knitting or snoozing, but others cheer and boo ardently while watching professional basketball on television. Nor are all grandfathers crotchety complainers with quavering voices or kindly patriarchs who fly kites with their grandsons. As many differences in personality, interest, financial status, and living styles exist in the older audience as among their young-adult grandchildren.

Public relations practitioners should remember these characteristics of seniors:

- With the perspective of long experience, they often are less easily convinced than young adults, demand value in the things they buy, and pay little attention to fads.

- They vote in greater numbers than their juniors and are more intense readers of newspapers and magazines. Retirees also watch television heavily.

- They form an excellent source of volunteers for social, health, and cultural organizations because they have time and often are looking for something to do.

- They are extremely health-conscious, out of self-interest, and want to know about medical developments. A Census Bureau study showed that most people over age 65 say they are in good health; not until their mid-80s do they frequently need assistance in daily living.

Financially, the elderly are better off than the stereotypes suggest. The poverty rate among older Americans (9.8%) is slightly below that of the population at large (12.5%). The Census Bureau found that people ages 65 to 74 have more discretionary income than any other group, with median assets of $108,885. In many instances, their homes are completely paid for, and they hold 70 percent of the country's assets.

Although they are poor customers for household goods, they eat out frequently and do much gift buying. They travel frequently. In fact, seniors account for about 80 percent of commercial vacation travel, especially cruises. All public relations personnel working in the restaurant, travel, and tourism industry should be particularly cognizant of this audience and how to effectively communicate with them.

Reaching Racial and Ethnic Groups

Historically, the United States has welcomed millions of immigrants and assimilated them into the cultural mainstream. They bring a bubbling mixture of personal values, habits, and perceptions that are absorbed slowly, sometimes reluctantly. The questions of assimilation—how much, how little?—somewhat pertains to all immigrant groups, whether they are from Ireland, Poland, Cuba, or the Philippines. It also pertains to two minorities that have a long history in the United States: African Americans and Native Americans. This diversity is a great strength of the United States, but also a source of friction and, at times, negative stereotyping.

Recently, the easily identifiable ethnic groups—primarily Hispanics, African Americans, Asian Americans, and Native Americans—as a whole have been growing five times faster than the general population, with nonwhite ethnic groups now comprising a majority in some states. The U.S. Census Bureau predicts that by the year 2010, Hispanics and African Americans will make up 14.6 and 12.5 percent of the U.S. population, respectively, for a total of 27.1 percent, and Anglos 67.3 percent. Asian Americans and Native Americans will provide the remaining percentage. According to the Census Bureau, even greater changes will occur by 2050. Notably, Hispanics will comprise nearly one-fourth of the U.S. population. (See Figure 11.1.)

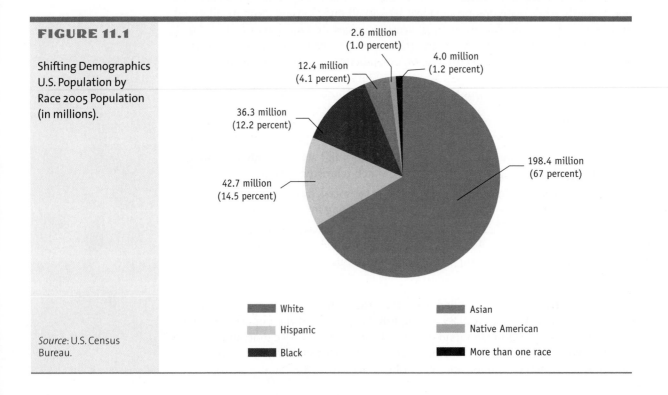

FIGURE 11.1

Shifting Demographics U.S. Population by Race 2005 Population (in millions).

2.6 million (1.0 percent)

4.0 million (1.2 percent)

12.4 million (4.1 percent)

36.3 million (12.2 percent)

42.7 million (14.5 percent)

198.4 million (67 percent)

White
Hispanic
Black
Asian
Native American
More than one race

Source: U.S. Census Bureau.

Such statistics place a strong focus on diversity and multiculturalism in the workplace (internal publics) as well as how public relations and marketing experts communicate with these groups as citizens and consumers. The stakes are high. In terms of disposable income, significant amounts of money are involved. The buying power of Hispanics was estimated at $863 billion in 2007, according to the Selig Center for Economic Growth at the University of Georgia. This represents, says the center, the first year that Hispanics controlled more personal income than any other U.S. minority group. Given the growth of the Hispanic community, some experts predict that their buying power will be in excess of $1 trillion by 2010. African American buying power in 2007 was an estimated $800 billion. Asian Americans have about $600 billion of disposable income, whereas Native Americans—the smallest of the four minority groups—have about $53 billion in buying power, according to the Selig Center.

Hispanic-owned businesses also are multiplying in the United States. These offer new client possibilities, not only for Hispanic-owned firms, but also for general public relations firms that adapt their services to Hispanic needs. A Pew Hispanic Center report showed a 30 percent increase in the number of Hispanic companies in the United States during the five-year period from 1997 to 2002. Further, Hispanics owned 1.6 million firms. The largest share of minority business revenue, however, was earned by Asians, who owned 1.1 million businesses. In general, Asian Americans are the most affluent and well-educated minority group. Of the 14 million Asians in the United States, half of those over age 25 have at least a bachelor's degree and 20 percent have a master's degree or higher. In addition, the median household income is over $65,000. For Indian-Asian Americans, many of whom are in the high-technology industry, the median family income is $69,000, according to the U.S. Census Bureau.

A basic point to remember, however, is that minority populations form many target audiences, not a massive monolithic group whose members have identical interests, education, and income levels. Asian Americans in San Francisco have different cultures and concerns from Hispanics in Miami. To be more precise, even the common terms for minority groups, such as *Asian American*, miss the cultural diversity among that racial group. Indeed, there are 17 major Asian groups and each has its own language and culture. India is a totally different culture than Thailand or China. There are also major cultural and even language differences among the peoples of Mexico, Central America, and even within the 12 nations of South America. All, however, are classified as "Hispanic."

There are even generational differences within each group. For example, the lifestyles, values, and interests of fourth-generation Korean Americans in Los Angeles are dramatically different than those of Koreans who have recently arrived in the United States. Thus, the practitioner must define the audience with particular care and sensitivity, taking into account race but increasingly considering the cultural and ethnic self-identity of many target audience segments. For example, as a mild form of protest against the broad ethnic category, Asian, young people in the United States whose roots go back to India use the long hyphenation: Asian-from-the-subcontinent-of-India as a tongue-in-cheek distinction.

Understanding Cultural Values

Although the sensitive communicator needs to take into consideration the differences in nationality, language, generational differences, and cultural values, there are some general guidelines. Fernando Figueredo, head of the multicultural practice for Porter Novelli, says there are some unique characteristics shared by the top three minority groups—Hispanics, African Americans, and Asian Americans.

on the job
A MULTICULTURAL WORLD

A Cruise Ship Line Builds Brand Affinity With African Americans

African Americans are traveling in greater numbers and the competition for their business is intense. Royal Caribbean International, working with Fleishman-Hillard public relations, decided on a cause-marketing strategy that would benefit the local community.

The format was a free, live art auction series held on docked cruise ships in Los Angeles, Baltimore, and Miami. It showcased art donated by nationally acclaimed African American artists and all proceeds supported summer art programs in those cities for African American teens.

The auctions generated more than $20,000 for local art programs and, at the same time, generated extensive coverage in the African American media. In terms of establishing a brand awareness, 95 percent of the attendees said they were likely to take a Royal Caribbean

A work by an African American artist that was part of the Royal Caribbean's art auction to benefit local art programs for Black teenagers.

cruise. Other African American groups also have inquired about holding charitable events aboard the ships. See a copy of the media advisory sent to the media in Chapter 14, page 377.

Figueredo, writing in *The Strategist*, said, "These include a deep family network with a strong mother or father figure, music, food, religion, and strong bonds between friends and family." He also says that multicultural consumers tend to be more loyal to brands that make an attempt to reach them in ways that are culturally relevant. He continues, "Whether through advertising, in-store promotions, or special festivals and events, reaching consumers in their culture has a strong impact on new and repeat purchases."

A strong community relations program is one way to effectively reach ethnic audiences. Indeed, many major corporations such as McDonald's, Coke, and Pepsi have spent considerable money and time developing community-based programs. Merrill Lynch, for example, reached the affluent Hispanic market in South Florida with a Hispanic art festival. See also the Multicultural box on this page about an African American art auction sponsored by Royal Caribbean Cruises.

Other companies, such as Allstate and American Airlines, have sponsored community-based events during the Asian Lunar New Year celebration that is significant for many Asian cultures. "Marketing to Asians during the Lunar New Year is one of the most important mechanisms for PR pros to recognize, show respect for, and strengthen brand relationships with Asian consumers," says Saul Girlin, executive vice president of K&L marketing services.

Language is also important. Although campaigns in both English and another language are expensive, research shows that the extra effort pays off, in particular, for the Hispanic community. A study by Roslow Research Group, for example, found that messages in Spanish were 61 percent more effective than those just in English. Another study by *Yankelovich Hispanic Monitor* found that 69 percent of Hispanics get more information on a product when it is presented in Spanish. Figueredo, who used these studies in his *Strategist* article, notes that

Proyecto E.R.A.S.E. ALERTA CONTRA EL ASMA
¿Su hijo tiene asma?

Esté alerta ante los siguientes signos para saber si su hijo está en riesgo.

1. Tose mientras duerme
2. Tiene dificultad para respirar o tose continuamente mientras está despierto
3. Hace ruido al respirar mientras está despierto o dormido
4. Falta mucho a la escuela por problemas respiratorios
5. Se cansa fácilmente en la escuela
6. No quiere participar en los deportes o los juegos porque está muy cansado

Asegúrese de que le practiquen pruebas a su hijo y que reciba tratamiento para el asma a través del Proyecto E.R.A.S.E.

This poster, in Spanish, was used by Fleishman-Hillard public relations during its campaign with New York City schools to raise awareness among students and their parents about the symptoms of asthma. In English, the poster is titled, "Asthma Alert: Does your child have asthma?" The entire E.R.A.S.E. campaign is highlighted in Chapter 4.

using Spanish helped build brand awareness and loyalty even for those consumers with strong English-speaking skills. An example of using Spanish in a campaign is the E.R.A.S.E. program in New York City schools, which was highlighted in Chapter 4. See the Insights box on this page.

Figueredo gives five basic concepts that should be considered when developing a communications campaign for multicultural consumers:

1. Organize a team with an inherent understanding of the customs and values of the various demographic groups you are trying to reach.
2. Understand that consumers of diverse cultural backgrounds respond better to messages that are culturally relevant.
3. Remember that consumers of diverse cultural backgrounds are extremely loyal and once your products and services become part of their lives, there is a very good chance you will keep them.
4. Use the primary language of the audience. A large portion of your target audience prefers to communicate in their primary language, even if they also have strong English skills.
5. Use spokespersons who represent the audience. The spokesperson must be able to be a good communicator and be sensitive to the issues that are important to the audience.

Using Ethnic Media

The expanding minority populations have been accompanied by an increase in the number and strength of the media through which messages can be delivered. Spanish-language media, in particular, has dramatically increased in recent years. There are now more than 2,453 unique U.S. Hispanic media outlets, including more

on the job
A MULTICULTURAL WORLD

Paramount Reaches Out to Hispanic Audiences

Although about 25 million Hispanics annually go to the movies, each seeing an average of 10 films a year, the film industry has been slow to produce films tailored to this market.

Paramount Studios, however, sought to address this situation by producing a comedy, *Nacho Libre*, during the summer of 2006. The film features Jack Black as a cook in a Mexican monastery/orphanage who turns to *lucha libre*—Mexico's popular form of pro wrestling—to raise money for the orphans. Shot in Mexico with a local cast and crew, the film costars Mexican telenovela star Ana de la Reguera as Sister Encarnción, Nacho's love interest.

The studio launched an extensive advertising and public relations campaign to promote the movie among Hispanics. It hired a consultant in Hispanic marketing, HM Communications, to focus mainly on the Mexican American market. Although about two-thirds of U.S. Hispanics are of Mexican heritage, one of the "don'ts" of marketing is treating the audience as homogeneous.

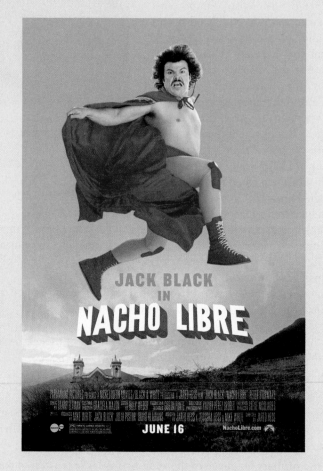

With this in mind, Paramount took Ms. De la Reguera on a media and promotional tour of cities with big Mexican American populations. Her status as a Mexican soap star drew considerable media attention and large audiences in such cities as San Antonio and Dallas.

The film's advertising campaign was segmented to various elements of the Hispanic population. For young males, the ads focused on the more ridiculous, comic moments. For families, they featured the heroic nature of the lead, Nacho. In one poster, orphans surround Nacho. For television, the studio made trailers for Spanish-language networks, including Univision and Telemundo.

Paramount, in selecting other marketing partners, avoided stereotypes such as tie-ins with the American fast-food chain Taco Bell. Julia Pistor, one of the film's producers, told the *Wall Street Journal*, "We didn't want it to be the 'Three Amigos! A Mexican Movie,'" referring to the 1986 Mexican bandit farce starring Steve Martin, Chevy Chase, and Martin Short.

than 1,200 print publications, more than 1,000 television and radio outlets, 200 Internet-only outlets, and 20 AP-style wire services and news syndicates. Three Spanish-language television networks, Univision, Telemundo, and Telefutura, serve millions of viewers on a national level. Major Hispanic newspapers include *La Opinion* (Los Angeles), *El Nuevo Herald* (Miami), and *Diario La Prensa* (New York). On the radio side, there's KSCA (Los Angeles), WCMQ (Miami), and WSKQ (New York). Major Spanish-speaking Web sites include Yahoo!Telemundo.com, QuePasa.com, and Univision.com. See the On the Job box on page 286 about the promotion of the movie *Nacho Libre* to the Hispanic audience.

Radio is an especially important way to reach this ethnic group. Surveys show that the average Hispanic person listens to radio 26 to 30 hours a week, about 13 percent more than the general population. Another Hispanic station in Los Angeles, KLVE-FM, has the largest audience, more than any English-language station.

Television also has a large, rapidly expanding Hispanic audience. The Nielsen rating service in 2004 estimated the number of Hispanic households in the United States with television sets at 10.57 million. Such households are defined as those in which the head of the household is of Hispanic descent. Univision, the predominant Spanish-language Television network, claims to reach three-fourths of Hispanic viewers. Since it signed up to be rated in early 2006, Univision consistently has ranked fourth or fifth among all broadcast networks in the 18–34 demographic according to the Nielsen National Television Index. The Spanish-language television network Telemundo is also making impressive market share gains.

The Asian American press, because of language diversity and culture, also is fairly numerous but highly concentrated. California, for example, is home to 70 percent of the nation's more than 650 Asian American–focused television channels, radio stations, and newspapers. For example, television newscasts on KTSF reaches 82,000 Cantonese speakers each night in the area around San Francisco, a region with a 19.2% Asian population.

The African American media, in contrast, is less robust. One possible reason is that African Americans have a longer history in the United States and English is their native language, as opposed to Hispanics and Asian Americans. Currently, there are only about 175 Black newspapers in the United States, but the Black Entertainment Television Network has a large national audience, as do such magazines as *Ebony* and *Essence*. Yet, a substantial number of possibilities exist for public relations messages for a Black audience, including the Internet. See the PR Casebook on page 296 about a health Web site for the Black community.

Business Wire's "Black PR Wire" lists more than a thousand Black-owned publications, media, and journalists. In addition to this circuit, Business Wire is also able to distribute a news release to all Asian publications in the United States, as well as most Asian nations.

Other specialty distribution firms include U.S. Asian Wire, and the Hispanic PR Wire. Although this book has emphasized the three major minority groups in the United States, it should be noted that there are any number of other foreign-language publications in the United States. The *Gale Directory*, for example, lists publications in 48 languages other than English.

Public relations people should give particular attention to how minorities are portrayed in any communications effort. All Muslims are not terrorists, nor are all Hispanics manual laborers. And all Asians are not rich or techies. A good example of racial insensitivity was the traditional figure of Aunt Jemima on packages of Quaker Oats food products. Her image was widely regarded in the black community

on the job
ETHICS

Don Imus: Racist or Just a Victim of Political Correctness?

It took about eight days in April 2007 for Don Imus to be fired from his talk show on CBS radio, "Imus in the Morning," after he called the Rutgers University women's basketball team a bunch of "nappy-headed hos." The phrase, which most of his two million viewers probably didn't know, contained a racial element, a gender element, and even a class element as it implied that the team (the majority of which were Black) were thuggish and ghetto compared to the winning team in the NCAA championships, the Tennessee Lady Vols.

The National Association of Black Journalists (NABJ) immediately asked for an apology, and Black leaders such as Jesse Jackson and Al Sharpton called for his resignation. Even members of the National Association for the Advancement of Colored People (NAACP) mounted a protest outside NBC headquarters in New York, which simulcast Imus on its MSNBC channel. The media also picked up the story. David Carr, who writes a media column for the *New York Times*, called the remark "the kind of unalloyed racial insult that might not have passed muster on a

low-watt AM station in the Jim Crow South."

Imus apologized for his remark on his show, saying, "Want to take a moment to apologize for the insensitive and ill-conceived remark. Our characterization was thoughtless and stupid, and we're sorry." He also appeared on several other talk shows to apologize and even offered to personally apologize to the Rutgers team. But this time, after years of so-called shock-jock commentary and insulting any number of public figures with coarse language, the apology didn't work. Many critics felt he had stepped over the line by insulting a group of hard-working female Black athletes who had achieved much by coming in second during the NCAA tournament.

CBS first suspended him for two weeks, but events moved even faster. MSNBC decided not to carry Imus, and major advertisers such as Procter & Gamble, General Motors, and American Express decided to pull their advertising from the show on the advice of their public relations counsel. CBS then fired him. His firing, however, ignited a national debate on the use of racial slurs by shock jocks, rap musicians,

Don Imus

comedians, and even politicians. Some DJs called the Imus firing a "witch hunt" that fostered censorship and threatened the expression of free speech. Others said such speech in a democratic society fostering diversity and multiculturalism was unacceptable and Imus deserved to be fired.

What do you think? Should Imus have been fired for his remark? If you were public relations counsel for a large advertiser, would you recommend that the organization cancel its advertising? Why or why not?

as a patronizing stereotype. To change this perception, Quaker Oats cooperated with the National Council of Negro Women to honor outstanding African American women in local communities, who then competed for a national award. At the local award breakfasts, all food served was Aunt Jemima brands, and Quaker Oats officials participated in the programs. The project generated an atmosphere of mutual understanding.

Racial slurs of any kind increasingly are not tolerated by minorities or society in general. See the Ethics box about the firing of talk show commentator Don Imus on page 288.

Other Emerging Audiences

As American society changes, newly defined audiences continually are emerging. Public relations professionals must be aware of emerging audiences and pay attention to them. The following sections deal with four such audiences: evangelical Christian groups, the gay/lesbian community, the disabled, and women.

Catholic and Evangelical Groups

Catholic and evangelical Christian religious groups are growing and bonding together in new constellations. Movies such as *The Passion of the Christ* and *The DaVinci Code* served as a focal point around which such groups expressed their values and concerns. According to Hallmark Cards, the Christian retail market is estimated at $3.75 billion in 2006, up from $2.6 billion in 1991. Sales of books with Christian themes, excluding Bibles, has increased fourfold since 1980, and Christian music now accounts for a 4.8% market share. From a marketing public relations point of view, it is clear that products and services structured around religious themes sell.

The Gay/Lesbian Community

At the opposite end of the sociopolitical spectrum, the gay community shows similar growth as an emerging demographic. According to a yearly census conducted by Jeff Garber, president of OpusComm Group, the SI Newhouse School of Public Communications at Syracuse University, and Scarborough Research, between 22 and 30 million gay, lesbian, bisexual, and transgendered people (GLBT) live in the United States Gay households have a median income of $65,000 per year and typically are highly educated. Witeck-Combs Communications and MarketResearch.com estimate that GLBT individuals spend between $450 and $513 billion per year. Because this figure includes all purchases, it cannot be compared directly to the market for Christian-themed products, but does suggest the buying power of this demographic group.

The Greater Philadelphia Tourism Marketing Corporation (GPTMC), for example, tapped into this buying power when it decided to launch a "Get Your History Straight and Your Nightlife Gay" campaign in order to generate more tourism for the city. It produced a 36-page trip planner for gays. Gay and lesbian media and travel professionals were contacted, news releases were sent to gay/lesbian publications, and two familiarization trips for journalists were done. The campaign got widespread coverage in the gay and mainstream press, including the *Daily Show with Jon Stewart*. The campaign's Web site usage increased 1,000 percent and more than 1,000 hotel packages were sold. For another example of a gay campaign, see the Multicultural box on page 290.

Media targeted to gay and lesbian consumers have grown over the last two decades. Magazines such as *Out* and *Advocate*, and the cable network Logo, focus

on the job
A MULTICULTURAL WORLD

A Real Fairy-Tale Wedding for Gays

In April 2007, Walt Disney Co. announced that gay couples could buy the company's expensive and lavish Fairy-Tale Wedding package, allowing them to exchange vows at Disney's theme parks and on its cruise ships. Disney incurred the wrath of religious conservatives such as the Southen Baptist Convention, which had imposed an eight-year boycott of Disney for its practice of providing health benefits to same-sex partners. The move by Disney acknowledges an increasingly diverse marketplace that requires attention, even though public relations staff must walk a tightrope in attempting to serve varied and often conflicting audiences.

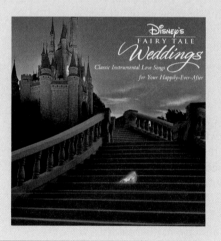

exclusively on gay themes. Mainstream television shows featuring gay themes, such as *Will & Grace* and *Queer Eye for the Straight Guy*, and the 2005 film *Brokeback Mountain* have attracted gay and straight audiences alike.

According to Garber, the gay community has high brand loyalty. They tend to purchase products that target advertisements to gay consumers and support gay issues. Subaru pioneered gay-specific advertising in 1996 with a campaign targeting lesbian consumers using gay tennis star Martina Navratilova as a spokesperson. The Internet travel site Orbitz, Absolut Vodka, and Ford have concentrated on attracting gay audiences. The *Gay Press Report* noted that, in 2005, advertising with gay-specific content accounted for more than 50% of all ads in gay and lesbian publications for the first time in 2005, up from slightly less than 10% in 2003.

In a more recent development, gays are even being incorporated into mainstream commercials. Unilever, for example, decided to hire three actors to play a girl's best gay friends in a campaign to introduce Sunsilk shampoo to the United States. They will be positioned as style experts and write advice columns in magazines, such as *Cosmopolitan*, diagnosing consumers' hair problems.

The Disability Community

The disability community, like all other groups, is very diverse. There are those who are in wheelchairs, blind, or even deaf, but there also are people who have learning, hearing, and speech disabilities. Many recognize they are disabled, but others—such as aging baby boomers—are often in denial that their hearing, eyesight, and mobility are gradually diminishing.

Although disabled individuals are only a fraction of the total population, public relations practitioners should be sensitive to their needs and how to effectively communicate with them. Often, one feels uncomfortable around the disabled. As Barbara Bianchi-Kai, a specialist in disability marketing, wrote in *The Strategist*, "We're afraid of offending the person through our actions or our language choices."

She goes on to say that it's okay to use the word *deaf* instead of *hearing disabled*, but it's more proper to use *mobility impaired* or *physically disabled* for people who have difficulty moving. It's not okay to use such terms as *crippled*.

As in any communication, language and the medium are key elements. Deaf people, for example, use American Sign Language (ASL) as their first language. If you can't communicate in ASL, it's best to write brochures, newsletters, or even specialized

Web pages at a third-grade level. Printed materials should be graphics-heavy and text-light. Sight-impaired individuals, on the other hand, not only require bold graphics but at least 18-point type in all printed materials.

Bianchi-Kai says the best medium to reach a variety of disability groups at the same time is television. Closed-captioning makes it accessible to deaf people, and those with speech or mobility disabilities are also easily reached.

The crafting of key messages is important. Many people, particularly those who are aging, don't know or are unwilling to admit that they have a disability such as hearing loss. For such audiences, the message has to be about innovation and making life easier instead of about buying a hearing aid out of necessity.

Women

Diversity also includes gender. Women of all nationalities and ethnic groups have always been an important audience for such corporations as Procter & Gamble that manufacture numerous household products.

Indeed, Ketchum communications makes the point, "Today's women hold an overwhelming share of consumer purchasing influence, making more than 80 percent of household purchase decisions, and spending over $3.3 trillion annually." Given these statistics, it is no surprise that women are also emerging as "influentials" in a variety of campaigns. In Chapter 1, for example, the campaign of the Abundant Forests Alliance targeted married women with children as the prime audience for conveying messages about preserving and using forest lands.

The Ketchum research, conducted by the University of Southern California's Annenberg Strategic Public Relations Centre, also found that women aged 25 to 54 were not only "super consumers" but were much faster than men to embrace some new media, such as social networking sites, and also to use corporate Web sites.

Other research studies have identified a segment called "supermoms" in terms of opinion leadership and word-of-mouth influence. These women, about 5.4 percent of mothers, have such characteristics as (1) they have at least 75 friends with whom they keep in touch, (2) they give their friends advice on what to buy and restaurants to try, (3) they spend at least nine hours a week on the Internet, and (4) they participate in online chats and discussion. Given this data, companies such as Procter & Gamble and Georgia Pacific's Dixie Brand have used these supermoms to get their opinions and also to sample new products, with the idea that their word-of-mouth influence will motivate other women to buy the product.

The research also found that three-fourths of the supermoms are employed outside the home. But women in the workplace are also a diverse group with differing ideas about work ethics, dress codes, and willingness to put in long hours. Sociologists say that, for the first time, there are actually four generations of women (and men) in the workplace, which often requires some management sensitivity and diversity training. Baby boomers and seniors, for example, often have a different work ethic than Generation X and Y women, who seem to be less committed to working long hours or making the extra effort. There's also a generational gap in terms of dress codes. Younger women prefer to dress more casually and to some, more provocatively, which upsets the baby boomers and seniors who grew up with a more formal dress code.

> "More seminars and workshops are focusing on the fact that diversity in the workplace isn't just about race or gender, it's also about age.
>
> — *Jeffrey Zaslow*, reporter for *The Wall Street Journal*

Reaching Global Audiences

The global audiences in Russia, China, India, Latin America, and Europe draw the attention of public relations professionals as trade (and public relations) expands on a global basis. Public relations professionals must overcome language barriers, learn local business customs, and consider social differences to practice culturally appropriate and locally acceptable public relations.

China offers a good example. It is a growing market undergoing revolutionary political, social, and industrial changes. Since it reopened to Western markets in 1978, the growth of business opportunities in China has been phenomenal. Despite the challenges of government regulation, American and European companies have embraced the Chinese market to take advantage of business opportunities.

Awareness of local customs and business practices is necessary, however. "There are cultural differences that you have to become attuned to," said Cynthia He, an investment relations manager with the search engine company Baidu in China during an interview with Asia edition *Time* magazine reporter Bill Powell.

> I've been at meetings when I've been very blunt in pointing something out, and there will be an awkward second or two of silence, and then someone will politely say, 'Well, that's a very American way of looking at it,' which is another way of saying, hey, will you tone it down a bit!

Chinese value their long-held traditions, and personal influence exists in every angle of business, society, and media systems. If a public relations practitioner wants to distribute news releases, they may need to get to know the reporters in person as a natural part of the process. In China, as in other Asian nations, the exchange of gifts is a normal procedure in the conduct of business. Asian culture, for the most part, also is concerned about "losing face." That means that criticism or severe questioning of an individual in front of others is not accceptable.

Russia is another cultural challenge. In the 1990s, corruption was common as so-called public relations technologists emerged, funneling millions of dollars into journalists' hands in exchange for favorable press. Overloading the press with rumor and hearsay about rival politicians or corporations, a technique known as *black public relations*, was also a frequent strategy.

With the new millenium, however, Russian public relations professionals began to recognize the benefit of modern public relations approaches. The German manufacturer Bosch, for example, launched a major campaign to convince Russians of the advantage of owning a dishwasher. By enlisting artists and musicians as advocates, Bosch increased sales by 70% in a brief period. An art installation entitled "A Monument to the Amount of Time Wasted on Washing Up," was particulary successful at helping define public need for a dishwasher. An art installation in the United States or Canada would probably be ineffective in convincing consumers to buy such a product, but because of cultural differences, it was successful in Russia.

Companies occasionally misstep in entering the international markets. Budweiser's decision to purchase the exclusive rights for beer sales at the 2006 World Cup held in Germany created an uproar among Germans, who are fiercely loyal to their native beer. German politician Fritz Maget made headlines by proclaiming that Budweiser was the "worst beer in the world," and that the Germans "have a duty of public welfare and must not poison visitors to the World Cup." The derision of German consumers probably will not hurt Budweiser's global reputation long term. Because media readily

on the job

A MULTICULTURAL WORLD

Women as a Special Audience: Breast Cancer Awareness in Pakistan

The Women's Empowerment Group, a nongovernmental organization (NGO) in Pakistan, had a major public relations challenge. Statistics showed that the country has the highest rate of breast cancer of any Asian nation. However, Pakistan's conservative Muslim society made public discussion of anything related to women's breasts a very sensitive topic. Indeed, the majority of Pakistani women are reluctant to be examined by doctors because of shyness and social customs.

Given this situation, the Women's Empowerment Group sought to break the taboos by first enlisting the support of the first lady, Begum Sehba Musharraf, and the prime minister's wife to launch the first-ever nationwide Breast Cancer Awareness Campaign. Its primary objectives were to (1) make breast cancer an acceptable topic in the public domain of Pakistan, (2) create widespread awareness about breast cancer among urban and rural women, (3) and promote understanding and the practice of self-diagnosis.

The tactics used included: (1) distribution of easy-to-read brochures through utility bills, health clinics, and women's colleges; (2) news releases, articles, and interviews in the press; (3) establishment of a bilingual, interactive Web site for women to get information and exchange information; (4) live discussion programs on FM radio and national television; (5) establishment of support groups; and (6) seminars and workshops for women's groups in various cities.

Because of the prominent spokespersons and the distribution of culturally sensitive promotional materials, the campaign was able to overcome the constraints of a conservative Islamic society and make breast cancer part of the national health agenda. Several governmental ministries became partners in the campaign for breast cancer awareness, and the Ministry of Health in Punjab even started a pilot project to train 3,700 local health volunteers to teach breast self-examination to women. Extensive coverage about the campaign and breast cancer appeared in local print, broadcast, and electronic media. International news outlets, such as BBC, also covered the story.

---

cover conflict, Budweiser garnered more exposure than if the German beer loyalists had not gone on the attack. Time will tell whether the American company actually gains brand recognition from the controversy.

Diversity, as one can see, has many faces around the world. In some Middle East nations, it's unacceptable to talk with an unaccompanied woman. At the same time, in Argentina, it is the custom for men and women to give each other a kiss on the cheek even on a first meeting. Media relations in Japan and Korea require a lot of wining and dining of journalists, whereas such practice is frowned on in the United States. In India, cows are sacred in the Hindu religion, so it's not a good idea to order a steak with Indian friends. At the same time, don't order a pork chop in Saudi Arabia because Muslims consider pork unclean. There is also the matter of "pay for play," which was discussed in Chapter 3. In many nations such as Indonesia, it's common practice to pay a journalist for writing a story about your client or employer. See Chapter 19 for more information on bridging the cultural divide and conducting international public relations.

The key strategic point for public relations professionals is to maintain sensitivity to different cultures and be equipped with different languages when entering international arenas to deal with global audiences. See the Multicultural World box on page 293 about a culturally sensitive campaign conducted in Pakistan.

Matching the Audience with the Media

This chapter has already outlined aspects of using ethnic media to reach specialized audiences, but all these groups also use what might be described as "mainstream" media. In other words, a local daily newspaper or a television news program has an audience representing the whole spectrum of ages, nationalities, and ethnic groups in that community.

Consequently, it's important for a public relations professional to thoroughly understand the array of printed, spoken, visual, and new media methods available so wise choices are made for selecting the right medium, or media, to use for reaching key audiences. The following are some general guidelines for understanding the characteristics of various media so a better job can be done matching the audience with the appropriate media. More specific guidance on producing materials for various media are given in Chapters 14 to 16 under Part Four, Tactics.

All forms of media, of course, are pervasive in our lives. Americans, for example, spend an average of 4.5 hours a day watching television, more time than they spend on any other medium. According to the Census Bureau's annual *Statistical Abstract of the United States*, radio is second followed by the Internet and then newspapers. All together, the Census Bureau has calculated that Americans in 2007 spent an average of 3,518 hours using the media, which is an increase of about 200 hours from the 2000 data.

A breakdown of all those hours is interesting.

- 1,555 hours watching television (broadcast and cable)
- 974 hours listening to the radio
- 195 hours using the Internet
- 175 hours reading a newspaper
- 122 hours reading magazines
- 106 hours reading books
- 86 hours playing video games

These figures, of course, are averages and there's great diversity of media usage. Young people, for example, spend considerably more time on the Internet than their parents, and data shows that people over 50 watch more TV than people who are 20.

Media usage was also the topic of a research report, "Media Myths & Realities," published by Ketchum communications and the Annenberg Strategic Public Relations Center. One myth, according to the report, is the perception that traditional media are dead. The survey, which polled 1,490 adults and 500 corporate communicators, found that the top four media in terms of usage—in descending order—were (1) local TV news, (2) major network news, (3) local newspapers, and (4) cable TV news. Blogs came 12th on a list of 15 media. Even 50 percent of respondents in the 18–24 age group indicated that they rely on newspapers for information, as compared to almost 85 percent of the 65+ group.

> All media is local and personal. Consumers are looking for authenticity and trust, and local media is one channel they turn to for it.
>
> —— *Nicholas Scibetta,* SVP of Ketchum

The key findings of the Ketchum/Annenberg study are:

◆ Public relations practitioners should use local print and broadcast media to reach diverse publics. Such media have high credibility among the public.

◆ Campaigns should incorporate concepts of word-of-mouth communications to reach influentials in each targeted public. Social networking Web sites are a good vehicle.

◆ Information should be provided when the audience is most receptive. Asian Americans, for example, are more receptive to travel and leisure messages during the Asian Lunar New Year's celebrations.

◆ Celebrity endorsements have low credibility among consumers, but they can provide a "triggering effect" in terms of getting audience attention.

◆ Women, particularly those in the 25 to 54 age group, use traditional media but also use the Internet more frequently than men to make purchasing decisions.

In some campaigns, the most cost-effective results come from use of a single medium. Other campaigns work best when several types of media are used. Wise selection of media, based on the audience sought and the money available, is an important skill for public relations practitioners to develop. Here are some other characteristics to keep in mind as you plan a communications campaign:

◆ Print media are the most effective for delivering a message that requires absorption of details and contemplation by the receiver. Printed matter can be read repeatedly and kept for reference. The Internet, perhaps more like traditional print sources than like broadcast media, is the fastest to deliver breaking news. Newspapers also are fast and have the most widespread impact. Magazines, although slower, are better directed to special-interest audiences. Books take even longer but can generate strong impact over time.

◆ Television has the strongest emotional impact of all media. Its visual power makes situations seem close to the viewer. The personality of the TV communicator creates an influence that print media cannot match.

◆ Radio's greatest advantages are flexibility and the ability to reach specific target audiences. Messages can be prepared for and broadcast on radio more rapidly than on television, at much lower cost. Because there are nine times as many radio stations as TV stations, audience exposure is easier to obtain, but the audiences reached are smaller.

◆ Use of online media, once considered a supplemental method of reaching a generally well-educated, relatively affluent audience, is expanding exponentially. Currently, somewhere between 70 and 75 percent of U.S. households have Internet access. About 16% of the world's population has Internet access, with a growth rate of about 183% between 2000 and 2005. In the foreseeable future, it is likely that electronic media delivery systems, such as the Internet and wireless communications, will overtake print media and even television as the primary source of information. Articles and other media content from the Internet can be downloaded or saved for future reference.

Again, see Chapters 14–16 in Part 4 of this book, which concentrates on how to produce a variety of public relations materials for diverse audiences.

PRCASEBOOK

Tailoring News Releases to Black Newspapers Shows Promise

The National Cancer Institute funds a news service in the Missouri School of Journalism that shapes breaking news about cancer to be particularly relevant to readers of Black newspapers in communities with high disparities between African American and Caucasian residents for cancer incidence and outcomes. The service tailors its news releases to the individual Black newspaper by providing local statistics and contact information. Each release also provides action steps, commonly called *mobilizing information*, to improve health in the Black community. The service has met with success by serving the needs of print editors and reporters. Ozioma has garnered extremely high usage by the text newspapers in the study and has led to changes in the extent and quality of coverage of cancer in the black newspapers. Given that the local Black paper is a highly trusted source viewed as holding the values and well-being of its community of readers paramount in importance, Ozioma serves as a good example of the way niche media can be employed to reach a specific, at-risk audience in a health public relations effort.

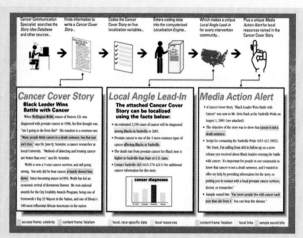

Diagram of process from science news release to local pick-up by Black paper.

These two clips illustrate how different the framing of cancer news can be, even within the same media channel such as a newspaper. Mainstream daily newspapers tend to focus on "new science" in cancer research and care. On the other hand, Black newspapers focus more on what cancer means to local individuals and to the newspaper's community of readers.

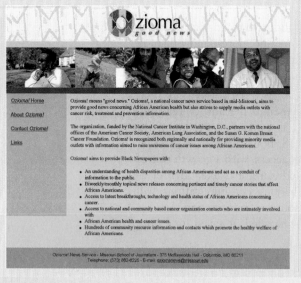

SUMMARY

Diverse and Multicultural Nature of the Public Relations Audience

Audiences are not monolithic. They are a complex mingling of groups with diverse cultural, ethnic, religious, and economic attributes. Through technology and research, it's now possible to segment audiences a number of ways that helps the public relations communicator understand the characteristics of the audience and how to best communicate with them. Audiences are increasingly visually oriented, increasingly taking control of how they want to receive information, and tend to polarize on controversial issues.

Reaching Diverse Age Groups

Audiences are generational and each have different values, interests, and needs. Public relations practitioners must understand youth groups such as Generation X and Y, as well the coming tidal wave of baby boomers who are reaching retirement. Baby boomers and seniors tend to be relatively affluent and constitute the majority of the travel and tourism business. Each group, however, prefers to receive information via different media channels. Although youth prefers information online and via cell phones, seniors still prefer traditional media such as daily newspaper and television news.

Reaching Racial and Ethnic Groups

The demographics of the United States is becoming more multicultural. Hispanics, by 2050, will constitute about 25 percent of the population. Other major groups are African Americans, and Asian Americans. Each group has its own cultural values that must be understood by professional communicators. In general, however, the various ethnic groups are strongly family-oriented and community-minded. The ethnic media in the country is rapidly developing, and there are many Spanish-speaking media outlets. In conducting campaigns for the Hispanic audience, Spanish is often the preferred language even if individuals have strong English-comprehension skills.

Other Emerging Audiences

Other emerging audiences include Catholic and evangelical groups, the gay/lesbian community, the disabled, and women. These groups, in varying degrees, constitute important consumer groups that attract the attention of marketers. A number of companies now advertise in gay publications. Women, particularly those in the 25 to 54 age group, are influential in word-of-mouth campaigns.

Reaching Global Audiences

The global economy makes it necessary for public relations professionals to consider the cultures and values of many diverse nations. Conducting a public relations program abroad takes a great deal of sensitivity. China, in particular, represents a major market.

Matching the Audience with the Media

Americans spend about 3,500 hours a year consuming various media. Watching television and listening to the radio consumes the most time, but using the Internet has now surpassed reading the newspaper. Print media, however, is effective for retaining information. Radio is best for its mobility. The Internet is good for fast-breaking news and researching for specific information.

CASE ACTIVITY What Would You Do?

The latest innovation in suncare packaging is spray-on sunscreens, which come in an ozone-free canister that sprays a clear mist that coats the skin without any rubbing. Dermatologists say the spray-on sunscreen offers the same protection as lotions. They also have the additional advantage of being easy to apply, which means that individuals will be more likely to coat every part of the body rather than just dabbing a little lotion on the arms, nose, or shoulders.

Banana Boat brand is currently marketing its Ultra-Mist sunblock, but it's interested in developing a tailored campaign directly oriented to Hispanic women, aged 18 to 25.

Market research indicates that this group is particularly interested in products that help them maintain a lighter skin tone. Traditionally, darker-skinned Hispanics were considered part of the lower classes because they worked in the fields.

Banana Boat retains your public relations firm to develop a public relations program that will effectively build awareness and visibility for its Ultra-Mist product in the Hispanic community. What would you do in terms of using ethnic media? What about traditional media? What kinds of events or promotions would you plan? Would you consider social networking Web sites?

QUESTIONS for Review and Discussion

1. Public relations practitioners are cautioned not to think of audiences as monolithic, but very diverse. Why?

2. How can technology be used to segment audiences?

3. What are some characteristics of Generation Y?

4. What is the baby boomer generation, and what are some of this group's characteristics?

5. Why is the senior audience so important in the United States? What are some characteristics of this audience?

6. What is the fastest-growing ethnic group in the United States?

7. How do you think the various changes in the racial and ethnic makeup of the United States will impact the future practice of public relations?

8. What are some of the cultural values of such groups as Hispanics, African Americans, and Asian Americans?

9. What are some guidelines for developing a communications campaign for multicultural audiences?

10. Describe some of the ethnic media that reaches a Hispanic audience.

11. What are some characteristics of the gay/lesbian community?

12. Why are women considered an important audience for public relations and marketing personnel?

13. If you're doing public relations in China, what are some guidelines for working in Chinese culture?

14. How much time do Americans spend consuming various forms of media?

15. Some say traditional media is dead. Do you agree? Why or why not?

16. Why is television a good way to reach diverse and multicultural publics, including the disabled?

SUGGESTED READINGS

"America by the Numbers: Special Report." *Time*, October 30, 2006, special insert.

"Asian Lunar New Year Ideal Time To Show Cultural Understanding." *PRWeek*, February 26, 2007, p. 11.

Barnes, Brooks. "Behind the Fall of Imus: A Digital Brush Fire." *Wall Street Journal*, April 13, 2007, pp. A1, A10.

Bianchi-Kai, Barbara. "Marketing to the Disability Community." *The Strategist*, Fall 2005, pp. 37–49.

Bush, Michael. "A Genuine Connection: Cause-Related Initiatives to Reach Multicultural Audiences." *PRWeek*, May 14, 2007, p. 29.

Elliott, Stuart. "Hey, Gay Spender, Marketers Spending Time With You." *New York Times*, June 26, 2006, p. C8.

Galloway, Chris. "Cyber-PR and 'Dynamic Touch.'" *Public Relations Review*, November 2005, Vol. 31, No. 4, pp. 572–577.

Getting Beyond Stereotypes: Grassroots PR Campaign Works to Give Media a Truer Picture of Native Americans. *Ragan's Media Relations Report*, January 2005, pp. 3, 7.

Iacono, Erica. "Women Under the Influence." *PRWeek*, February 12, 2007, p. 17.

Longpre, Marc. "A Youthful Approach." *PRWeek*, May 7, 2007, p. 17.

Kirat, Mohammed. "Promoting Online Media Relations: Public Relations Departments' Use of Internet in the UAE." *Public Relations Review*, Vol. 33, No. 2, June 2007, pp. 166–174.

McQuire, Craig. "Creating PSAs That Really Talk to Teens." *PRWeek*, April 9, 2007, p. 14.

McGuire, Craig. "Hitting Home With Baby Boomers." *PRWeek*, June 12, 2006, p. 18.

Nolan, Hamilton. "Paths toward Global Growth." *PRWeek*, April 3, 2006, p. 13.

Poniewozik, James. "Who Can Say What." *Time*, April 23, 2007, pp. 32–38.

Roberts, Sam. "Fatter, Taller and Thirstier Americans." *New York Times*, December 15, 2006, p. A5.

Schmelzer, Randi. "The Asian Answer." *PRWeek*, March 13, 2006, p. 17.

Schwadron, Terry. "76 Million Reasons to Reconsider What Is Typical for Those Over 60." *New York Times*, April 11, 2006, p. F3.

"Special Diversity Issue." *The Strategist*, Fall 2005. Entire issue devoted to articles about diversity and multiculuralism.

Ward, David. "Generation X Proves Elusive Target." *PRWeek*, August 15, 2005, p. 9.

Zaslow, Jeffrey. "A New Generation Gap: Differences Emerge Among Woman in the Workplace." *New York Times*, May 4, 2006, p. C3.

Public Relations and the Law

A Sampling of Legal Problems

The law and its many ramifications are somewhat abstract to the average person. Many people may have difficulty imagining exactly how public relations personnel can run afoul of the law or generate a suit simply by communicating information.

To bring things down to earth and to make this chapter more meaningful, we provide here a sampling of recent government regulatory agency cases and lawsuits that involved public relations materials and the work of practitioners:

◆ Porter Novelli sued two employees who left to start another public relations firm, claiming that they had planned the new firm on company time and took a client with them.

◆ A public relations counselor was quizzed in a California courtroom regarding his role in writing a misleading news release stating that all of the Oakland Raiders's games were sold out for the season. The lawsuit was between the football team and the Oakland Coliseum.

◆ Bonner & Associates and its client, the Pharmaceutical Research and Manufacturers of America, were charged with violating Maryland's lobbying disclosure laws. A citizens group claimed that the firm used "deceptive tactics in the guise of a consumer-based organization to do the bidding of the pharmaceutical industry."

◆ The Securities and Exchange Commission (SEC) fined a former employee of Ogilvy PR Worldwide $34,000 for passing "material, nonpublic information" to his father, who used the information to purchase stock in Wells Fargo Bank before it was publicly announced that it was acquiring another company.

◆ The Federal Trade Commission (FTC) filed charges against three national diet firms after they failed to provide factual evidence in their advertising and publicity that clients actually achieved weight-loss goals or maintained them.

◆ A Chicago man sued for invasion of privacy after he appeared in a video news release for a cholesterol-lowering drug because the company and video producer didn't tell him the actual purpose of the taping.

◆ The Los Angeles city attorney filed a civil suit against Fleishman-Hillard charging that the LA office inflated invoices, claimed work that was not done, and double-charged for other activities when the firm worked for the city's Department of Water and Power.

◆ An 81-year-old man sued the United Way of America for using his picture on campaign posters and brochures without his permission.

These examples provide some idea of the legal pitfalls that a public relations person may encounter. Many of the charges were eventually dismissed or settled out of court, but the organizations paid dearly for the adverse publicity and the expense of defending themselves.

Public relations personnel must be aware that they can be held legally liable if they provide advice or tacitly support an illegal activity of a client or employer. This area of liability is called *conspiracy*. A public relations person can be named as a coconspirator with other organizational officials if he or she:

◆ Participates in an illegal action such as bribing a government official or covering up information of vital interest to the public health and safety

◆ Counsels and guides the policy behind an illegal action

♦ Takes a major personal part in the illegal action

♦ Helps establish a "front group" whereby the connection to the public relations firm or its clients is kept hidden

♦ Cooperates in any other way to further an illegal action

These five concepts also apply to public relations firms that create, produce, and distribute materials on behalf of clients. The courts have ruled on more than one occasion that public relations firms cannot hide behind the defense of "the client told me to do it." Public relations firms have a legal responsibility to practice "due diligence" in the type of information and documentation supplied by a client. Regulatory agencies such as the FTC (discussed shortly) have the power under the Lanham Act to file charges against public relations firms that distribute false and misleading information.

Libel and Defamation

Public relations professionals should be thoroughly familiar with the concepts of libel and slander. Such knowledge is crucial if an organization's internal and external communications are to meet legal and regulatory standards with a minimum of legal complications.

Traditionally, *libel* was a printed falsehood and *slander* was an oral statement that was false. Today, as a practical matter, there is little difference in the two, and the courts often use *defamation* as a collective term.

Essentially, defamation is any false statement about a person (or organization) that creates public hatred, contempt, ridicule, or inflicts injury on reputation. A person filing a libel suit usually must prove that:

♦ the false statement was communicated to others through print, broadcast, or electronic means;

♦ the person was identified or is identifiable;

♦ there is actual injury in the form of money losses, loss of reputation, or mental suffering; and

♦ the person making the statement was malicious or negligent.

In general, private citizens have more success winning defamation suits than do public figures or corporations. With public figures—government officials, entertainers, political candidates, and other newsworthy personalities—there is the extra test of whether the libelous statements were made with actual malice (*New York Times v. Sullivan*).

Corporations, to some degree, also are considered "public figures" by the courts for several reasons: (1) They engage in advertising and promotion offering products and services to the public, (2) they are often involved in matters of public controversy and public policy, and (3) they have some degree of access to the media—through regular advertising and news releases—that enables them to respond and rebut defamatory charges made against them.

This is not to say that corporations don't win lawsuits regarding defamation. A good example is General Motors, which filed a multimillion-dollar defamation suit against NBC after the network's *Dateline* news program carried a story about gas tanks on GM pickup trucks exploding in side-impact collisions.

on the job
ETHICS

Mattel Recalls Dora and Elmo

Concern for product safety and possible lawsuits caused Mattel to recall one million Fisher-Price toys in August of 2007 after it was found that the toys contained excessive levels of lead paint. The toys, many featuring Nickelodeon and Sesame Street characters, were made by a contract manufacturer in China.

The recall, costing about $30 million, utilized a number of public relations tactics to inform the public. This included answering all media inquiries, sending news alerts to the print and broadcast media, messages to bloggers, and calls to consumer affairs offices at the state and federal level. No advertising was used. In addition, Mattel posted an easy-to-use chart on its Web site with the name, number, and image of the products being recalled.

At stake for Mattel was the reputation of its Fisher-Price toys for quality and safety. Any toy recall becomes a big issue in the public's mind, of course, because it's about children. Branding and public relations experts gave Mattel high marks for initiating the recall and maintaining a high degree of transparency regarding the situation. Allen Adamson, managing director of Landor Associates, told *Advertising Age*, "You need to be upfront, direct, and very proactive. The louder they send out this message, the better it is for their brand."

Mattel's recall came several months after poisonous pet food made in China was taken off U.S. shelves in a massive recall after a number of pets had died. Voluntary recalls of tainted toys or even food is the legal and ethical thing to do, but it raises the additional question of why Mattel and the pet food companies didn't certify the safety of their imported products before they were distributed to stores around the nation.

What do you think is a better and more ethical public relations strategy for maintaining a company's reputation: (1) Issuing voluntary recalls after the product has been sold in stores, or (2) ensuring the safety of their products before selling them?

GM's general counsel, in a news conference, meticulously provided evidence that NBC had inserted toy rocket "igniters" in the gas tanks, understated the vehicle speed at the moment of impact, and wrongly claimed that the fuel tanks could be easily ruptured. Within 24 hours after the suit was filed, NBC caved in. It agreed to air a nine-minute apology on the news program and pay GM $2 million to cover the cost of its investigation.

Increasingly, corporations are using fraud and contract law to sue news organizations, instead of pursuing harder-to-prove libel claims. In *Food Lion v. Capital Cities/ABC* (1995), for example, the grocery chain was awarded $315,000 after it sued ABC News for fraud and trespassing; two TV producers had lied on job applications and hid cameras in their wigs to report an exposé on alleged health violations at several stores. In another case, a federal judge in Cincinnati ruled that a *Business Week* reporter lied and breached a contract with a credit-reporting agency while writing a cover story on privacy.

Avoiding Libel Suits

There is little investigative reporting in public relations, but libel suits can be filed against organizational officials who make libelous accusations during a media interview, send out news releases that make false statements, or injure someone's reputation.

Some executives have been sorry that they lost control during a news conference and called the leaders of a labor union "a bunch of crooks and compulsive liars." Suits have been filed for calling a news reporter "a pimp for all environmental groups." Such language, although highly quotable and colorful, can provoke legal retaliation, merited or not.

Accurate information, and a delicate choice of words, must be used in news releases. For example, a former employee of J. Walter Thompson advertising agency claimed she was libeled in an agency news release that stated she had been dismissed because of financial irregularities in the department she headed. Eventually, the $20 million lawsuit was dismissed because she couldn't prove that the agency acted in a "grossly irresponsible manner."

In situations involving personnel, organizations often try to avoid lawsuits by saying that an employee left "for personal reasons" or to "pursue other interests," even if the real reason was incompetence or a record of sexual harassment. News releases and product publicity should also be written in accordance with FTC and SEC regulations, to be discussed shortly.

Another potentially dangerous practice is making unflattering comments about the competition's products. Although comparative advertising is the norm in the United States, a company must walk a narrow line between comparison and "trade libel," or "product disparagement." Statements should be truthful, with factual evidence and scientific demonstration available to substantiate them. Companies often charge competitors with overstepping the boundary between "puffery" and "factual representation."

An organization can offer the opinion that a particular product or service is the "best" or "a revolutionary development" if the context clearly shows that the communication is a statement of opinion attributed to someone. Then it is classified as "puffery" and doesn't require factual evidence.

Don Sneed, Tim Wulfemeyer, and Harry Stonecipher, in a *Public Relations Review* article, say that a news release should be written to indicate clearly statements of opinion and statements of fact. They suggest that:

1. opinion statements be accompanied by the facts on which the opinions are based,
2. statements of opinion be clearly labeled as such, and
3. the context of the language surrounding the expression of opinion be reviewed for possible legal implications.

The Fair Comment Defense

Organizations can do much to ensure that their communications avoid materials that could lead to potential lawsuits. By the same token, organizations are somewhat limited in their ability to use legal measures to defend themselves against criticism.

Executives are often incensed when an environmental group includes their corporation on its annual "dirty dozen" polluters or similar lists. Executives are also unhappy when a broadcast consumer affairs reporter flatly calls the product a "rip-off."

A corporate reputation may be damaged and product sales may go down, but a defamation case is difficult to win because, as previously mentioned, the accuser must prove actual malice. Also operating is the concept of *fair comment and criticism*.

This defense is used by theater and music critics when they lambaste a play or concert. Fair comment also means that when companies and individuals voluntarily display their wares to the public for sale or consumption, they have no real recourse against criticism done with honest purpose and lack of malicious intent.

A utility company in Indiana, for example, once tried to sue a citizen who wrote a letter to a newspaper criticizing it for seeking a rate hike. The judge threw the suit out of court, stating that the rate increase was a "matter of public interest and concern" even if the letter writer didn't have all the facts straight.

Invasion of Privacy

An area of law that particularly applies to employees of an organization is *invasion of privacy*. Public relations staff must be particularly sensitive to the issue of privacy in at least four areas:

- employee newsletters,
- photo releases,
- product publicity and advertising, and
- media inquiries about employees.

Employee Newsletters

It is no longer true, if it ever was, that an organization has an unlimited right to publicize the activities of its employees. In fact, Morton J. Simon, a Philadelphia lawyer and author of *Public Relations Law*, wrote, "It should not be assumed that a person's status as an employee waives his right to privacy." Simon correctly points out that a company newsletter or magazine does not enjoy the same First Amendment protection that the news media enjoy when they claim "newsworthiness" and "public interest." A number of court cases, he says, show that company newsletters are considered commercial tools of trade.

This distinction does not impede the effectiveness of newsletters, but it does indicate editors should try to keep employee stories organization-oriented. Indeed, most lawsuits and complaints are generated by "personals columns" that may invade the privacy of employees. Although a mention that Joe Doaks honeymooned in Hawaii or that Mary Worth is now a great-grandmother may sound completely innocent, the individuals involved—for any number of reasons—may consider the information a violation of their privacy. The situation may be further compounded into possible defamation by "cutesy" editorial asides in poor taste.

In sum, one should avoid anything that might embarrass or subject an employee to ridicule by fellow employees. Here are some guidelines to remember when writing about employee activities:

- Keep the focus on organization-related activities.
- Have employees submit "personals" in writing.
- Double-check all information for accuracy.
- Ask: "Will this embarrass anyone or cause someone to be the butt of jokes?"
- Don't rely on secondhand information; confirm the facts with the person involved.
- Don't include racial or ethnic designations of employees in any articles.

Photo Releases

Ordinarily, a public relations practitioner doesn't need a signed release if a person gives "implied consent" by posing for a picture and is told how it will be used. This is particularly true for "news" photographs published in internal newsletters.

Public relations departments, however, should take the precaution of (1) filing all photographs, (2) dating them, and (3) giving the context of the situation. This precludes the use of old photos that could embarrass employees or subject them to ridicule. In other cases, it precludes using photographs of persons who are no longer employed or have died. This method also helps to make certain that a photo taken for the employee newsletter isn't used in an advertisement. If a photo of an employee or customer is used in product publicity, sales brochures, or advertisements, the standard practice is to obtain a signed release.

Product Publicity and Advertising

As already noted, an organization must have a signed release on file if it wants to use the photographs or comments of employees and other individuals in product publicity, sales brochures, and advertising. An added precaution is to give some financial compensation to make a more binding contract.

Chemical Bank of New York unfortunately learned this lesson the hard way. The bank used pictures of 39 employees in various advertisements designed to "humanize" the bank's image, but the employees maintained that no one had requested permission to use their photos in advertisements. Another problem was that the pictures had been taken up to five years before they began appearing in the series of advertisements.

> If I used my mother in an ad, I'd get her permission—and I almost trust her 100 percent.
>
> —*Jerry Della Femina,*
> advertising executive

An attorney for the employees, who sued for $600,000 in damages, said, "The bank took the individuality of these employees and used that individuality to make a profit." The judge agreed and ruled that the bank had violated New York's privacy law. The action is called *misappropriation of personality*, which is discussed later in this chapter. Jerry Della Femina, an advertising executive, succinctly makes the point: Get permission. "If I used my mother in an ad," he said, "I'd get her permission—and I almost trust her 100 percent."

Written permission also should be obtained if the employee's photograph is to appear in sales brochures or even in the corporate annual report. This rule also applies to other situations. A graduate of Lafayette College sued the college for using a photo of his mother and him at graduation ceremonies, without their permission, in a financial aid brochure.

Media Inquiries about Employees

Because press inquiries have the potential of invading an employee's right of privacy, public relations personnel should follow basic guidelines as to what information will be provided on the employee's behalf.

In general, employers should give a news reporter only basic information.

DO PROVIDE:

1. confirmation that the person is an employee,
2. the person's title and job description, and
3. date of beginning employment, or, if applicable, date of termination.

DO NOT PROVIDE EMPLOYEE'S:

1. salary,
2. home address,
3. marital status,
4. number of children,
5. organizational memberships, and
6. job performance.

If a reporter does seek any of this information, because of the nature of the story, several methods may be followed.

First, a public relations person can volunteer to contact the employee and have the person speak directly with the reporter. What the employee chooses to tell the reporter is not then a company's responsibility. Second, many organizations do provide additional information to a reporter if it is included on an optional biographical sheet that the employee has filled out. In most cases, the form clearly states that the organization may use any of the information in answering press inquiries or writing its own news releases. A typical biographical form may have sections in which the employee can list such things as memberships in community organizations, professional affiliations, educational background, past titles and positions, and even special achievements. This sheet should not be confused with the person's official employment application, which must remain confidential.

If an organization uses biographical sheets, it is important that they be dated and kept current. A sheet compiled by an employee five years previously may be hopelessly out of date. This is also true of file photographs taken at the time of a person's employment.

Copyright Law

Should a news release be copyrighted? How about a corporate annual report? Can a *New Yorker* cartoon be used in the company magazine without permission? What about reprinting an article from *Fortune* magazine and distributing it to the company's sales staff? Are government reports copyrighted? What about posting a video clip from Comedy Central on the Internet? What constitutes copyright infringement?

These are some of the bothersome questions that a public relations professional should be able to answer. Knowledge of copyright law is important from two perspectives: (1) what organizational materials should be copyrighted and (2) how correctly to utilize the copyrighted materials of others.

In very simple terms, *copyright* means protection of a creative work from unauthorized use. A section of the U.S. copyright law of 1978 states: "Copyright protection subsists . . . in the original works of authorship fixed in any tangible medium of expression now known or later developed." The word *authorship* is defined in seven categories: (1) literary works; (2) musical works; (3) dramatic works; (4) pantomimes and choreographic works; (5) pictorial, graphic, or sculptural works; (6) motion pictures; and (7) sound recordings. The word *fixed* means that the work is sufficiently permanent or stable to permit it to be perceived, reproduced, or otherwise communicated.

Thus, a copyright does not protect ideas, but only the specific ways in which those ideas are expressed. An idea for promoting a product, for example, cannot be

on the job
A MULTICULTURAL WORLD

New Harry Potter author, Li Jingsheng, wrote a final Harry Potter novel for his son, Dongwei, and posted it online. Pirated bound copies of his book sold on Beijing streets.

Have You Read "Harry Potter and the Hiking Dragon"?

Public relations professionals, in order to do their jobs, must understand the legal concepts of copyright and intellectual property, but literary license seems to flourish in China. A wholly unauthorized version of *Harry Potter and the Deathly Hallows* came out 10 days before the official worldwide English version, and the story line had nothing in common with J. K. Rowling's best-seller.

In fact, there are more than a dozen unauthorized Harry Potter titles on the Chinese market that mix characters, add new ones, and even include plots from kung-fu epics. Some sample titles: *Harry Potter and the Chinese Empire*, *Harry Potter and the Showdown*, and *Harry Potter and the Leopard-Walk-Up-to-Dragon*.

The *New York Times* did a translation of the *Dragon* book's publisher summary:

Harry becomes a fat, hairy dwarf after being caught in a 'sour and sweet rain'; he loses all his magic and can get it back only by obtaining the magic ring. After he does, Harry becomes a dragon that fights evil. Voldemort has an even more powerful brother who makes trouble for Harry.

As *New York Times* reporter Howard French points out, "The global Harry Potter publishing phenomenon has mutated into something altogether Chinese: a combination of remarkable imagination and startling industriousness, all placed in the service of counterfeiting, literary fraud, and copyright violation."

Even in the United States and Europe, which have strict laws about copyright and protection of intellectual property, it's worth remember-

> **"** You are not supposed to use the name of Harry Potter anywhere else other than J. K. Rowling's own books. **"**
> ———*Sun Shunlin*, director of a Chinese publishing house

ing that Harry Potter and his friends (including his enemies) can't be used in any way, shape, or form on behalf of a client or employer without the express permission of his creator, J. K. Rowling.

---

copyrighted—but brochures, drawings, news features, animated cartoons, display booths, photographs, recordings, videotapes, corporate symbols, slogans, and the like that express a particular idea can be copyrighted. It should be noted, however, that the Supreme Court did rule in 1991 that directories, computer databases, and other compilations of facts may be copied and republished unless they display "some minimum degree of creativity."

Under current law, a work is automatically copyrighted the moment it is "fixed" in tangible form. Although such a "work" doesn't have to carry a notice of copyright, many organizations take the extra precaution of using the letter "c" in a circle (©), followed by the word *copyright* and citing the year of copyright to discourage unauthorized use.

A more formal step, providing full legal protection, is official registration of the copyrighted work within three months after creation. This is done by depositing two copies of the manuscript (it is not necessary that it has been published), recording, or artwork with the Copyright Office of the Library of Congress. Registration is not a condition of copyright protection, but it is often helpful in a court case against unauthorized use by others.

A copyright, under current U.S. law, protects original material for the life of the creator plus 70 years for individual works and 95 years from publication for copyrights held by corporations. It is often called the "Mickey Mouse" law because Congress in 1998 extended copyright protection to its current level after extensive lobbying from Walt Disney Company. Its copyright on its Mickey Mouse character would have expired in 2003 under the previous 50-year rule. The length of copyright protection varies by nation. In Europe, copyright protection only lasts 50 years, which has caused some conflict with American recording companies who don't want the work of such artists as Elvis Presley in the public domain because they will lose royalties. In other nations, such as China, copyright is widely abused. See the Multicultural Box on page 307 about Harry Potter's adventures in China.

Fair Use versus Infringement

Public relations people are in the business of gathering information from a variety of sources, so it is important to know where fair use ends and infringement begins. See Insights box Plagiarism versus Copyright Infringement on page 309.

Fair use means that part of a copyrighted article may be quoted directly, but the quoted material must be brief in relation to the length of the original work. It may be, for example, only one paragraph in a 750-word article and up to 300 words in a long article or book chapter. Complete attribution of the source must be given regardless of the length of the quotation. If the passage is quoted verbatim, quote marks must be used.

It is important to note, however, that the concept of fair use has distinct limitations if part of the copyrighted material is to be used in advertisements and promotional brochures. In this case, permission is required. It also is important for the original source to approve the context in which the quote is used. A quote out of context often runs into legal trouble if it implies endorsement of a product or service.

The copyright law does allow limited copying of a work for fair use such as criticism, comment, or research. However, in recent years, the courts have considerably narrowed the concept of "fair use" when multiple copies of a copyrighted work are involved.

A landmark case was a successful lawsuit in 1991 by book publishers against Kinko's, a national chain of photocopying stores. The chain was charged with copyright *infringement* because it reproduced excerpts from books without permission and sold them in anthologies to college students. Although Kinko's argued "fair use" for educational purposes, the court rejected this defense. The court settlement cost Kinko's $500,000 in damages and almost $1.5 million in legal fees.

Organizations that have a single subscription to a newsletter and then circulate it via in-house e-mail also violate the law. Atlas Telecom paid a $100,000 settlement after admitting that it electronically distributed about a dozen telecommunications newsletters to its employees. According to the suit filed by Phillips Publishing, Inc., the company made hundreds of copies by reproducing the newsletters on the in-house database.

Such lawsuits can be avoided if an organization orders quantity reprints from the publisher and pays a licensing fee that permits it to make paper or electronic copies.

on the job INSIGHTS

Plagiarism versus Copyright Infringement

Copyright infringement and plagiarism differ. You may be guilty of copyright infringement even if you attribute the materials and give the source, but don't get permission from the author or publisher to reproduce the materials.

In the case of plagiarism, the author makes no attempt to attribute the information at all. As the guide for Hamilton College says, "Plagiarism is a form of fraud. You plagiarize if you present other writers' words or ideas as your own." Maurice Isserman, writing in the *Chronicle of Higher Education,* further explains, "Plagiarism substitutes someone else's prowess at explanation for your own efforts."

The World Wide Web has increased the problems of plagiarism because it is quite easy for anyone, from students to college presidents, to cut and paste entire paragraphs (or even pages) into a term paper or speech and claim it as their own creation. Of course, students also can purchase complete term papers online, but that loophole is rapidly shrinking as more sophisticated software programs, such as www.turnitin.com, can scan the entire Internet for other sources that use the same phrases used in a student's research paper.

John Barrie, founder of Turnitin, told the *Wall Street Journal* that ". . . 85 percent of the cases of plagiarism that we see are straight copies from the Internet—a student uses the Internet like a 1.5 billion-page cut-and-paste encyclopedia." Most universities have very strong rules about plagiarism, and it is not uncommon for students to receive an "F" in a course for plagiarism. In the business world, stealing someone else's words and expression of thought is called *theft of intellectual property* and lawsuits are filed.

Source: Dennis L. Wilcox. *Public Relations Writing and Media Techniques,* 5th ed. Boston: Allyn & Bacon, 2005, p. 77.

Dow Jones, publisher of the *Wall Street Journal,* has a whole department (www.djreprints.com) that arranges reprints that can be used in print, e-mail, PDF, or Web link formats. In the case of using entire articles or book chapters from a variety of sources, individuals and organizations can get permission and pay a royalty fee to the Copyright Clearance Center (www.copyright.com), which has been established to represent a large number of publishers.

Government documents (city, county, state, and federal) are in the public domain and cannot be copyrighted. Public relations personnel, under the fair use doctrine, can freely use quotations and statistics from a government document, but care must be exercised to ensure that the material is in context and not misleading. The most common problem occurs when an organization uses a government report as a form of endorsement for its services or products. An airline, for example, might cite a government study showing that it provides the most service to customers, but neglect to state the basis of comparison or other factors.

Photography and Artwork

The copyright law makes it clear that freelance and commercial photographers retain ownership of their work. In other words, a customer who buys a copyrighted photo owns the item itself, but not the right to make additional copies. That right remains with the photographer unless transferred in writing.

In a further extension of this right, the duplication of copyrighted photos is also illegal. This was established in a 1990 U.S. Federal District Court case in which the Professional Photographers of America (PPofA) sued a nationwide photofinishing firm for ignoring copyright notices on pictures sent for additional copies.

Freelance photographers generally charge for a picture on the basis of its use. If it is used only once, perhaps for an employee newsletter, the fee is low. If, however, the company wants to use the picture in the corporate annual report or on the company calendar, the fee may be considerably higher. Consequently, it is important for a public relations person to tell the photographer exactly how the picture will be used. Arrangements and fees then can be determined for (1) one-time use, (2) unlimited use, or (3) the payment of royalties every time the picture is used.

Computer manipulation of original artwork can also violate copyright. One photographer's picture of a racing yacht was used on a poster after the art director electronically changed the numbers on the sail and made the water a deeper blue. In another case, a photo distribution agency successfully sued *Newsday* for unauthorized use of a color image after the newspaper reconstructed the agency's picture using a computer scanner, then failed to credit the photographer. FPG International was awarded $20,000 in damages, ten times the initial licensing fee of $2,000. In sum, slightly changing a copyrighted photo or a piece of artwork can be considered a violation of copyright if the intent is to capitalize on widespread recognition of the original art.

This was the case when the estate of the late children's author, Dr. Seuss, won a $1.5 million judgment against a Los Angeles T-shirt maker for infringement of copyright. The manufacturer had portrayed a parody of Dr. Seuss's Cat in the Hat character smoking marijuana and giving the peace sign. In another situation, the Rock and Roll Hall of Fame filed a copyright suit against a freelance photographer who snapped a picture of the unique building at sunset and sold posters of his work without paying a licensing fee.

Similarly, sports logos are registered trademarks, and a *licensing fee* must be paid before anyone can use logos for commercial products and promotions. Teams in the National Football League (NFL) and the National Basketball Association (NBA) earn more than $3 billion annually just selling licensed merchandise, and the sale of college and university trademarked goods is rapidly approaching that mark. Schools such as Notre Dame, Michigan, and Ohio State rake in more than $3 million a year in royalties from licensing their logos to be placed on everything from beer mugs to T-shirts. The penalty for not paying a licensing fee is steep. The NFL, during Super Bowl week, typically confiscates about $1 million in bogus goods and files criminal charges against the offending vendors.

The Rights of Freelance Writers

Although the rights of freelance photographers have been established for some years, it was only recently that freelance writers gained more control over the ownership of their work.

In the now famous *Reid* Case (*Community for Creative Nonviolence v. Reid*), the U.S. Supreme Court in 1989 ruled that writers retained ownership of their work and that purchasers of it simply gained a "license" to reproduce the copyrighted work.

Prior to this ruling, the common practice was to assume that commissioned articles were "work for hire" and the purchaser owned the copyright. In other words, a magazine could reproduce the article in any number of ways and even sell it to another publication without the writer's permission.

Under the new interpretation, ownership of a writer's work is subject to negotiation and contractual agreement. Writers may agree to assign all copyright rights to the work they have been hired to do or they may give permission only for a specific one-time use.

In a related matter, freelance writers are pressing for additional compensation if an organization puts their work on CD-ROM, online databases, or the Internet's World Wide Web. They won a major victory in 2001 when the Supreme Court (*New York Times v. Tasini*) ruled that publishers, by making articles accessible through electronic databases, infringed the copyrights of freelance contributors.

Public relations firms and corporate public relations departments are responsible for ensuring compliance with the copyright law. This means that all agreements with a freelance writer must be in writing, and the use of the material must be clearly stated. Ideally, public relations personnel should negotiate multiple rights and even complete ownership of the copyright.

Copyright Issues on the Internet

The Internet and World Wide Web raise new issues about the protection of intellectual property. Two issues regarding copyright are: (1) the downloading of copyrighted material and (2) the unauthorized uploading of such material.

The Downloading of Material   In general, the same rules apply to cyberspace as to more earthbound methods of expressing and disseminating ideas. Original materials in digital form are still protected by copyright. The fair-use limits for materials found on the Internet are essentially the same as the fair use of materials disseminated by any other means.

Related to this is the use of news articles and features that are sent via e-mail or the Web to the clients of clipping services. An organization may use such clips to track its publicity efforts, but it can't distribute the article on its own Web site or intranet without permission and a royalty payment to the publication where the article appeared.

The Uploading of Material   In many cases, owners of copyrighted material have uploaded various kinds of information with the intention of making it freely available. Some examples are software, games, and even the entire text of *The Hitchhiker's Guide to the Galaxy*. The problem comes, however, when third parties upload copyrighted material without permission. Consequently, copyright holders are increasingly patrolling the Internet and World Wide Web to stop the unauthorized use of material.

A good example is Viacom, which constantly monitors such sites as Google's YouTube for unauthorized postings of video clips from its various televison programs on MTV or CBS. Under the 1998 Digital Millennium Copyright Act, Internet businesses such as YouTube are immune from liability for material posted by its users, but are required to take down any infringing material after it is notified by the copyright owner. In one year alone, YouTube removed 230,000 clips at the request of Viacom— so that's why a viewer may see a video one day and have it disappear the next day. The posting of illegal video clips continues to dog the industry, causing a great deal of lobbying for more protective legislation and even major lawsuits. In 2007, for example, Viacom filed a $1 billion copyright infringement suit against Google.

Some other examples:

◆ Dutton Children's Books threatened a lawsuit against a New Mexico State University student for using Winnie the Pooh illustrations on his home page.

◆ Paramount Pictures sent warning notes to *Star Trek* fans against using the Internet to disseminate photos from the TV series.

◆ Corbis Corporation, which has millions of photos for licensing or purchase, threatened legal action against a retirement community for using a photo of an elderly couple on its Web site without paying the licensing fee.

Copyright Guidelines

A number of points have been discussed about copyright. A public relations person should keep the following in mind:

◆ Ideas cannot be copyrighted, but the expression of those ideas can be.

◆ Major public relations materials (brochures, annual reports, videotapes, motion pictures, position papers, and the like) should be copyrighted, if only to prevent unauthorized use by competitors.

◆ Although there is a concept of fair use, any copyrighted material intended directly to advance the sales and profits of an organization should not be used unless permission is given.

◆ Copyrighted material should not be taken out of context, particularly if it implies endorsement of the organization's services or products.

◆ Quantity reprints of an article should be ordered from the publisher.

◆ Permission is required to use segments of television programs or motion pictures.

◆ Permission must be obtained to use segments of popular songs (written verses or sound recordings) from a recording company.

◆ Photographers and freelance writers retain the rights to their works. Permission and fees must be negotiated to use works for other purposes than originally agreed on.

◆ Photographs of current celebrities or those who are now deceased cannot be used for promotion and publicity purposes without permission.

◆ Permission is required to reprint cartoon characters, such as Snoopy or Garfield. In addition, cartoons and other artwork or illustrations in a publication are copyrighted.

◆ Government documents are not copyrighted, but caution is necessary if the material is used in a way that implies endorsement of products or services.

◆ Private letters, or excerpts from them, cannot be published or used in sales and publicity materials without the permission of the letter writer.

◆ Original material posted on the Internet and the World Wide Web has copyright protection.

◆ The copyrighted material of others should not be posted on the Internet unless specific permission is granted.

Trademark Law

What do the names Diet Coke, iTunes, Dockers, eBay, Academy Awards, and even Mr. Peanut have in common? They are all registered trademarks protected by law.

A *trademark* is a word, symbol, or slogan, used singly or in combination, that identifies a product's origin. According to Susan L. Cohen, writing in *Editor & Publisher*'s annual trademark supplement, "It also serves as an indicator of quality, a kind of shorthand for consumers to use in recognizing goods in a complex marketplace." Research

FedEx® Is Not Synonymous With Overnight Shipping.

That's why you can't FedEx or Federal Express your package. Neither FedEx® nor Federal Express® are nouns, verbs, adverbs or even participles. They are adjectives and identify our unique brand of shipping services. So if you want to send a package overnight, ask for FedEx® delivery services.

When you do, we think you'll know why we say "Why Fool Around With Anyone Else?"® After all, FedEx is "Absolutely, Positively the Best in the Business."® Help us protect our marks. Ask us before you use them, use them correctly, and, most of all, only ask for FedEx® delivery services.

FedEx

Be absolutely sure.

www.fedex.com

© 1998 Federal Express Corporation

Protection of trademarks requires corporate diligence. Some companies deliver warning messages through advertisements in trade magazines, as in this FedEx example.

indicates, for example, that 53 percent of Americans say brand quality takes precedence over price considerations.

The concept of a trademark is nothing new. The ancient Egyptians carved marks into the stones of the pyramids, and the craftsmen of the Middle Ages used guild marks to identify the source and quality of products.

What is new, however, is the proliferation of trademarks and service marks in modern society. Coca-Cola may be the world's most recognized trademark, according to some studies, but it is only one of almost one million active trademarks registered with the federal Patent and Trademark Office. And, according to the International Trademark Association, the number keeps going up at a rapid rate.

The Protection of Trademarks

There are three basic guidelines regarding the use of trademarks:

- Trademarks are proper adjectives and should be capitalized and followed by a generic noun or phrase (e.g., *Kleenex tissues* or *Rollerblade skates*).
- Trademarks should not be pluralized or used in the possessive form. Saying "American Express's credit card" is improper.
- Trademarks are never verbs. Saying "The client Express Mailed the package" violates the rule.

In addition, organizations take the step of designating brand names and slogans with various marks. The registered trademark symbol is a superscript, small capital "R" in a circle—®. "Registered in U.S. Patent and Trademark Office" and "Reg. U.S. Pat. Off" may also be used. A "TM" in small capital letters indicates a trademark that isn't registered. It represents a company's common-law claim to a right of trademark or a trademark for which registration is pending. For example, 3M™ Post-it® Notes.

A *service mark* is like a trademark, but it designates a service rather than a product, or is a logo. An "SM" in small capitals in a circle—Ⓢⓜ—is the symbol for a registered service mark. If registration is pending, the "SM" should be used without the circle.

These symbols are used in advertising, product labeling, news releases, company brochures, and so on to let the public and competitors know that a name, slogan, or symbol is protected by law. See the FedEx ad on page 313 for an example of how organizations publicize their trademarks and service marks.

Public relations practitioners play an important role in protecting the trademarks of their employers. They safeguard trademarks and respect other organizational trademarks in the following ways:

♦ Ensure that company trademarks are capitalized and used properly in all organizational literature and graphics. Lax supervision can cause loss of trademark protection.

♦ Distribute trademark brochures to editors and reporters and place advertisements in trade publications, designating names to be capitalized.

♦ Educate employees as to what the organization's trademarks are and how to use them correctly.

♦ Monitor the mass media to make certain that trademarks are used correctly. If they are not, send a gentle reminder.

♦ Check publications to ensure that other organizations are not infringing on a registered trademark. If they are, the company legal department should protest with letters and threats of possible lawsuits.

♦ Make sure the trademark is actually being used. A 1988 revision of the Trademark Act no longer permits an organization to hold a name in reserve.

♦ Ensure that the trademarks of other organizations are correctly used and properly noted.

♦ Avoid the use of trademarked symbols or cartoon figures in promotional materials without the explicit permission of the owner. In some cases, to be discussed, a licensing fee is required.

Organizations adamantly insist on the proper use of trademarks in order to avoid the problem of having a name or slogan become generic. Or, to put it another way, a brand name becomes a common noun through general public use. Some trade names that have become generic include *aspirin, thermos, cornflakes, nylon, cellophane,* and *yo-yo.* This means that any company can use these names to describe a product.

The Problem of Trademark Infringement

Today, when there are thousands of businesses and organizations, finding a trademark not already in use is extremely difficult. The task is even more frustrating if a company wants to use a trademark on an international level.

A good example is what happened to Nike at the 1992 Olympic Games in Barcelona. The athletic shoe manufacturer paid millions to be an official sponsor of the games, and it planned to introduce a new line of clothes at the event. There was a snag, however. A Spanish high court ruled that the Beaverton, Oregon, firm's

$50 million for the rights to license his name and likeness. According to the *Wall Street Journal*, Ali's name and image currently generates about $4 million to $7 million annually in licensing fees and endorsements.

The legal doctrine is the *right of publicity*, which gives entertainers, athletes, and other celebrities the sole ability to cash in on their fame. The legal right is loosely akin to a trademark or copyright, and many states have made it a commercial asset that can be inherited by a celebrity's descendents. One California artist, for example, was sued by the heirs of the Three Stooges because he made a charcoal portrait of the famous acting team and reproduced it on T-shirts and lithographs.

Legal protection also extends to the use of "sound-alikes" or "look-alikes." Bette Midler won a $400,000 judgment against Young & Rubicam (later affirmed by the Supreme Court on appeal) after the advertising agency used another singer to do a "sound-alike" of her singing style in a rendition of the song "Do You Wanna Dance?" for a Ford commercial. The court ruled: "When a distinctive voice of a professional singer is widely known and is deliberately imitated in order to sell a product, the sellers have appropriated what is not theirs."

Regulations by Government Agencies

The promotion of products and services, whether through advertising, product publicity, or other techniques, is not protected by the First Amendment. Instead, the courts have traditionally ruled that such activities fall under the doctrine of commercial speech. This means that messages can be regulated by the state in the interest of public health, safety, and consumer protection.

Consequently, the states and the federal government have passed legislation that regulates commercial speech and even restricts it if standards of disclosure, truth, and accuracy are violated. One consequence was the banning of cigarette advertising on television in the 1960s. A more difficult legal question is whether government can completely ban the advertising or promotion of a legally sold product such as cigarettes or alcohol.

Public relations personnel involved in product publicity and the distribution of financial information should be aware of guidelines established by major government agencies such as the Federal Trade Commission (FTC), the Securities and Exchange Commission (SEC), and even the Federal Communications Commission (FCC).

Federal Trade Commission

The Federal Trade Commission has jurisdiction to determine that advertisements are not deceptive or misleading. Public relations personnel should also know that the commission has jurisdiction over product news releases and other forms of product publicity, such as videos and brochures.

In the eyes of the FTC, both advertisements and product publicity materials are vehicles of commercial trade—and therefore subject to regulation. In fact, Section 43(a) of the Lanham Act makes it clear that anyone, including public relations personnel, is subject to liability if that person participates in the making or dissemination of a false and misleading representation in any advertising or promotional material. This includes advertising and public relations firms, which also can be held liable for writing, producing, and distributing product publicity materials on behalf of clients.

An example of an FTC complaint is one filed against Campbell Soup Company for claiming that its soups were low in fat and cholesterol and thus helpful in fighting heart disease. The commission charged that the claim was deceptive because publicity and advertisements didn't disclose that the soups also were high in sodium, a condition that increases the risk of heart disease.

The Campbell Soup case raises an important aspect of FTC guidelines. Although a publicized fact may be accurate in itself, FTC staff also considers the context or "net impression received by the consumers." In Campbell's case, advertising copywriters and publicists ignored the information about high sodium, which placed an entirely new perspective on the health benefits of the soup.

> " There is a trend toward potential claims, including PR firms, for their role in disseminating a message that is misleading or . . . has omitted material facts. "
>
> —*Michael Lasky,* partner in the New York law firm of Davis & Gilbert

Hollywood's abuse of endorsements and testimonials to publicize its films also has attracted the scrutiny of the FTC. It was discovered that Sony Pictures had concocted quotes from a fictitious movie critic to publicize four of its films. And 20th Century Fox admitted that it had hired actors to appear in "man in the street" commercials to portray unpaid moviegoers.

More recently, the FTC has been focusing on the marketing of food and beverages to children. In 2007, the agency subpoenaed 44 food marketers asking for detailed reports on how much they spend promoting their products to children and adolescents to determine whether more federal regulations might be required.

FTC investigators are always on the lookout for unsubstantiated claims and various forms of misleading or deceptive information. Some of the words in promotional materials that trigger FTC interest are *authentic, certified, cure, custom-made, germ-free, natural, unbreakable, perfect, first-class, exclusive,* and *reliable*.

In recent years, the FTC also has established guidelines for "green" marketing and the use of "low-carb" in advertisements and publicity materials for food products. The following general guidelines, adapted from FTC regulations, should be taken into account when writing product publicity materials:

- Make sure the information is accurate and can be substantiated.
- Stick to the facts. Don't "hype" the product or service by using flowery, nonspecific adjectives and ambiguous claims.
- Make sure celebrities or others who endorse the product actually use it. They should not say anything about the product's properties that cannot be substantiated.
- Watch the language. Don't say "independent research study" when the research was done by the organization's staff.
- Provide proper context for statements and statistics attributed to government agencies. They don't endorse products.
- Describe tests and surveys in sufficient detail so the consumer understands what was tested under what conditions.
- Remember that a product is not "new" if only the packaging has been changed or the product is more than six months old.
- When comparing products or services with a competitor's, make certain you can substantiate your claims.
- Avoid misleading and deceptive product demonstrations.

Companies found in violation of FTC guidelines are usually given the opportunity to sign a consent decree. This means that the company admits no wrongdoing but agrees to change its advertising and publicity claims. Companies may also be fined by the FTC or ordered to engage in corrective advertising and publicity.

Securities and Exchange Commission

The megamergers and the IPOs (initial public offerings) of many new companies in the 1990s made the Securities and Exchange Commission a household name in the business world. This federal agency closely monitors the financial affairs of publicly traded companies and protects the interests of stockholders.

SEC guidelines on public disclosure and insider trading are particularly relevant to corporate public relations staff members who must meet those federal requirements. The distribution of misleading information or failure to make a timely disclosure of material information may be the basis of liability under the SEC code. A company may even be liable if, while it satisfies regulations by getting information out, it conveys crucial information in a vague way or buries it deep in the news release.

A good example is Enron, the Houston-based energy company that became a household word overnight when it became the largest corporate failure in U.S. history. The company management was charged with a number of SEC violations, including the distribution of misleading news releases about its finances. According to congressional testimony, the company issued a quarterly earnings news release that falsely led investors to believe that the company was "on track" to meet strong earnings growth in 2002. Three months later, the company was bankrupt. Later, in criminal trials, Enron's CEO, Jeffrey Skilling, was sentenced to 24 years in prison. The head of investor relations, Mark Koenig, received 18 months for aiding and abetting securities fraud.

The SEC has volumes of regulations, but the three concepts most pertinent to public relations personnel are as follows:

1. **Full information must be given on anything that might materially affect the company's stock.** This includes such things as (1) dividends or their deletion, (2) annual and quarterly earnings, (3) stock splits, (4) mergers or takeovers, (5) major management changes, (6) major product developments, (7) expansion plans, (8) change of business purpose, (9) defaults, (10) proxy materials, (11) disposition of major assets, (12) purchase of own stock, and (13) announcements of major contracts or orders. In a somewhat unusual situation, computer giant HP was investigated by the SEC for not disclosing the reasons why a prominent member of the board of directors resigned because he disagreed with the board chair, Patricia Dunn, about a decision to "spy" on other board members to discover possible leaks of proprietary information.

2. **Timely disclosure is essential.** A company must act promptly (within minutes or a few hours) to dispel or confirm rumors that result in unusual market activity or market variations. The most common ways of dispensing such financial information are through use of electronic news release services, contact with the major international news services (Dow Jones Wire), and bulk faxing.

3. **Insider trading is illegal.** Company officials, including public relations staffs and outside counsel, cannot use inside information to buy and sell company stock. The landmark case on insider trading occurred in 1965, when Texas Gulf Sulphur executives used inside information about an ore strike in Canada to buy stock while at the same time issuing a news release downplaying rumors that a rich find had been made. (To review the highest-profile inside trader case in recent history, see the PR Casebook on Martha Stewart, page 320.)

PRCASEBOOK

A Suggested Recipe for Martha Stewart: Litigation Public Relations

The practice of litigation public relations started in the 1990s. The O. J. Simpson murder trial gave the practice high visibility as both sides extensively used public relations to influence public perceptions—and even the jury pool—about the character of the defendant.

Since then, a number of public relations firms have started litigation practices to help both celebrities and organizations deal with criminal charges and class-action suits that can severely damage reputations and even the bottom line. In essence, litigation public relations is a form of reputation management.

As James Haggerty, author of *Winning Your Case with Public Relations*, writes, "Communication is now central to the management of modern litigation. It can mean communicating to external audiences, such as the media, or to internal audiences, like employers, investors, shareholders, and others with a vested interest in the organization." He continues, ". . . while you can have a victory in the courtroom of public opinion without a victory in the courtroom, your legal victory doesn't amount to much if, in the process, you sacrifice reputation, corporate character, and all of the other elements that make up an organization's goodwill in the marketplace."

Martha Stewart, the queen of home decorating and cooking, didn't win in the court of law or in the courtroom of public opinion. She was sentenced to five months in prison (plus five months' home confinement) in 2004 for lying to federal investigators about a stock sale and possible insider trading. On the courthouse steps after the conviction, Stewart told the press, "Whatever happened to me personally shouldn't have any effect whatsoever on the great company Martha Stewart Living Omnimedia."

Unfortunately, that wasn't the case. Stewart didn't realize that the whole business was based on her persona. As Steven Fink, a crisis communication consultant, noted, "People are buying her products because they have a positive impression of the public image of Martha Stewart. If that image becomes damaged, it can hurt her business in a serious way."

And it was serious. Although the revenues and stock price of her company declined during the pretrial period, total revenues dropped 33 percent in the three months following the conviction. The television program *Martha Stewart Living* lost half of its viewers after the verdict, and

Martha Stewart reads a prepared statement after being convicted of lying to federal prosecutors about a stock sale based on insider information.

revenues from the program dropped 50 percent, causing the show to be suspended.

Public relations experts say that the basic concepts of litigation public relations practice could have saved Stewart, or at least resulted in a less painful outcome. Stewart, for example, stonewalled the media, even though there was intense public interest because of her celebrity status. Indeed, the public relations firm Hill & Knowlton found that 80 percent of Americans are willing to suspend judgment if an organization responds quickly to an accusation. Other studies have found that nearly three times as many people presumed an organization to be innocent when the company responded to all allegations, as opposed to saying "no comment."

Stewart was also faulted for not following any of the basic rules of crisis communications. According to *PRWeek*, Stewart "resisted making even the slightest apologetic gesture as she was accused, tried, and convicted of Wall Street shenanigans." It also didn't help her reputation and image when she showed up for court with a $5,000 designer purse, which the media gleefully reported in full.

Some pundits predicted that Stewart would never recover her reputation as the queen of home decorating, but she emerged from jail a more humble person and gained a degree of public sympathy. When she was a guest on Fox News in April 2006, David Asman summarized her comeback:

Well, if you thought Martha Stewart was down for the count, think again. Since her release from prison, her business is back, and so is her stock, scoring deal after deal, with Sirius Satellite Radio, a new magazine, designing upscale homes, also grabbing six Emmy nominations for daytime TV. Now the Martha Stewart brand will be in Macy's, inking a deal to stock a line of home furnishings.

The courts are increasingly applying the *mosaic doctrine* to financial information. Maureen Rubin, an attorney and professor at California State University, Northridge, explains that a court may examine all information released by a company, including news releases, to determine whether, taken as a whole, they create an "overall misleading" impression. One such case was *Cytryn v. Cook* (1990), in which a U.S. District Court ruled that the proper test of a company's adequate financial disclosure was not the literal truth of each positive statement, but the overall misleading impression that it combined to create in the eyes of potential investors.

As a result of such cases, investor relations personnel must also avoid such practices as:

◆ Unrealistic sales and earnings reports

◆ Glowing descriptions of products in the experimental stage

◆ Announcements of possible mergers or takeovers that are only in the speculation stage

◆ Free trips for business reporters and offers of stock to financial analysts and editors of financial newsletters

◆ Omission of unfavorable news and developments

◆ Leaks of information to selected outsiders and financial columnists

◆ Dissemination of false rumors about a competitor's financial health

The SEC also has regulations supporting the use of "plain English" in prospectuses and other financial documents. Companies and financial firms are supposed to make information understandable to the average investor by removing sentences littered with lawyerisms such as *aforementioned*, *hereby*, *therewith*, *whereas*, and *hereinafter*. The cover page, summary, and risk factor sections of prospectuses must be clear, concise, and understandable. A SEC booklet gives helpful writing hints such as (1) make sentences short; (2) use *we* and *our*, *you* and *your*; and (3) say it with an active verb. More information about SEC guidelines can be accessed at its Web site: www.sec.gov/.

Fair Disclosure Regulation   The SEC has another regulation regarding Fair Disclosure (known as *Reg FD*). Although regulations already existed regarding "material disclosure" of information that could affect the price of stock, the new regulation expanded the concept by requiring publicly traded companies to broadly disseminate "material" information via a news release, Webcast, or SEC filing.

According to the SEC, Reg FD ensures that all investors, not just brokerage firms and analysts, will receive financial information from a company at the same time. Schering-Plough, a drug maker, was fined $1 million by the SEC because the company disclosed "material nonpublic information" to analysts and portfolio managers without making the same information available to the public.

Sarbanes-Oxley Act   The most recent legislation is the Sarbanes-Oxley Act, which was made law in 2002 as a result of the Enron and Worldcom financial scandals. The Enron scandal alone cost investors an estimated $90 billion.

Officially known as the Public Company Accounting Reform and Investor Protection Act, its purpose is to increase investor confidence in a company's accounting procedures. Chief executive officers (CEOs) and chief financial officers (CFOs) must now personally certify the accuracy of their financial reports and are subject to criminal proceedings if they are not accurate.

The law also forbids companies from giving personal loans to officers and directors, and it places more independent fiscal responsibility on boards of directors to ensure that the company is adhering to good corporate governance and accounting practices. One of the first executives to be charged under the act was Richard Scrushy, former CEO of HealthSouth Corp. According to prosecutors, he was involved in a $2.7 billion accounting fraud at the company.

The jury is still out, however, as to whether the Sarbanes-Oxley Act will ensure that the public actually receives more detailed financial information from public companies. The act is still being clarified and challenged in the courts, and attorneys have a powerful role in deciding what can and can't be released. Woody Wallace, head of an investor relations firm, told *O'Dwyer's PR Services Report*, "Most attorneys are conservative and are going to cut down what's being said. Less information and less useful information is being given out. News releases become cursory." How public relations personnel and attorneys work together will be discussed shortly.

Federal Communications Commission (FCC)

The FCC is primarily involved in the licensing of radio and television stations, allocating frequencies, and ensuring that the public airwaves are used in the public interest. However, on occasion, the commission's policies and procedures directly impact the work of public relations personnel who distribute video news releases (VNRs) on behalf of employers and clients.

The controversy about proper *source attribution* of VNRs by television stations was somewhat discussed in Chapter 3, but political debate still continues about FCC's ruling in 2005 that broadcasters must disclose to viewers the origin of video news releases produced by the government or corporations when the material runs on the public airways. The agency didn't specify what form such disclosure should take, but broadcasters argued that the FCC was curtailing their First Amendment rights. FCC commissioner Jonathan Edelstein disagreed, saying the issue was not free speech, but about identifying who is actually speaking. He told the *Washington Post*, "We have a responsibility to tell broadcasters they have to let people know where the material is coming from. Viewers are hoodwinked into thinking it's really a news story when it might be from the government or a big corporation trying to influence the way they think."

The issue of source attribution came about as a result of critics complaining that VNRs produced by the Bush administration and aired as part of local television reports was "government propaganda." In addition, public relations firms came under fire from citizen watchdog groups who say the actual client for a VNR is often obscured. For example, television stations used a VNR that featured two prominent "debunkers" of global warming under the rubric of the "TCS Daily Science Roundtable," which was actually owned by a Republican public relations firm that included ExxonMobil as a client.

Both the broadcast and public relations industry have joined together to call for voluntary controls and disclosure instead of "government intrusion" into the news process. Both industries have also adopted codes of practice (discussed in Chapter 3), but this didn't stop the FCC in October 2007 from fining a television station in Pennsylvania $40,000 and Sinclair Broadcast Group $36,000 for airing programs by Armstrong Williams in which he promoted the U.S. Department of Education's No Child Left Behind program. He failed to disclose that he was paid $240,000 by the federal agency as part of a contact awarded to Ketchum communications back in 2005, thus violating the FCC's rules about sponsorship identification. This case is also discussed in Chapter 3.

Fines have also been levied by the FCC in terms of enforcing regulations about indecency on the airwaves. The triggering event was Janet Jackson's "wardrobe malfunction" at the 2004 Super Bowl halftime show when Justin Timberlake ripped off a piece her black leather top, exposing her right breast for an instant. The "malfunction," of course, got more media coverage and public discussion than the game itself. The FCC was not amused; it levied a $550,000 fine on CBS television (a division of Viacom) for airing the incident.

In another case, the agency fined Clear Channel Communications, the largest radio station chain in the United States, $1.75 million over indecency complaints against Howard Stern and other radio personalities. As a result of all this, live television programs have a short delay before the signal is transmitted just in case someone does something "indecent" or uses the "F" word. Public relations personnel also are feeling the heat as broadcasters express more caution booking talk show guests who discuss sexual and reproductive health.

Other Federal Regulatory Agencies

Although the FTC and the SEC are the major federal agencies concerned with the content of advertising and publicity materials, public relations professionals should be familiar with the guidelines of two other major agencies: the Food and Drug Administration (FDA) and the Equal Employment Opportunity Commission (EEOC).

The Food and Drug Administration

The FDA oversees the advertising and promotion of prescription drugs, over-the-counter medicines, and cosmetics. Under the federal Food, Drug, and Cosmetic Act, any "person" (which includes advertising and public relations firms) who "causes the misbranding" of products through the dissemination of false and misleading information may be liable.

The FDA has specific guidelines for video, audio, and print news releases on health-care topics. First, the release must provide "fair balance" by telling consumers about the risks as well as the benefits of the drug or treatment. Second, the writer must be clear about the limitations of a particular drug or treatment, for example, that it may not help people with certain conditions. Third, a news release or media kit should be accompanied by supplementary product sheets or brochures that give full prescribing information.

Because prescription drugs have major FDA curbs on advertising and promotion, the drug companies try to sidestep the regulations by publicizing diseases. Eli Lilly & Co., the maker of Prozac, provides a good example. The company sponsors ads and distributes publicity about depression. And the Glaxo Institute for Digestive Health conducts information campaigns about the fact that stomach pains can be an indication of major problems. Of course, Glaxo also makes the ulcer drug Zantac.

Another public relations approach that has come under increased FDA scrutiny is the placement of celebrities on television talk shows who are being paid by the drug companies to mention the name of a particular drug while they talk about their recovery from cancer, a heart attack, or depression. Some programs, such as *Today*, have now banned such guests.

Equal Employment Opportunity Commission

Diversity in the workplace has dramatically increased in recent years and the EEOC is charged with ensuring that workers are not discriminated against on the basis of their religion, ethnic background, gender, or even their English skills.

Employers, for example, need to accommodate the religious needs of their employees. The focus has been on Muslims who pray five times a day and have attire related to their religion, but Jews must also be allowed to be absent from the workplace on various Holy days. At the same time, EEOC guidelines also call for employers to ensure that employees don't express their religious views at work or impose their beliefs on others. In other words, a company's policy about harassment also needs to include wording covering religion.

> "Employers must understand that discriminatory English-only rules can hurt productivity, morale, and ultimately their bottom line."
>
> ——*Kimberlie Ryan,* Denver attorney

The EEOC also gets involved in the contentious issue of language. Federal law doesn't prevent employers from requiring workers to speak only English if it is justified by business necessity or safety concerns, but a blanket policy of English-only can get an employer in trouble if it forbids workers to speak another language during breaks, or the language spoken doesn't make a difference in the performance of the job. English-only advocates argue that multilingualism in the workplace encourages newcomers to retain their own language and that English-speakers feel slighted when fellow workers talk to each other in their native langue. On the other hand, Denver attorney Kimberlie Ryan told the *Wall Street Journal,* "This is not about whether people should learn English; it's about not using language as a weapon of harassment."

Being sensitive to diversity of the workplace, plus a thorough understanding of EEOC guidelines, is a requirement for anyone working in employee communications. Public relations personnel often work closely with human resources to offer workshops and educational materials on diversity to educate the employees to be more tolerant and understanding of each other. It is much cheaper than a series of lawsuits charging discrimination.

Corporate Speech

The First Amendment of the U.S. Constitution guarantees "freedom of speech," but exactly what speech is protected has been defined by the courts over the past 200 years, and is still being interpreted today. However, there is a well-established doctrine that commercial speech doesn't have the same First Amendment protection as other forms of speech.

Essentially, the government may regulate advertising that is

◆ false,

◆ misleading,

◆ deceptive, or

◆ that promotes unlawful goods and services.

The courts also have ruled that product news releases, brochures, and other promotional vehicles intended to sell a product or service constitute commercial speech.

Another area, however, is what is termed *corporate speech*. Robert Kerr, author of *The Rights of Corporate Speech: Mobil Oil and the Legal Development of the Voice of Big Business*, defines corporate speech as "media efforts by corporations that seek to affect political outcomes or social climate—in contrast with 'commercial speech,' which promotes products or services."

The courts, for the most part, have upheld the right of corporations and other organizations to express their views on public policy, proposed legislation, and a host of other issues that may be of societal or corporate concern. Organizations often do so through op-ed articles, letters to the editor, postings on their Web site, and even news releases.

Some landmark Supreme Court cases have helped establish the concept of corporate free speech. In 1978, for example, the Court struck down a Massachusetts law that prohibited corporations from publicizing their views on issues subject to the ballot box. Then, in 1980, the Court ruled that a New York Public Utilities Commission regulation prohibiting utilities from making statements of public policy and controversy was unconstitutional. Six years later, the Court ruled that the California Public Utilities Commission could not require PG&E to include messages from activist consumer groups in its mailings to customers. The utility argued that inclusion of such messages (called "bill stuffers") impaired the company's right to communicate its own messages.

Nike's Free Speech Battle

The Supreme Court again became involved with corporate free speech in 2003 when it was petitioned by Nike, the shoe and sports clothes manufacturer, to redress a California Supreme Court decision that had ruled that the company's efforts to explain its labor policies abroad was basically "garden variety commercial speech."

The case, *Nike v. Kasky*, raised the thorny question of how to deal with the blurred lines that often separate "free speech" and "commercial speech." Marc Kasky, an activist, had sued Nike, claiming that the company had made false and misleading statements that constituted unlawful and deceptive business practices. Nike, on the other hand, claimed that it had the right to express its views and defend itself against allegations by activist groups that it operated sweatshop factories in Asia and paid subpar wages.

Does a corporation have the right of free speech? Nike took its case to the U.S. Supreme Court after the California court ruled that Nike's defense of its labor practices abroad was simply "commercial speech." Here, protesters unfurl banners opposing Nike's position.

The California Supreme Court disagreed. In its decision, it wrote, . . . "when a corporation, to maintain and increase its sales and profits, makes public statements defending labor practices and working conditions at factories where its products are made, those public statements are commercial speech that may be regulated to prevent consumer deception."

The U.S. Supreme Court, however, was less certain about the "commercial" nature of Nike's public relations campaign. Although it didn't make a decision and sent the case back to the California courts, Eugene Volokh, professor of law at UCLA, noted in a *Wall Street Journal* op-ed piece that Justice Stephen Breyer made an important point. According to Volokh, "Because the commercial message (buy our shoes) was mixed with a political message (our political opponents are wrong), and was presented outside a traditional advertising medium, it should have been treated as fully protected."

Nike, rather than face the California courts again, decided to settle the case with Kasky for $1.5 million that would go to the Fair Labor Association to monitor American factories abroad, particularly in Asia. A number of groups that supported Nike's effort to defend corporate free speech, including PRSA and the Arthur W. Page Society, were somewhat disappointed that the conclusion of the case left many unanswered questions about the right of corporations to speak out on issues and even defend themselves against the charges of activist groups.

Employee Speech in the Digital Age

A modern, progressive organization encourages employee comments and even criticisms. Many employee newspapers and e-bulletin boards even carry letters to the editor because they breed a healthy atmosphere of two-way communication and make company publications more credible. In an era of digital communications and increased legal litigation, however, organizations are increasingly setting guidelines and monitoring what employees say online. The following is a discussion of employee e-mail, surfing the Internet, blogging and even guidelines for being an "avatar" on sites such as Second Life.

Employee E-Mail

The monitoring of employee e-mail by management is well established. A survey by Forrester Consulting for Proofpoint, a maker of e-mail security products, found that almost 50 percent of large companies audit outbound e-mail by their employees. Another 32 percent had actually fired an employee within the last year for breaking e-mail rules.

A number of court decisions have reinforced the right of employers to read employees' e-mail. Pillsbury, for example, fired a worker who posted an e-mail message to a colleague calling management "back-stabbing bastards." The employee sued, but the court sided with the company. In another case, Intel got a court injunction against a former employee who complained about the company in e-mails sent to thousands of employees. The Electronic Frontier Foundation, a group devoted to civil liberties in cyberspace, worried about violation of First Amendment rights. The company, however, contended that it wasn't a matter of free speech, but trespassing on company property.

Employers are increasingly monitoring employee e-mail for two reasons. First, they are concerned about being held liable if an employee posts a racial slur, engages in sexual harassment online, and even transmits sexually explicit jokes that would cause another employee to feel that the workplace was a "hostile" environment. Second, companies are concerned about employee e-mails that may include information that the organization considers proprietory such as trade secrets, marketing plans, and development of new products that would give the competition an advantage. In other words, you should assume that any e-mails you write at work are subject to monitoring and that you can be fired if you violate company guidelines.

Surfing the Internet

Employees should also be careful about using the World Wide Web at work. According to a recent survey by the American Management Association (AMA), more than 75 percent of American employers monitor personal web surfing at work. And more than 25 pecent of the companies have actually fired someone for doing it. Other studies, of course, show that Web surfing at work for personal reasons is done by the majority of employees—and many even think of the Internet in the same context as using the lowly telephone.

> " A New Jersey court found that employers were not just permitted but actually obliged to monitor employee Internet use. "
>
> ——*Patti Waldmeir,* columnist for the *Financial Times*

Employers, of course, are concerned about loss of productivity when employees sit at their desks surfing the Internet or even playing video games. Potential liability, however, is another big factor. Companies can and do get sued for what their employees do online. Office workers accessing porn sites, instant messaging of smutty and racial jokes, and posting desktop wallpaper from *Playboy* magazine are all lawsuits waiting to happen when other workers are offended and even file complaints with the Equal Opportunity Employment Commission (EEOC). According to the *Financial Times*, "A New Jersey court found that employers were not just permitted but actually obliged to monitor employee Internet use."

Employee Blogs

Many organizations now encourage employees to have a blog as a way of fostering discussion on the Internet and getting informal feedback from the public. In some large companies, even top executives have a blog. In most cases, the blog prominently features their association with the business and gives information (and images) about the employer. As John Elasser, editor of *Public Relations Tactics*, says, "Some of that content may be innocuous; other types may be embarrassing or come back to haunt the company in litigation."

Consequently, it is important for the business to have a clear policy that provides guidelines for what rank-and-file employees, as well as executives, can say or not say on their blogs or a posting on another blog. The public relations staff often prepares the general guidelines and trains employees about such matters as the proper use of corporate trademarks, avoiding unfair criticism of other employees or the competition, the use of copyrighted material, or even what topics are particularly sensitive because of pending lawsuits or business negotiations. Bloggers also have an obligation to inform readers that they are employees of the organization, not just an interested average citizen.

Other general rules of netiquette are listed in Chapter 13. In addition, the Electronic Frontier Foundation has a "Legal Guide for Bloggers" at its Web site, www.eff.org/bloggers/lg.

Virtual Online Communities

A newer innovation is virtual online communities, such as Second Life, Entropia, Universe, and There.Com. Although these communities are used by gambling parlors and pornographers, they are also increasingly home to multinational companies advertising their brands and hoping to promote communication among employees worldwide.

IBM, realizing the potential for hosting meetings with clients and partners, has published guidelines for more than 5,000 of its employees who inhabit Second Life and other worlds. Some of its basic rules are (1) don't discuss intellectual property with unauthorized people, (2) don't discriminate or harass, and (3) be a good netizen. IBM, whose employees are often parodied as cogs in matching navy suits, doesn't have a dress code for its employee avatars, but it does suggest being "sensitive to the appropriateness of your avatar or persona's appearance when you are meeting with IBM clients or conducting IBM business."

Liability for Sponsored Events

Public relations personnel often focus on the planning and logistics of an event; they must also take steps to protect the organization from liability and possible lawsuits.

Plant Tours and Open Houses

Plant tours should not be undertaken lightly. They require detailed planning by the public relations staff to guarantee the safety and comfort of visitors. Consideration must be given to such factors as

1. logistics,

2. possible work disruptions as groups pass through the plant,

3. safety, and

4. amount of staffing required.

A well-marked tour route is essential; it is equally important to have trained escort staff and tour guides. Guides should be well versed in company history and operations, and their comments should be somewhat standardized to make sure that key facts are conveyed. In addition, guides should be trained in first aid and thoroughly briefed on what to do in case of an accident or heart attack. At the beginning the guide should outline to the visitors what they will see, the amount of walking involved, the time required, and the number of stairs. This warning tells visitors with heart conditions or other physical handicaps what they can expect.

Many of the points about plant tours are applicable to open houses. The additional problem is having large numbers of people on the plant site at the same time. Such an event calls for special logistical planning by the public relations staff, possibly including the following measures:

- arranging for extra liability insurance,
- hiring off-duty police for security and traffic control,
- arranging to have paramedics and an ambulance on site, and
- making contractual agreements with vendors selling food or souvenirs.

Such precautions will generate goodwill and limit the company's liability. It should be noted, however, that a plaintiff can still collect if negligence on the part of the company can be proved.

Promotional Events

These events are planned primarily to promote product sales, increase organizational visibility, or raise money for charitable causes.

Events that attract crowds require the same kind of planning as does an open house. The public relations person should be concerned about traffic flow, adequate restroom facilities, signage, and security. Off-duty police officers are often hired to handle crowd control, protect celebrities or government officials, and make sure no disruptions occur.

Liability insurance is a necessity. Any public event sponsored by an organization should be insured against accidents that might result in lawsuits charging negligence. Organizations can purchase comprehensive insurance to cover a variety of events or a specific event.

The need for liability insurance also applies to charitable organizations if they sponsor a 10-K run, a bicycle race, or a hot-air balloon race. Participants should sign a release form that protects the organization against liability in case of a heart attack or an accident. An organization that sponsored a 5-K "fun run" had the participants sign a statement that stated in part, ". . . I assume all risk associated with running in this event, including, but not limited to, falls, contact with other participants, the effects of the weather, including high heat/or humidity, traffic, and other conditions of the road."

Promotional events that use public streets and parks also need permits from the appropriate city departments. A 10-K run or a parade, for example, requires permits from the police or the public safety department to block streets. Sponsors frequently hire off-duty police to control traffic.

A music store in one California city found out about these needs the hard way. It allowed a popular rock group to give an informal concert in front of the store as part of a promotion. Radio DJs spread the word and, as a result, a crowd of 8,000 converged on the shopping center, causing a massive traffic jam. The city attorney filed charges against the store for creating a public disturbance and billed it $80,000 for police overtime pay to untangle the mess.

A food event, such as a chili cook-off or a German fest, requires a permit from the public health department and, if liquor is served, a permit from the state alcohol board. If the event is held inside a building not usually used for this purpose, a permit is often required from the fire inspector. In addition, a major deposit may be required as insurance that the organization will clean up a public space after the event.

The Attorney/Public Relations Relationship

Litigation is an integral part of today's business environment, In fact, it is estimated that 90 percent of American corporations are dealing with lawsuits at any given time. Indeed, Philip Rudolph, a partner in a Washington, D.C., law firm, is quoted in *PRWeek*; "The bounds of liability are beginning to stretch in ways that traditional lawyering does not address. You see companies being sued by their own customers over the lawful use of a legal product—such as obesity lawsuits brought against McDonald's."

In such an environment, it's important for public relations personnel and lawyers to work together to not only win in the court of law but in the court of public opinion. Indeed, a survey by Kathy R. Fitzpatrick, a public relations professor now at DePaul University, found that almost 85 percent of the public relations respondents said their relationship with legal counsel was either "excellent" or "good." Researchers at the University of Houston and the University of Missouri, in separate studies, also found that lawyers and public relations practitioners report cooperative relationships.

Winning in the court of public opinion is the responsibility of the public relations professional, and such work is the practice of "litigation public relations." A good example of how this works is how Daimler Chrysler integrates public relations and legal counsel. First, both public relations personnel and legal staff serve on joint committees that review possible litigious situations. Second, when a lawsuit is filed, the integrated team formulates strategies to ensure that key company messages about the lawsuit are distributed to the media and the public.

In one case, even before a Texas trial judge dismissed a $2 billion products liability suit because attorneys for the plaintiffs had falsified evidence, a Daimler Chrysler team was on a nationwide media tour to explain their side of the case. Resulting headlines were "Chrysler Takes Fight to Lawyers" and "Chrysler Group Puts Texas Lawyers on Trial." In another case, when a jury ruled in favor of Chrysler in a wrongful death suit, the automaker regularly gave its perspective on the case to the media to ensure fair and balanced coverage during the trial.

Public relations firms specializing in litigation are also retained if a celebrity gets into legal trouble, whether it be Martha Stewart, Paris Hilton, or football player Michael Vick. See the Insights boxes on pages 320 and 331.

The cooperation between lawyers and public relations counsel has been strengthened in recent years by court rulings that conversations between the two can be considered attorney–client privilege if certain conditions are met. U.S. District Court

on the job INSIGHTS

Litigation PR: Quarterbacking for Michael Vick

High-profile personalities, on occasion, not only need legal counsel but also experts in litigation public relations. Michael Vick, quarterback for the Atlanta Falcons, faced federal charges in July 2007 connected with running a dogfighting operation in Virginia.

The charges against Vick generated widespread media coverge and a great deal of public outrage, particularly from animal lovers. In short order, the National Football League (NFL) suspended him and several companies stopped selling his endorsed products. Nike, for example, suspended Vick's contract without pay and withdrew his products at Nike-owned stores, saying that cruelty to animals was "inhumane and abhorrent." Reebok, owned by Germany's Adidas AG, also suspended sales of its Vick-branded jerseys, saying that it found the accusations

Quarterback Michael Vick.

against Vick "too disturbing to ignore."

At this point, attorneys for Vick called in Sitrick & Co. to handle public relations and help the defense team quell the outpouring of negative

publicity. Vick's lawyers, via Sitrick, noted at a news conference, "We'd like to remind the public that these are only allegations, not facts. This case will be tried in the courts, not the media." Vick, who entered a not-guilty plea at a preliminary hearing, also used the public relations firm to issue a statement that apologized to his teammates and asked that the public to withhold judgment.

Public relations, however, has its limitations. Vick pleaded guilty to federal dogfighting charges and was given a 23-month sentence. At the time of his guilty plea, Vick again made a contrite statement of apology to his teammates and "all the young kids out there for my immature acts." The court of law has finished its business, but the verdict is still out in the court of public opinion whether Vick can save his football career and restore his reputation.

Judge Lewis Kaplan in New York, for example, ruled that client–attorney privilege exists if five conditions are met. Each of the following points must be checked off says Kaplin before the next point can be considered: "(1) confidential communications . . . (2) between lawyers and PR consultants . . . (3) hired by the lawyers to assist them in dealing with the media in cases as this . . . (4) that are made for the giving or receiving of advice . . . (5) directed at handling the client's legal problems are protected by the attorney–client privilege." Other legal experts, however, say that attorney–client privilege is better protected if outside legal counsel actually employs a litigation public relations firm as a consultant instead of using internal public relations staff.

PRSA's *Tactics* suggests six "keys to winning in the court of law—and public opinion." They are:

◆ Make carefully planned public comment in the earliest stages of a crisis or legal issue.

◆ Understand the perspective of lawyers and allow them to review statements when an organization is facing or involved in litigation.

- Public relations practitioners need to guard against providing information to the other side of the legal case.
- Public relations professionals should counsel and coach the legal team.
- Build support from other interested parties, such as industry associations or chambers of commerce.
- Develop a litigation communication team before you need it.

Because the collaboration between lawyers and public relations practitioners is so important, a number of steps can be taken by an organization to ensure that the public relations and legal staffs have a cordial, mutually supportive relationship:

- The public relations and legal staffs should report to the same top executive, who can listen to both sides and decide on a course of action.
- Public relations personnel should know basic legal concepts and regulatory guidelines in order to build trust and credibility with the legal department.
- Both functions should be represented on key committees.
- The organization should have a clearly defined statement of responsibilities for each staff and its relationship to the other. Neither should dominate.
- Periodic consultations should be held during which materials and programs are reviewed.
- The legal staff, as part of its duties, should brief public relations personnel on impending developments in litigation, so press inquiries can be answered in an appropriate manner.

SUMMARY

A Sampling of Legal Problems

There are a number of ways that a public relations practitioner may get caught up in a lawsuit or a case with a government regulatory agency. Practitioners may also be held legally liable if they provide advice or support the illegal activity of a client.

Libel and Defamation

There is now practically little difference between libel and slander; the two are often collectively referred to as *defamation*. The concept of defamation involves a false and malicious (or at least negligent) communication with an identifiable subject who is injured either financially or by loss of reputation or mental suffering. Libel suits can be avoided through the careful use of language. Some offensive communications will fall under the "fair comment" defense; an example of this would be a negative review by a theater critic.

Invasion of Privacy

Companies cannot assume when publishing newsletters that a person waives his or her right to privacy due to status

as an employee. It is important to get written permission to publish photos or use employees in advertising materials, and to be cautious in releasing personal information about employees to the media.

Copyright Law

Copyright is the protection of creative work from unauthorized use. It is assumed that published works are copyrighted, and permission must be obtained to reprint such material. The "fair use" doctrine allows limited quotation, as in a book review. Unless a company has a specific contract with a freelance writer, photographer, or artist to produce work that will be exclusively owned by that company (a situation called "work for hire"), the freelancer owns his or her work. New copyright issues have been raised by the popularity of the Internet and the ease of downloading, uploading, and disseminating images and information.

Trademark Law

A *trademark* is a word, symbol, or slogan that identifies a product's origin. These can be registered with the U.S. Patent and Trademark Office. Trademarks are always capitalized and used as adjectives rather than nouns or verbs. Companies vigorously protect trademarks to prevent their becoming common nouns. One form of trademark infringement may be "misappropriation of personality," the use of a celebrity's name or image for advertising purposes without permission.

Regulations by Government Agencies

Commercial speech is regulated by the government in the interest of public health, safety, and consumer protection. Among the agencies involved in this regulation are the Federal Trade Commission (FTC), the Securities and Exchange Commission (SEC), the Food and Drug Administration (FDA), and the Equal Employment Opportunity Commission (EEOC).

Corporate Speech

Organizations, in general, have the right to express their opinions and views about a number of public issues. However, there is still some blurring of lines between what is considered "commercial speech" and "free speech," as illustrated by the Nike case.

Employee Speech in the Digital Age

Employees are limited in expressing opinions within the corporate environment. E-mail and surfing the Internet, for example, are subject to monitoring. Employees can be fired (or former employees sued) for revealing trade secrets or harassing fellow employees. Companies are also setting guidelines for employee blogs and participating in virtual online communities such as Second Life.

Liability for Sponsored Events

Plant tours, open houses, and other promotional events raise liability issues concerning safety and security. Liability insurance is a necessity. Permits may also be required for the use of public streets and parks and for serving food and liquor.

The Attorney/Public Relations Relationship

Because of all the issues discussed in this chapter, a cooperative relationship must exist between public relations personnel and legal counsel. It helps if both groups report to the same top executive and both are represented on key committees. Public relations practitioners should also be aware of legal concepts and regulatory guidelines and receive briefings from the legal staff on impending developments. A new practice area is litigation public relations.

CASE ACTIVITY What Would You Do?

Expresso Unlimited, a chain of coffee shops, has hired you as director of public relations and marketing. Some of your ideas include (1) a series of advertisements showing pictures and quotes from satisfied customers; (2) hiring a freelance photographer to build up a photo file for use in possible magazine articles, brochures, newsletters, and advertising; (3) reprinting and distributing various magazine articles that have been written about the company; (4) starting an employee newsletter with emphasis on employee features and "personals"; (5) including in the newsletter and advertisements cartoons about coffee drinking from various publications, including the *New Yorker*; (6) citing a government study that rates the quality of coffee beans from around the world, and pointing out that Expresso Unlimited uses only the highest-quality beans; (7) writing a news release that quotes a survey showing that 8 out of 10 serious coffee drinkers prefer Expresso Unlimited; and (8) creating a home page on the Internet that would include pictures of famous people drinking a cup of coffee.

Prepare a memo outlining the legal and regulatory factors that should be considered in implementing the above activities.

QUESTIONS for Review and Discussion

1. Why do public relations staff and firms need to know the legal aspects of creating and distributing messages?
2. How can a public relations person take precautions to avoid libel suits?
3. What is the concept of fair comment and criticism? Are there any limitations?
4. What precautions should a public relations person take to avoid invasion-of-privacy suits?

5. If an organization wants to use the photo or comments of an employee or a customer in an advertisement, what precautions should be taken?

6. When the media call about an employee, what kinds of information should the public relations person provide? What other approaches can be used?

7. What basic guidelines of copyright law should public relations professionals know about?

8. What rights do photographers and freelance writers have regarding ownership of their works?

9. How do public relations people help an organization protect its trademarks?

10. What is "misappropriation of personality"?

11. What should public relations people know about the regulations of the Federal Trade Commission?

12. What should public relations personnel know about the regulations of the Securities and Exchange Commission?

13. Review the Nike case about corporate free speech. Do you agree or disagree that organizations should have full First Amendment rights to answer charges from activist groups and present their opinions on various public issues? What about Nike? Do you agree with the California Supreme Court that Nike's defense of its labor practices abroad was simply "commercial" speech?

14. The casebook on Martha Stewart discusses litigation public relations. Do you think she could have done a better job of handling her reputation after being charged with lying to federal investigators about inside stock trading?

15. The FCC is clamping down on the television stations for using video news releases (VNRs) from public relations sources without telling the viewers the source of the video footage. What is your opinion about the VNR controversy? Should government get involved in this issue?

16. What is the difference between plagiarism and copyright infringement?

17. Many companies contend that they have the right to read the e-mail of employees. What do you think? Is this a violation of privacy and employee free speech?

18. If an organization is sponsoring an open house or a promotional event, what legal aspects should be considered?

19. What should be the relationship between public relations staff and legal counsel in an organization? In what ways do public relations firms assist organizations when they are involved in litigation and court trials?

SUGGESTED READINGS

Bunker, Matthew D., and Bolger, Bethany. "Protecting a Delicate Balance: Facts, Ideas, and Expression in Compilation Copyright Cases." *Journalism & Mass Communications Quarterly,* Vol. 80, No. 1, 2003, pp. 183–197.

Doyne, Karen. "Litigation PR Vital to Winning in Court of Public Opinion." *PRWeek,* July 7, 2004, p. 2.

Fitzpatrick, Kathy R., and Palechar, Michael J. "Disclosing Special Interests: Constitutional Restrictions on Front Groups." *Journal of Public Relations Research,* Vol. 18, No. 3, 2006, pp. 203–224.

Goldsborough, Reid. "Blogging and the Law: Letting Loose is Not Without its Risks." *PRSA Tactics,* August 2005, p. 11.

Gower, Karla K. *Legal and Ethical Restraints on Public Relations.* Long Grove, IL: Waveland Press, 2003.

Hazley, Greg. "PR, Legal Need to Play on Same Team." *O'Dwyer's PR Report,* December 2005, pp. 1, 12–13.

Jordan, Miriam. "Testing 'English Only' Rules: Employers Who Require Workers to Speak English Can Face Discrimination Suits." *Wall Street Journal,* November 8, 2005, pp. B1, 13.

Koppel, Nathan. "A Battle Erupts Over the Right to Market Marilyn." *Wall Street Journal,* April 10, 2006, pp. A1, A11.

Karnitschnig, Matthew. "Media Titans Pressure YouTube Over Copyrights." *Wall Street Journal,* October 10, 2006, p. B1.

Langston, R. Carter. "Public Relations and the Law: Six Keys to Winning in the Court of Law—and Public Opinion." *Public Relations Tactics,* March 2006, p. 14.

McGuire, Craig. "At the Lawyer's Right Hand: A Growing Number of Companies Now Have Units to Handle Their Litigation." *PRWeek,* January 22, 2007, p. 13.

Nolan, Hamilton. "Press subpoenas are wake-up call for PR." *PRWeek,* May 15, 2006, p. 10.

Parkinson, Michael G., and Parkinson, L. Marie. *Law for Advertising, Broadcasting, Journalism, and Public Relations.* Mahwah, NJ: Lawrence Erlbaum Associates, 2002.

Reber, Bryan, Gower, Karla, and Robinson, Jennifer. "The Internet and Litigation Public Relations." *Journal of Public Relations Research,* Vol. 18, No. 1, 2006, pp. 23–44.

Rundle, Rhonda. "Critical Case: How an E-mail Rant Jolted a Big HMO." *Wall Street Journal,* April 24, 2007, pp. 1, 16.

Silver, David. "Managing the Litigation PR Process in the Court of Public Opinion." *The Strategist,* Summer 2006, pp. 42–43.

Vara, Vauhini. "Photo Firms Hunt Copyright Violators." *Wall Street Journal,* October 19, 2005, p. A4.

CHAPTER

13

New Technologies in Public Relations

Working Smart Using New Tools

For public relations, the advances and the innovations in technology merit a chapter dedicated to the tools of the profession, but at the outset it is important to keep in mind that the key to success with any tool remains a smart, highly skilled user. The communication explosion of new technologies offers fascinating opportunities for success in public relations that will be covered throughout the chapter, but such tools should never replace thoughtful strategic planning and carefully crafted communication of program elements.

> *Once a nice add-on, digital prowess is now key to an agency's capabilities.*
> ——*PRWeek*

According to a study commissioned by *pr reporter*, use of new technologies is the leading trend in public relations. Digital devices of all kinds enable the more advanced and ambitious practitioner to stay on top of the latest events in the external communication environment. And new technologies provide more precise and instantaneous delivery of messages to those publics impacting competitive success or stemming crisis costs for the practitioner's employer. Similarly, tried-and-true media relations is more targeted and thereby well-received by journalists. According to the Middleberg/Ross Survey of journalists nationwide, the Internet is a rapidly growing means of receiving news releases, story ideas, and even audio and photo files from public relations sources.

But more important than the shift to new tech pitches to media is the direct access to key publics that does not require the challenges and frustrations of working with media gatekeepers. Through the Web, thousands of companies, organizations, media, and individuals tell the world about themselves, sell their wares, and promote their ideas, communicating with tens of millions of netizens worldwide. Many of the emerging technologies are interactive, affording the two-way communication that is so vital in professional public relations. Instead of depending on the programs the television networks and cable systems provide, for example, viewers can order pay-per-view movies onto their screen or move seamlessly between television programming and high-speed Internet access on their television sets. News media, music, movies, Internet videos from YouTube and others, gaming and advert gaming, and Web browsing are now delivered through the Internet to entertainment PCs and then transmitted via wireless systems to every room in the home. The home computer increasingly serves not only in its familiar roles as a workstation and instant messaging tool, but as the information and entertainment portal for the family. This mainstream use of the Internet increases the audience for public relations messages as we move from workplace use of the Internet to our reliance on Internet-delivered content in the home, as well as on the go with increasingly powerful handheld devices such as personal digital assistants (PDAs) and smart phones.

Despite the ubiquity of the Internet, a huge digital divide exists across the globe, which poses a strategic problem if communication resources are devoted exclusively or predominantly to new media channels. Key publics may be missed altogether. Caveats aside, the Internet is the most intriguing of the new electronic methods that are changing mass communication in general and providing public relations practice with innovative tools. Other digital technologies have revolutionized the management of public relations.

This chapter examines how such recent developments and new technologies can be applied to accomplish public relations objectives. As you can see in Table 13.1, these

on the job
ETHICS

Who Is Concerned about the Digital Divide?

The following editorial in *Monde Diplomatique* expresses concern about the global digital divide. Read the statement and consider the questions presented.

The Internet became available to the public only a decade ago. In that short time, it has revolutionized political, economic, social, and cultural life to such an extent that we can now reasonably speak of the new Internet world order in telecommunications. Nothing is as it was before. For a large proportion of the world's people the speed and reliability of computer networks has changed their manner of communication, study, shopping, news, entertainment, political organization, cultural life, and work. The growth of Internet-based activities and e-mail has put the computer at the center of a network, relayed via a new generation of do-everything phones, that has transformed all areas of social activity.

But this remarkable transformation has largely been to the advantage of Western countries, already the beneficiaries of previous industrial revolutions. It is now exacerbating the digital gap between those who have an abundance of information technologies and the many more who would have none. Two figures give a sense of the inequality: 91 percent of the world's users of the Internet are drawn from only 19% of the world's population. The digital gap does as much to accentuate and aggravate the north-south divide as the traditional inequality between rich and poor—20 percent of the population of the rich countries own 85 percent of the world's wealth. If nothing is done cyber technologies will leave the inhabitants of the least advanced countries outside, especially in sub-Saharan Africa, where scarcely 1 percent of people have access, and those are mostly men.

Who is responsible for this digital divide? Should we really be concerned about the lack of Internet access in countries that have so many other basic infrastructure problems? Can the Internet be used as a development tool, offering developing countries a way to leapfrog forward in making progress toward filling basic needs?

Most important, what role can you envision for public relations professionals as part of the solution to the digital divide?

new technologies have had an impact on the media, and consequently, on public relations practice.

The Computer

Computers reside in smart devices used by public relations professionals, such as personal organizers, calendars, and contact lists on personal BlackBerrys, Palm Pilots, or many smartphones; and even on computerized wristwatches. Computer chips enable the automation of office procedures so that tasks can be completed faster and more extensively than the old do-it-by-hand methods were capable of accomplishing.

As a research tool, computers make an immense amount of information easily accessible through secondary analysis of data. E-mail and chat forums enhance environmental scanning and issues management. Three skills that are essential to success in public relations—project management, time billing, and digital presentation—all are made more efficient and flexible through the use of computers.

Computer software such as Spin Control and Vocus are used in public relations to manage the media relations process. Such programs help the public relations professional

UNHCR goodwill ambassador Angelina Jolie sits and speaks with Sudanese women who have crossed the border into Tine, Chad, after fleeing fighting in the Darfur region of Sudan. The United Nations High Commission on Refugees effectively uses its Web site to show the activities of its high-profile ambassadors and give status reports from the field.

develop media contact databases, track mail and phone pitches to those contacts, and record news coverage obtained from the media relations effort.

Some functions crucial to public relations practice that Vocus software delivers are:

- Target key journalists who could write about your company or your competition
- Keep track of all your conversations and interactions with journalists in one central location
- Send out personalized press releases to journalists in under ten minutes and view their interactive responses
- Eliminate expensive clipping services with delivery of your news in real time
- Produce clip books and reports in seconds

Table 13.1

Pros and Cons of New Media in Public Relations

TRADITIONAL MASS MEDIA	NEW MEDIA
Geographically constrained: Local or regional targets	Distance insensitive: Topic, need, or interest targeting worldwide
Hierarchical: Series of gatekeepers/editors	Flattened: One to many and many to many
Unidirectional: One-way dissemination	Interactive: Feedback, discussion, debate, and response to requests by person or machine
Space/time constraints: Limited pages and airtime	Fewer space/time constraints: Large, layered capacity for information
Professional communicators: Highly trained to professional standards	Nonprofessional: Anyone with limited training or professional values may participate
High access costs: Startup and production costs prohibitive	Low access costs: More affordable, but expensive computer programming talent required initially
General interest: Large audiences and broad coverage	Customized: Narrowcasts, even individually tailored
Linearity of content: News hierarchy	Nonlinearity of content: Hypertext links enable nonlinear navigation
Feedback: Slow, effortful, and limited	Feedback: E-mail and online chat are immediate and easy
Ad-driven: Big audiences and revenue	Diverse funding sources: Varied but limited revenue
Institution-bound: Corporate ownership	Decentralized: Grassroots efforts
Fixed format: Predictable in format, time, and place	Flexible format: Emerging but fluid formats; multimedia
News, values, journalistic standards: Conventional	Formative standards: Currently obscure

Source: Adapted from *pr reporter,* May 17, 1999.

Most important, the computer should be viewed as the vehicle that can carry the practitioner into the maze of the Internet and World Wide Web. Communication and information resources abound in the online world, making life for public relations professionals more interesting and efficient.

The Internet

Created in the late 1960s by researchers who were seeking a way to link computers in separate cities, the Internet was initially an academic–government tool. It came into public use in the early 1990s; tie-ins developed between the American system and those in more than 150 other countries.

The Internet and Public Relations

The Internet gives public relations practitioners a multifaceted form of worldwide communication, primarily involving message exchange by e-mail, information delivery and persuasion through the Web, and extensive access to audiences for strategic research opportunities.

The following are the primary uses of the Internet by public relations professionals:

◆ **E-mail distribution.** E-mail includes messages to individuals; newsletters to staff members; transmission of news releases, photos, and pitch letters to media offices; and dispatch and receipt of copy between public relations firms and clients, including fully formatted documents using software such as Adobe Acrobat. Most e-mail systems

An example of how public relations firms use the Internet is the home page of Edelman Public Relations Worldwide. It offers a variety of information about clients.

now accept hypertext e-mail that presents images in full color when the e-mail is opened. Professional Training Associates, a newsletter publisher, was able to send its direct mail postcard on the Internet to selected editors and reporters. The postcard announced a new Web site entitled Hard@Work with a whimsical shot of the publisher and editor perched on a rock in the middle of a stream.

> Wikis and collaboration is a space we and many people in the industry are using now as opposed to just sticking to dry e-mail.
>
> ——*Jordan Chanofsky,* CEO at Fusion Public Relations

- **Web sites.** These sites provide a way for organizations to tell Internet users what they do, to publicize projects, and to advocate policies. Edelman Public Relations Worldwide, for example, gives information about its clients. Ketchum offers recipes from its food-product clients. And Manning Selvage & Lee created a hilarious site for Philips Norelco called shaveeverywhere.com as part of a product launch for the Bodygroom shaver targeted at 25–34-year-old men who could do with a little less body hair. See the Casebook on page 341.

Companies have begun to use special Web sites called *wikis* as collaborative space where ideas or guidelines can be shared and developed with employees or opened up to media contacts and bloggers, those who maintain journals online. Conceivably, a wiki could be developed to address an emerging issue that an organization faces, providing information and perhaps setting an agenda for discussion of the issue.

- **Blogs, Moblogs, and Vlogs.** The term *blog* is a contraction of two words, *Web* and *log*. A blog is a regularly updated online diary that also features links to news items and stories on the Web. The individual running the site is called a *blogger*, which cynics say now includes virtually everyone. This person typically is a pundit who wishes to express his or her views on the news. Some bloggers are professional journalists. A blog also serves as a public forum for active give-and-take with the blogger, which may afford more opportunities for public relations professionals than the online journal itself. Blogs serve as an excellent forum for public discourse about an issue such as global warming. *Moblogging* using cell phones with cameras is the latest rage. With moblogging, content is posted to the Internet from a mobile or portable device, such as a cellular phone or PDA. One of the latest developments in the online diary/forum area is *video logs* or *vlogs*. For example, the Natural Resources Defense Council and Environmental Countdown recently hired a highly appealing video personality, Amanda Congdon of the vlog Rocketboom, to anchor its environmental Web site.

- **RSS—Really Simple Syndication.** An emerging technology may very well supplant the majority of printed news releases sent to reporters and editors. *RSS* is a Web-based process of searching and gathering together news and information that is then fed to the user's computer or wireless device such as a cell phone. Essentially, software called an *RSS reader* is loaded onto the device and preferences for topics and sources are set. The reader then searches and delivers information to the user. Journalists increasingly look to RSS as a customized source that enables them to reduce irrelevant media pitches and many recommend that any good public relations person will set up an RSS feed to put releases and stories out there for the journalist's RSS reader to find. Many Web sites do not offer RSS feeds, but major news organizations and companies offer their content in RSS format so that the readers can obtain it for delivery

PRCASEBOOK

Online Campaign Convinces Men to "Take it all off"

Philips Norelco successfully launched a new product for men in 2006, the Bodygroom, designed to easily remove body hair through a creative campaign that effectively used a Web site to generate buzz about the new product.

The Web site, www.ShaveEverywhere.com, featured Robe Guy (also called Innuendo Guy) who explains the benefits of using Bodygroom on the back, underarms, and other body parts that are bleeped out. For example, he credits the device for giving him an "extra optical inch on my BLEEP." As Bob Walker explains in a *New York Times Magazine* article, "It's easy to decode the bleeps, even without the images of peaches and carrots that pop up on the screen."

It's not exactly Comedy Central material, but it was a huge hit among the target audience of men aged 24 to 45. The Web site attracted more than one million unique visitors in the first month alone, and another million during the next six months. In fact, the site was so successful that Philips Norelco released a second online video full of bawdy bleeping, which was a spoof involving outrageously hairy men prowling the Coney Island Boardwalk in the pre-Bodygroom era.

Satellite radio also played an important role. The Bodygroom was launched on the *Howard Stern Show* because the show's demographics fit the target audience. After researching the program format, Manning Selvage & Lee (MS&L) public relations engaged entertainer Jodie Moore to demonstrate the merits of the new product. She groomed Beetle Juice, one of the show's well-known characters, on the air in a 35-minute segment. The show was also aired on Howard Stern on Demand and the segment was e-mailed and linked to a wide number of other Web sites. The show generated about three million impressions (size of potential audience) and 300,000 visitors to the ShaveEverywhere Web site in just the first week.

Although the online campaign was the central focus, MS&L also generated media coverage and buzz through events and placement of stories in magazines such as *FHM* and *Men's Health*. One event was "Shave Your Kiwis" at the Sundance Film Festival, where celebrities were asked to defuzz Kiwis (a nod to one of the more sensitive body parts) to earn a donation to a nonprofit that supports the independent film industry. Another event was a home and housewares show where a "Shave the Brave" charity shave-off was held between the Chicago Fire Department and the New York Fire Department. The match featured three "hairy" firefighters from each city using BodyGroom to take it all off.

The campaign was an outstanding success. Philips Norelco went from 0% to 70% share of the electric bodygrooming category and contributed to a 33 percent increase in the company's grooming sales from 2005 to 2006. On Amazon.com, it became the number-one product sold in its health and personal care section.

The ShaveEverywhere.com site has been written about on more than 1,500 blogs and there are currently more than 13,000 links pointing to it. In fact, the company claims that 60 percent of Bodygroom buyers say they learned about the product from the site. No print or television advertising was used in the entire campaign. *PRWeek* awarded Philips Norelco and MS&L the "Best Use of the Internet/New Media" award in 2007, and the campaign also received PRSA's Silver Anvil for best campaign in consumer markerting. A news release about a Bodygroom survey was shown in Chapter 5.

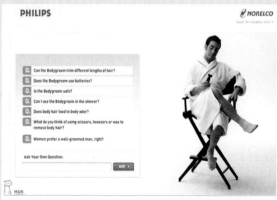

The Philips Norelco home page for its new product, Bodygroom, featuring the Robe Guy.

Dilbert derides not only the trendy nature of blogging, which may be eroding the credibility and utility of blogs, but also the ease with which genuine Web journaling can be counterfeited by the unscrupulous.

to users. Strategic communicators can not only deliver RSS feeds, but can make wise use of the RSS platform to track activity of competitors and to monitor issues that might grow into conflicts of crisis dimensions for their employer or client. Two recommended, free RSS readers are NewsDesk (www.wildgrape.net) and Dogpile Search Tool (www.dogpile.com). NewsGator is an inexpensive RSS feeder that integrates RSS news into your e-mail program if you use Microsoft Outlook for e-mail. With News-Gator, a public relations professional can readily set up a news watch using keywords, with stories on the watch topic delivered as e-mail.

◆ **Podcasting.** In the same way that text content such as online newspaper and magazine stories can be delivered to a user, so can radio, television, and even film content make its way to a digital device. A computer or a PDA or an MP3 player can play the audio or video file when it is convenient for the user. The term *podcast* is associated with the Mac iPod, but the range of devices runs the full gamut. The podcast consumer can either select a particular program for download or can set up a regular delivery of a program automatically whenever a new one is created. The term refers both to the content and to the process, with the author of the product called the *podcaster*. Public relations professionals increasingly will become podcasters by making files available on a Web site. Those who are able to create audio news releases or video products that can then be delivered to highly targeted audiences will have an additional tool for reaching key publics with compelling multimedia content.

◆ **Brochureware.** Although this term is used ironically by those who envision Web sites as a unique new channel, much of the content on Web sites is little more than an online version of the brochures and collateral materials that organizations provide to stakeholders. Public relations professionals should increasingly capitalize on the interactive and multimedia characteristics that distinguish Web communication from traditional print materials. Over time, interactivity and video clips will distinguish brochureware from its print predecessor, adding to the mix of communication tools available to the public relations professional.

Here are specific examples of how the Internet is used in public relations practice:

◆ Organizations increasingly set up Web sites to serve informational needs of reporters, especially during a crisis or a breaking news situation. The Starr Report

Companies, such as Purina, are increasingly using Podcasts to reach audiences about pet care and, of course, their products.

investigation of President Clinton's affair with Monica Lewinsky was released to the Web for wide and immediate dissemination. News organizations then made it available on their own Web sites, where an estimated 24.7 million people read parts of it in a matter of days, still one of the most galvanizing Web events to date.

♦ Xerox's public relations Web site offers answers to any question—any question at all. In response to an online question, the offbeat site reported its calculation that it would take 33,661 years to vacuum the state of Ohio! A mention in *People* magazine and various TV news features resulted.

♦ At least 400 health-care organizations and companies distribute medical information over their Web sites. Two examples include the American Medical Association, which provides information for physicians and patients about treatments, medical developments, and other health-care news, and the National Alliance of Breast Cancer Organizations (NABCO), which provides current information about breast cancer research and treatment, events, and links to other Web sites.

Greenpeace, the activist environmental organization, uses its Web site to publicize its confrontations at sea with vessels whose work it opposes. Here, a Greenpeace ship tries to block passage of a Norwegian whaling vessel. The Web site carries news reports and background information from the Greenpeace point of view.

◆ Companies such as Boeing and HP have used Webcasting to increase coverage of important news conferences by broadcasting video footage over the Web via Medialink's Web site, Media Portal.

◆ The University of Wisconsin's Technology Enhancing Cancer Communication (TECC) (chess2.chsra.wisc.edu/tecc) offers support for cancer patients and their loved ones who provide care for them. Interactive technologies link people facing similar cancer challenges across distance and time to facilitate effective cancer communication between patient, partner/ caregiver, and clinical teams. TECC explores how computers can be used to help those dealing with cancer or caring for loved ones with cancer.

◆ The governor of Hawaii used a Webcast to address critics and field questions from concerned citizens regarding a teachers' strike and lockout. At a minimal direct cost of $100, an enormous audience, estimated at 30,000, was reached. Facing a crisis in the schools, Governor Cayetano communicated directly to the audience, generating both advance and follow-up coverage and ongoing access to the archived Webcast online.

Key Aspects of the Internet

Public relations professionals should keep in mind the following important facts about the Internet:

◆ Its reach is worldwide. A message intended for local or regional use may draw reactions, good or bad, from unexpected places.

◆ The content of the Internet is virtually uncontrolled. Anyone can say or show anything without passing it through "gatekeepers," the editors and producers who approve the material that reaches the public through traditional media channels. Lack of editorial control permits unfettered freedom of speech, but it also permits distribution of unconfirmed, slanted, or even potentially libelous material. *Tactics*, which is published by PRSA, welcomes this freedom from editorial control. It asserts: "PR pros can now get messages out without passing them through the filter of editors and journalists. Traditional media gatekeepers have lost their power in today's print-and-click world."

◆ Issue tracking, a major component of professional public relations management, can be more thorough using the Internet and far more immediate. Services such as NewsEdge monitor Web-based news and wire services, then alert users when relevant topics appear in Internet news sources. By monitoring the Internet, practitioners can keep track of what competitors, opponents, and the general audience are saying. Thus informed, practitioners can better shape their own tactics and messages as well as respond in real time to forestall erroneous or unbalanced stories from gaining momentum without correction. A PR Newswire executive recalled how a story released by his service at 7:30 A.M. prompted an e-mail response by a public relations person. The result was a factually corrected release on PR Newswire by 7:35 A.M.

on the job

A MULTICULTURAL WORLD

The United Nations High Commission for Refugees Draws on the Web for Global Reach

The global digital divide does not cause the human tragedies that result in refugee camps. However, the digital revolution may be part of the solution by making the world small enough that we all become aware and involved with the plight of refugees.

The United Nations High Commissioner for Refugees (UNHCR.ch) Web site seeks to increase public awareness of the global refugee problem. The site includes maps, photographs, and print and video news about people who have abandoned their homes to escape war and persecution. A *Refugees Magazine* is available as well as UNHCR screensavers. Interviews with the director of UNHCR can be viewed on demand.

International sponsors are helping local newspapers mount Web editions of their papers so that refugees can assess when conditions are favorable for a return to their homelands. Spokespersons provide testimonials and video from refugee camps. Angelina Jolie has been particularly

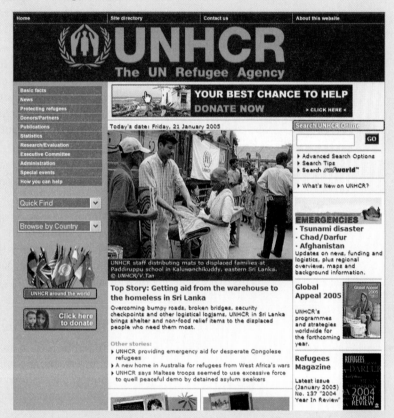

active in the work of the UNHCR, taking time to appear in videos and to conduct online chat sessions with interested persons around the world.

Source: Courtesy of UNHCR Public Information Section.

New Tech and Online Research   The Internet introduces several innovations in existing research methodologies:

◆ Hybrid Surveys—phone to drive people to Web-based survey instruments enable random sample and tracking of participation for response rates

◆ Online Focus Groups—in the recent past, focus groups were convened in-person. But when appropriate participants are located across the country or the globe, convening the focus group in a chat room on the Internet can be highly effective. Anonymity increases candor and reduces groupthink.

◆ Online Experiments—the latest versions of software for online survey research enable the presentation of digital exhibits (text, video, Web sites) such as public service announcements (PSAs) in health communication. By varying the persuasive strategy or production values of the PSA, experimental comparisons can be made between alternative versions.

◆ Copy Testing or Message Testing—using the same capability to present digital exhibits, collateral materials such as brochures and mailers or video news releases can be tested for audience response.

◆ Online Theater Research—in a further refinement made possible by the Internet, audiences can be recruited to view a speech or video with simple instructions to the participants. Use your mouse to drag a cursor back and forth to express greater or lesser favorability as the speech or video is played. This dynamic research protocol to capture real-time response to a video enables public relations strategists and copywriters to identify what passages resonate with an audience.

◆ Web Usability Research—using inexpensive software and a Web cam. The software captures the face of the Web user, records audio comments about the Web site and Web pages, while also documenting every cursor movement and click on the screen.

◆ 3-Dimensional Text Mapping—huge volumes of text such as transcripts of online focus groups derived from capture of all chat exchanges can be analyzed using software called CatPac. The software creates a three-dimensional map showing what concepts or terms are associated. For example, a company name may align with certain terms that essentially provide a mental map of participant perceptions of the company.

> **❝** One group [of University of Colorado fans] concocted a fake Facebook page for an amorous coed named "Jeanne," then had Jeanne cyberflirt with K-State's Cartier Martin. He gave her his number. . . . Next thing Martin knew, Colorado fans were tormenting him with calls to his cell phone. **❞**
>
> ———*Rick Reilly, Sports Illustrated*

Internet Problems

In addition to its multiple benefits, the global spiderweb of interlocking computer networks also offers some challenges. The following should be kept in mind when planning Internet communication programs:

◆ Increasingly, search engines are prioritizing search results based on fee payments from companies and organizations, biasing search results.

◆ Although the Internet allows many voices to be heard, increasing diversity of opinions in the public forum of ideas and lifestyles, there is still a fairly high skill level required to set up a functional Web site. Web development for marginal groups such as those representing workers or the less powerful in society remains a challenge. However, when compared with the cost of controlling a printing press, opportunities for diverse viewpoints should increase over time.

◆ Controversial security problems and legal questions of copyright infringement, libel, invasion of privacy, and pornography remain unsolved.

on the job INSIGHTS

Creating Winning Web Sites

A Web site can serve as a controlled, yet credible, tool for organizations to disseminate messages. National surveys indicate that audiences hold Web-based information in high regard. Internet information, according to one survey of over 1,000 respondents by professors at the University of California at Santa Barbara, was as credible as TV, radio, and magazines, but less credible than newspapers. Researchers say that this high credibility perhaps explains why Web information is seldom double-checked with other sources by the audience.

Web sites also enable strategic targeting of messages to audiences. Responsible practitioners can get the word out to key publics using links to customized Web pages tailored to the particular public. However, according to Stuart Esrock and Greg Leichty, most corporate Web sites are used to service investors, customers, and, to a lesser extent, the media. Consequently, the com-

munication potential of Web sites has not yet been fully tapped.

To date, according to Candace White and colleagues at the University of Tennessee, most Web site planning is done by trial and error, with little formal research and evaluation. Practitioners report Web site development as a low priority on to-do lists because of skepticism about the site's effectiveness, inefficient evaluation methods, and lack of control over the site.

Opportunities for a broader range of publics should be developed as support for Web sites increases and public relations practitioners become more assertive in taking control of Web sites. Given the enormous and burgeoning audience for Web sites, as well as key target audiences, creating more effective Web sites will be essential for public relations departments.

Louis Falk of Florida International University offers some no-nonsense advice for Web site development:

- Make it fast. Be sure that a page loads in less than eight seconds.

- Use a functional, balanced design. Make sure that the site works on all major Web browsers, such as Internet Explorer and Firefox. Place the most important information on the left side of the page. Use standard colors that work consistently on many different browsers and machines. Offer an easy and logical interaction, making good use of internal search engines.

- Make sure there are no dead links.

- Include contact information.

- Identify your purpose(s). Public information differs dramatically from e-commerce, for instance.

- Keep it fresh. Not only should information be current, you also should check the site's performance on a regular basis.

- Register with major search engines. This ensures that you can be found.

- Cyberheckling. The humorist Rick Reilly, who writes weekly for *Sports Illustrated*, brought to light a rather unfriendly practice in sports that could become a problem in other walks of life. The use of embarassing information from Facebook pages or creation of bogus Facebook entries are only two of the ways sports fans get at the opposition. False Wikipedia entries have temporarily besmirched athletes such as golfer Fuzzy Zoeller, "documenting" his consumption of copious amounts of booze along with Vicodin. Lawsuits followed this particular heckler.

- The transitory, intangible nature of electronic content can lead to an historical perspective, with online users considering current affairs content to be a transitory stream of information that is overwritten regularly as Web sites are updated. Fortunately, projects such as Wayback Machine capture truly vast chunks of the Web for historical and legal archiving.

◆ Malicious and irritating practices nag at online users. The Internet offers many opportunities for spammers to clutter e-mail channels with bogus or dubious offers. Unsolicited advertising on the Web adds to this clutter, making the messages sent by public relations professionals less effective. Online users are perhaps most decisively impacted by those who program viruses to take down servers or disrupt personal computer systems.

◆ Astroturfing online. When purportedly grassroots organizations actually turn out to be sponsored organizations, the efforts of these artificial movements are often called *astroturfing*. With the rise of community, or user-generated, amateur content such as blogs and video produced for sites such as YouTube, the potential for astroturfing abuses proliferates. For example, a satirical video about presidential candidate and Senator Hillary Clinton became wildly popular on YouTube. It turned out that the video deriding Clinton's vote for the Iraq war was actually produced by an operative in the rival Barack Obama campaign—who was subsequently fired. To gauge how important the work of rogue videographers can be, consider that a YouTube clip showcasing the "flip-flop" of Republican presidential hopeful Mitt Romney on key issues such as abortion was countered within eight hours by a rebuttal video, according to the *Washington Post*.

In sum, the Internet is an evolving form of mass communication. Public relations tools based on the Internet are frequently conceived, developed, and hyped for their features. Many will end up on the tech scrap heap; however, the winners can equip the adept professional with a competitive edge.

Other Computer Applications

The well-known physicist and thinker Stephen Hawking predicts that computer applications such as artificial intelligence will one day universally supercede human brainpower. The dazzling future aside, immediate application of the new technologies in public relations are well worth adopting right now. Promising new media tools are listed in Table 13.2.

Dictation and Voice Generation

Most computers being sold today have the memory and processing speed needed to recognize human speech. The software program Dragon Naturally Speaking not only recognizes the user's speech, but also improves its recognition accuracy by taking into account corrections the user makes in the dictated text on the computer screen. Over time, the program becomes more accurate in converting speech to word processing, presentation, Web, database, or spreadsheet content. Computer commands also may be spoken, including the command "Read Text," which prompts the computer to generate speech by reading the written text to the user. One important boon of this new technology may well be a reduction in painful repetitive motion syndrome injuries caused by hours of keyboarding. Conversational exchanges with Web sites will create a virtual presence for sites offering counseling or other special interactive services to users. In general, professionals capitalizing on dictation and voice generation should use the new tools to create a positive virtual presence, a more personal and responsive experience for members of the public. However, most such uses remain in the imagination of cutting-edge practitioners at this point. Radio news monitoring services such as Radio

on the job INSIGHTS

Getting Reporters to Use Your Web Site

According to the Nielsen Norman Group, professionals should conduct usability studies of their Web sites, especially to understand the problems and concerns of ordinary users and journalists. Nielsen Norman says that journalists frequently go to company Web sites as they start to work on a story. Reporters look to:

- Find a public relations contact.
- Check basic facts about a company.
- Discover a company's perspective on events.
- Check financial information.
- Download images to illustrate stories.

Typical steps taken by reporters include:

1. Getting to your site.
   - Tip: Submit the site to major search engines, such as Google.

   - Tip: Avoid Flash or Shockwave features that may not work or could bog down the reporter's research.

2. Finding the news.
   - Tip: Don't lose reporters in the forest.
   - Tip: Clearly and prominently label information meant for reporters (e.g., Media; Press; News).

3. Looking for contact information.
   - Tip: Reporters in the Nielsen Norman Group study had a low success rate in finding the phone number for the public relations contact.
   - Tip: Put contact information on every page of your site, especially the phone number, to help journalists get answers quickly.

4. Researching a product, event, or person.

   - Tip: Dedicate an easy-to-find link to press releases.
   - Tip: Make releases searchable and sortable by topic or date.
   - Tip: Avoid pop-up windows for press releases—they imply skimpy information.
   - Tip: Link to third-party resources that provide credible supplements to the company's story.

5. Fact checking.
   - Tip: Provide fact sheets, executive biographies, financial data, and product information.

6. Looking at pictures.
   - Tip: Reporters like graphics, and they convey much about a company.
   - Tip: Don't overdo it; make sure the images are useful and not just "eye candy."

Keyword Search (see Television, Radio, and Web Monitoring Services on pp. 354) are adopting the technology to automate searches of broadcast transcripts.

Expert Systems

One modest form of artificial intelligence—expert system programming—has made its mark in the business world. Expert systems identify a limited domain of expertise and then emulate the decision making that an expert would undertake. Someday public relations professionals will use expert systems to assist with special-event planning, issue evaluation, and other domains of expertise in the field.

Public Relations Management Tools

- Public relations professionals can use project-scheduling software such as Microsoft Project and MacProject to quickly create and modify Gantt charts, track

Table 13.2

Some New Tools in Public Relations Practice

NEW TECH TOOL	PR FUNCTION	TYPICAL AUDIENCE	TECHNIQUES/FEATURES
Internet	Media relations	Media contacts	Pitching stories and sending digital media kits
	Activism	Media	Evens the resource field for activist groups
	Crisis management	Media and internal audiences	Preemptive tool against investigative hatchet job
	Event or product promotion	Widespread, often teens or trendsetters	Guerrilla (subtle) and viral (self-generating) dissemination
Intranet	Internal communication	Employees and password-access outsiders	Enables confidential communication and rumor research
Online newswires (e.g., Newstream.com)	Investor relations	Investors and financial media in 6,000 online newsrooms	Submit to Business Wire and index with Yahoo! company news
Webcasting services such as Medialink	Meetings and media relations	Varied	Enables a large, geographically dispersed audience to participate online
Web searching	Issues tracking	Management	Search by client or industry name
Web site development	E-commerce and public information	Customers and constituents	Offer products and services
Online monitoring services (e.g., Dialog NewsEdge and Briefme.com)	Issues and crisis management	Practitioner receives news alerts	Enables monitoring of both slow-boil and breaking news about own organization
CD-ROM	Media relations	Media	Digital media kit or reporter's resource
	Employee communication	Employees	Interactive, audiovisual training and notification
Satellite and radio media tours	Publicity	Viewers and listeners	Overcomes distance barriers in media appearances
Web research	Audience analysis and message testing	Colleagues and clients	Online surveys, focus groups, secondary research, and usability studies
Media database software (e.g., prPowerBase)	Release distribution/tracking	Media	Access and use Bacon's and other major databases
Research software (e.g., Publics, SPSS)	Formative and evaluative research	Client	Enables targeted audiences and tailored messages
Presentation software (e.g., PowerPoint)	Briefings	Varied	Multimedia features and last-minute changes
Calendar software (e.g., Sidekick, Outlook)	Project and event coordination	Varied	Set up team meetings and recurring appointments
Project management software (e.g., Microsoft Project)	Production and campaign planning/tracking	Colleagues and clients	Enables control of complex projects
Time tracking and billing software (e.g., Timeslips)	Management	Colleagues and clients	Track time for productivity analysis and billing of services

NEW TECH TOOL	PR FUNCTION	TYPICAL AUDIENCE	TECHNIQUES/FEATURES
Media management software (e.g., Vocus, Spinware)	Media relations	Media	Track media contacts and coverage, online press center
Creativity tools (e.g., Visio, Photoshop, Quark)	Materials production	Readers and viewers	Design and layout of materials
Netbusiness card	Firm visibility and marketing	Clients	Registered users appear in all major online Yellow Pages

A wide range of technologies serve important functions of modern public relations and often are directed at particular audiences. Some of these technologies are just emerging, others are more commonly used.

resources, and monitor progress toward the completion of a project. (See Chapter 6 for a sample Gantt chart.) Special software such as Timeslips streamlines the time-billing process and allows professionals to use the computer as a timer and recorder of billable hours. Particularly in the public relations agency world, time tracking to capture precious billable hours is an essential task that can be made less burdensome with software.

Desktop Publishing

Computers can be used to create professional-looking newsletters and graphically illustrated material on a personal computer right in the office.

This "just-in-time" printing enables a sense of immediacy in content without sacrificing appearance. Desktop publishing saves both money and time. Less than $5,000 will buy all the components necessary to produce high-quality newsletters and graphics in-house: a personal computer, a word-processing program, a graphics program, page-making software, and a magazine-quality laser printer. Producing materials in-house reduces the fuss and expense of involving a commercial printer, especially when turnaround times are short and production standards are not excessively high. For the best possible publication quality, however, the advisable approach is to deliver the files to a professional printer for production using a suite of design, photo, and layout tools such as those included in Adobe In-Design.

Mailing Lists

Up-to-date mailing lists are vital in public relations work. Lists of names are typed into database programs such as Microsoft Works or ACT! contact management software and stored in computer memory. The capability to select groups of names from the master list assists the practitioner in reaching target audiences. For example, when introducing its new models, Ford sought to generate ample publicity for more than 2,000 of its dealers located in rural areas. The automaker created a computer file on each dealer that included the address, phone number, and name of the local spokesperson. By combining this file with its standard news release, Ford created 9,600 customized news releases. Every release mentioned a local dealer by name and used local dealer data in the release. The releases also were sent to customers based on a carefully culled mailing list of potential customers in the dealer's territory.

Public relations departments and firms may compile their own computer lists of media contacts or purchase databases from press-directory companies, such as Bacon's

MediaSource software, which provides postal addresses, e-mail addresses, and phone data for nearly 30,000 editors on CD-ROM or at a password-protected Web site. Online services are now the norm because of the need to update the positions and contact information for reporters and editors who regularly change news beats, positions, or even employers.

Online Conferences

Online conferences, which can be likened to a chat room or instant-messaging session (i.e., a series of typed messages exchanged among members of a work group), are increasingly valuable in public relations. Practitioners use their computers to "converse" with clients and suppliers or to participate in forums on professional matters with their peers. The transcript of the exchange can be retained in computer memory or printed for documentation of negotiations with a client or establishment of common ground with a public.

Because of the ubiquity of personal computers, online conferences are becoming commonplace. Mobile computing with laptop, mini-notebook, and palm-sized PDAs makes out-of-office conferences during business travel an important part of the business communication landscape. Free software such as Netmeeting is available for online conferencing. More sophisticated applications are available for those with more advanced needs.

With the rise in telephone services over the Internet, named VoIP for Voice over Internet Protocol, voice conferences have become less expensive. Traditionally, conference participants would call in to a toll-free 800-number that charges the conference host a significant fee. Callers provide a passcode and enter the conversation. Now, VoIP services such as Skype (www.skype.com) enable computer-to-computer voice calls as well as computer chat for no charge. Recently, Skype released its own conference calling function, enabling up to 100 participants to call in using Skype. This is an excellent tool for functions such as briefing public relations teams and clients about emerging issues, conducting problem-solving sessions, and gaining consensus on what stance along the contingency continuum the organization will take regarding a public.

Graphics, Design, and Photography

The use of computers to design eye-catching colored graphics—drawings, graphs, charts, and text—has emerged as a stellar new technology in public relations practice. Recent developments in computer software make such graphics feasible and widely used, even in one-person public relations offices.

Attractive graphics give visual impact to annual reports and employee publications, as well as to video programs and presentations. Imaginative visual effects may be obtained with only a modest investment of time and money. Representations of people, designs, and charts add visual zest that stimulates audiences. Increasingly, public relations departments and firms employ such graphics to dress up transparencies or digital presentations. (Presentation software is discussed in Chapter 16.)

High-quality digital cameras, easily identified by their larger camera bodies and compatibility with conventional SLR lenses, generate RAW images at 8 MB each for professional-quality shots that can be manipulated in virtually all the ways that film processing has always made available for special effects and retouching. For as little as $4,000, camera body, excellent specialized lenses, and sophisticated flash systems enable small public relations firms to deliver superb photos to Web and print platforms. Even large-scale posters can be printed in high resolution and color saturation by specialty photoprint services from digital files. Specifications, technical proofing, and final print order are all accomplished online.

Facsimile Transmission

Increasingly, the lines between Facsimile (Fax) and e-mail have blurred. It is now possible to use services that will convert an e-mail message into a broadcast fax that can be delivered to the physical fax machines of the target public. Similarly, incoming faxes to a professional's phone number can be received and forwarded as e-mail to the traveling public relations person. Public relations professionals use a fax, or its equivalent in the form of a scanned document attached to an e-mail, to send a news release, a draft of a client's newsletter, instructions from headquarters to a branch office, or any number of documents. By using broadcast fax, a sender can transmit a single document to hundreds of recipients simultaneously. A corporation, for example, can distribute a news release swiftly and equally to competing news media. In another application, a customer can call a major vendor such as PR Newswire or Business Wire via toll-free 800 number, request a piece of information, and receive it by fax within minutes.

A word of caution: Discretion should be used in faxing news releases to editors. Send only those you consider to be truly important and urgent. Editors complain, often quite sharply, about the amount of "junk fax" they receive.

News Release Delivery

More than a dozen American companies deliver news releases electronically to large newspapers and other major news media offices. The news releases are fed into computers at the receiving newsrooms and examined by editors.

The difference between news release delivery firms and the traditional news services such as the Associated Press is this: Newspapers, radio, and television stations pay large fees to receive the reports of the news services, which maintain staffs of editors and reporters to gather, analyze, select, and write the news in a neutral style. In contrast, the news release delivery companies are paid by creators of news releases to distribute the news releases to the media, who pay nothing to receive them. These delivery services are prepaid transmission belts, not selectors of material. However, they do enforce editing standards and occasionally reject releases as unsuitable.

One of the largest news release delivery companies is Business Wire. Using electronic circuits and satellite communications, the company can simultaneously reach more than 1,600 media points in the United States and Canada and more than 500 in Europe, Latin America, East Asia, and Australia. In addition, Business Wire provides rapid dissemination of financial news releases to more than 600 securities and investment firms worldwide. The company sends an average of 600 news releases daily for a roster of more than 9,000 clients.

Electronically delivered news releases have an advantage over the conventional variety. Releases transmitted by satellite tend to receive closer, faster attention from media editors than those arriving by mail.

> " . . . in the last few months, acceptance of the Internet as part of broadcast PR campaigns has spread and a push toward content generated specifically for the web has emerged. "
>
> ——*Greg Hazley, O'Dwyer's PR Report*

Another large news release delivery company, PR Newswire, was the first to distribute its releases by satellite. PR Newswire's computers distribute releases and official statements from more than 7,500 organizations directly into newsroom computers. PR Newswire releases are entered into several commercial databases.

Video and Audio News Release Distribution

Satellite transmission also makes the fast distribution of video news releases (VNRs) possible. The picture-and-voice releases are sent primarily to cable television networks, local cable systems, and local television stations. Nearly 30 companies produce and distribute hundreds of VNRs for clients. Only relatively few of the most newsworthy, technically superior VNRs succeed in obtaining airtime. (See Chapter 15 for a discussion of VNRs.) Successful VNRs usually feature video footage that would be difficult for a station to obtain, as demonstrated by the following examples:

- ◆ A VNR sponsored by OshKosh B'Gosh bib overalls quotes the winner of its Search for the Oldest Bib Overall contest, 89-year-old Claude Mehder, who owns a pair of circa-1901 bibs: "We'll keep having kids, as long as the bib overalls hold up."
- ◆ Ringling Brothers & Barnum & Bailey circus clowns helped *PC Computing* magazine conduct the Notebook Torture Test of laptop computers.
- ◆ "The Car of the Future," a VNR distributed by D. S. Simon Productions, included DVD video screens, on-board message systems, global positioning, and a home security monitor.

Voice-and-sound news releases for use on radio also are distributed by satellite.

Television, Radio, and Web Monitoring Services

> " We should be able to tell someone within 10 to 15 minutes where and when they're being talked about. "
>
> ——*Robb Wexler,* president of National Aircheck

Chapter 11 made the point that audiences consume news and current affairs content delivered by traditional television channels, but also on Webcasts and hot new video services such as YouTube. Arguably, public relations has been print-bound, especially in the capture of media coverage by collecting newspaper and magazine clips. TV is transitory and the Web even more so. It sounds impossible to search and collect video from the hundreds of TV, radio, and Webcasts every day across the country. But a number of services, such as Burrelle's MediaConnect Portal and Medialink's Teletrax and Mediavision, now provide almost instantaneous capture and aggregation of telecasts for clients. National Aircheck provides a similar service for radio. Minutes after evening newscasts across the country, the professional can review all video or audio matching search terms or images. The collected newscasts can be delivered by e-mail or made available on a password-protected Web portal. Considering the audience shift to visual media and the profound effects that come from seeing events, not just reading about them, these services should increasingly become a standard part of every monitoring and evaluation component for public relations campaigns.

Teleconferencing

The most spectacular use of satellite transmission for public relations purposes is *tele-conferencing*, which is also called *videoconferencing*. A public relations professional can easily arrange a teleconference by employing a firm that specializes in this service. In the United States, some 20,000 sites are equipped to handle such events.

With teleconferencing, groups of conferees separated by thousands of miles can interact instantaneously with strong visual impact, saving time and transportation costs. In one 5-year period, the Boeing Company used teleconferencing for 5,699 meetings and eliminated the need for more than 1.5 million miles of travel.

Figure 13.1 shows, in schematic form, how satellite transmission works. Guests at receiving locations view the presentation on large screens. Regular telephone circuits back to the point of origin enable the guests to ask follow-up questions.

Here are examples of teleconferencing in operation:

◆ Ford Motor Company has installed a $10 million system connecting more than 200 Ford locations in North America. It provides customer and vendor relations as well as regular sales training events. Other companies have similar systems.

◆ A Midwestern magazine company incurred major costs for expensive executive travel on short notice to its parent company in New York, with as many as five flights a week. The costs for installation of a Picturetel system were recovered in a matter of months. The system's robotic camera can switch from a wide-angle shot of all participants at a large conference table to a full-screen shot of each speaker.

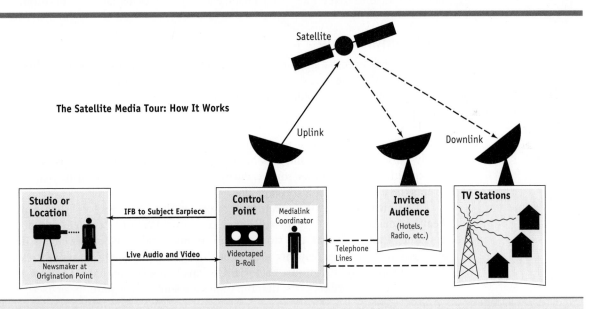

FIGURE 13.1

This diagram explains how a media satellite tour is conducted, enabling the person being interviewed to remain in one place while appearing on screens in other cities.

Source: MediaLink, Inc.

The speaker's microphone activates the camera to "zero in" on him or her while speaking, providing a fairly naturalistic meeting environment in all locations.

♦ The Whirlpool Corporation in the United States and an N. V. Philips division in the Netherlands needed to explain their new $2 billion joint-venture agreement. So they held an international teleconference for their respective stockholders and employees, the media, and financial analysts.

♦ Hill and Knowlton, on behalf of several government agencies, arranged a two-hour conference between Cairo, Egypt, and five U.S. cities that permitted several hundred U.S. investors to talk directly with high-ranking Egyptian officials about private investment in that nation.

♦ To introduce a newly developed hepatitis B vaccine, Merck Sharp & Dohme used a teleconference beamed to more than 400 locations where doctors, health-care workers, and reporters had gathered. After watching the presentation, the invited guests telephoned questions to a panel of experts.

To decide whether a teleconference will be cost-effective, a public relations practitioner should obtain quotes from vendors based on all expenses involved and then compare those figures with the price of travel, lodging, and entertainment if all employees or invited guests were brought to a central conference location.

Those who use teleconferencing emphasize that it is most effective for reaching large audiences for such purposes as introducing a product, conducting a sales meeting, or announcing new corporate policies. However, teleconferencing does lack the personal warmth that comes from a handshake and a face-to-face conversation.

Webconferencing

The Web has become a less expensive alternative for videoconferencing. In its most basic form, Webconferencing is a "see-you-see-me" technology. Users with cameras and microphones mounted on their computers can engage in an Internet version of videophone.

Increasingly, professionals are able to use the Web for interactive Webcasts that primarily serve for the dissemination of information. For example, a press conference might be Webcast to any and all who log in to the event online. The participants can ask questions of the news source during the conference by e-mail. Seminar-style events can attract a worldwide audience.

The Health Media Research Laboratory at the University of Michigan (www.healthmedia.umich.edu) regularly offers real-time Webcast seminars about cancer research. Past Webcasts are stored in an archive and can be viewed on demand. Discussion among participants takes place using AOL Instant Messenger. A recent Webcast topic was "Fractional Factorial Designs," suggesting that the term *narrowcast* also may be appropriate, given that the topics are sometimes quite specialized.

Satellite Media Tours

Instead of having a celebrity—an actor or author, for example—crisscross the country on an expensive, time-consuming promotional tour, public relations sponsors increasingly use the so-called satellite tour. In a time of crisis, imagine the value in having a leader make a personal plea for calm or for consideration of all the facts in a case by interacting with trusted local media figures.

on the job INSIGHTS

Building Relationships Online

Many definitions of public relations embrace the concept of relationship management, often emphasizing mutual benefit in the relationship between an organization and its publics. These definitions also take a longer-term perspective that stresses loyalty built on trust and loyalty between parties. The unique features of new media, particularly the interactivity and decentralization of communication, afford public relations practitioners special opportunities to build beneficial relationships for the organization.

In a study funded by the Institute for Public Relations, Maria Len-Rios found that stronger relationships can result from more extensive use of an organization's Web site. Minor mistakes in content or online service are more likely to be forgiven, and loyal users will accept a more assertive program of e-mail offers and messages. These so-called push strategies include everything from requests for assistance with a charitable cause to online sales offers to e-mail reminders for employees or members.

With precision public relations, practitioners narrowly target key publics. Online channels facilitate this narrow targeting through the creation of messages based on each customer's individual characteristics. Provided permission is granted, e-mail and customized Web content can be tailored to the individual. As the relationship between an organization and an individual matures, more personalized or tailored messaging can be directed to that individual without violating the rules for appropriate online communication.

The interactivity of the Internet is particularly relevant to public relations. Building relationships through an interactive Web site will ultimately serve to improve the corporate image and align corporate policy with public opinion. This two-way symmetrical communication reflects change on the part of the organization to accommodate the public.

Some examples of such two-way communication include the following:

♦ Personalized satellite radio is available in luxury cars. With personalized satellite radio, music programming is tailored to personal tastes. Personalized news and current affairs will be offered in the near future, enabling drivers to save stories or forward stories to others.

♦ The natural spread of ideas, which is often called *viral marketing*, and tactics to spur social movements work well when push e-mail and tailored messages are directed to "e-fluentials," according to Burson-Marsteller. (See www.efluentials.com for more on e-fluentials.)

♦ Amazon.com offers each customer a personalized greeting and information on new books and products based on the customer's past activity on the Amazon Web site. For a regular and loyal user, this is likely to be viewed as a convenience, not an imposition.

With a satellite tour, the personality is stationed in a television studio and reporters interview him or her by satellite from their home studios. Two-way television is used, permitting a visual dialogue. Each station's reporter is put through to the personality at a specified time; thus a series of interviews, 5 to 10 minutes each, can be done in sequence. Corporations also employ satellite media tours to promote their products or services, often using a well-known performer or other "name" figure as a spokesperson. (See Figure 13.1.)

Before his paralyzing spinal injury, actor Christopher Reeve, most famous for his film role as Superman, set an endurance record by doing 45 consecutive interviews at one sitting. Tiresome mentally and physically, no doubt, but much faster and cheaper than visiting all those cities! See Chapter 15 for more information on satellite media tours (SMT).

Other Tools

Numerous other electronic tools are used regularly in public relations practice. New instruments based on digital transmission appear frequently.

Cell Phones

Using cellphones, public relations professionals can be available anytime and at any place. This is a double-edged sword, meaning that work matters are only a melodious ringtone away.

In health-care public relations, cellular phones are being used to provide treatment reminders and to organize activist and support groups. In addition, the nearly ubiquitous presence of cell phones in teen and young adult populations affords opportunities for clever public relations professionals to reach this important target audience. (See page 340, for further discussion of cell phones and flash mob activity.)

Personal Digital Assistants

In business settings, the Palm Pilot, BlackBerry and Treo, along with smartphones and pocket PCs running the full Microsoft software suite, provide portable management of traditional information such as e-mail, calendars, tasks, and contacts. The Windows Mobile 2005 operating system enables the latest generation of these wireless devices to use PowerPoint for presentations and Excel to review or revise budgets and spreadsheets on the fly. In addition, personal digital assistants or PDAs also offer striking new business functions such as the electronic exchange of business cards by infrared beam between Bluetooth-enabled handhelds. Most of these devices also offer Web browsing and Instant Messaging (IM) capabilities. Because developing nations do not have extensive landlines and electrical infrastructure, PDAs are one "leapfrog technology" to enable professionals to skip earlier technologies. One of the authors is working in South Africa on health and risk communication efforts delivered through PDAs to traditional healers serving HIV-AIDS patients.

Memory: The CD-R/RW, DVD-R/RW, and Flash Memory

The multimedia versions of the familiar music CD and the movie DVD offer an enormous capacity for message delivery in public relations; up to 300,000 pages of text, color pictures, and graphics can be stored on a single DVD. Because of their high storage capacity, CDs and DVDs have been the common "coinage" in public relations firms for the transfer of Web pages, graphics, and entire publications among account or project team members.

CDs and DVDs with a "/RW" are rewritable and can be used to backup professional work. It only takes one computer crash for overly confident young professionals to realize the importance of backing up creative copy and irreplaceable records that a public relations client is expecting to use. More recently, dedicated backup systems, essentially huge external hard drives holding 100s of gigabites of memory, are a wise investment for one-click backup of an entire computer.

Now that materials can be delivered digitally to customers over the Internet or other wireless communication networks, some question the utility of CDs and DVDs. However, many people prefer a tangible product over virtual information. Public relations practitioners should keep this human need for tangible communication products

PDAs and cell phones equipped with Microsoft's Windows Mobile enables users to receive everything from email and RSS feeds to electronic issues of magazines and newspapers. A person, on a long flight, can even download a favorite television program or a movie.

in mind when deciding how much information to provide exclusively in digital form. A "press disc," the CD/DVD version of a media kit, is being used, but reporters make little use of the novelty. A more efficient use of the disc technique is to distribute information to specific target audiences. For example, corporations may distribute their annual reports to stockholders on CD or DVD.

Informational brochures can be placed on discs and mailed to target audiences. Buick, for example, mailed 20,000 discs to users of Apple personal computers to tell them about its new models. Recipients of the Buick disc were able to interact with the information presented. By pushing a few buttons, a user could load the trunk with luggage and ask questions about mileage, standard equipment, and how the Buick compared with other auto makes.

Even business cards have joined the digital age. Up to 600 megabytes of information can be placed on a small, circular CD that fits in the tray of the computer's CD-ROM drive. An agency can use a CD business card to present all collateral materials about the firm as well as sample campaigns, including video and audio clips, on one 25-megabyte business card (www.avo-card.com).

New technologies often have a limited lifespan. Increasingly, discs are being supplanted by flash memory sticks the size of a five-pack of gum that plug into the USB port of most modern computers. These memory sticks serve as portable, external hard drives that hold enormous amounts of data, the equivalent of DVD capacity. Flash memory can be used to read and write large amounts of data for backups or for the delivery of very large files, such as multimedia presentations and photo layouts, to clients.

Electronic Blackboards

Blackboards with chalk now belong to the past; companies with farflung personnel or clients are gravitating to the use of electronic whiteboards. A person can write on a whiteboard with a liquid marker during a presentation, and the image on the whiteboard is then electronically scanned so that it can be saved or printed for future reference. The electronic whiteboard image also can be transmitted to Webconference participants in real time or after a presentation is complete.

A Peek into the Future

Although it is unwise to predict the future in general, it is even more questionable in the fast-changing world of new media technologies. Nevertheless, it can be useful to anticipate what imminent technological advances may mean for public relations professionals.

User Generated Content: Social Media and Web 2.0

Social media describes the online technologies and practices that people use to share content, opinions, insights, experiences, perspectives, and media itself. Facilitating or, even to some extent, orchestrating this process of community building will become an important strategy in public relations. Social media can take many different forms, including text, images, audio, and video. The social media sites typically use tools that some view as a second generation or Web 2.0 version of software and Web site functions. Web 2.0 loosely describes Internet features that facilitate collaboration and sharing between users such as:

- Wikis: Wikipedia
- Social networking: MySpace and Facebook
- Presence apps: Twitter and Jaiku
- Video sharing: YouTube
- Virtual Reality: Second Life
- Events: Upcoming
- News aggregation: Digg and Reddit
- Photo sharing: Flickr and Zooomr
- Livecasting: Justin.tv
- Episodic online video: Stickham, YourTrumanShow
- Episodic online audio: this WEEK in TECH (TWIT)
- Media sharing: Izimi and Pownce
- Social bookmarking: del.icio.us
- Online gaming: World of Warcraft

Text100 has created a virtual presence in Second Life, where "avatars" can learn how to write a news release or watch a video about the firm. *PRWeek* awarded the firm with the "PR Innovation of the Year 2007," for not only "talk[ing] the talk, but also walk[ing] the walk" in terms of public relations firms taking the initiative to explore new opportunities in what is called "social media."

These tools, several of which have been covered in the chapter, enable a high degree of user participation and user generation of content, such as the creation and editing of a humorous video making a political statement on YouTube or the writing of political opinion on a blog with editorial management of reader postings in response.

Skeptics question the claim that these Internet features constitute a sea change in the way people relate with each other or even a social revolution. Critics go further, claiming that the terms *social media* and *Web 2.0* are mainly marketing ploys for public relations firms and service companies. Certainly, long after the buzz surrounding the terms is gone, the reality for public relations will be to include strategies that encourage or build on these tools. Professionals will find ways to harness the human urge to relate to each other on the Web and to create or assemble compelling content that is shared with others.

The challenge in our field will be to avoid manipulating social media in ways that alienate users or lead to backlash. The PRSA ethics code provides much of the needed guidance in admonitions against false front organizations and plants of content that mislead. By masquerading as the spontaneous expression of an individual using a social media tool, the deliberate and duplicitous work of a public relations professional on behalf of a paying client is a betrayal that will seldom go unpunished online—harsh criticism, negative publicity, even banishment will follow. On the other hand, forthright and transparent use of social media for public relations objectives will be accepted as part of the mix of ideas and positions that are shared online. Other developments:

◆ **Think digital, but not necessarily online.** Many public relations tools will involve specialized digital devices or media that are not online or that are used more frequently off-line. For example, digital tablets and digital ink enable online content to be downloaded overnight so that the user can carry the lightweight device on a commuter train. Page loads are instantaneous because there is no download delay, and voice recognition/generation features enable commands and replies. News and other content can be read to the user by the tablet, making better use of professional travel time.

◆ **Forget Papyrus—and even drop paper.** As already noted, computer processing is not limited to traditional devices. Thin, lightweight tablets hardly larger than a yellow notepad can link to the Internet and carry the computing power of full-sized desktop computers. These devices recognize the user's handwriting and respond to touch commands on the screen, enabling notetaking and small group activity in public relations offices. An even more portable medium is reaching the consumer market. E-ink enables computer functions on a sheet of material the size and thickness of a typical plastic placemat at a dining table. Applications for public relations remain to be realized, but as a portable computer and a reading device, the potential communication angles should be very interesting.

◆ **Wireless broadband.** Cable and other high-capacity services such as satellite and DSL service often are collectively referred to as *broadband services*. Broadband enables online public relations professionals to meet the eight-second rule for loading time while offering broadcast-quality video and unlimited information stores to media, investors, and other publics. Cell and dish satellite companies have now broken the broadband barrier, meaning that wireless computers and cell devices will browse and communicate at speeds comparable to desktop machines on cable or DSL service today. These broadband speeds enable the Internet to offer the previously mentioned telephone service called VoIP (Voice over Internet Protocol) at low cost, especially for international calling.

◆ **Virtual presence.** Increased online capacity through broadband services will enable public relations professionals and Webmasters to create virtual environments and emulate the bricks-and-mortar presence of their organizations. Special boxes are becoming commercially available that will generate scents to accompany other elements of virtual reality to give users a sense of presence in a world created by the organization. Activist groups could convey pollution conditions. E-commerce sites could offer a restaurant aura (sounds, aroma, clientele, layout, view) to help users decide where to make a reservation or what food suits their fancy for takeout.

◆ **Virtual worlds.** Second Life is one of the most popular and well developed of the 3-D online digital worlds where many people spend time. Nearly 6 million residents spend $1.5 million actual U.S. dollars on services within the virtual world. Some individuals are making their entire living in the Second Life economy. Special events, a staple of public relations, occur daily, including support groups for chronic and acute pain, community fairs and fundraisers, live evening programs of religious groups, and Earth Day celebrations. Kansas educators convene and share ideas in a place called Oz Island, an allusion to the Wizard of Oz. The potential for public relations activities and messages reaching highly targeted audiences in Second Life is only beginning to be realized. *PRWeek's* annual award for PR Innovation of the Year 2007 went to Text 100 Public Relations for building a virtual office in Second Life, celebrating the company's 25th anniversary in the new virtual space that included hundreds of employees. See illustration on page 361.

◆ **Processing speed and memory capacity.** With continuing increases in computer chip capacity and speed, public relations professionals will enjoy digital tools in the future that are unimagined now. According to a National Public Radio program entitled *Talk of the Nation*, "Science Friday," computer processors will be 25 times faster within five years. Quantum computing researchers are manipulating the spin of electrons in atoms to compute and record data at rates 1,000 times what we know today. Artificial intelligence to assist with crises, issues management, complex event management, and visual design will become commonplace. Multimedia and unusual hybrid media will meet public relations objectives such as on-demand information and virtual presence, which are currently constrained by machine limitations.

The future holds many changes and advances in communication tools and channels. However, each tool requires an "operator" with good managerial judgment and excellent people skills. In the midst of a new age of electronic wonders, most public relations triumphs will continue to hinge on human creativity.

SUMMARY

The Communications Explosion
In the 1990s, the Internet grew from a means of exchanging scientific information in a relatively small community to become a global communications tool for the masses, blending telephone, television, and the computer into an information superhighway. Three key factors have contributed to the communication explosion: fiber-optic cable, the digital transmission of sound and pictures, and wireless technologies.

The Computer
The computer is not just a tool to handle office procedures; it is also the on-ramp to the Internet.

The Internet
One of the primary uses of the Internet is for communication, both in the form of e-mail and in information delivery and research opportunities. Its reach is worldwide, but keep in mind that Internet content is virtually uncontrolled. Users can become frustrated in trying to find information online. There are also problems with security and copyright infringement.

Other Computer Uses
Public relations practitioners use computers in the following tasks: dictation and voice generation, expert system programming, processing of news releases, e-mail, desktop publishing, mailing list generation, online conferencing, graphics production, and facsimile transmission. They also use computers as management tools.

Satellite Transmission
Major newspapers use satellites to transmit material to regional printing plants. A number of companies deliver news releases via satellite, including audio and video releases. Teleconferencing is a rapidly growing application of satellite transmission; approximately 20,000 U.S. sites are equipped to use this technology, saving companies time and money on business travel.

Other Tools
Other electronic tools include cell phones, personal digital assistants, CDs and DVDs, and electronic blackboards.

A Peek into the Future
Future trends may include the use of off-line digital devices, the growth of broadband and wireless broadband services, the development of "virtual presence" capabilities, and expanded processing speeds and memory capacity. All of these wonders will still require traditional managerial judgment and people skills.

CASE ACTIVITY What Would You Do?

Ashland Community Hospital is deeply involved in health education as part of its approach to preventive care. In the past, the hospital has distributed leaflets about various diseases and conducted community seminars on such topics as how to stop smoking, the importance of physical fitness, and how to detect early signs of cancer.

The hospital can use new technologies to expand its potential in health education. Write a proposal on how the hospital could use the Internet, the World Wide Web, e-mail, CDs and DVDs, and faxes to disseminate health-care information to the community.

QUESTIONS for Review and Discussion

1. What part of the Internet has home pages? What does the term *home page* mean?
2. What is the Internet, and what are some of its most promising uses in public relations?
3. Define the following terms: *broadband, virtual presence, brochureware, listservs, Webcasting,* and *artificial intelligence.*
4. How do you think public relations professionals should address the tangibility factor when pitching stories to reporters?
5. What is the difference between a news release delivery system such as Business Wire and a news service such as the Associated Press?
6. Teleconferencing is growing in popularity. Explain how it operates. How does it differ from Webconferencing?

How do you think the two will merge as a result of broadband Internet service?

7. Authors frequently participate in satellite media tours. How do they work, and why do many authors prefer them to traditional book promotion tours?
8. What impact do you think the tailoring of messages to individual audience members will have on public relations? Will it make our work more difficult? Noticeably more effective? Less ethically sound?
9. As a public relations practitioner, how might you use online computer conference calls?
10. Do you think that new technologies will facilitate or hamper creativity in public relations?

SUGGESTED READINGS

Altus, Celeste. "Intranets Keep Teams on Same Page Worldwide." *PRWeek,* September 4, 2006, p. 9.

Barkow, Tim. "Blogging for Business: Do You Really Want Your Employees to Have Their Own Blogs At Work?" *The Strategist,* Fall 2004, pp. 40–42.

Bush, Michael. "New-media tools foster greater comms efficiency." *PRWeek,* March 6, 2007, www.prweek.com/us/search/article/637115/.

Frank, John N. "Blogs Offer New Way for PR Pros to Speak with Clients." *PRWeek,* October 18, 2004, p. 9.

Hazley, Greg. "PR Taps Into 'Net Video.'" *O'Dwyer's PR Report,* April 2007, pp. 1, 14, 16, 40.

Hiebert, Ray E. "Commentary: New Technologies, Public Relations, and Democracy." *Public Relations Review,* Vol. 31, 2005, pp. 1–9.

Ivry, Sara. "Now on YouTube: The Latest News from Al Jazeera, in English." *New York Times,* July 4, 2006, www.nytimes.com.

Iacono, Erica. "Newswires 2.0." *PRWeek,* September 11, 2006, p. 17.

Kiousis, Spiro, and Daniela V. Dimitrova. "Differential Impact of Web Site content: Exploring the Influence of Source (Public Relations versus News), Modality, and Participation on College Student's Perceptions." *Public Relations Review,* June 2006, Vol. 32, No. 2, pp. 177–179.

McKenna, Ted. "Popular vlogger joins environmental effort." *PRWeek,* September 25, 2006, p. 2.

"More Abuse for the Much-maligned Press Release: Is RSS Becoming the Preferred Way to Receive News?" MRR Online, Ragan's eNewsstand, October 13, 2006, www.raganenewsstand.com.

O'Brien, Keith. "A Digital State of Play." *PRWeek,* April 23, 2007, pp. 4–5.

O'Brien, Keith. "Growth of MVNOs Making 'Third Screen' More Targeted." *PRWeek,* April 10, 2006, p. 6.

Parker, Laura. "Courts Are Asked to Crack Down on Bloggers, Websites. Those Attacked Online Are Filing Libel Lawsuits." *USA Today,* October 3, 2006, p. 1A.

Porter, Lance V., and Sallot, Lynne M. "Web Power: A Survey of Practitioners' World Wide Web Use and Their Perceptions of Its Effects on Their Decision-Making Power." *Public Relations Review,* Vol. 31, 2005, pp. 111–119.

Porter, Lance V., Trammell, Kaye, Chung, Deborah, and Kim, Eunseong. "Blog Power: Examining the Effects of Practitioner Blog Use on Power in Public Relations." *Public Relations Review,* Vol. 33, No. 1, March 2007, pp. 92–95.

Quain, John R. "Fine-tuning Your Filter for Online Information." *New York Times Circuits,* October 13, 2006, www.nytimes.com/ref/technology/circuits/03basi.html.

Regalado, Antonio, and Searcey, Dionne. "Where Did that Video Spoofing Gore's Film Come From?" *Wall Street Journal Online,* August 3, 2006. online.wsj.com.

Reber, Bryan H. "How Activist Groups Use Websites in Media Relations: Evaluating Online Press Rooms." *Journal of Public Relations Research,* Vol. 18, No. 4, 2006, pp. 313–333.

Taylor, Maureen, and Perry, Danielle C. "Diffusion of Traditional and New Media Tactics in Crisis Communication." *Public Relations Review,* Vol. 31, 2005, pp. 209–217.

CHAPTER 14

News Releases, Media Alerts, and Pitch Letters

The News Release

The *news release*, also called a *press release*, has been around since Ivy Lee issued a news release back in 1906 for the Pennsylvania Railroad, it continues to be the most commonly used public relations tactic. Basically, a news release is a simple document whose primary purpose is the dissemination of information to mass media such as newspapers, broadcast stations, and magazines.

A great deal of the information that you read in your weekly or daily newspaper originates from a news release prepared by a publicist or public relations practitioner on behalf of a client or employer. Gary Putka, the Boston bureau chief of the *Wall Street Journal*, admits that "a good 50 percent" of the stories in the newspaper come from news releases. Another study, by Bennett & Company (Orlando), found that 75 percent of the responding journalists said they used public relations sources for their stories.

The media rely on news releases for several reasons. First, the reality of mass communications today is that reporters and editors spend most of their time processing information, not gathering it. Second, no media enterprise has enough staff to cover every single event in the community. Consequently, a lot of the more routine news in a newspaper is processed from information provided by public relations practitioners. As one editor of a major daily once said, public relations people are the newspaper's "unpaid reporters."

It must be remembered, however, that a news release is not paid advertising. News reporters and editors have no obligation to use any of the information from a news release in a news story. News releases are judged solely on newsworthiness, timeliness, interest to the readers, and other traditional news values. Lisa Barbadora, director of public relations and marketing for Schubert Communications, provides the following list of tips for "news-centered" releases in an article by Jerry Walker in *O'Dwyer's PR Report*:

 ◆ Use short, succinct headlines and subheads to highlight main points and pique interest. They should not simply be a repeat of the information in the lead-in paragraph.

 ◆ Don't use generic words such as "the leading provider" or "world-class" to position your company. Be specific, such as "with annual revenues of."

 ◆ Don't describe products using phrases such as "unique" or "total solution." Use specific terms or examples to demonstrate the product's distinctiveness.

 ◆ Use descriptive and creative words to grab an editor's attention, but make sure they are accurate and not exaggerated.

 ◆ Don't highlight the name of your company or product in the headline of a news release if it is not highly recognized. If you are not a household name, focus on the news instead.

 ◆ Tell the news. Focus on how your announcement affects your industry and lead with that rather than overtly promoting your product or company.

 ◆ Critique your writing by asking yourself, "Who cares?" Why should readers be interested in this information?

 ◆ Don't throw everything into a release. Better to break your news into several releases if material is lengthy.

 ◆ Don't use lame quotes. Write like someone is actually talking—eliminate the corporatese that editors love to ignore. Speak with pizzazz to increase your chances of being published.

◆ Target your writing. Create two different tailored releases that will go out to different types of media rather than a general release that isn't of great interest to either group.

◆ Look for creative ways to tie your announcement in with current news or trends.

◆ Write simply. Use contractions, write in active voice, be direct, avoid paired words such as "clear and simple," and incorporate common action-oriented phrases to generate excitement. Sentences should be no longer than 34 words.

◆ Follow the *Associated Press Stylebook* and specific publications' editorial standards for dates, technical terms, abbreviations, punctuation, spellings, capitalization, and so on.

◆ Don't use metaphors unless they are used to paint a clearer picture for the reader.

◆ Don't overdo it. It's important to write colorfully, to focus on small specific details, to include descriptions of people, places, and events—but do not write poetry when you want press.

◆ Don't be formulaic in your news release writing. Not every release must start with the name of the company or product. Break out of the mold to attract media attention.

◆ Don't expect editors to print your entire release. Important information should be contained in the first two paragraphs.

◆ Make it clear how your announcement is relevant for the editors' readers.

Planning a News Release

Before writing a news release, a number of questions should be answered to give the release direction and purpose. A planning worksheet should be used to answer the following questions:

◆ What is the key message? This should be expressed in one sentence.

◆ Who is the primary audience for the release? Is it for consumers who may buy a product or service? Or is it for purchasing agents in other companies? The answer to this question also affects whether the release is sent to a daily community newspaper or to a trade magazine.

◆ What does the target audience gain from the product or service? What are the potential benefits and rewards?

◆ What objective does the release serve? Is it to increase product sales, to enhance the organization's reputation, or to increase attendance at an event?

These planning questions are answered from a public relations perspective, but the next step is to structure the content and format of a news release. This is discussed further in the next several sections.

The Content of a News Release

A news release, as already noted, is written like a news story. The lead paragraph is an integral and important part of the text, because it forms the apex of the journalistic "inverted pyramid" approach to writing. This means that the first paragraph succinctly summarizes the most important part of the story and succeeding paragraphs fill in the details in descending order of importance.

There are three reasons why you should use the inverted pyramid structure. First, if the editor or reporter doesn't find anything interesting in the first three or four lines of the news release, it won't be used. Second, editors cut stories from the bottom. In fact, Business Wire estimates that more than 90 percent of news releases are rewritten in much shorter form than the original text. If the main details of the story are at the beginning, the release will still be understandable and informative even if most of the original text has been deleted.

A third reason for using the inverted pyramid is that readers don't always read the full story. Statistics show, for example, that the average reader spends less than 30 minutes a day reading a metropolitan daily newspaper. This means that they read a lot of headlines and first paragraphs, and not much else.

Here are some other guidelines for the content of a news release:

♦ Double-check all information. Be absolutely certain that every fact and title in the release is correct and that every name is spelled properly. Check the copy for errors in grammar, punctuation, and sentence structure. Make sure trademarks are noted.

on the job
ETHICS

What to Write, or Not Write

A common activity of public relations practitioners is to write news releases on behalf of a client or employer.

At times, the content and choice of words in a news release can be an ethical dilemma. Consider the following two scenarios:

♦ The president of a small business software company wants to get some publicity and visibility in the business press. He asks you to write a news release announcing that the company has recently received major contracts from large corporations such as General Electric, AT&T, Starbucks, and ExxonMobil. The president then adds, "We only have a contract with AT&T right now, but we've been talking to the other companies, and it's a pretty sure thing that they will sign on." Given this information, would you go ahead and write the news release? Why or why not?

♦ A top-level executive has been fired by a company for manipulating accounts and claiming more sales for her division than could be documented. The media is calling about the executive's departure, so the president asks you to write a short news release that the executive has resigned "to pursue other business opportunities." Would you go ahead and write the news release? Why or why not?

♦ Eliminate boldface and capital letters. Avoid boldfacing key words or sentences and don't place the name of the organization in all capital letters.

♦ Include organization background. A short paragraph at the end of the news release should give a thumbnail sketch of the organization. It may be a description of what the organization does or manufactures, how many employees it has, or whether it is a market leader in a particular industry. This helps journalists unfamiliar with the organization to get a sense of its size, scope, and major products.

♦ Localize whenever possible. Most studies show that news releases with a local angle get published more often than generic news releases giving a regional or national perspective. Airlines, for example, "localize" news releases about the total number of passengers and revenues by breaking down such figures by specific cities and making that the lead paragraph for releases sent to journalists in those cities. Insurance companies also do "hometown" releases by mentioning local agents in the copy.

Beyond the practical aspects of content are ethical considerations about writing a particular news release. See the Ethics box on this page to examine some of these questions.

Format of a Print News Release

The traditional print news release follows a basic format, which is illustrated in the Sunkist news release on this page.

This news release from Sunkist Growers is a good example of how to format a print news release.

FOR IMMEDIATE RELEASE

**KIDS 'TAKE A STAND' ON THE FIRST DAY OF SUMMER
SELLING LEMONADE FOR CHARITIES NATIONWIDE**

**Sunkist's "Take a Stand" Program to Distribute 10,000 Lemonade Stands
In Response to Overwhelming Demand**

SHERMAN OAKS, Calif. (June 21, 2006) – To celebrate the official first day of summer, Sunkist announced that it has extended its "Take a Stand" program, doubling its distribution to now give away 10,000 free lemonade stands for kids to raise money for a charity of their choice. With more than 5,000 "Take a Stand" pledges already submitted by kids from every state in the country, Sunkist was inspired to double its efforts and give even more kids the opportunity to take some time from their summer vacations to help their local communities.

To receive a complimentary lemonade stand, parents and their young philanthropists must submit their "Take a Stand" pledges online at http://www.sunkist.com/takeastand. With their parent's or legal guardian's permission, kids ages 7-12 are eligible to receive a stand after they submit their brief, 100-word pledge describing how they plan to operate their stand to benefit a charity. The additional stands will be released throughout the summer, while supplies last.

In its third year, Sunkist "Take a Stand" kicked off this year with a live concert by GRAMMY® Award winning country star and "Take a Stand" national spokesperson Billy Dean. The program gives parents a great tool to teach their kids the importance of philanthropy and volunteerism. At the same time, the kids are given an opportunity to learn how to run a business and feel great about helping to raise money for a charity that is of interest to them.

Kids have raised money for a variety of local and national charities – from helping their school or church to cancer research and hurricane relief efforts. The decision is left up to the kids to decide which charity will benefit from their hard squeezed lemonade sales.

-more-

6500 Wilshire Blvd., Suite 1900 Los Angeles, CA 90048 Ph. 323-866-6000 Fax 323-866-6001

The major components are as follows:

◆ Use standard 8.5-by-11 inch paper. It should be white or on the organization's letterhead.

◆ Identify the sender (contact) in the upper-left or right corner of the page and provide the sender's name, address, and telephone number. Many releases also include a fax number and an e-mail address.

◆ After the contact information, write For Immediate Release if the material is intended for immediate publication, which is usually the case. Some practitioners discard the phrase because they say that all news releases are automatically assumed to be for immediate release.

◆ Leave 2 inches of space for editing convenience before starting the text.

◆ Provide a boldface headline that gives the key message of the release so the editor knows exactly what the release is about at a glance.

◆ Provide a dateline, for example: Minneapolis, MN: September 21, 2008. This indicates where the news release originated.

◆ Start the text with a clearly stated summary that contains the most important message you want to convey to the reader, even if he or she only reads the first paragraph. Lead paragraphs should be a maximum of three to five lines.

◆ Leave at least a 1.5-inch margin. Double-space the copy to give editors room to edit the material.

◆ Use a 10- or 12-point standard type, such as Times Roman or Courier, because they are easy to read.

◆ Never split a paragraph from one page to the next. Place the word *more* at the bottom of each page.

◆ Place an identifying slug line and page number at the top of each page after the first one.

Format of an Internet News Release

The format and content of news releases for distribution via e-mail and the Internet is somewhat different than the traditional 8.5-by-11, double-spaced format that is mailed or faxed to media outlets. A news release that is sent via e-mail, for example, is single-spaced. Another difference is that the contacts are usually listed at the end of the news release instead of at the top. See page 384 for an electronic news release from Heinz Company that was sent via an electronic news service, which will be discussed shortly.

B. L. Ochman, writing in *The Strategist*, suggests that you should "think of the electronic news release as a teaser to get a reporter or editor to your Web site for additional information." He makes the following suggestions:

◆ Use a specific subject line that identifies exactly what the news release is about.

◆ Make your entire release a maximum of 200 words or less, in five short paragraphs. The idea is brevity so that reporters see the news release on one screen and don't have to scroll. If a journalist has hundreds of e-mails in his or her inbox, scrolling becomes a real chore.

◆ Write only two or three short sentences in each of the five paragraphs.

◆ Use bulleted points to convey key points.

on the job

A MULTICULTURAL WORLD

Sensitivity Required for Global News Releases

News releases are now distributed internationally, but there are cultural differences, sensitive political issues, and language that must be taken into consideration.

In terms of cultural differences, news releases are perceived differently in various nations. In Latin America, for example, editors are highly suspicious of news releases that describe new products or services as "best," "world-class," or even "cutting edge." In Russia, editors are highly skeptical of anything coming from a U.S. source and won't be interested unless the release is highly oriented to Russia. "Asian general media is more tolerant of technical releases than are Europeans or Latin Americans," according to Colleen Pizarev, PR Newswire's VP of international distribution.

Political issues are another pitfall. The writer of a news release for the Chinese press, for example, should avoid making any mention of such hot topics as human rights, dissent, freedom, Taiwan, or even refer to the company's commitment to corporate social responsibility (CSR). By the same token, a company sending a news release to the Taiwanese media must be careful not to mention anything about its business in China. Another aspect about China—it has a highly regulated system and all news stories must be government-sanctioned. In other words, news releases can't be distributed directly to media; they first must go through official censorship channels.

Language is another consideration. News releases should be translated into the national language of the country. In India, for example, English is widely used but many organizations also translate news releases into Hindi if they are sending the release to regional and local publications. In Singapore, it's best to have news releases in English and Chinese. China presents a problem because there are several versions of Chinese. Mandarin is extensively used in the southern part of the nation, but simplified Chinese is used in the north. Even English-speaking nations must be considered in terms of adopting spelling. A news release in the United Kingdom or Australia, for example, should use the Queen's English. This means "organisation" instead of "organization," and "honours" instead of "honors."

Global public relations firms, with offices in many nations, often serve their clients by having local staffs write, translate, and distribute media materials. One key factor, according to *PRWeek* reporter Tanya Lewis, is to adapt a global release by providing local contacts and including quotes from local representatives of the company. Lewis also advises, "Don't use phrases/words that would cause confusion when translated." The number "six," for example, is better than saying "half dozen."

◆ Above the headline or at the bottom of the release be sure to provide a contact name, phone number, e-mail address, and URL for additional information.

◆ Never send a release as an attachment. Journalists, because of possible virus infections, rarely open attachments.

Ochman concludes, "Write like you have 10 seconds to make a point. Because online, you do."

Electronic news releases, also called *e-releases*, can be e-mailed to journalists, posted on an organization's Web page or newsroom, and distributed via electronic news services. Releases distributed on a global basis need special sensitivity, which is outlined in the Multicultural World box on this page. The various distribution methods of news releases will be discussed shortly.

Publicity Photos

The cliché is that a picture is worth a thousand words. For this reason, both print and electronic news releases are often accompanied by a photo. News releases about personnel often include a head-and-shoulder picture (often called a *mug shot*) of a person named in the release. New product news releases often include a photo of the product in an attractive setting. See the publicity photo on this page that was distributed by a grower and distributor of lettuce.

Studies show that more people "read" photographs than read articles. The Advertising Research Foundation found that three to four times as many people notice the average one-column photograph as read the average news story. In another study, Wayne Wanta of the University of Missouri found that articles accompanied by photographs are perceived as significantly more important than those without photographs.

Like press releases, publicity photos are not

Food publicity photos often show a savory dish prepared with the product. Boggiatto Produce, Inc. shows how its Romaine lettuce can be used to make a Caesar Chicken Pizza. Its press kit, prepared by Railing and Associates, contains a CD of other attractive dishes and recipes that food editors can use.

published unless they appeal to media gatekeepers. Although professional photographers should always be hired to take the photos, public relations practitioners should supervise their work and select what photos are best suited for media use. Here are some additional suggestions:

Quality   Photos must have good contrast and sharp detail so that they reproduce in a variety of formats, including grainy newsprint. Digital photography is the norm, and in many cases editors download digital photos from an organization's Web site. But a beautiful photo on the computer screen may not come out the same way when it is printed.

Most Web sites use images at 72 dpi (dots per inch) for fast download, but print publications need photos at 300 dpi in JPEG or GIF files. Consequently, electronic news services and corporate online press rooms usually have a protected site that provides high-resolution photos for registered journalists. Photos also are supplied to editors on CD or DVD. In general, never send photos as an attachment unless the journalist has specifically requested it.

Subject Matter   A variety of subjects can be used for publicity photos. Trade magazines, weekly newspapers, and organizational newsletters often use the standard "grip-and-grin" photo of a person receiving an award or the CEO shaking hands with a visiting dignitary. This has been a staple of publicity photos for years, and there is no sign that they are going out of fashion despite being tired clichés. Another standard approach is the large group photograph, which is appropriate for the club newsletter, but almost never acceptable for a daily newspaper. A better approach is to take photos of groups of three or four people from the same city and send only that photo to editors in that specific city.

Composition   The best photos are uncluttered. Photo experts recommend (1) tight shots with minimum background, (2) an emphasis on detail, not whole scenes, (3) and limiting wasted space by reducing gaps between individuals or objects. At times, context also is important. Environmental portraits show the subject of the photo in his or her normal surroundings—for example, a research scientist in a lab.

Action   Too many photos are static, with nothing happening except someone looking at the camera. It's better to show people doing something—talking, gesturing, laughing, running, or operating a machine. Action gives the photo interest. The exception is the standard product photo.

Scale   Another way to add interest is to use scale. Apple, for example, might illustrate its newest iPod by having Steve Jobs hold the device while surrounded by large stacks of CDs, showing how much music could be stored on it.

Camera Angle   Interesting angles can make the subject of a photo more compelling. Some common methods are shooting upward at a tall building to make it look even taller or an aerial shot giving the viewer an unusual perspective.

Lighting   Professional photographers use a variety of lighting techniques to ensure that the subject is portrayed, quite literally, in the best light. Product photos, for example, always have the light on the product and the background is usually dark or almost invisible. Background is important. If the executives at a banquet are all wearing dark suits, the photographer shouldn't line them up in front of a dark red curtain, because there will be no contrast. Also, outdoor shots require using the sun to advantage.

Color   Today, with digital cameras and flash cards, almost all publicity photos are in color. Because of new printing technologies, many publications now use color on a regular basis. Daily newspapers, for example, regularly use color publicity photos in the food, business, sports, and travel sections. Publications have differing requirements. Some want photos that can be downloaded via Web sites; others want CD or DVD, and still others want color 35-mm color slides. Again, the general rule is to have several formats available and send what the publication or Web news site needs.

Mat Releases

A variation of the traditional news release is what is called the *mat feature release*. They were originally called "mat" because they were sent in mat form ready for the printing press. Today, these materials are distributed in a variety of formats including word documents, jpegs, and pdfs.

The format of mat release is somewhat different than the traditional news release because a feature angle is usually used instead of a lead that gives a key message. They also are in the format of a standing column headline such as *Healthy Eating, Cooking Corner*, or *Vacations of a Lifetime*.

The concept is to provide helpful consumer information and tips about a variety of subjects in an informative way with only a brief mention of the nonprofit or corporation that has distributed the release via firms such as Family Features (www.familyfeatures.com) and the North American Precis Syndicate (www.napsinfo.com). These canned features show up in thousands of weekly newspapers and many dailies in the food, travel, fashion, automotive, and business sections. For example, a recipe feature titled "Chicken and Rice: Always a Winning Combination" distributed by NAPS for Rice-a-Roni generated more than 1,400 newspaper articles in 40 states with a total readership of 75 million.

On occasion, a mat release is included as one tactic in a public relations campaign. Sunkist Growers, for example, used a mat release as part of its promotion of its Take a Stand campaign (see Chapter 6). The lead of the mat release was as follows:

> This summer parents are finding clever ways to teach their kids valuable life lessons—through lemonade. Instead of letting your kids waste away their summer vacations playing video games, encourage them to start up a small business by running a good old-fashioned lemonade stand.

The mat release continued by mentioning how kids could sign up for the "Take a Stand" program and get a free lemonade stand. It then gave kids tips on how to run a stand and increase neighborhood lemonade sales. A sidebar accompanying the mat release gave the recipe for "real old-fashioned lemonade." Contrast this mat release with the Sunkist news release shown on page 370.

Another approach is a regular column that features an expert. Nestlé, for example, distributes a column via Family Features called "Mix it Up With Jenny." The column, under the byline of Jenny Harper, who is identified as a senior culinary specialist for the Nestlé Test Kitchens, offers seasonal recipes that, of course, include ingredients made by Nestlé. One column, distributed in the spring to daily and weekly newspapers, discussed desserts that could be prepared quickly for graduation parties.

A more sophisticated mat release is an entire color page layout that a newspaper can select and publish with no cost. Family Features has pioneered this concept, and a good example is the full-color page about receiving a puppy for Valentine's Day, which is shown on this page. This entire feature, offered at no cost to newspapers, was paid for by Purina, a manufacturer of pet food. The feature, however, makes only a passing reference to Purina so the entire piece reads like a feature page actually prepared by the newspaper.

Newspapers and other publications are given a catalogue of available features by Family Features or NAPS via the Web, and editors then chose which ones they want to receive. The Purina feature, for example, was "06627: Furry Valentines With Wet Noses. Materials courtesy of Purina." Mat services also provide video and audio features to the broadcast industry. Many newspapers, with reduced staffs, find the features provided by editorial services such as Family Features a cost-effective way of filling space at virtually no cost to them.

06627: Furry Valentines With Wet Noses
All materials courtesy of: Purina

To order, download at www.FamilyFeatures.com or contact Media Communications at support@familyfeatures.com or 1-888-824-3337

An innovative approach to the standard mat news release is an entire newspaper page written and designed around a particular theme. This release, distributed by Family Features Editorial Syndicate on behalf of Nestlé Purina PetCare Company, uses the theme of Valentine's Day to give information about how to select and care for a new puppy.

Media Alerts and Fact Sheets

On occasion, the public relations staff will send a memo to reporters and editors about a news conference or upcoming event that they may wish to cover. Such memos also are used to let the media know about an interview opportunity with a visiting expert or alert them that a local person will be featured on a network television program. These *media alerts* also are referred to as *media advisories*. They may be sent with an accompanying news release or by themselves. See the media alert issued by Royal Caribbean about its African American art auction on this page. This campaign was highlighted in Chapter 11.

The most common format for media alerts is short, bulleted items rather than long paragraphs. A typical one-page advisory might contain the following elements: a one-line headline, a brief paragraph outlining the story idea, some of journalism's five Ws and H, and a short paragraph telling the reporter who to contact for more information or to make arrangements. The following is the text of a media advisory from Old Bay Seasonings, which includes information about satellite feeds from the event.

Media alerts are used to inform the media about an upcoming event. All the relevant information is given in bullet form in an effort to encourage print and broadcast coverage of the event. See Chapter 11 about the Royal Caribbean's outreach to the African American community.

MEDIA ALERT

Royal Caribbean Rolls Out the Red Carpet to Celebrate Cultural Arts
This fall, Royal Caribbean International® will host live onboard art auctions benefiting the next generation of African-American artists

WHAT: Beginning this fall, Royal Caribbean International® will collaborate with art institutes in three major U.S. cities to celebrate the culture and rich legacy that African Americans have made within the arts arena by hosting live art auctions onboard its spectacular ships docked at local piers. The art featured during the onboard auctions is donated by national and local African-American artists.

Proceeds from these auctions will support summer arts programs for aspiring African-American artists who are in high school in the Baltimore, Los Angeles and Miami areas. Partnering art organizations will host the summer programs at their facilities and implement the hands-on curricula.

The events are complimentary and open to the public. Space is limited and availability is on a first-come, first-served basis. In addition to national and local African-American artists, we have invited community officials, prominent artists, educators, business professionals, alumni from local Historically Black Colleges and Universities and church associations, along with a host of other individuals.

WHY: This community-based initiative is the beginning of what will become a longstanding effort on Royal Caribbean's part to encourage cultural arts. On this day, we will celebrate the African-American art experience, while nurturing the vision that dwells within so many existing and aspiring African-American artists.

WHO: Dianne Williams, Manager, Multicultural Marketing, Royal Caribbean International is available for telephone or in person interviews prior to and during the art auction events.

Nationally and internationally renowned artists Synthia Saint James, Jeffrey Kent and Mari Hall are available for interviews to speak about the legacy of the arts within the African-American community and fostering the arts among youth.

WHEN:
- Los Angeles — Sunday, Oct. 16:   Vision of the Seas®
- Baltimore — Sunday, Oct. 23:   Grandeur of the Seas®
- Miami — Saturday, Nov. 5:   Navigator of the Seas®

Time: 11:30 a.m. – 4:00 p.m. Event takes place while ship is in port.

WHERE: Phone and on-site interviews aboard Royal Caribbean's premiere cruise ships can be arranged. To attend art auction please call 1-800-728-0031 or visit www.royalcaribbean.com/artauctions. For more information check out www.royalcaribbean.com/gopack.

CONTACT: **Lonnetta Ragland** at 816-512-2348 or raglandl@fleishman.com.

Media Alert

Who:	Old Bay Seasoning, a unique blend of a dozen herbs and spices and a Chesapeake Bay cooking tradition for over 60 years, conducted a search for America's seafood lovers and Old Bay fans.
	More than 1,600 people across the country entered the contest by briefly describing in 100 words or less why they are America's biggest seafood fanatics and Old Bay fans and providing their favorite unusual uses for Old Bay.
What:	Ten lucky finalists from across the country were selected to vie for a $10,000 grand prize in the first-ever Old Bay Peel and Eat Shrimp Classic—a 10-minute, timed tournament to see who can peel and eat the most Old Bay-seasoned shrimp.
When:	The contest will kick off Labor Day Weekend on Friday, August 30, from 11:30 A.M. to 12:30 P.M.
Where:	Harborplace Amphitheater (outdoors) 200 East Pratt Street Baltimore, Maryland.
Special Guest:	Tory McPhail, executive chef at Commander's Palace restaurant in New Orleans and rising star in the culinary industry, will be master of ceremonies for the event.
Contact:	Amanda Hirschhorn, Hunter Public Relations 212/679.6660, ext. 239, or ahirschhorn@hunterpr.com Event-day cell: 914/475.4074

SATELLITE FEED INFORMATION FOLLOWS
Friday, August 30
Feed Time: 3:30–3:45 P.M. ET (Fed in Rotation)
Coordinates: C-Band: Telstar 4 (C)/Transponder 11/AUDIO 6.2 & 6.8
DL FREQ: 3920 (V)

Fact sheets are another useful public relations tool. Fact sheets are often distributed to the media as part of a media kit or with a news release to give additional background information about the product, person, service, or event.

Fact sheets are usually one to two pages in length and serve as a "crib sheet" for journalists when they write a story. A fact sheet about an organization may use headings that provide (1) the organization's full name, (2) products or services offered, (3) its annual revenues, (4) the number of employees, (5) the names and one-paragraph biographies of top executives, (6) the markets served, (7) position in the industry, and (8) any other pertinent details.

A variation on the fact sheet is the FAQ (Frequently Asked Questions). HP, for example, supplemented an Internet news release on its new ScanJet printer with a FAQ that answered typical consumer questions about the new product. Norelco's Bodygroom (see Chapter 5) product information fact sheet is more reflective of the campaign's creative theme and is shown on page 378.

Media Kits

A *media kit*, which is sometimes referred to as a *press kit*, is usually prepared for major events and new product launches. Its purpose is to give editors and reporters a variety of information and resources that make it easier for the reporter to write about the topic.

PHILIPS NORELCO BODYGROOM

Norelco gets up close and personal with its latest grooming gadget that removes unwanted hair below the chin… even below the belt!

Norelco BODYGROOM BG2020

Recommended Retail Price: $39.99

Availability: Target and Amazon.com in April 2006

For Additional Information Visit:
www.norelco.com

Features:	Benefits:
Take it ALL Off	Specifically designed for all body parts below the chin – it grooms unwanted hair from legs, chest, back, groin area and more!
Feelin' Good	Chromium Steel trimmer blades combined with a hypoallergenic shaving foil leave even the most sensitive skin smooth with less irritation.
Make it Your Own	Three interchangeable attachment combs trim hair different lengths because sometimes we don't want to take it all off!
Rechargeable and cordless	Can be charged for 50 minutes of cordless trimming time.
We got your back	Full Two Year Warranty

Fact sheets telling the specifics of a new product are often included in media kits so reporters have basic information at their fingertips. This fact sheet for a new men's razor was prepared by Manning Selvage & Lee and matches the tone of its campaign on behalf of client Philips Norelco. See Chapter 5 for more details about this campaign.

The basic elements of a media kit are (1) the main news release; (2) a news feature about the development of the product or something similar; (3) fact sheets on the product, organization, or event; (4) background information; (5) photos and drawings with captions; (6) biographical material on the spokesperson or chief executives; and (7) some basic brochures. All information should be clearly identified; it's also important to prominently display contact information such as e-mail addresses, phone numbers, and Web site URLs.

The contents of a media kit are traditionally placed inside a custom-designed folder. The folder will vary based on the size of budget. Pillsbury designed a folder that was the shape of a large chocolate chip cookie with a bite taken out of it to launch its new Big Deluxe Classics cookies. Another creative approach was a wine-box-style media kit that Heinz used to introduce its personalized ketchup bottle labels. This campaign is featured in the PR Casebook on page 379. Other organizations, such as Cirque du Soleil, just use a standard folder with its name emblazoned on it.

The typical media kit folder is 9-by-12 inches and has four surfaces: a cover, two inside pages (with pockets to hold news releases, etc.), and a back cover that gives the name and address of the organization. Another common feature is to have a slot on the inside page that holds a business card of the public relations contact person.

PRCASEBOOK

Creative Media Kit Launches Ketchup Campaign

How about a personalized bottle of Heinz Ketchup for your birthday or wedding? That's now possible thanks to the innovative public relations campaign that introduced Heinz Personalized Labels to the world. Heinz wanted to tap the "vanity" market and worked with Jack Horner Communications (JHC) to come up with a creative campaign to attract media attention and coverage.

A creative approach to a media kit. Jack Horner Communications, on behalf of client Heinz, sent editors a wine-box-style kit to introduce the ketchup's personalized labels' Web site. One story appeared in *USA Today*.

The campaign centerpiece was a creative, eye-catching media kit that was sent to 250 selected media and blog contacts. According to Horner Communications,

> The media kit consisted of a wine box-style carrier with the tagline "Next Time, Celebrate with a Bottle of Red." As media opened the box, they found a 14-ounce glass bottle of ketchup with a message on the label reading, "What Will You Say?" and the Web site address, www.myheinz.com. A pull-down menu on the inside of the box provided sample sayings to get reporters creative juices flowing. All press materials were also contained within the "wine box."

In addition, a news release was distributed nationally via BusinessWire to all media.

The public relations firm gave special attention to morning shows. JHC researched and developed customized individual ketchup bottles with sayings that would be appropriate for each show's hosts. For *Good Morning America*, a personalized label was made saying "Diane & Robin, a Perfect Pair." In the case of Steve Doocy, cohost of *Fox & Friends*, he even displayed the media kit on the air and commented about its creativity. Diane Sawyer, some weeks after the launch, presented actor Jack Black with a personalized "It's a Boy" Heinz Ketchup bottle on the air, thanking "our friends at Heinz."

The campaign was a success. Public relations was the sole means of communicating the launch of the Heinz Personalized Labels and the Web site. With only a $40,000 budget, JMC was able to generate 145 million branded media impressions featuring the Web address on *Good Morning America*, *Fox & Friends*, Comedy Central, and CNNMoney.com. Newspapers included the *Washington Post*, *USA Today*, and the *New York Times*.

In terms of the bottom line, Heinz sold 12,000 personalized ketchup bottles in the first month after the launch, and a total of 35,000 bottles were sold in the first year. Sales of Heinz ketchup also increased 12 percent in the fiscal quarter that the campaign was implemented. The campaign received PRSA's 2007 Silver Anvil Award in the category of marketing consumer products.

A good example of a well-designed media kit that fits the organization's products and personality was one done by Crayola to celebrate its 100th anniversary with a 25-city bus tour. The kit was a self-mailer that unfolded into a large round sheet 2 feet in diameter that featured artwork done with a rainbow of crayon colors. The kit also included a colorful news release (localized for each city) and two background articles on the history of the company. One piece of interesting trivia: "Since 1903, more than 120 billion crayons have been sold throughout the world. End-to-end they would circle the earth 200 times."

E-Kits

Compiling and producing a media kit is time consuming and expensive. It's not uncommon for press kits to cost $8 to $10 each by the time all of the materials have been produced. Much of the cost is in printing the kits.

> " The days of a thousand press kits are gone. Instead, well-designed online press kits can have an ongoing shelf life with constantly updated content. "
>
> ——*Tom Bucktold* of Business Wire

Consequently, Weber Shandwick has predicted the end of paper media kits. A 2004 poll by the firm of 1,500 media outlets found that 70 percent of them prefer what is called *e-kits*. Instead of bulky folders stuffed with printed information, the trendline is for putting all this information on the organization's online newsroom or on a CD. E-kits have the advantage of easy storage, ability to forward, easy conversion to any desired format for publication, the added features of video and audio, Web links, RSS feeds, and the elimination of newsroom clutter.

Cost savings for the organization also is a big factor. Patrick Pharris, founder of Electronic Media Communications gave *PR News* a good example. The company developed an Internet media kit for a client with eight documents, five photos, and a PR Newswire distribution for $4,000. If the same material would have been printed in a traditional media kit, the cost would have been about $16,000. HP, for a trade show, also used an e-kit that saved the company about $20,000 in printing costs.

Not every journalist, however, likes the digital approach. Daniel Cantelmo, writing in *Public Relations Quarterly*, quotes one senior editor for a high-technology magazine who said, "In 5 or 10 minutes, I can go through 25 printed press kits . . . and pick out exactly what I need. If I had to go through 25 CDs or online press kits, it would take hours. I don't have the time." Because of editors like him, e-kits probably will never totally replace the traditional media kit. In many cases, public relations firms and organizations continue to produce and distribute both a printed kit and a CD, often in the same package. The idea, again, is to provide whatever format the particular editor or journalist wants.

Pitch Letters

As previously noted, getting the attention of media gatekeepers is difficult because they receive literally hundreds of news releases and media kits every week.

Consequently, many public relations practitioners and publicists will write a short letter or note to the editor that tries to grab their attention. In the public relations industry, this is called a *pitch*. A standard pitch regarding the Sunkist Growers "Take a Stand" campaign is shown below. It was attached to the media kit and lets the editor know, in brief form, about the program. Notice that the writer also promises to follow-up with the editor about a possible story.

Dear (name),

With schools letting out and summer approaching fast, parents are presented with the challenge of finding fun and meaningful ways for their kids to pass the time. This summer, instead of watching TV and playing video games, why not get your kids started on the path of becoming an entrepreneur? What better way for kids to spend the dog days of summer than to learn how to run a business and raise money for charity through an old-fashioned lemonade sale!

In its third year, the Sunkist "Take a Stand" Program encourages kids, ages 7–12, across the country to get involved in their communities and raise money for a charitable cause that's near and dear to their hearts.

In 2005, Sunkist gave away more than 2,000 free lemonade stands to kids who wanted to give back to their communities through the "Take a Stand" Program. From those 2,000 stands alone, participants reported raising an estimated $400,000 for hundreds of charities nationwide.

The "Take a Stand" Program is back by popular demand and Sunkist is giving away an unprecedented 5,000 lemonade stands in 2006. So far this year, Sunkist has received pledges from kids in every state who will be coming soon to a neighborhood corner near you.

And getting involved is as easy as logging on to www.sunkist.com/takeastand and submitting a "Take a Stand" pledge. Sunkist will then send a free, limited edition Sunkist Summer Fun Lemonade Stand and Juicer Kit complete with tools kids need to be successful, while supplies last.

With summer vacation on the horizon, now is the perfect time to report on how kids in your area are getting involved in your local community. Enclosed is a press kit with additional information on the "Take a Stand" Program, including lemonade recipes and som fun facts on lemons.

I'll be following up with you soon to discuss your interest in a story on the "Take a Stand" Program. In the meantime, if you have any questions or are interested in finding out if kids in our area are setting up a lemonade stand, please contact me directly at (phone), or at (email).

Thanks for your time and consideration.

Kind regards,

(name)

On behalf of Sunkist Growers, Inc.

Public relations people also use pitches to ask editors to assign a reporter to a particular event, to pursue a feature angle on an issue or trend, or even to book a spokesperson on a forthcoming show. If you are doing a pitch by e-mail, however, here are some specific guidelines:

◆ Use a succinct subject line that tells the editor what you have to offer; don't try to be cute or gimmicky.

◆ Keep the message brief; one screen at the most.

◆ Don't include attachments unless the reporter is expecting you to do so. Many reporters, due to virus attacks, never open attachments unless they personally know the source.

◆ Don't send "blast" e-mails to large numbers of editors. E-mail systems are set up to filter messages with multiple recipients in the "To" and "BCC" fields, a sure sign of spam. If you do send an e-mail to multiple editors, break the list into small groups.

◆ Send tailored e-mail pitches to specific reporters and editors; the pitch should be relevant to their beats and publications.

◆ Personally check the names in your e-mail database to remove redundant recipients.

♦ Give editors the option of getting off your e-mail list; it will make your list more targeted to those who are interested. By the same token, give editors the opportunity to sign up for regular updates via RSS feeds or from your organization's Web site. If they cover your industry, they will appreciate it.

♦ Establish an e-mail relationship. As one reporter said, "The best e-mails come from people I know; I delete e-mails from PR people or agencies I don't recognize."

> " Media relations specialists should not send out a pitch without knowing the reporters and publications in advance. "
>
> ———*David B. Oates,* strategy and planning manager of ContentOne communications

Pitching is a fine art, however, and public relations personnel must first do some basic research about the publication or broadcast show that they want to contact. It's important to know the kinds of stories that a publication usually publishes or what kinds of guests appear on a particular talk show. Knowing a journalist's beat and the kinds of stories they have written in the past also is helpful. Another important point: If you are making a telephone pitch, make sure you call when the reporter or editor is not on deadline.

The media expresses great interest in trends, so it's also a good idea to relate a particular product or service with something that is already identified as part of a particular fashion or lifestyle. Fineberg Publicity, a New York firm, convinced *Hard Copy* to do a 3-minute segment on its client Jockey International. The news hook was the "slit skirt" trend in the fashion industry and how women were buying stylish hosiery to complement their skirts. The segment showed celebrities wearing Jockey's hosiery products.

The best pitches show a lot of creativity and are successful in grabbing the editor's attention. *Ragan's Media Relations Report* gives some opening lines that generated media interest and resulting stories:

♦ "How many students does it take to change a light bulb?" (A pitch about a residence hall maintenance program operated by students on financial aid.)

♦ "Would you like to replace your ex-husband with a plant?" (A pitch about a photographer who is expert at removing "exes" and other individuals out of old photos.)

♦ "Our CEO ran 16 Boston Marathons . . . and now he thinks we can walk a mile around a river." (A pitch about a CEO leading employees on a daily walk instead of paying for expensive gym memberships or trainers.)

Distributing Media Materials

News releases, photos, and media advisories are distributed via five major methods: (1) first-class mail, (2) fax, (3) e-mail, (4) electronic wire services, and (5) Web-based newsrooms.

Mail

A widely used distribution method, even in the Internet age, is still regular first-class mail or express shippers such as DHL or FedEx. Even though it is slower than electronic distribution, mail is quite adequate for distribution of routine materials to local and regional media, particularly small weekly shoppers and newspapers.

Some editors even prefer mailed releases, which they can easily review and often discard into the nearest wastebasket. Their preference, in part, is due to the exponential increase in e-mails that has engulfed almost everyone. According to one media survey by

Jim Rink, an online newsletter publisher, one survey respondent said, ". . . I get hundreds of e-mails weekly and I seldom read any but those from people I know," he said.

In other words, it's not yet a paperless society. Many organizations and public relations firms continue to print news releases and media kits even when they have companion electronic versions. The main objective should be to give editors and reporters whatever format they desire.

Fax

Although facsimile machines have been declared artifacts of another age, the news of their death may be premature. A fax is as quick as a telephone call and has the advantage of providing information in both written and graphic form.

A fax is best used for announcing late-breaking news, announcing a hastily organized news conference, or providing a one-page media alert about an upcoming event. It is possible to send "broadcast" or "bulk" faxes to every media outlet in the country within minutes.

Editors, however, aren't particularly fond of bulk fax because it clogs up their machines in the same way that a mailbox or e-mail box gets overstuffed with junk mail. Fax, however, is still used when individuals want to get an actual copy of something instead of taking the time to download and print it from their computers. Also, in the age of e-mail, some public relations professionals say an editor will pay more attention to a single fax than a mailbox with 200 e-mails in it.

E-Mail

Despite the major problem of overstuffed inboxes, most surveys show that editors and reporters prefer to receive public relations materials via e-mail. Almost 60 percent of the journalists in Bennett & Co.'s 2004 media survey said they prefer to get information in such a manner. Seven out of 10 even said they read every e-mail they get except for obvious spam. And Vocus, a public relations measurement and evaluation firm, found that an even higher percentage of journalists prefer e-mail—almost 85 percent—over fax or regular mail.

The key to successful e-mail is having a good subject line. It's also recommended that you never send attachments to a journalist unless he or she specifically requests them. Viruses have led to distrust of attachments. The alternative is to give the journalist links to Web-based material in the regular e-mail message.

Here are some tips for e-mailing journalists with news releases and other materials. Other guidelines for writing e-mail news releases were listed on page 371.

- ◆ Don't send HTML e-mail messages.
- ◆ Don't send attachments unless specifically requested to do so.
- ◆ Use extended headlines at the top of the news release that give the key message or point.
- ◆ Keep it short. Reporters hate to scroll through multiple screens.
- ◆ Use blind copy distribution. No reporter wants to know that they are part of a mass mailing.
- ◆ Continually update e-mail addresses.

An increasing problem is antispam software. Public relations professionals are finding that their news releases are being blocked as the software becomes more sophisticated. For this reason, reporters who cover specific corporations on a regular basis are now signing up for daily RSS feeds sent out by the organization.

Electronic News Services

Almost all organizations of any size now use an electronic wire service (also mentioned in Chapter 13) to distribute news releases, photos, and advisories. This is particularly true for corporate and financial information that must be released, according to SEC guidelines, to multiple media outlets at exactly the same time.

The two major newswires are Business Wire (www.businesswire.com) and PR Newswire (www.prnewswire.com). Each organization transmits about 18,000 news releases monthly to daily newspapers, broadcast stations, ethnic media, financial networks, and online news services. Other speciality electronic news services reaching multicultural audiences include Hispanic PRWire, USAsian Wire, and Black PRWire.

Heinz used a "smart" news release to tell about how it honors couples with a 57th wedding anniversary. These releases, distributed by electronic news services such as Business Wire, regularly embed links to photos, videos, and even major search engines.

Heinz to Honor 5,700th Wedding Anniversary Couple

Heinz Rings in Marriages from 1950; Celebrates Winning Couple with Custom Wedding Bell

Smart Multimedia Gallery▶▶

June 19, 2007 - This year, Heinz will present its 5,700th bell to one lucky couple, along with a $5,700-anniversary party. Since 1999, Heinz has celebrated couples who have been married for 57 years by presenting them with a commemorative bell. (Photo: Business Wire)

PITTSBURGH–(BUSINESS WIRE)–The H. J. Heinz Company (NYSE:HNZ) will help one lucky couple ring in their 57th wedding anniversary with the giveaway of the 5,700th Heinz 57th Wedding Anniversary Bell, which Heinz anticipates issuing later this summer. Since its inception in 1999, the Heinz 57th Wedding Anniversary Bells program has celebrated couples who have been married for 57 years by presenting them with a commemorative porcelain bell adorned with the iconic Heinz 57 Keystone.

Couples who are in their 57th year of marriage need only to send a copy of their marriage certificate and a letter signed by both husband and wife to "Happy 57th Anniversary," H. J. Heinz Company, P.O. Box 57, Pittsburgh, Pa., 15230-0057.

According to the U.S. Census Bureau, 1,667,000 couples said their "I Do's" in 1950.

A Renewed Commitment

Later this summer, Heinz will announce the winning couple and will honor them with a commemorative, custom made bell engraved with the Heinz 57 Keystone, which will be presented by a Heinz senior executive. The bell presentation honoring the couple will take place at a $5,700-wedding anniversary party in their hometown — an opportunity for the husband and wife to renew their wedding vows — in front of 57 of their closest family members and friends.

"For the past eight years, Heinz has connected with thousands of happily married couples who have celebrated their 57th wedding anniversary," said William R. Johnson, Chairman, President and CEO of H. J. Heinz Company. "This program emphasizes loyalty, tradition and commitment, and we are happy to continue it and celebrate the 5,700th couple."

More Than Just 57 Varieties

When Henry J. Heinz coined the legendary slogan "57 Varieties" in 1896, after already 27 years in business, Heinz's portfolio of products exceeded more than 57 varieties; however, the tagline quickly became synonymous with the iconic Heinz brand. Today, several thousand Heinz products can be found on grocery store shelves and in restaurants around the globe, with leading brands such as Ore-Ida®, Weight Watchers® Smart Ones®, Bagel Bites® and Plasmon infant nutrition, to name a few.

"57 Varieties" symbolizes an American icon and tradition. The idea of honoring couples, who have been married for 57 years, was originally suggested by loyal consumers who recalled a similar program where celebrating couples received a gift pack of 57 Heinz products. The program was discontinued as the Heinz product line grew and became difficult to sample.

ABOUT HEINZ: H. J. Heinz Company, offering "Good Food Every Day"™ is one of the world's leading marketers and producers of nutritious foods in ketchup, condiments, sauces, meals, soups, snacks and infant foods. Heinz provides superior quality, taste and nutrition to people eating at home, at restaurants, at the office and "on-the-go." Heinz is a global family of leading brands, including Heinz® ketchup, sauces, soups, beans, pasta and infant foods (representing over one third of Heinz's total sales), Ore-Ida® potato products, Weight Watchers® Smart Ones® entrees, Boston Market® meals, T.G.I. Friday's® snacks, and Plasmon infant nutrition. Heinz has number-one or number-two brands on five continents, showcased by Heinz® ketchup, The World's Favorite Ketchup®. Information on Heinz is available at www.heinz.com.

Available for interviews:

No paper is involved; the release is automatically entered into the appropriate databases and search engines, which can be accessed not only by editors and reporters throughout the world but also the general public. Editors select releases that are newsworthy to them, write a headline, and then push another key to have it automatically set for publishing or broadcast. Of course, they can easily click on the delete key, too.

Wire services are making the news release more sophisticated. Business Wire, for example, now has "smart" news releases that can be embedded with visuals and audio. An example is the Heinz news release on page 384. A reporter also can click various hyperlinks to get more information and photographs or charts. Tags can also be embedded in news releases that give key words that can be picked up by more than 300 social networks, such as YouTube.com, Yahoo, and Google. According to Craig McGuire writing in *PRWeek*, "BusinessWire can convert a traditional news release into a search-engine optimized page of Web content that includes photos, graphics, video and multimedia, logo branding, keyword links, formatting, and social media tags." This is best illustrated by Figure 14.1, which shows the various components of a news release from Business Wire.

National distribution of a "smart" release can cost up to $1,000, but a basic 400-word news release transmitted to all major media in the United States is about $650. If you want the entire planet to get the news release, it costs about $7,000. In sum, electronic news services provide a cost-effective way of directly reaching thousands of media across the nation and even the globe with a single click.

Online Newsrooms

"An online pressroom is the media's front door to the company," writes *PRWeek* reporter Sherri Deatherage Green. Most major organizations have a press room or a newsroom as part of their Web site. With a few clicks, a journalist can access everything from the organization's executive profiles to the most recent news releases. They also can download high-resolution photos and graphics, videos, and background materials such as position papers and annual reports.

> "An online pressroom is the media's front door to the company."
>
> ——*Sherri Deatherage Green,* reporter for *PR Week*

A company's online press room is accessed on a regular basis by reporters who cover a particular industry or group of companies. In fact, one survey of journalists by TEK Group International found that 70 percent of them visit online newsrooms "often" or "very often."

Sometimes the company will let reporters know via e-mail that a particular item is available on the company's site. Because there are billions of Web pages, extra effort must be made to ensure that reporters are aware of the Web site and what's on it. A good online newsroom, at minimum, should have (1) current and archived news releases, (2) the names, phone numbers, and direct e-mail addresses of public relations contacts, (3) photographs, and (4) product information.

In the 24/7 news cycle that exists today, it's important that a company keep its Web site up-to-date. Reporters seeking information usually look first at the organization's Web site and online newsroom. In the case of a major news development or crisis that involves the organization, such as a product recall or a crisis such as a plant explosion, it's also vital that the organization post updates on an hourly basis.

Surveys have found that journalists go first to an organization's Web site for information in the case of a crisis. It's also important that the materials posted on a Web site are not just copies of the printed materials. They must be reformatted and offer short summaries, extensive links, and strong visual elements. All documents, however, should have a "printer-friendly" version.

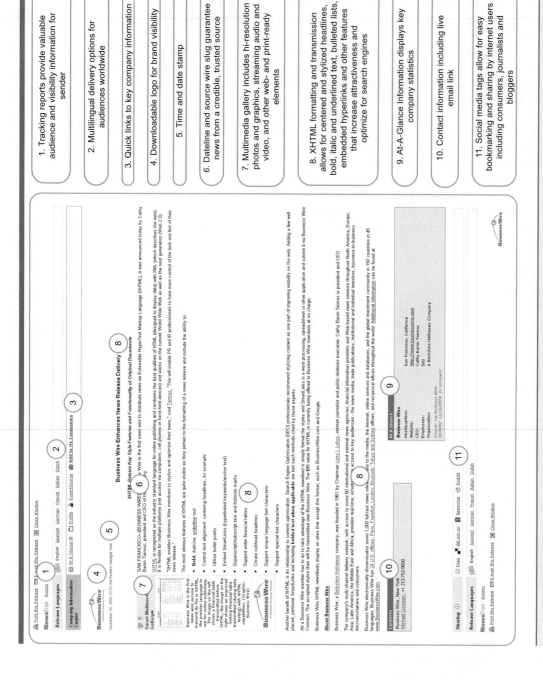

1. Tracking reports provide valuable audience and visibility information for sender

2. Multilingual delivery options for audiences worldwide

3. Quick links to key company information

4. Downloadable logo for brand visibility

5. Time and date stamp

6. Dateline and source wire slug guarantee news from a credible, trusted source

7. Multimedia gallery includes hi-resolution photos and graphics, streaming audio and video, and other web- and print-ready elements

8. XHTML formatting and transmission allows for centered and stylized headlines, bold, italic and underlined text, bulleted lists, embedded hyperlinks and other features that increase attractiveness and optimize for search engines

9. At-A-Glance Information displays key company statistics

10. Contact information including live email link

11. Social media tags allow for easy bookmarking and sharing by internet users including consumers, journalists and bloggers

FIGURE 14.1

The modern news release, distributed via electronic news services, are now embedded with links to photo galleries, social media sites, search engines, and so on. Special graphic prepared by Business Wire, San Francisco, for this textbook.

Other tips, given by *PRWeek*'s Green, are (1) keep the online newsroom content somewhat simple; don't use software or animation that might not be compatible with reporters' computers, (2) post high-resolution photos and graphics that can be used for publication, and (3) link the pressroom to the company home page.

SUMMARY

The News Release
The news release is the most commonly used public relations tactic. News releases are sent to journalists and editors for possible use in the news columns, and they are the source for a large percentage of articles that are published. News releases must be accurate, informative, and written in journalistic style.

Publicity Photos
Publicity photos often accompany news releases to make a story more appealing. Photos must be high resolution and well composed. A photo can be made more interesting by manipulating the camera angle and lighting and by showing scale and action. Color photos are now commonly used in most publications.

Mat Releases
A mat release is a form of a news release but primarily with a feature angle instead of hard news. They provide consumer information and tips in an objective manner with only a brief reference to the nonprofit or corporation that has distributed the information via a distribution firm such as Family Features. These canned features appear in the food, travel, automotive, and business sections of a newspaper.

Media Advisories and Fact Sheets
Advisories, or alerts, let journalists know about an upcoming event such as a news conference or photo or interview opportunities. Fact sheets give the 5 Ws and H of an event in outline form. Fact sheets also can be used to provide background on an executive, a product, or an organization.

Media Kits
A media kit, or press kit, is typically a folder containing news releases, photos, fact sheets, and features about a new product, an event, or other newsworthy projects undertaken by an organization. Many media kits are now produced in CD format to save costs.

Pitch Letters
Public relations personnel "pitch" journalists and editors with story ideas about their employer or client. Such pitches can be letters, e-mails, or even telephone calls. A good pitch is based on research and a creative idea that will appeal to the editor.

Distribution of Publicity Materials
Publicity materials can be distributed in five ways: (1) mail, (2) fax, (3) e-mail, (4) electronic wire services, and (5) Web pressrooms. Each has its advantages and disadvantages. Increasingly, publicity materials are distributed electronically.

CASE ACTIVITY What Would You Do?

A new university library will open next month. The $100 million building is an eight-story wonder of glass and steel beams designed by the famous architectural firm, BK Skinner and Associates. The library has over 125 commissioned works of art and 2,500 Internet plug-ins for students with their laptops. In addition, the library has several computer labs for students and meeting rooms that can be used by the university and community organizations. And, in a special coup, author J. K. Rowling of *Harry Potter* fame will be the guest of honor at the official opening.

Write a general news release about the new library and its planned grand opening. Second, write a pitch letter to the local media encouraging them to do feature stories about the new library in advance of the opening. Third, write a media alert letting the media know that J. K. Rowling will be available for interviews on a particular day. Fill in the appropriate quotations and information that you deem necessary.

QUESTIONS for Review and Discussion

1. What role do news releases play in the news process, and what ultimately appears in the newspaper or in the broadcast news show?

2. How should a news release be formatted? Why is the inverted pyramid structure used in news releases?

3. List at least six guidelines for writing a news release.

4. How does an e-mail news release differ from a standard news release?

5. Why is it a good idea to include a photograph with a news release? What six factors should be considered with regards to a publicity photo?

6. What is a mat release? How is it different than a regular news release?

7. What's the difference between a media advisory and a fact sheet?

8. What's a media kit? What does a media kit typically contain?

9. Before pitching an item to a journalist or editor, why is it a good idea to first do some basic research on the individual, the publication, or the talk show?

10. Various methods can be used to deliver publicity materials to the media. Name the methods and compare their relative strengths and weaknesses. Some experts believe that e-mail is the ultimate distribution channel. Do you agree or disagree?

11. If you had a news release to distribute to daily newspapers in your region, what method would you use? Why?

SUGGESTED READINGS

Applegate, Edd. "Mistakes Made in Companies' Press Releases." *Public Relations Quarterly,* Winter 2005, pp. 25–27.

Green, Sherri Deatherage. "All the News That's Fit to Download." *PRWeek,* April 26, 2004, p. 18.

Hulin, Belinda. "What Do Editors Think? The Craft of Good Writing." *Public Relations Tactics,* February 2004, p. 19.

Lewis, Tanya. "What's Mandarin for 'Press Release?'" *PRWeek,* February 12, 2007, p. 18.

Lewis, Tanya. "Newswires Search for the Right Words." *PRWeek,* November 20, 2006, p. 18.

Lipp, Danielle. "Crafting the Picture-Perfect Pitch." *PRWeek,* April 30, 2007, p. 14.

McGuire, Craig. "Newswires Strive to Bolster Releases." *PRWeek,* July 23, 2007, p. 18.

McGuire, Craig. "The New, Lightweight Press Kit." *PRWeek,* May 15, 2006, p. 18.

McGuire, Craig. "A Picture Tells a Thousand Words." *PRWeek,* April 24, 2006.

Oates, David B. "A Pitch Must Keep the Editor in Mind." *Public Relations Tactics,* December 2003, p. 13.

Seitel, Fraser P. "The Art of Pitch Emails." *O'Dwyer's PR Report,* May 2007, pp. 48–49.

Ward, David. "Journalists at Your Fingertips." *PRWeek,* June 19, 2006, p. 18.

Wilcox, Dennis L. *Public Relations Writing & Media Techniques,* 5th ed. Boston: Allyn & Bacon, 2005.

Woodall, Ibrey. "Journalists Relay What is Expected from an Online Newsroom." *Public Relations Tactics,* July 2006, p. 18.

Wylie, Ann. "Yes, You Can Make Your Press Releases Creative." *Public Relations Tactics,* May 2004, p. 15.

Radio,
Television,
and the Web

The Reach of Radio and Television

Broadcasting and its various forms, which now include Webcasting, are important because they reach the vast majority of the American public on a daily basis. More than 13,000 radio stations in the United States, for example, reach about 150 million Americans on an average day. A large percentage of this audience is reached in their cars; the average American now commutes nearly 50 minutes each workday.

The more than 800 televisions stations in the United States also reach a mass audience. The National Association of Broadcasters (NAB) says that local television news also attracts about 150 million viewers. And, despite the advent of the Internet, Nielsen Media Research reports that the average U.S. household still watches more than eight hours of television per day. A survey by the Radio and Television News Directors Foundation also showed that almost 70 percent of adults list local television news as their primary source of information. The Hispanic broadcast media also reaches a large and influential audience. See the Multicultural World box on page 404.

Writing and preparing materials for broadcast and digital media, however, requires a special perspective. Instead of writing for the eye, a practitioner has to shift gears and think about adding audio and visual elements to the story. This section discusses the tactics used by public relations personnel, when they use radio, television, and the Web on behalf of their employers and clients.

Radio News Releases

Radio news releases in the industry are called *audio news releases* or ANRs. They differ in several ways from print media releases. The most important difference is that a radio news release is written for the ear. The emphasis is on strong, short sentences that average about 10 words that can be easily understood by a listener.

The second major difference is that an ANR is more concise and to the point. Instead of a print news release that may run 400 or more words, a standard one-minute ANR is about 160 words. The timing is vital, because broadcasters must fit their message into a rigid time frame that is measured down to the second.

A third difference is writing style. A print news release is more formal and uses standard English grammar and punctuation. Sentences often contain dependent and independent clauses. In a radio release, a more conversational style is used, In such a style, partial or incomplete sentences are OK. The following are some guidelines from the Broadcast News Network on how to write a radio news release:

- Time is money in radio. Stories should be no longer than 60 seconds. Stories without actualities (soundbites) should be 30 seconds or less.
- The only way to time your story is to read it out loud, slowly.
- A long or overly commercial story is death. Rather than editing it, a busy radio newsperson will discard it.
- Convey your message with the smallest possible number of words and facts.
- A radio news release is not an advertisement; it is not a sales promotion piece. A radio news release is journalism—spoken.
- Announcers punctuate with their stories; not all sentences need verbs or subjects.
- Releases should be conversational. Use simple words and avoid legal-speak.
- After writing a radio news release, try to shorten every sentence.

◆ Listeners have short attention spans. Have something to say and say it right away.

◆ Never start a story with a name or a vital piece of information. While listeners are trying to figure out the person speaking and the subject matter, they don't pay attention to the specific information.

Format   A radio news releases can be sent to stations for announcers to read, but the most effective approach is to send the radio station a recording of the news announcement. One approach is for someone with a good radio voice to read the entire announcement; the person doing the reading may not be identified by name. This, in the trade, is called an *actuality*.

A second approach is to have an announcer, but also include what is called a *soundbite* from a satisfied customer or a company spokesperson. This approach is better than a straight announcement because the message comes from a "real person" rather than a nameless announcer. This type of announcement is also more acceptable to stations, because the radio station's staff can elect to use the whole recorded announcement or take the role of announcer and just use the soundbite.

An example of an effective ANR was one produced for the American Psychological Association (APA). The APA, using the firm News Generation, got soundbites from a number of researchers presenting papers on topical issues at its national convention. One soundbite, for example, was about the differences in how men and women hear and smell. A number of radio stations used the ANR, reaching a potential audience of 20 million.

The following is a 60-second ANR that includes a soundbite from a spokesperson. It was produced by Medialink for its client, Cigna Health Systems, and distributed to radio stations via satellite.

Worried at Work

New Survey Shows American Workers Are Stressed Out But Can Take Simple Steps to Ease Workplace Tension

SUGGESTED ANCHOR LEAD: If you're feeling stressed out at work, you're not alone. A new survey shows economic uncertainty, dwindling retirement savings, and ongoing terrorist concerns have American workers increasingly stressed out. But as Roberta Facinelli explains, employees and employers alike can do things to counteract all this tension.

SCRIPT: If you're like most American workers, you're facing increased stress on and off the job. In fact, according to a new nationwide study conducted by employee assistance experts at CIGNA Behavioral Health, almost half of employees surveyed have been tempted to quit their jobs over the past year, have quit, or are planning to soon, given the series of pressures they're facing. But according to CIGNA's Dr. Jodi Aronson Prohofsky, there are things you can do to ease workplace tension.

CUT (Aronson Prohofsky): Simple changes in your lifestyle can help reduce stress. Exercising more often, volunteering, making time to read or engaging in a favorite hobby are all easy steps we can take. Many of us also take time out for reflection and meditation to deal with daily pressures.

SCRIPT: Employees often find workplace support programs a good place to start, so check with your employer. Many provide programs such as counseling services, flexible work schedules as well as nutrition and health programs—all of which can help reenergize stressed out workers to achieve a better work–life balance. I'm Roberta Facinelli.

SUGGESTED ANCHOR TAG: If you're interested in learning more about workplace stress reduction tips, visit www.cignabehavioral.com.

The Cigna script is an example of an ANR that gives information and tips to the listener in a conversational way. It contains helpful information about how to reduce stress and is not overly commercial. Cigna is mentioned in the context of the story, but primarily as a source of information. A station newsperson, no doubt, would find the subject current and newsworthy for the station's audience.

Production and Delivery   Every ANR starts with a carefully written and accurately timed script. The next step is to record the words. When recording, it is imperative to control the quality of the sound. A few large organizations have complete recording studios, some hire radio station employees as consultants, but most organizations use a professional recording service.

Professional recording services have state-of-the-art equipment and skilled personnel. They can take a script, edit it, eliminate words or phrases that will not be understandable, record it at the proper sound levels, and produce a finished tape suitable for broadcasting.

Radio news stories and features can be produced in multiple copies on cassette or CD-ROM. The most common method, and the most economical, is to burn the recording to CD. In addition, the MP3 or iPod format for digital files is increasingly popular.

Radio stations, like newspapers, have preferences about how they want to receive audio news releases. One survey by DWJ Television found that almost 75 percent of the radio news directors prefer to receive actualities by phone. This is particularly true for late-breaking news events in the station's service area. When a forest fire threatened vineyards in California's Napa Valley, a large winery contacted local stations and offered an ANR with a soundbite from the winery's president telling everyone that the grape harvest would not be affected. About 50 stations were called, and 40 accepted the ANR for broadcast use.

Organizations sending ANRs for regional or national distribution usually use satellite or the World Wide Web after sending the station's news director an e-mail notification that an ANR is available on a particular topic or issue. Radio stations can also receive a ANR by dialing an 800 number.

Use of ANRs   Producing ANRs is somewhat of a bargain compared with producing materials for television. Ford Motor Company, for example, spent less than $5,000 for national distribution of a news release on battery recycling as part of Earth Day activities. More than 600 radio stations picked up the ANR, and about 5 million people were reached.

Despite their cost-effectiveness, an ANR should not be sent to every station. Stations have particular demographics. A release about the benefits of vitamin supplements for senior citizens isn't of much interest to a rock music station. In other situations, market research will indicate key markets and geographic areas that are most appropriate for the subject of the ANR.

The use of ANRs is increasingly popular with radio stations. Thom Moon, director of operations at Duncan's American Radio Quarterly, told *PRWeek* that he thinks the major reason for this is the consolidation of ownership in radio broadcasting, which has resulted in cost-cutting and fewer news personnel.

Jack Trammell, president of VNR-1 Communications, echoed this thought. He told *pr reporter*, "They're telling us they're being forced to do more with less. As long as radio releases are well produced and stories don't appear to be blatant commercials, newsrooms are inclined to use them." Trammell conducted a survey of radio stations and found that 83 percent of them use radio news releases. And 34 percent said such releases give them ideas for local stories. The news editors look for regional interest (34 percent), health information (23 percent), and financial news (11 percent). They also like technology stories, children's issues, politics, seasonal stories, and local interest issues.

Public Relations Tactics gives some additional tips from Trammell:

- **Topicality.** Stories may fail every other judgment criteria and still get airtime simply because they offer information on a hot topic. Newsroom maxim: News is about issues that matter to the majority of our listeners or viewers.

- **Timeliness.** Stories should be timed to correspond with annual seasons, governmental rulings, new laws, social trends, and so on.

- **Localization.** Newsrooms emphasize local news. A national release should be relevant to a local audience. Reporters are always looking for the "local angle."

- **Humanization.** Show how real people are involved or affected. Impressive statistics mean nothing to audiences without a human angle.

- **Visual appeal.** Successful stories provide vibrant, compelling soundbites that subtly promote, but also illustrate and explain.

Radio Public Service Announcements

Public relations personnel working for nonprofit organizations often prepare *public service announcements* (PSAs) for radio stations.

A PSA is defined by the FCC as an unpaid announcement that promotes the programs of government or voluntary agencies or that serves the public interest. In general, as part of their responsibility to serve the public interest, radio and TV stations provide airtime to charitable and civic organizations to make the public aware of and educate them about such topics as heart disease, mental illness, and AIDs.

> " In PSAs, speak to the common man . . . Make it as simple as possible. "
> ———*Christiane Arbesu,* VP of production, MultiVu

Profit-making organizations do not qualify for PSAs despite their claims of "public service," but sometimes an informational campaign by a trade group qualifies. For example, the Aluminum Association received airtime on a number of stations by producing a PSA about how to recycle aluminum cans. Before the announcement was released, the association received an average of 453 calls a month. Five months after the PSA began appearing, the association had received 9,500 calls at its toll-free number. The PSA was used in 46 states, and 244 stations reported 16,464 broadcasts of the announcement.

Format and Production   Radio PSAs are written in uppercase and double-spaced. Their length can be 60, 30, 20, 15, or 10 seconds. And, unlike radio news releases, the standard practice is to submit multiple PSAs on the same subject in various lengths. To prepare PSAs in various lengths, the writer should use the following guidelines setting margins for a 60-space line:

2 lines = 10 seconds (about 25 words)

5 lines = 20 seconds (about 45 words)

8 lines = 30 seconds (about 65 words)

16 lines = 60 seconds (about 125 words)

The idea is to give the station flexibility in using a PSA of a particular length to fill a specific time slot. DWJ Television explains: "Some stations air PSAs in a way that relates length to time of play, for example, placing one length in their early news shows and another in the late news shows. Supplying both lengths allows a campaign to be heard by those who only watch one of these shows."

PSAs can be delivered in the same way as radio news releases. Scripts can simply be mailed to the station for reading by announcers. Another popular approach is to mail stations a CD with announcements of varying lengths. Once a recording is made, it also can be transmitted via telephone.

Here is a basic PSA produced by the American Red Cross, which shows how the same topic can be treated in various lengths:

20 seconds

Ever give a gift that didn't go over real big? One that ended up in the closet the second you left the room? There is a gift that's guaranteed to be well received. Because it will save someone's life. The gift is blood, and it's desperately needed. Please give blood. There's a life to be saved right now. Call the American Red Cross at 1-800-GIVE LIFE.

60 seconds

We want you to give a gift to somebody, but it's not a gift you buy. We want you to give a gift, but not necessarily to someone you know. Some of you will be happy to do it. Some of you may be hesitant. But the person who receives your gift will consider it so precious, they'll carry it with them the rest of their life. The gift is blood and, every day in America, thousands of people desperately need it. Every day, we wonder if there will be enough for them. Some days, we barely make it. To those of you who give blood regularly, the American Red Cross and the many people whose lives you've saved would like to thank you. Those of you who haven't given recently, please help us again. There's a life to be saved right now. To find out how convenient it is to give blood, call the American Red Cross today at 1-800-GIVE-LIFE. That's 1-800-GIVE-LIFE.

Another PSA script, showing sound and music, is shown in the Insights box on page 395.

Use of Radio PSAs   Almost any topic or issue can be the subject of a PSA. Stations, however, seem to be more receptive to particular topics. A survey of radio station public affairs directors by West Glen Communications, a producer of PSAs, found that local community issues and events were most likely to receive airtime, followed by children's issues. About 70 percent of the Advertising Council's PSA campaigns, for example, now address issues that affect children from asthma, obesity, and even underage drinking. Stations also express an interest in PSAs about health/family, medical, technology, and business.

The majority of radio stations also prefer PSAs that include a local phone number rather than a national toll-free number. Therefore, many national groups distribute scripts to chapters that can be "localized" before they are sent to radio stations. Note should be made that PSAs are sent to the public affairs director of a station, not the news department.

Other studies have shown that an organization needs to provide helpful information in a PSA and not make a direct pitch for donations. PSAs often tell people about the organization and direct listeners to a phone number or Web site where they can learn more information—and make a donation.

on the job INSIGHTS

Adding Music and Sound to a PSA

You can make your radio PSA more interesting if you take the time to incorporate music and other sounds (SFX) into the speaker's script (VO). The Santa Clara County (California) Network for a Hate-Free Community distributed this PSA in a CD format to radio stations in the area.

Don't Teach Hate (60 Seconds)

MUSIC: MUSIC BOX VERSION OF "WHEELS ON THE BUS"

SFX: BABY TALK, CHILDREN LAUGHING

VO: AT SIX WEEKS BABIES LEARN TO SMILE.

SFX: BABY COOING

VO: BY SIX MONTHS THEY WILL RESPOND TO DIFFERENT COLORS.

SFX: BABY LAUGHING

VO: AT SIXTEEN MONTHS, THEY DEVELOP A SENSE OF SELF.

SFX: BABY SAYS "MINE!"

VO: AT WHAT AGE DO THEY LEARN TO HATE?

SFX: (PAUSE—MUSIC STOPS)

SFX: HORN HONKS, BRAKES SLAM.

ANGRY MAN'S VOICE: JEEZ, FREAKIN' FOREIGNERS, TOO DAMN STUPID TO OPERATE A CAR. YOU OKAY, BACK THERE, SPORT?

(MUSIC UP)

BABY'S VOICE: "M OKAY DADDY.

VO: THEY LEARN TO HATE WHEN YOU TEACH THEM. YOUR CHILDREN ARE LISTENING AND THEY'RE LEARNING FROM YOU. INSULTS AND SLURS BASED ON RACE, RELIGION, DISABILITY, GENDER OR SEXUAL ORIENTATION TEACH CHILDREN IT'S OKAY TO HATE. HATE IS THE ENEMY IN SANTA CLARA COUNTY AND YOU ARE ON THE FRONT LINE.

To report a hate crime or to receive services, call the Santa Clara County Network for a Hate-Free Community at (408) 792-2304.

Radio Media Tours

Another public relations tactic for radio is the *radio media tour* (RMT). Essentially, a spokesperson conducts a series of around-the-country, one-on-one interviews with a series of radio stations from a central location. A public relations practitioner (often called a *publicist* in such a situation) prebooks telephone interviews with DJs, news directors, or talk show hosts around the country, and the personality simply gives interviews over the phone that can be broadcast live or recorded for later use.

A major selling point of the RMT is its relatively low cost and the convenience of giving numerous short interviews from one central location. Laurence Moskowitz, president of Medialink, told *PRWeek*, "It is such an easy, flexible medium. We can interview a star in bed at his hotel and broadcast it to the country. Radio is delicious."

A major multinational pharmaceutical concern, Schering-Plough, used an RMT to point out that most smokers in the United States fail to recognize the warning signs of chronic bronchitis. Of course, the company makes a drug for such a condition. The RMT was picked up by 88 stations with an audience of more than 2.8 million. The RMT was part of a campaign that also used a *satellite media tour* (SMT) for television stations. SMTs are discussed in the next section.

Public relations practitioners setting up a RMT, however, need to do their homework. As Richard Strauss, president of Strauss Radio Strategies, told *PRWeek*, "It's not enough just to know the show exists. Listen to the show, understand the format, read the host's bio, and know past guests to gain some kind of familiarity." Another guideline is to tie the RMT to an event, premiere, holiday, or current news that provides a link to the listening audience. "For example, seat-belt safety campaigns are most effective around Thanksgiving and the Fourth of July, when Americans take to the roads in record numbers," says Curtis Gill of News Generation, a firm that arranges RMTs for clients.

Timing is also a consideration. Most interviews are on morning talk shows between the hours of 8 A.M. and noon. This means that the spokesperson, either an expert or a known celebrity, must be prepared to give early morning interviews to cover all the time zones. Other experts also give the tip that an organization should select a spokesperson with some endurance—they might be giving one interview after another for three or four hours.

Television

There are four approaches for getting an organization's news and viewpoints on local television. The first approach is to simply send the same news release that the local print media receive. If the news director thinks the topic is newsworthy, the item may become a brief 10-second mention by the announcer on a news program. A news release may also prompt the assignment editor to think about a visual treatment and assign the topic to a reporter and a camera crew for follow-up.

A second approach is a media alert or advisory informing the assignment editor about a particular event or occasion that would lend itself to video coverage. Media alerts, which were discussed in Chapter 14, can be sent via e-mail, fax, or even regular mail.

The third approach is to phone or e-mail the assignment editor and make a pitch to have the station do a particular story. The art of making a pitch to a television news editor is to emphasize the visual aspects of the story.

The fourth approach is to produce a *video news release* (VNR) package that, like an ANR, is formatted for immediate use with a minimum of effort by station personnel. The VNR also has the advantage of being used by numerous stations on a regional, national, or even global basis.

> " Today's VNRs are much more than just broadcast placement tools. They are being targeted to a variety of audiences through Web syndication, strategic placements in broadcast, cable, and site-based media in retail outlets and hospitals. "
>
> ——*Tim Bahr,* managing director of MultiVu, a broadcast production firm

Video News Releases

An estimated 5,000 VNRs are produced annually in the United States. Large organizations seeking enhanced recognition for their names, products, services, and causes are the primary clients for VNRs. The production of VNRs can be more easily justified if there is potential for national distribution and multiple pickups by television stations and cable systems. Increasingly, costs are also justified because a VNR package can be reformatted for an organization's Web site or even as part of a multimedia news release distributed by an electronic news service.

A typical 90-second VNR, says one producer, costs a minimum of $20,000 to $50,000 for production and distribution. Costs vary, however, depending on the number of location shots, special effects, the use of celebrities, and the number of staff required to produce a high-quality tape that meets broadcast standards.

Because of the cost, a public relations department or firm must carefully analyze the news potential of the information and consider whether the topic lends itself to a fast-paced, action-oriented visual presentation. A VNR should not be produced if there's nothing but talking heads, charts, and graphs. Another aspect to consider is whether the topic will still be current by the time the video is produced. On average, it takes four to six weeks to script, produce, and distribute a high-quality VNR. In a crisis situation or for a fast-breaking news event, however, a VNR can be produced in a matter of hours or days.

An example of a fast response with a VNR is Pepsi. Within a week of news reports that syringes and other sharp objects had been found in cans of Diet Pepsi, the soft-drink company produced and distributed a VNR showing that the insertion of foreign objects into cans on their

When some customers claimed they had found syringes in Pepsi cans, the company distributed a video news release (VNR) showing that the intrusion into its high-speed bottling process was virtually impossible. The claim proved to be a hoax.

high-speed bottling lines was virtually impossible. This VNR, because of its timely nature and high public interest, reached a total of 186 million viewers and helped avoid a massive sales decline of Pepsi products.

Format   The traditional VNR package is like a media kit prepared for print publications, which was discussed in the last chapter. It has various components that enable the television journalist everything they need to produce a television news story. According to MultiVu, a production firm, this includes the following:

- 90-second news report with voiceover narration on an audio channel separate from that containing soundbites and natural sound.
- A B-roll. This is the video only, without narration, giving a television station maximum flexibility to add their own narration or use just a portion of the video as part of a news segment.
- Clear identification of the video source.
- Script, spokespeople information, media contacts, extra sound bites, and story background information provided electronically.

Conceptualizing and writing a VNR script is somewhat complicated because the writer has to visualize the scene, much like a playwright or screenwriter. In addition, it's important to keep what Jack Trammell, president of VNR-1 Communications, says are the "five gospels" of the television newsroom: ". . . topicality, timeliness, localization, humanization, and visuality." Adam Shell, in *Public Relations Tactics*, describes the required skills:

> Producing a VNR requires expert interviewing skills, speedy video editing, creative eye for visuals, and political savvy. The job of the VNR producer is not unlike that of a broadcast journalist. The instincts are the same. Engaging soundbites are a result of clever questioning. Good pictures come from creative camera work. A concise, newsworthy VNR comes from good writing and editing. Deadlines have to be met, too.

And then there's all the tiny details and decisions that have to be made on the spot. Not to mention figuring out subtle ways to make sure the client's signage appears on the video without turning off the news directors.

Perhaps the best way to illustrate some of Shell's comments is to show the first two pages of a typical VNR script prepared by Medialink for Beringer Vineyards.

Medialink

VISUAL	AUDIO
FADE IN: **Suggested Anchor Lead-in:**	Despite the economy and world events, things are going "GRAPE" in California's wine country. The "CRUSH," officially underway in the heart of wine country, is the most exciting time of year. Grapes generate (help generate) billions of dollars in travel, tourism, jobs and sales. Especially in the Napa Valley where wine makers consistently create some of the world's finest wine. The buzz this year? A later than usual harvest may produce even higher quality wines. As Mother nature places the finishing touches on this year's grape harvest, wine lovers are out in force, pursuing their passion in restaurants, hotels and wine tasting rooms. If the bottom line is good taste, Elizabeth Anderson uncorks some vintage secrets. **NAT SOT (:04 approx)** **NARRATION** Coming to a glass near you…
Pour Nouveau-Beringer	The grapes of California's crush.
Crush, picking-harvest	92% of America's wine is produced in California…some of the world's best in Napa Valley.
Wine, grapes	Beringer's Nouveau, the first wine of the 2002 vintage, will beat all California wines to market. Of the Golden State's 847 wineries, this landmark is the oldest in Napa Valley…bottling award-winning magic for 125 years.
Napa beauty shot	
Wine picking, crush-harvest.	
Nouveau, Beringer beauty shots, famous	**NAT SOT Beringer Winemaker**
Exteriors, wine is poured.	"The grapes are ready…just the right sugar content."
See Beringer name of famous real estate	
Historical video (from tv cmxl)	
B-roll to complement what he says	
Continuously show various vineyards – St. Clements, Stags Leap	
Barrels, caves	
Dissolve to: Beringer and awards <u>See</u> 4	

Medialink

VISUAL	AUDIO
winery of the year awards -- better than saying it -- articles, visuals, awards, Beringer	
Winemaker walks and tastes grapes in vineyards	**NARRATION** Beringer's legendary winemaker knows the secret to good taste.
ON CAMERA	**SOT - Winemaker**
B-roll to compliment what he says	"Making perfect wine means growing, harvesting and crushing perfect grapes at the right time in the best
Continuously show various	climate, using unique barrels & caves and land that, naturally, have the ideal temperature for storing/aging
Vineyards-various, St. Clements, Stags Leap	wine. Ingredients that cant be duplicated! Of California's wine country, Napa is a small region.but
Barrels, caves	produces the best and most critically acclaimed wines. Due to a later than usual harvest this year, the wines
Napa region visual.	are expected to be <u>even better</u>. Just some reasons why we consistently capture top winery awards over
Beauty shots grapes, and wine. Sunrise, sunset	our traditional European competitors."
Workers in field.	
Awards, articles or Beringer & industry	
Tourism: wining, dining, purchasing	
Lots of Nat Sot (natural sound)	
Harvest, Tourists, restaurant type activity	
Wine-sipping, etc. dissolve to:	
	NAT SOT :03 (harvest-crush-machinery)
	NARRATION
Crush activity. Grapes splash into camera	The crush proves good things come in small packages: grapes are the state's 3rd leading
Agricultural activity	crop.providing 145-thousand jobs and a $33 billion dollar bottom line.
Regional shots, tourists, perhaps purchasing wine.	NAT SOT (cheers!)
Wining, dining. Tourism, tourists in wine room	If California were a nation, it would be the 4th leading wine-producing country behind Italy, France and
Crowds toast, hear Japanese tourists toast	Spain. Even in a tough economy, in their language.

The script of a video news release requires thinking about the visuals at the same time that you write copy and plan for interview excerpts. This two-column format, showing visual and audio components, shows how a script is written.

Production   Although public relations writers can easily handle the job of writing radio news releases and doing basic announcements for local Television stations, the production of a VNR is another matter. The entire process is highly technical, requiring trained professionals and sophisticated equipment.

PRCASEBOOK

Hurricane Katrina: A VNR Helps Pregnant Women and Babies

In the aftermath of Hurricane Katrina, the March of Dimes mounted a major effort to aid pregnant women and sick or premature babies.

The organization, through its many volunteers, provided care for more than 120 babies who were transported to the Women's Hospital of Baton Rouge, Louisiana. Other volunteers collected maternity clothes, cribs, and baby essentials for the displaced mothers. In addition, the charitable group put a fleet of "Mom Vans" on the roads of the Gulf Coast to help mothers and babies in shelters and rural areas who did not have access to medical care.

DS Simon Productions
Storyboard for March of Dimes B-Roll During Hurricane Aftermath
Help the Babies of Katrina

More than 100 premature newborns were evacuated to Baton Rouge during Katrina, and the March of Dimes helped reunite them with their families.

The shelter in Baton Rouge housed more than 6,000 in one large room on cots. Everyone slept side by side, some on cots, others -- including pregnant women -- slept on the floor.

Eight-months pregnant, Crystal Sulliven walked from New Orleans with her one-year-old son to a Baton Rouge shelter. There she received help from the March of Dimes.

Ingrid Olivas fled New Orleans while eight-months pregnant with her first child. She told her story in English and Spanish of receiving pre-natal vitamins, clothes and help relocating from the March of Dimes.

March of Dimes volunteers distributed clothes to pregnant women and children at crowded shelters. They also provided pre-natal vitamins, diapers and other supplies for families with young children.

March of Dimes volunteers like Liza Cooper worked to help move pregnant women and families with newborn babies into smaller shelters. Stress is one known cause of premature birth, and they wanted to alleviate some of the stress on pregnant women during Katrina's aftermath.

In order to continue this assistance, however, the March of Dimes needed to increase public awareness and raise more money. It turned to D S Simon to do an English and Spanish-language VNR that was tagged "Help the Babies of Katrina." A bilingual producer, Sylvan Solloway, took charge of the project and took a camera crew to Jackson, Mississippi, to shoot footage and interview the homeless mothers.

One segment told about how an eight-months pregnant woman walked from New Orleans with her one-year-old son to a March of Dimes shelter in Baton Rouge, a distance of more than 80 miles. Another story was about a woman who received prenatal vitamins, clothes, and help in relocating from New Orleans. See the storyboard of the B-roll.

The production company distributed a B-roll (video without spoken narration) to 700 newsrooms, and about 300 phone calls were made as follow-up. In addition, the D S Simon media team arranged media interviews for March of Dimes president Jennifer Howse. She appeared on such programs as "Fox and Friends" and Telemundo National.

The effort, at a cost of about $20,000, reached nearly 4.5 million viewers. More important, the VNR helped generate about $50,000 in donations and was a contributing factor to helping the March of Dimes win a $500,000 grant from the U.S. Office of Minority Health. The campaign was recognized by *O'Dwyer's PR Report* for excellence in public communications.

Consequently, public relations departments and firms usually outsource production to a firm specializing in scripting and producing VNR packages. Public relations personnel, however, usually serve as liaison and give the producer an outline of what the VNR is supposed to accomplish. The public relations person also will work with the producer to line up location shots, props, and the individuals who will be featured. See the PR Casebook on page 400 about a VNR produced for the March of Dimes.

Medialink, a major producer and distributor of VNRs, gives some tips about the production of VNRs that best meet the needs of Television news directors:

◆ Give Television news directors maximum flexibility in editing the tape using their own anchors or announcers. This can be done by producing the VNR on split audio (the announcer track on one audio channel and the natural sound of the VNR on another). This way, the news director has the option of "stripping" the announcer's voice and inserting the voice of a local reporter or announcer.

◆ Produce the VNR with news footage in mind. Keep soundbites short and to the point. Avoid commercial-like shots with sophisticated effects.

◆ Never superimpose your own written information on the actual videotape. Television news departments usually generate their own written notes in their own typeface and style.

◆ Never use a stand-up reporter. Stations do not want a reporter who is not on their own staff appearing in their newscast.

◆ Provide Television stations with a local angle. This can be done by sending supplemental facts and figures that reflect the local situation. This can be added to the VNR when it is edited for broadcast.

◆ Good graphics, including animation, are a plus. Stations are attracted to artwork that shows things in a clear, concise manner.

Delivery   The VNR package should also include two or three minutes of B-roll, or background pictures, for use by the Television news producer in repackaging the story. Typical B-roll includes additional interviews, soundbites, and file footage. A Nielsen

Media Research survey of 130 Television news directors, for example, found that 70 percent wanted a VNR with B-roll attached.

An advisory will accompany the VNR package or will be sent to news directors before the actual satellite transmission of the video to the station. The advisory, in printed form, should contain the basics: the key elements of the story, background and description of the visuals, editorial and technical contacts, satellite coordinates, and date/time of the transmission. Many stations prefer to receive this advisory by fax instead of e-mail or wire service. A fax is on printed paper and can be passed around the newsroom so many staffers can see it.

Satellite distribution is the most cost-effective way of distributing VNRs on a national or even global scale. In addition, it is the preferred method of most news directors. Virtually every television station in the country has at least one satellite receiving dish. Other methods include digital store-and-forward systems such as Pathfire, MPEG-2 delivery via the Internet, and Web distribution, which will be discussed shortly. Mail distribution also is used to send stock footage, standard video shots of a company's production line, headquarters, or other activities that a station can store until the company is in the news. Then, as the anchor gives the current news, the viewers see the stock footage on the screen.

Use of VNRs   Larry Moskowitz, president of Medialink, says every television station in the United States uses VNRs in their newscasts. He told a radio talk show host, "We determined prima facie and scientifically and electronically that every TV station in America has used and probably uses regularly this material from corporations and organizations that we provide as VNRs, or B-roll." West Glen Communications estimates that 90 percent of the stations use VNRs.

These optimistic statistics, however, are tempered by the reality that TV stations today receive so many VNRs that they are overwhelmed. Consequently, the competition is intense, and unless the VNR meets multiple criteria, it won't be used. Even if it is used, public relations departments and firms must be realistic about audience reach. A well-done VNR, according to surveys, usually gets 40 to 50 station airings with an audience of 2 to 3 million people. In other words, for every VNR that gets millions of viewers, there are hundreds that don't.

Ethical Uses of VNRs   Video News Releases have come under fire because television stations often use them without source attribution. Watchdog groups have complained to the Federal Communications Commission (FCC) that stations using VNR content, without telling the viewers about the source, were presenting "fake news." The Center for Media and Democracy, for example, conducted a six-month probe and found that 46 stations in 22 states aired unsourced video material supplied by VNR production firms on behalf of clients.

The controversy over the use of VNRs by television stations also put the spotlight on the public relations industry. The issue is whether public relations firms and the VNR producers are adequately labeling VNR packages that identify the sponsor or client. As a consequence, the Public Relations Society of America and the National Association of Broadcast Communicators (NABC) issued a new standard for VNRs: "All prepackaged materials should contain a complete disclosure of the sources of information, the transparent identification of individuals or organizations who paid for, sponsored or initiated the production of the materials, and an explicit revelation of interests/points of view represented in the materials." The NABC code is discussed in Chapter 3.

Unfortunately, even when public relations practitioners apply these standards, they cannot stop television stations from stripping the source out and using the VNR or the B-roll as a product of their own reporting.

Television Public Service Announcements   Television stations, like radio stations, use PSAs on behalf of governmental agencies, community organizations, and charitable groups. In fact, a survey by News Broadcast Network found that the typical Television station runs an average of 137 PSAs per week as part of its commitment to public service.

Many of the guidelines for radio PSAs, which were discussed previously, apply to television PSAs. They must be short, to the point, and professionally produced. Television is different, however, in that both audio and visual elements must be present. Even a simple PSA, consisting of the announcer reading text, is accompanied by a photo or artwork that is shown on the screen at the same time. A good example is the 30-second television PSA from Rotary International on this page.

A slightly more sophisticated approach is to have a spokesperson, such as a celebrity, talk directly into the camera for 30 seconds. In the trade, such a PSA is known as a *talking head.* This means that the format is relatively simple; it involves just one person speaking to the camera. There are no other visual cues such as other scenes or action. This approach seems to work particularly well if a celebrity is used. Ogilvy Public Relations Worldwide, for example, produced a PSA for the Centers for Disease Control and Prevention to build awareness about preventative colorectal cancer screenings. The PSAs featured celebrities such as Katie Couric and Morgan Freeman, both with personal ties to the cancer.

A more complex approach is to involve action and a number of scenes to give the PSA more movement and visual appeal. A good example is a PSA that was created for the American Cancer Society. The objective was preventing teenage smoking. The writer, Jeff Goldsmith, created a parody using the motif of a television game show, "Cancer for Cash." One scene shows three showgirls spinning a coffin on stage to select questions for contestants. The person who got the right answer got "cancer cash" for chemotherapy treatments.

Rotary International distributes a variety of television PSAs on CD format to television stations and cable operators. This is the storyboard for one PSA.

vo Does peace really have a chance within our lifetime? At Rotary, we believe it does. We've created programs at universities around the world dedicated solely to teaching peace to a new generation. There is a new symbol for peace. Rotary. Humanity in motion.   Symbols :30

on the job
A MULTICULTURAL WORLD

Reaching Out to the Hispanic Audience

The numbers tell the story. Hispanics are the largest and fastest-growing minority in the country and, by 2050, will constitute about 25 percent of the U.S. population. This gives public relations professionals a special impetus to include this audience when executing a campaign that includes radio and televison.

The Hispanic audience is important for several reasons. First, Latino consumers spend more than $685 billion annually on goods and services. A second reason is the average household size of 3.4 persons; this makes the Latino audience attractive to retailers of such goods as clothes, telephone services, and groceries.

Radio and television are particularly good communication channels for the Hispanic audience. First, in terms of Hispanic media, there are now about 600 Spanish-language radio stations and 75 Hispanic Television stations in the U.S. In addition, Univision is now the fifth-largest network in the United States.

Second, research studies show that the Hispanic audience outpaces the general population in terms of listeners and viewers. Hispanics, for example, average 24 hours a week listening to radio and one out of every three radio stations in the top 10 media markets are Hispanic. In terms of television, Hispanics view an average of one hour daily more than non-Hispanic whites. Seventy percent watch both English and Spanish programs.

This means that the full range of radio and television tactics, such as news releases, PSAs, media tours, and video news releases (VNRs) should be prepared with the Hispanic audi-

> Make sure that the PSAs are scripted, reviewed, and voiced by fluent native Spanish speakers.
>
> ———*Raul Martinez*, Strauss Radio Strategies

ence in mind. That means more than simply translating an English version of the same material into Spanish. As a monograph from Medialink says, "A direct translation from English to Spanish, in many cases, simply does not make sense from a grammatical and syntax perspective." The suggestion is practically start from scratch and to have translations done by someone completely fluent in Spanish.

Radio and television media tours, called RMTs and SMTs, have their own special requirements. It is important to have a Hispanic spokesperson who speaks Spanish as his or her native language.

Although Spanish is the common denominator, it's also important to have spokespersons who appeal to different age groups. A good example is television PSAs prepared by Strauss Radio Strategies on behalf of the Hispanic Heritage Awards Foundation (HHAF). Celebrity spokespersons included Gloria Estefan, Carlos Ponce, Jon Secada, and Shalim, as well as Television personalities Judy Reyes from NBC's *Scrubs* and sports announcer Andres Cantor.

Another tip from Strauss Radio Strategies is to remember that many Hispanic radio and television stations operate on a shoestring budget and don't have the latest technologies. So, instead of satellite transmission, it's often necessary to distribute VNRs and PSAs by CD and an e-mail MP3 file. In terms of pitching radio and television stations, a public relations person fluent in both English and Spanish is highly recommended.

Satellite Media Tours

The television equivalent to the radio media tour is the *satellite media tour* (SMT). Essentially, an SMT is a series of prebooked, one-on-one interviews from a fixed location (usually a television studio) via satellite with a series of television journalists or talk show hosts. (See also Chapter 13.) Interviews via satellite are regularly seen on a number of network news shows, including CNN News and PBS: The News Hour with Jim Lehrer.

The SMT concept started several decades ago when companies began to put their CEOs in front of television cameras. The public relations staff would line up reporters in advance to interview the spokesperson via satellite feed during allocated time frames of one to five minutes. This way, journalists could personally interview a CEO in New York even if they were based in San Francisco or Chicago. For busy CEOs, the satellite was a time-efficient way to give interviews.

Today, the SMT is a staple of the public relations and television industry. In fact, a survey by West Glen Communications found that nearly 85 percent of the nation's television stations participate in satellite tours.

The easiest way to do an SMT is to simply make the spokesperson available for an interview at a designated time. Celebrities are always popular, but an organization also can use articulate industry experts. In general, the spokesperson sits in a chair or at a desk in front of a television camera. Viewers usually see the local news anchor asking questions and the spokesperson on a large screen, via satellite, answering them in much the same way that anchors talk to reporters at the scene of an event.

Another popular approach to SMTs is to get out of the television studio and do them on location. When the National Pork Producers Council wanted to promote outdoor winter grilling, its public relations staff hired a team from Broadcast News Network to fire up an outdoor grill in Aspen, Colorado, and put a celebrity chef in a parka to give interviews, via satellite, while he cooked several pork recipes. E & J Gallo Winery was also creative about using a location to promote its products to the blue-collar crowd. The SMT site was a tailgate party at Giants Stadium in San Francisco where, instead of hot dogs and beer, the menu was shrimp and wine. Habitat for Humanity, on the other hand, used one of its home building sites for an SMT.

Anecdotal evidence, however, indicates that four out of five pitched satellite media tours don't get aired. You can increase the odds if you follow these "do's" and "don'ts" compiled by *PRWeek:*

Do

- Include a relevant angle for the stations in every market you pitch.
- Use an interesting, visually appealing background or set. It often makes the difference between your SMT getting on the air or not.
- Get stations involved by sending them items that will help them perform and promote the interview.
- Respect producers' wishes when they tell you they will get back to you. Incessant follow-up will only annoy those who you are trying to convince.
- Localize your SMT. If local audiences aren't going to be interested, neither are the producers airing the story.
- Be clear in your pitch. Provide producers with the who, what, when, and why right away.
- Use credible, knowledgeable spokespersons who project confidence and are personable.

Don't

- Let the SMT become a commercial. If producers think there is the possibility of too many product mentions, they won't book it.
- Be dishonest with producers about the content of your SMT.
- Pitch your SMT to more than one producer at a station.

- Be conservative with amount of talent. A boring medical SMT will pack more punch if you present a patient along with the doctor.
- Surprise the producer. Newscasts are planned to the minute and unexpected events (spokesperson cancels) will not be appreciated.

News Feeds   A variation on the SMT is a news feed that provides video and sound-bites of an event to Television stations across the country via satellite. The news feed may be live from the event as it is taking place (real time) or it could be video shot at the event, edited, and then made available as a package.

In either case, the sponsoring organization hires a production firm to record the event. Major fashion shows, which take place in New York or Europe, often arrange for video feeds to media outlets around the world. Major auctions also send video feeds to media outlets and even gatherings of interested buyers. DWJ Television, for example, was hired by Christie's to cover the auction of 56 outfits worn by women at Academy Award ceremonies. Stations could air the entire auction or simply make a video clip for use in later newscasts. In the case of Pokemon's party at a park in New York City, which was outlined in Chapter 6, a news feed was arranged so stations and Pokemon fans across the country could also participate. News feeds also are regularly used when the president gives a news conference or a company makes a major announcement at a news conference or trade show. Another form of the news feed, of course, is the Webcast, which will be discussed shortly.

Personal Appearances

Radio and television stations increasingly operate on round-the-clock schedules. They require vast amounts of programming to fill the time available.

Thus far, this chapter has concentrated on how to prepare and generate timely material for newscasts. This section focuses on how to get spokespersons on talk and magazine shows. In these cases, your contact is no longer the news department, but the directors and producers of such programs. The most valuable communication tools in reaching these people are the telephone and the persuasive pitch letter, as discussed earlier in this chapter.

Before contacting directors and producers, however, it is necessary for the public relations staff to do their homework. They must be totally familiar with a show's format and content, as well as the type of audience that it reaches. Media directories are available, such as Bacon's, that give key information about specific programs, such as the names and addresses of producers, the program format, audience demographics, and the purpose of the show.

A second approach, and one that is highly recommended, is to actually watch the program and study the format. In the case of a talk or interview show, what is the style of the moderator or host? What kinds of topics are discussed? How important is the personality or prominence of the guest? How long is the show or a segment? Does the show lend itself to product demonstrations or other visual aids? The answers to such questions will help determine whether the show is appropriate for your spokesperson and how to tailor a pitch letter to achieve maximum results.

Talk Shows

Radio and television talk shows have been a staple of broadcasting for many years. KABC in Los Angeles started the trend in 1960, when it became the first radio station in the country to convert to an all-news-and-talk format. Today, more than 1,110 radio stations have adopted the format. Stations that play music also may include talk shows as part of their programming. In fact, it is estimated that there are now more than 4,000 radio talk shows in the United States.

The same growth applies to television. Phil Donahue began his show in 1967. Today, there are more than 20 nationally syndicated talk shows and a countless number of locally produced talk shows. For the past decade, the number one syndicated daytime talk show has been the *Oprah Winfrey Show*, attracting about 8 million viewers on a daily basis. On the network level, three shows are the Holy Grail for publicists: NBC's *Today*, ABC's *Good Morning America*, and CBS's *Early Show*. Collectively, these three shows draw about 14 million viewers between 7 and 9 A.M. every weekday. Another popular venue, particularly for entertainers promoting their most recent film or show, is the late night shows such as *The Tonight Show with Jay Leno* and *Late Night with David Letterman*.

Late-night TV shows are virtually a non-stop promotion of a celebrities' latest book, movie, television program, album, or even political agenda. Here, host Jay Leno of the *Tonight Show* interviews Paula Abdul, a pop star and judge on the popular show, *American Idol*.

The advantage of talk shows is the opportunity to have viewers see and hear the organization's spokesperson without the filter of journalists and editors interpreting and deciding what is newsworthy. Another advantage is to be on the program longer than the traditional 30-second soundbite in a news program.

When thinking about booking a spokesperson on a local or syndicated talk show, here's a checklist of questions to consider:

♦ Is the topic newsworthy? Is there a new angle on something already in the news?

♦ Is the topic timely? Is it tied to some lifestyle or cultural trend?

♦ Is the information useful to viewers? How to and consumer tips are popular.

♦ Does the spokesperson have viewer appeal? A celebrity may be acceptable, but there must be a natural tie-in with the organization and the topic to be discussed.

♦ Can the spokesperson stay on track and give succinct, concise statements. The spokesperson must stay focused and make sure that the key messages are mentioned.

♦ Can the spokesperson refrain from getting too commercial? Talk show hosts don't want guests who sound like an advertisement.

> " We expect our hosts (spokespersons) to be able to put the products in a newsworthy context and answer unexpected questions. "
>
> ———*Michael Friedman*, EVP of DWJ Television

Consideration should also be given to the characteristics of an ideal guest from the media's perspective. Gresham Strigel, a senior producer, shared his thoughts with *Bulldog Reporter*, a media placement newsletter:

♦ Guests should be personable and approachable when producers conduct preinterviews on the phone. They are forthright but not aggressive. "If you're wishy-washy, non-committed, or stilted, you're not going much further."

◆ Guests should have strong opinions. "We don't call certain people back because they have been trained not to say anything. The stronger your position is, and the higher up it is, the more media attention you're going to get. Nobody likes guests who play it safe."

◆ Guests should be passionate about the subject. "We don't want people who are robotic—who just spit out facts. If you convey passion about what you're talking about, you jump off the screen."

◆ Guests should be able to debate without getting personal or mean-spirited. "Smile. . . . Audiences like to see someone who is comfortable on-screen—someone who is happy to be there."

◆ Guests should have engaging, outgoing personalities. "Talking heads and ivory-tower types don't do well on television. They're better suited for print, where their personality—or lack of it—can't turn audiences off."

Magazine Shows

The term *magazine* refers to a television program format that is based on a variety of video segments in much the same way that print magazines have a variety of articles. These shows may have a guest related to the feature that's being shown, but the main focus is on a video story that may run from 3 to 10 minutes. At the network level, CBS's *60 Minutes* is an example of a magazine program.

Many human-interest magazine shows are produced at the local level. A sampling of magazine shows in one large city featured such subjects as a one-pound baby who survived, a treatment for anorexia nervosa, a couple who started a successful cookie company, remedies for back pain, tips on dog training, a black-belt karate expert, blue-collar job stress, and the work habits of a successful author.

Most, if not all, of these features came about as the result of someone making a pitch to the show's producers. The objective of the segments, at least from the perspective of the people featured, is exposure and the generation of new business. The tips on dog training, for example, featured a local breeder who also operated a dog obedience school. The karate expert ran a martial arts academy, and even the story of the one-pound baby was placed by a local hospital touting its infant-care specialty.

Booking a Guest

The contact for a talk show may the executive producer or assistant producer of the show. If it is a network or nationally syndicated show, the contact person may have the title of *talent coordinator* or *talent executive*. Whatever the title, these people are known in the broadcasting industry as *bookers* because they are responsible for booking a constant supply of timely guests for the show.

One common approach in placing a guest is to place a phone call to the booker briefly outlining the qualifications of the proposed speaker and why this person would be a timely guest. Publicists also can write a brief one-page letter or send an e-mail telling the booker the story angle, why it's relevant to the show's audience, and why the proposed speaker is qualified to talk on the subject. In many cases, the booker will ask for video clips of the spokesperson on previous TV shows or newspaper clips relating to press interviews. It's important to be honest about the experience and personality of the spokesperson, so the booker isn't disappointed and the public relations professional retains his or her credibility for another day.

on the job
ETHICS

Should Guests on TV Talk Shows Reveal Their Sponsors?

Actress Lauren Bacall, appearing on NBC's *Today*, talked about a dear friend who had gone blind from an eye disease and urged the audience to see their doctors to be tested for it. She also mentioned a drug, Visudyne, that was a new treatment for the disease.

Meanwhile, over at ABC's *Good Morning America*, actress Kathleen Turner was telling Diane Sawyer about her battle with rheumatoid arthritis and mentioned that a drug, Enbrel, helped ease the pain. A month later, Olympic gold medal skater Peggy Fleming appeared on the show to talk about cholesterol and heart disease. Near the beginning of the interview, Fleming said, "My doctor has put me on Lipitor and my cholesterol has dropped considerably."

What the viewing audience didn't know was that each of these celebrities was being paid a hefty fee by a drug company to mention its product in prime time. Indeed, even the talk show hosts apparently didn't know until the *New York Times* wrote an investigative piece on drug companies using "stealth marketing" tactics to get product mentions on regular news and talk shows.

This raises a dilemma for public relations personnel who often book guests on various radio and television talk shows. Should you tell the show's producer up front that a celebrity is under contract as an endorser of a particular product? If you do, it may mean that your spokesperson won't be booked, because programs such as NBC's *Today* tend to shy away from what is called "stealth marketing."

What are your responsibilities? What is the responsibility of the talk show hosts? Should the public know that Peggy Fleming is appearing as an endorser of a product?

In recent years, there has been some controversy over guests who are invited because they are celebrities and have large audience appeal. However, once they get on the show, it turns out that they are endorsers of various products. See the Ethics box on this page. In general, talk shows book guests three to four weeks in advance. Unless a topic or a person is extremely timely or controversial, it is rare for a person to be booked on one or two day's notice. Public relations strategists must keep this in mind as part of overall campaign planning.

Product Placements

Television's dramas and comedy shows, as well as the film industry, are good vehicles for promoting a company's products and services. It is not a coincidence that the hero of a detective series drives a Dodge Viper or that the heroine is seen boarding a United Airlines flight.

Such product placements, sometimes called *plugs*, are often negotiated by product publicists and talent agencies. This is really nothing new. *IPRA Frontline* reports, "In the early 1900s, Henry Ford had an affinity for Hollywood and perhaps it is no coincidence that his Model T's were the predominant vehicle appearing in the first motion pictures of the era."

Product placements, however, came of age with the movie *E.T.* in the early 1980s. The story goes that M&M Candies made a classic marketing mistake by not allowing

Reality shows are filled with product placements, such as Coke's presence on *American Idol*.

the film to use M&Ms as the prominently displayed trail of candy that the young hero used to lure his big-eyed friend home. Instead, Hershey's Reese's Pieces jumped at the chance, and the rest is history. Sales of Reese's Pieces skyrocketed, and even today, more than 20 years after the film's debut, the candy and *E.T.* remain forever linked in popular culture and the minds of a whole generation of *E.T.* fans.

Since E.T. went home, product placements have proliferated in television shows and movies. Reality shows such as *Survivor*, *The Apprentice*, and *American Idol* have recently been in the forefront of product integration into television and have even changed the landscape of product placements by charging hefty fees for manufacturers to have their products featured.

The *Wall Street Journal* explained how America's #1 show, *American Idol*, engages in product placement:

The series launched in summer 2002 with a few sponsors, namely Coca-Cola Co., which paid to have a big Coke cup sitting in front of the three judges in every episode. . . . In the current season, Fox abandoned any pretense at subtlety. The Coke cups are still there . . . , but now Coca-Cola's famous logo appears prominently onscreen for part of each show; fizzy bubbles fill a screen behind contestants as they describe what song they will sing each week. . . . And each episode is loaded with other hard sells for a truckload of other merchandise, ranging from Cingular phones and text-messaging services to Kenny Rogers' new CD.

In other series, such as *The Sopranos*, the product placement is more subtle but still blatant in terms of brand name-dropping. Carmela drives a new Porsche Cayenne and Tony has a Cingular wireless phone. Clothing manufacturers and other retailers are particularly active in product placements because studies show that today's youth gets most of their fashion ideas from watching television shows. This is why Buffy the Vampire Slayer wore jeans from the Gap.

Automakers are particularly active in product placements. Jack Bauer drives a Ford Expedition on *24*. Horatio Caine arrives in a Hummer on *CSI: Miami*. Perhaps the most successful product placement in recent years was Pontiac's decision to make a deal with Oprah Winfrey for her first show of the season. Everyone in the studio audience—all 267 of them—received a free Pontiac G6. It cost General Motors almost $8 million, but the automaker reached an estimated 8 to 9 million viewers and reaped a flood of media publicity throughout the United States and the world for its new model. Comparatively speaking, GM thought it was a good deal; advertising in national markets would have cost even more. And it would not have been as credible as Oprah saying to her nationwide audience that Pontiac was a great car.

Another opportunity for product exposure on television is on game shows. *The Price Is Right*, for example, uses a variety of products as prizes to contestants. In one episode, for example, the prize was a tent, a camp table and chairs, and lanterns. It was a great, low-cost product placement for Coleman for less than $200.

Public relations specialists should always be alert to opportunities for publicity on television programs and upcoming movies. If the company's service or product lends itself to a particular program, the normal procedure is to contact the show's producers directly or through an agent who specializes in matching company products with the show's needs.

In some cases, it's a matter of mutual benefit. A television series needs a resort location, for example, and the resort makes an offer to house and feed the cast in exchange for being featured on the program. At other times, it's a matter of whether Pepsi or Coke is used in the scene, and there's often a negotiated fee. A 20-second product placement in *Desperate Housewives*, at the height of its popularity, went for $400,000—about the same cost as a 30-second commerical on the program. Such fees place product placement more in the category of advertising and marketing than in public relations.

Issues Placement

A logical extension of product placements is convincing popular television programs to write an issue or cause into their plotlines. Writers for issue-oriented shows such as *The West Wing*, *ER*, and *Law & Order* are constantly bombarded with requests from a variety of nonprofit and special-interest groups. The most visible issues may be health related. For example, Fox's medical drama *House* even has a location on its Web site (www.fox.com/house/features/research/) that allows research into medical topics featured by episode.

The National Campaign to Prevent Teen Pregnancy, for example, works very hard to get the issue of teen pregnancy placed into television programming. The WB's *Seventh Heaven* included an episode in which the Camden family supported Sandy as she went into labor. *The George Lopez Show* on ABC discussed teen pregnancy when George and Angie's teenage daughter, Carmen, planned to get pregnant to keep her boyfriend. Many social and health organizations also lobby the producers of daytime soap operas to write scripts in which the major characters deal with cancer, diabetes, drug abuse, alcoholism, and an assortment of other problems.

The idea is to educate the public about a social issue or a health problem in an entertaining way. Someone once said, "It's like hiding the aspirin in the ice cream." Even the federal government works with popular television programs to write scripts that deal with the dangers and prevention of drug abuse. All of this has not escaped the notice of the drug companies; they are now exploring the opportunities for getting their products mentioned in plotlines, too.

The flip side of asking scriptwriters to include material is asking them to give a more balanced portrayal of an issue. The health-care industry, for example, is concerned about balance in such programs as *ER*. The popular program deals with a variety of health issues and, in many cases, health maintenance organizations (HMOs) are portrayed in an unfavorable light. Even the American Bar Association gets upset about the portrayal of lawyers in some series. Consequently, these organizations often meet with the program's scriptwriters to educate them about the facts so the program is more balanced.

Ultimately, however, the programs are designed as entertainment. Scriptwriters, like newspaper editors, make their own evaluations and judgments.

DJs and Media-Sponsored Events

Another form of product placement is agreements with radio stations to promote a product or event as part of their programming. The most common example is a concert promoter giving DJs 10 tickets to a "hot" concert that are then awarded as prizes to listeners who answer a question or call within 30 seconds.

A nonprofit group sponsoring a fund-raising festival also may make arrangements for a radio station (or television station) to cosponsor an event as part of the station's own promotional activities. This means that the station will actively promote the festival on the air through PSAs and DJ chatter between songs. The arrangement also may call for a popular DJ to broadcast live from the festival and give away T-shirts with the station's logo on them. This, too, is good promotion for the festival and the radio station, because it attracts people to the event.

The station's director of promotions or marketing often is in charge of deciding what civic events to sponsor with other groups. The station will usually agree to a certain number of promotional spots in exchange for being listed in the organization's news releases, programs, print advertising, and event banners as a sponsor of the event. Such terms are spelled out in a standard contract, which is often supplied by the radio or television station.

Stations will not necessarily promote or cosponsor every event. They must be convinced that their involvement will benefit the station in terms of greater public exposure, increased audience, and improved market position.

The Web

This section has emphasized radio and television, but it would be incomplete if the Internet was not mentioned as a major vehicle for distributing information and also reaching millions of people.

One important development has been the advent of Web-based news sites. There are more than 6,000 news sites, and the number grows each day. In addition, according to West Glen Communications, "more than 50 percent of the 110 million users of the Internet in the United States use this medium as a source of news and information."

MSNBC.com, for example, reaches 4 million viewers a day, which no daily newspaper in the United States can match. Dean Wright, editor-in-chief of MSNBC.com, told *Jack O'Dwyer's Newsletter*, "No one would seriously suggest that the daily newspaper is irrelevant. But the Web is something that can't be ignored. The message I have for PR pros is, if you want to reach out to a highly desirable demographic—people at work—then you must include the Web in your plans."

Elizabeth Shepard, editor-in-chief of Epicurious.com and Concierge.com, agrees. She says Epicurious.com, the longest-running and largest food site on the Internet, gets 20 million page views per month. She told *Jack O'Dwyer's Newsletter*, "People contact me about new restaurant openings or special tasting menus, new wines that are launching in the U.S., or special distribution of wines in certain areas." Needless to say, such a Web site is an excellent publicity opportunity for restaurants and wineries.

Many Web sites, of course, are extensions of a particular newspaper, magazine, radio or television station, or even television network. That means that the materials used by these traditional media may also wind up on their Web sites. Articles from *Gourmet*, *Bon Appetit*, and *Parade*, for example, can be found on Epicurious.com, but most of these sites also have editors who are looking for original material. Public relations practitioners should not neglect such sites in today's world.

Podcasts

The editors of the *New Oxford American Dictionary* affirmed what many public relations practitioners already knew—podcasting is a hot and rapidly growing communication trend. That's why the dictionary's editors chose "podcasting" as their 2005 Word of the Year. The definition of *podcasting*, "a digital recording of a radio broadcast or similar program, made available on the Internet for downloading to a personal audio player," was included in the *New Oxford American Dictionary* beginning in its 2006 editions.

Podcasting had been the domain of techies and early adopters, but it got a boost into the mainstream in June 2005 when Apple added a podcast directory to its iTunes Web site. Podcasts are now listed in several online directories such as podcast.net, podcast-directory.com, ipodder.org, and podcastingnews.com. They are also available on the Web sites of various corporations and non-profit agencies. Podcasts are a valuable public relations tool because they allow organizations to link active and interested members of their publics to deliver entertaining, unedited, and often long-format messages lasting up to 10 minutes.

Podcasts are used by a variety of organizations to reach diverse audiences with highly targeted messages. The Disneyland Resort, for example, gives up-to-date information about upcoming events and attractions. The Propane Education & Research Council (PERC) used podcasts for public education about the role propane can play in the aftermath of a disaster. PERC made podcasts available at PropaneCast.com and featured stories such as homeowners who used propane generators to power their homes after Hurricane Katrina.

The basic concept, as in the discussion of mat news releases in Chapter 14, is to provide helpful consumer information instead of making a podcast a long *commercial*. Tom Biro, director of new media strategies at MWW Group, wrote in *Public Relations Tactics*, "It's not about putting a 15- or 30-minute commercial on someone's iPod—it's about service marketing." He says a good example is Purina's weekly podcast "where animal experts discuss anything from pet insurance to training."

Another podcast phenomenon has been dubbed "momcasts," but the podcasts are really family-focused. Two mothers host an Internet show that is podcast on MommyCast.com. This podcast provides a forum for sponsorship by organizations that are targeting busy parents. Georgia-Pacific, for example, sponsored the podcast on behalf of its Dixie brand of paper goods. Uncle Ben's brand promoted the health benefits of whole grains on MommyCast.com.

In a similar vein, Whirlpool brands sponsored a weekly American Family podcast that promised, "The discussion-based podcast will address matters that impact families with diverse backgrounds and experiences. The podcast will feature real, everyday people and/or subject-matter experts." Audrey Reed-Granger, Whirlpool Brand's director of public relations, told *PRWeek*, "We're in touch with our consumers; we know what they need and want. For busy moms, there's more to life than appliances. Sometimes, women and families just want to commiserate. Sometimes, just laugh." Podcasts allow public relations pros to easily reach these niche targets.

> **"** Podcasting is the perfect vehicle to position your client as an expert, but not to sell a product. **"**
>
> ———*Sheri Baer,* broadcast director of the Hoffman Agency based in San Jose, CA

Blogs

Weblogs, or *blogs*, have become an integral part of the Internet. Essentially, blogs are regularly updated online personal journals with links to items of interest on the Web.

Technorati, a blog-tracking organization, estimated in 2007 that there were about 61 million blogs and about 175,000 being created each day.

Most bloggers are amateurs, but many are professional journalists who like to express their opinions, observations, and criticisms about almost everything. And, although the mass majority of bloggers are obscure, others have risen in prominence and have a large following. Political candidates have also recognized the power of influential bloggers and court them with the same diligence as the mainstream media.

Increasingly, a number of public relations practitioners are becoming bloggers on behalf of their employers and clients because, as one professional says, "They (blogs) let businesses take their message right to the public without the TV network news or the local newspaper having to act as a mouthpiece." Jason Kottke, a San Francisco Web designer and blogger, told *PRWeek*:

> A clever Weblog can combine the information dissemination of a traditional Web site with the communication you get with direct mail, e-mail, or an e-mail newsletter. The frequent updates, along with looser writing style adopted by many Webloggers gives your customers the impression that you're having a conversation with them instead of just shoving information at them in a press release form.

Public relations personnel also are starting to pitch Weblogs. One public relations firm didn't think a client's minor software upgrade was worth a news release, but staff did send an e-mail to some bloggers covering the industry and got a favorable response. The Heritage Foundation, a conservative think tank, also took the time to e-mail 175 political bloggers and found that most of them would be interested in receiving information from the organization.

Lloyd Trufelman and Laura Goldberg of Trylon Communications, wrote in *Public Relations Tactics*:

> The most important thing a publicist can do before pitching a blogger is to carefully read his or her blog. Unlike beat reporters at typical news outlets, bloggers are extremely idiosyncratic in choice of subject matter and slant. In order to begin a conversation with one—and it should be viewed as a conversation, rather than a pitch—it is vital that you are well-acquainted with the interests of the blogger. Many of them still consider their sites to be personal forums for their views and perspectives, and are wary of corporate or PR interference.

Trufelman and Goldberg offered these tips:

- Do not spam bloggers
- Be aware of their likes and dislikes before contacting them
- Conventional pitch letters may be offensive
- E-mail is the preferred means of contact
- Be completely open and honest about why you are contacting bloggers
- Disclose your affiliation
- Keep pitches short and link any published story or item you might want the blogger to consider
- Do not ask bloggers to link to your client's site or the latest press release.

Another aspect of blogs, which causes headaches for public relations staffs, is what the writers may say about a company or its products. As *Ragan's Media Relations Report* says, "A prominent blogger who trashes a product, service, or company can do serious damage to sales or public image. Bloggers also frequently post links to mainstream or other news articles—making the reach of offending news coverage that much greater."

Consequently, it is recommended that public relations personnel monitor Weblogs that reach large numbers of consumers or that cover a particular industry. Oftentimes, the information being disseminated is untrue or distorted, and it's necessary for the organization to set the record straight. At other times, a blog site may be an excellent opportunity to place positive information about the organization.

Many organizations are setting up their own blogs as a means of answering critics or getting information out quickly. David Krejci, vice president of Web relations for Weber Shandwick, wrote in *Public Relations Tactics* that he recommends that his clients inject their voice into the blog conversation by writing their own blogs. He poses the question, What if an explosion happens at your company's factory? "Any employee with a camera can shoot images of the occurrence and have it online in minutes. How well and how quickly would your client respond? A company with a blog: minutes." He suggests letting your client or CEO know that "blogs represent a compelling alternative to mainstream media for some audiences, that media consumption is increasingly fragmented, that mainstream media often look to blogs for information."

Organizational Webcasts

It has been previously noted that public relations materials, such as news releases, media kits, fact sheets, brochures, and so on, are commonly posted on an organization's Web site. Many organizations also operate online pressrooms or newsrooms to provide information for journalists who need photos, executive profiles, or the most recent annual report.

Now, most organizations also are posting SMTs, news feeds, and online news conferences on the Internet to reach an ever-expanding audience through continuous audio and video, which is called *Webcasting*.

Webcasts also can be used for live events such as news conferences and new product introductions that are made available in real time to online journalists, consumers, employees, or other key audiences. Such access makes it easier for journalists to cover the organization and get the information they need. Marc Wein, president of Murray Hill Studios in New York, told *Public Relations Tactics*, "We did one press conference where almost nobody showed up; we did a live stream onto the Web and we had dozens of reporters watching it." Jeff Wurtz, SVP of business development for News Broadcast Network, agrees. He says, "Online press conferences are by far your client's most cost-effective means of getting their story out in a clearly articulated, consistent message—at a fraction of the cost of a traditional, in-person press conference."

In general, a Webcast of a news conference or an earnings report should run about 40 minutes, with an additional 15–20 minutes for Q & A. Anything longer than this runs the risk of losing audience attention. Again, the basic idea is to keep Webcasts informative and educational and avoid overcommercialization. Webcasts should be announced and promoted to target audiences through e-mail, snail mail, and even other Web sites several weeks before the event.

SUMMARY

The Reach of Radio and TV

In today's society, radio and television reach the vast majority of people on a daily basis.

Radio News Releases

These releases, unlike those for print media, must be written for the ear. A popular format is the audio news release

(ANR) that includes an announcer and a quote (soundbite) from a spokesperson. Radio news releases should be no longer than 60 seconds.

Public Service Announcements

Both radio and television stations accept public service announcements (PSAs) from nonprofit organizations that wish to inform and educate the public about health issues or upcoming civic events. PSAs are like advertisements, but stations don't charge to air them. Television PSAs require visual aids.

Broadcast Media Tours

A radio media tour (RMT) and a television satellite media tour (SMT) happen when an organization's spokesperson is interviewed from a central location by journalists across the country. Each journalist is able to conduct a one-on-one interview for several minutes.

Video News Releases

The video news release (VNR) is produced in a format that television stations can easily use or edit based on their needs. VNRs are relatively expensive to produce, but they have great potential for reaching large audiences.

News Feeds

With a news feed, an organization arranges for coverage of a particular event, and television stations across the country can watch it in "real time" or receive an edited version of it for later use.

Personal Appearances

Public relations personnel often book spokespersons on radio and television talk shows. The guest must have a good personality, be knowledgeable, and give short, concise answers.

Product Placements

Producers are increasingly making deals with companies to feature their products on television shows or movies. Nonprofit organizations also lobby to have scripts mention key health messages and deal with various social issues.

Web Sites and Streaming Media

Public relations personnel should not overlook Web news sites for placement of publicity. Podcasts have quickly become a public relations campaign staple. In addition, the popularity of Weblogs, or blogs, means that public relations personnel should also harness them as a tactic for reaching an audience. Organizations are increasingly using Webcasts to transmit news conferences and interact with journalists.

CASE ACTIVITY What Would You Do?

Home Depot, for the past decade, has been a supporter of the Olympic Job Opportunity Program (OJOP), which allows Olympic athletes to work part-time during training and receive full-time pay and benefits. Currently, there are about 40 Olympic athletes working for Home Depot in stores across the nation.

Home Depot is proud of its assistance to Olympic athletes and wants to gain some visibility among the public

for its contribution. Your public relations firm is retained to come up with some ideas for doing a satellite media tour (SMT) and also produce a Video News Release (VNR) package that would attract the interest of television stations. Write a short memo about what you would do for a SMT. In addition, write a memo giving a storyboard for a VNR, including visuals. See the B-roll storyboard on page 400 or the VNR script on page 398 for some ideas about format.

QUESTIONS for Review and Discussion

1. Why should public relations personnel consider radio and television as major tools in reaching the public?
2. Radio news releases must be tightly written. What's the general guideline for the number of lines and words in a 30-second news release? What other guidelines should be kept in mind when writing a radio news release?
3. How does an audio news release (ANR) differ from a standard print news release?

4. Review the audio news release on page 391 from Cigna Health Care Systems. What aspects of this release illustrate good guidelines for writing an effective release?
5. What is a public service announcement (PSA)? How does it differ from a standard radio news release?
6. What is the advantage of a radio media tour (RMT) or a satellite media tour (SMT) to the organization and journalists? Are there any disadvantages?

7. What are some guidelines for a successful SMT?

8. List four ways that an organization can get its news and viewpoints on local television.

9. What are the format and characteristics of a video news release (VNR)? What is a B-roll?

10. What's a news feed, and how is it used in public relations?

11. What makes an ideal radio or television talk show guest/spokesperson?

12. What three television talk shows are the Holy Grail of public relations?

13. Companies increasingly are working with television programs and film studios to get their products featured as part of a program or movie. What do you think of this trend?

14. How can a public relations person work with radio and television stations on joint promotions?

15. How is the Web used in public relations?

16. A new online trend is Weblogs, or blogs. Why should public relations personnel pay attention to these sites?

17. What is a podcast? How can it be used in public relations?

SUGGESTED READINGS

Calabro, Sara. "Pitching a VNR: Winning over Television's Gatekeepers." *PRWeek*, January 19, 2004, p. 18.

Casalino, Christie. "Satellite Media Tours: Gaining Exposure With Proper Disclosure." *PRWeek*, October 3, 2005, p. 18.

Casalino, Christie. "How to Tune Into Radio Producers." *PRWeek*, April 25, 2005, p. 18.

Chabria, Anita. "The Power of Placement." *PRWeek*, January 31, 2005, p. 13.

Foley, Kevin. "NABC Tackles Threat Posed by Activists." *O'Dwyer's PR Report*, April 2007, pp. 10–11.

Hazley, Greg. "VNRs, Oversight Rank Among Top PA Issues." *O'Dwyer's PR Report*, February 2007, pp. 1, 19–20.

Iacono, Erica. "Broadcast Tools Find Second Home." *PRWeek*, May 1, 2006.

Iacono, Erica. "PR Can Take Lead in Product Placement." *PRWeek*, June 5, 2006, p. 14.

Iacono, Erica. "Lights, Camera, and the Power of TV." *PRWeek*, May 29, 2006, p. 15.

Iacono, Erica. "Latest VNR Flap Puts Onus on Media." *PRWeek*, April 17, 2006, p. 6.

Lewis, Tanya. "Reaching Any Audience With a Webcast." *PRWeek*, May 14, 2007, p. 30.

Lewis, Tanya. "The Language of Motivation." *PRWeek*, December 11, 2006, p. 26.

McCauley, Kevin. "Broadcast PR Firms Fight Back in Fake News Battle." *O'Dwyer's PR Report*, November 2006, pp. 10–11.

McQuire, Craig. "Going Beyond the Talking Heads." *PRWeek*, October 2, 2006, p. 18.

McQuire, Craig. "PSAs That Speak the Right Language." *PRWeek*, March 27, 2006, p. 18.

McQuire, Craig. "Targeting PSAs to a Multicultural Audience." *PRWeek*, June 13, 2005, p. 14.

Thomas, Bob. "How to Bullet-Proof an SMT." *O'Dwyer's PR Report*, April 2006, p. 10.

Ward, David. "The Mid-Morning Treasure Trove." *PRWeek*, July 10, 2006, p. 18.

Media Interviews, News Conferences, and Speeches

TOPICS COVERED IN THIS CHAPTER INCLUDE:

Media Interviews

The previous two chapters on tactics have emphasized the preparation and production of publicity materials that are distributed to the media. This chapter focuses on how a great deal of organizational information is disseminated through the spoken word in the form of media interviews, news conferences, and a variety of presentations to target audiences.

The ability of a person to answer a journalist's questions in a concise manner or give a major speech to an audience requires thought and preparation. Andrew D. Gilman, president of CommCore in New York City, emphasizes the need for preparation. He says, "I would no more think of putting a client on a witness stand or through a deposition without thorough and adequate presentation than I would ask a client to be interviewed by a skillful and well-prepared journalist without a similar thorough and adequate preparation."

Preparing for a Media Interview

In all interviews, the person being questioned should say something that will inform or entertain the audience. The public relations practitioner should prepare the interviewee to meet this need. An adroit interviewer attempts to develop a theme in the conversation—to draw out comments that make a discernible point or illuminate the character of the person being interviewed. The latter can help the interviewer—and his or her own cause as well—by being ready to volunteer specific information, personal data, or opinions about the cause under discussion as soon as the conversational opportunity arises.

In setting up an interview, the public relations person should obtain from the interviewer an understanding as to its purpose. Armed with this information, the practitioner can assemble facts and data for the client to use in the discussion. The practitioner also can aid the client by providing tips about the interviewer's style.

Some interviewers on the radio talk shows that have proliferated in recent years ask "cream puff" questions, whereas others bore in, trying to upset the guest into unplanned admissions or embarrassment. Thus, it is especially important to be well acquainted with the interviewer's style, whether it be Larry King before a national audience of millions or a local broadcaster. Short, direct answers delivered without hesitation help a guest project an image of strength and credibility. It also provides better quotes or soundbites, which is valued by the media.

Print Differs from Broadcast

A significant difference exists between interviews in print and those on radio and television. In a print interview, the information and character impressions the public receives about the interviewee have been filtered through the mind of the writer. The person interviewed is interpreted by the reporter, not projected directly to the audience. On radio and television, however, listeners hear the interviewee's voice without intervention by a third party. During a television interview, where personality has the strongest impact of all, the speaker is both seen and heard. Because of the intimacy of television, a person with a weak message who projects charm or authority may influence an audience more than one with a strong message who does not project well. A charismatic speaker with a strong message can have enormous impact. See Chapter 15 for more information on radio and television talk shows.

Know When to Say No

When an organization or individual is advocating a particular cause or policy, opportunities to give newspaper interviews are welcomed, indeed sought after. Situations arise, however, when the better part of public relations wisdom is to reject a request for an interview, either print or electronic. Such rejection need not imply that an organization has a sinister secret or fails to understand the need for public contact.

For example, a corporation may be planning a fundamental operational change involving an increase in production at some plants and the closing of another, outdated facility. Details are incomplete, and company employees have not been told. A reporter, either suspecting a change or by sheer chance, requests an interview with the company's chief executive officer.

Normally, the interview request would be welcomed, to give the executive public exposure and an opportunity to enunciate company philosophy. At this moment, however, public relations advisers fear that the reporter's questions might uncover the changes prematurely, or at least force the executive into evasive answers that might hurt the firm's credibility. So the interview request is declined, or delayed until a later date, as politely as possible.

An alternative approach would be for the chief executive officer to grant the interview, with the understanding that only topics specified in advance would be discussed. Very rarely is such an approach acceptable, however, because reporters usually resent any restrictions and try to uncover the reasons for them.

The Print Interview

An interview with a newspaper reporter may last about an hour, perhaps at lunch or over coffee in an informal setting. The result of this person-to-person talk may be a published story of perhaps 400 to 600 words. The interviewer weaves bits from the conversation together in direct and indirect quotation form, works in background material, and perhaps injects personal observations about the interviewee. The latter has no control over what is published, beyond the self-control he or she exercises in answering the questions. Neither the person being interviewed nor a public relations representative should ask to approve an interview story before it is published. Such requests are rebuffed automatically as a form of censorship.

> " Being concise and staying on message is a skill spokespeople need to learn. "
>
> ——*Cindy Sullivan*, director of communications for Cymfony, a media analysis company

Magazine interviews usually explore the subject in greater depth than those in newspapers, because the writer may have more space available. Most magazine interviews have the same format as those in newspapers. Others appear in question-and-answer form. These require prolonged taped questioning of the interviewee by one or more writers and editors. During in-depth interviews, the interviewee should answer the questions, but refrain from going off on tangents.

Radio and Television Interviews

The possibilities for public relations people to have their clients interviewed on the air are immense. The current popularity of talk shows, both on local stations and syndicated satellite networks, provides many opportunities for on-air appearances in which the guest expresses opinions and answers call-in questions. (See Chapter 15.)

A successful radio or television broadcast interview appearance has three principal requirements:

1. **Preparation.** Guests should know what key message should be emphasized.

2. **Concise speech.** Guests should answer questions and make statements precisely and briefly. They shouldn't hold forth in excessive detail or drag in extraneous material. Responses should be kept to 30 seconds or less, because seconds count on the air. The interviewer must conduct the program under severe time restrictions.

3. **Relaxation.** "Mike fright" is a common ailment for which no automatic cure exists. It will diminish, however, if the guest concentrates on talking to the interviewer in a casual person-to-person manner, forgetting the audience as much as possible. Guests should speak up firmly; the control room can cut down their volume if necessary.

A public relations adviser can help an interview guest on all of these points. Answers to anticipated questions may be worked out and polished during a mock interview in which the practitioner plays the role of broadcaster. A tape recording or videotape of a practice session will help the prospective guest to correct weaknesses.

All too often, the hosts on talk shows know little about their guests for the day's broadcast. The public relations adviser can overcome this difficulty by sending the host in advance a fact sheet summarizing the important information and listing questions the broadcaster might wish to ask. On network shows such as David Letterman's, nationally syndicated talk shows such as Oprah Winfrey's, and local programs on metropolitan stations, support staffs do the preliminary work with guests. Interviewers on hundreds of smaller local television and radio stations, however, lack such staffs. They may go on the air almost "cold" unless provided with volunteered information.

News Conferences

At a news conference, communication is two-way. The person speaking for a company or a cause submits to questioning by reporters, usually after a brief opening statement. A news conference makes possible quick, widespread dissemination of the sponsor's information and opinions through the news media. It avoids the time-consuming task of presenting the information to the news outlets individually and ensures that the intensely competitive newspapers and electronic media hear the news simultaneously.

Most news conferences—or *press conferences*, as they frequently are called—are positive in intent; they are affirmative actions to project the host's plans or point of view. A corporation may hold a news conference to unveil a new product whose manufacture will create many new jobs, or a civic leader may do so to reveal the goals and plans for a countywide charity fund drive she will head. Such news conferences should be carefully planned and scheduled well in advance under the most favorable circumstances.

Public relations specialists also must deal frequently with unanticipated, controversial situations. A business firm, an association, or a politician becomes embroiled in difficulty that is at best embarrassing,

News conferences can be held almost anywhere, and they give the media a collective opportunity to interview a celebrity or newsmaker. Here, Justin Timberlake answers a reporter's question while pop singer and actor Beyonce Knowles looks on.

possibly incriminating. Press and public demand an explanation. A bare-bones printed statement is not enough to satisfy the clamor and may draw greater press scrutiny of the stonewalling organization. A well-prepared spokesperson may be able to achieve a measure of understanding and sympathy by issuing a carefully composed statement when the news conference opens.

No matter how trying the circumstances, the person holding the news conference should create an atmosphere of cooperation and project a sincere intent to be helpful. The worst thing he or she can do is to appear resentful of the questioning. The person never should succumb to a display of bad temper. A good posture is to admit that the situation is bad and that the organization is doing everything in its power to correct it, the approach described by Professor Timothy Coombs at Wayne State University as the "mortification" strategy. (Further discussion of crisis public relations appears in Chapter 10.)

Rarely, an organization or public person caught in an embarrassing situation foolishly attempts to quiet public concern by holding a news conference that really isn't a news conference. The host reads a brief, inadequate statement, then refuses to answer questions from reporters. This practice alienates the press.

Two more types of news conferences are held. One is spontaneous, arising out of a news event: the winner of a Nobel Prize meets the press to explain the award-winning work or a runner who has just set a world's record breathlessly describes his feelings. The other type is the regularly scheduled conference held by a public official at stated times, even when there is nothing special to announce. Usually this is called a *briefing*—the daily State Department briefing, for example.

Planning and Conducting a News Conference

First comes the question, "Should we hold a news conference or not?" Frequently the answer should be "No!" The essential element of a news conference is news. If reporters and camera crews summoned to a conference to receive information of minor news value to their readers or listeners, they go away disgusted. Their valuable time has been wasted—and it is valuable. If editors send reporters to a conference that has been called merely to satisfy the host's sense of self-importance, they resent it. One guideline for deciding whether a news conference is warranted: Realistically assess whether the information can just as effectively be distributed through a news release or media kit.

Every news outlet that might be interested in the material should be invited to a news conference. An ignored media outlet may become an enemy, like a person who isn't asked to a party. The invitation should describe the general nature of the material to be discussed so an editor will know what type of reporter to assign.

What hour is best? This depends on the local media situation. If the city has only an afternoon newspaper, 9:30 or 10 A.M. is good, because this gives a reporter time to write a story before a midday deadline. If the city's newspaper publishes in the morning, 2 P.M. is a suitable hour.

Another prime goal of news conference sponsors is the early evening newscasts on local television stations, or even network TV newscasts if the information is important enough. A conference at 2 P.M. is about the latest that a television crew can cover and still get the material processed at a comfortable pace for inclusion in a dinner-hour show. This time period can be shortened a little in an emergency.

A warning: A public relations representative in a city with only an afternoon newspaper who schedules a news conference after that paper's deadline, yet in time for the news to appear on the early evening television newscasts, makes a grave blunder. Newspaper editors resent such favoritism to television and have long memories. Knowledge of, and sensitivity to, local news media deadlines are necessary.

Here are two pieces of advice from longtime public relations specialists to persons who hold news conferences:

1. The speaker should never attempt to talk off-the-record at a news conference. If the information is so secret that it should not be published, then the speaker shouldn't tell it to reporters. Many editors forbid their reporters to honor off-the-record statements, because too often the person making them is merely attempting to prevent publication of material that is legitimate news but might be embarrassing. Any statement made before a group will not stay secret long, anyway.

2. The speaker should never lie! If he or she is pushed into a corner and believes that answering a specific question would be unwise, it is far better to say, "No comment" in some form than to answer falsely. A person caught in a lie to the media suffers a critical loss of credibility.

Preparing the Location

At a news conference, public relations representatives resemble producers of a movie or television show. They are responsible for briefing the spokesperson, making arrangements, and ensuring that the conference runs smoothly. They stay in the background, however.

Bulldog Reporter, a West Coast public relations newsletter, suggests the following checklist for a practitioner asked to organize a news conference. The time factors given are normal for such events as new product introductions, but conferences concerning spot news developments for the daily press and electronic media often are called on notice of a few days or even a few hours.

♦ Select a convenient location, one that is fairly easy for news representatives to reach with minimal travel time.

♦ Set the date and time. Times between midmorning and midafternoon are good. Friday afternoons are deadly, as are days before holidays.

♦ When possible, issue an invitation to a news conference about six to eight weeks ahead of time, but one month is acceptable. The invitation should include the purpose of the conference, names of spokespersons, and why the event has significant news value. Of course, the date, time, and location must be provided.

♦ Distribute a media release about the upcoming news conference when appropriate. This depends on the importance of the event.

♦ Write a statement for the spokesperson to give at the conference and make sure that he or she understands and rehearses it. In addition, rehearse the entire conference.

♦ Try to anticipate questions so the spokesperson can readily answer difficult queries. Problem/solution rehearsals prepare the spokesperson.

♦ Prepare printed materials for distribution at the conference. These should include a brief fact sheet with names and titles of participants, a basic news release, and basic support materials. This is sometimes called a *media kit*.

♦ Prepare visual materials as necessary. These may include slides, transparencies, posters, or even a short videotape.

◆ Make advance arrangements for the room. Be sure that there are enough chairs and leave a center aisle for photographers. If a lectern is used, make certain that it is large enough to accommodate multiple microphones.

◆ Arrive 30 to 60 minutes early to double-check arrangements. Test the microphones, arrange name tags for invited guests, and distribute literature.

Some organizations provide coffee and sweet rolls for their media guests as a courtesy. Others find this gesture unnecessary because most of the newspeople are in a hurry. Liquor should not be served at a regular news conference. Such socializing should be reserved for the press party, discussed in the next section.

At some news conferences, still photographers are given two or three minutes to take their pictures before questioning begins. Some photographers complain that, thus restricted, they cannot obtain candid shots. If free shooting is permitted, as usually is the best practice, the physical arrangements should give the photographers operating space without allowing them to obstruct the view of reporters.

A practitioner should take particular care to arrange the room in such a way that the electronic equipment does not impede the print reporters. Some find it good policy for the speaker to remain after the news conference ends and make brief on-camera statements for individual TV stations, if their reporters request this attention. Such statements should not go beyond anything the speaker has said to the entire body of reporters.

A final problem in managing a news conference is knowing when to end it. The public relations representative serving as backstage watchdog should avoid cutting off the questioning prematurely. To do so creates antagonism from the reporters. Letting a conference run down like a tired clock is almost as bad. A moment comes when reporters run out of fresh questions. A speaker may not recognize this. If not, the practitioner may step forward and say something like, "I'm sorry, but I know some of you have deadlines to make. So we have time for just two more questions."

Online News Conferences

The previous section has discussed a news conference as an event at a particular location, but journalists around the world can also "attend" if arrangements are made to have the event streamed via the Internet as a Webcast (discussed in Chapter 15). Today, many online news conferences are better attended because journalists can view and even ask questions while sitting at their desks.

In fact, if a news conference is for reporters across the country covering a particular industry, a Webcast with company officials speaking to reporters via the Internet is not only more cost efficient but more effective.

Media Tours and Press Parties

In the typical news conference, the purpose is to transmit information and opinion from the organization to the news media in a businesslike, time-efficient manner. Often, however, an organization wishes to brief the media or get to know journalists and editors on a more personal basis. There are two approaches. One is the media tour and the other is the dinner or cocktail party. Both require intense attention every possible detail and an ability to juggle multiple logistics.

Media Tours

There are three kinds of media tours. The most common is a trip, often disparagingly called a "junket," during which editors and reporters are invited to inspect a company's manufacturing facilities in several cities, ride an inaugural flight of a new air route, or watch previews of the television network programs for the fall season in Hollywood or New York. The host usually picks up the tab for transporting, feeding, and housing the reporters. Many publications, however, insist on paying transportation and housing to avoid any potential conflict of interest. In either case, a public relations staff should give reporters the option of being a paid guest of the organization or paying for their own transportation and housing.

A variation of the media tour is the *familiarization trip*. "Fam trips," as they are called, are offered to travel writers and editors by the tourism industry (see Chapter 22). Convention and visitor bureaus, as well as major resorts, pay all expenses in the hope that the writers will report favorably on their experiences. Travel articles in magazines and newspapers usually result from a reporter's "fam trip."

In the third kind of media tour, widely used in high-technology industries, the organization's executives travel to key cities to talk with selected editors; for example, top Apple Computer executives toured the East Coast to talk with key magazine editors and demonstrate the capabilities of the new Apple iMac computer. Depending on editors' preferences, the executives may visit a publication and give a background briefing to key editors, or a hotel conference room may be set up so that the traveling executives may talk with editors from several publications at the same time.

Press Parties

This gathering may be a luncheon, a dinner, or a cocktail party. Whatever form the party takes, standard practice is for the host to rise at the end of the socializing period and make the "pitch." This may be the launch of a new product, a brief policy statement followed by a question-and-answer period, or merely a soft-sell thank-you to the guests for coming and giving the host an opportunity to know them better. Guests usually are given press packets of information, either when they arrive or as they leave. Parties giving the press a preview of an art exhibit, a new headquarters building, and so forth are widely used. See the PR Casebook on page 426 about a press party held by Hanes.

> " An event must help prepare me to write a story. "
> ———*Lisa McLaughlin,* reporter for *Time* magazine

The advantages of a press party to its host can be substantial under the proper circumstances. During conversation over food or drink, officials of the host organization become acquainted with media people who write, edit, or broadcast material about them. Although the benefit from the host's point of view is difficult to measure immediately, the party opens the channels of communication.

Also, if the host has an important policy position to present, the assumption—not necessarily correct—is that editors and reporters will be more receptive after a social hour. The host who expects that food and drink will buy favorable press coverage may receive an unpleasant surprise. Conscientious reporters and editors will not be swayed by a free drink and a plate of prime rib followed by baked Alaska. In their view, they have already given something to the host by setting aside a part of their day for the party. They accept invitations to press parties because they wish to develop potential news contacts within the host's organization and to learn more about its officials.

PRCASEBOOK

A Press Party to Create "Buzz"

A press party coupled with an event is a common tactic for public relations practitioners. Hanes, the clothing company, held an unusual event to promote a new line of women's undergarments. In April 2006, Hanes and spokesperson Jennifer Love Hewitt hosted a "Panti-monium" launch party in Hollywood and declared 2006 the Year of Panti-monium to market a new line of underwear. The event was meant to help generate buzz about the new line. Invited guests included celebrities; consumer, entertainment, and lifestyle reporters; producers; agents; and other Hollywood types. Guests were treated to manicures, massages, and champagne as models exhibited Hanes intimate apparel.

The Hanes press party included models wearing the new line of underwear and celebrity spokesperson Jennifer Love Hewitt.

Gifts in the form of pen, note pad, or a company paperweight are often given to reporters attending a press party, but anything costing more than a token amount should be avoided. Some large newspapers will not even permit their staffs to accept token gifts. (Ethics are discussed extensively in Chapter 3.) See the Ethics box on page 427 about a press junket sponsored by Disneyland.

The Art of Speechwriting

Work in public relations also requires excellent knowledge of interpersonal communications, and one form of this is speechwriting. Other forms of face-to-face communications include giving speeches and presentations.

Public relations practitioners frequently are called on to write a speech for their employers or clients. As speechwriters, their role is a hidden one. They labor silently to produce the words that may sparkle like champagne when poured forth by their employers from the lecterns of conventions, civic banquets, and annual meetings.

In the White House, the wraps of anonymity usually are drawn around the writers who churn out speeches and statements for the President of the United States. A president utters a memorable phrase and gets the credit, but a high-level speechwriter probably created it. Michael J. Gerson, for example, is credited with what many say was President Bush's best speech, made to a joint session of Congress after the September 11 attacks. There is nothing disreputable about this. Presidents, as well as CEOs of corporations, have more urgent tasks than to think up catchy phrases. The speechwriter finds personal satisfaction in creating competent speeches for someone else.

on the job
ETHICS

Press Party at Disney World Criticized

Disney World in Florida threw a press party to celebrate its anniversary, and more than 10,000 journalists showed up. The park offered to pay the entire expense of any invited journalist who wanted to come, but it was also aware that many media outlets had policies about their news staff accepting such offers. Therefore, Disney public relations staffers sent invitations outlining three options:

1. Disney World and its travel-promotion partners would pay all of the journalist's travel, lodging, and food costs.

2. Disney World would pay $150 daily to a visiting journalist, and

his or her employer could reimburse the journalist for anything over that amount.

3. A journalist's employer could pay all of his or her expenses.

The *New York Times,* however, editorialized that the journalists who accepted the free trip "debased" journalism and gave the public impression that the entire press was "on the take." The *St. Petersburg Times* called the party "junket journalism" and also castigated Disney World for trying to "buy the press." Smaller newspapers and broadcasting stations were less outraged. They said their journalists could not attend such an event if Disney had

not offered to pay all or part of the expenses.

Disney World did receive a large amount of favorable news stories about the park as a result of the anniversary celebration, except for the media-ethics dispute. The total cost was about $7.5 million to host all the journalists, according to *Editor & Publisher.*

Did Disney and its public relations staff do anything wrong in terms of inviting the journalists? Do you think Disney should be criticized for trying to "buy the press"? Why or why not? Is this a public relations ethics concern, or primarily one of ethics for the mass media?

Most large corporations employ speechwriters, some of whom receive annual salaries in the six figures. Smaller organizations often use professional freelance writers who command anywhere from $1,000 to $10,000 for a speech. Still other organizations simply have speeches written in-house by their own public relations staff, which often has other duties in addition to speechwriting.

Research Is the First Step

Speechwriting doesn't take place in a vacuum. If you are given a speechwriting assignment, several preliminary steps must be taken before a speech outline can even be started. The first step is to research the intended audience of the speech. Who? What? Where? When? How many people? What time of day? Purpose of the meeting? Length of speech? Purpose of the talk? Other speakers on the program? A speechwriter finds answers to these questions by talking with the organizers of the event or meeting. Don't accept vague answers; keep asking follow-up questions until you have a complete picture.

A good description of the event and the audience will help to determine the tone, structure, and content of the speech so that the speech is relevant to the audience. A good example of defining an audience is when an EDS corporate executive was asked to give a keynote address for a meeting of the Association of American Chambers of

Speechwriters are in demand and well paid. This ad from Saudi Aramco is an example of opportunities in the field.

Commerce of Latin America in Lima, Peru. Beth Pedison, executive speechwriter for EDS, analyzed the intended audience in the following way:

> Intended Audience: 400 top Latin American and Caribbean business executives, government leaders, and Chamber representatives. Because the audience came from diverse industries, countries, and company sizes, their familiarity with information technology varied widely. We didn't want to talk down to those who were technologically savvy, or talk over the heads of those who were not technologically proficient. English was the business language of the conference and the speech, although most everyone in the audience spoke English as a second language. Therefore, we needed to keep sentence structure simple, and avoid the use of colloquialisms, contractions, or U.S.-centric language.

The second research step is to know everything about the executive who's going to give the speech. A good speechwriter will take the time to determine the speaker's speech pattern by listening to how he or she talks to other groups and subordinates. The purpose is to see how the speaker's mind works, what words or phrases are favored, and what kind of opinions are expressed. In addition to listening, it's also a good idea to go over material that the executive has written or, if written by others, that the executive or client admires in terms of style and method of presentation.

Another part of this research is to have lengthy conversations with the speaker before writing a rough draft of the talk. In an informal setting, you and the speaker should discuss the speech in terms of the audience being addressed, the objective, the theme, the kind of facts and statistics that should be gathered, and the major points that need to be included. In this way, the speechwriter is better able to think like the speaker and write a speech that fits the person's beliefs and speech pattern.

This is how Marie L. Lerch, director of public relations and communication for Booz Allen & Hamilton, described her work with the company's chairman for a diversity awards speech to company employees:

> The central message, "Do the Right Thing," has been Mr. Stasior's core theme throughout his tenure as chairman. I worked with him to adapt the theme to the issue of diversity; researched quotes and other materials that would add color and emphasis to the message; and interviewed him to flesh out his ideas and words on the subject. With notes and research in hand, I developed a first draft of the speech, which Mr. Stasior and I revised together in its final form.

Objectives and Approach

Preparing a speech takes a great deal of energy and time on the part of the speechwriter and the speaker. Therefore, it's important to determine what the speech is supposed to accomplish. In other words, what information and opinions should the audience have when the speech is concluded?

Everything that goes into a speech should be pertinent to the key objectives of the speech. Material that does not help to attain the objectives or communicate key message points should not be used. Whether the objective is to inform, persuade, activate, or commemorate, that objective should be uppermost in the speechwriter's mind.

A good example of setting objectives was done by Melissa Brown, a freelance speechwriter, who was commissioned to write a speech for the president of the Grocery Manufacturers of America (GMA), who was going to speak at the International Food and Lifestyles Media Conference in Cincinnati. The topic of the speech was "The Changing Challenges Facing the Food Industry."

The objectives of the speech were as follows:

> **The most important thing . . . is to know the client and to know the audience.**
>
> ———*John Schacter,* senior consultant at Porter Novelli

- ◆ Give food writers useful, research-based information on the lifestyles of American consumers, thus positioning GMA as a good source of statistics/information.

- ◆ Neutralize misinformation presented by opponents of biotechnologically developed food products, presenting the industry's side of the story and exposing the lack of credentials of a major voice in the opposition.

- ◆ Provide information on the good work the industry has accomplished in addressing environmental issues, in particular, packaging and solid waste.

- ◆ Demonstrate to GMA board that the association is speaking out on the issues that affect their businesses.

- ◆ Frame the arguments other food industry spokespeople can use in other opportunities within their companies and with the press.

The approach might be described as the *tone* of the speech. A friendly audience may appreciate a one-sided talk, with no attempt to present both sides of an issue. For example, a politician at a fund-raising dinner of supporters does not bother to give the opposition's views. Also, an executive talking to the company's sales force does not need to give the pros and cons of competing products.

Many speaking engagements, however, take place before neutral audiences such as a civic club (Lions, Rotary, Kiwanis) and any other number of civic groups where the audience may have mixed views or even a lack of knowledge about a particular subject. The Lifestyles Media Conference, mentioned earlier, is such a speaking engagement. Some of the people in the audience will be strong supporters or opponents of foods created through biotechnology.

In such a case, it is wise to take a more objective approach and give an overview of the various viewpoints. The speech can still advocate a particular position, but the audience will appreciate the fact that you have included other points of view. From the standpoint of persuasion, a speaker also will have more control over how the opposition view is expressed, instead of an audience member bringing it up.

Hostile or unfriendly audiences present the greatest challenge. They are already predisposed against what you say, and they tend to reject anything that does not square with their opinions. Remember the old saying: "Don't confuse me with the facts—my mind is already made up." The best approach in this situation is for the speaker to find some common ground with the audience. This technique lets the audience know that the speaker shares or at least understands some of their concerns.

Writing the Speech

After determining the objectives and approach, the next step is to write an outline of the speech. Such an outline has three main parts: the opening, the body, and the closing.

The opening is the part of the speech that must get the audience's attention, establish empathy and a relationship, and point toward a conclusion. A good approach is to tell the audience what the topic is, why it is important to them, and the direction you plan to take in addressing it.

The body of the speech presents the evidence that leads to the conclusion. The outline should list all of the key points. In this section, the speechwriter will list quotes from acknowledged experts in the field, facts and figures, and examples that support the speaker's theme or point of view. The conclusion summarizes the evidence, pointing out what it means to the audience.

The outline should be discussed with the speaker to ensure that the approach is acceptable and that all of the necessary facts, statistics, and quotes are assembled. Oftentimes, the speechwriter may have to do some additional research or track down some obscure fact that the speaker wants to use.

Once the outline is approved, the speechwriter writes a first draft of the speech. The speechwriter should keep in mind the time constraints on the speech. It's no use writing a 45-minute speech if the request by the host organization is for a 20-minute speech. Some guidelines on the length of speeches will be given shortly.

A speech is built in blocks that are joined by transitions. The following pattern for assembling the blocks provides an all-purpose organizational structure on which most speeches can be built:

Beginning

1. Introduction (establish contact with the audience).
2. Statement of the main purpose of the speech.

Middle

3. Development of the theme with examples, facts, and anecdotes. Enumeration of individual points is valuable here. It gives a sense of structure and controlled use of time.
4. Statement of secondary theme, if any.
5. Enunciation of the main point that the speaker has been building up to. This main point is the heart of the speech.
6. A pause at this plateau, with an anecdote or two. This is the soft place where the audience absorbs the point just made.

End

7. Restatement of the theme in summary form.
8. A brief, brisk conclusion.

Word choice, which is based on the nature of the audience, is an important part of the first draft.

The words used in the text of a speech can make a major difference in how well the audience can follow the speech and easily understand it. Here are some guidelines for selecting the right words:

◆ **Use personal pronouns.** "You" and "we" make the talk more conversational and lets the listeners know that the speaker is talking to them.

- **Avoid jargon.** Every field has its own vocabulary of specialized words. Don't use words and acronyms that are unfamiliar to your audience. You may know what "ROI" means, but many people in audience may not.

- **Use simple words.** Don't say "print media" when you mean "newspapers." Don't say "possess" when "have" means the same thing.

- **Use round numbers.** Don't say "253,520,000 Web sites"; say "more than 250 million Web sites."

- **Use contractions.** Instead of "do not," say "don't." Say "won't" instead of "would not." It makes the speech more conversational.

- **Avoid empty phrases.** Don't say "In spite of the fact" when "since" or "because" works just as well.

- **Use active verbs.** Say "I think" instead of "It is my conviction that. . . ."

- **Don't dilute expressions of opinion.** It blunts the crispness of your talk if you use waffling terms such as "Of course, it's only my opinion but . . ." or "It seems to me. . . ."

- **Avoid modifiers.** Words such as "very" or "most" should be deleted.

- **Use direct quotes.** Identify the name or source first, and then give a direct quote. For example, "John Baskin, a reporter for the *New York Times*, wrote. . . ."

- **Vary sentence length.** In general, short sentences are best. However, occasionally break up a series of short sentences with some longer ones.

- **Use questions.** Such an approach often gets the audience more involved. "Does anyone here know the average family income in the United States?" You can also ask rhetorical questions: "What would you do in such a situation?"

- **Make comparisons and contrasts.** "An extra 1 percent in sales tax will provide enough money to build three new branch libraries."

- **Create patterns of thought.** It's all right to restate and rephrase to create a particular pattern of emphasis. Senator Hillary Clinton once used this phrasing in one of her speeches: "If women are healthy and educated, their families will flourish. If women are free from violence, their families with flourish. If women have a right to work . . . their families will flourish."

Experienced speechwriters caution that you should not feel dejected if the first, second, or even third draft comes back in tatters. It is only through this process that the speech becomes the natural expression of the speaker's personality. This is the ideal process. The most successful speakers take the time to work with their speechwriters. Unfortunately, too many executives fail to understand this.

A report prepared by Burson-Marsteller offers reasons why business people have trouble explaining themselves to the public. The report noted:

> All too often the chief executive expects a speech to appear magically on his desk without any contribution on his part. He feels too busy to give the speech the attention it deserves. In the end, he becomes the victim of his own neglect. He stumbles through a speech which, from start to finish, sounds contrived. And then he wonders why nobody listened to what he said.

Coaching the Speaker

In addition to writing a speech, a speechwriter often serves as a coach for the speaker. Whether the speech is memorized (rare) or read, a coach helps the speaker rehearse and polish the delivery so that he or she becomes totally familiar with it. The tone of voice, emphasis given to certain words or phrases, pauses, gestures, and rate of delivery are all important. Nonverbal communication is an essential part of the speech, and the section on page 435 gives some guidelines for the speaker to come across as friendly, assured, and self-confident.

Some speakers prefer to have certain phrases underlined and to have detailed cues in the script, such as "pause," "look at the audience," or "make point with arm raised." Others don't want such cues; it's a matter of preference.

Format is also a matter of personal preference. Some people prefer to have the speech double-spaced; others want triple spacing. A few like to have the speech in all capital letters, but the standard practice is caps and lowercase with heads and subheads in boldface type. A speech is often printed in large type, 14 to 20 points, so the speaker can easily read it, even in a dim light.

The speaker should be sufficiently familiar with the note cards or prepared text to permit abridgment on brief notice. Such advance thinking is particularly important for a speaker at a luncheon meeting. All too often, the meal is served late or the group takes an excessive amount of time discussing internal matters or making general announcements, leaving a speaker far less time than originally planned.

The same thing can happen at an evening banquet. For example, the awards ceremony may take longer than expected, and the speaker is introduced at 9:15 P.M., three hours after everyone has sat down to dinner. In this instance, the most applause is for the speaker who realizes the time and makes a brief speech.

Giving a Speech or Presentation

Writing a speech focuses almost exclusively on content. Giving a speech or presentation is all about delivery. Public relations practitioners in the course of their daily work may not give many formal speeches to large audiences, but they do give any number of presentations to their employers and clients about proposed new programs, progress on current programs, or the results of a particular campaign.

Much that has already been said about writing a speech also is applicable to giving a speech or presentation. You still need to know the audience and objective of the speech. Is it to inform, persuade, celebrate, amuse, or entertain? An informative speech might tell the audience how something was done. A persuasive speech attempts to motivate the audience into doing something—approving the new plan, volunteering to serve on a task force, or writing their local legislator. A celebratory speech is designed to honor some person or event. If it's a retirement party, you can be somewhat amusing and offer some platitudes that no doubt will be well received.

Appealing to the Ear

The average speech or presentation has only one brief exposure—the few minutes during which the speaker is presenting it. There is no chance to go back, no time to let it slowly digest, no opportunity for clarification. The message must be clearly understood at the time it is given.

Public relations personnel are usually accomplished writers, but they must realize that speaking is quite another form of communication. As Louis Nizer, a writer, once said, "The words may be the same, but the grammar, rhetoric, and phrasing are different. It is a different mode of expression—a different language."

With a speech, you have to build up to a major point and prepare the audience for what is coming. The lead of a news release attempts to say everything in about 15 or 20 words right at the beginning. If a speaker were to use the same form as a news release, most of the audience probably would not hear the main point of the speech. When a speaker begins to talk, the audience is still settling down. Therefore, the first words of a speech often are devoted to setting the stage: thanking the host, making a humorous comment, or saying how nice it is to be there. Here's the opening of the EDS speech for the Association of American Chambers of Commerce in Latin America:

> Hello. I am glad to be with you at this important event. I am enthusiastic about the event's theme, "The Transformation of the Americas," as well as the topic for this panel, "Opportunities Created by Advances in Information Technology," because I truly believe we are in a major transformation, and tremendous opportunities abound.

People's minds wander during a speech. As your speech progresses, it's a good idea to restate and summarize the key points. One platitude of the speaking circuit, and a valid one, is to "tell them what you are going to tell them, tell it to them, and then tell them what you have told them." In this way, an audience is given a series of guideposts as they listen to the presentation.

Keeping the Audience in Mind

It has already been noted that the first step in speechwriting is determining the composition of the audience. This also is true if you are the speaker. A talk before a professional group can be more relevant if you prepare for it by doing some preliminary research.

Talk to some members of that particular profession. Get an idea of the issues or problems they face. Another approach is to go online to the site of the organization, whether it's local or international, and see what is posted. Some speakers may even visit the local library and look through some issues of the organization's national magazine. Of course, the organization's contact who invited you should be consulted about the group and what they are expecting from your talk.

Your familiarity with the organization can pay dividends in terms of making relevant references to the group within the context of the talk. This can help you choose examples, quotes, and stories that are meaningful—and appreciated.

Audiences usually remember only a small part of what they hear. The speaker therefore must make sure they hear things that stick in their minds. A vague generality has little or no chance of being understood or remembered. A speaker can issue the vague call for more transparency and financial accountability in corporations, but the audience will better remember the point if he or she is more specific, for example, calling for new federal regulations that would severely penalize corporations for failing to write annual reports that a sixth grader could understand.

In most cases, the person who is asked to speak is perceived to be an expert on a given subject. Consequently, the audience wants the benefit of that person's thoughts, analysis, and even opinions on a particular situation or issue. They don't want platitudes or statements that are vague and self-evident.

Here are some tips about keeping the audience in mind:

- **Know your listeners.** Think about such demographics as age, income, education, occupation, and gender.

on the job
A MULTICULTURAL WORLD

A Chinese Approach to Speechwriting

An important speech takes a lot of preparation and polishing, but President Jiang Zemin's opening speech to the Communist Party's 16th Congress was an extraordinary effort. More than 900 people labored in a yearlong effort to compose the speech, which ran 70 pages.

Preparation for the speech started with meetings in 16 provinces to talk about what should be in the speech. A large number of Chinese citizens were canvassed, and a first draft of the speech was prepared for comment by President Jiang and other officials of the Communist Party. About six months later, a team

of writers worked for eight days to polish the "masterpiece."

The speech, which took more than two hours to deliver, apparently was a big hit. More than 1.1 million copies of the speech were sold in Beijing alone, according to the Xinhua News Agency.

- ◆ **Use their language.** Use terms and expressions that are familiar to the audience.
- ◆ **Use visuals.** Audiences remember better if information is presented in visual form, such as charts or bulleted slides.
- ◆ **Use humor carefully.** Avoid side comments and jokes that may offend. The safest humor is a story that a speaker tells about himself or herself.
- ◆ **Watch your facts.** Be absolutely certain that the information is accurate.
- ◆ **Focus on the benefit.** Any speech must tell listeners what they will gain from the ideas presented.

Length of the Presentation

With regard to the length of a presentation, the axiom "less is best" is a good one. Most speeches and presentations, except those given at an academic conference or technical seminar, should be 20 to 30 minutes in length. A 20-minute speech is about 2,500 to 3,000 words, or about 10 pages double-spaced. The general rule is that a speaker can read about 150 to 160 words per minute.

If there is only one major speaker, a luncheon speech at a civic club usually is 20 to 30 minutes. If there are several speakers and business is conducted, a guest speaker often may speak for only 15 to 20 minutes. Many organizations that meet for breakfast or lunch have strict rules on ending a meeting at a specific time, and a speaker going beyond that time does so at his or her peril.

Evening talks at banquets also require brevity. A keynote speaker, as already noted, may be only part of a long program that includes a number of speakers and awards. The audience is tired, so the best advice is to talk for no more than 15 or 20 minutes. In China, however, a speech may go on for several hours. See the Multicultural World box on this page.

Nonverbal Communication

Don't read a speech with your eyes glued to the lectern. It is important to look frequently at the audience and establish eye contact, which is another reason for being totally familiar with your text or note cards. Experts recommend that a speaker should look at specific people in the audience for several seconds before moving on to another part of the audience. Eye contact, according to research studies, is a major factor that establishes a speaker's rapport and credibility with an audience.

Nonverbal communication is just as important as what is said. Veteran speaker Jack Pyle offers the SPEAK method as an approach to nonverbal communication. The following is adapted from his remarks to *pr reporter*.

The art of public speaking requires the speaker to be animated, enthusiastic, and to use gestures to make an important point. Here, US Senator Barack Obama speaks after receiving an award from at the Rock the Vote awards dinner in Washington, D.C. The nonprofit group works to register new voters and increasing political power for young people.

◆ **S = Smile.** It's one of your best communication tools; it makes a good first impression and helps others want to hear what you have to say.

◆ **P = Posture.** Stand straight, and don't slouch or lean on the podium. It signals that the speaker is not confident in what he or she is saying.

◆ **E = Eye Contact.** A person who is believable and honest "looks you straight in the eye." Don't stare, but look at someone in the audience for about three seconds before moving on.

◆ **A = Animation.** Show your interest in the subject with energy and animation. Be enthusiastic. "A" also is for attitude. Make sure you feel good about yourself and what you are saying. A good attitude, in today's public skepticism of corporate CEOs, is one of humility. Martha Stewart, charged with lying to federal investigators about insider trading, didn't learn this lesson until after she was convicted.

◆ **K = Kinetics (motion).** Use your arms to make gestures that support your words. Use your hand to emphasize a point; occasionally move to the side of the podium as if you are personally talking to someone in the audience.

Nervous gestures, on the other hand, are distracting. Don't play with your hair, fiddle with a pen, fondle your necklace or tie, pull on your ears, or keep moving your leg or foot. Posture also is a gesture. Don't hunch over the podium; stand up straight. Pay attention to your facial expression; smile at your audience, express enthusiasm, and show that you are deeply interested in the subject. Audiences pick up on nonverbal cues and assess the speaker accordingly.

> " A smile translates everywhere. It relaxes your audience. "
>
> ———*Karen Freidman,* media training coach based in Philadelphia

Visual Aids

A banquet speaker, making an after-dinner speech, usually delivers his or her message without visual aids. Many speeches and presentations, however, benefit from the use of visual aids to present information in a memorable way. Consider the following research findings:

◆ Sight accounts for 83 percent of what we learn.

◆ When a visual is combined with a voice, retention increases by 50 percent.

- Color increases a viewer's tendency to act on information by 26 percent.
- Use of video increases retention by 50 percent and accelerates buying decisions by 72 percent.
- The time required to present a concept can be reduced by up to 40 percent with visuals.

It is important to understand the advantages and disadvantages of each visual aid technique to determine what is most effective for a given situation. If the presentation is at a workshop or seminar where the objective is to inform and educate an audience, a PowerPoint presentation may be the best approach. If, on the other hand, the workshop has the objective of generating ideas and audience discussion, perhaps an easel with a blank pad of paper is the only visual aid required.

A major speech for a large convention, however, may be more effective if one uses 35-mm slides and video clips. This was the case when Hector Ruiz, president of AMD, addressed the annual meeting of high-technology manufacturers in Las Vegas. He used three short videos in his talk to illustrate how AMD partnered with other companies to solve their particular problems and, along the way, create new products.

PowerPoint   The leading presentation software is Microsoft's PowerPoint. In fact, Microsoft estimates that more than 30 million PowerPoint presentations are made every day. *USA Today* business writer Kevin Maney said it best when he wrote, "PowerPoint users are inheriting the earth. The software's computer-generated, graphic-artsy presentation slides are everywhere—meetings, speeches, sales pitches, Web sites. They're becoming an essential to getting through the business day as coffee and Post-It notes."

In fact, PowerPoint presentations have become so common that one study flatly claimed that it was ". . . a way of life, considering that more than 90 percent of computer-based presentation visuals in the United States are created using it." Not everyone is happy with this situation. Many public relations professionals say the program has been overused to the point that audiences have begun to groan when someone fires up the LCD projector with yet another PowerPoint presentation.

PowerPoint, however, is a very versatile software program from the standpoint of preparing information that can be used in a variety of ways. Here are some of the ways it can be used:

- **Use your computer monitor.** A desktop or laptop computer is the ideal way to show the presentation to one or two individuals. The laptop or notebook presentation is popular on media tours and when talking one-to-one with a journalist or financial analyst.

- **Harness your laptop to a computer projector.** If you are reaching a larger audience, technology has now advanced so you can show a PowerPoint presentation on a large screen in a meeting hall.

- **Post PowerPoint presentations on the Web.** You can post an entire slide presentation to the organization's Web site or intranet.

- **Make overhead transparencies.** A PowerPoint presentation can be downloaded and printed on clear plastic sheets, called *transparencies*. Some speakers, for example, carry a set of transparencies just in case the computer projector (LCD) malfunctions. Also, a speaker should not always count on an LCD projector being available.

◆ **Print pages.** "Hard" copies of a presentation can be distributed to members of the audience. The software allows the creator to place thumbnails of each slide on the left column of a printout and give a place for individuals to take notes on the right side of the page.

◆ **Create 35-mm slides.** A PowerPoint presentation can also be converted to 35-mm slides and then shown using a slide projector and a carousel slide tray. This approach is a good backup in case the organization or meeting room doesn't have an LCD projector. Using a slide projector also means that a speaker doesn't have to bring a laptop computer or worry about connections between the LCD projector and the laptop, which can be tricky at times.

◆ **Create CDs and DVDs.** Many organizations put PowerPoint presentations on CDs or, increasingly, on DVDs, so they can be easily sent to media reporters, customers, and field personnel, who can then view them at a convenient time.

Whatever the medium, some design rules about the composition of a PowerPoint slide should be kept in mind.

One key rule is to keep it simple. If the slide is too cluttered with text, borders, and even clip art, it cuts down on readability and retention. Peter Nolan, writing in *Public Relations Tactics*, says, "The last thing any presenter wants is to have the audience reading a heavy text slide rather than paying attention to what is being said. Presentation slides should support the speaker with a few key words or easily understood graphics."

A good solution to Nolan's concern is the 4 by 4 rule. Use no more than four bullets and no more than four or five words for each bullet. Others, such as Cornelius Pratt, formerly of Michigan State University, recommend a "triple-seven" rule: no more than seven bullets, no more than seven words per bullet, and no more than seven lines per bulleted slide. This is not to say that every slide should look exactly the same. Transitional slides, those bridging from one topic or major point to another, may consist of only one or two words or perhaps a photo or piece of clip art. In general, the axiom holds—less is better.

In terms of type size, the standard rule is 24- to 28-point type for all words. Anything smaller will be difficult to see from the back of the room. There should also be about a 2-inch margin around any copy; this ensures that any text will fit the configuration of a slide projector and a 35-mm slide, if that medium is used. PowerPoint has text boxes that supply the right amount of space around the text.

Color also is an important consideration. PowerPoint has hundreds of colors available on its palette, but that doesn't mean you should use all of them. Multiple colors for the background and text only distract the audience and give the impression of an incoherent presentation. Maney, from *USA Today*, says ". . . people spend too much time messing with the PowerPoint and not enough time messing with the message."

In other words, keep it simple. Use clear, bold fonts for colors that contrast with the background. According to research, a dark blue background conveys a corporate approach. Green works well when feedback is desired, and reds motivate the audience to action. Yellows and purples are not recommended for most business presentations. In general, black is the best color for text, but remember the contrast rule. Black type on a dark blue or red background won't be readable. Other experts recommend earth tones and middle-range colors for a slide's background so there is a maximum contrast between the text (black or another dark color) and the background.

Slide Presentations   PowerPoint presentations, as previously mentioned, can be converted to 35-mm slides. This format is often used for presentations in school classrooms and at civic club meetings where an LCD projector may not be readily available. The carousel projector may not be high-tech, but it is still found in many civic meeting rooms and classrooms.

A 35-mm slide presentation, like a PowerPoint presentation, needs a script that is coordinated with the slides. Speakers using a slide presentation often write their speeches in a two-column format, with the slide number or description on the left side and the text on the right side, in much the same manner that a video news release (VNR) is formatted (see page 398). This allows the speaker to coordinate his or her slides with what is being said. There's nothing worse than a slide showing one thing and the speaker talking about something else.

The timing of the slides in a presentation varies. It's possible to make a good presentation with just a few slides. In fact, Pratt recommends one PowerPoint or 35-mm slide with text every five minutes. Others, however, say that a 35-mm slide presentation with a lot of photos could have about 100 slides changed at the rate of 4 or 5 per minute. The general guideline is that a slide should be on the screen long enough for the audience to digest and understand it. Photos, of course, take less time than text.

Transparencies   The traditional workhorse in the seminar or workshop is the overhead projector. Organizations still use transparencies—often created using PowerPoint software—in training sessions and other situations where a high-tech approach is not really needed. An overhead projector is much cheaper than equipping multiple rooms with LCD projectors. Transparencies also are relatively inexpensive and can be made on a photocopy machine at the last minute.

The same rules apply to formatting and text size. Use 24- to 28-point type, keep the text to four or five lines per page, and use a 2-inch margin. One common problem with transparencies is that speakers often turn their back on the audience while they read the text on the screen.

Charts and Graphs   These also can be formatted in PowerPoint and enlarged onto large poster boards or projected onto the screen. Common charts are pie charts or bar graphs. The main rule is to keep them relatively simple so they can be readily understood by the audience.

Flip Charts   Another visual aid is the flip chart, information on poster boards or a large-page tablet mounted on an easel. This format is used in small group presentations. The speaker uses the flip-chart as an integral part of his or her presentation as new pages are flipped or new posters are exposed to the audience. As previously mentioned, meetings designed to solicit audience ideas and feedback use a blank pad on the easel to display ideas. A more sophisticated approach is the "smart" whiteboard, which allows anything written on it to be electronically transferred to a printer or even to computers in front of everyone in the group.

Speaker Training

Giving speeches and presentations is an important part of an organization's outreach to its key publics. A talk by an executive is an effective medium for building relationships through face-to-face interaction. It adds a human dimension to any organization, and it also offers the chance for interaction between a speaker and the audience.

Speeches, therefore, should be an integral part of an organization's overall public relations program. Indeed, public relations personnel are often involved in training speakers and seeking appropriate forums where key publics can be reached.

Executive Training

Today, the public is demanding more disclosure and accountability from organizations, which is forcing many executives to mount the speaker's platform.

Ned Scharff, a longtime speech writer at Merrill Lynch & Co., says it best in an article for *The Strategist:* "If the . . . CEO is to excel as a leader, he or she cannot avoid giving speeches. People have a deep-seated need to see and hear their leaders actively expressing vision and conviction. The more trying the circumstances, the greater the need." Indeed, a survey by Burson-Marsteller of corporate communications executives found that a company CEO typically gets about four speaking invitations a week.

As a consequence, more executives are taking courses designed to improve their public speaking skills. Cincinnati Gas & Electric, for example, holds seminars of this kind for both executives and middle managers. Other companies also have rushed into formal speech training for executives so they can represent the organization at various conferences and seminars. An articulate CEO can do much to increase the visibility of the organization and position it as a leader in the industry.

Outside consultants specializing in speech training are often hired to work with an executive on how to give speeches, because this is almost becoming a prerequisite for anyone seeking the top job in an organization. In the past, a brilliant engineer or research scientist could become a CEO but, today, that person would also need to be an excellent speaker.

Media Training

In one survey of executives, *pr reporter* found that over half spend 10 hours or more each month meeting with outside groups. In addition, the majority average 20 speeches a year, about two-thirds spend time on press conferences, and another third appear on television talk shows.

This aspect of conducting news conferences and having to deal with multiple one-on-one requests from print and broadcast for interviews has also made media training a top priority of many organizations. And it's not only for CEOs. Increasingly, plant and store managers are being given media training because local media will call them before calling corporate headquarters in some distant city.

Many consultants, often former print and broadcast journalists, offer media training. However, most organizations rely on their own in-house public relations department or their outside public relations firm to provide such training.

The idea is that executives and middle managers don't know much about how the mass media operates and how to conduct a media interview. In many cases, it is the responsibility of the public relations professional to tell them such things as how to answer a question in 15 seconds or less.

Public relations practitioners often train executives to do media interviews by playing the role of a reporter in a mock interview. They start by asking some basic questions so the executive can get comfortable; then they will start asking more complex and controversial questions to give the executive some experience in handling such inquiries. At times, executives become very agitated about such questions, but it's better to do this in a mock interview than in a real one. Another common approach is to videotape the executive answering questions so that he or she can hear the tone of his or her voice and view the kind of nonverbal communication he or she is using.

Media training can be divided into two parts: what to say and how to say it. Public relations personnel are most effective in helping executives crystallize what they want to say. Another consideration is what to say that will advance organizational objectives. Media trainers tell executives to be concise and to keep on message—to make sure that one or two key points get through to the audience.

How to say it is another matter. Print journalists often summarize and synthesize a whole conversation. Broadcast journalists, on the other hand, often edit a videotape and take a particular statement that may or may not be in context. Media training helps executives understand the difference and deal with it.

Another aspect of media training is to educate executives how news is produced and processed. Few executives, for example, realize that a reporter's story is often edited and changed by a newspaper's copy desk or that the headline is written by someone else other than the reporter. Executives also have trouble understanding why a 20-minute interview videotaped by a camera crew winds up as a 20-second story on the air.

Publicity Opportunities

The number of people a speech or presentation reaches can be substantially increased through publicity.

Before the Event   Whenever anyone from your organization speaks in public, the public relations staff must make sure that the appropriate media are notified in advance. This often takes the form of a media advisory, which was discussed in Chapter 14.

An *advisory* is simply a short note or memo, via letter or e-mail, alerting a media outlet that an organizational representative will be speaking on a particular topic on a certain date at a particular time and location. In a brief sentence or two, a public relations staffer will say why the talk is important and offer a good news angle. It may be tied to a particular issue or trend in society.

If it's a major policy speech by the CEO, an advance text is often sent to the media and selected reporters covering that particular beat. An advance text, however, should have an embargo date. In other words, the media is requested to not use the story until after the speech has been given. There are two reasons for this. First, news stories about the speech may reduce attendance at the event. Second, accidents happen, and the speech may be cancelled for some reason. The media would be embarrassed covering a speech that was never given.

If the speech is a major one, it's also possible to arrange with a production company to do a Webcast of the speech so reporters across the country can listen to it in real time. This was discussed in Chapter 15.

After the Event   After a major speech has been given, the work of the public relations staff is just beginning. Public relations practitioners prepare audio, video, and print news releases about the speech for distribution to appropriate media. Television stations, in particular, appreciate a short video clip that can be used on the next newscast. See the Insights box on page 441 about how to write a news release about a speech.

A number of other tactics are possible. One is the conversion of the speech into an op-ed article for newspapers and magazines. Another is the speech reprint, packaging the speech (with some editing) into a brochure that can be mailed to customers, employees, and opinion leaders in a particular industry. Excerpts can be posted, with video clips, on the organization's Web site.

on the job INSIGHTS

The Speech as News Release

The audience reach of a speech is multiplied many times when a news release is distributed that summarizes the speaker's key message. A speech news release follows many of the same structural guidelines outlined in Chapter 14, but there are some specific concepts that you should keep in mind.

"The key to writing stories about speeches is to summarize the speech or to present one or two key points in the lead sentence," says Douglas Starr, a professor of journalism and public relations at Texas A&M University.

In an article for *Public Relations Tactics*, Starr says a speech news release should follow a particular format. He says, "Answers to the questions—

Who, Said What, to Whom—must be in the lead of every speech story. Answers to the questions—Where, When, How, Why—may be placed in the second paragraph."

The most common mistake inexperienced writers make is to tell readers that a speaker spoke about a topic instead of saying what the speaker said about the topic. An example of the first approach is "Susan Jones, president of XYZ corporation, spoke about environmental regulations." A better approach would be, "Susan Jones, president of XYZ Corporation, says rigid environmental regulations are strangling the economy." See the difference?

The second sentence or paragraph of a speech news release usu-

ally describes the event where the speech was given, the location, the attendance, and the reason for the meeting. It is unnecessary, however, to give the title of a person's speech or even the theme of the convention or meeting. They are meaningless to the reader.

The third and subsequent paragraphs may contain speaker quotes, additional facts or figures, and other relevant information that helps provide context for the speech. When attributing quotes, "said" is the preferred verb. However, some writers vary this by using the terms *stated*, or *added*. Starr suggests you stay away from such attribution terms as *discussed*, *addressed*, and *spoke*, because they don't say anything.

Source: Dennis L. Wilcox. *Public Relations Writing and Media Techniques*, 5th ed. Boston: Allyn & Bacon, 2005, p. 493.

Another possibility is submitting the speech to the publication *Vital Speeches of the Day*. Some organizations even make arrangements for the speech to be printed as part of the *Congressional Record*.

SUMMARY

Media Interviews

A face-to-face interview with a print or broadcast journalist is a good way to communicate an organization's perspective. Before being interviewed, however, the individual should have a clear idea of what the journalist needs and how key messages of the organization can be effectively communicated. Public relations personnel often brief and prepare executives for various interviews.

News Conferences

A news conference is a way that an organization can distribute information to multiple journalists at the same

time. It is a format for journalists to ask questions. News conferences should only be held when there is news that requires elaboration and clarification.

Media Tours and Press Parties

These activities are designed to build a relationship with journalists and to offer them the opportunity to visit plant sites or other locations. Media tours should have news value and not be just a "junket" or "vacation" for journalists.

The Art of Speechwriting

This is a systematic process that requires research into the prospective audience and a thorough understanding of the speaker's beliefs and how he or she expresses them. The objectives and key message points must be decided upon. First an outline is done and then a draft of the speech is written.

Writing a Speech
The writing style and word choice must be designed for the ear. Writing should be conversational, concise, and clear. Simple sentences are preferred, and words should paint pictures in the minds of the audience. All speeches have a beginning, a middle, and an end.

Giving a Speech or Presentation
Unlike journalistic writing, in which the most important point is in the lead paragraph, a speech builds up to a main point. Before speaking before a group, it's wise to find out as much as you can about the group and its interests. Nonverbal communication is an important part of any presentation. A speaker should be enthusiastic, maintain eye contact with the audience, smile, and use gestures appropriately. Most speeches should be between 20 and 30 minutes long.

Visual Aids Help a Speech
People retain more information if they can hear and see it at the same time. The most common presentation software is PowerPoint, which can be used in a variety of ways. The major point is to keep slides simple and uncluttered. Other visual aids can include 35-mm slides, transparencies, charts and graphs, and flip charts.

Speaker Training
Public relations personnel often train executives to give effective speeches and presentations. Such appearances give the organization a human face and help build relationships. Another area is media training. Executives and middle managers must know how the media operates and how to give succinct, short answers.

Publicity Opportunities for Speakers
The audience for a speech can be expanded through publicity, such as news releases, media advisories, speech reprints, op-ed articles, and video clips of the speech on the organization's Web site. The speech also can be Webcast to journalists in real time or delayed for later viewing.

CASE ACTIVITY What Would You Do?

Speechwriting is a highly refined skill. The president of a local company has hired you to write a 15-minute speech that he plans to present at the monthly meeting of the American Management Association. This group, consisting of corporate managers, wants to hear the president's views on the pros and cons of outsourcing various corporate functions, such as accounting, customer service, and management information systems (MIS), to locations such as India, where labor costs are cheaper. The president is a busy man, but he does tell you that he thinks outsourcing is an excellent way to keep American business and industry competitive. Taking the audience into consideration, do some research and draft a speech for the president. You should aim to write a speech that is five pages, doubled-spaced.

QUESTIONS for Review and Discussion

1. What preliminary steps should be taken before conducting a media interview?
2. What are the differences between a print and a broadcast interview?
3. What are the eight aspects of organization for an effective speech?
4. Why should an executive work with a speechwriter on drafting and formatting a particular speech or presentation?
5. How does writing a speech differ from writing a news release or even a brochure?
6. Give at least five tips about the use of words in a speech.
7. Every speaker engages in nonverbal communication. What is nonverbal communication? Can you give some examples?
8. Why is it necessary to know the demographics and interests of your audience before you speak? How do you find this information?

9. How long is a typical speech? How long is the text of a 20-minute speech?
10. What gestures should you avoid when giving a speech?
11. Is there any evidence that visual aids improve the effectiveness of a presentation?
12. Identify at least three ways that PowerPoint software can be used.
13. What are some general guidelines for using Power-Point slides?
14. Why do executives and middle managers need media training?
15. What can you do before and after a speech is given to generate media publicity and expand the audience for the speech?
16. Do public relations practitioners always have to honor a media request for an interview with the CEO? Why or why not?
17. What are the logistics of organizing a news conference?
18. How do press parties and media tours differ?
19. Should organizations pick up the tab for journalists who go on a media tour? What about giving journalists gifts?

SUGGESTED READINGS

Bush, Michael. "Hanes goes Hollywood for its 'Panti-monium' launch party," *PRWeek*, May 8, 2006, p. 3.

Friedman, Karen. "Culture Club: Tips for Speaking with International Audiences." *Public Relations Tactics*, February 2005, p. 29.

Friedmann, Lynne. "Who Let the Dogs Out? What They Don't Teach You About Running a News Conference." *Public Relations Tactics*, May 2006, p. 19.

Hedges, Kristi. "Be Ready to Meet the Press: The Keys to Effective Media-Training Program." *Public Relations Tactics*, May 2005, p. 22.

Ketchner, Kathy. "Preparing for Better Presentations." *Public Relations Tactics*, February 2004, p. 27.

Lukaszewski, James. "Overcoming the Commonplace: The Seven Serious Weaknesses Found in Most Media Training." *Public Relations Tactics*, February 2006, p. 10.

Lukaszewski, James. "Talking Business: The Secrets, Strategies and Skills To Making Powerful and Purposeful Presentations." *Public Relations Tactics*, November 2005, p. 14.

McKenna, Ted. "The Power from the Podium." *PRWeek*, March 12, 2007, p. 14.

Nolan, Hamilton. "The Funny Thing About Speechwriting." *PRWeek*, March 6, 2006, p. 18.

Nolan, Hamilton. "Good Ways to Deliver Bad News." *PRWeek*, March 7, 2005, p. 18.

Sietel, Fraser. "Researching the Speech." *O'Dwyer's PR Services Report*, May 2005, p. 52.

Stolberg, Sheryl. "Clock Ticking, Speechwriters for Bush Seek Perfect Pitch." *New York Times*, December 20, 2006, p. A10.

Sullivan, Cindy. "He Said, She Said: The Seven Habits of an Effective Spokespeson." *Public Relations Tactics*, May 2005.

Ward, David. "Short, Sweet, and to the Point." *PRWeek*, February 5, 2007, p. 18.

CHAPTER 17

Corporations

Today's Modern Corporation

Today, giant corporations have operations and customers around the world. International conglomerates control subsidiary companies that often produce a grab bag of seemingly unrelated products under the same corporate banner. These companies deal with a number of governments at many levels. Their operations affect the environment, control the employment of thousands, and have an impact on the financial and social well-being of millions.

The large size of these corporations, however, also brings remoteness. A corporation has a "face" in terms of its products, logo, and brand being readily visible in advertising and billboards from Azerbaijan to Zimbabwe and all the nations in between. However, the average consumer really can't comprehend organizations such as Wal-Mart, with $312 billion in worldwide sales, or MobilExxon, with $371 billion in global sales. These figures boggle the mind, and they represent more than the combined gross national product (GNP) of many nations.

As a result, the public is distrustful of the power, influence, and credibility of such giant corporations and business in general. When U.S. gasoline prices rise rapidly, for example, suspicion spreads that the oil companies have conspired to gouge the public, a distrust that the oil companies never fully allay. Major corporate financial scandals and the misdeeds of corporate executives also take their toll.

For example, fewer than 3 in 10 Americans (27 percent) feel that most large U.S. corporations are trustworthy, according to a recent Roper survey. And a Gallup poll reveals that business leaders and stockbrokers have joined used car dealers in the category of "least trusted" individuals in American society. Gallup polls also indicate that 82 percent of the public believes that the top executives of larger corporations receive outrageous salaries in the millions of dollars and, at the same time, improperly use corporate funds to fund lavish lifestyles.

Public perceptions of greed and corporate misdeeds are reinforced by stories in the media. Hundreds of stories were written about celebrity CEO Martha Stewart's indictment, trial, and conviction for lying to federal investigators about a stock sale, but other executives from such corporations as Enron, WorldCom, Adelphia, and Tyco were also in the news for falsifying financial records or raiding the corporate treasury. By early 2007, the number of prosecutions for white-collar crime became a major business news topic involving other major corporations with household names. The CEO of telecommunications giant Quest became the latest in a line of corporate princes who were sentenced to spend their golden years in a penitentiary.

The Role of Public Relations

The extensive negative publicity about corporations and business in general over the past several years has made it imperative that companies make a special effort to regain public credibility and trust. Thus, the concept of *corporate social responsibility* (CSR) is now high on the priority list of executives and their public relations staffs who are charged with improving the reputation and citizenship of their employers.

Indeed, the public relations profession has taken steps to outline a plan of action for rebuilding public trust in business. A coalition of 19 U.S.-based organizations—including the Council of Public Relations Firms, the International Association of Business Communicators, and the National Investor Relations Institute—published a white paper in 2003 titled *Restoring Trust in Business: Models for Action*.

"These are people who deal with trust issues all the time," says James Murphy, global managing director of communications for Accenture, and chair of the coalition. "Therefore, we're in a good position to address them." The 10-page white paper asked American businesses and their leaders to act in three main areas:

1. adopt ethical principles,
2. pursue transparency and disclosure, and
3. make trust a fundamental precept of corporate governance.

Copies of the report were sent to *Fortune* 500 CEOs and to the 50,000 public relations professionals represented by member groups in the coalition.

The importance of public relations in CSR is explained by Jack Bergen, senior vice president of marketing and communications for Siemens Corporation. He told *PRWeek*:

> We are the eyes and ears of an organization. The best way to be socially responsible is to have your eyes and ears trained on all the stakeholders, to know what they want and need from the company. These are classic public affairs issues and the idea that they should be handled by anyone else would show a lack of understanding.

A number of strategies and tactics can be used to implement CSR, which involves corporate performance as well as effective communications. One of the more important ones is the role of the public relations executive in counseling the CEO.

The public relations executive serves as a link between the chief executive and the realities of the marketplace and the organization, according to Mark Schumann, global communications practice leader with Tower Perrin. He told an international IABC conference that CEOs are often "disconnected" and surrounded by other executives who simply agree with whatever the CEO says. Schumann told *PRWeek*, ". . . everyone sucks up and lies to them." Schumann believes corporate public relations professionals should be the ". . . playwright and director, but we also need to be the toughest critics" to ensure that the CEO comes across as concerned and involved with employees and customers.

Corporations seek a better reputation for a variety of reasons. First, responsible business practices ward off increased government regulation. As a result of major financial scandals such as Enron, the U.S. Congress passed additional laws regarding accounting practices and disclosure (see discussion about the Sarbanes-Oxley Act in Chapter 12). Second, there is the matter of employee morale; companies with good policies and a good reputation tend to have less employee turnover. Corporate reputation also affects the bottom line. A survey of executives by the Center for Corporate Citizenship with the Hitachi Foundation, for example, found that 82 percent of the respondents believe that good corporate citizenship contributes to meeting the organization's financial objectives. In addition, 53 percent say corporate citizenship is important to their customers.

Being a good corporate citizen is an admirable goal, but corporations also face a number of pressures and counterpressures when making decisions and forming policies. General Electric, one of the world's largest corporations, with a market value of about $340 billion, once outlined four key factors that have to be considered at all times when making a decision:

- **Political.** How do government regulations and other pressures affect the decision?
- **Technological.** Do we have the engineering knowledge to accomplish the goal?

♦ **Social.** What is our responsibility to society?

♦ **Economic.** Will we make a profit?

The following sections discuss various facets of today's modern corporation and kinds of activities that require the expertise and counsel of public relations professionals.

Media Relations

Reporting by the media is a major source of public information and perceptions about the business world and individual companies. In recent years, the news hasn't been all that favorable.

Major financial scandals and other negative coverage can cause a corporation's reputation to plummet. Wal-Mart, once ranked number one in corporate reputation, saw its position drop to seventh in the space of six months after coverage regarding the hiring of illegal immigrants and the filing of a class-action suit that claimed that it discriminated against female employees.

As a result, corporate executives are somewhat defensive about how journalists cover business, because they feel that too much emphasis has been given to corporate misdeeds. One survey of executives, by Jericho Communications, found that almost half of the respondents agreed with the statement that a "CEO must view the media as an enemy." Another 60 percent said an executive can best avoid controversy by "limiting exposure to the media" and through "secrecy and tighter control of information."

Many corporate executives take this approach because they have several continuing complaints about media coverage. These include inaccuracy, incomplete coverage, inadequate research and preparation for interviews, and antibusiness bias. One survey by the American Press Institute, for example, found about a third of the CEOs polled were dissatisfied with the business news they found in their local newspapers.

> " You (executives) should communicate factually, frequently, and consistently. Use this time wisely, say the journalists, to position yourself. "
>
> ———*Don Middleburg,*
> Euro RSCG

Business editors and reporters state in response that often they cannot publish or broadcast thorough, evenhanded stories about business because many company executives, uncooperative and wary, erect barriers against them. Writers complain about their inability to obtain direct access to decision-making executives and being restricted to using news releases that don't contain the information they need. Journalists assert, too, that some business leaders don't understand the concept of objectivity and assume that any story involving unfavorable news about their company is intentionally bad.

Journalists also say it's a major mistake for corporate executives to slash public relations and communications during times of financial scandal and economic downturn. A survey of journalists conducted by Middleberg Euro RSCG, a public relations firm, and the Columbia University Graduate School of Journalism, found that journalists also believe corporations should focus on delivering more fact-driven messages. Don Middleberg, director of the survey, told *PRWeek,* "You (executives) should communicate factually, frequently, and consistently. Use this time wisely, say the journalists, to position yourself."

Public relations practitioners serving businesses stand in the middle. They must interpret their companies and clients to the media, while showing their chief executive and other high officials how open, friendly media relations can serve their interests.

One major interest that executives have is corporate reputation, and this is often tarnished or enhanced by the type of media coverage that an organization receives.

One survey by Hill & Knowlton, for example, found that Canadian CEOs believe that print and broadcast media criticism is the biggest threat to their company's reputation; even ahead of such things as disasters and allegations by the government about employee or product safety.

At the same time, surveys show that the media is probably the most effective way for an organization to get its message across and to achieve business goals. A *PRWeek* survey of CEOs, for example, found that:

- more than 80 percent of the respondents said conducting media interviews was the most effective way for the company to spread its message,
- followed by attending or speaking at industry conferences and tradeshows.
- In third place was meeting with key industry and financial analysts;
- fourth place was "authoring op-eds, bylined articles, or letters-to-the-editor." (Media and speaker training for executives was discussed in Chapter 16.)

Customer Relations

Customer service, in many respects, is the front line of public relations. A single incident, or a series of incidents, can severely damage a company's reputation and erode public trust in its products and services. Customer satisfaction is important because of word of mouth. A person who has a bad experience, surveys indicate, shares his or her story with an average of 17 people, whereas a person with a good experience will tell an average of 11 people.

The rapid growth of the Internet and blogs, however, has considerably changed the math. Today, a dissatisfied customer is capable of informing thousands, or even millions, of people in just one posting. One somewhat embarrassing example is what happened to Comcast. A customer videotaped a Comcast repairman sound asleep on the couch in his home and posted it on www.Snakesonablog.com. The clip was then picked up by a technology blog and then was also shown on a MSNBC program. In no time, about 200,000 people saw the video and Comcast was embarrassed enough to immediately send a team of technicians to the customer's home to fix the problem. The video, however, reached an even greater audience with a story about the video in the *New York Times*, which noted that the repairman had fallen asleep while he tried to get through to the cable company's repair office on the phone.

Further illustrating the problem, *Pittsburgh Post-Gazette* reporter Teresa Lindeman wrote:

> . . . companies that consider ignoring tales of dissatisfied customers might want to take a look at a study released yesterday by the Wharton School of the University of Pennsylvania. Researchers there found that more than 50 percent of Americans said they wouldn't go to a store if a friend had a bad shopping experience there. Even worse, when someone has a problem, it gets embellished with every retelling, and pretty soon that store has a really, really big problem.

Product recalls, in particular, test the patience of consumers and bring into question the credibility of the entire company for providing safe and quality products. Mattel, in the summer of 2007, had to recall more than 20 million toys because such famous icons as Barbie, Elmo, and Dora the Explorer were tainted with lead paint used by Chinese subcontractors. Earlier in the year, the RC2 company issued a recall of 1.5 million Thomas the Tank Engine wooden trains and other components that were contaminated with paint containing lead.

Mattel had to immediately begin a crisis communications program to reassure customers, particularly parents, that the company took product safety seriously and were taking steps to ensure the quality of its products. The CEO of Mattel appeared on a number of television news and talk show programs to explain the company's efforts, and full-page ads in the nation's press announced a three-point safety check of paint used on its toys: "(1) All paint must be tested before it is used on our toys. No exceptions; (2) We have significantly increased testing and unannounced inspections at every stage of production; and (3) We are testing every production run of finished toys to ensure compliance before they reach you." It also posted additional information about toy safety and recalls on www.mattel.com/safety/us/.

Julie Andres, director of corporate communications for Mattel, told *PRWeek* that she hoped all these efforts would keep Mattel's reputation intact. She added, "We definitely will take a look at our reputation management and hope we can continue to build trust with parents and communicate openly when we have issues and when we don't."

The Toy Industry Association (TIA) also sprang into action. It announced a year-long campaign to educate the media and consumers about a variety of topics, including how to buy proper toys for children. According to Julie Livingston, senior director of marketing communications for TIA, "There are obviously serious problems with the system, and they are going to be addressed immediately. We're doing everything we can to make sure of that, including working with government officials, major retailers, and our members."

The massive toy recall even shook consumer confidence in big retailers such as Wal-Mart, which is widely known for selling low-priced toys made in China. The retail giant also had to take steps to reassure its customers that their safety came first after one survey indicated that 56 percent of consumers believed Wal-Mart "was more interested in profits than people." For more insight on how to handle a product recall, see the PR Casebook about Dell on page 450.

Traditionally, customer service has been separate from the communications or public relations function in a company. Bob Seltzer, a leader in Ruder Finn's marketing practice, told *PRWeek*, "I defy anyone to explain the wisdom of this. How a company talks to its customers is among, if not the, most critical communications it has." Rande Swann, director of public relations for the Regional Airport Authority of Louisville, Kentucky, agrees. He says, "Our reputation is probably based more on how we serve our customers than any other single thing. If we don't have a reputation for great service, we don't have travelers."

Increasingly, however, corporations are realizing that customer relations serves as a telltale public relations barometer. Many public relations departments now regularly monitor customer feedback in a variety of ways to determine what policies and communication strategies need to be revised. One common method is to monitor customer queries to the organization's Web site. Indeed, most companies have a link for "contacting us" on its Web site. Another method is the content analysis of phone calls to the customer service center.

> " Ignoring complaints can ultimately damage a company's reputation. "
> ———*Andy Hopson,*
> Burson-Marsteller executive

This sharing of information is valuable from the standpoint of getting public relations professionals involved in active listening

PRCASEBOOK

Dell Computers Turns Lemons into Lemonade

Imagine that years ago, your little neighborhood lemonade stand sold a dozen cookies to valued customers up and down the street. You soon discovered that the cookies were made with rancid walnuts. You have a problem—a major product recall is required to save your good reputation, even though you did not make the cookies—your brother did!

Dell Computers faced exactly the same problem, but on a slightly larger, global scale! The company learned that as many as 4.2 million Sony-made batteries carrying the Dell brand name in its laptops could overheat and fail—or even explode in a customer's lap. By employing a systematic issues management process, Dell dealt with the problem ahead of all other major notebook sellers who also used batteries made by Sony.

Dell acted almost immediately on the basis of only six incidents, resisting the human inclination to ignore the problem or to shift blame to Sony. Corporate communication and investor relations staff (CorpComm/IR) took a proactive approach, focusing on the central message that Dell's paramount concern was the safety of its customers. No excuses were made and no blame-shifting occurred. By focusing on customer safety, Dell turned the problem into an opportunity to show its commitment to customers and customer safety, as well as its enormous database capability for serving individual customers during the recall process. Dell's neighborhood encompassed the globe, but worked much like a lemonade stand recall on a single street.

The planned recall announcement was leaked to the press, requiring Dell to accelerate its plans by 12 hours, including launching the recall Web site early. Public relations staff engaged top-tier media, such as the *New York Times,* CNBC, and leading regional media, to ensure a wide distribution of the key messages. Dell executives were placed on *Today* and Bloomberg TV that same day,

with subsequent global coverage on outlets such as BBC World News. Frequent and regular dialogue with target audiences was enhanced through the blogosphere. A blog entry was posted on an external blogsite as well as an in-house Web site called One Dell Way. The vice president of Global Corporate Communications/Investor Relations sent an update to some of Dell's top investors and financial analysts who cover Dell. Industry analysts who had been briefed by CorpComm/IR served as key partners in educating customers. The day of the announcement, Dell received more than 50 million hits on www.dellbattery-program.com, responded to more than 135,000 phone calls, and received more than 150,000 battery replacement orders. Dell shipped the first replacement units the day it announced the recall.

Dell won a 2007 Silver Anvil Award from PRSA for successfully handling the largest global recall in the history of consumer electronics by doing the following:

- practicing proactive issues management
- maintaining a focused and positive message
- thoroughly executing both traditional and new media efforts for dissemination and monitoring
- backing up its communicated promises with good service to customers
- and serving the needs of three audiences that this chapter identifies as crucial to corporate success
  - customers
  - employees
  - shareholders

It is fair to say that the computer giant took the proverbial positive approach: When Dell received lemons, it made lemonade.

so they can strategize on what steps a company should take to ensure a good reputation among customers. As Andy Hopson, CEO of Burson-Marsteller's northeast region, told *PRWeek,* "Ignoring complaints can ultimately damage a company's reputation."

Public relations professionals also pay attention to consumer surveys. One such mechanism is the American Customer Satisfaction Index, which is the definitive benchmark of how buyers feel about what business is selling to them. The index, which has been tracking customer satisfaction for 200 companies in 40 industries for over a decade, has found that a company offering the lowest prices may not necessarily get the highest satisfaction rating. Wal-Mart, for example, only scores 75 out of 100 points, compared with the national average of 74.4 for all companies.

Reaching Diverse Markets

The United States is becoming more diverse every year, which is now being recognized by corporate marketing and communications departments. As racial and ethnic minorities continue to increase in number and become more affluent, they will constitute a larger share of the consumer marketplace. By the close of 2007, for example, it was estimated that buying power among Hispanics increased 315 percent over rates at the time of the census in 2000. The increase among Asians will be 287 percent, and among African Americans 170 percent. See also Chapter 11 about diverse audiences.

According to Gina Amaro, director of multicultural and international markets for *PR Newswire*, "Companies that focus solely on one audience when creating products are missing an enormous opportunity. Furthermore, companies that do not incorporate a multicultural marketing and PR campaign to communicate these products and services to their many niche audiences will miss even larger opportunities."

Many public relations firms have set up specialty practices for multicultural marketing and communications. Edelman Worldwide, for example, has a diversity practice that assists companies. One client, Unilever, hired Edelman to organize a Hispanic marketing communications campaign for six of its personal care products, including Dove Soap. Other examples of multicultural public relations campaigns are given throughout this book in Multicultural World boxes.

Companies also have set up departments to reach minority audiences. Wells Fargo Bank, for example, organized an Emerging Markets division to help increase home ownership among minority families. Part of this initiative is a Hispanic Customer Service Center in Las Cruces, New Mexico, which provides specialized services to Spanish-speaking homebuyers in 16 states. In addition to translating brochures and other information into Spanish, bilingual customer service representatives are available to answer e-mail and telephone inquiries. Bank of America also has a program, which was highlighted in Chapter 1.

Yahoo! also has recognized the potential of the Hispanic market. It began Yahoo! en Español, which is now the top online destination for U.S. Hispanics. Special features, such as music, news, and various promotions, are designed exclusively for this audience. Gina Amaro of PR Newswire agrees with this approach. She says that it is vitally important to build relationships with niche audiences by communicating to them in their language and culture.

As with many initiatives in public relations, there are two sides to most arguments. Efforts to accommodate Spanish speakers are met with criticism from some quarters. Those who feel illegal immigration is out of control criticize bilingual efforts in education and marketing. Clearly, public relations is strategic conflict management much of the time and the astute professional keeps a vigilant eye on seemingly innocent, positive communication programs that may stir controversy.

Consumer Activism

A dissatisfied customer can often be mollified by prompt and courteous attention to his or her complaint or even an offer by the company to replace the item or provide some discount coupons toward future purchases. A more serious and complex threat to

> " The people from PETA are not going to be satisfied unless we go out of business, but there are consumers less radical than PETA who are still concerned about animal-handling practices. "
>
> ——*Tyson* Foods spokesperson

corporate reputation, which can also affect sales, are consumer activists who demand changes in corporate policies.

Tyson Foods, a major American producer of meat and poultry products, was accused of inhumane treatment of animals by various animal rights groups, such as the People for the Ethical Treatment of Animals (PETA). The corporate response was to establish an office of animal well-being to assure retailers and consumers that it takes humane animal handling seriously.

Ed Nicholson, Tyson's director of media and community relations, told *PRWeek*, "The people from PETA are not going to be satisfied unless we go out of business, but there are consumers less radical than PETA who are still concerned about animal-handling practices." The new wellness office, headed by a veterinarian, will oversee audits of animal-handling practices and make them available to customers on request.

KFC also has been targeted by PETA and other animal rights groups, whose efforts have received extensive media publicity. The charges of inhumane animal treatment and how chickens are slaughtered can and do affect consumer buying decisions, especially when activists are outside a franchise wearing T-shirts that say "KFC Tortures Animals." In such a situation, the public relations staff has the difficult job of defending the company against what it believes are unfounded allegations and to also, at the same time, assure the public that KFC's policies do provide for the humane slaughter of its chickens.

Consequently, when it came to light that a KFC subcontractor was mistreating chickens, the company immediately called the abuse by workers appalling and told the subcontractor to clean up its act—or lose its contract. In this instance, because of a quick response, the media was able to include KFC's response in the story about the abuses, which were documented on videotape.

Coca-Cola also has reputation problems. Some activist groups charged the giant bottler with contributing to childhood obesity by selling its products in schools. Karl Bjorhus, director of health and nutrition communications for the bottler, told *PRWeek*, "We have been listening and trying to understand what people's concerns are."

As a result, the company partnered with the American Beverage Association and the Alliance for a Healthier Generation to voluntarily shift to lower calorie and healthier beverages in school vending machines. The shift was announced in 2006 and is scheduled to be completed in the 2009–2010 school year. In a company news release, Don Knauss, president of Coca-Cola North America, said:

> By combining our product offerings with the nutrition and physical education programs we support, such as Live It!, Triple Play and Copa Coca-Cola, we can help put schools at the forefront of the efforts to create a healthier generation. . . .

Corporations face a variety of challenges today from advocacy groups quite adept at generating media coverage for their particular cause. Here, the People for the Ethical Treatment of Animals (PETA) demonstrate outside a Kentucky Fried Chicken restaurant in Hong Kong to protest what they claim is the restaurant chain's cruel treatment of chickens.

We feel strongly that by advocating these new guidelines, and accelerating the shift to low-calorie and nutritious beverages for the school environment, we can also strengthen our industry's ability to counter the perception by our critics that some of our products don't fit into a balanced diet. It's a perception that is simply not true. Our broad range of beverages will continue to be a part of occasions where the need for hydration, refreshment, nutrition and celebration go hand-in-hand with physical activity, fun and enjoyment.

The responsibility for achieving balanced lifestyles is shared by everyone. We can all work together to encourage choices that include a balanced and nutritious mix of foods, beverages and physical activity. Everyone has a role to play. With today's announcement, we're joining in to do our part.

Another activist group had other concerns. One campaign, Stop Killer Coke, claimed that Coca-Cola was using paramilitary thugs in Colombia to intimidate workers and prevent unionization. The company said the charges were "false and outrageous," but that didn't stop the campaign's organizers from spreading the word to colleges, high schools, and unions. As a result, at least six colleges booted Coke beverages off their campuses, and several food co-ops decided to stop selling Coke products. In such a situation, even false allegations can affect the sales of a product. For a related problem, see the Ethics box on page 454.

In today's climate of media attention to health-related topics such as obesity, every food product company is suspect. McDonald's was the subject of a movie documentary, *Super Size Me*, in which the producer decided to eat three meals a day at McDonald's for several months. He of course details how all the "junk food" made him overweight and prone to major health problems.

In this case, McDonald's reaction was aggressive. Walt Riker, vice president of corporate communications, told *PRWeek*,

> We're responding aggressively because the film is a gross misrepresentation of what McDonald's is about. The scam in the movie is that he has given the impression of that he only ate three basic meals a day, but the reality is that he stuffed himself with 5,000 to 7,000 calories, which is two or three times the recommended amount.

According to *PRWeek*, "McDonald's has been engaging the media in interviews and the company has made its global nutritionist, Cathy Kapica, available." Kapica appeared on CNN and CNBC, and gave a number of newspaper interviews about the film producer's "extreme behavior." The company also distributed a VNR and an ANR giving its views on smart choices in diet and exercise. It also sent briefing materials to its 2,700 franchises so they could talk to local media in an informed way.

Ford Motor Company also faced reputation and trust problems with consumers after Bluewater, an environmental group, took out full-page ads in various newspapers accusing the automaker of continuing to make "America's worst gas guzzlers." The ads went on to say, "Don't Buy Bill Ford's Environmental Promises. Don't Buy His Cars."

At the strategic level, a company weighs the potential impact of the charges or allegations on potential customer reaction and possible effect on sales before deciding on a course of action.

> " We're responding aggressively because the film is a gross misrepresentation of what McDonald's is about. The scam in the movie is that he has given the impression that he only ate three basic meals a day, but the reality is that he stuffed himself with 5,000 to 7,000 calories, which is two or three times the recommended amount. "
>
> ———*Walt Riker*, VP of McDonald's

on the job
ETHICS

Congressional Committee Criticizes Yahoo's Ethics

"While technologically and financially you are giants, morally you are pygmies." This is what Rep. Tom Lantos (D-CA) told the CEO of Yahoo at a hearing of the House Foreign Affairs Committee investigating Yahoo's operations in China.

The issue was Yahoo's cooperation with the Chinese government to turn over the name and email account of a journalist that the government said had violated "state secrets" by using the Internet to send information to an overseas Web site. The journalist, Shi Le, got 10 years in prison. As the *Wall Street Journal* commented, "In China, privacy takes a back seat to laws governing criticism of the government . . ."

Yahoo executives said they had no choice in the matter because they must obey the laws of the country where they do business. They also say that Yahoo's employees in China could face prosecution for violating Chinese law. There, of course, is also the business side. China, with its one billion citizens, is a very lucrative market for companies such as Yahoo, Microsoft, and Google.

Congressional critics and human rights activists, however, say U.S. companies operating overseas should adhere to American values such as freedom of speech and right of assembly, even in such nations as China that don't share those values. An editorial in the *San Jose* (CA) *Mercury News*, located in Yahoo's backyard, flatly stated, "U.S. firms shouldn't abandon values overseas."

The Yahoo situation highlights the risk that comes with overseas operations. On one hand, the huge Chinese market cannot be ignored. Yet, companies who cooperate with repressive governments also face a potentially high cost in negative publicity and criticism for lack of ethics. Thus, gains in China may be offset by backlash from American consumers and investors. On the day after the Congressional hearing, for example, Yahoo's stock dropped five percent when the stock market was generally up.

Yahoo got the message. The company, in an effort to stem the negative publicity in the aftermath of the Congressional hearing, announced that it had settled a lawsuit with the family of the imprisoned journalist and would pay the legal costs of appealing his case. In addition, Yahoo announced it would set up a fund that would provide humanitarian and legal aid to dissidents who have been imprisoned for expressing their opinions online. Jerry Yang, president of Yahoo, issued a statement, "We are committed to making sure our actions match our values around the world."

What's your assessment? Do you think Yahoo's cooperation with the Chinese government to track down a pro-democracy activist was ethical? Or is it more important to obey the laws of the country even if you disagree with them? From a public relations viewpoint, do you think Yahoo helped restore its ethical reputation by settling a lawsuit and setting up a fund to provide legal aid to dissidents who have been imprisoned?

This threat appraisal concept was discussed in Chapter 10. Activist consumer groups are a major challenge to the public relations staff of an organization. Do you accommodate? Do you stonewall? Do you change policy? A discussion of issues management is in Chapter 10, but here are some general guidelines from Douglas Quenqua, which appeared in *PRWeek*, on how to be proactive.

Do

◆ Work with groups who are more interested in solutions than getting publicity.

◆ Offer transparency. Activists who feel you're not open aren't likely to keep dealing with you.

◆ Turn their suggestions into action. Activists want results.

Don't

◆ Get emotional when dealing with advocacy groups.

◆ Agree to work with anyone making threats.

◆ Expect immediate results. Working with adversaries takes patience—establishing trust takes time.

Consumer Boycotts

The *boycott*—a refusal to buy the products or services of an offending company—has a long history and is a widely used publicity tool of the consumer movement.

PETA, for example, announced that consumers should boycott Safeway until it improved conditions for farm animals. The key aspect of theater for this protest was Safeway's annual stockholders' meeting in which activists would unfurl a banner saying, "Safeway means animal cruelty." It had, as *PRWeek* says, "all the makings of a PR person's worst nightmare."

Safeway headed off a boycott by negotiating. Just days before the annual meeting, the company's public affairs staff began working with PETA and quickly announced new standards for monitoring conditions with meat suppliers. Instead of a protest, PETA supporters showed up at the annual meeting with a large "Thank You" sign for entering stockholders. In addition, PETA ended its 20-state boycott of the chain. The director of public affairs for Safeway said the boycott didn't have any effect on sales, but PETA took a different track. Its director told *PRWeek*, "It's just a truism that you don't want your corporation targeted by activists. My hunch is the timing of the call (from Safeway public affairs) was not purely coincidental."

The success of consumer boycotts is mixed. Various activist groups have boycotted Procter & Gamble for years without much effect because the company makes so many products under separate brand names that consumers can't keep track of what P&G makes. On the other hand, a single product name is more vulnerable.

Activists point out that a boycott doesn't have to be 100 percent effective in order to change corporate policies. Even a 5 percent drop in sales will often cause corporations to rethink their policies and mode of operations. Nike got serious about sweatshop conditions abroad only after activist groups caused its stock and sales to drop. Nike was losing market share, so it decided to formulate new policies for its subcontractors abroad and become active in a global alliance of manufacturers to monitor working conditions in overseas factories.

Employee Relations

Employees have been called the organization's "ambassadors." Consequently, the public relations department, often working with the human resources department, concentrates on communicating with employees just as vigorously as it does on delivering the corporate story to the outside world. A workplace that respects its management, has pride in its products, and believes it is being treated fairly is a key factor in corporate success.

Surveys indicate, however, that the success of communication efforts varies widely among organizations. According to a survey of 1,000 U.S. workers by Towers Perrin, 20 percent believe their organization does not tell them the truth. About half of the respondents say their company generally tells employees the truth, and about the same percentage believe that their employers try too hard to "spin" the truth. Another finding: Almost half believe they get more reliable information from their direct supervisors than they do from senior executives.

The extensive media coverage of corporate scandals also has taken its toll in terms of employee perceptions. A Fleishman-Hillard survey of workers, for example, found that 80 percent believe that greed is driving corporate scandals. The majority also agreed that corporations care more about stock value than customers' needs. On the plus side, however, more than 70 percent of the respondents thought the information they received from their employer was "adequate" to "very comprehensive."

The value of credible and trustworthy communications cannot be underestimated. Mark Schumann of Towers Perrin told *Public Relations Tactics*, "Regardless of the topic, an organization will find it difficult to motivate, engage, and retain their most talented employees if their messages are not believed." Don Etling of Fleishman-Hillard told *PRWeek*, "We look at internal communications as something that affects performance, whether you have two or 200 employees. Companies that do a good job of explaining their values, not just to their partners, investors, and clients, but also to their employees, seem to enjoy better results. . . . Companies really need to look at this as a performance issue."

A good example of successful corporate policies that build employee loyalty is the annual survey by *Working Mother* magazine that compiles a list of the 100 best companies for working mothers. An analysis of these companies, compared with other organizations, shows the following:

- 100 percent of the 100 best companies offer flextime, versus 55 percent companies nationwide.
- 99 percent of the 100 best offer an employee assistance program, versus 67 percent nationwide.
- 98 percent of the 100 best offer elder-care resource and referral services, versus 20 percent nationwide.
- 96 percent of the 100 best offer child-care resource and referral services, versus 18 percent nationwide.
- 94 percent of the 100 best offer compressed workweeks, versus 31 percent nationwide.
- 93 percent of the 100 best offer job-sharing, versus 22 percent nationwide.

Many employee issues must be addressed by the company, and public relations professionals often are involved in counseling not only what policies should be created but how they should be implemented and communicated. One such issue is health and medical benefits. Company information about benefits should be written in plain English instead of legalese so employees thoroughly understand what is covered. If there is a change in a health plan, the company must spend time and effort, often through small group meetings, to explain the changes and why they are necessary.

Another issue is sexual harassment. This worries both employees and management for both legal and ethical reasons. The U.S. Supreme Court ruled in *Monitor Savings Bank v. Vinson* (1986) that a company may be held liable in sexual harassment suits even if management is unaware of the problem and has a general policy condemning any form of verbal or nonverbal behavior that causes employees to feel "uncomfortable" or consider the workplace a "hostile environment."

Organizations, to protect themselves from liability and the unfavorable publicity of a lawsuit, not only must have a policy, they must also clearly communicate the policy to employees and conduct workshops to ensure that everyone thoroughly understands what might be considered sexual harassment. What about off-color jokes at the water cooler or via e-mail? Yes. What about a *Playboy* calendar in someone's cubicle? Certainly yes. What about a coworker constantly asking you for a date? Absolutely yes. See Chapter 12 about company monitoring of employee e-mails.

Layoffs and Outsourcing

Layoffs present a major public relations challenge to an organization. Julie Hood, an editor of *PRWeek*, says it best: "The way in which a company handles job reductions can have a significant impact on its reputation, its share price, and its ongoing ability to recruit and maintain good staff. And that presents a major challenge for communication departments."

Although human resource (HR) departments are most involved in layoffs, it's also a situation in which the expertise of the public relations department is harnessed to ensure employee understanding and support. One cardinal rule is that a layoff is never announced to the media before employees are first informed. Another cardinal rule is that employees should be informed in person by their immediate supervisor—the traditional "pink slip" or an e-mail message is unacceptable. Employees who are being retained should also be called in by their immediate supervisor to let them know their status.

The rumor mill works overtime when there is uncertainty among employees about their job security, so it's also important for the company to

When internal public relations programs fail to build and maintain a positive relationship between employer and employee, the inevitable tensions and conflicts between management and worker can erupt into protests and group actions that damage both the reputation and bottom line of corporations.

publicly announce the layoffs and the impact as quickly as possible. Companies should be very forthright and upfront about layoffs; this is not the time to issue vague statements and "maybes" that just fuel the rumor mill.

Companies that are interested in their reputation and employee trust also make every effort to cushion the layoff by implementing various programs. Merrill Lynch, for example, laid off 6,000 employees by giving them the option of "voluntary separation" in exchange for one year's pay and a percentage of their annual bonus. Other companies offer out-placement services, the use of office space, and other programs. Such programs do much to retain employee goodwill even as workers are being laid off.

A more contentious issue, which has become an emotional and political football in recent years, is the matter of outsourcing white-collar jobs to such nations as India. The practice is commonly called *offshoring*, and many American companies are now using lower-paid professionals in India and other Asian nations to do everything from customer service to software engineering and accounting. Recently, a weekly newspaper in the United States outsourced news coverage of the city commission, which webcasts all of its proceedings. Reporters in India now cover that beat.

Prior to this, labor unions and human rights groups had raised the issue of sweat-shop labor in which women and children were being exploited in Third World facto-ries. This time, however, offshoring is being framed by the media as a middle-class job drain that's taking a toll on educated workers. Jim Martinez of GCI public relations says the issue is the "perfect storm" generated by a number of political and economic factors coming together at the same time.

The increasing practice of offshoring presents major internal communication challenges for public relations departments. How do you explain the corporate policy? How do you overcome employee suspicion that their jobs are vulnerable because a software engineer in India works for half of what U.S. workers are paid?

Companies and various business associations have tried to show that offshoring doesn't really cause job losses in the United States or that outsourcing makes the com-pany more competitive and actually creates more U.S. jobs. The American Electronics Association (AEA) issued a report saying that offshoring is just the reality of the global economy, and it's unfair to blame it as the main cause of job losses. It remains to be seen whether U.S. employees are convinced.

Minorities in the Workforce

As discussed earlier, the United States is becoming more diverse. This brings intensi-fied problems of language and cultural differences to the workplace. Traditionally, senior executives have been white males, although there has been some advancement of females and racial/ethnic groups in the executive suite.

The greatest change, of course, has been in the composition of rank-and-file employ-ees. As more minorities join the workforce, often coming from different cultures and reli-gious faiths, an employer must be sensitive to their needs. English as a second language is one hurdle; public relations staffs must be sure that employee communications are written in plain English and that basic words are used to communicate key messages.

In today's world, companies must embrace diversity and also actively recruit eth-nic minorities and people of color. A failure to do so can cause major public relations problems for an organization. If a large minority group in the community believes a company fails to hire enough of its members, the result may be a product boycott, ral-lies at corporate headquarters, and even lawsuits—which usually are given extensive coverage in the media. Such situations should never arise if the company has good policies in place and it remains sensitive to employee concerns.

When it fails to do so, the cost in money and corporate reputation can be great. Texaco, Inc., provides a notorious example. After lingering in federal court for more than two years, a suit against the oil company by 1,300 employees charging racial dis-crimination was blown wide open by disclosure of tapes recorded secretly at meetings of company executives. The executives were heard using racial slurs against employees and discussing the destruction of documents the employees might use in their suit. Eleven days later, Texaco agreed to pay $176 million to settle the case—the largest settlement ever in a racial discrimination suit.

Investor Relations

Another major component of keeping a company's health and wealth is communicat-ing with shareholders and prospective investors. *Investor relations* (IR) is at the center of that process.

The goal of investor relations is to combine the disciplines of communications and finance to accurately portray a company's prospects from an investment standpoint. Some key audiences are financial analysts, individual and institutional investors, shareholders, prospective shareholders, and the financial media. Increasingly, employees are an important public, too, because they have stock options and 401 plans.

Individuals who specialize in investor or financial relations, according to salary surveys, are the highest-paid professionals in the public relations field. One reason for this is that they must be very knowledgeable about finance and a myriad of regulations set down by the SEC on initial stock offerings (IPOs), mergers, accounting requirements, the contents of quarterly financial reports, and public disclosure of information. A company going public for the first time, for example, is required by the SEC to observe a "quiet period" when company executives are not allowed to talk about the offering to analysts or the financial press to avoid "hyping" the stock.

Google's initial public offering (IPO) of its stock on the New York Stock Exchange had to be delayed because CEO and founder Marc Benioff made some comments about the stock offering in a major magazine interview during the SEC's mandated "quiet period." The foul-up gave Google a rocky start in terms of positioning the stock and building a good impression among Wall Street analysts. See Chapter 12 for more information about the SEC.

Mergers also require the expertise of investor relations professionals in order to satisfy FTC antimonopoly rules and also to keep the various publics informed. The acquisition of Wild Oats, the second-largest organic and fine-food grocery chain in the country, by the largest chain, Whole Foods, was put into jeopardy when it was learned that the CEO of Whole Foods had been making anonymous postings on the Internet denigrating Wild Oats to drive down the purchase price. The deal was ultimately approved, but the image of Whole Foods as a "wholesome" organization was besmirched and the acquisition was delayed while the SEC conducted an investigation. Later, the Whole Foods board of directors announced a policy that no executive should make comments on the Internet unless he or she properly identified themselves.

Investor relations staff must be very comfortable with numbers, as they primarily communicate with institutional investors, individual investors, stockbrokers, and financial analysts. They are also sources of information for the financial press such as the *Wall Street Journal*, *Barron's*, and the *Financial Times*. In their jobs, they make many presentations, conduct field trips for analysts and portfolio managers, analyze stockholder demographics, oversee corporate annual reports, and prepare materials for potential investors.

This employment ad by Kimberly-Clark illustrates the type of communication professionals who are needed to guide a company's internal and external communications.

Marketing Communications

Many companies use the tools and tactics of public relations to support the marketing and sales objectives of their business. This is called *marketing communications* or *marketing public relations.*

Thomas L. Harris, author of *A Marketer's Guide to Public Relations*, defines marketing public relations (MPR) as "The process of planning, executing, and evaluating programs that encourage purchase and consumer satisfaction through credible communication of information and impressions that identify companies and their products with the needs, wants, concerns, and interests of consumers."

In many cases, marketing public relations is coordinated with a company's messages in advertising, marketing, direct mail, and promotion. This has led to the concept of *integrated marketing communications* (IMC) in which companies manage all sources of information about a product or service in order to ensure maximum message penetration. This approach was first discussed in Chapter 1 as a major concept in today's modern public relations practice.

In an integrated program, for example, public relations activities are often geared to obtaining early awareness and credibility for a product. Publicity in the form of news stories builds credibility, excitement in the marketplace, and consumer anticipation. These messages make audiences more receptive to advertising and promotions about the product in the later phases of the campaign. Indeed, there is a growing body of support that public relations is the foundation stone for branding and positioning a product or service.

The potato industry decided to reintroduce its product, which had taken a hit because of the popularity of low-carb diets such as Atkins and South Beach. The United States Potato Board partnered with Fleishman-Hillard to launch an integrated communication campaign. The campaign used advertising in the *New York Times*, *Washington Post*, and *USA Today* to generate interest within the media. The ads focused on the FDA nutrition label and endorsements by nutritionists who identified the potato's key nutrition benefits and introduced the "healthy potato" campaign theme.

Simultaneously, press kits were distributed, an exclusive appeared in the *New York Times*, and a nutritionist briefed food and nutrition editors. The United States Potato Board's Web site was redesigned to be more consumer friendly, its URL was changed to healthypotato.com, and new recipes were featured. A partnership was developed with Weight Watchers to inform that organization's dieters of the potato as a health food and to co-release a VNR. Registered dieticians were enlisted as regional spokespersons. And a registered dietician testified before the congressional Dietary Guidelines Advisory Committee as the committee reviewed the nation's dietary standards.

The campaign was evaluated as a success.

◆ It reached 140 million people with the combination of advertising and publicity.

◆ A senior editor at *Cooking Light* magazine commended the campaign before a meeting of the International Association of Culinary Professionals.

◆ The new congressional nutritional guidelines were favorable for the potato.

The objectives of marketing communications, often called *marcom* in industry jargon, are accomplished in several ways.

Product Publicity

The cost and clutter of advertising have mounted dramatically, and companies have found that creative product publicity is a cost-effective way of reaching potential customers. Even mundane household products, if presented properly, can be newsworthy and catch media attention.

Clorox, for example, generated many news articles and broadcast mentions for its Combat cockroach killer by sponsoring a contest to find America's five worst cockroach-infested homes. And Dove Deodorant sponsored a Most Beautiful Underarms pageant at Grand Central Station in New York. Miss Florida won the crown. The contest received airtime on *Today*, *Fox & Friends*, and mention on the news shows of 400 television stations.

A company also can generate product publicity by sponsoring a poll. The Clor-Trimeton Allergy Index has measured pollen counts since 1984. Polls, in order to get media attention, can be somewhat frivolous and even unscientific. *Food & Wine* magazine, along with America Online, did such a survey and announced to the world that the supermarket checkout line is the most popular choice for where to meet a mate. It also found that whipped cream is the sexiest food, but that chocolate mousse is better than sex.

Product Placement   A product that appears as part of a movie or television program is a form of product placement. As was discussed in Chapter 15, a brand is built by exposure in multiple films and television shows.

Increasingly, product placements are the result of fees paid to film studios and television producers. At times, there is a trade-off; Gap, for example, volunteers to provide the entire wardrobe for a television show, which reduces the cost of production for the producer and also gives the clothing firm high visibility.

On occasion, the filmmaker has a story line that requires a specific product. Tom Hanks, for example, played a FedEx man stranded on a deserted island in *Cast Away*. *Where the Heart Is* was a tale of a pregnant teen living in an Oklahoma Wal-Mart. Both corporations gave their permission for portrayal of its product. In another situation, the movie *Harold and Kumar Go to White Castle* gave the White Castle chain national visibility. The film producers originally wrote the screenplay for Krispy Kreme doughnuts, but that company refused permission, because the two characters in the movie smoke marijuana and are somewhat slovenly characters. That didn't bother White Castle.

Stuart Elliott and Julie Bosman, writing in the *New York Times*, explained the allure of product integration:

> [Opportunities to promote products inside television shows] . . . come in the form of what is called branded entertainment or product integration. They include mentioning brands in lines of dialogue, placing products in scenes so they are visible to viewers, and giving advertisers roles in plots of shows, whether it is a desperate housewife showing off a Buick at a shopping mall or a would-be apprentice trying to sell a new flavor of Crest toothpaste.
>
> The goal of branded entertainment is to expose ads to viewers in ways that are more difficult to zip through or zap than traditional commercials. Devices like digital video recorders and iPods are making it easier than ever to avoid or ignore conventional sales pitches.

Cause-Related Marketing

Companies in highly competitive fields, where there is little differentiation between products or services, often strive to stand out and enhance their reputation for CSR by

on the job INSIGHTS

Selection Criteria for Corporate Sponsorships

Corporations are inundated with requests from organizations to sponsor everything from rock concerts to museum exhibits and sporting events. Consequently, each corporation selects sponsorships that best support its marketing and public relations objectives. A company considering a sponsorship should ask these questions:

◆ Can the company afford to fulfill the obligation? The sponsorship fee is just the starting point. Count on doubling it to have an adequate total event budget.

◆ Is the event or organization compatible with the company's values and mission statement?

◆ Does the event reach the corporation's target audience?

◆ Is there enough time before the event to maximize the company's use of the sponsorship?

◆ Are the event organizers experienced and professional?

◆ Is the event newsworthy enough to provide the company with opportunities for publicity?

◆ Will the event be televised?

◆ Will the sales force support the event and use it to leverage sales?

◆ Does the event give the company a chance to develop new contacts and business opportunities?

◆ Can the company live with the event on a long-term basis while its value builds?

◆ Is there an opportunity for employee involvement? Corporate sponsorships can be used to build employee morale and teamwork.

◆ Is the event compatible with the "personality" of the company's products?

◆ Can the company reduce the cash outlay and enhance the marketing appeal by trading off products and in-kind services?

◆ Will management support the event? If the answer is yes to the previous questions, the likelihood of management support of the sponsorship is fairly high.

---

engaging in *cause-related marketing*. In essence, this means that a profit-making company collaborates with a nonprofit organization to advance its cause and, at the same time, increase sales. A good example is Dannon yogurt brand, which tells customers that 1.5 percent of its sales goes to support the National Wildlife Federation.

Companies supporting worthy causes have good customer support. One study, by Cone/Roper, found that 79 percent of Americans feel companies have a responsibility to support causes as part of its corporate citizenship. More important, 81 percent said they were likely to switch brands, when price and quality were equal, to support the cause.

Sometimes, a corporation will organize its own cause. Bristol-Myers Squibb, for example, organized a bicycle Tour of Hope to raise funds for cancer research and to help cancer survivors be more proactive in their care. Spectrum Science Public Relations was engaged to organize, promote, and publicize the cross-country tour. Cycling clubs and cancer advocacy groups were contacted to generate supporters for local rides, and a nationwide search was conducted to find avid cyclists who had a strong connection to cancer, either through relatives or their work.

Twenty-six cyclists were ultimately selected. They received two months of personal training and were given custom-made Trek racing bikes, the same model used by Lance Armstrong, seven-time champion of the Tour de France. The tour started in

Los Angeles and finished in Washington, D.C. John Seng, Spectrum president, told *PRWeek*, "It wasn't just about driving awareness, but motivating people to show their care and concern." More than $1.3 million was raised, 40,000 Cancer Promises were signed to find a cure for cancer, and almost 2,000 riders participated in the Tour of Hope.

Selecting a charity or a cause event to support involves strategic thinking. A chain of pet care stores, for example, would be better served by sponsoring projects with the Humane Society of America than contributing a percentage of its sales to the American Cancer Society. By the same token, a company such as Bristol-Myers Squibb that makes drugs to treat cancer would find such a relationship a good fit. Here are some tips for conducting cause-related marketing:

- Look for a cause related to your products or services or that exemplifies a product quality.
- Consider causes that appeal to your primary customers.
- Choose a charity that doesn't already have multiple sponsors.
- Choose a local organization if the purpose is to build brand awareness for local franchises.
- Don't use cause-related efforts as a tactic to salvage image after a major scandal; it usually backfires.
- Understand that association with a cause or nonprofit is a long-term commitment.
- Realize that additional budget must be spent to create public awareness and build brand recognition with the cause.

Corporate Sponsorships

A form of cause-related marketing is corporate sponsorship of various activities and events such as concerts, art exhibits, races, and scientific expeditions. The ultimate corporate sponsorship is the Olympics, which is discussed in the Multicultural box on page 465.

According to IEG, Inc. (www.sponsorship.com) companies spend about $10 billion annually sponsoring activities ranging from the Indianapolis 500, the Kentucky Derby, the Academy Awards, PGA golf tournaments, and even the road show of Britney Spears or Madonna. Many of these events, unlike causes, are money-making operations in their own right, but a large part of the underwriting often comes from sponsorships provided by other corporations. Sports sponsorships are further discussed in Chapter 22.

The popularity of sponsored events is due to several reasons. These events

1. enhance the reputation and image of the sponsoring company through association,
2. give product brands high visibility among key purchasing publics,
3. provide a focal point for marketing efforts and sales campaigns, and
4. generate publicity and media coverage.

Sponsorships can be more effective than advertising. Visa International, for example, spends about $200,000 annually sponsoring the USA-Visa Decathlon Team, or about the price of a 30-second prime-time television commercial. Speedo, the swimwear manufacturer, sponsors the U.S. Olympic swim team, but also gets its name before millions of television viewers, because most swimmers from other nations also wear Speedo swim caps and suits. In the Sydney games, about 70 percent of the gold medalists in swimming wore Speedo gear. This translates to brand dominance in sales.

Local stadiums and concert halls almost everywhere now have corporate names. An obscure technology company, 3COM, got reams of national publicity when Candlestick Park in San Francisco became 3COM Park. Naming rights to the new baseball stadium in San Francisco went to SBC. The facility is now called AT&T Park after SBC changed its name. In Philadelphia, Lincoln Financial Group—not exactly a household name—snapped up naming rights for the new stadium for the Eagles pro football team. The company's reasoning: Its name becomes recognized as a major brand by those attending Eagles games and the 10 to 12 million fans who watch home games on television.

Naming rights, however, are not forever, and the fortunes of high-flying corporations can change. Enron got great visibility by putting its name on the stadium of the Houston Astros, but its collapse into financial scandal caused the team to quickly disassociate itself from its corporate partner. Today, Minute Maid has its name emblazoned in stadium lights.

The demographic characteristics of potential customers determine, for the most part, what events a company will sponsor. Manufacturers of luxury products usually sponsor events that draw the interest of affluent consumers. That's why Lexus, a luxury car, sponsors polo championships. Tennis also has fairly affluent demographics, so Volvo sponsors tennis tournaments. General Motors GMC division, however, is interested in selling pickup trucks, so it sponsors a 15-city country-western music tour. See the Insights box on page 462 for more guidelines on corporate sponsorships.

On occasion, a company will sponsor an event for the primary purpose of enhancing its reputation among opinion leaders and influential decision makers. Atofina Chemicals, for example, usually sponsors events that advance science education. However, it did agree to sponsor an exhibit of Degas's ballet-themed works at the Philadelphia Art Museum to highlight the company's history as a Paris-based corporation. One objective was to increase employee pride. The company's 1,200 employees in Philadelphia and their families were invited to an exclusive showing at the museum before the exhibit was open to the public. In addition, the company used the exhibit and museum as a centerpiece for entertaining customers and their significant others. It also organized events for and donations of products to the Philadelphia High School for the Creative and Performing Arts.

Environmental Relations

Another aspect of CSR that is coming to the forefront in the first decade of the 21st century is increased corporate concern for the environment and the maintenance of sustainable resources.

The 1990s saw major clashes and confrontations between corporations and activist nongovernmental organizations (commonly referred to as NGOs) about a host of environmental and human rights issues. The trend line in the 21st century, however, is for more cooperation and partnerships among former adversaries. Dialogue between corporate public relations officers and senior representatives of Environmental Defense and Greenpeace occurs with increasing frequency and civility. Companies have realized that simply making claims to an environmental conscience, which is derisively called *greenwashing* by environmental groups, is not effective. In a recent *O'Dwyer's PR Report*, E. Bruce Harrison, corporate communications expert on environmental

on the job
A MULTICULTURAL WORLD

Olympic Torch Faces Ill Political Winds

Public relations staff at Coca-Cola and Samsung, two major corporate sponsors of the Olympic movement, faced an issues management challenge for the 2008 torch run to Beijing. The problem was not the incredibly long, complicated torch route of 137,000 kilometers over 130 days spanning five continents and scaling Mount Everest that was planned by the Chinese government.

The real problem was Taiwan, which posed a greater obstacle than the world's highest mountain. Taiwan, claiming its independent status from China, refused to be a part of the torch route, asserting that setting the torch itinerary to go directly from Taiwan to Hong Kong was meant to symbolize a domestic segment in the itinerary. The plan implied the torch should go from one island province to the next as it approached mainland China.

"It is something that the government and people cannot accept," Tsai Chen-wei, the head of Taiwan's Olympic Committee stated. The episode underscores the deep mistrust between the two antagonists in an unresolved civil war going back to the Communist overthrow of China by Mao.

Public relations challenges aside, both Coca-Cola and Samsung were convinced from prior experience that they have much to gain from the sponsorship. As official sponsors of the 2004 Olympic games, which cost about $40 million per sponsor, Samsung integrated its brand presence into interactive experiences, bus wraps, airport luggage carts, and other signage. Both sponsors also operated extensive hospitality centers for athletes and visiting dignitaries, positioning the companies as exemplary global citizens. Worldwide brand recognition also follows from such major sponsorhips.

The 2004 Olympics marked the first time that the Olympic torch went around the world—traveling 78,000 kilometers in 78 days—before a runner made the final lap and ignited the cauldron at the opening ceremonies in Athens before a live audience of 72,000 and a global television audience of 4 billion.

Almost 4,000 torchbearers carried the flame to previous host cities and, for the first time, the flame visited Africa and Latin America. An estimated 260 million people saw the flame during the relay, which made Coca-Cola and Samsung very happy corporate sponsors.

Performers celebrate the one year countdown to the Olympics in Beijing's Tiananmen Square.

Gabriel Kahn, a reporter for the *Wall Street Journal*, pointed out that:

> The sponsors . . . turn each stop along the relay into a golden marketing opportunity. Both Samsung and Coke get to choose some of the relay runners for each city. Their corporate logos emblazon all sorts of torch-related paraphernalia. And as the relay entourage winds it way through each city, Coke and Samsung trucks leave behind a stream of pennants, pins, and sodas."

Elli Panagiotopoulou Giokeza, writing in IPRA's *Frontline*, explains why corporate sponsors are attracted to the Olympics: "The sponsorship of the Olympic Games

(CONTINUED)

is a great communication tool, which not only extends the corporate visibility of the companies involved, but also provides them with the possibility to increase their relationship with the consumer and their respective trade audiences."

Another reason is given by Josh McCall in *PRWeek:* "The Olympics continue to be among the most prominent platforms for branding on the planet." One study, for example, showed that half of U.S. consumers thought Olympic sponsors were industry leaders. These enormous marketing gains rely heavily on effective public relations. Strategic management of potential conflict on behalf of high-profile sponsors, such as the Taiwan–China diplomacy challenge, must be accomplished to avoid "marketing blowback" for event sponsors who are placing enormous bets that all will go well.

issues, noted three constructive developments in corporate public relations about the environment:

1. more environmental reports that show flaws and shortfalls as well as attainments
2. fewer glossy, feel-good photos with kids and animals
3. more collaboration with green groups.

Many companies, such as Shell, are now issuing annual corporate responsibility reports and working with environmental groups to clean up the environment, preserve wilderness areas, and even replace exploited natural resources.

Home Depot is a good case study. Between 1997 and 1999, the giant chain of homebuilding supplies was the target of environmentalists, who picketed hundreds of Home Depot stores. They were concerned that the company, the world's largest retailer of lumber, was causing the massive destruction of forests around the world by not ensuring that its supplies didn't come from endangered forests. The protests received extensive media coverage and the company, quite frankly, was worried about a consumer backlash and sliding sales.

In 2001, Home Depot conducted an assessment of the "state of the world's forests." The company's wood purchasing policy states: "To set our purchasing directives through 2010, we are conducting our second review of the state of the world's forests, to be completed in 2005–2006."

The company says it has increased the number of products certified by the Forest Stewardship Council, "whose mission is to promote environmentally appropriate, socially beneficial and economically viable management of the world's forests."

In addition to working with the Forest Stewardship Council, Home Depot partners with the World Wildlife Fund, The Nature Conservancy, and other organizations "to promote responsible forestry and curb illegal logging."

The company correctly perceived the potential problem as an issue that needed to be addressed (see discussion of issues management in Chapter 10). As a first step, the company agreed to stop using products from endangered forests and backed up its decision by slashing its imports from Indonesia, where loggers were practically clearcutting tropical forests, by 90 percent. It also pressured Canada to declare logging off-limits in the Great Bear Rainforest in British Columbia. In another effort, it mediated an agreement between timber companies and environmentalists in Chile to preserve natural forests and establish guidelines for the sustainable farming of new trees.

The partnership between Home Depot and environmental groups is a win-win situation. The company gets credit for being environmentally concerned, which results in less negative publicity and more customer loyalty. The environmental groups, in turn, have more power to accomplish their objectives. Randy Hayes, president of the Rainforest Action Network, told the *Wall Street Journal*, "If you've got Home Depot carrying your water, you're going to get a lot farther than as just an environmental group."

Other large corporations around the world are forging alliances with various NGOs to preserve the environment, promote human rights, and provide social/medical services. The following are some examples of long-term CSR programs:

- The Royal Dutch/Shell Group wants to abolish child labor. Shell companies in 112 nations have procedures in place to prevent the use of child labor.

- Unilever, the food and consumer products company, is helping to restore a dying river estuary in the Philippines. The campaign is one of several programs by the company's global Water Sustainability Initiative.

- Volvo Corporation is working with the UN High Commissioner for Human Rights on a project addressing discrimination in the workplace.

- LM Ericsson, a Swedish telecommunications company, has a program to provide and maintain mobile communications equipment and expertise for humanitarian relief operations.

- Merck, the pharmaceutical giant, is a partner with the Bill and Melinda Gates Foundation on a five-year AIDS project in Botswana and is selling its drugs at cost in developing nations.

Corporate Philanthropy

Another manifestation of CSR is *corporate philanthropy*. This, in essence, is the donation of funds, products, and services to various causes. The range is everything from providing uniforms and equipment to a local Little League baseball team to a multi-million dollar donation to a university for upgrading its programs in science and engineering. In many cases, the organization's public relations department handles corporate charitable giving as part of its responsibilities.

In 2006, American corporations and their foundations gave $12.7 billion to a variety of causes. Although there is a common perception that corporate philanthropy provides the lion's share of donations, the actual percentage is very small. Of the $295 billion total given that year, only 4.5 percent was from corporations. The largest amount of money given, 75.6 percent, was given by individuals. See Chapter 20 on nonprofits for more information on charitable contributions.

Corporations, of course, have long used philanthropy to demonstrate community goodwill and to polish their reputations as a good citizen. There's also evidence that corporate giving is good for business and retaining customers. As previously noted, the Hill & Knowlton survey found that 76 percent of Americans claim to take corporate citizenship into consideration when purchasing products. At the same time, 76 percent of the respondents believe that companies participate in philanthropic activities to get favorable publicity, whereas only 24 percent believe corporations are truly committed to the causes they support.

> " Never do it for publicity. Do it for building your business, your brand equity, and your stakeholder relations. "
> ———*Cone/Roper* research firm

Getting good publicity, no doubt, is a factor, but companies should not believe that this is the ultimate objective. Cone/Roper, a survey organization, says companies should be very careful about bragging about their good deeds, because the public will be skeptical about the motivation. Instead, companies should concentrate on the people they help, and the programs they showcase should be more than "window dressing." The research firm further states, "Never do it for publicity. Do it for building your business, your brand equity, and your stakeholder relations."

It also should be noted that companies don't give to anything and everything. A series of small grants to a wide variety of causes doesn't really help any particular charity, and it dilutes the impact of the contributions. Home Banc Mortgage Corporation, for example, used to give $300,000 annually in small grants to a variety of causes, but it eventually decided that the available funds could have more impact (and visibility) if only one or two causes were heavily funded. Consequently, the company now gives most of its charitable funds to Habitat for Humanity, a nonprofit that builds homes for low-income families.

In Home Banc's case, funding Habitat for Humanity is a strategic decision to funnel contributions into a cause directly related to home ownership, which is the business of the mortgage company. HP also is strategic in deciding where to place its charitable contributions. It expends considerable money on a scholarship program and summer jobs for minority and female engineering and computer science majors. Another major initiative is gifts of its computers, medical equipment, and test equipment to institutions of higher learning. The company's giving philosophy is clearly stated: "HP giving to colleges and universities meets university needs for products while attracting higher skilled workers to the industries we support."

Strategic philanthropy is defined by Paul Davis Jones and Cary Raymond of IDPR Group as "the long-term socially responsible contribution of dollars, volunteers, products, and expertise to a cause aligned with the strategic business goals of an organization." Such giving, they say, can reap a number of benefits for the corporation, including:

- Strengthened reputation and brand recognition
- Increased media opportunities
- Improved community and government relations
- Facilitation of employee recruitment and retention
- Enhanced marketing
- Access to research and development
- Increased corporate profitability

Corporate philanthropy, despite its potential benefits, does have its limitations. A large grant by a corporation, for example, cannot offset a major financial scandal or the negative publicity of a class-action suit for discrimination of female employees. Philanthropy, as Philip Morris found out, also can't erase public concern about the promotion and marketing of tobacco products. Wal-Mart, faced with community opposition to "big-box" stores, probably won't change the opponent's minds by giving several million dollars to local schools.

Another downside to corporate philanthropy can arise when special interest groups object to the cause that's being funded. Pro-life groups, for example, often target companies that give grants to Planned Parenthood and ask their supporters to boycott the company's products. Bank of America was caught in a controversy when it decided to stop funding the Boy Scouts of America because of the group's refusal to admit gays. Although gay activists were pleased by the action, a storm of protest arose from other bank customers who supported the Boy Scouts. Many canceled their accounts and encouraged others to do the same.

According to Paul Holmes, a columnist for *PRWeek*, there's even a Washington, D.C., group called the Capital Research Center that seeks to "end the liberal bias in corporate philanthropy." It objects to company donations to "antibusiness" charities such as the National Wildlife Federation.

All this leaves corporations somewhat in a quandary about what charities are "safe" and which ones might raise controversy and protests at annual stockholder meetings. There's also the consideration of what special groups are most influential or have the ability to cause headaches for the corporation through boycotts, pickets, and demonstrations. In bottom-line terms, the corporation also thinks about what decision would be best in terms of keeping its overall customer base. Pro-life groups had originally forced Dayton-Hudson Corporation, a department store chain, to cancel its contributions to Planned Parenthood, but the company reversed its decision after hundreds of irate customers sent in cut-up credit cards.

Despite the possible downsides and controversies, corporate philanthropy is a good tool for enhancing reputation, building relationships with key audiences, and increasing employee and customer loyalty. It also serves the public interest in many ways.

When the world's largest aquarium—the Georgia Aquarium in Atlanta—needed to transport two Beluga whales from Mexico City, Atlanta-based UPS came to the rescue with specially built tanks, an equipped cargo plane, and ground transportation. The safe and humane shipping of the 12-foot-long, 1,600-pound whales gave UPS an opportunity to provide a public service for its hometown, but also garnered the package carrier local, national, and international news coverage.

SUMMARY

Today's Modern Corporation

Today, giant corporations have operations and customers around the globe. The public is often distrustful of these large entities because of their perceived wealth and power. Corporate financial scandals in recent years have further eroded public trust.

The Role of Public Relations

Corporations must make special efforts to win back public credibility and trust, and the concept of corporate social responsibility (CSR) is high on the list of priorities. Public relations professionals are on the front line in this effort, counseling companies to be more transparent in their operations, to adopt ethical principles of conduct, and to improve corporate governance.

Media Relations

The public's perception of business comes primarily from the mass media. Consequently, it is important for organizations to effectively tell their story and build a rapport with business editors and reporters by being accessible, open, and honest about company operations and policies.

Customer Relations

Customer service, in many ways, is the front line of public relations. Customer satisfaction is important for building loyalty and telling others about the product or the reputation of the company. Public relations professionals solicit customer feedback as often as possible and act to satisfy customers' needs for communication and service.

Reaching a Diverse Market

The U.S. population is becoming more diverse, and companies are now establishing communication programs, as well as marketing strategies, to serve this growing audience.

Consumer Activism

In today's society, any number of special interest groups exert pressure on corporations to be socially responsible. Companies cannot avoid activist groups; they must engage in dialogue to work out differences. Oftentimes, the public relations staff is the mediator. Consumer boycotts also require public relations expertise to deal effectively with a group's demands.

Employee Relations

Emloyees are the "ambassadors" of a company and are the primary source of information about the company to their friends and relatives. Employee morale is important, and a good communications program—coupled with enlightened company policies—does much to maintain high productivity and employee retention.

Layoffs and Outsourcing

The cardinal rule, from a public relations standpoint, is to first talk to employees in person before announcing a layoff to the public. Many companies ease the impact of a layoff by providing a severance package. Offshoring is a rising concern of American workers, and companies must be sensitive to possible criticism.

Minorities in the Workplace

The American workforce is diverse. Companies must take this into consideration when planning employee communication campaigns.

Investor Relations

Public relations professionals who work in investor relations must be knowledgeable about communications and finance. It's the highest-paying field in public relations, but the practitioner must have extensive knowledge of government regulations.

Marketing Communications

Increasingly, companies take an integrated approach to campaigns. Public relations, marketing, and advertising staffs work together to complement each other's expertise. Product publicity and product placement are part of marketing communications. Cause-related marketing involves partnerships with nonprofit organizations to promote a particular cause. Another aspect of marketing communications is corporate sponsorships.

Environmental Relations

A new trend line is for corporations and activist organizations to have a dialogue and engage in collaborative efforts to change situations that damage the environment or violate human rights.

Corporate Philanthropy

Companies give about $12 billion a year to worthy causes. It's important to select a charity that is complementary to the organization's business and customer profile. In general, corporate philanthropy is part of an organization's commitment to be socially responsible.

CASE ACTIVITY What Would You Do?

The Tour de France bicycle race is one of the most-watched sporting events in Europe and throughout the world. The three-week race draws an estimated 15 million watchers along the route and 100 million television viewers worldwide.

Each of the competing teams has a corporate sponsor, which places its logo on the riders' clothes, and top-ranking riders receive television coverage and appear in newspapers and magazines around the world, generating even greater exposure for their sponsors.

That's the good news. The bad news is that individual riders and even whole teams have received considerable negative publicity because of doping and using other banned drugs to enhance performance. This places spon-

sors in an awkward position when athletes they fund are accused of doping and consequently eliminated from the race. As one sponsor said, "This (drug use) is something they wouldn't allow in their workplace."

Your company is currently a sponsor of a team in the Tour de France, but the CEO has expressed concern about continuing because its $6 million investment doesn't really help the image or reputation of the company if a rider or an entire team—all wearing the company logo—are accused of using drugs and kicked out of the race as television cameras and photographers cover their humiliation. As vice president of corporate communications and marketing, what would be your recommendation? Continue as a sponsor or pull out? Explain your rationale.

QUESTIONS for Review and Discussion

1. What are the characteristics of today's modern corporation? Why is there so much public suspicion and distrust? Is there any evidence to support the public's perceptions?
2. What is the concept of corporate social responsibility (CSR), and why is it important to today's corporations? What is the role of public relations professionals in this concept?
3. General Electric says that a corporation must consider four factors when making any decision. What are they?
4. Corporate executives indicate that they are wary of the media. What reasons do they give? Do you think their concerns are valid? Journalists also are critical of business executives. What are their complaints?
5. Why is it important for corporate executives to have a good relationship with the mass media?
6. Traditionally, customer relations and public relations have been separate corporate functions. Do you think the two functions should be merged? Why or why not?
7. Why is it important for companies to consider diversity in their marketing and public relations strategies?
8. Consumer activists are very vocal about the misdeeds of corporations. How should a company react to charges and allegations from activist groups such as PETA? What factors would go into your decision making?
9. If an activist group has called for the boycott of a particular company's products, would you be inclined to stop buying the product? Why or why not? Under what circumstances would you join a boycott against a company?
10. Why is employee relations so important to a company's image and reputation?
11. What employee policies do *Fortune*'s 100 best companies have that distinguish them from other corporations?
12. How should a company tell its employees about a layoff?
13. How can a company benefit from meeting the needs of a diverse workforce?
14. Many companies give workers time off with pay to volunteer on local charitable projects. Would you be more inclined to work for such a company? Why or why not?
15. Give some examples of product publicity and product placement.
16. What is cause-related marketing? Give some examples. What guidelines should be considered when partnering with a cause?
17. Give four reasons why corporate sponsorship of concerts, festivals, and even the Olympics is considered a good marketing and public relations strategy.
18. Corporations, throughout the 1990s, had frequent clashes with environmental and human rights groups. Today, there seems to be more cooperation and collaboration. Why do you think this has occurred?
19. Corporate philanthropy is now very strategic; companies support organizations and causes that have a direct relationship to their business. Do you think all this makes corporate philanthropy too self-serving? Why or why not?

SUGGESTED READINGS

Chen, Yi-ru Regina. "The Strategic Management of Government Affairs in China: How Multinational Corporations in China Interact with the Chinese Government." *Journal of Public Relations Research*, Vol. 19, No. 3, 2007, pp. 283–306.

Creamer, Matthew. "Offshoring Reputation." *PRWeek*, April 5, 2004, p. 13.

Hall, Margrete R. "Corporate Philanthropy in Corporate Community Relations: Measuring the Relationship-Building Results." *Journal of Public Relations Research*, Vol. 18, No. 1, 2006, pp. 1–21.

Harrison, E. Bruce. "The Drying of Corporate Greenwash." *O'Dwyer's PR Report*, June 2007, pp. 1, 12.

McCauley, Kevin. "ExxonMobil Funds Anti-Warming Groups." *O'Dwyer's PR Services Report*, February 2007, pp. 1, 13.

McGuire, Craig. "Public Conversations: Companies Are Increasingly Recognizing the Importance of Communications Efforts in the IPO Process." *PRWeek*, April 23, 2007, p. 13.

Nolan, Hamilton. "Alternate Annual Reports Are Essential in Digital Age." *PRWeek*, April 23, 2007, p. 11.

Park, Dong-Jin, and Berger, Bruce K. "The Presentation of CEOs in the Press, 1900–2000: Increasing Salience, Positive Valence, and a Focus on Competency and Personal Dimensions of Image." *Journal of Public Relations Research*, Vol. 16, No. 1, 2004, pp. 93–125.

Stein, Andi. "Employee Communications and Community: An Exploratory Study." *Journal Of Public Relations Research*, Vol. 18, No. 3, 2006, pp. 249–264.

Wan, Hua-Hsin, and Schell, Robert. "Reassessing Corporate Image—An Examination of How Image Bridges Symbolic Reationships with Behavioral Relationships." *Journal of Public Relations Research*, Vol. 19, No. 1, 2007, pp. 25–45.

Politics and Government

TOPICS COVERED IN THIS CHAPTER INCLUDE:

Government Relations

A specialized component of corporate communications is government relations. This activity is so important that many companies, particularly in highly regulated industries, have separate departments of government relations. The reason is simple. The actions of governmental bodies at the local, state, and federal level have a major impact on how a business operates.

Government relations specialists, often called *public affairs specialists,* have a number of functions: They gather information, disseminate management's views, cooperate with government on projects of mutual benefit, and motivate employees to participate in the political process.

As the eyes and ears of a business or industry, and even the nonprofit sector, practitioners spend much time gathering and processing information. They monitor the activities of many legislative bodies and regulatory agencies to keep track of issues coming up for debate and possible vote. Such intelligence gathering enables a corporation, an industry, or nonprofit groups to plan ahead and, if necessary, adjust policies or provide information that may influence the nature of government decision making.

Monitoring government takes many forms. Probably the most active presence in Washington, D.C., and many state capitals is the trade association that represents a particular industry. A Boston University survey once showed that almost 70 percent of the responding companies monitored government activity in Washington through their trade associations. Second on the list were frequent trips to Washington by senior public affairs officers and corporate executives; 58 percent of the respondents said they engaged in this activity. Almost 45 percent of the responding firms reported that they also had a company office in the nation's capital.

Government relations specialists spend a great amount of time disseminating information about the company's position to a variety of key publics. Spoken tactics may include an informal office visit to a government official or testimony at a public hearing. In addition, public affairs people are often called on to give a speech or write one for a senior executive.

Written tactics may include writing letters and op-ed articles, preparing position papers, producing newsletters, and placing advocacy advertising. Although legislators are a primary audience, the Foundation for Public Affairs reports that 90 percent of companies also communicate with employees on public policy issues, whereas another 40 percent communicate with retirees, customers, and other publics such as taxpayers and government employees.

The importance of effective governmental relations to the economic well-being of a company is best summarized by a *New York Times* writer:

> Public relations executives can rightly point out that, with the cacophony of interests clamoring for attention in Washington, there is a role for professional advice on how to insure that one's message is heard. With the expanding role of Congress and the increasing complexity of government, this probably is true now more than ever. There are undoubtedly times that public relations firms can help journalists, politicians and clients.

Corporations, membership organizations, and industry-wide trade groups are also actively engaged in lobbying and making campaign contributions, which are discussed next.

Lobbying

The term *lobbyist* originally was used to describe the men who sought favors from President Abraham Lincoln, who conducted affairs of state in the lobby of the Willard Hotel near the White House. President Ulysses S. Grant continued the tradition of conducting business in the hotel's lobby while he had a cigar and a brandy.

Today, lobbying is closely aligned with governmental relations or public affairs, and the distinction between the two often blurs. This is because most campaigns to influence impending legislation have multiple levels. One level is informing and convincing the public about the correctness of the organization's viewpoint, which the public affairs specialist does.

Lobbying is a more specific activity. *Webster's New World Dictionary* defines a lobbyist as "a person . . . who tries to influence the voting on legislation or the decisions of government administrators." In other words, a lobbyist directs his or her energies to the defeat, passage, or amendment of proposed legislation and regulatory agency policies.

Lobbyists can be found at the local, state, and federal levels of government. California, for example, has about a thousand registered lobbyists who represent more than 1,600 special-interest groups. The interests represented in Sacramento include large corporations, business and trade groups, unions, environmental groups, local governments, nonprofit groups, school districts, and members of various professional groups. Lobbyists usually outnumber legislators in any state capitol. New York State's 212 lawmakers are outnumbered 18 to 1 by lobbyists; in Florida, it's about 13 to 1.

The number and variety of special interests multiply at the federal level. One directory of Washington lobbyists lists about 30,000 individuals and organizations. The interests represented include virtually the entire spectrum of U.S. business, educational, religious, local, national, and international pursuits.

The diversity of those groups can be illustrated with the debate about managed health care and patient rights. Opposing new regulations are (1) insurance companies, (2) HMO trade groups, (3) the United States Chamber of Commerce, (4) the National Federation of Independent Business, and (5) the American Association of Health Plans. These groups are concerned about higher costs to employers, increased government control of health care delivery systems, and more litigation and lawsuits.

Groups supporting patient rights include (1) a broad coalition of consumer groups, (2) the American Medical Association, and (3) the Trial Lawyers of America. However, all of this organized and planned communication effort can be overwhelmed by popular culture. Michael Moore's latest film, *Sicko*, an exposé on health care and the pharmaceutical industry in America, has created both a media and a public policy agenda that ensures health care's place as an issue in the 2008 presidential election campaign. It also ensures that millions will be spent by various interests to influence any legislation. Between 1998 and 2004, for example, various groups spent about $55 million on health care lobbying.

Another example of conflicting interests and major lobbying is national energy legislation. It's an epic battle pitting such major players as automakers, oil companies, electric utilities, coal producers, and even corn farmers against each other. Major cattle feedlots, for example, are against subsidies for corn-based ethanol because it will raise the price of feed. Meanwhile, the automakers are lobbying against more stringent fuel economy standards because it would force them to retool their plants at a high cost.

PR CASEBOOK

Google™ Goes to Washington

Google, as one of the most successful start-ups in recent history, saw no particular reason why it needed to have a presence in Washington. Its political awakening, however, came in early 2006 when the company's executives were severely criticized by a congressional committee about its business dealings with China.

Google, along with Microsoft, Cisco Systems, and Yahoo, was accused of aiding and abetting China's government in the censoring of search results and imperiling the safety of Chinese Internet surfers. "Can you say in English that you are ashamed of what you and your company have done?" Democratic representative Tom Lantos demanded. Other committee members mocked the company's motto, "Do no evil," as a meaningless slogan. See the ethics box in Chapter 17 for more information on this issue.

At that point, it dawned on Google that Congress and federal regulators could have a significant effect on Google's bottom line and expansion plans. In short order, Google hired about a dozen staffers and put several prominent lobbying firms on retainer to represent the company in the halls of Congress and at the hearings of various federal agencies. One immediate pressing issue was a looming battle with telecommunications companies who were lobbying for legislation that would enable them to levy extra fees on big users of Internet bandwidth. Although Google claimed that this was bad for consumers, it was also worried that higher fees could cause declining audiences for YouTube, which delivered Web video clips to consumers billions of times each month.

There were also other issues that required lobbying. Some members of Congress were concerned about Google's proposed $3.1 billion deal for the ad services company Double Click. Some wanted the Federal Communications Commission (FCC) to block the deal on the grounds that it would give Google too much control over delivering ads to Web sites. There was also the issue of privacy; consumers were worried about leaks in personal information, and federal authorities wanted the search engine to assist in criminal investigations. Copyright issues were also on the docket. Media companies were lobbying for stricter copyright regulations to keep Google

> " It's been the growth of Google as a company and as a presence in the industry that has prompted our engagement in Washington. "
>
> ———*Alan Davidson*, legal counsel for Google

from posting on YouTube materials taken from television programs and movies.

Google was also engaged in a fierce lobbying battle with telecommunication giants such as AT&T and Verizon over its plan to offer up to $4.6 billion for a swath of the nation's airwaves, which were being auctioned by the federal government. Google wanted the airwaves to provide more Internet services and, eventually, to enable consumers to buy any wireless phone on the open market and then select their own wireless provider. Needless to say, the giant phone companies were completely opposed to such an idea and lobbied the FCC to prevent Google from buying the airwaves.

Although Google is now actively participating in traditional lobbying, the company is also bringing its own brand of lobbying to the nation's capital. Google staffers, for example, meet with both Democratic and Republican campaign operatives to tell them how they can use cost-effective online ads and other free services from Google to help their candidates win. One Google service provides details about people who visit a campaign Web site and where they live. Google also sets up seminars and briefings for congressional staff and teaches attendees how to use the search engine more

Google has expanded its governmental relations and public affairs presence by inviting presidential candidates to its headquarters in Mountain View, California, to talk to employees. Here, John Edwards answers a question from the floor.

Another bipartisan approach is to invite political candidates, particularly presidential candidates, to Google's headquarters in Mountain View, California, to participate in forums for Google employees and the media. Most presidential candidates have made the trek, and Google has garnered a great deal of media coverage. Most news photographs of the candidate, for example, also have the Google logo in the background.

Google, however, still has a way to go before becoming a major beltway player. In 2006, it spent only $800,000 on outside lobbyists compared to $9 million by Microsoft and $1 million by Yahoo. The total of these three firms, however, was far less than AT&T's $20 million spent on lobbying. Google's political action committee (PAC), which channels employee donations to political candidates, is also somewhat puny. In 2006, Google employees donated only $31,000 to political candidates, compared to Microsoft's $1.36 million and AT&T's $3 million.

Given the high stakes, however, no one doubts that Google will continue to build its Washington presence and put more resources into the fine art of lobbying.

effectively and even get satellite photos for lawmakers' presentations. The idea is to build relationships and friends on both sides of the aisle to ensure that Google's point of view is not only heard but respected.

Organizations such as FedEx and Southwest Airlines, however, are lobbying for more fuel economy and cost-effective alternative fuels. The utility industry also supports alternative sources of energy, but wants the development of nuclear power plants included in any tax credits. The coal industry is opposed to more stringent standards about "clean" coal unless the government is willing to guarantee billions of dollars in loans for coal-to-liquid plants and long-term government purchases. As one senator remarked, "This is going to be the mother of all bills."

The Nature of Lobbying

Although the public perceives that only big business lobbies, a variety of special interests do it. *Fortune*, for example, ranked the top 25 lobbying groups in Washington in terms of influence, and the American Association of Retired Persons (AARP) was first on the list. The next four rankings, in descending order, were (1) the American Israel Public Affairs Committee, (2) the National Federation of Independent Business, (3) the National Rifle Association, and (4) the AFL-CIO. See the PR Casebook that starts on page 476 about a relative newcomer to the lobbying arena, Google.

These large and influential groups, of course, are only the tip of the iceberg. There are literally hundreds of other groups that lobby to influence government policy. Even the antiwar movement has moved to K Street, the address of Washington's most influential lobbying and public relations firms. One group, Americans Against Escalation in Iraq (A.A.E.I.) lobbies members of Congress to withdraw troops from Iraq and also conducts public information campaigns about the cost of the war. According to the

> **The advantage of lobbyists is that they are focused on an issue or two and can put together a compelling report.**
>
> ———*Prof. Rogan Kersh,*
> *NYU Wagner School*
> *of Public Service*

New York Times, it spent about $12 million in 2007 on a combination of grassroots organizing, polling, and television advertisements to get the United States out of Iraq.

According to *Times* writer Michael Crowley, "The playbook for opposing a war has changed markedly since the street-protest ethos of the anti-Vietnam movement. Tie-dyed shirts and flowers have been replaced by oxfords and BlackBerries."

Competing lobbying efforts, of course, often cancel each other out. All this still leaves legislators and regulatory personnel the responsibility of weighing the pros and cons of an issue before voting. Indeed, *Time* magazine notes that lobbyists representing all sides of an issue "do serve a useful purpose by showing busy legislators the virtues and pitfalls of complex legislation." A classic conflict is the debate between saving jobs and improving the environment. A coalition of environmental groups constantly lobbies Congress for tougher legislation to clean up industrial pollution or protect endangered species. Simultaneously, local communities and unions often argue that the proposed legislation would mean the loss of jobs and economic chaos.

The Problem of Influence Peddling

Although a case can be made for lobbying as a legitimate activity, deep public suspicion exists about former legislators and officials who capitalize on their connections and charge large fees for doing what is commonly described as *influence peddling*.

Indeed, the roster of registered lobbyists in Washington includes a virtual "who's who" of former legislators and government officials from both Democratic and Republican parties. According to the watchdog group Center for Public Integrity, more than 12 percent of current lobbyists are former executive and legislative branch employees. This includes more than 200 former members of Congress and 42 former agency heads. The Ethics in Government Act forbids government officials from actively lobbying their former agencies for one year after leaving office. Critics say that it has had little or no impact.

A good case study is the U.S. Department of Homeland Security. When Tom Ridge became director of the White House Office of Homeland Security after the 9/11 attack, he brought together a number of trusted aides to help set up the office. Then, when he became the first Secretary of Homeland Security in President Bush's cabinet, many of his senior aides left government and started new careers as lobbyists for companies seeking contracts with the department, which has a $40 billion budget to spend.

Many members of Congress also become lobbyists immediately after leaving office. A good example is former representative J. C. Watts (R-OK) who announced the formation of a group of lobbying and public affairs firms exactly one day after leaving office. High-ranking members of Watts's congressional staff moved with him to his new offices to begin their careers as lobbyists of their former colleagues.

Even congressional staff members who know intimately the structure and operations of key committees begin second careers as lobbyists. Ann Eppard, an administrative assistant for 22 years to Congressman Bud Shuster, a Republican from Pennsylvania, set up shop after he became chair of the House Transportation Committee. In short order, she had clients such as Federal Express and the American Road and Transportation Builders Association, which had vital interests before the committee.

on the job
A MULTICULTURAL WORLD

The Risks of Polishing Venezuela's Image

In recent years, it has become increasingly common for countries to hire lobbying groups to represent their interests in Washington, D.C. In 2003, Venezuela, for example, hired Patton Boggs to help improve relations with the U.S. government, entering into a contract worth $1.2 million annually. Venezuela faced some enormous public relations challenges, as the American public's perception of it was less than favorable. Liberals in the United States were disturbed by the uneven distribution of wealth. Many conservatives, including members of the Bush administration, perceived Venezuela's populist president, Hugo Chavez, as a threat. Evangelical leader Pat Robertson went so far as to call for Chavez's assassination in 2005, blasting Venezuela as "a launching pad for communist infiltration and Muslim extremism all over the continent" on a 700 Club broadcast.

After a series of brainstorming sessions, Patton Boggs decided to focus on a two-pronged public relations approach. On one hand, they sought to persuade the U.S. government and citizens to not interfere in the internal politics of Venezuela. On the other, Patton Boggs concentrated on getting across the message that the country's oil wealth was now being spent to improve the lives of all Venezuelans. They recommended that Lumina Strategies and Underground Advertising be hired to handle media relations and advertising to disseminate the strategic messages. Print ads, placed in the *New Yorker, New York Times, Economist, International Herald Tribune,* and *Roll Call* (a congressional publication), heralded the country's progress.

The Public Relation campaign was not without critics, however. The *New York Times* reported that Venezuela is "pitching itself as an egalitarian nirvana where petrodollars are funneled straight to the poor." An opposition group of Venezuelan exiles, displaced when Chavez took power in 2002, has countered the Venezuelan government's message, arguing that Chavez's regime threatens the region's stability and that the claim of egalitarianism is a myth. They have lobbied Congress aggressively to place economic sanctions on the country.

Chavez's subsequent actions, however, have turned American public opinion against Venezuela. In June 2006, the Patton Boggs newsletter featured an article on Chavez's interruption of oil shipments to the U.S., calling it a "blatant political risk." Although offering little explanation, their Web site no longer lists Venezuela among current foreign sovereign clients.

The case raises some pertinent ethical questions for public relations agencies serving foreign clients. Is it possible that Patton Boggs and other public relations agencies may face sanctions, litigation, or loss of reputation because of their work on behalf of a country that opposes U.S. policy? Or, like lawyers, do Public Relation firms have a responsibility to represent their clients to the best of their ability, no matter who they are?

Such connections, and the "cashing in" on them, give the press and public the uneasy feeling that influence peddling is alive and well in the nation's capital. It also gives credence to the cliché, "It's not what you know, but who you know." See the Multicultural box on this page about a Washington firm taking Venezuela as a client.

Regulation of Lobbying

Various legislative efforts to curtail the influence of lobbyists have a history going back at least 60 years. In 1995, during the Clinton administration, Congress passed a comprehensive reform bill after a number of polls indicated that the public believed lobbyists had runaway influence in Washington.

One key provision was an expanded definition of who is considered to be a "lobbyist." The new law defined a lobbyist as "someone hired to influence lawmakers, government officials or their aides, and who spends at least 20 percent of his or her time representing any client in a six-month period." Another key provision requires lobbyists to register with Congress and disclose their clients, the issue areas in which lobbying is being done, and roughly how much is being paid for it. Violators faced civil fines of up to $50,000.

The tougher restrictions on lobbyists also applied to eating and drinking. Under the law, lobbyist-paid lavish lunches and drawn-out dinners were forbidden. Receptions at which finger food is served are allowed. Lobbyists call this the *toothpick rule*. The law also prohibited a lobbyist from buying a meal for a lawmaker unless at least 25 people from an organization attend. That is considered a "widely attended event" at which a lobbyist could not monopolize a lawmaker's time. There were also new rules for gifts and travel. Senators, their aides, and other Senate officers are barred from accepting gifts worth more than $50 and from accepting privately paid travel to "recreational events."

Congress again revised and updated lobbying rules in 2007 in the aftermath of a major scandal involving one of Washington's top lobbyists, Jack Abramoff, who *Time* described in a cover article as "The man who bought Washington." He was convicted of fraud, tax evasion, and bribing public officials. Caught in the web of Abramoff's influence peddling were several high-profile legislators, including House leader Tom DeLay, who lost his title and also resigned from office after it was revealed that he and an aide went on an expense-paid golfing junket to Scotland.

The 2007 legislation prohibited lawmakers and aides from accepting any gifts, meals, or trips from lobbyists. It also abolished the practices of discounted rides on private planes, requiring senators as well as candidates for the Senate or the White House to pay full charter rates for trips. House members are barred from accepting free trips on private planes. In addition, the new legislation required lawmakers to disclose the names of lobbyists who raise $15,000 or more in contributions during any six-month period through bundling of donations.

The restrictions on food and drink were kept in the new legislation. Dinners were out, but it was OK to offer a legislator "light appetizers and drinks, or soda and cookies." Lobbyists even complained that the incentive of offering free pizza to congressional staffers who attended a session on some impending legislation was probably out of the question. There was a loophole, however. A more elaborate meal could be served if the situation was a "widely attended event." Aerospace contractors, for example, hosted legislators at luxurious receptions in Paris during a trade show under the guise that the event was "widely attended," according to the *New York Times*.

Lobbyist Jack Abramoff, described by Time magazine as "The man who bought Washington," leaves the courthouse after his indictment. His excesses, which included bribery, caused Congress to pass new legislation to regulate lobbying.

Although federal officials were forbidden to lobby their former agencies and the White House for at least a year after leaving office, the 2007 legislation was also extended to members the legislative branch. Former senators would have to wait two years before lobbying Congress; ex-House members would have to wait one year. It remains to be seen whether all these new rules can be enforced.

Grassroots Lobbying

Grassroots lobbying is now an $800 million industry, according to *Campaigns and Elections*, a bimonthly magazine for "political professionals." What makes it so attractive to various groups is that there are virtually no rules or regulations.

The tools of such lobbying are advocacy advertising, toll-free phone lines, bulk faxing, Web sites, and computerized direct mail aimed at generating phone calls and letters from the public to Congress, the White House, and governmental regulatory agencies.

One major firm, Bonner & Associates, has a highly sophisticated communications system that includes banks of telephones and computers that can call or send letters to thousands of citizens within hours. For example, the American Bankers Association hired Bonner to kill a congressional bill that would lower credit card interest rates. The firm orchestrated 10,000 phone calls from citizens and community leaders to 10 members of the House Banking Committee. The bill died in committee.

Grassroots lobbying also involves coalition building. The basic idea is to get individuals and groups with no financial interest in an issue to speak on the sponsor's behalf. The premise is that letters and phone calls from private citizens are more influential than arguments from vested interests.

A good example comes from another Bonner campaign. In this case, Congress was considering an auto pollution bill opposed by car manufacturers. The auto companies sought opposition to the bill from beyond the auto industry. Key legislators soon began hearing from disabled and elderly people who were convinced the bill would force the industry to build cars too small to hold walkers and wheelchairs and from Little League parents worried that fuel-efficient station wagons would not accommodate a whole team. The bill was defeated.

Although public involvement in legislative issues is admirable, critics say grassroots lobbying, with its orchestration of public feedback, often slips into the category of unethical behavior. Much grassroots lobbying, for example, is done under the cover of front groups (see Chapter 3). This is called *stealth lobbying*, because the public isn't told what vested interests are behind a particular campaign.

In one example, APCO Associates organized the Mississippians for a Fair Legal System (M-Fair) to solicit public support for tort reform. What the public didn't know was that the sponsoring organization, the American Tort Reform Association, included large tobacco and chemical companies, which wanted legislation limiting liability for dangerous or defective products.

Such "grassroots" campaigns make public interest groups wonder whether they really shouldn't be called "Astroturf" campaigns, since the "grass" is artificial. Michael Pertschuk, codirector of the Advocacy Institute in Washington, D.C., told *O'Dwyer's PR Services Report*, "Astroturf groups are usually founded with corporate seed money that is funneled through PR firms." An example is the group National Smokers Alliance, organized by Burson-Marsteller with seed money from Philip Morris.

Guidelines for Grassroots Lobbying   Legitimate coalitions of companies, associations, and citizens are effective grassroots tools, but "misleading front groups and sneak attacks are recipes for trouble," says Jay Lawrence, senior vice president of Fleishman-Hillard public relations.

Lawrence gives these tips for effective grassroots lobbying in *O'Dwyer's PR Services Report:*

- **Target the effort.** Few campaigns need to reach every congressman or state legislator.
- **Go after "persuadables."** Narrow the audience by concentrating on fence-sitters.
- **Build coalitions on economic self-interest.** Go after individuals and organizations who would be financially affected.
- **Think politically.** Find people who know legislative decision-makers or have some connection with them.
- **Letters are best.** Personal letters are the most effective—far better than postcards, mailgrams, and petitions. The best letters are short and simple.
- **Make it easy.** Provide sample drafts of letters, as well as pens, paper, and even stamps.
- **Arrange meetings.** The best single communication is a meeting in the official's home district with a group of interested constituents.
- **Avoid stealth tactics.** If you can't say up front whose interest you are promoting and why, it is a good idea to take another look at the effort.

Election Campaigns

Public affairs activities and lobbying, either in the halls of Congress or at the grassroots level, are year-round activities. During election years, either at the congressional or presidential level, an army of fund-raisers, political strategists, speechwriters, and communications consultants are mobilized to help candidates win elections.

The high cost of running for office in the United States has made fund-raising virtually a full-time, year-round job for every incumbent and aspirant to office. In fact, American-style campaigning is the most expensive in the world. According to *The Economist,* a colossal $4 billion was spent on the 2004 congressional and presidential races—a third more than was spent in the 2000 election. Of that amount, paid advertising by the two major presidential candidates topped $600 million. This was despite the advent of the McCain-Feingold Campaign Finance Act that was passed in 2002, which will be discussed shortly.

It's difficult to comprehend such large figures, but the *New York Times,* in an analysis of costs associated with just the preliminaries of the 2008 presidential campaign, gave some insight into how much money is raised and how it is spent. For openers, the 17 presidential candidates running for president had already spent $150 million by June 30, 2007—about 18 months before the 2008 November election. Mitt Romney was the big spender with $32.3 million, which helped position him as a major contender. John McCain was second with $23.2 million; Barack Obama came in third with $22.7 million. Fourth was Hillary Clinton, spending about $18 million to advance her candidacy. Rudi Giuliani was also in the running with $17.3 million in expenditures.

These filings with the Federal Election Commission (FEC) also indicated the type of expenditures that candidates must make to become president. John McCain, for example, paid $4.6 million to consultants, and Barack Obama reported the salaries of

508 people on his campaign staff. Meanwhile, Mitt Romney spent $300 on makeup for his first debate, and Hillary Clinton's staff spent $1,286 on pizza. Mitt Romney favors Best Western hotels and spent $9,057 for rooms in the six-month period. Obama is a Holiday Inn person, spending $39,218 for rooms. Of course, rallies need entertainment. Senator McCain paid $1,600 for a group called the Mad Bavarian Band to play in New Hampshire, and Senator Obama paid $1,700 for a band called Double Funk Crunch to play at a rally in California.

There are, of course, major costs in terms of chartered planes, buses, rented halls, banners, posters, advertising, and telecommunications. Consequently, presidential candidates and their staffs expend a considerable amount of time and energy doing fund-raising. Early in the primary campaign, presidential hopefuls Barack Obama and Mitt Romney put themselves in serious contention for the Democratic and Republican nominations with early and dramatic fund-raising success, challenging front-runners with greater name recognition such as Hillary Clinton and John McCain in their respective party races. Romney and Obama each raised over $20 million in the first quarter of 2007 alone.

Candidates retain professionals to organize fund-raising activities. A standard activity in Washington, D.C., and other major cities across the country is the luncheon, reception, or dinner on behalf of a candidate. The *Wall Street Journal*, for example, reported that 14 such events were held on a typical day in October, raising $650,000 for congressional incumbents. At the presidential level, the stakes increase. In the 2004 election, for example, President Bush collected $4 million at a $2,000 per person dinner in Manhattan while his running mate, Dick Cheney, collected more than $1.6 million on the same day at separate events in Virginia and Massachusetts.

Attending such events are individual donors and lobbyists for various organizations. Although a chicken dinner or a cheese platter with crackers and champagne are not exactly worth $2,000 a person in literal terms, the idea is to show support of the candidate and to have contact with him or her. No business is actually discussed, but the occasion gives both individuals and lobbyists for special interests an opportunity to show the "flag" and perhaps influence legislation or personnel appointments at a later date after the election—if the candidate wins.

Some consultants specialize in direct mail and telemarketing. They are assisted by firms that specialize in computer databases and mailing lists. Aristotle Publishers, for example, claims to have records on 128 million registered voters. A candidate can get a tailored list of prospects using any number of demographic variables, including party affiliation, voting record, contribution record, age, geographic location, and opinions on various issues.

The Internet has become a standard tool for fund-raising and reaching supporters. One use of the Internet is for research. The *Wall Street Journal*, for example, reported in 2004 that a Kerry support organization in Concord, New Hampshire, was able to track down Democratic women voters, aged 18 to 30, who were interested in abortion rights. Within seconds, the computer was able to generate the names of 812 local women and also give a street map marking their addresses. Members of Planned Parenthood and other Kerry supporters followed up with door-to-door visits on behalf of the presidential candidate.

Although the Internet was first used for fund-raising and building grassroots support during the 2000 presidential election, its effectiveness wasn't proved until the 2004 election. Former Vermont governor Howard Dean, an early leader in the Democratic primaries, used the Internet to build a grassroots network and raise money. Although Dean eventually lost to John Kerry in the primaries, he and his campaign

> "The Internet is making it much easier for people to participate in politics and much easier for them to donate money.
>
> —Simon Rosenberg, president of NDN, a Democratic advocacy group

consultants, including some very savvy Web designers, set the standard. The Kerry organization, for example, went on to establish its own Web presence for fund-raising and raised more than $75 million after the primaries. In the 2008 election, all presidential candidates extensively used the Internet for fund-raising. Many candidates used YouTube to upload videos and other information. Blogs about the candidates were also aggegated by Yahoo for interested political junkies and voters.

Experts say that the Internet's major value is in organizing people and getting them in contact with each other in a very cost-efficient way. Ultimately, however, winning elections still requires a great amount of one-on-one contact. Mark Macarato, co-chair in Nashville for Dean, told *PRWeek*,

> When you don't have money for mailings and fund-raisers and you're outside the Democratic power structure, the net is just a wonderful tool to get things rolling. The Internet is a very efficient way to connect people, replacing the inefficient tool of a phone call. What is changed is the ability to organize quickly and efficiently. . . . But you need old-fashioned shoe-leather campaigning to take it from there.

Other groups of consultants and technicians also are employed by candidates in election campaigns. They are writers of position papers, speechwriters, graphic artists, computer experts, Webmasters, media strategists, advertising experts, radio and television producers, public affairs experts, pollsters, and public relations specialists. A highly visible and critical job is done by advance people who spend many hours organizing events, arranging every detail, and making sure there's a cheering crowd—with signs—when the candidate arrives. On a single day, for example, a presidential candidate may give five to seven talks at rallies in multiple states.

Campaign Finance Reform

The high cost of political campaigning and the heavy reliance of candidates on the large donations by individuals, corporations, labor unions, and other special interest groups led to the passing of the McCain-Feingold Act in 2002 that set limits on contributions.

Essentially, the legislation, which was reaffirmed in 2003 by the U.S. Supreme Court, divided contributions into three areas:

◆ **Soft Money.** National political parties are prohibited from accepting large, unlimited contributions from corporations, unions, and individuals. State and local party committees can accept up to $10,000 from individuals for get-out-the-vote and voter registration efforts in federal elections, as long as those efforts do not refer to any clearly identified federal candidate and all the money is raised locally.

◆ **Hard Money.** Individuals can now give a total of $95,000 in each two-year election cycle to all federal candidates, political parties, and political action committees (PACs) combined. That includes maximum contributions of $2,000 per election directly to a candidate and $25,000 to a political party per year.

◆ **Issue Advertising.** Advertising in support of a specific candidate must be paid for only with regulated hard money. Ads that fall into this category cannot be broadcast within 30 days of a primary or 60 days of a general election.

527s Become a Major Issue

Although McCain-Feingold drastically reduced the amount of "soft" money given to candidates and political parties, it had some unintended effects. One effect was the migration of soft money to other "independent" partisan organizations.

These organizations are called 527s, which refers to Section 527 of the Internal Revenue Code, which allows them to retain nonprofit status while running "issue" ads as long as they are not directly coordinated with the national political parties or candidates they support. In addition, 527s could not directly endorse a particular candidate.

The Democratic Party was the first to use a 527 group. One early group, formed during the Clinton administration, was MoveOn.org, a liberal online group, that originally raised money and support for President Clinton's defense when he was impeached by the U.S. House of Representatives and then acquitted by the U.S. Senate. Another group, America Coming Together (ACT) was a liberal, pro-Democratic group organized to do advocacy advertising and voter mobilization work. Although not directly affiliated with the Democratic Party, members of this group knocked on 21 million doors, placed 39 million phone calls, mailed 72 million pieces of literature, and placed a number of ads attacking George W. Bush's policies. In one 3-month period, ACT raised $24 million for its activities.

It didn't take the Republican Party long to figure out that third-party partisan groups were also an opportunity to launch attack ads against Democratic candidate John Kerry without having to take responsibility for the content. The first major 527 was Swift Boat Veterans for Truth, later named the Swift Vets and POWs for Truth. In short order, the group spent $22 million for ads on television and in newspapers. One television ad, for example, showed a series of veterans questioning Kerry's service medals in Vietnam and his participation in the Paris peace talks. The last veteran flatly states, "John Kerry cannot be trusted."

A planned side effect of such advertising was the media coverage they generated. The allegations of the Swift Boat Veterans, for example, became a major campaign issue, and the media devoted countless news stories to the group and its charges. Advocacy groups know that shrill ads grab media attention and stories. A group only has to place attack ads on a few small stations and cable outlets at a minimum cost, and the resulting news media stories will carry the message to a national audience.

It has been estimated that third-party partisan groups spent about $500 million in the 2004 presidential campaign trying to influence voters. Such expenditures raised new concerns about the influx of enormous amounts of unregulated money into the political process. There was also the crucial question as to how "independent" these 527 organizations were from the major political parties. The Swift Boat Veterans group, according to a report in the *New York Times*, showed ". . . a web of connections to the Bush family, high-profile Texas political figures, and President Bush's chief political aide."

In 2006, the Federal Election Commission (FEC) ruled that several 527 groups had violated the law by soliciting contributions and then spending the money with the express purpose of electing or defeating a particular candidate. Three groups were fined: Swift Boat Veterans, $300,000; League of Conservation Voters, $180,000; and MoveOn.org, $150,000. Michael E. Toner, chair of the FEC, told the *New York Times*, "Going forward to 2008, 527 groups are on clear notice: organizations whose sole purpose is to influence the presidential election will have to register with the FEC and follow hard-dollar limits."

The issue of advocacy, however, remains contentious. There is concern about free speech and First Amendment rights, so a continued debate no doubt will be the order of the day. The McCain-Feingold Act went all the way to the Supreme Court because various groups believed restrictions on contributions abridged their freedom of speech.

Public Affairs in Government

Since the time of the ancient Egyptians 5,000 years ago, governments have always engaged in what is known in the 21st century as public information, public relations, and public affairs.

The Rosetta Stone, discovered by Napoleon's troops and used by scholars as the key to understanding Egyptian hieroglyphics, turned out to be a publicity release for the reign of Ptolemy V. Julius Caesar was known in his day as a master of staged events in which his army's entrances into Rome after successful battles were highly orchestrated.

There has always been a need for government communications, if for no other reason than to inform citizens of the services available and the manner in which they may be used. In a democracy, public information is crucial if citizens are to make intelligent judgments about the policies and activities of their elected representatives. Through information, it is hoped that citizens will have the necessary background to participate fully in the formation of government policies.

The objectives of government information efforts were summarized some years ago by William Ragan, former director of public affairs for the United States Civil Service Commission:

1. Inform the public about the public's business. In other words, communicate the work of government agencies.

2. Improve the effectiveness of agency operations through appropriate public information techniques. In other words, explain agency programs so that citizens understand and can take actions necessary to benefit from them.

3. Provide feedback to government administrators so that programs and policies can be modified, amended, or continued.

4. Advise management on how best to communicate a decision or a program to the widest number of citizens.

5. Serve as an ombudsman. Represent the public and listen to its representatives. Make sure that individual problems of the taxpayer are satisfactorily solved.

6. Educate administrators and bureaucrats about the role of the mass media and how to work with media representatives.

Skills Needed for Work in Public Affairs

Work in public affairs, including governmental relations, is a specialty area of public relations that requires certain skills and abilities. The following list is adapted from an article by Doug Pinkham, president of the Public Affairs Council in Washington, D.C., in the organization's newsletter:

◆ **Knowledge of how public relations and public affairs supports business goals.** You need to measure and evaluate your programs, not on the basis of clips or bills lobbied, but whether you have improved the reputation of the company among key stakeholders.

◆ **A knack for discerning which opponents to take seriously.** In the Internet age, anyone can be an activist and set up a Web site. A search on Google, for example, will reveal 1.3 million hits for the word "boycott." You need the ability to evaluate which activist groups are credible, and those that aren't. In too many cases, corporations have caused more media attention by refuting charges that few people took seriously in the first place.

◆ **Ability to integrate all communications functions.** You need to coordinate the efforts of multiple corporate departments during a crisis situation.

◆ **Understanding how to control key messages.** The development of key messages, representing all divisions and companies of the corporate parent, should be centralized at company headquarters. If message development is decentralized, consumers may get mixed messages.

◆ **Ability to have influence without being too partisan.** Build relationships with both Democrats and Republicans; don't favor one party over another.

◆ **Talent for synthesizing, filtering, and validating information.** Today's problem is information overload. You need the ability to extract the nuggets of relevant information and position your department as the one that can make sense out of all the noise.

◆ **Aptitude for information technology.** Elections, legislative battles, and even reputations are now being won and lost because of the Internet. Every public policy or public relations campaign needs an online strategy. You need to be Web-savvy to build networks of supporters, communicate with thought-leaders, keep employees informed, and get your message to key audiences.

◆ **Global perspective.** American companies need to learn more about other countries where they manufacture or market their products and services. You need to build relationships with local communities and entire nations so that everyone benefits from economic growth.

◆ **Sustain strong personal relationships.** Public relations is not a direct-mail business. Success demands a commitment to individual service and personal integrity. You also need to develop a reputation for intelligence and credibility. Reporters, political leaders, and other stakeholders are deluged with news and opinion; they rely on those individuals who they respect on a personal level.

"Public Information" versus "Public Relations"

Although many of the objectives described by Ragan would be considered appropriate goals in almost any field of public relations, in government such activities are never referred to as "public relations." Instead, various euphemisms are used. The most common titles are:

◆ public information officer
◆ director of public affairs
◆ press secretary
◆ administrative aide
◆ government program analyst.

In addition, government agencies do not have departments of public relations. Instead, the FBI has an External Affairs Division; the Interstate Commerce Commission has an Office of Communications and Consumer Affairs; and the Environmental

Protection Agency has an Office of Public Awareness. The military services usually have Offices of Public Affairs.

Such euphemisms serve to reconcile two essentially contradictory facts:

1. The government needs to inform its citizens, and
2. it is against the law to use appropriated money for the employment of "publicity experts."

As early as 1913, Congress saw a potential danger in executive branch agencies' spending taxpayer dollars to sway the American public to support programs of various administrations. Consequently, the Gillett Amendment (Section 3107 of Title V of the United States Code) was passed. It stated, "Appropriated funds may not be used to pay a publicity expert unless specifically appropriated for that purpose." The law was reinforced in 1919 with prohibition of the use of any appropriations for services, messages, or publications designed to influence a member of Congress. Another law that year required executive agencies to utilize the U.S. Government Printing Office so that publications could be more closely monitored than in the past. Restrictions also prohibit executive departments from mailing any material to the public without a specific request.

Congress was clearly attempting to limit the authority of the executive branch to spend taxpayer money on public relations efforts to gain support for pet projects of the president. Some presidents chafed at this, but others thought it was entirely proper that the government should not be in the business of propagandizing the taxpayers. President Eisenhower, for example, ordered all executive branch agencies to dispense with field office information activity. The only problem was the great number of public and press requests for information. Consequently, information offices lost their titles but continued their dissemination functions under such titles as "technical liaison officers" for the Corps of Engineers and "assistant to the director" in the Bureau of Reclamation.

In 1972, alarmed by Richard Nixon's expansion of the White House communications staff, Congress reaffirmed prior legislation by stating that no part of any appropriation bill could be used for publicity or propaganda purposes designed to support or defeat legislation before Congress.

Although most citizens would agree that government should not use tax money to persuade the public of the merits or demerits of a particular bill or program, there is a thin line between merely providing information and using information as a lobbying tool. If a public affairs officer for the Pentagon testifies about the number of surface-to-air missiles deployed by Iran or North Korea, does this constitute information or an attempt to influence congressional appropriations? Or, to use another example, is a speech by the Surgeon General about the dangers of passive smoking information only or support of legislation that would ban cigarette smoking from all federal buildings?

While ascertaining the difference between "public relations" and "public information" may be an interesting semantic game, the fact remains that the terms *public relations* and *publicity* are seldom used by a government agency.

Scope of Federal Government Information

The U.S. government is said to be the world's premier collector of information. It also is maintained, without much disagreement, that the government is one of the world's greatest disseminators of information.

Ascertaining the exact size of the government's "public relations" effort, however, is like trying to guess the number of jelly beans in a large jar. One major difficulty is forming a standard definition of what constitutes "public affairs" activity.

The General Accounting Office (GAO) once estimated that probably $2.3 billion was spent each year by federal agencies and the White House on "public relations" activity. Others, often critics of government public relations, have estimated that between 10,000 and 12,000 federal employees are involved in what might be called "public relations" work. It is said, for example, that the Department of Defense has about 1,000 people working in public affairs/information jobs.

Such figures, however, give a false impression of government agencies in general. At the Commerce Department, for example, there are 25 public affairs people out of 36,000 employees. The Immigration and Naturalization Service has eight public affairs officers in a staff of 24,000. The Customs Department has 15 public affairs officers in a staff of 18,000. *O'Dwyer's PR Services Report* says, "That translates to 1/10 of one percent of its workforce."

Advertising is another governmental activity. Federal agencies spend several hundred million dollars a year on public service advertising, primarily to promote military recruitment, government health services, and the U.S. Postal Service. The following sections discuss the public affairs efforts of federal agencies, Congress, and the White House.

Government Agencies   Public affairs officers (PAOs) and public information specialists engage in tasks common to the public relations department of corporations. They typically answer press and public inquiries, write news releases, work on newsletters, prepare speeches for top officials, oversee the production of brochures, and plan special events. Senior-level public affairs specialists also try to counsel top management about communications strategies and how the agency should respond to a crisis situation.

One of the largest public affairs operations in the federal government is operated by the U.S. Department of Defense, which is the cabinet-level agency that oversees the armed forces. Its operations vary from the mundane to the exotic. One of the longest-running public relations efforts has been the preparation and distribution of "hometown" releases by the military. The Fleet Home Town News Center, established during World War II, sends approximately a million news releases annually about the promotions and transfers of U.S. Navy, Marine Corps, and Coast Guard personnel to their hometown media.

A more exotic assignment for a military public affairs officer is to give background briefings and escort journalists who want to cover military operations on the battlefield. A large number of PAOs were assigned as escorts when the military initiated the policy of "embedding" journalists within military units during the invasion of Iraq. In recent years, the Pentagon and its PAOs have

Government entities, such as the United States Postal Service, gain visibility through a variety of public relations activities. Lance Armstrong, six-time winner of the Tour de France, is sponsored by the postal service. Sporting events, in particular, are densely populated by sponsor logos that appear on billboards, programs, and even the clothing of the contestants.

on the job ETHICS

Pay for Play: U.S. Military Plants Favorable Stories in the Iraqi Press

It is a dilemma to define what constitutes public information versus propaganda. Does the nature of war on terror justify using questionable means, or should public relations efforts, no matter what the situation, be guided by ironclad ethical standards? Such situations are not necessarily as cut and dry as they may appear. Fighting an enemy that does not adhere to the conventional rules of warfare may require different public relations approaches.

In November 2005, the *Los Angeles Times* reported that the Pentagon and U.S. military had contracted with the Lincoln Group to plant more than 1,000 "good-news" stories in several Iraqi and Arab papers. The contract specified that the public relations firm, which is based in Washington, D.C., was to inform the Iraqi people of American goals and the progress being made in rebuilding the country to gain public support. Lincoln paid stipends of a few hundred dollars per month for local journalists to write positive stories and paid the editors of papers such as *Azzaman* and *al Sabah* between $40 to $2,000 to publish articles prepared by Lincoln

staffers, soldiers at "Camp Victory," and military public relations officers.

According to *New York Times* reporters Jeff Gerth and Scott Shane, the contract further stipulated that the Lincoln group would compensate "temporary spokespersons" and disseminate "alternative or diverting messages which divert media and public attention" to "deal instantly with the bad news of the day." In most cases, the source of the articles and opinion pieces was not revealed, nor was it made clear that the spokespersons represented the views of the United States and the "Coalition of the Willing."

For the most part, the military and U.S. government defended their actions. Lt. Col. Steven A. Boylan argued that such pay for play was necessary because the Iraqi papers "normally don't have access to those kinds of stories." Michael Rubin, formerly of the Coalition Provisional Authority, stressed the need for "an even playing field" because the insurgents use deceptive messages.

Gen. Peter Pace, however, expressed concern that planting stories without attribution may "be

detrimental to the proper growth of democracy." According to the *New York Times*, national security advisor Stephen J. Hadley reported that President Bush is also "very troubled" by the disclosure. Nevertheless, a 2006 Pentagon review of the secret program found it to be "appropriate," though it recommended establishing guidelines regarding the attribution of authorship.

Journalists have widely denounced the practice of pay for play. "Ethically, it's indefensible," said Patrick Butler, vice president of the International Center of Journalists in Washington. Likewise, the Public Relations Society of America has issued a condemnation of the practice. Pamela Keaton, director of public affairs for the congressionally funded Institute for Peace, worried about the long-term effects of what she sees as a propaganda campaign: "I think there are places where we need to draw the line—and one of them is using the news media for psyops purposes. It will get to the point where the news media won't trust anybody, and the people won't trust what's being quoted in news articles."

been on the firing line, so to speak, because of American military operations in Afghanistan and Iraq. See the Ethics box on this page about the ethics of paying Iraqi journalists for favorable news coverage.

A major operation of the Pentagon is assisting Hollywood with the production of movies. More than 20 public information specialists are assigned as liaisons with the film and television industry. They review scripts and proposals, advise producers on military procedures, and decide how much assistance, if any, a film or TV show portraying the military should receive.

The film *Black Hawk Down*, for example, received military assistance by providing boot-camp training to the actors, technical advisors, eight choppers, and more than 100 soldiers—a package worth about $2 million. The movie *Pearl Harbor* also got considerable help, including the use of an aircraft carrier. Not all films portraying the military, however, get assistance. The Pentagon turned down a request from the producers of *Broken Arrow* because it featured John Travolta as a deluded air force pilot who steals two nuclear missiles with ease.

Other federal agencies also conduct campaigns to inform citizens. In many cases, a public relations firm is selected through a bidding process to execute the campaign. Some recent examples of campaigns are as follows:

◆ The Centers for Disease Control and Prevention (CDC) launched a campaign, with the assistance of Ogilvy PR Worldwide, to inform Americans about who was most vulnerable to getting influenza and who should get the flu vaccine. Also see the Insights box on page 492 about a TB campaign.

◆ The Department of Commerce retained Edelman Worldwide to launch a campaign to lure more foreign visitors to the United States.

◆ The National Endowment for the Arts (NEA) retained Edelman's Washington office to coordinate promotion and public relations for a national tour bringing Shakespeare productions to local communities.

◆ The Federal Trade Commission (FTC) launched a campaign to inform Americans about Internet privacy and security. An animated turtle mascot, Dewie, was part of the campaign.

◆ The Department of Health and Human Services awarded a $9 million, three-year contract to Ogilvy Public Relations Worldwide for work on its pandemic preparedness campaign to tell citizens about influenza and how to protect themselves.

◆ Edelman Worldwide handled media relations related to the much-anticipated release of the Iraq Study Group in December 2006. Forty staffers helped arrange and oversee group and one-on-one interviews with the press.

◆ U.S. Customs and other border agencies launched an information campaign about new passport regulations about traveling between the United States and Mexico, Canada, and the Caribbean.

◆ Weber Shandwick received a $5 million contract from the U.S. Mint to publicize the launch of the $1 coin featuring U.S. presidents.

◆ Burson-Marsteller received a $5 million, five-year contract from the Treasury Department's Bureau of Engraving for a public education and awareness effort to publicize the new $5 and $100 notes. Retailers and foreign exchanges will be informed about new security features to avoid counterfeiting.

◆ The Department of Defense awarded the Rendon Group a $6.4 million contract to do "strategic communications" in Iraq. A few months later, the Lincoln Group received another $6 million contract to support military public relations efforts in Iraq. See Ethics box on page 490.

◆ The U.S Army contracted with McCann Erickson advertising and its sister public relations firm, Weber Shandwick, to conduct a $200 million campaign to recruit volunteers. Outreach included minority communities, NASCAR sponsorships, and Web sites.

Federal agencies, on occasion, also stumble and reap negative publicity. The Federal Emergency Management Agency (FEMA), still recovering from a poor image

on the job
INSIGHTS

The Centers for Disease Control's National Immunization Program

The Centers for Disease Control (CDC), located in Atlanta, Georgia, operates the National Immunization Program (NIP). The program mission is to provide "consultation, training, promotional, educational, epidemiological, and technical services to assist health departments in planning, developing and implementing immunization programs." The NIP supports the establishment of vaccine supply contracts, assists with immunization programs, and tracks possible outbreaks of disease through strategic communication efforts.

The CDC's public awareness and educational programs focus on alerting the public about possible threats. NIP's programs are publicized through PSAs, news releases, radio and television programs, pamphlets, and posters. Information about immunization is directly distributed through local health departments, hospitals, and doctors' offices. The NIP's Web site is particularly effective. A section entitled "In the Spotlight . . . for the Public" offers daily updates about disease outbreaks, potential threats, and immunization schedules. Other links on the homepage provide information aimed at different target populations including parents of young children, adolescents, and the aging.

The CDC uses a variety of public relations strategies to reach the public, such as posters distributed to public health agencies. "World TB Day" poster, CDC, 2005.

Additional links direct visitors to sections devoted to frequently asked questions, statistics, and surveys and offers fact-driven and hands-on public information. A section entitled "Media" provides links to press releases, media resources, and academic research, whereas a section for health care providers offers vaccine guidelines, information kits, and software tools for both health professional and patient training guides.

because of communications foul-ups in the aftermath of Hurricane Katrina in New Orleans, suffered another embarrassment in October 2007. The agency called a news conference to discuss progress on a series of forest fires in Southern California, but when no reporters showed up because they were only given 15-minutes notice,

FEMA's director of public affairs allowed agency employees to pose as journalists and ask questions of FEMA's deputy director. The news media denounced the "fake news conference," and the agency's public affairs director was fired.

The controversy over the U.S. Office of Education's decision to pay a TV commentator/pundit $240,000 to promote the Bush Administration's No Child Left Behind legislation was covered in Chapters 3 and 11. See also the ethics box in this chapter about the U.S. military paying Iraqi journalists.

Two U.S. Department of State activities, public diplomacy and the Voice of America (VOA), are discussed in the next chapter. These tools are used to build relationships with other nations and their citizens.

Congressional Efforts   The House of Representatives and the Senate are great disseminators of information. Members regularly produce a barrage of news releases, newsletters, recordings, brochures, taped radio interviews, and videotapes—all designed to inform voters back home about Congress.

Critics complain that most materials are self-promotional and have little value. The franking privilege (free postage) is singled out for the most criticism. The late Senator John Heinz, a Republican from Pennsylvania, once distributed 15 million pieces of mail, financed by taxpayers, during one election year. Obviously, the franking privilege is a real advantage for an incumbent.

All members of Congress also employ a press secretary. According to Edward Downes of Boston University,

> Capitol Hill's press secretaries play a significant role in the shaping of America's messages and consequent public policies. In their role as proxy for individual members, the press secretaries act as gatekeepers, determining what information to share with, and hold from, the media; thus, they have command over news shared with the citizenry.

White House Efforts   At the apex of government public relations efforts is the White House. The president receives more media attention than all the federal agencies and Congress combined. It is duly reported when the president visits a neighborhood school, tours a housing development, meets a head of state, or even chokes on a pretzel while watching a football game.

All presidents have taken advantage of the intense media interest to implement public relations strategies that would improve their popularity, generate support for programs, and explain embarrassing policy decisions. And each president has had his own communication style.

Ronald Reagan, by most accounts, was considered the master communicator. He was extremely effective on television and could read a teleprompter with perfect inflection. He understood the importance of using symbolism and giving simple, down-to-earth speeches that often ended with "God bless you." Reagan's approach was the use of the carefully packaged sound bite and staged event. Terrance Hunt, an Associated Press reporter who covered the Reagan years, says the former president's funeral in 2004 recalled the high style and stagecraft of his presidency. "Presidential appearances were arranged like movie scenes with Reagan in the starring role. There was a heavy emphasis on staging and lighting," says Hunt.

George H. W. Bush (senior) was no Ronald Reagan as a public speaker, but he did project enthusiasm for his job and had a friendly, but formal, working relationship with the White House press corps. Bill Clinton, on the other hand, was more populist in his communication style. He was at home with today's information technology, experts

A key element of any presidency is the carefully staged photo op. Here, President Bush speaks about the No Child Left Behind legislation with the appropriate signage behind him.

say, and made effective use of television talk shows. Clinton was most effective when he talked one-on-one with an interviewer or a member of the audience.

George W. Bush's style is more like Ronald Reagan's "down-home" style. He is plainspoken, uses short declarative sentences, is self-effacing in speeches to groups across the nation, and does a good job of staying "on message." He comes across as sincerely committed to his beliefs, even in the face of protracted fighting against insurgents in Iraq and record lows in opinion polls. President Bush also has adopted Reagan's approach to stage-craft and symbolism.

A team of television and video experts makes sure every Bush appearance is well choreographed for maximum visual effect. The attention to detail ranges from having audience members behind Bush being asked to take off their ties so they look more like ordinary taxpay-ers who would benefit from his tax cut to arranging the television angle at Mount Rushmore so Bush's head would be aligned with the four former presidents carved in granite on the mountain. For the anniversary of the 9/11 terrorist attack, the White House rented three barges of giant Musco lights to illuminate the Statue of Liberty in the background while President Bush gave his speech. According to the *New York Times*, "It was the ultimate patriotic backdrop for Mr. Bush who spoke from Ellis Island."

The staged event that got the most press, and criticism, was Bush's appearance on the aircraft carrier *Abraham Lincoln* in 2003 when he announced the overthrow of the Hussein regime and the successful occupation of Iraq. The White House staff planned his arrival in a flight suit and his early evening speech so that the setting sun cast a golden glow on his face. In addition, ship crew members were arranged in coordinated shirt colors over Bush's right shoulder while the banner "Mission Accomplished" was positioned to capture the president in a single shot. In this situation, however, the photo op later became a source of amusement and sarcasm because, in actuality, the overthrow of the Hussein government was just the beginning of long, protracted conflict.

The Bush administration's concept of stagecraft also manifested itself in tight control over information and limited media access, except when it could be totally controlled. Bush, for example, gave substantially fewer press conferences, interviews, and other media events than either Bill Clinton or George H. W. Bush. According to Ken Auletta, a respected chronicler of the communications industry, Bush was wary of the press and thought journalists as a whole were too liberal to do a decent job of objectively covering the White House.

Another aspect of Bush's communications style was his insistence that everyone in the administration stay on message. Michael Deaver, previously mentioned, told Auletta, "This is the most disciplined White House in history." Thanks to e-mail, everyone in the administration speaks with one voice, partly because everyone gets the daily "talking point" every morning when they come to work. Although "staying on message" is generally considered a good strategy in public relations, critics say Bush "stayed on message" even when the facts didn't support the message.

All presidents, of course, have assistance in their constant quest to be popular, sell their policies, and be perceived as effective leaders. On every White House staff are experts in communications strategy, media relations, speech writing, and staging the perfect event. In addition, advance people plan every presidential appearance and trip in meticulous detail. They confirm that the person who heads the receiving line is politically correct and that the sound system works. They make arrangements for the press, organize the cheering crowds, select the people in the front rows, select the best symbolic photo opportunity, decide where the television cameras will be positioned, and plan the president's entrance and exit to the last second. The Secret Service, responsible for protecting the president, also does a detailed analysis of the site and the guests. Nothing is left to chance.

The top public relations person in the White House is the Director of Communications. In the first two years of the Bush administration, that individual was Karen Hughes, who also became a special counselor to the president. Her job was to advise the president on communications strategy, and she is generally acknowledged as the architect of the "compassionate" side of Bush's basic conservatism. It was her decision, for example, to have President Bush visit a local mosque to show support for Muslims just days after the 9/11 terrorist attack. The event was a symbolic attempt to assure Muslims in America and around the world that the "war on terrorism" was not a war on Islam.

Hughes also helped Bush set the tone for his speeches. For example, she was instrumental in formulating Bush's speech to the joint session of Congress about America's planned reaction to terrorist attack. Some aides pressed for a bellicose declaration of war on terrorists, but Hughes intervened and shaped the "reassurance theme" that he ultimately used to great effect. In fact, many analysts said it was one of President Bush's best speeches.

Hughes left her powerful position in 2003 for a return to Texas and her family, but she remained close to the president as a frequent advisor and loyalist. Tucker Eskew, former head of the White House Office of Global Communications, told *PRWeek* that Hughes was unique in the Bush Administration: "She's a message crafter, master of ceremonies, and mother-confessor all rolled into one," he said. In 2005, Hughes returned to Washington to be Bush's undersecretary of state for public affairs, charged with winning the "hearts and minds" of foreign audiences. She served in this position until November 2007. See Chapter 19 for more details.

The most visible person, on a daily basis, is the president's press secretary, who has the high-pressure duty of briefing reporters on a daily basis. Tony Snow, affable former Fox news journalist, maintained high levels of candor and good humor as the lightning rod in presidential news conferences, earning respect from the White House press corps. He however, resigned in July 2007 because of health problems. His replacement was Dana Perino, the second woman to ever hold the position of presidential press secretary.

Ari Fleischer, Bush's press secretary during his first term, said the role of the press secretary ". . . is to faithfully articulate what the president thinks and why he thinks it. That's what a press secretary ultimately does for a living. A substantial part of it is trying to help the press, but never forgetting that you represent and work for the president."

Despite the pressure-cooker environment of being grilled by a roomful of aggressive, competitive reporters every day—often on live television—the job of press secretary to the president has

> **" I want to do something more relaxing—like dismantle live nuclear weapons. "**
>
> ——Quip from *Ari Fleischer,* on his resignation as presidential Press Secretary

its rewards. Former press secretary Marlin Fitzwater, who served George Bush senior and Ronald Reagan, says, "It's the greatest job in the world and worth taking no matter how much trouble your President is in. Now, you may die in the job, it may ruin your life and reputation. But it still will have been the greatest experience in your life." Most former press secretaries also give the advice, "keep a sense of humor."

State Information Services

Every state provides public information services. In California, the most populous state, there are about 175 public information officers (PIOs) in about 70 state agencies. On a daily basis, PIOs provide routine information to the public and the press on the policies, programs, and activities of the various state agencies.

State agencies also conduct a variety of public information and education campaigns, often with the assistance of public relations firms that have been selected through a bidding process. A state agency, for example, will issue a request for proposal (RFP) and award a contract on the basis of presentations from competing firms.

One program area is health and safety. The Florida Department of Health took a somewhat creative approach to the risk of pandemic influenza without even mentioning the word. Research indicated that the public didn't believe the risk was real, so the approach was to emphasize basic hygiene practices with a "Fifth Guy" campaign based around the fact that one in five people don't wash their hands after using the restroom, cover their mouth when they cough, or stay home when they are sick. Herle Communications Group hired an actor to play "the fifth guy" for a morning-show media tour around the state. There was also a Web site, videos uploaded to YouTube.com, and a MySpace presence.

The California Department of Health Services (DHS) also runs various campaigns on a variety of health issues, such as encouraging immunization shots for children, screening for breast cancer, and preventing teen pregnancy. The California Highway Patrol (CHP) also conducts safety campaigns. One recent campaign was an effort to increase seat-belt use and decrease drunk driving accidents among African Americans. Statistical data indicated that this audience was less likely to use seat belts and more likely to die in an alcohol-related crash. According to the CHP, leaders in the African American community supported the campaign and didn't find it to be discriminatory.

In Virginia, the Department of Health launched a campaign to reduce the number of instances of statutory rape and other forms of sexual coercion. The campaign had the slogan "Isn't She a Little Young" with the tagline "Sex with a minor. Don't go there." The health department used billboards and sent 255,000 postcards, posters, coasters, and napkins to bars and restaurants in the state.

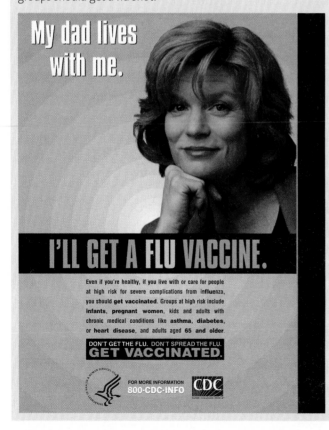

Governmental agencies promote health and safety in a number of public information campaigns. This poster by the Centers for Disease Control advocates that people in daily contact with risk groups should get a flu shot.

Other state campaigns have targeted litter. The Texas Department of Transportation conducted an antilitter campaign with the slogan "Don't Mess With Texas." Research showed that most of the litter on the highways was from people under the age of 24. Therefore, the campaign was pitched to this audience through videos and high school assembly programs. In California, the slogan was "Don't Trash California." Ogilvy PR Worldwide received a $6.5 million contract to conduct a multicultural, statewide effort in English, Spanish, and Asian languages. Radio spots and billboards were used to reach the driving public.

States also promote tourism through advertising and public relations campaigns. Tourism and conventions are the second-largest industry in Wisconsin, so the Department of Tourism concentrates on branding Wisconsin as a destination for cheese lovers (350 types of cheese are produced here) and beer drinkers ("Beer Capital of the U.S."). The Illinois Department of Commerce and Economic Opportunity also is interested in tourism and recently awarded a $6.5 million contract to Edelman Worldwide to develop it. Pennsylvania spends between $8 million and $12 million annually promoting tourism.

Another area is economic development. Delaware, a small state with less than 800,000 people, hired a public relations firm to conduct a $600,000 campaign to attract business investment. The public relations firm used the slogan "It's good being first," referring to Delaware being the first state to adopt the U.S. Constitution. The public relations firm admitted it was a difficult assignment. The firm's president told *PRWeek*, "As opposed to having a bad image, Delaware simply has no image at all."

Meanwhile, down in Florida, the Department of Citrus tapped Golin/Harris International to reemphasize the role of orange juice in breakfasts. The citrus industry is a $9 billion business in Florida and employs 90,000 workers. Consequently, the state wants to position orange juice as an essential part of breakfast for the American family. The slogan: "The best start under the sun."

City Information Services

Cities employ information specialists to disseminate news and information from numerous municipal departments. Such agencies may include the airport, transit district, redevelopment office, parks and recreation, convention and visitors bureau, police and fire, city council, and the mayor's office.

The information flow occurs in many ways, but all have the objective of informing citizens and helping them take full advantage of opportunities. The city council holds neighborhood meetings; an airport commission sets up an exhibit showing the growth needs of the airport; the recreation department promotes summer swimming lessons; and the city's human rights commission sponsors a festival promoting multiculturalism.

Cities also promote themselves to attract new business. *PRWeek* reports, "The competition for cities and wider regions to attract businesses is as intense as ever, experts say, with an estimated 12,000 economic development organizations vying for the roughly 500 annual corporate moves/expansions that involve 250 or more jobs each." Bob Marcusse, president of the Kansas City Area Development Council, told *PRWeek*, "The stakes are so high because success means millions of dollars in taxes, it means wealth creation, it means jobs. It is the lifeblood of the community."

Consequently, many cities pump millions of dollars into attracting new business through a variety of communication tools that include elaborate brochures, placement of favorable "success" stories in the nation's press, direct mail, telemarketing, trade fairs, special events, and meetings with business executives.

Cities also promote themselves in an effort to increase tourism, which is further discussed in Chapter 22. An example of city information efforts is the campaign by the

Panama City (Florida) Convention and Visitors Bureau to position itself as a prime destination for college students during spring break. According to *PRWeek*, the bureau spent about $300,000 promoting the city through posters, news releases, brochures, advertising, and special events to let students know that they were welcome. Indeed, the "spring breakers," as they are called, pumped about $135 million into the local economy.

Improving the image of a city is also an objective. Gary, Indiana, long a city in decline because of steel mill closings, bid $1.2 million to play host to the Miss U.S.A. beauty pageant. It was hoped that the pageant, televised nationally, would bring recognition and some degree of prestige to the city. The mayor told a *New York Times* reporter that the pageant "has the ability to build local pride in the city and the psychology of the public in a positive way. If you don't have that, nothing else you do is going to work."

Although beauty pageants are a good "hook" for creating short-time national visibility and tourism for a city, extensive information efforts are also needed when a natural disaster strikes. When Des Moines, Iowa, was flooded several years ago and the city's water supply became contaminated, the city conducted an aggressive information campaign to keep the public informed of flood developments and hold anxiety to a minimum.

Criticism of Government Information Efforts

Although the need for government to inform citizens and publicize programs is accepted in principle, many skeptics are critical about the cost and true purpose of such activities. Such criticism reached a high point during the Bush presidency because his administration spent literally billions of dollars on "public information" campaigns to publicize various presidential initiatives.

Between 2003 and early 2006, the Bush administration spent over $1.6 billion on hundreds of contracts with advertising and public relations firms to promote its position on issues such as energy policies, the Medicare prescription plan, and the No Child Left Behind Act. In addition, the Department of Defense spent another $1.1 billion on advertising and public relations. Democratic legislators such as Nancy Pelosi and Henry Waxman, among a chorus of others, criticized the expenditures as "covert propaganda." Federal law, for example, prohibits the government from engaging in propaganda to support a partisan cause.

The Bush administration, say critics, crossed the line in its campaign to promote the No Child Left Behind legislation. It became a major issue in the mainstream press when it was revealed that conservative commentator Armstrong Williams was paid $240,000 to promote the legislation on his syndicated radio and television shows without disclosing that he was being paid. A large chorus of legislators and journalists expressed outrage about the "pay for play" scheme and called for an investigation concerning the improper use of taxpayer money to pay for "propaganda" campaigns.

Also getting a black eye in the controversy was Ketchum, a major public relations firm that had received a $1 million contract from the U.S. Office of Education to promote No Child Left Behind. Part of the contract included the $240,000 payment to Williams. In addition, Ketchum was commissioned to produce and distribute VNRs that promoted the legislation. A controversy then erupted whether these VNRs were misleading because the U.S. Office of Education was not adequately identified as the sponsor of the material. The result was a 2005 ruling by the General Accounting Office (GAO) that federal money could be spent on such communication vehicles as VNRS but that they must openly acknowledge the government's role in their production.

Budget hawks in Congress also worry about cost and intent of other government information programs. Brad Sherman (R-CA) told the *Los Angeles Daily News*, "There's a growing tendency to spend money to make government look good. It's hard for me to think this is the best possible use of taxpayer's dollars." Congressional lawmakers were even more critical of a proposal to spend $10 million over a five-year period to boost the image of AmeriCorps as an effective volunteer service organization. House Majority Whip Roy Blount (R-MO) said, "AmeriCorps should be spending its taxpayer funds to help the needy. The good they can do for Americans in need with their $10 million PR budget will be its own positive message."

Others, including journalists, criticize public information activities because legislators are notorious for sending reams of useless news releases that often just promote themselves. Such abuse, coupled with snide news stories about the cost of maintaining government "public relations" experts, rankle dedicated public information officers (PIOs) at the various state and federal agencies who work very hard to keep the public informed with a daily diet of announcements and news stories. One PIO for a California agency said, "I'd like to see the press find out what's going on in state government without us."

Indeed, a major source of media hostility seems to stem from the fact that reporters are heavily dependent on handouts. In one study, almost 90 percent of a state government's news releases were used by daily and weekly newspapers. The textbook *Media: An Introductory Analysis of American Mass Communications* by Sandman, Rubin, and Sachsman puts it succinctly: "If a newspaper were to quit relying on news releases, but continued covering the news it now covers, it would need at least two or three times more reporters."

> " I'd like to see the press find out what's going on in state government without us. "
>
> ——A PIO officer for a California state agency

News releases, however, are only one aspect of helping the media do their job. The city of Homestead, Florida, spent $70,000 on facilities and staff just to handle the deluge of reporters who descended on the city in the aftermath of Hurricane Andrew. And cities across the country also spent considerable amounts of money providing news facilities for visiting reporters when presidential candidates come to town. Public information efforts also are justified in terms of cost efficiency. The U.S. Department of Agriculture public affairs office receives hundreds of inquiries every year. Two-thirds of the requests can be answered with a simple pamphlet, brochure, or a link on its Web site.

There is also the argument about how much the public saves through preventive public relations. The taxpayers of California spend about $7 billion annually to deal with the associated costs of teenage pregnancy, so $5.7 million spent on a successful education campaign could save the state considerably more in reduced welfare costs. Michigan's $100,000 expenditure to educate citizens about recycling aerosol cans does much to reduce the costs of opening more landfills.

An Associated Press reporter acknowledged in a story that government information does have value. He wrote:

> While some of the money and manpower goes for self-promotion, by far the greater amount is committed to an indispensable function of a democratic government— informing the people.
>
> What good would it serve for the Consumer Product Safety Commission to recall a faulty kerosene heater and not go to the expense of alerting the public to its action? An informed citizenry needs the government to distribute its economic statistics, announce its antitrust suits, tell about the health of the president, give crop forecasts.

SUMMARY

Corporate Public Affairs

A major component of corporate communications is public affairs, which primarily deals with governmental relations at the local, state, national, and even international levels. Public affairs specialists build relationships with civil servants and elected officials and also monitor governmental actions that may affect the employer or client. Trade groups, primarily based in state capitals or Washington, D.C., have public affairs specialists representing various professions and industries.

Lobbying

A public affairs specialist primarily provides information about the organization's viewpoint to the public and government entities. A lobbyist has a more specialized function to work directly for the defeat, passage, or amendment of proposed legislation and regulatory agency policies. In recent years, there has been public concern about "influence peddling" in terms of former legislators and other officials becoming lobbyists and "cashing in" on their knowledge and connections. To curb abuse, several laws have been passed (1995 and 2007) to regulate lobbyists.

Election Campaigns

The cost of running for office in the United States is the highest in the world. An army of specialists, including public relations experts, are retained by major candidates to organize and raise money for election campaigns. In recent years, the Internet has played an important role in raising money, generating high visibility for candidates, and increasing the number of registered voters.

Campaign Finance Reform

The large amount of "soft money" given to candidates was curtailed by the McCain-Feingold Act, and individuals and groups have restrictions on how much can be given to candidates, state parties, and national parties. However, 527 groups are a loophole in this law. These partisan organizations, which have no official connection to the candidate or the political party, were a major force in the 2004 presidential elections in terms of placing numerous "attack" ads.

Public Affairs in Government

Governments, since the ancient Egyptians, have always engaged in campaigns to inform, motivate, and even persuade the public. In the United States, Congress forbids federal agencies from "persuading" the public, so the emphasis is on "public information" efforts. All agencies of the federal government employ public affairs officers and public information specialists. Members of Congress also engage in extensive "information" efforts to reach their constituents.

The White House

The apex of all government information and public relations efforts is the White House; the president's every move and action is chronicled by the mass media. Presidents throughout history have used this media attention to lead the nation, convince the public to support administration policies, and get reelected. The White House press secretary probably has the most stressful and demanding job in terms of dealing with the press on a daily basis.

State Information Services

Various states employ public information officers to tell the public about the activities and policies of various agencies. In addition, agencies conduct a number of campaigns to inform the public about health and safety issues. Another initiative is to promote the state as a tourist destination.

City Information Services

All major cities employ public information specialists to tell citizens about city services and promote economic development.

Criticism of Government Information Services

Major expenditures by the Bush administration to promote its programs caused a wave of criticism from journalists and legislators. However, most government information progams are needed to inform the public about programs and services offered by any number of agencies. In addition, preventive information campaigns often save government millions of dollars a year by reducing litter, teen pregnancy, and smoking.

CASE ACTIVITY What Would You Do?

Fake News or Information?

Video news releases are a standard public relations tactic, but the use of them by the Bush administration has stirred major controversy and criticism. The *New York Times* has called VNRs distributed by government agencies "fake news," and is concerned that the public is not being told that a particular video clip or narration originated from a government agency.

Public relations executives, including government agency officials, contend that all government-produced VNRs are clearly identified as to the source. "Talk to the television stations that ran it without attribution," says William A. Pierce, spokesperson for the Department of Health and Human Services. He is further quoted in the *New York Times*, "This is not our problem. We can't be held responsible for their actions." Rick Rice, a California governmental agency official, points out that VNRs are just like printed news releases and, ultimately, a journalist decides what to use—and even attribute.

What do you think? First, is it a legitimate information function of governmental agencies to produce VNRs? Second, if government-produced VNRs are aired, who has the ultimate responsibility to ensure that the public knows the source of the news item?

QUESTIONS for Review and Discussion

1. What is the difference between someone working in corporate public affairs (governmental relations) and a lobbyist?

2. What skills are needed for work in corporate public affairs?

3. The public, in general, has low esteem for lobbyists. Do you think the perception is justified? Why or why not?

4. Lobbyists for the food industry are very involved in trying to influence federal guidelines for good nutrition. What's at stake for them and the industries they represent?

5. Many lobbyists are former legislators and government officials. Do you think they exercise undue influence in the shaping of legislation? Why or why not?

6. What were the major points of the lobbying reform act? Do you think the law has curtailed excessive "influence-peddling"? Why or why not?

7. Name some guidelines for ethical grassroots lobbying.

8. The issue has been raised about the use of "front groups" in grassroots lobbying efforts. Do you think the public has a right to know what special interests are funding many of these efforts?

9. Summarize the major parts of the McCain-Feingold Act. Do you think this law has effectively curtailed unregulated large gifts to candidates and parties?

10. Fund-raisers play a crucial role in elections. Would you like to be a political fund-raiser? Why or why not?

11. How did Howard Dean use the Internet in the Democratic primaries? Do you think the Internet will play an even more important role in the 2008 elections?

12. The major issue of the 2004 presidential election was the activities of 527s. Explain what these groups are and how they operated during the election. What's your opinion of 527s? Should the Federal Election Commission (FEC) ban them? Why or why not?

13. Why do government agencies engage in "public information" efforts instead of "public relations" activities? Are there any laws involved? If so, what are they?

14. The Pentagon was criticized for stonewalling information regarding abuse of Iraqi prisoners. Do you think the criticism was justified? Why or why not? What about commanders asking soldiers to sign form letters supporting the war and sending them to their hometown newspapers?

15. Federal agencies engage in any number of public information campaigns. What is your opinion on this? Are these campaigns just a waste of taxpayer dollars, or are they legitimate and necessary?

16. The office of White House Press Secretary is one of the most demanding jobs in communications. Why is it so demanding, and would you ever aspire to hold this job? Why or why not?

SUGGESTED READINGS

Andrews, Edmund. "As Congress Turns to Energy, Lobbyists Are Out in Force." *New York Times*, June 12, 2007, p. A14.

Auletta, Ken. "Fortress Bush: How the White House Keeps the Press Under Control." *New Yorker*, January 19, 2004, pp. 53–65.

Bowen, Shanon A. "Narratives of the SARS Epidemic and Ethical Implications for Public Health Crises." *International Journal of Strategic Communication*, Vol. 1, No. 2, 2006, pp. 73–91.

Barstow, David, and Stein, Robin. "Under Bush, a New Age of Prepackaged TV News." *New York Times*, March 13, 2005, www.nytimes.com/2005/03/13/politics.

Broder, John M., and Risen, James. "Blackwater Mounts a Defense With Top Talent from Capital." *New York Times*, November 1, 2007, p. 1, A8.

Cooper, Michael, and Luo, Michael. "Where the Campaign Money Goes." *New York Times*, July 18, 2007, pp. A1, A11.

Crowley, Michael. "Can Lobbyists Stop the War?" *New York Times Magazine*, September 9, 2007, pp. 56–59.

Delaney, Kevin, and Schatz, Amy. "Google Goes to Washington With Its Own Brand of Lobbying." *Wall Street Journal*, July 20, 2007, pp. A1, A14.

Kirkpatrick, David. "Tougher Rules Change Game for Lobbyists." *New York Times*, August 7, 2007, pp. A1, A12.

Lipton, Eric. "FEMA Aide Loses New Job Over Fake News Conference." *New York Times*, October 30, 2007, p. A4.

Liu, Brooke Fisher, and Horsley, J. Suzanne. "The Government Communication Decision Wheel: Toward a Public Relations Model for the Public Sector." *Journal of Public Relations Research*, Vol. 19, No. 4, 2007, pp. 377–393.

Luce, Edward. "Cash and the Candidacy: Policy Comes a Poor Second in America's Billion-Dollar Battle." *Financial Times*, May 31, 2007, p. 9.

Martinelli, Diana Knott. "Strategic Public Information: Engaging Audiences in Government Agencies' Work." *Public Relations Quarterly*, Spring 2006, pp. 37–41.

McKenna, Ted. "A Call to Arms: The Latest Recruitment Effort by the U.S. Army." *PRWeek*, June 7, 2007, p. 17.

Tumulty, Karen. "The Man Who Bought Washington." *Time*, January 16, 2006, pp. 30–39.

Wang, Jian. "Managing National Reputation and International Relations in the Global Era: Public Diplomacy Revisited." *Public Relations Review*, June 2006, Vol. 32, No. 2, pp. 91–96.

Wise, Kurt. "Lobbying and Relationship Management: The K Street Connection." *Journal of Public Relations Research*, Vol, 19, No. 4, 2007, pp. 357–376.

Zielbauer, Paul von. "Propaganda Fear is Cited in Account of Killings of Iraqis." *New York Times*, May 6, 2007, pp. A1, 12.

Global Public Relations

TOPICS COVERED IN THIS CHAPTER INCLUDE:

What Is Global Public Relations?

Global or *international public relations*, may be defined as the planned and organized effort of a company, institution, or government to establish and build relationships with the publics of other nations. These publics, in turn, may be defined as the various groups of people who are affected by, or who can affect, the operations of a particular firm, institution, or government.

International public relations may also be viewed from the standpoint of its practice in individual countries. Although public relations is commonly regarded as a concept developed in the United States at the beginning of the 20th century, some of its elements, such as countering unfavorable public attitudes by means of disclosure of operations through publicity and annual reports, were practiced by railroad companies and at least one shareholding corporation in Germany as far back as the mid-19th century, to mention only one such country. (See Chapter 2.)

Even so, it is largely American techniques that have been adapted to national and regional public relations practices throughout the world, including many totalitarian nations. Today, although in some languages there is no term comparable to *public relations*, the practice has spread to most countries, especially those with industrial bases and large urban populations. This is primarily the result of worldwide technological, social, economic, and political changes and the growing understanding that public relations is an essential component of advertising, marketing, and diplomacy.

Global Corporate Public Relations

This section explores the new age of global marketing and emphasizes that differences in language, laws, and cultural mores must be overcome when companies conduct business in other countries. We also discuss how U.S. public relations firms represent foreign interests in this country as well as U.S. corporations in other parts of the world. Aspects of public relations practice in some other nations are delineated.

The New Age of Global Marketing

For decades, hundreds of corporations based in the United States have been engaged in international business operations, including marketing, advertising, and public relations. These activities swelled to unprecedented proportions during the 1990s, largely because of new communications technologies, development of 24-hour financial markets almost worldwide, the lowering of trade barriers, the growth of sophisticated foreign competition in traditionally "American" markets, and the shrinking cultural differences that are bringing the "global village" ever closer to reality.

Today almost one-third of all U.S. corporate profits are generated through international business. In the case of Coca-Cola, probably the best-known brand name in the world, international sales account for 70 percent of the company's revenues. In addition, large U.S.-based public relations firms such as Burson-Marsteller and Edelman now generate between 30 and 40 percent of their fees serving foreign clients (see Chapter 4).

At the same time, overseas investors are moving into American industry. It is not uncommon for 15 to 20 percent of a U.S. company's stock to be held abroad. The United Kingdom, for example, has a direct foreign investment in the United States exceeding $122 billion, followed by Japan and the Netherlands with nearly half that sum each, according to the U.S. Department of Commerce.

Fueling the new age of global public relations and marketing are satellite television, computer networks, electronic mail, fax, fiber optics, cellular telephone systems, and emerging technologies such as integrated services digital networks (ISDN), which enable users to send voice, data, graphics, and video over existing copper cables. For example, Hill and Knowlton has its own satellite transmission facilities, and the General Electric Company has formed an international telecommunications network, enabling employees to communicate worldwide using voice, video, and computer data simply by dialing seven digits on a telephone. Using three satellite systems, Cable News Network (CNN) is viewed by more than 200 million people in more than 140 countries. England's BBC world service also reaches an impressive number of nations, including the 40+ members of the British Commonwelth. A number of newspapers and magazines are also reaching millions with international editions. *Cosmopolitan*, to cite one example, has 50 foreign editions. And, of course, the *Wall Street Journal* and the *Financial Times* have daily editions in the United States, Europe, and Asia.

Differences in language, laws, and cultural mores among countries (to be discussed shortly) are a continuing challenge in cultural sensitivity. There also is a need for both managers and employees to learn to think and act in global terms as quickly as possible. Already, Burson-Marsteller, with offices in many countries, has been spending more than $1 million a year on training tapes and traveling teams of trainers and seminars to foster a uniform approach to client projects.

Much of the new business jousting takes place on West European terrain, where a recently expanded European Union (EU) attracts enormous attention. In recent years, public relations expenditures have increased significantly. The growth has been precipitated in part by expansion of commercial television resulting from widespread privatization, the desire of viewers for more varied programming, satellite technology, and slowly developing EU business patterns. Rupert Murdoch's SkyB satellite channel reaches about 10 million households, and Europeans now have access to cable systems for television, the Internet, pay-per-view movies, and sporting events. On the print side, the business press has been growing about 20 percent every year, and there are about 15,000 trade publications in Western Europe.

Although the EU promoted the phrase "a single Europe," corporations and public relations firms still face the complex task of communicating effectively to 400 million people in 25 countries speaking multiple languages.

Language and Cultural Differences

Companies operating in other nations are confronted with essentially the same public relations challenges as those in the United States. The objective is to successfully compete and also to manage conflict, but the task is more complex on an international and intercultural level.

Public relations practitioners need to recognize cultural differences, adapt to local customs, and understand the finer points of verbal and nonverbal communication in individual nations. Experts in intercultural communication point out that many cultures, particularly non-Western ones, are "high-context" communication societies. This means that the meaning of the spoken word is often implicit and based on the environmental context and the relationship rather than on explicit, categorical statements. The communication style of Asian and Arab nations, for example, is "high context."

This is in contrast with the European and American communication styles, which are considered "low context." Great emphasis is placed on exact words, and the receiver is expected to derive most of the meaning from the written or verbalized statements, not from nonverbal behavior cues. Legal documents produced in the West are the ultimate in explicit wording.

The concept of low- and high-context communication styles is manifested in several ways. Americans, for example, tend to be very direct (and often blunt) in their communication style. In high-context cultures, Americans often are perceived as verbose, opinionated, and very focused on getting to the point as soon as possible. They also are clock watchers, get upset if meetings don't start on time, and carry day planners as if they were bibles.

The communication style in a high-context culture is quite different. Group harmony is more important than take-charge individualistic traits, a social relationship must be built before business is conducted, a handshake takes the place of a legal contract, and being on time to a meeting isn't all that important. One aspect of high-context Asian cultures is "loss of face." Individuals don't want to offend, so a person will never say "no" outright. A Japanese executive, for example, will suck air through his or her teeth and exclaim, "Sa! That will be very difficult" when they really mean "no."

There also are other cultural differences. Geert Hofstede, a company psychologist for global giant IBM, studied national/cultural differences among employees around the world back in the 1970s and came up with five basic cultural dimensions. Today, students still rely on his typology to understand various national cultures. Professors David Guth and Charles Marsh of the University of Kansas summarized Hofstede's cultural dimensions in their book, *Adventures in Public Relations: Case Studies and Critical Thinking*:

1. *Power distance* measures how tolerant a society is about unequally distributed decision-making power. In other words, management makes all the decisions and there is little input from rank-and-file employees. Countries with a high acceptance of power distance include Mexico and France. Countries with a low acceptance include Austria and the United States.

2. *Individualism*, as contrasted with *collectivisim*, pits loyalty to one's self against loyalty to a larger group. Countries in Asia and Latin America gravitate toward collectivism, whereas the United States, Canada, and most European countries gravitate toward individualism.

3. *Masculinity/femininity* contrasts competitiveness (traditionally masculine) against compassion and nurturing (traditionally feminine). Masculine nations include the United States, Germany, and Japan. Feminine nations include Sweden and Spain.

4. *Uncertainty avoidance* measures how well a society tolerates ambiguity. Nations that have difficulty functioning in uncertainty include Germany. Nations that tolerate ambiguity include Great Britain and the United States.

5. *Long-term/short-term orientation* measures a society's willingness to consider the traditions of the past and carry them into the future. China and other East Asian nations tend to have long-term orientations. The United States has a short-term orientation.

Language, of course, is another challenge. The following are some examples of the type of language problems that have been reported in various newspaper and magazine articles:

◆ A British executive staying at a hotel in New York was embarrassed because he asked the front desk for a "rubber," which is an eraser in England. The hotel staff thought he wanted a condom.

◆ A producer of calzones, which are cheese- and meat-filled turnovers, had a major marketing problem in Spain because, in Spanish, *calzone* means "underwear."

◆ The Milk Processor Association found that the catchy phrase "Got Milk?" didn't translate too well into Spanish. The literal translation was "Are You Lactating?"

◆ The "thumbs up" gesture in the United States means "well done" or "good job." In other cultures, it can be considered offensive and should be avoided. Also, the thumb-and-forefinger "OK" sign is an obscene gesture in many cultures.

Cultural differences provide additional pitfalls, as shown by the following examples:

◆ In China, tables at a banquet are never numbered. The Chinese think such tables appear to rank guests or that certain numbers are unlucky. It's better to direct a guest to the "primrose" or "hollyhock" table.

◆ Americans are fond of using first names, but it's not proper business etiquette in Europe and Asia unless you have been given permission.

◆ Early morning breakfast meetings are not done in Latin America; by the same token, a dinner meeting may not start until 9 or 10 P.M.

◆ In Thailand, patting a child on the head is seen as a grave offense because the head is considered sacred. Also, it's considered a crime to make disrespectful remarks about the royal family, particularly the king.

◆ In Latin America, a greeting often includes physical contact by hugging the individual or grabbing them by the arm. Men and women commonly greet each other with a kiss on the cheek in Argentina and Chile.

◆ News releases in Malaysia should be distributed in four languages to avoid alienating any segment of the press.

◆ Gift-giving is common in Asian cultures. Executives, meeting for the first time, will exchange gifts as a way of building a social relationship.

◆ In Muslim nations, particularly in the Middle East, men should not stand near, touch, or stare at any woman. Conservative dress for women, even foreign visitors, is required.

All of these illustrations indicate that Americans and others not only must learn the customs of the country in which they are working, but they also should rely on native professionals to guide them. See the Multicultural World box on page 509 about Starbucks in China. Media materials and advertising must be translated, and the best approach is to employ native speakers who have extensive experience in translating ad copy and public relations materials. An example is the FedEx news release on page 508.

Representing Foreign Corporations in the United States

Corporations and industries in other countries frequently employ public relations and lobbying firms to advance their products, services, and political interests in the United States. In fact, in a six-year period from 1998 to mid-2004, the Center for Public Integrity (a nonprofit watchdog group) reported that 700 companies, with headquarters in about 100 nations, spent more than $520 million lobbying the U.S. government. The center's analysis continues, "Over that time, those companies employed 550 lobbying

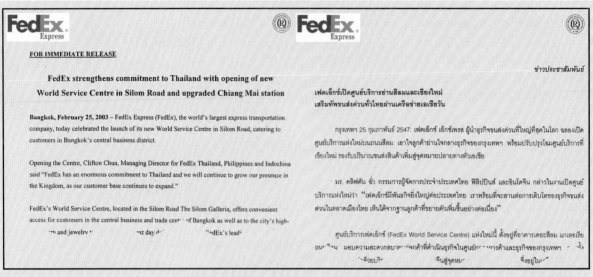

International public relations requires the translation of news releases into several languages. Here, the first part of this FedEx announcement is in English. Also shown is the same announcement in Thai. (MDK consulting/Bangkok)

firms and teams of 3,800 lobbyists, more than 100 of whom were former members of Congress." (More details can be found at www.public-i.org.)

Companies from the United Kingdom (UK) top the list, spending more than $180 million betweeen 1998 and 2004. This included BP (British Petroleum) and the pharmaeutical giant GlaxoSmithKline, which have extensive operations in the United States. GlaxoSmithKline, for example, consistently lobbies on Medicare and Medicaid reform issues. BP, on the other hand, lobbies on matters relating to environmental standards and oil and gas issues. Companies from Germany are second on the list, spending about $70 million on lobbying. The major spender is Daimler Chrysler Corporation. Swiss corporations are third with about the same expenditures, and Japanese companies are fourth with about $60 million during the six-year period.

Even companies that don't directly operate in the United States engage in lobbying. They seek to ensure an advantageous trade policy in international trade agreements, of which the United States is a major player. According to the Center for Public Integrity, "Not surprisingly, international trade was by far the most common issue foreign companies reported lobbying on, followed by defense and taxation."

Carl Levin, vice president and senior consultant, Burson-Marsteller, Washington, D.C., gives five major reasons for a foreign corporation to retain a public relations counsel in the United States

- ◆ *To hold off protectionist moves threatening their company or industry.* Companies from India, for example, are concerned that Congress may place restrictions on U.S. firms that outsource various activities such as customer service to India and other nations.

- ◆ *To defeat legislation affecting the sale of a client's product.* African nations, for example, strive to change legislation that favors American-grown cotton and places high tariffs on African-produced cotton.

- ◆ *To provide ongoing information on political, legal, and commercial developments in the United States that could bear on the client's business interests,* Nations such as Iran,

on the job

A MULTICULTURAL WORLD

Starbucks in China: Cultural Sensitivities and the Power of the Blog

Should Starbucks have a shop in the Forbidden City, the hallowed 600-year-old home of China's emperors? In a classic case of conflict management, Starbucks became the topic of a Web crusade to be expelled from China's national icon because many Chinese believe it offends their national culture to have a U.S.-based company selling coffee in the compound.

Although Starbucks has had a small outlet in the Forbidden City since 2000, the pressure for closing the shop began in early 2007 when 29-year-old news anchor Rui Chenggang wrote on his blog that Starbucks "is really too inappropriate for the world's impression of the Forbidden City. This isn't globalization, this is the erosion of Chinese Culture." In the space of a week, his posting had been viewed more than a half-million times, and his demand to shut the café turned into a national cause. Indeed, the Chinese use of the Internet to express their opinions is giving foreign corporations major headaches. China is home to 132 million Internet users, second only to the United States. And according to one government estimate, there are 20 million Chinese bloggers, of whom more than 3 million write actively.

Rui Chenggang even e-mailed the president of Starbucks suggesting that the store be removed from the Forbidden City. Starbuck's CEO, Jim McDonald, responded, "We have shown and continue to show our respect for local history, culture and social customs, and have made a serious effort to fit within the environment of the Forbidden City." According to the *Wall Street Journal,* the Starbucks shop doesn't even have its logo on a sign outside the shop, which is housed next to the national museum store.

Starbucks officials declined further comment, but Geoffrey Fowler, a reporter for the *Wall Street Journal,* writes that government officials often heed online protests and make changes. A KFC store at Beihai Park, a scenic imperial garden north of the Forbidden City, was closed after a local political advisory board objected.

In sum, Starbucks is going through the contingency continuum outlined in Chapter 10. Should the company be a strong advocate for keeping its kiosk open in the Forbidden City, or should it move toward more accommodation and resolution? According to Fowler, "Even blog crisis advisors don't entirely agree on how companies should respond to bloggers in these cases." He quotes Sam Flemming, the chief executive of Shanghai-based blogging consultancy, CIC, which works for Pepsi and Nike Inc. "And then you should react quickly. Consumers feel like they should be listened to. If they feel like they're being ignored, it makes things even worse."

Source: Fowler, Geoffrey. "It's Called the Forbidden City for a Reason." *Wall Street Journal,* January 19, 2007, p. B1.

Sudan, and Burma are greatly affected when the U.S. government places sanctions on doing business or investments in the country.

◆ *To support expansion of the client's markets in the United States.* Unilever, a competitor of Procter & Gamble in the home products area, has extensively promoted its products such as Dove in the American market.

◆ *To deal with a crisis situation that threatens the financial health or reputation of an organization.* China, for example, stepped up public relations activities in the United States to restore its reputation after Mattel recalled millions of toys manufactured in Chinese plants.

Representing U.S. Corporations in Other Nations

Many U.S. corporations are global in scope in terms of employees, products, manufacturing plants, and distribution centers. In fact, the four largest public companies in the world in descending order of market value are American-based: ExxonMobil ($362 billion), General Electric ($348 billion), Microsoft ($279 billion), and Citigroup ($234 billion).

These giant corporations, including hundreds of other U.S. companies, also engage in extensive public relations and lobbying activities in other nations for virtually the same five reasons that Levin lists in the previous section. The total amount expended on public relations and lobbying abroad, however, is not known because U.S. companies don't have to report such expenditures to the U.S. government.

Public relations professionals who work for these giants, as well as a host of other American companies, are automatically in the field of international public relations, because their work involves many nations. Many of these corporations also retain global public relations firms such as Burson-Marsteller and Hill & Knowlton to provide services from offices in major cities around the world. The global scope of public relations firms was discussed in Chapter 4.

American companies, at the start of the 21st century and in the aftermath of the 9/11 terrorist attacks in 2001, face a number of challenges abroad in terms of competing with other large corporations headquartered in other nations, dealing with sustainable development, being boycotted by nations that disagree with American foreign policy, and being good corporate citizens at the local and national level.

David Drobis, a former senior partner and chair of Ketchum, outlined some of these challenges in a talk to the International Communications Consultancy Organization (ICCO). According to Drobis, one major challenge is to better communicate the economic advantages of globalization to the world's people. The *Economist*, for example, has called globalization a massive communications failure because the public and private sectors have done such a poor job communicating the benefits, being transparent about their activities, and building important alliances.

Drobis believes that public relations professionals are the best-suited group to explain the benefits of globalization. These benefits must be communicated to three key groups. The first group is the companies themselves. Companies must realize that international capitalism has a bad connotation in many parts of the world because it's perceived as nothing more than "a byword for oppression, exploitation, and injustice by rapacious multinationals."

Companies, Drobis says, have done little to correct this view despite the efforts of a few highly responsible companies who have outstanding programs. He continues,

> companies must take into consideration a broad group of stakeholders as they pursue their business goals globally. And by doing so, there are tangible and intangible business benefits. In this way, good corporate citizenship is not a cost of doing business, but rather a driver of business success. What's good for the soul is also good for business. . . .

Trade is now a global enterprise, but not everyone is happy about it. Here, protestors demonstrate against the World Trade Organization (WTO) and its policies. Today, as never before, international organizations and corporations must pay attention to public opinion on a global basis.

[Studies show] that companies that pursue initiatives—be they related to the environment, labor standards, or human rights—are rewarded with improved business success in a number of areas, including shareholder value, revenue, operational efficiencies, higher employee morale and productivity, and corporate reputation.

The second group that must be informed of the benefits of globalization is nongovernmental organizations (NGOs). Although many NGOs are outright hostile to all private enterprise, American companies must realize that NGOs can become an important seal of approval for brands. Indeed, major mainstream NGOs such as the World Wildlife Fund and Greenpeace are working with corporations on sustainable development programs. The *Financial Times* notes, "A new type of relationship is emerging between companies and NGOs, where NGOs act as certification bodies, and, in many cases, permitting the use of their logos, showing that products and services are being produced in a socially responsible and environmentally friendly ways."

The third group is international institutions such as the World Trade Organization (WTO), the World Bank, the International Monetary Fund (IMF), or even the United Nations. Drobis says these organizations are unfairly criticized as being undemocratic, but fairly criticized for being nontransparent. An article in *Foreign Affairs* puts it this way: "To outsiders, even within the same government, these institutions can look like closed and secretive clubs. Increased transparency is essential. International organizations can provide more access to their deliberations, even after the fact."

Drobis, in giving advice to American companies doing business abroad, concludes that the era of "relationship building" is over. Instead, he says, the 21st century is one of "confidence building" in the international arena so various publics not only trust corporations to do the right thing, but believe globalization is a benefit to hundreds of millions of poor people around the globe. On a more basic level, American corporations use public relations as part of the marketing mix to market its products and services around the globe.

International Government Public Relations

This section explores how and why the governments of most nations seek to influence the opinions and actions of governments and people in other countries. Many employ U.S. public relations firms for this purpose.

Influencing Other Countries

The governments of virtually every country have one or more departments involved in communicating with other nations. Much effort and millions of dollars are spent on the tourism industry, attracting visitors whose expenditures aid the local economy. Even larger sums are devoted to lobbying efforts to obtain favorable legislation for a country's products; for example, Costa Rica urged the U.S. Congress to let its sugar into the nation at favorable rates.

Conflict and war also generates public relations efforts by nations to make their case in the world court of public opinion. See the Insights box on Israel versus the Palestinians on page 512. Israel has also been active on the public relations front as a result of the Lebanon war in 2006.

Information Efforts by the United States   The American government is the major disseminator of information around the world. This is called *public diplomacy*, because

on the job
INSIGHTS

The Image War: Israel versus the Palestinians

The Israeli–Palestinian conflict has produced any number of news stories and photos showing Israeli soldiers, tanks, helicopters, and guided missiles being used against a relatively unarmed Palestinian population. As Israel's minister of information, Nachman Shai, said, "We looked like Goliath and they looked like David."

This has caused some concern for the Israeli government, particularly as it affects opinion in the United States, because it is important to have the continuing support of the American population and the government. That support is in danger if public opinion shifts to increased sympathy for the Palestinian cause.

Consequently, Israel has been active, encouraging the Jewish community in the United States to be more proactive in explaining the

Israeli side of the conflict. In addition, a New York public relations firm has been hired to place Israel's representatives in various media outlets. According to Steve Rubenstein, from Rubenstein Associates, "We felt people were missing the whole truth and that if we could show a fuller picture visually, it would be easier to make the Israeli case."

The Palestinians are also beginning to realize how decisive the battle for public opinion is, and various Arab groups, such as the Arab-American Anti-Discrimination Committee (ADC), have stepped up publicity efforts to inform Americans about the Palestinian side of the conflict. The group has taken full-page ads in daily newspapers across the country and written op-ed articles. Another group, the Council of American–Islamic Relations (CAIR),

also places ads in American publications to improve the image of Arabs living and working in the United States.

More recently, when the Hamas organization won the Palestinian general election in 2006, it immediately signed a $180,000 contract with a public relations consultant to persuade Europeans and Americans that it was not a group of religious fanatics who promoted suicide bombings against and hatred of Israel. Nashat Aqtash, the public relations consultant and also a teacher at Birzeit University in Ramallah, told the *Manchester Guardian,* "Hamas has an image problem. The Israelis were able to create a very bad image of the Palestinians in general and particularly Muslims and Hamas. My contract is to project the right image."

it is an open communication process primarily intended to present American society in all its complexity so citizens and governments of other nations can understand the context of U.S. actions and policies. Another function is to promote the American values of democracy, free trade, and open communication around the world.

The United States Information Agency (USIA), created in 1953 by President Dwight Eisenhower, was the primary agency involved in shaping America's image abroad. USIA, in many ways, was the direct descendant of George Creel's Committee on Public Information (CPI) during World War I and Elmer Davis's Office of War Information, in World War II (see Chapter 2).

Following World War II, the new threat, of course, was the outbreak of the Cold War with the Soviet Union and the Communist bloc nations in Eastern Europe. The Cold War was a war of words on both sides to win the "hearts and minds" of governments and their citizens around the world. Some USIA activities included (1) the stationing of public affairs officers (PAOs) at every American embassy to work with local media, (2) publication of books and magazines, (3) distribution of American films and TV programs, (4) sponsorship of tours by American dance and musical groups, (5) art shows, (6) student and faculty exchange programs such as the Fulbright program, and (7) sponsorship of lecture tours by American authors and intellectuals.

CHAPTER 19 · Global Public Relations 513

At the height of the Cold War, USIA had a budget of about $900 million and 12,000 employees. When the Soviet Union imploded in the early 1990s, the fortunes of the USIA began to fall as Congress and other critics decided that the United States didn't need such a large public profile in the world. As a result, the agency was abolished in 1999 and most of its functions were transferred to the U.S. Department of State under an undersecretary of state for public affairs and diplomacy. The staff was cut 40 percent and funding for projects decreased sharply.

The 9/11 terrorist attack on the United States created a new impetus to "sell" America and the U.S. decision to invade Afghanistan and Iraq. Once again, the cry was to "win the hearts and minds" of the world's people and to gain public, as well as international support, for U.S. actions. The effort, however, was somewhat diffused and confused because the Pentagon and the White House undertook public diplomacy efforts rather than the U.S. State Department.

The 9/11 Commission, in its 2004 final report, called for centralization of U.S. diplomacy efforts, a more robust and targeted program, and a drastic increase in funding of diplomatic exchanges and campaigns. Currently, the budget for the State Department's public diplomacy programs worldwide is $850 million (2007), an increase of $173 million from 2005 levels. Many communications experts, however, are critical of such a miniscule budget for global public diplomacy. The Pentagon's budget, in contrast, is $480 billion. See the PR Casebook on page 514 for more information on U.S. public diplomacy efforts abroad.

Broadcast Efforts   The Voice of America (VOA), created in 1948, was part of USIA for several decades. When USIA was dismantled and moved to the State Department, VOA was placed under the control of an independent federal agency, the Broadcasting Board of Governors (BOG). The idea was to have a firewall between the agency and the administration to ensure that VOA would continue to be an objective news service with credibility around the world. Article One of the VOA, for example, states that it should be a "reliable and authoritative source of news" and the news should be "accurate, objective, and comprehensive."

Its core work has traditionally been broadcasting news, sports, and entertainment around the world via shortwave. This is still done, but VOA has also established AM and FM radio transmitters throughout the world to reach an even broader audience. In addition, the agency supplies many radio and television stations throughout the world with various news, music, and talk programs free of charge. The VOA also offers audio streaming on World Wide Web. According to the Broadcasting Board of Governors, the worldwide audience for VOA is about 115 million who listen or watch in 45 different languages. VOA, for example, is broadcasting television programming by satellite six hours a day to Iran in the Persian language.

> " U.S. sponsored radio and TV broadcasts remain critical weapons in the struggle for freedom around the world. "
>
> ———*James K. Glassman,* chair of the Broadcasting Board of Governors

VOA is the major voice of the United States abroad, but the government isn't always happy with its strict adherence to journalistic standards and objectivity. Consequently, the government also operates other radio and television services that are more proactive in advancing U.S. interests and foreign policy. Radio Free Europe was started in 1949 to reach the nations of Eastern Europe under the thumb of the Soviet Union. Radio Liberty was also started, under CIA funding, to broadcast directly to the citizens of the Soviet Union. The Soviet response during the Cold War was to jam these broadcasts because they were American "propaganda." Although both services still exist, they have significantly fewer staff and do less broadcasting.

PRCASEBOOK

U.S. "Public Diplomacy" Faces Major Obstacles

Perhaps the easiest part of the war on terrorism was the toppling of the Taliban regime in Afghanistan and the removal of Saddam Hussein's government in Baghdad. Most experts agree, however, that the toughest part is winning the war of worldwide public opinion.

The U.S. government is now engaged in a war of ideas. As the *Economist* points out, "It has to persuade America, its allies and Muslims around the world that its fight is against terror, not Islam." Many experts are less optimistic about winning this part of the war. One Arab expert told the Associated Press, "The U.S. point of view is not unknown to the Arab people, they just don't buy it." According to the *New York Times*, "Many Muslims say American policy favors Israelis over Palestinians and needs to be altered before sentiments will change."

John Paluszek, senior counsel of Ketchum, puts it more bluntly. He wrote in *PR Week*, "It's the policy, stupid." He continues, "It is policy—and related action—that matters most in successful PR. Recent opinion polls tell us that it's current American foreign policy, not traditional American values, that is unacceptable to many people in the Middle East." Indeed an Advisory Group on Diplomacy for the Arab and Muslim World appointed by Congress concluded, "much of the resentment toward America stems from our policies" and "In this time of peril, public diplomacy is absurdly and dangerously underfunded."

Although funding is a major problem, critics also say that the limited monies available have been poorly spent. One project that received considerable criticism was a multimillion dollar advertising campaign initiated by Charlotte Beers, a former CEO of two major advertising agencies. She was named Undersecretary of Public Diplomacy and Public Affairs in 2001. Almost immediately she decided on using advertising as a major tool to win "hearts and minds." Her idea was a series of television commercials with the theme "shared values" that would show Muslim men and women leading happy and productive lives in a religion-tolerant America. As one critic dryly noted, "It was like this was the 1930s and the government was running commercials showing happy blacks in America."

Although the ads were used in Indonesia, the world's largest Muslim nation, most television stations in the Middle East refused to accept the ads because they were considered nothing but "propaganda." Also, of the Muslims featured in the ads, none of them were Arabs.

American public diplomacy has taken a severe beating since the invasion of Iraq. Here, Pakistani Muslim protestors chant anti-American slogans during a protest in Islamabad.

After about five weeks, the State Department suspended the advertising program, and Charlotte Beers, barely 18 months into her job, resigned for "health reasons." Her successor, Margaret Tutwiler, lasted only five months.

President Bush, in 2005, then appointed Karen Hughes to the public diplomacy and public affairs position. She is one of the president's most trusted confidantes and most observers believed her access to the president was a positive development for a renewed—and more effective—public diplomacy effort on the part of the United States to win the war for favorable worldwide public opinion. Her high status in the Bush administration was evident at her swearing-in ceremony. On hand was the president, Laura Bush, Condoleezza Rice, four cabinet secretaries, and the chair of the Joint Chiefs of Staff.

Shortly after her appointment, Hughes took a three-country visit to the Middle East on a "listening tour" that met with mixed results. She also initiated rapid response teams of State Department specialists to monitor the Arab press and electronic media to counter misinformation and distortions. Other initiatives have been to meet with Muslim leaders in the United States and even to do an interview on Al Jazeera, the popular Arabic satellite television station often accused by administration officials of being anti-American.

Meanwhile, global opinion polls show that the image of America abroad continues to decline. The Pew Research Center, a group based in Washington, D.C., has conducted an annual survey since 2002 to access America's image abroad. In its 2006 survey of 16,700 citizens in 15 nations, it found approval of American policies continued to drop. In Spain, for example, only 23 percent of the respondents had a favorable view of America, down from 41 percent the previous year. In Turkey, only 12 percent said they had a favorable opinion, down from 23 percent the previous year. There were also declines in such nations as India, Russia, and Indonesia. According to the *New York Times*, "Although strong majorities in several nations expressed worries about Iran's nuclear intentions, in 13 of 15 countries polled, most people said the war in Iraq posed more of a danger to world peace. Russians held that view by a 2 to 1 margin."

A similar 2006 poll by Harris, in association with the *Financial Times,* found that Europeans see the United States as the greatest threat to global stability. The newspaper, reporting the survey of 5,000 people in five Western European nations (United Kingdom, France, Germany, Spain, and Italy) continued, "Some 36 percent identified the U.S. as the greatest threat to global stability, while 30 percent named Iran and 18 percent selected China."

There is some good news, according to the *Economist*. It reported, "The Pew survey shows that respondents are able to distinguish between a country, its people, and its government. The American people are more popular than America the country, while Mr. Bush's ratings are far lower than both."

Karen Hughes, as America's chief image officer, continues to be upbeat. She told the *New York Times*, "Ed Murrow [*the legendary CBS newsman and former director of the United States Information Agency*] once famously said that there's no cash register that rings when a mind is changed. But I think over the long haul we can begin to shape a better perception in the Middle East." The other major challenge, however, is to improve America's image throughout the rest of the world. That task may be next to impossible, according to the Pew survey, as long as American troops are in Iraq. Hughes, citing some progress, resigned in November 2007.

More recently, Congress has set up radio and television services focusing on Iraq and the Middle East. Radio Sawa, for example, injects news tidbits written from an American perspective into a heavy rotation of American and Middle Eastern pop music. A similar radio service aimed at Iranian youth is Radio Farda. On the television side, the U.S. government has started Alhurra, which, according to the *New York Times*, is "a slickly produced Arab-language news and entertainment network that will be beamed by satellite from a Washington suburb to the Middle East." According to the U.S. government, 71 percent of adults in Iraq tune in each week to Alhurra and Radio Sawa, which broadcast 24 hours a day in the Arabic language. It is the American government's answer to the popular pan-Arab television service, Al Jazeera.

In Afghanistan, Ashna Radio from VOA and Radio Azadi from Radio Free Europe each broadcast 12 hours daily of news and information, reaching around 50 percent of the population.

It should be noted that the VOA, including such services as Radio Sawa, are not directed at U.S. citizens. By design, under the United States Information and Educational Exchange Act of 1948, Congress prohibits the government from directing its public diplomacy efforts toward its own citizens. There were congressional fears of the government propagandizing its own citizens.

U.S. Firms Working for Foreign Governments

For fees ranging upward of $1 million per year, several hundred American public relations firms work in this country for other nations. In recent years, for example, Hill and Knowlton has represented Indonesia and Morocco; Burson-Marsteller has represented

Argentina, Costa Rica, Hungary, and Russia (the latter mainly in trade fairs); and Ruder, Finn & Rotman has represented El Salvador, Israel, and Japan. Doremus & Company, clients have included Egypt, Iran, Jordan, the Philippines, Saudi Arabia, and Tunisia.

In many cases, the objective is to influence U.S. foreign policy, generate tourism, create favorable public opinion about the country, or encourage trade.

The Countries' Goals   What do these countries seek to accomplish? Burson-Marsteller's Carl Levin says that they pursue several goals, including:

♦ To advance political objectives

♦ To be counseled on the United States' probable reaction to the client government's projected action

♦ To advance the country's commercial interests—for example, sales in the United States, increased U.S. private investment, and tourism

♦ To assist in communications in English

♦ To counsel and help win understanding and support on a specific issue undermining the client's standing in the United States and the world community

♦ To help modify laws and regulations inhibiting the client's activities in the United States.

Under the Foreign Agents Registration Act (FARA) of 1938, all legal, political, fund-raising, public relations, and lobbying consultants hired by foreign governments to work in the United States must register with the Department of Justice. They are required to file reports with the Attorney General listing all activities on behalf of a foreign principal, compensation received, and expenses incurred.

Action Programs   Normally hired by an embassy after open bidding for the account, the firm first gathers detailed information about the client country, including past media coverage. Attitudes toward the country are ascertained both informally and through surveys.

The action program decided on will likely include the establishment of an information bureau to provide facts and published statements of favorable opinion about the country. In many cases, a nation may also use paid issue advertising publications such as the *New York Times*, *Washington Post*, and *Wall Street Journal*, that reach a high percentage of opinion leaders and elected officials. The Republic of Kazakhstan, for example, placed full-page ads in major American newspapers after its national elections to reinforce public perceptions that it was a democracy. The ad's headline: "Today, Kazakhstan has another asset besides oil, gas and minerals. Democracy."

Appointments also are made with key media people and other influentials, including educators, business executives, and leaders of various public policy groups. In many cases, the primary audiences are key members of congressional committees, heads of various governmental agencies, and even the White House staff. These people are often invited to visit the client country on expense-paid trips, although some news media people decline on ethical grounds. (Ethical questions will be discussed in more detail shortly.)

Gradually, through expert and persistent methods of persuasion (including lobbying), public opinion may be changed, favorable trade legislation may be passed, foreign aid may be increased, or there's an influx of American tourists.

Problems and Rewards   The toughest problems confronting the firm are often as follows:

◆ Deciding to represent a country, such as Uzbekistan or Zimbabwe, whose human rights violations may reflect adversely on the agency itself

◆ Persuading the heads of such a nation to alter some of its practices so that the favorable public image sought may reflect reality

◆ Convincing officials of a client country, which may totally control the flow of news internally, that the American press is independent from government control and that they should never expect coverage that is 100 percent favorable

◆ Deciding whether to represent a nation such as Belarus, in which the autocratic head of state, Aleksandr Lukashenko, has drastically reduced civil liberties and crushed any opposition.

Why, then, do these firms work for other governments? Perhaps even those that are unpopular? Said Burson-Marsteller's Carl Levin: "I do not think it is overreaching to state that in helping friendly foreign clients we also advance our national interests. And we help in ways that our government cannot." A case in point is China, which has ramped up its public relations and lobbying efforts in recent years to counter criticisms (and fears) in the United States about its growing economic and military power. It hired the Patton Boggs firm, for example, to lobby on a wide range of issues before Congress, including trade tariffs, intellectual property, currency exchange rates, and Taiwan. Public relations firms were also retained to fend off congressional criticism in 2005 when China made a bid for a small U.S. oil company, Unocal. No amount of public relations, however, was able to stem public and congressional concern—bordering on xenophobia—that a "foreign company" was buying a "strategic resource." China withdrew its offer.

In another situation, Qorvis Communications has represented Saudi Arabia since 9/11 and earned about $13 million for its efforts in a recent 12-month period. The account, however, has not been without controversy. Several senior officers of Qorvis resigned, according to newspaper reports, because they were uncomfortable working on the Saudi account.

The following is a representative sample of contracts signed by American public relations firms to work on behalf of foreign clients, as reported in *O'Dwyer's Newsletter*:

◆ **The Glover Park Group**: $600,000 contract with the government of Turkey to devise overall communications and media strategy aimed at the American public. The firm also "will advise the Turks on their relationship with the White House and Congress."

◆ **GoodWorks International**: $180,000 contract with the government of Rwanda to promote U.S. investment in the country. According to the contract, the firm will ". . . focus greater public attention on the tremendous improvements on the economic, political, and social aspects since 1994, when the genocide unfolded."

◆ **Fleishman-Hillard and its sister firm, DDB Advertising**: $40 million contract with the Egyptian Tourist Agency to promote tourism and U.S. investment.

◆ **Fahmy Hudome International**: $750,000 contract with the government of Libya to help develop long-term U.S.–Libyan relations.

◆ **Ketchum Communications**: Multimillion dollar contract with the Russian government to improve the country's image. Ketchum advised the Kremlin on communications with Western media during Vladimir Putin's presidency when he hosted the Group of Eight (G8) summit during 2006–2007. More recently, Ketchum was one of several firms retained by Gazprom, the Russian gas giant, to improve its international image.

 ◆ **A&R Partners**: $250,000 contract with the Australian Tourism Commission to promote travel to the country.

 ◆ **Hill & Knowlton**: $3.8 million contract for work in Afghanistan to persuade farmers not to grow poppies; it's estimated that 85 percent of the world's heroin comes from Afghan poppies. The contract is with the U.S. State Department.

The Rise of NGOs

Hundreds of nongovernmental organizations (NGOs) depend on international support for their programs and causes. Such organizations as Greenpeace, Amnesty International, Doctors Without Borders, Oxfam, and a large number of groups opposed to globalization have been effective in getting their message out via the World Wide Web, e-mail, and demonstrations.

One study by StrategyOne, the research arm of Edelman Worldwide, showed that media coverage of such organizations more than doubled over a four-year period, and NGOs were perceived by the public to be more credible than the news media or corporations when it came to issues such as labor, health, and the environment.

Thought leaders, for example, trust NGOs more than government or corporations because they consider their motivation to be based on "morals" rather than "profit." Public Affairs Council president Doug Pinkham said the StrategyOne report should be taken as a "wake-up call" by large corporations that have failed to embrace greater social responsibility and transparency. Pinkham told *PRWeek*, "The next five to ten years will be challenging for companies that operate on a world stage with the rise of technologically enabled activism."

Indeed, there is increasing evidence that giant corporations are cooperating with activist NGOs to form more socially responsible policies. Citigroup, for example, adopted new policies to reduce habitat loss and climate change after the Rainforest Action Network (RAN) urged customers to cut up their Citicards and plastered the Internet with nasty jibes against named executives.

Public Relations Development in Other Nations

On a global basis, public relations as an occupation and a career has achieved its highest development in the industrialized nations of the world—the United States, Canada, Western Europe, and parts of Asia. It emerges more readily in nations that have multiparty political systems, considerable private ownership of business and industry, large-scale urbanization, and relatively high per capita income levels, which also impacts literacy and educational opportunities.

China has experienced explosive growth in public relations as it has become industrialized and embraced a relatively free market economy. As discussed in Chapter 1, the growth of public relations activity in China has been tremendous in the past decade. Public relations revenues for the past several years have experienced double-digit gains, and China is now the second-largest market in Asia after Japan. It is expected that the Beijing Olympics in 2008 will further increase China's image and influence in the world.

The United States and other European nations began exporting their public relations expertise to the People's Republic of China during the mid-1980s. Hill & Knowlton, active in Asia for more than 30 years, began its Beijing operation in a hotel room with three U.S. expatriates and a locally hired employee. Today, almost every global public relations firm has a Beijing office to represent U.S. and European companies in the Chinese market.

In addition, global public relations firms and advertising agencies are now buying stakes in successful Chinese firms. Omnicom Group of New York, for example, bought a majority stake in Unisono Fieldmarketing, which has 2,000 full- and part-time employees. The French advertising holding company, Publicis Groupe, purchased an 80 percent stake in the Shanghai-based Betterway Marketing Solutions. Geoffrey Fowler, a reporter for the *Wall Street Journal*, wrote, "Newly acquired Chinese agencies are likely to help the multinationals as they push beyond China's wealthy coastal cities into its interior, increasingly an important commercial battlefield. China has more than 100 cities with a population exceeding one million."

Indeed, homegrown Chinese firms in advertising, public relations, and marketing have developed to the point that they have lured business away from the large international firms. They offer low cost and wide reach. In the public relations area, Chinese firms have advanced beyond product publicity and now offer services in analyst, government, community relations, and even sports marketing.

> " Journalists in China are arguably the worst paid, so to offset the reality of public transportation woes, you are expected to provide a media travel allowance. "
>
> ——*Cindy Payne,* director of Asia-Pacific Connections

Media relations in China, however, is somewhat different than in most Western nations. There is the tradition that reporters receive "transportation money" for covering events and going to interview company representatives. According to an article in the *Financial Times*, a reporter covering an event gets about $27 in a "red envelope" for transportation. A television crew can receive up to $200. A representative of China's Public Relations Association told the *Financial Times*, "You cannot say we encourage or discourage this practice." See the Ethics box on page 520 about "pay for play" in Russia.

Other nations and regions, to varying degrees, also have developed larger and more sophisticated public relations industries within the past decade. Here are some thumbnail sketches from around the globe:

◆ **Africa.** South Africa is a relatively mature market with a long tradition of public relations education, professional development for practitioners, and large corporations with international outreach. Nigeria, the most populous nation in Africa, has made some strides in developing its public relations industry.

◆ **Australia, Singapore,** and **Hong Kong.** These are relatively mature public relations markets, offering a variety of services ranging from financial relations to media relations and special event promotions. More attention is given to overall strategic planning and integrating communications for overall corporate objectives. A major growth area in Singapore is in the hospitality and service industry as the island nation adds new resorts and casinos.

◆ **Brazil.** This is the largest economy in South America, and there are about 1,000 public relations firms in the country, primarily in the São Paulo area. To date,

on the job ETHICS

Got a News Release? Please Include Cash

Paying a reporter or an editor to publish or broadcast a news release has long been a common practice in many parts of the world, especially in emerging nations where salaries are low.

In Russia, the practice of paying for placement is called *zakazukhi* (bought articles), and the International Public Relations Association (IPRA) has announced the formation of an international committee to eliminate the practice. According to IPRA president Alasdair Sutherland, "The credibility of any publication can only be based on its independent objectivity. As long as the practice of illicit paid-for-editorial continues in any marketplace, the local public can never have confidence in what they read."

The issue of *zakazukhi* in Russia was brought into the open when a public relations firm in Moscow, Promaco, issued a fictitious news release to see how much various publications would charge to publish

it as a news item. According to the *Economist,*

Of the 21 publications tested, one published the news release for free (but without checking its accuracy). Four asked for more information, and did not run stories. Three said they would run the article as an advertisement. But 13 papers and magazines offered to run it as an article, for fees ranging from around $135 at *Tribuna,* a paper backed by Gazprom, the national gas company, to more than $2,000 in the official government newspaper, *Rossiskaya Gazeta. . . .*

Sutherland, who is also an executive at Manning Selvage & Lee public relations, said

IPRA has long been aware of this unethical practice in a number of marketplaces around the world, especially in some where the concept of a free press is comparatively 'new.' . . . We urge both Russian and international public relations clients not to support this illegal practice in

the future. According to our code, no IPRA member is permitted to use such methods.

Russian editors were less than embarrassed. According to the *Economist,* "The editor of *Noviye Izvestiya* said it made no difference to readers whether articles were paid for or not." Another editor suggested that public relations firms were really to blame. When the newspaper wants to run the news release as an advertisement, the public relations firms just take their business elsewhere.

What do you think? If you were doing public relations for an American or European firm in Moscow, would you go along with the local custom of *zakazukhi?* Or would you refuse to pay the media for using your news release? How about the common practice in China of giving reporters "transportation" money for attending a news conference?

few global public relations firms have established a presence, primarily because Brazilian corporations still spend a disproportionate amount of their budgets on advertising campaigns. Issues management, public affairs, internal communications, and marketing communications are still somewhat undeveloped fields.

◆ **India.** The Indian market, with more than 1 billion people, is a major market for products, services, and public relations expertise. There are at least 1,000 large and small public relations firms serving the subcontinent, but training and educating qualified practitioners continues to be a major problem.

◆ **Japan.** Business and industry are still in the stage of perceiving public relations as primarily media relations. Public relations firms and corporate communications departments work very closely with the more than 400-plus reporters' clubs that filter and process all information for more than 150 newsgathering organizations. See the next column for an ad by a Japanese public relations firm.

◆ **Mexico.** Traditionally, small public relations firms dominated the market and provided primarily product publicity. With the North American Free Trade Agreement (NAFTA), international firms have established operations with more sophisticated approaches to strategic communications.

◆ **Middle East.** The Middle East consists of 22 nations and more than 300 million people. In general, the public relations industry is relatively immature, unstructured, and lacking in trained personnel. There is government-censored media and fear of transparent communications. Dubai, which is in the United Arab Emirates, in recent years has positioned itself as a major business center and has attracted many international companies. In such a situation, it's expected that public relations services will expand.

◆ **Russian Federation** and **Former Republics.** The rise of a market economy and private enterprise has spurred the development of public relations activity, but the continuing stagnation of the Russian economy has stunted its development. The press and journalists are still very dependent on supplemental income, and news articles can still be "bought" without much effort. See the Ethics box on page 520. In a more recent development, Russia's giant oil and energy company Gazprom signed a multimillion dollar contract with a consortium of several global public relations firms (including Moscow-based PBN) to improve the image of the state-controlled gas monopoly after it was badly dented by "gas wars" with former Soviet Republics.

Public relations is now an international enterprise and every country has its own industry. This ad is for a Japanese public relations firm.

◆ **Serbia.** The country retained the most population after the breakup of the former Yugoslavia, and Belgrade remains the economic hub of the region. Most public relations activity is at the media relations level, but organizations are also applying concepts of marketing communications and corporate social responsibility. A great deal of public relations effort is being done to promote tourism and the travel industry. See the Multicultural box on page 522 about the Belgrade Beer Fest. Governmental efforts, to a large degree, is focused on attracting foreign investment and gaining eventual membership in the European Union (EU).

◆ **Thailand.** This nation has a great deal of foreign investment and is becoming an assembly center for automobiles. It's the primary hub in Southeast Asia for international tourism, and a number of public relations firms, advertising firms, and corporations have well-qualified staffs to handle media relations, product publicity, and

on the job

A MULTICULTURAL WORLD

A Beer Fest Puts Belgrade on the Map

Europeans usually head for the countryside during the summer months, and Belgrade, Serbia, is no exception. All this changed in August 2003, however, when billboards and flyers around the city announced a four-day beer festival to be held beneath the imposing Kalemegdan fortress at the confluence of the Sava and Danube rivers.

Thousands of people showed up for good beer and music, and the annual fest was launched much to the elation of Serbians, who haven't had much to celebrate since the Balkan wars of the 1990s, in which Belgrade was even bombed by NATO forces. The Belgrade Cultural Network (BCN), a nongovernmental organiza-

tion, worked closely with business and government agencies to promote the beer fest, with the objective of putting the city on the map as a tourist destination.

By 2005, the beer fest was a five-day event attracting more than 250,000 people through promotions in the electronic, print, and outdoor media. In addition, the fest's Web site, www.belgradebeerfest.com, was visited by 50,000 people in a 45-day period. In terms of beer, 32 different brands (local and foreign) were served and attendees consumed 420,000 liters, or about 105,000 gallons.

Word-of-mouth and media testimonials increase attendance every year. In 2006, the *Independent* news-

paper in the United Kingdom included the Belgrade Beer Fest on its list of the top 20 events worth attending. In 2007, the beer fest doubled its physical capacity to accommodate even more beer drinkers and music fans. According to the organizers, "Thousands of TV reports, interviews, and newspaper articles about the Belgrade Beer Fest have been published since the launch of the fest."

Dejan Grastic, vice president of BCN, told one newspaper reporter, "Diligency and hard work can successfully transform Serbia's image. We expect a significant turnout of tourists from the entire Europe and we will do our best to make this year's festival the best so far."

The Belgrade Beer Fest attracts 250,000 annually.
Photo courtesy of Belgrade Cultural Network.

special event promotion. However, it lacks a cohesive national organization of public relations practitioners that promotes professional development. More recently, the country has suffered image problems abroad as the result of a military coup in late 2006. The deposed prime minister, Thaksin Shinawatra, isn't giving up without a

on the job
INSIGHTS

Giving the "Ugly American" a Makeover

Business for Diplomatic Action Inc., a nonprofit organization, works with U.S. companies to improve the reputation of the United States in the world. To that end, it has compiled guidelines on how business travelers (as well as tourists) should behave abroad. Here are some tips from its brochure, "World Citizens Guide":

Read a map: "Familiarize yourself with the local geography to avoid making insulting mistakes." Knowledge of current events and public issues are a real plus.

Dress up: "In some countries, casual dress is a sign of disrespect."

Talk small: "Talking about wealth, power, or status—corporate or personal—can create resentment." Bragging about how great America is a real turnoff.

No slang: "Even casual profanity is unacceptable."

Slow down: "We talk fast, eat fast, move fast, live fast. Many cultures do not."

Listen as much as you talk: "Ask people you're visiting about themselves and their way of life."

Speak lower and slower: "A loud voice is often perceived as bragging."

Religious restraint: "In many countries, religion is not a subject for discussion."

Political restraint: "Steer clear . . . if someone is attacking U.S. politicians or policies. Agree to disagree."

Learn some words: "Learning some simple phrases in the host country's language is most appreciated."

Source: McCarney, Scott. "Teaching Americans How to Behave Abroad." *Wall Street Journal,* April 11, 2006.

fight. He hired Edelman's New York office to help arrange meetings with the international news media to engage in strategic conflict management for him.

Opportunities in International Work

The 1990s, according to many experts, represented a new golden age of global marketing and public relations. The opening of the European Market, coupled with economic and social reforms in East European countries and the former Soviet Union, hastened the reality of a global economy.

All of these developments led Jerry Dalton, past president of the PRSA, to say: "I think more and more American firms are going to become part of those overseas markets, and I expect a lot of Americans in public relations will be living overseas." Indeed, Dalton believes that the fastest-growing career field for practitioners is international public relations. He adds: "Students who can communicate well and are fluent in a foreign language may be able to write their own ticket." But the coming of the "global village," as Marshall McLuhan once described it, still means that there will be a multiplicity of languages, customs, and values that public relations professionals will have to understand. See the Insights box on this page giving tips for American citizens traveling abroad.

Gavin Anderson, chairman of Gavin Anderson & Company, a pioneer in international public relations penned the following observatons some years ago—but the message is still relevant today:

> Practitioners of either global or international public relations are cultural interpreters. They must understand the business and general culture of both their clients (or employers) and the country or countries in which they hope to do business. Whether as an outside or inhouse consultant, the first task is to tell a U.S. company going abroad (or a foreign party coming to the United States) how to get things done. How does the market work? What are the business habits? What is the infrastructure? The consultant also needs to understand how things work in the host country, to recognize what will need translation and adaptation . . .
>
> The field needs practitioners with an interest in and knowledge of foreign cultures on top of top-notch public relations skills. They need a good sense of working environments, and while they may not have answers for every country, they should know what questions to ask and where to get the information needed. They need to know where the potential dangers are, so as to not replenish the business bloopers book.

The decision to seek an international career should be made during the early academic years, so that a student can take multiple courses in international relations, global marketing techniques, the basics of strategic public relations planning, foreign languages, social and economic geography, and cross-cultural communication. Graduate study is an asset. See the employment ad from Cathay Pacific on this page. Students should also study abroad for a semester or serve an internship with a company

There are a number of employment opportunities in international public relations. Here, Hong Kong–based Cathay Pacific seeks a communications manager for North America.

CATHAY PACIFIC

COMMUNICATIONS MANAGER, AMERICAS

Cathay Pacific Airways, Asia's premier international airline, is now seeking candidates to fill the position based in Los Angeles.

Responsibilities:
- Effectively communicate and generate goodwill with key organizations to positively affect their behavior, especially toward purchasing our company's products and services.
- Maintain and develop key media relationships. Coordinate interviews between influential media contacts and company's key personnel.
- Act as the company's spokesperson. Create and distribute press releases.
- Increase visibility of our company in N. America through special events and activities.
- Maintain good internal staff communications. Handle crisis communications effectively.
- Effectively keep our company's name in front of key publics through innovative and concentrated community support opportunities.
- Support the company's N. America Marketing & Sales initiatives.

Requirements:
- Minimum 5 years experience in Public Relations with important projects involved.
- Ability to communicate effectively at all levels with superior oral and written skills.
- College degree with strong PC knowledge.
- Superior independent work capability.
- Excellent decision-making, problem-solving, time management and organization skills. Must be detailed oriented.

We offer a unique package of benefits including attractive salary plus profit sharing; company sponsored insurance, travel benefits, pension & 401k option.

Forward resume immed to Personnel & Administration Manager via Fax 1-310-615-0042 or email: usa#personnel@cathaypacific.com.

or organization in another nation as a desirable starting point. Students may also apply for the Fulbright student progam that funds travel and study abroad. Another opportunity is a student foreign study scholarship offered by Rotary International.

A note of caution. American students should not assume they have an "inside" advantage working for an American-based global corporation. Increasingly, global corporations are looking at a worldwide pool of young talent—and Europeans are often excellent candidates because they know several languages and are more accustomed to intercultural communications. Hewlett-Packard is one example; it prefers to hire European- or American-trained Russians for its corporate communications efforts in Moscow and the Russian Federation.

Taking the U.S. Foreign Service Officers' examination is the first requirement for international government careers. Foreign service work with the innumerable federal agencies often requires a substantial period of government, mass media, or public relations service in the United States before foreign assignments are made.

SUMMARY

What Is Global Public Relations?
Public relations now takes place on a global scale, with relationships being built with the publics of all nations. Although some elements of public relations were being practiced in Europe over a hundred years ago, American techniques are those most commonly adapted for use throughout the world.

International Corporate Public Relations
In the new age of global marketing, public relations firms represent foreign interests in the United States as well as the interests of American corporations around the world. This means that the practitioner must deal with issues of language and cultural differences, including subtle differences in customs and etiquette and even ethical dilemmas involving bribery.

International Government Public Relations
Most governments seek to influence the international policies of other countries as well as the opinions and actions of the public. These communications can range from promoting tourism to attempts to influence trade policies. The U.S. government refers to its international information effort as "public diplomacy," the attempt to enhance understanding of our culture and promote our foreign policy objectives. The Voice of America radio broadcasts are part of this program. There are also U.S. public relations firms working for foreign governments, helping them advance their political objectives and commercial interests, counseling them on probable U.S. reactions to their proposed actions, and assisting in communications in English.

The Rise of NGOs
Among nongovernmental organizations depending on international support for their causes are Greenpeace, Amnesty International, Doctors Without Borders, Oxfam, and the International Red Cross. Such organizations are widely believed to be more credible than the news media on such issues as labor, health, and the environment, partly because they are perceived to lack the self-interest ascribed to governments and corporations.

Public Relations in Other Nations
Public relations is a well-developed industry in many nations around the world. China, in particular, has a rapidly expanding industry that is getting more sophisticated every year.

Opportunities in International Work
As global marketing and communications have expanded in recent years, so too have opportunities for international public relations work. Fluency in foreign language is a valued skill but not a prerequisite; also important are backgrounds in international relations, global marketing techniques, social and economic geography, and cross-cultural communication.

CASE ACTIVITY What Would You Do?

Turkey has a problem. The country was on track to becoming the fastest-growing destination for Americans prior to 9/11. That projection was derailed by the terrorist attacks and the subsequent invasion of Afghanistan and Iraq, which caused many Americans to think twice about visiting a Muslim nation—even if it had a secular government and a strong European orientation.

Yet, Turkey remains a virtual treasure house of art, culture, and cuisine that would appeal to seasoned travelers looking for a new experience and destination. To this end, the Turkish Culture and Tourism Office has retained your public relations firm to conduct a media relations program in the American press (and, to some extent, the European media) to increase awareness of Turkey as a desirable tourist destination.

Research and interviews with Turkish tourism authorities indicate that segmentation of various audiences would be more fruitful than a general campaign. Travelers interested in food and wine, for example, might be reached by articles about the cuisine of Turkey. Music lovers might be interested in the new jazz sounds coming from Turkish musicians, and even shoppers looking for vintage jewelry and other exotic products (such as carpets) in the famous bazaars of Istanbul would be a good, specialized public. Then, of course, there are the history buffs who would be interested in visiting the sites of ancient civilizations.

Now that you know the possible interests of several target audiences, develop a public relations plan that will use appropriate media and events for these various audiences. Your plan should outline possible feature stories for print and broadcast media, as well as the venues for special events.

QUESTIONS for Review and Discussion

1. What is meant by international public relations? What are some reasons for its growth in recent decades?

2. How does public relations fit into the mix of global marketing operations?

3. What are some difficulties that a corporation is likely to encounter when it conducts business in another country?

4. What objectives do foreign nations seek to accomplish by hiring U.S. public relations firms to represent them in America?

5. International surveys indicate that citizens in other nations have a low approval rating of the United States and its policies. What "public diplomacy" efforts could the United States undertake to change these negative perceptions?

6. The U.S. government conducted an extensive program of "public diplomacy" as part of the war on terrorism. Do you think it was effective? Why or why not?

What suggestions do you have for U.S. public diplomacy efforts?

7. What is the Russian practice of *zakazukhi*? Why does the IPRA consider it a bad practice?

8. Why is Israel worried about its image in the United States and other nations?

9. International public relations requires knowledge of a nation's history and political sensitivities. It also requires a knowledge of proper manners and cultural sensitivity. What advice is given for business executives who travel abroad?

10. What kinds of ethical dilemmas do public relations firms face when they are asked to do work for a particular nation?

11. What does the abbreviation "NGO" mean? How has the new information technology enabled NGOs to expand their influence?

12. What opportunities exist for someone who wants to specialize in international public relations as a career?

SUGGESTED READINGS

Anderlini, Jamil, and Dickie, Mure. "Cash Handouts to Journalists Skew Chinese Media Coverage." *Financial Times,* August 3, 2007, p. 2.

"Anti-Americanism: The View from Abroad." *Economist,* February 19, 2005, pp. 24–25.

Badler, Dick. "10 Rules for Building a Successful Global Corporate Communications Organization." *The Strategist,* Winter 2004, pp. 18–21.

Freitag, Alan R. "Ascending Cultural Competence Potential: An Assessment and Profile of U.S. Public Relations Practitioners' Preparation for International Assignments." *Journal of Public Relations Research,* Vol. 14, No. 3, 2002, pp. 207–227.

Giridharadas, Anand. "Lobbying in the U.S., Indian Firms Present an American Face." *New York Times,* September 4, 2007, pp. C1, 11.

Glassman, James K. "Media Is Only Half the Battle." *Wall Street Journal,* September l4, 2007, p. A13.

Knowlton, Brian. "Global Image of the U.S. Is Worsening, Survey Finds." *New York Times,* June 14, 2006, p. A14.

Lee, Suman. "An Analysis of Other Countries International Public Relations in the U.S." *Public Relations Review,* June 2006, Vol. 32, No. 2, pp. 97–103.

Longpre, Marc. "A World of Opportunity." *PRWeek,* July 2, 2007, pp. 12–18.

Mateas, Margo M. "Spotlight on Diversity: Managing Diversity in Virtual Teams across the Globe." *Public Relations Tactics,* Vol. 11, No. 8, 2004, p. 20.

McKenna, Ted. "Hughes Tackles a Shaky Image." *PRWeek,* July 23, 2007, p. 6.

Paluszek, John. "How Do We Fit Into the World?" *The Strategist,* Winter 2004, pp. 6–11.

Payne, Cindy. "Asia Inside and Out: How North American Companies Can Extend Their Reach Into Asia's Highly Lucrative Markets." *Public Relations Tactics,* August 2007, p. 21.

Rieff, David. "Their Hearts and Minds? Why the Ideological Battle Against Islamists Is Nothing Like the Struggle Against Communism." *New York Times Magazine,* September 4, 2005, pp. 11–12.

Stateman, Alison. "Diplomatic Link: The Private Sector's Role in U.S. Public Diplomacy." *The Strategist,* Spring 2005, pp. 40–42.

Wang, Jian. "Managing National Reputation and International Relations in the Global Era: Public Diplomacy Revisited." *Public Relations Review,* June 2006, Vol. 32, No. 2, pp. 91–96.

Yardley, Jim. "No Spitting on the Road to Olympic Glory, Beijing Says." *New York Times,* April 17, 2007, p. A10.

Yeatman, C. Perry, and Berdan, Stacie N. *Get Ahead by Going Abroad: A Woman's Guide to Fast-Track Career Success.* www.getaheadbygoingabroad.com.

CHAPTER 20

Nonprofit Organizations

The Role of Public Relations

A broad area of public relations work, and the source of many jobs, is the nonprofit organization. There are an estimated 1.4 million charities and religious organizations in the United States, and they range from small city historical societies to religious orders and gigantic international foundations that disperse million-dollar grants.

The crucial point about nonprofit organizations is that they are tax exempt. The federal government grants them this status because they enhance the well-being of their members, as with trade associations, or enhance the human condition in some way, as with environmental work or medical research. Many nonprofit organizations could not survive if they were taxed, because they face the unending public relations task of raising money to pay their expenses and finance their projects.

Basic Needs of Nonprofits

Mothers Against Drunk Driving (MADD) seems to have little in common with the American Red Cross or the National Academy of Songwriters, yet all three engage in the same types of tasks in order to succeed:

◆ All three create communication campaigns and programs such as special events, Internet Web sites, brochures, and radio and television appearances that stimulate public interest in organizational goals and invite public participation.

◆ They develop a strong staff to handle the work. Recruiting volunteers and keeping them enthusiastic are essential.

◆ These organizations establish a realistic fund-raising goal and a plan to attain it.

The significance of these factors will become evident as we examine the various types of nonprofit organizations. For convenience, such organizations can be grouped roughly as membership groups, advocacy agencies, or social organizations.

Membership Organizations

A membership organization consists of people with a common interest, in either business or social life. The purpose of a membership organization is mutual help and self-improvement. These organizations often use the strength of their common bond to improve community welfare, endorse legislation, and support socially valuable causes.

Trade Associations

At last count, there were about 6,000 trade and professional associations in the United States. Because federal laws and regulations often can affect the fortunes of an entire industry, about one-third of these groups are based in the Washington, D.C., area. There, association staffs can monitor congressional activity, lobby for or against legislation, communicate late-breaking developments to the membership, and see government officials on a regular basis.

The membership of a trade association usually consists of manufacturers, wholesalers, retailers, or distributors in the same field. Memberships are held by corporate entities, not individuals. The following are a few examples of trade associations:

◆ Electronic Industries Association
◆ National Soft Drink Association
◆ National Association of Home Builders

Although individual members may be direct rivals in the marketplace, they work together to promote the entire industry, generate public support, and share information of general interest to the entire membership.

By representing its entire industry, an association often is more effective as a news source than is an individual company. When a news situation develops involving a particular field, reporters often turn to the spokesperson of its association for comment.

Labor Unions

The size and political clout of labor unions have declined in recent decades. In 1983, union membership was 21 percent of the American workforce. By 2006, union membership had declined to 12 percent.

Traditionally, union membership was strongest in the manufacturing sector but that has radically changed in recent years. The National Education Association (NEA), comprised of teachers, is now the largest union with 2.8 million members. Second largest is the Service Employees International Union with 1.8 million members. The American Federation of State, County, and Municipal Employees (AFSCME), the International Brotherhood of Teamsters, and the United Food and Commercial Workers (UFCW) each have 1.4 million members. In contrast, the United Auto Workers (UAW) now has 600,000 members.

Nevertheless, labor unions still are very much a part of the American scene, from players in the National Basketball Association to UPS employees scurrying with deliveries in our communities. The image of labor unions, however, is not always favorable. The public often has the perception that unions are money hungry, inflexible, lacking in concern for the public interest, and at times arrogant also created a severe image problem. Media coverage often shows union members in negative, adversarial positions that sometimes inconveniences the public.

The union movement is relying on public relations tools to counter some of these negative stereotypes and to position themselves as deeply concerned about healthcare in the workplace, preservation of employee pension benefits, and job security. The NEA has also initiated public service initiatives such as a Read Across America program to emphasize its motto, "Great public schools for every child."

Unions also continue to exert influence in the political arena. In every national political

Rallies with large signs are one tactic that labor unions use to raise public awareness and generate media publicity.

campaign, unions spend millions of dollars in support of candidates they regard as friendly. Some of this money goes directly to candidates, but significant amounts are devoted to "issue ads" that do not explicitly endorse an individual. Major sums of union money also are spent on lobbying efforts, but business interests spend significantly more to influence legislation. See Chapter 18.

> If we're trying to promote ourselves and to change public policy, we have to project a sense of what we're about.
>
> ——*Gary Hubbard,* USW director of public affairs

Like corporations, union managements employ public relations when communicating with their internal audiences. They must keep their memberships informed about what they receive in return for their dues, including social and recreational programs and the representation to company management that the union leadership supplies.

Professional Associations

Members of a profession or skilled craft organize for mutual benefit. In many ways, their goals resemble those of labor unions in that they seek improved earning power, better working conditions, and public acceptance of their role in society.

Because professional organizations do not engage in collective bargaining between employers and employees as labor unions do, they instead place their major emphasis on setting standards for professional performance, establishing codes of ethics, determining requirements for admission to the field, and encouraging members to upgrade skills through continuing education. In some cases, professional organizations have quasi-legal power to license and censure members. In most cases, however, professional groups use the techniques of peer pressure and persuasion to police their membership.

In general, professional associations are national in scope with district, state, or local chapters. Many scientific and scholarly associations, however, are international, with chapters in many nations. Organizations such as the Public Relations Society of America (PRSA) and the International Association of Business Communicators (IABC) are classified as professional associations.

Public relations specialists for professional organizations use the same techniques as their colleagues in other branches of practice. And like their counterparts in trade groups and labor unions, many professional associations maintain a Washington office or one in their state capital and employ lobbyists to advocate positions. One of the most politically active groups is the American Medical Association (AMA).

The lobbying power exercised in Washington by major professional associations is especially evident in the efforts of the AMA. With 220,000 physician members, the AMA has developed a grassroots effort to apply both public and backstage pressures to shape medical liability reform, also called "tort reform," in Congress to the association's advantage. The AMA argues that medical liability settlements are excessive. The AMA provides a Physician Action Kit, expert testimony to Congress, talking points for members to use when speaking about medical liability reform, and a paper confronting the myths of medical liability reform in addition to sponsoring letter-writing campaigns.

Public relations activity on behalf of individual professionals is a relatively new development. Traditionally, lawyers and medical doctors did not advertise or seek to publicize themselves in any way. The taboo arose in part from the rules and regulations of the professional societies. Until recently, many medical societies prohibited their members from hiring public relations firms.

Many attorneys and physicians still feel uncomfortable about advertising their services, but competition for clients and patients is breaking down the traditional taboos. A survey by *Attorneys Marketing Report,* for example, shows the majority of lawyers using Yellow Pages advertising. In descending order of frequency, they also use: (1) entertainment of clients, (2) brochures, (3) seminars, and (4) newsletters.

With the rise of general practitioners promoting their services for elective procedures such as laser removal of hair or dark blemishes as a supplemental revenue stream, the competitive market will most likely mean even more public relations activity for professionals. The *Wall Street Journal* observed another trend: "Medical associations are also hiring public relations firms to publicize new or controversial techniques. 'Fat suctioning' was the focus of a press briefing publicized by Doremus & Co. for the American Society of Plastic and Reconstructive Surgeons."

Chambers of Commerce

A *chamber* is an association of businesspersons, often joined by professionals, who work to improve their city's commercial climate and to publicize its attractions. State chambers of commerce and, nationally, the Chamber of Commerce of the United States provide guidance to local chambers and speak for business interests before state legislatures and the federal government.

Often, the chamber of commerce is the public relations arm of city government. The chamber staff often produces the brochures and maps sent to individuals who seek information about visiting the city or who are considering moving to the area. Attracting conventions and new businesses to the city also is an important part of chamber work.

Chambers also conduct polls and compile statistics about the economic health of the city, including data on major industries, employment rates, availability of schools and hospitals, housing costs, and so on. Chambers of commerce play the role of community booster: They spotlight the unique characteristics of a city and sing its praises to anyone who will listen. Chambers often coin a slogan for a city, such as "Furniture Capital of Indiana." Chambers tend to be boosters of business growth.

Advocacy Groups

The environment holds a high place on the public agenda, primarily because of vigorous campaigns by environmental organizations. By promoting recycling, eliminating toxic waste sites, purifying the air and water, and preserving natural resources, such organizations strongly influence the collective conscience. Organizations that fight for social and human rights causes also achieve significant impact, both positive and negative. See the Insights box on page 533 about the activities of the Darfur Coalition.

Environmental Groups

Greenpeace, an organization that operates in 30 countries, including the United States, with 5 million members, is perhaps the best known of the confrontational groups. Television viewers are familiar with the daredevil efforts of some members in small boats to stop nuclear warships and Japanese whaling boats. In 2007, one media attention-getting project was the building of a Noah's Ark on Mount Ararat to call attention to global warming and possible flooding from the meltdown of ice and snow at the north and south poles.

Other major environmental groups include the Rain Forest Action Network, the National Wildlife Federation, and The Nature Conservancy.

on the job
A MULTICULTURAL WORLD

Save Darfur Coalition Uses Multiple Strategies

The situation in the Darfur region of the Sudan has raised considerable international concern and outrage. It is estimated that more than 400,000 people have died and millions have been displaced because of Sudanese government policies that have encouraged renegade militias to rape women, destroy villages, and disrupt international relief efforts.

A coalition of human rights groups, however, launched an advertising and public relations campaign to raise public awareness about the "genocide" in Darfur and to put pressure on corporations that have investments in Sudan. One approach has been a series of one-page advertisements in leading newspapers such as the *Wall Street Journal* and the *New York Times* calling for citizens to give donations and write members of Congress to condemn Sudan and to support an international peacekeeping force.

A second strategy was to put pressure on American corporations and state pension funds to divest of any business dealings or investments in Sudanese companies. Fidelity Investments and Berkshire Hathaway, for example, were targeted because their various investment funds held large stakes in PetroChina. Its parent

The Save Darfur Coalition rallies outside a Fidelity office.

company, the China National Petroleum Corporation (CNPC), has invested $5 billion in the state-run Sudanese oil industry. The coalition, claiming that investments in PetroChina helped fund the renegade militias, organized a series of rallies and protests at Fidelity offices. In Omaha, the headquarters of Warren Buffet's Berkshire Hathaway, print ads and billboards calling for divestment were used during the investment fund's annual meeting of stockholders. "It's time for these companies not to be just market leaders, but moral leaders," said Darfur Coalition executive director David Rubenstein.

The coalition also enlisted NAACP chapters throughout the nation to lobby state-run pension programs to stop their association with Fidelity if the firm didn't divest itself of PetroChina shares. Fidelity SVP of media relations and public affairs Anne Crowley, however, told *PRWeek* that the firm didn't support or fund the "tragedy in Sudan" and fully complies with U.S. laws that block direct investments in companies owned or controlled by the Sudanese government.

Celebrity spokespersons were also used by the Darfur Coalition. Actress Mia Farrow gave media interviews and wrote op-eds to support the cause. Other celebrities, such as George Clooney, have also been active promoting the cause.

Social Issue Organizations

Several other widely known organizations are similar to the environmental groups in structure, but with social and behavioral goals. They use public relations methods such

PRCASEBOOK
Men Get the Message to End Rape

Rape is a very high-incidence crime. One in four U.S. women will be raped in her lifetime, and on average a woman is raped every 54 minutes in California. These shocking statistics motivated the California Coalition Against Sexual Assault (CALCASA) to launch a campaign primarily directed at teenage males. "Our goal was to engage young men to stand up and speak out against sexual violence," according to Chris Kuchenmeister of Paine Public Relations in Los Angeles.

The centerpiece of the joint advertising and public relations campaign was the theme "My Strength is Not for Hurting"; posters, buttons, brochures, and radio public service announcements were used to deliver its message to the somewhat elusive audience of young males. The poster campaign, for example, showed close-ups of young couples with such messages as "So when she said NO, I said OK," and "So when I wanted to and she didn't, WE DIDN'T: Men Can Stop Rape." A typical poster is shown on this page. The print materials and radio announcements were made available in English and Spanish, and parents, counselors, and educators could download the materials at www.MyStrength.org Web site. CALCASA (www.calcasa.org) also made available ringtones for cell phones, screen savers, links to rape crisis centers throughout the state, and other resource materials about such topics as date rape and rape prevention strategies.

Paine Public Relations and CALCASA representatives didn't just rely on publicity materials, but also hired a "MyStrength" team of "cool, young bilingual men to be the campaign's face and voice." Actor Dorian Gregory (from *Charmed*) was the celebrity spokesperson, but other "cool" young men went on the road to deliver the message to local media and high schools. The teams reached thousands of young Californians at student assemblies in high schools and distributed 200,000 brochures and other print materials. In addition, the message was featured in 150 print, broadcast, and online media stories. According to Robert Coombs, director of public affairs for CALCASA, "To get through to men 14 to 18 is tough . . . we've done a good job."

This is one of 12 posters produced, in both English and Spanish, for the MyStrength campaign. © 2005 Men Can Stop Rape, Inc. Photo by Lotte Hansen. For more information about the campaign, visit www.mystrength.org.

PRWeek, in critiquing the campaign, noted "The statewide outreach program met its goals and got the MyStrength message out to a multicultural audience. It also managed to open dialogue about a topic that can be controversial as well as uncomfortable for a variety of people."

as those used by the California Coalition Against Sexual Assault (CALCUSA) which is highlighted on page 534.

Mothers Against Drunk Driving (MADD) is one such group. The antiabortion Right to Life movement and the pro-choice National Organization for Women (NOW), bitter enemies, frequently clash in rival public demonstrations. Animal rights groups such as People for the Ethical Treatment of Animals (PETA) at times resort to extreme confrontational tactics such as raiding animal research laboratories and seeking to shame the wearers of fur. The group's campaign against the dairy industry takes a different tack—humor and parody—on the Web site at www.milksucks.com.

Other groups, such as the American Family Association, pressure advertisers to drop sponsorship of television shows that they consider contrary to family values. As a result of massive letter-writing campaigns by this group, Coca-Cola and Procter & Gamble decided to cancel commercials on programs targeted for objectionable content. Members of the AFA also pressured Pepsi into canceling its Madonna ads after seeing the star's video clip for her song "Like a Prayer."

Given the pervasive use of cell phones across the globe, it is no surprise that user-generated cell phone ringtones are an emerging tactic for social action. Mobile-Active.org is an activist network that facilitates cell-based tactics such as ringtones that make a personal statement. One example is the download of sounds of endangered animals, such as a Beluga whale, as a conversation-starter about the loss of biodiversity.

Other Activist Groups

The work of major organizations that receive frequent national attention is illustrative of intense efforts by relatively less prominent associations as well. The National Rifle Association influences Congress and state legislatures through lobbying and campaign contributions. The Christian Coalition fights abortion with public statements, mailings, and telephone calls, and works through the right wing of the Republican Party. Christian church denominations sometimes adopt an activist role. The Southern Baptist Convention mounted a boycott of Disney corporation and all of its subsidiaries in protest of sex and violence in Disney entertainment productions. The boycott was also motivated by "gay days" at Disney's theme parks.

Methods of Operation

The principal ways that environmental organizations work to achieve their goals are lobbying, litigation, mass demonstrations, boycotts, and reconciliation.

♦ **Lobbying.** Much of this is done at state and local government levels, because environmental problems often can be resolved there. For example, approximately 150 organizations campaigned for laws to forbid smoking in public places and to restrict the sale of tobacco. The campaign has had numerous successes.

♦ **Litigation.** Through litigation, organizations file suits seeking court rulings favorable to their projects or attempting to block unfavorable projects. The Sierra Club did so in a years-long action that resulted in a decision by the U.S. Fish and Wildlife Service declaring the northern spotted owl a threatened species. The American Horse Council contends against changes in insurance laws that would discourage many horse enthusiasts who would not be covered in the event of a horse-related accident.

♦ **Mass demonstrations.** Designed to demonstrate public support for a cause and, in some cases, to harass the operators of projects to which the groups object, mass demonstrations require intricate public relations organizational work. Organizers

on the job ETHICS

Working Within the System or Selling Out?

The Multicultural World box on page 533 highlights the activities of the Darfur Coalition to put pressure on corporations and state pension funds to divest of any stock in companies that have investments in the Sudan. Indeed, a common strategy of advocacy groups is to put pressure on corporations through rallies, protests, and even public appeals to boycott companies whose policies are not considered "socially responsible."

The causes and issues vary. Environmental groups concerned about global warming asked Home Depot to stop advertising on the Fox network because several of its commentators and talk show hosts believed global warming didn't exist. The advocacy groups reasoned that if Home Depot was really committed to a "green" agenda, as it claimed, it

should not support a network that wasn't also committed to solving the problem of global warming. In another case, activists have pressured college campuses to kick Coca-Cola off campus because environmentalists in India and elsewhere claim that bottling plants are depleting scarce water supplies for many villages.

In other situations, an ethical question is raised if an environmental or human rights organization accepts contributions from certain corporations. The environmental group Keep America Beautiful (KAB), for example, accepts contributions from Anheuser-Busch and Coca-Cola, whose bottles and cans, detractors say, cause the most clutter in parks and waterfronts in the first place. KAB responds that there is nothing wrong with corporations acting in their own enlightened

self-interest by supporting the quiet constructive work of environmental groups.

What ethical guidelines, from a public relations perspective, should a corporation follow? In the case of Darfur, Fidelity says it is operating within the framework of current U.S. law and making investment decisions based on the best interests of its investors, not social issues. Home Depot takes the position that placing advertising on Fox Network reaches potential customers in an effective way. Coca-Cola says it also provides jobs and helps the economy of India. As for KAB, is it being unethical to take money from corporations who are also making products that can cause litter? In another situation, should a university take a major donation from a tobacco company?

must obtain permits, inform the media, and arrange transportation, housing, programs, and crowd control. A mass demonstration of farmers dependent on irrigation water from drought-threatened rivers in Klamath Falls, Oregon, culminated with the arrival on a truck trailer of a gigantic metal pail, the symbol of the grassroots movement.

◆ **Boycotts.** "Hit them in the pocketbook" is the principle underlying use of the boycott to achieve a goal. Some boycotts achieve easily identifiable results. Others stay in effect for years with little evident success. One environmental success story occurred when the Rainforest Action Network boycotted Burger King for buying Central American beef raised in cleared rain forests. The fast-food chain agreed to stop such purchases. See Chapter 17 for more information on consumer boycotts and their effectiveness.

◆ **Reconciliation.** Some environmental organizations find good results by cooperating with corporations to solve pollution problems. The Environmental Defense Fund joined a task force with McDonald's to deal with the fast-food chain's solid waste problem, leading to a company decision to phase out its polystyrene packaging.

A willingness to accommodate an activist group or ignore them can often raise ethical considerations. See the box on page 536 about such situations.

Fund-Raising

Direct mail fund-raising and publicity campaigns are basic tools of advocacy groups. Raising money to conduct their programs is an unending and costly problem for them. Greenpeace, for example, once sent out 4.5 million pieces of mail a month for this purpose. With so many groups in the field, competition for donations is intense. Some professional fund-raisers believe that as a whole, the groups depend too much on direct mail and should place more emphasis on face-to-face solicitation. Ironically, while some environmental groups advocate preservation of forests, they also create mountains of waste paper by sending millions of "junk mail" letters to raise funds for their organization.

Social Organizations

The term *social* includes social service, health, cultural, philanthropic, and religious groups serving the public in their various ways. Because communication is essential for their success, they require active, creative public relations programs.

Because these organizations are not profit oriented, the practice of public relations on their behalf differs somewhat from that in the business world. Traditionally, nonprofit social agencies have been seen as the "good guys" of society—high-minded, compassionate organizations whose members work to help people achieve a better life. Recently, that perception has changed in some cases.

Numerous agencies have been caught by the recent American urge to scrutinize all aspects of the government and social establishment. Famous organizations usually regarded as sacrosanct have found themselves in trouble. The Girl Scouts of America was accused of having such heavy overhead expense for its annual national cookie sale that the girls themselves received little direct benefit. The Boy Scouts of America ran into difficulty for barring homosexuals from membership. Nevertheless, a national survey of 2,553 U.S. citizens by the D.C.-based Independent Sector found high confidence in the efficiency and effectiveness of charitable organizations.

For many nonprofit groups, obtaining operating funds is a necessity that dominates much of their effort. Without generous contributions from companies and individuals whose money is earned in the marketplace, nonprofit organizations could not exist. As an indication of the scope of philanthropy in the United States, and of the money needed to keep voluntary service agencies operating, American contributions to charity were $295 billion in 2006, according to the Giving Institute (see Figure 20.1). Additional funds are donated to specialized nonprofit organizations that do not fall under the "charity" mantle, and still more are contributed by federal, state, and local governments. Competition among nonprofit agencies for their share of donations is intense.

This ad, placed in *PRWeek*, gives an indication of what experience and skills a nonprofit organization seeks in a public relations executive.

In general terms, nonprofit social organizations are of two types: *services,* typified nationally by the Visiting Nurse Association and the Boys Clubs of America; and *causes,* whose advocacy role is exemplified by the National Safety Council and the National Association for the Advancement of Colored People (NAACP). Organizations frequently have dual roles, both service and advocacy.

Categories of Social Agencies

For purposes of identification, nonprofit social organizations and their functions may be grouped into seven categories:

1. **Social service agencies.** These organizations serve the social needs of individuals and families in many forms. Among prominent national organizations of this type are Goodwill Industries, the American Red Cross, the Boy Scouts and Girl Scouts of America, and the YMCA. Local chapters carry out national programs. Service clubs such as the Rotary, the Kiwanis, the Lions, and the Exchange Club also raise significant amounts of money for charitable projects.

2. **Health agencies.** Many health agencies combat a specific illness through education, research, and treatment, whereas others deliver generalized health services in communities. Typical national organizations include the American Heart Association, the American Cancer Society, and the National Multiple Sclerosis Society.

3. **Hospitals.** Public relations work for hospitals is a large and expanding field. The role of hospitals has taken on new dimensions. In addition to caring for ill and injured patients, hospitals conduct preventive health programs and provide other health-related social services that go well beyond the traditional institutional concept. Hospitals may be tax-supported institutions, nonprofit organizations, or profit-making corporations.

4. **Religious organizations.** The mission of organized religion, as perceived by many faiths today, includes much more than holding weekly worship services and underwriting parochial schools. Churches distribute charity, conduct personal guidance programs, provide leadership on moral and ethical issues in their communities, and operate social centers where diverse groups gather. Some denominations operate retirement homes and nursing facilities for the elderly. At times, religious organizations assume political roles to further their goals. The nondenominational Salvation Army provides the needy with shelter, food, and clothing. It has a vigorous public relations program to earn its place at the top of the fund-raising ranks.

A recent study by the Brookings Institution, titled "Fiscal Capacity of the Voluntary Sector," stated in this regard: "Because religion occupies a stable, central role in American life, religious institutions will be looked to as a backup finance and delivery mechanism by other subsectors . . . particularly . . . in the human service field."

5. **Welfare agencies.** Most continuing welfare payments to persons in need are made by government agencies, using tax-generated funds. Public information officers of these agencies have the important functions of making certain that those entitled to the services know about them and improving public understanding of how the services function.

6. **Cultural organizations.** Development of interest and participation in the cultural aspects of life falls heavily into the hands of nonprofit organizations. So, in many instances, does the operation of libraries; musical organizations, such as symphony orchestras; and museums of art, history, and natural science. Such institutions frequently

receive at least part of their income from government sources; many are operated by governments. Even government-operated cultural institutions depend on privately supported organizations such as Friends of the Museum to raise supplementary funds.

7. **Foundations.** The hundreds of tax-free foundations in the United States constitute about 9 percent of total charitable giving. Money to establish a foundation is provided by a wealthy individual or family, a group of contributors, an organization, or a corporation. The foundation's capital is invested, and earnings from the investments are distributed as grants to qualified applicants. The public knows about such mammoth national organizations as the Ford Foundation, the Rockefeller Foundation, and the Bill & Melinda Gates Foundation. Many are probably not aware, however, of many smaller foundations, some of them extremely important in their specialized fields, that distribute funds for research, education, public performances, displays, and similar purposes.

Giving away money constructively is more difficult than most people realize. Again, public relations representation has a significant role. The requirements of a foundation must be made known to potential applicants for grants. Inquiries must be handled and announcements of grants made.

This summary shows the many diverse, personally satisfying opportunities that are available to public relations practitioners in the social agency fields.

Public Relations Goals

Every voluntary agency should establish a set of public relations goals. When doing so, its management should heed the advice of its public relations staff members, for they are trained to sense public moods and ultimately are responsible for achieving the goals. Emphasis on goals will vary, depending on the purpose of each organization. In general, however, nonprofit organizations should design their public relations to achieve the following objectives:

◆ Develop public awareness of the organization's purpose and activities.

◆ Induce individuals to use the services the organization provides.

◆ Create educational materials—especially important for health-oriented agencies.

◆ Recruit and train volunteer workers.

◆ Obtain funds to operate the organization.

The sections that follow discuss ways in which each of these goals can be pursued.

Public Awareness   The news media provide well-organized channels for stimulating public interest in nonprofit organizations and are receptive to newsworthy material from them. Newspapers usually publish advance stories about meetings, training sessions, and similar routine activities. Beyond that, much depends on the ingenuity of the public relations practitioner in proposing feature articles and photographs. Television and radio stations will broadcast important news items about organizations and are receptive to feature stories and guest appearances by organization representatives. Stories about activities are best told in terms of individuals, rather than in high-flown abstractions. Practitioners should look for unusual or appealing personal stories, such as a retired teacher helping Asian refugee children to learn English.

Creation of events that make news and attract crowds is another way to increase public awareness. Such activities might include an open house in a new hospital wing or a concert by members of the local symphony orchestra for an audience of blind children.

Novelty stunts sometimes draw attention to a cause greater than their intrinsic value seems to justify. For example, a bed race around the parking lot of a shopping center by teams of students at the local university who are conducting a campus fund drive for the March of Dimes could be fun. It would draw almost certain local television coverage and raise money, too.

Very serious, dramatic messages also can be widely dispersed by staging an event made for television coverage. A North Carolina sheriff was saddened and frustrated by the number of unwanted animals put to death in his county animal shelter. He arranged for telecast of the euthanasia death of a 35-pound collie mix during his local public affairs show, *Sheriff's Beat.* Response was tremendous in the area, with adoptions up 300 percent and markedly increased spaying and neutering by local veterinarians. The story garnered national coverage as well, raising awareness across the nation of the need to control dog and cat reproduction.

Publication and distribution of brochures explaining an organization's objectives, operation of a speaker's bureau, showings of films provided by general headquarters of national nonprofit organizations, and periodic news bulletins distributed to opinion leaders are quiet but effective ways of telling an organization's story.

Use of Services   Closely tied to creation of public awareness is the problem of inducing individuals and families to use an organization's services. Free medical examinations, free clothing and food to the urgently needy, family counseling, nursing service for shut-ins, cultural programs at museums and libraries, offers of scholarships—all of these and many other services provided by nonprofit organizations cannot achieve their full value unless potential users know about them.

Because of shyness or embarrassment, persons who would benefit from available services sometimes hesitate to use them. Written and spoken material designed to attract these persons should emphasize the ease of participation and, in matters of health, family, and financial aid, the privacy of the consultations. The American Cancer Society's widely publicized warning list of cancer danger signals is an example of this approach.

Creation of Educational Materials   Public relations representatives of nonprofit organizations spend a substantial portion of their time preparing written and audio-visual materials. These are basic to almost any organization's program.

The quickest way to inform a person about an organization is to hand out a brochure. Brochures provide a first impression. They should be visually appealing and contain basic information, simply written. The writer should answer a reader's obvious questions: What does the organization do? What are its facilities? What services does it offer me? How do I go about participating in its activities and services? The brochure should contain a concise history of the organization and attractive illustrations. When appropriate, it may include a membership application form or a coupon to accompany a donation.

Organizations may design logos, or symbols, that help them keep their activities in the public eye. Another basic piece of printed material is a news bulletin, usually monthly or quarterly, mailed to members, the news media, and perhaps to a carefully composed list of other interested parties. This bulletin may range from a single duplicated sheet to an elaborately printed magazine. A source of public relations support for national philanthropic organizations is the Advertising Council. This is a not-for-profit association of advertising professionals who volunteer their creative and technical skills for organizations. The council handles more than 30 public service campaigns a year for nonsectarian, nonpartisan organizations, chosen from 300 to 500 annual requests. Newspapers and radio and television stations publish or broadcast free of charge the advertisements the council sends them.

One of the best ways to tell an organization's story succinctly and impressively is with an audiovisual package. This may be a slide show or a video, usually lasting about 20 minutes, to be shown to community audiences and/or on a continuing basis in the organization's building.

Volunteer Workers   A corps of volunteer workers is essential to the success of almost every philanthropic enterprise. Far more work needs to be done than a necessarily small professional staff can accomplish. Recruiting and training volunteers and maintaining their enthusiasm so they will be dependable long-term workers are important public relations functions. Organizations usually have a chairperson of volunteers, who works with the public relations (often called community relations) director.

The statistics are impressive. One in five American adults volunteers time for charitable causes, according to a Bureau of Labor Statistics survey. The median weekly time volunteers contribute is slightly more than four hours. Yet the demand for more volunteers is intense.

What motivates people to volunteer? The sense of making a personal contribution to society is a primary factor. Volunteer work can fill a void in the life of an individual who no longer has business or family responsibilities. It also provides social contacts. Why does a former business leader living in a retirement community join a squad of former corporate executives who patrol its streets and public places each Monday, picking up wastepaper? The answer is twofold: pride in making a contribution to local well-being and satisfaction in having a structured activity that partially replaces a former business routine. For the same reasons, the retired executive spends another day each week as a hospital volunteer. These motives are basic to such volunteerism.

Social prestige plays a role, too. Appearing as a model in a fashion show that raises funds for scholarships carries a social cachet. So does selling tickets for a debutante ball, the profits from which go to the American Cancer Society. Serving as a docent, or guide, at a historical museum also attracts individuals who enjoy being seen in a prestigious setting. Yet persons who do well at these valuable jobs might be unwilling to stuff envelopes for a charity solicitation or spend hours in a back room sorting and mending used clothing for resale in a community thrift shop—jobs that are equally important. Such tasks can be assigned to those volunteers who enjoy working inconspicuously and dread meeting the public. Religious commitment is another powerful motivating force for volunteers.

Retirees Make Excellent Volunteers   Retired men and women, who are increasing in number, form an excellent source of volunteers. The Retired Senior Volunteers Program (RSVP) operates 750 projects nationwide, staffing them from its membership of 365,000. The largest organization of seniors, the American Association of Retired Persons (AARP), directs its members into volunteer work through its AARP Volunteer Talent Bank.

How to Recruit Volunteers   Recruiters of volunteers should make clear to potential workers what the proposed jobs entail and, if possible, offer a selection of tasks suitable

on the job INSIGHTS

Charitable Contributions Reach a New Level

Charitable giving is a well-established American institution, and a record $295 billion was given in 2006. This is an increase of almost $12 billion over 2005, according to the Giving USA Foundation.

The major sources of giving, according to the research conducted by the Center for Philanthropy at Indiana University, were as follows:

FIGURE 20.1

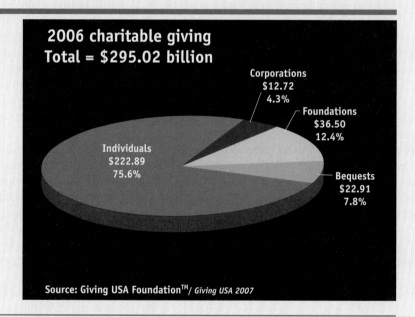

2006 charitable giving
Total = $295.02 billion

Corporations
$12.72
4.3%

Foundations
$36.50
12.4%

Individuals
$222.89
75.6%

Bequests
$22.91
7.8%

Source: Giving USA Foundation™/ *Giving USA 2007*

to differing tastes. A volunteer who has been fast-talked into undertaking an assignment he or she dislikes will probably quit after a short time.

The public relations practitioner can help in recruiting by providing information resources to explain the organization's purpose, to show the essential role its volunteers play, and to stress the sense of achievement and social satisfaction that volunteers find in their work. Testimony from successful, satisfied volunteers is an excellent recruiting tool.

Like all persons, volunteers enjoy recognition, and they should receive it. Certificates of commendation and luncheons at which their work is praised are just two ways of expressing appreciation. Hospital auxiliaries in particular keep charts showing how many hours of service each volunteer has contributed. Service pins or similar tokens are awarded for certain high totals of hours worked. Every organization that uses volunteers should be sure to say, "Thank you!"

The $295 billion in donations were distributed to a variety of organizations. According to Richard T. Jolly, chair of the Giving USA Foundation, "America's 1.4 million charitable and religious organizations provide a huge range of services that improve lives, from meeting immediate needs to funding medical research or creating endowments to assure the future of arts or educational institutions." The following is a breakdown of the various categories by distribution of funds:

FIGURE 20.2

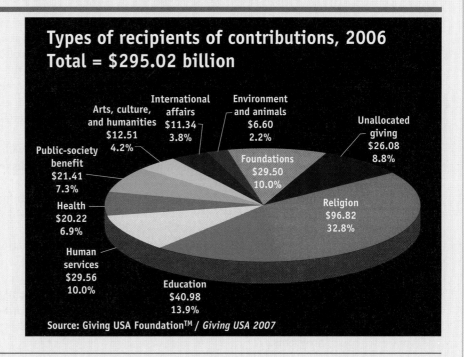

Types of recipients of contributions, 2006
Total = $295.02 billion

Arts, culture, and humanities $12.51 4.2%

International affairs $11.34 3.8%

Environment and animals $6.60 2.2%

Unallocated giving $26.08 8.8%

Public-society benefit $21.41 7.3%

Foundations $29.50 10.0%

Health $20.22 6.9%

Religion $96.82 32.8%

Human services $29.56 10.0%

Education $40.98 13.9%

Source: Giving USA Foundation™ / *Giving USA 2007*

Fund-Raising

At board meetings of voluntary agencies, large and small, from coast to coast, the most frequently asked question is "Where will we get the money?" Discussion of ways to maintain present programs and to add new ones revolves around that inevitable query.

Finding ways to pay the bills is a critical problem for virtually all nonprofit organizations, even those that receive government grants to finance part of their work. Fund-raising has been elevated to a highly developed art and science.

Although the largest, most publicized donations are made by corporations and foundations, the total of individual contributions far exceeds combined corporate and foundation giving, amounting to about 76 percent, about $223 billion, in annual U.S. philanthropic donations. See the sources of funding and the category of participants on page 542. Depending on their needs, voluntary organizations may try to catch minnows—hundreds of small contributions—or angle for the huge marlin—large gifts from big-money sources. Some national organizations raise

> ❝ If nonprofits don't become more sophisticated in their marketing approaches, they could be left behind. ❞
>
> ———*Sarah Evans*, VP of communications for the Prostate Cancer Foundation

massive sums. The Salvation Army, Catholic Charities USA, and the United Jewish Appeal are among the largest recipients.

Public relations representatives may participate directly in fund-raising by organizing and conducting solicitation programs or they may serve as consultants to specialized development departments of their organizations. Organizations often employ professional firms to conduct their campaigns on a fee basis. In that case, the organization's public relations representatives usually have a liaison function.

The Risks of Fund-Raising   Fund-raising involves risks as well as benefits. Adherence to high ethical standards of solicitation and close control of money-raising costs, so that expenses constitute only a reasonable percentage of the funds collected, are essential if an organization is to maintain public credibility. Numerous groups have suffered severe damage to their reputations from disclosures that only a small portion of the money they raised was applied to the cause they advocated, with the rest consumed by solicitation expenses and administrative overhead.

Fund-raising and administrative costs fluctuate widely among organizations, depending on circumstances, and it is difficult to establish absolute percentage standards for acceptable costs. New organizations, for example, have special start-up expenses. In general, an organization is in trouble if its fund-raising costs are more than 25 percent of what it takes in or if fund-raising and "administrative overhead" exceed 40 to 50 percent.

Some examples among respected national organizations include the following: The American Cancer Society applies about 78 cents of every dollar it raises to its anti-cancer work; solicitation costs approximate 12 cents and administrative overhead 10 cents. The American Heart Association applies 75 cents to its work, with 14 cents for solicitation and 11 cents for administration. The National Charities Information Bureau sets a standard that 70 percent of funds raised by a charity should go into programs.

Motivations for Giving   An understanding of what motivates individuals and companies to give money is important to anyone involved in fund-raising. An intrinsic desire to share a portion of one's resources, however small, with the needy and others served by philanthropic agencies is a primary factor—the inherent generosity possessed in some degree by almost everyone. Another urge, also very human, if less laudable, is ego satisfaction. Those who are motivated by it range from donors to large institutions who insist that the buildings they give be named for them, down to the individuals who are influenced to help a cause by the knowledge that their names will be published in a list of contributors. Peer pressure is a third factor; saying "no" to a request from a friend is difficult. The cliché about "keeping up with the Joneses" applies here, openly or subtly.

Although many companies truly desire to contribute a share of their profits to the community well-being, they also are aware that news of their generosity improves their reputations as good corporate citizens. Individuals and corporations alike may receive income tax deductions from their donations, a fact that is less of a motivating factor in many instances than the cynical believe.

Independent Sector commissioned the Gallup Poll to do a survey on volunteerism and giving. The survey found that 53 percent of those responding cited "assisting those who are less fortunate" as their personal motive for volunteering and giving.

The second most frequently cited reason was gaining a feeling of personal satisfaction; religion was third. Only 6 percent cited tax considerations as a major reason for giving.

Fund-raisers know that although many contributors desire nothing more than the personal satisfaction of giving, others like to receive something tangible—a plastic poppy from a veterans' organization, for example. This fact influences the sale of items for philanthropic purposes. When a neighbor high school girl rings the doorbell, selling candy to raise funds for a stricken classmate, multiple forces are at work—instinctive generosity, peer pressure (not to be known in the neighborhood as a tightwad), and the desire to receive something for the money given. Even when householders are on a strict diet, they almost always will accept the candy in return for their contribution rather than merely give the money.

The Competitive Factor   The soliciting organization also should analyze the competition it faces from other fund-raising efforts. The competitive factor is important. The public becomes resentful and uncooperative if approached too frequently for contributions. This is why the United Way of America exists: to consolidate solicitations of numerous important local service agencies into a single unified annual campaign.

The voluntary United Way management in a community, with professional guidance, announces a campaign goal. The money collected in the drive is distributed among participating agencies according to a percentage formula determined by the United Way budget committee.

Types of Fund-Raising   Philanthropic organizations raise funds in several ways:

- Corporate and foundation donations
- Structured capital campaigns
- Direct mail
- Sponsorship of events
- Telephone solicitations
- Use of telephone numbers with "800" and "900" area codes for contributors
- Commercial enterprises

Corporate and Foundation Donations   Organizations seeking donations from major corporations normally should do so through the local corporate offices or sales outlets. Some corporations give local offices a free hand to make donations up to a certain amount. Even when the decisions are made at corporate headquarters, local recommendation is important. Requests to foundations generally should be made to the main office, which will send application forms.

Corporations gave $12.72 billion in 2006 and much of that was in large sums for major projects. A directory, the *Guide to Corporate Giving*, published by the American Council for the Arts in New York, describes the contribution programs of 711 leading corporations. Corporations often fix the amount they will contribute each year as a certain percentage of pretax profits. This ranges from less than 1 percent to more than 2.5 percent. Organizations also make donations on a matching basis with gifts by their employees. The matching most commonly is done on a dollar-for-dollar basis; if an employee gives $1 to a philanthropic cause, the employer does the same. Some corporations match at a two-to-one rate or higher.

on the job
INSIGHTS

Writing a "Case for Support"

Charitable organizations requesting major funds from wealthy individuals, foundations, and corporations usually prepare a "case for support." The following is an outline of what should be contained in such a document.

Background of the Organization

The background information should include the organization's founding date, its purpose and objectives, what distinguishes the organization from similar organizations, and the evolution (development) of objectives and services.

Current Status of Organization's Services

The number of paid and volunteer staff, facilities, the number of clients served annually, current budget, a breakdown of how that budget is allocated, and geographical areas served should be included here.

Need for Organization's Services

The report should present factual and statistical evidence, the availability of similar services, evidence showing the seriousness of the problem, and the uniqueness of the program.

Sources of Current Funding

Public donations, foundations and corporations, and government funding should be listed.

Administration of the Organization

The report should discuss the background of the executive director and qualifications of key staff and the board of directors (including names and titles).

Tax Status of Organization

The tax status of the organization should be stated.

Community Support

Letters from satisfied clients, letters from community leaders, and favorable media coverage of programs will demonstrate community support.

Current Needs of the Organization

Specific programs, specific staffing, financial costs, the amount of financial support needed, and sources of possible funding should be discussed.

Benefits to the Community from the New or Expanded Program

The report should persuasively present the proposed benefits to the community.

Request for Specific Amount of Funds

This portion will explain the need for the donor's participation and benefits to the donor.

Corporations make contributions to charities in less direct ways, too, some of them quite self-serving. (The practice of cause-related marketing is explained in Chapter 17.) When applying for a charitable donation, an applicant should submit a "case for support" proposal that provides a comprehensive overview of the charitable group and the necessity of the fund-raising project. See the Insights box on this page for an outline on how to write a case for support.

Structured Capital Campaigns   The effort to raise major amounts of money for a new wing of a hospital, for an engineering building on a campus, or even for the reconstruction and renovation of San Francisco's famed cable car system is often called a *capital campaign.*

In a capital campaign, emphasis is placed on substantial gifts from corporations and individuals. One key concept of a capital campaign is that 90 percent of the total amount raised will come from only 10 percent of the contributors. In a $10 million campaign to add a wing to an art museum, for example, it is not unusual that the lead gift will be $1 or $2 million.

Capital campaigns require considerable expertise and, for this reason, many organizations retain professional fund-raising counsel. A number of U.S. firms offer these services; the most reputable ones belong to the Association of Fundraising Professionals (AFP), which can be reached at www.afpnet.org.

Traditionally, professional fund-raisers were paid by organizations for their work either in salary or by a negotiated fee. In a controversial decision, however, the National Society of Fund-Raising Executives changed its code of ethics in 1989 to permit its members to accept commissions based on the amount of money they raise.

The preparation for a capital campaign, whether managed by a professional counseling firm or by the institution's own development staff, is almost as important as the campaign itself. A fund-raising campaign usually is organized along quasi-military lines, with division leaders and team captains. In a typical campaign, there are teams of volunteers organized to solicit major businesses, various levels of individual prospects based on their wealth and ability to give, and even a team to get donations from rank-and-file employees.

> " In grant writing, you communicate messages, but you also create programs. "
> ———*Liz Rogers*, director of communications for OralHealth America

Donors often are recognized by the size of their gifts, and terms such as *patron* or *founder* are used. Major donors may be given the opportunity to have rooms or public places in the building named after them. Hospitals, for example, prepare "memorial" brochures that show floor plans and the cost of endowing certain facilities.

Direct Mail   Although direct mail can be an expensive form of solicitation because of the costs of developing or renting mailing lists, preparing the printed materials, and mailing them, it is increasingly competitive with advertising costs directed at similarly targeted audiences. An organization can reduce costs by conducting an effective local, limited direct mail campaign on its own if it develops an up-to-date mailing list of "good" names known to be potential donors and can provide enough volunteers to stuff and address the solicitation envelopes. Regional and national organizations, and some large local ones, either employ direct mail specialists or rent carefully chosen mailing lists from list brokers.

The abundance and diversity of mailing lists for rent are impressive. One company offers more than 8,000 different mailing lists. A common rental price is $40 per thousand names. Other lists cost more, depending on their special value. *Direct Mail List Rates and Data*, updated bimonthly by Standard Rate & Data Service, Inc., is a basic reference book for direct mail lists. The best lists contain donors to similar causes. Direct Media List Management Group, for example, offered a list of almost 1.5 million "aware" women who have contributed to at least one of 27 causes.

Direct e-mail campaigns also can be arranged at reasonable costs with companies that compile e-mail addresses similar to print mail lists. Such targeting greatly increases the predictable percentage of successful contacts from the mailing. A response of 1 percent on a mailing usually is regarded as satisfactory; 2 percent is excellent.

Take the following steps to make a profitable return on direct mail investments:

1. Make use of an attention-getting headline.
2. Follow with an inspirational lead-in on why and how a donation will benefit clients of the charitable agency.

3. Give a clear definition of the charitable agency's purpose and objectives.

4. Humanize the cause by giving an example of a child or family that benefited.

5. Include testimonials and endorsements from credible individuals.

6. Ask for specific action and provide an easy method for the recipient to respond. Self-addressed stamped envelopes and pledge cards often are included.

7. Close with a postscript that gives the strongest reason for reader response.

One marketing research firm enhanced direct-mail precision by identifying 34 human factors such as age, gender, education, and levels of economic well-being. It fed these factors into computers along with a list of 36,000 zip code markets and produced 40 neighborhood types. An organization interested in reaching one of these types—the supereducated top income level, for example—could use suitable mailing lists broken down to postal area routes.

Attractive, informative mailing pieces that stimulate recipients to donate are keys to successful solicitation. The classic direct-mail format consists of a mailing envelope, letter, brochure, and response device, often with a postage-paid return envelope.

Sponsorship of Events   The range of events a philanthropic organization can sponsor to raise funds is limited only by the imagination of its members. A particularly effective promotion was Heart Truth and its Red Dress icon, which is described on page 549.

Participation contests are a popular method. Walkathons and jogathons appeal to the current American emphasis on using the legs for exercise. Nationally, the March of Dimes holds an annual 32-kilometer WalkAmerica in 1,100 cities on the same day. Local organizations do the same in their own communities. Bikeathons are popular, too. The money-raising device is the same in all such events: Each entrant signs up sponsors who promise to pay a specified amount to the fund for each mile or kilometer the entrant walks, jogs, runs, or cycles.

The popularity of walkathons, however, is getting to the point that competing groups are virtually running into each other. In one day, for example, nonprofits in the Miami area held three competing runs. According to the *Wall Street Journal,* "Charity groups now find themselves not only competing for donor dollars, but also for participants and popular dates on which to hold their events." Despite the competition, *USA Track & Field* reports that $656 million was raised in 2005 by what *Wall Street Journal* reporter calls, "legions of sneaker-clad Samaritans."

Staging of parties, charity balls, concerts, and similar events in which tickets are sold is another widely used approach. Often, however, big parties create more publicity than profit, with 25 to 50 percent of the money raised going to expenses. Other methods include sponsorship of a motion-picture opening, a theater night, or a sporting event. Barbecues flourish as money-raisers in western cities. Seeking to attract donors from the under-30 age group, some organizations use the "fun" approach by raffling off such items as Madonna's sequined brassiere (for $2,500) and a T-shirt by artist Felix Gonzalez-Torres with the message "Nobody Owns Me" (for $50).

Sale of a product, in which the organization keeps a portion of the selling price, ranges from the church baked-goods stand, which yields almost 100 percent profit because members contribute homemade products, to the massive national Girl Scout cookie sale, which grosses about $375 million annually. A key to success in all charity-fund sales is abundant publicity in the local news media.

Direct solicitation of funds over television by telethons is used primarily in large cities. A television station sets aside a block of airtime for the telethon sponsored by a

on the job
INSIGHTS

Women and Heart Disease: The Red Dress Campaign

The number one killer of women in the United States is heart disease. Research by the National Heart, Lung, and Blood Institute (NHLBI), however, indicated that only about a third of the women surveyed were aware of this alarming statistic. Thus was born the Heart Truth project, which made the red dress the symbol of a campaign that was a partnership between governmental agencies, corporations, and nonprofit health groups.

Ogilvy Worldwide Public Relations was commissioned to execute a public relations campaign with the following objectives: (1) increase awareness that heart disease is the number one killer of women, (2) increase recognition of the Red Dress as the national symbol for women and heart disease awareness, (3) increase awareness of risk factors that cause heart disease, and (4) capitalize on the power of partnerships to spread the campaign's message.

Several major programs were launched. One was the debut of the Red Dress Collection each February on National Wear Red Day, featuring combined designs from top fashion designers modeled by celebrities and models. Another strategy was the active involvement of First Lady Laura Bush as the Heart Truth's spokesperson for media interviews and also attendance at national and local events across the country. There was also a traveling exhibit to major cities featuring a red dress display

The Heart Truth Red Dress campaign generated coverage in major magazines.

and real women's stories, along with free educational materials and health screenings. In Washington, D.C., an exhibit displaying red dresses from all seven living First Ladies was held at the John F. Kennedy Center for the Performing Arts. Ogilvy PR also helped coordinate hundreds of local events across the country that included health fairs, walks, rallies, teas, and red dress fashion shows.

The Heart Truth campaign partnered with a number of magazines such as *Newsweek, Glamour, Essence,* and *Woman's Day* to run articles, advertorial, and PSA placements. Laura Bush also appeared on all major

network morning shows to kick off the campaign and to promote National Wear Red Day. Her husband, George, also participated by signing an official presidential proclamation declaring February as American Heart Month at a signing ceremony in the White House, which was also widely covered in the media. Other materials prepared included a heart handbook for women, fact sheets, posters, broadcast PSAs, and the launch of a Web site, www.hearttruth.gov.

The campaign achieved its objectives. Awareness among women about heart disease as a major killer increased from 34 percent in 2001 to

(CONTINUED)

57 percent in 2007. Another 57 percent of women now recognize the Red Dress as the national symbol for women and heart disease awareness, up from 25 percent in 2005. In addition, the campaign generated more than 25 national grassroots community partnerships and more than 30 corporate sponsorships.

Media coverage was extensive. There were 12 national newspaper advertising inserts featuring Heart Truth with a combined circulation of 369 million. The Heart Truth logo or red dress was also included in the packaging of many products by various manufacturers of food items. Broadcast, newspaper, magazine, and online placements in major and local markets generated about 1.5 billion impressions. Color print PSAs placed in *Essence, Elle, Parenting, Health,* and other publications represented an advertising value of about $1 million. Health provider exhibits at 16 professional conferences reached almost 165,000 health professionals. In terms of informational materials, more than 1.2 million brochures and facts sheets have been distributed since the program's inception in 2002.

philanthropic organization. Best known of the national telethons is the one conducted annually by comedian Jerry Lewis for muscular dystrophy. More recently, the television program *American Idol* held an enormously successful fund-raising extravaganza involving established musical stars as well as stars whose careers were launched by the talent program.

Telephone Solicitations   Solicitation of donations by telephone is a relatively inexpensive way to seek funds but is of uncertain effectiveness. Many groups hold down their cost of solicitation by using a WATS (Wide Area Telephone Service) line that provides unlimited calls for a flat fee, without individual toll charges. Some people resent receiving telephone solicitations. If the recipient of the call is unfamiliar with the cause, it must be explained clearly and concisely—which is not always easy for a volunteer solicitor to do. The problem of converting verbal promises by telephone into confirmed written pledges also arises. The normal method is for the sponsoring organization to send a filled-in pledge form to the donor for signature.

Use of "800" or "900" Telephone Numbers   Toll-free telephone numbers with area codes of 800, permitting callers to phone an organization long distance without cost to themselves, have been in use for years. A 900 code has been added by the telephone companies that requires users to pay a fee for each call placed. The phone company takes a service charge from this fee, and the remainder goes to the party being called. Public television station WNET in New York used a 900 number in an annual pledge drive and received $235,000 in contributions through it.

Commercial Enterprises   Rather than depending entirely on contributions, some nonprofit organizations go into business on their own or make tie-ins with commercial firms from which they earn a profit. Use of this approach is growing, but it entails risks that must be carefully assessed.

Three types of commercial money-raising are the most common:

1. License the use of an organization's name to endorse a product and receive payment for each item sold. This is the approach of Bono's (PRODUCT) RED program, which is briefly described on page 551.
2. Share profits with a corporation to receive a share of its profits from sales of a special product, such as Newman's Own salad dressing.
3. Operate a business that generates revenue for the organization.

Celebrities often lend their name to charitable fund-raising. Here Bono and Oprah Winfrey leave a Gap store in Chicago after buying clothes as part of Bono's (PRODUCT) RED campaign. Retailers such as Gap, Apple, Converse, and American Express donate a percentage of profits on RED-branded products to combat disease in Africa. In return, they get the support of Bono and enhanced recognition as a socially responsible organization. There is also the promise of being considered more "hip" and attracting more customers who want to support worthy causes. The (PRODUCT) RED project was started by Bono in 2005 and, in the first six months of existence, the project generated $10 million for the Global Fund to Fight Aids.

Advocates describe commercial involvement by nonprofit organizations as creating wealth, not receiving it, but the risks for an organization are obvious. Entrepreneurship requires good business management, not always available in charitable organizations. Businesses can lose money as well as make it. Ill-advised lending of an organization's name to a shoddy product or a high-pressure telemarketing scheme can damage a charity's reputation.

Any nonprofit organization contemplating operation of a business should check the tax laws, which require that the enterprise be "substantially related" to the purpose of the nonprofit group.

Hospital Public Relations

The public relations staff of a hospital has two primary roles:

◆ to strengthen and maintain the public's perception of the institution as a place where medical skill, compassion, and efficiency are paramount, and

◆ to help market the hospital's proliferating array of services. Many hospitals have sought to redefine themselves as community health centers.

Basically, hospitals, like hotels, must have high room-occupancy rates to succeed financially. They supplement this fundamental source of income by creating and marketing supplementary services, an area that offers a challenge to public relations people. Typical of these supplementary services are alcoholism rehabilitation, childbirth and parenting education, hospices for the terminally ill, pastoral care, and physician referral services.

Hospital Audiences

Because hospitals sell a product (improved health), parallels exist between their public relations objectives and those of other corporations. They focus on diverse audiences, external and internal; involve themselves in public affairs and legislation because they operate under a mass of government regulations; and stress consumer relations. In the case of hospitals, this involves keeping patients and their families satisfied, as well as seeking new clients. Hospitals produce publications for external and internal audiences. They have an additional function that other corporate public relations practitioners don't need to handle—the development and nurturing of volunteer organizations.

Hospital public relations programs have four basic audiences: patients, medical and administrative staffs, news media, and the community as a whole. The four audiences overlap, but each needs a special focus. Careful scrutiny can identify significant subaudiences within these four—for example, the elderly; women who have babies or soon will give birth; victims of heart disease, cancer, and stroke who need support groups after hospitalization; potential financial donors to the hospital; and community opinion leaders whose goodwill helps to build the institution's reputation. Each group can be cultivated by public relations techniques discussed in this textbook.

The reputations of some hospitals have been damaged by the public's perception of them as cold institutions that don't care enough about individual patients. Complaints by patients about poor food and brusque nurses add to the problem.

Here are a few examples of methods hospitals use to project a positive image:

- ◆ Sponsorship of community health fairs, offering free screenings to detect symptoms of certain diseases and low-cost comprehensive blood tests.
- ◆ A "direct line" telephone system within the hospital on which patients and visitors can register complaints and suggestions 24 hours a day.
- ◆ Bingo games on a closed-circuit television system, for which patients pay a small fee and win cash prizes. This brightens the patients' day.

SUMMARY

The Role of Public Relations

Nonprofit organizations have been given tax-exempt status because their primary goal is to enhance the well-being of their members or the human condition. Fund-raising is a major public relations task in these groups.

Basic Needs of Nonprofits

Although there is a broad range of nonprofit organizations, they all create communications campaigns and programs, require a staff (including volunteers) to handle their work, and are involved in fund-raising.

Membership Organizations

A membership organization is made up of people with a common interest, either business or social. Such groups include trade associations, labor unions, professional associations, and chambers of commerce.

Advocacy Groups

Advocacy groups work for social causes such as the environment, civil rights, gun ownership, or the pro-choice movement. Their efforts include lobbying, litigation, mass demonstrations, boycotts, reconciliation, and public education. As with other nonprofits, fund-raising is an unending issue with these groups.

Social Organizations

Social service groups, health agencies, hospitals, religious organizations, welfare agencies, cultural groups, and foundations all fall into the category of social organizations. Their public relations goals include developing public awareness, getting individuals to use their services, creating educational materials, recruiting volunteers, and fund-raising. Fund-raising can take the form of corporate and foundation donations, structured capital campaigns, direct mail, sponsorship of events, telephone solicitations, the use of toll-free numbers, and commercial enterprises.

CASE ACTIVITY What Would You Do?

The Vision Council of America is a trade group representing the optical industry. Its three core membership groups are ophthalmologists, opticians, and optometrists.

The group decides to launch a consumer education program after research reveals a reluctance to take children for eye exams because parents rely on free in-school screenings. Additional research shows that 80 percent of learning before age 12 is accomplished through vision, yet traditional in-school vision screenings miss between 70 and 80 percent of children's vision problems.

Your public relations firm is retained to conduct a national consumer education program emphasizing the importance of annual eye exams for children. What would you suggest? Program elements that you should consider include key publics, message themes, time of year, strategies, and innovative communication tactics, especially technologies such as CD-ROM and the Web.

QUESTIONS for Review and Discussion

1. Trade associations, like other membership organizations, often have headquarters in Washington, D.C., or a state capital. Why?
2. What has caused the recent intensified scrutiny of nonprofit organizations?
3. Name the seven categories of social agencies.
4. What challenges do labor unions face today?
5. What are the differences and similarities among trade groups, labor unions, and professional associations?
6. What motivates people to serve as volunteer workers?
7. Describe four commonly used types of fund-raising.
8. Chambers of commerce often are described as the public relations arm of city government. Why?
9. Identify four methods advocacy groups use to further their causes.
10. What two principle roles does a hospital public relations staff fulfill?

SUGGESTED READINGS

Doty, Cate. "Who's the Most Charitable of Us All? Celebrities Don't Always Make the Cut." *New York Times*, September 10, 2007.

Gingerich, Jon. "Computer Makers go Green for Good PR." *O'Dwyer's PR Report*, February, 2007, p. 9.

Goldberg, Jeffrey. "Selling Wal-Mart—Can the Company Co-opt Liberals?: Wal-Mart Has Hired Democratic P.R. Experts to Help Improve its Reputation on such Issues as Low Wages, Miserly Benefits, Sex Discrimination, and Union Busting." *New Yorker*, April 2, 2007. tinyurl.com/33177b

Hoggan, James. "Think Tanks: Giving PR a Bad Name." *O'Dwyer's PR Report*, February, 2007, p. 8.

Hand, Mark. "Nonprofit Sharing: PR Pros in the Nonprofit Area Often Have to Do More With Less." *PRWeek*, January 9, 2006, p. 19.

Kelly, Kathleen S. *Effective Fund-Raising Management*. Mahwah, NJ: Lawrence Erlbaum, 1998.

Kinnick, Katherine N., Krugman, Dean M., and Cameron, Glen T. "Compassion Fatigue: Communication and Burnout toward Social Problems." *Journalism and Mass Communication Quarterly*, Vol. 73, No. 3, Autumn 1996, pp. 687–707.

McKenna, Ted. "A Show of Support." *PRWeek*, July 2, 2007, p. 21.

Nolan, Hamilton. "State of the Unions." *PRWeek*, June 26, 2006, p. 25.

Russell, Jacob. "Hunger vs. the Arts." *Wall Street Journal,* October 14, 2006, pp. P1, 8–9.

Strom, Stephanie. "What's Wrong With Profit?" *New York Times*, November 13, 2006, pp. E1, 12.

Ward, David. "Media Maintains Its Interest in Art: Many Opportunities Exist for Media Coverage of Art, but PR Pros Must Overcome the Intense Competition and a Lack of Attention Paid to Unknown Artists." *PRWeek*, August 23, 2004, p. 11.

Waxman, Sharon. "So Many Causes, So Little Time for the Hollywood Do-Gooder." *New York Times*, November 13, 2006, p. A14.

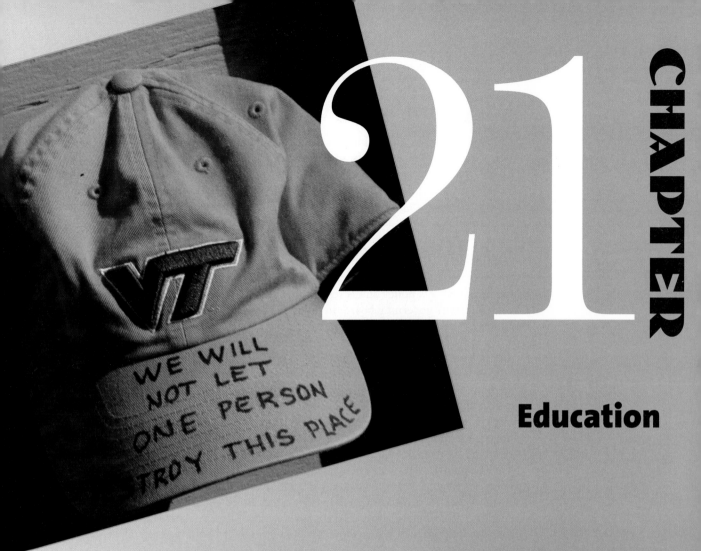

21 CHAPTER

Education

Colleges and Universities

Higher education is big business in the United States. California, the most populous state, with 36 million residents, spends about $20 billion annually on four-year public colleges and universities. It's also a business that has millions of customers. Almost 17.5 million students are enrolled at more than 4,000 American colleges and universities. Almost every one of these institutions has personnel working in such activities as public relations, marketing communications, and fund-raising.

Development and Public Relations Offices

The president (or chancellor) is the chief public relations officer of a college or university; he or she sets policy and is responsible for all operations, under the guidance of the institution's governing board. In times of a crisis, the leadership of the president is particularly crucial.

In large universities, the vice president for development and university relations (that person may have some other title) supervises the office of development, which includes a division for alumni relations, and also the office of public relations; these functions are combined in smaller institutions. Development and alumni personnel seek to enhance the prestige and financial support of the institution. Among other activities, they conduct meetings and seminars, publish newsletters and magazines, and arrange tours. Their primary responsibilities are to build alumni loyalty and generate funding from private sources.

The public relations director, generally aided by one or more chief assistants, supervises the information news service, publications, and special events. Depending on the size of the institution, perhaps a dozen or more employees will carry out these functions, including writing, photography, graphic design, broadcasting, and computer networking. Figure 21.1 shows the organization of a public affairs staff at Stanford University.

In addition, scores of specialists at a large university perform diverse information activities in agricultural, medical, engineering, extension, continuing education, and other such units, including sports.

News Bureaus

The most visible aspect of a university public relations program is its news bureau. Among other activities, an active bureau produces hundreds of news releases, photographs, and special columns and articles for the print media. It prepares programs of news and features about faculty activities and personalities for stations. It provides assistance and information for reporters, editors, and broadcasters affiliated with the state, regional, and national media. The staff responds to hundreds of telephone calls from members of the news media and the public seeking information. In a crisis situation, the intense media attention can be almost overwhelming. See the Insights box on page 558 about the killing of 33 students at Virginia Tech.

Serving the Publics

To carry out their complex functions, top development and public relations specialists must be a part of the management team of the college or university. At some institutions this is not so, and the public relations program suffers. Ideally, these leaders should attend all top-level meetings involving the president and other administrators, learning

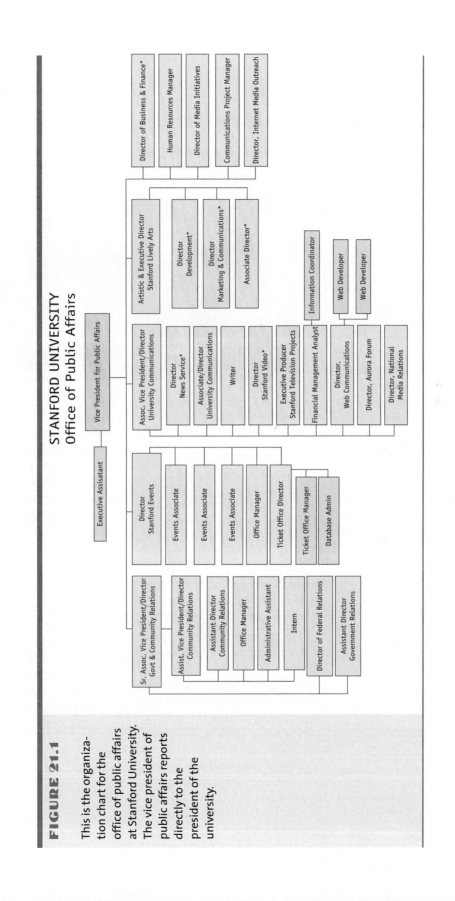

FIGURE 21.1

This is the organization chart for the office of public affairs at Stanford University. The vice president of public affairs reports directly to the president of the university.

STANFORD UNIVERSITY
Office of Public Affairs

Vice President for Public Affairs

Executive Assisatant

Sr. Assoc. Vice President/Director Govt & Community Relations
- Assist. Vice President/Director Community Relations
- Assistant Director Community Relations
- Office Manager
- Administrative Assistant
- Intern
- Director of Federal Relations
- Assistant Director Government Relations

Director Stanford Events
- Events Associate
- Events Associate
- Events Associate
- Office Manager
- Ticket Office Director
- Ticket Office Manager
- Database Admin

Assoc. Vice President/Director University Communications
- Director News Service*
- Associate/Director University Communications
- Writer
- Director Stanford Video*
- Executive Producer Stanford Television Projects
- Financial Management Analyst
- Information Coordinator
  - Web Developer
  - Web Developer
- Director, Web Communications
- Director, Aurora Forum
- Director, National Media Relations

Artistic & Executive Director Stanford Lively Arts
- Director Development*
- Director Marketing & Communications*
- Associate Director*

Director of Business & Finance*
Human Resources Manager
Director of Media Initiatives
Communications Project Manager
Director, Internet Media Outreach

557

on the job
INSIGHTS

Virginia Tech Endures Massacre; Lessons Evident for Public Relations

On April 16, 2007, the Virginia Tech campus was rocked by a shooting spree that left 33 dead and many wounded.

At the height of the intense media coverage, there were 600 reporters and four or five acres of satellite trucks on the campus, which practically overwhelmed the university's communications staff.

A 300-page report released by a state panel at the end of August 2007 criticized Virginia Tech administration and law enforcement for failing to follow recommended security procedures and ignoring serious warning signs about the mental health of the assailant, Seung-Hui Cho. Family members of victims voiced frustration that Virginia Tech had not imposed a lockdown after the first deadly shooting of two students, which occurred hours before the mass killing.

Any such report is bound to reflect the brilliant insights made possible only in hindsight. And the most positive approach to such reports is to learn from the analysis of events that took place in the chaos of the moment. In that spirit, the International Association of Campus Law Enforcement Administrators, Inc. (IACLEA)

encourages campus public safety departments throughout the U.S. to carefully review this report and identify lessons that can be learned from these tragic events. These lessons include recommendations in the report calling for campuses to conduct threat and risk assessments, *regular review and updating of*

emergency response plans, review of communications procedures and equipment. . . .

For college public relations professionals, several lessons emerge:

◆ The first is simply that communication on today's campuses is more important than ever before. Campuses are now working to instill a more caring and a more vigilant culture that identifies those troubled students who could be a danger to themselves and others.

◆ A distinction should be made between proactive and reactive performance of public relations staff. While Virginia Tech should have done more to create a campus culture that would prevent mass violence, the administration, campus police force, and public relations staff earned high marks for honest, heartfelt, and responsible handling of the crisis communication in the immediate aftermath of the tragedy.

◆ The crucial lapse in performance resulted from the failure to

make the university relations department at Virginia Tech an integral part of management plans for response to any violent act such as rape, attempted murder, or murder on campus. Professional organizations such as IACLEA recommend an ironclad rule that violent acts trigger a communication crisis response. Public relations personnel should send mass e-mails and use traditional media such as radio and loudspeakers to notify students and staff of a lockdown order. New media techniques such as text messages to student cell phones and emergency announcements on popular Web sites at Virginia Tech also could have precluded the massacre that took place in a classroom building.

The point is not to direct blame at communication professionals on the Virginia Tech campus, but to recognize the role of public relations and to raise our standards of performance to deal with future situations.

the whys and wherefores of decisions made and lending counsel. Only then can they satisfactorily develop action programs and respond to questions from the publics those programs concern. They are indeed the arms and voice of the administration.

Faculty and Staff   As noted in previous chapters, every sound public relations program begins with the internal constituency. Able college presidents involve their faculty in decision making to the fullest extent possible, given the complexities of running a major institution. It is a maxim that the employees of a company or institution serve as its major public relations representatives because they come into contact with so many people. Good morale, a necessity, is achieved in large measure through communication.

College administrators communicate with their faculty and staff members through e-mail and internal newsletters and newspapers; journals describing research, service, and other accomplishments (which also are sent to outside constituencies); periodic meetings at which policies are explained and questions answered; and in numerous other ways.

Faculty and staff members who fully understand the college's philosophy, operations, and needs generally will respond with heightened performance. For example, when the University of Georgia sought to obtain $2.5 million in contributions from its faculty members as part of an $80 million bicentennial enrichment campaign, they responded with a generous outpouring of nearly $6 million—a signal to outside contributors that helped ensure the success of the program.

Students   Because of their large numbers and the many families that they represent, students make up the largest public relations arm—for good or bad—that a university has. The quality of the teaching they receive is the greatest determinant of their allegiance to the institution. However, a sound administrative attitude toward students, involving them as much as possible in decisions that affect their campus lives, is extremely important. So are other forms of communication, achieved through support of student publications and broadcast stations and numerous other ways. When, upon graduation, they are asked to join the university's alumni association, chances are good that, if they are pleased with their collegiate experience, many will support the university in its future undertakings. A public relations effort directed at students is thus essential.

Alumni and Other Donors   The loyalty and financial support of alumni are crucial to the ongoing operations of a college or university. Alumni are considered the major foundation of any fund-raising effort because of their immediate association with the institution. Consequently, colleges and universities cultivate their loyalty and support through events and monthly magazines. The alumni magazine from Iowa

Universities constantly communicate with alumni to build loyalty and potential financial support. This is the cover of one such alumni publication. Reprinted with permission of the Iowa State University Alumni Association and *Visions* magazine. Photo by Jim Heemstra.

State University on page 559 is a good example. Donors who are not alumni also are cultivated for major gifts based on their interest in a particular field or discipline.

Indeed, fund-raising has increased dramatically at most public and private universities in recent years as costs have risen and allocations from state legislatures and federal agencies have dramatically declined. Total nongovernmental financial support for higher education was $41 billion in 2006, according to Giving U.S.A., an annual tally of charitable contributions published by the A.A.F.R.C. Trust for Philanthropy, a unit of the American Association of Fundraising Counsel. This amount represents 14 percent of the total charitable giving in the United States, which was $295 billion. See page 543 in Chapter 20 for a breakdown.

In addition to annual operating fund campaigns, universities are increasingly conducting long-range capital campaigns for large amounts of money. In 2007, at least 28 American universities were in the process of raising $1 billion or more. For example, Johns Hopkins University had a goal of $3.2 billion by 2008, Brown University had a goal of $1.4 billion by 2010, and the University of Maryland had a goal of $1 billion by 2011.

Such large amounts, coupled with annual alumni campaigns, have caused a major demand for experienced fund-raisers. Indeed, Brent Keltner, vice president of Eduventures, told the *Chronicle of Higher Education*, "The rapid growth of university fundraising is creating a new set of operational challenges and a growing appetite for a new type of development professional."

The competition for qualified development personnel is also causing a rise in salaries. The median annual salary of a chief development officer at a university offering doctoral degrees is $190,204 as of 2006, according to the annual survey by the *Chronicle of Higher Education*. In contrast, the median salary of a chief public relations officer is $132,290 at doctoral institutions. Salaries at four- and two-year institutions are somewhat lower.

Colleges and universities raise money for a variety of purposes. This may include such projects as recruiting new faculty, buying equipment, building student residence halls, providing scholarships, remodeling classrooms, and upgrading campus computer networks. New York University, for example, is planning to add 125 new faculty to its 625-member arts and sciences faculty over a five-year period. Money also will be spent on laboratories, offices, and housing for the new professors.

Many institutions employ students to participate in fund-raising phonathons. At the University of Michigan, students called 970,000 alumni and raised $8.3 million during a nine-month period. Computerized dialing systems are often used. At most institutions, letters are mailed to specific graduating classes over the names of members who have agreed to be class agents for that purpose.

Year-by-year contributions are sought, as are bequests and annuities. In return, the colleges publish honor rolls listing donors, invite contributors to join honorary clubs (the President's Club, for example), and name rooms and buildings for the largest givers. Columbia University, for example, received a $400 million gift from John W. Kluge, one of its alumni. He had received a scholarship to attend Columbia back in the 1930s and went on to own an extensive radio and television empire. He always felt grateful for the aid he received, so Kluge has earmarked his gift for student financial aid.

Universities often use matching grants to make a donor's contribution go further— and thus make giving more attractive. For instance, a donor in Dallas who wanted to remain anonymous contributed $8 million toward the establishment of faculty enrichment chairs at the University of Texas at Austin. The sum was matched by foundations, and the entire $16 million, in turn, was matched by the university, making possible the establishment of 32 new chairs. Such support is essential in order for good universities to become great universities.

Influential alumni and other important friends of colleges and universities also are encouraged, through personal contact and correspondence, to provide political clout with legislative bodies and boards of regents in support of the institutions' financial and other objectives. Such support also is important in the recruitment of students with outstanding academic, athletic, or other achievements.

Government   State and federal governments often hold the vital key to whether universities receive sufficient monies to maintain facilities, faculty, and programs. Most large institutions have someone who regularly monitors the state legislature on appropriations and issues ranging from laboratory experiments on animals to standardized tests and taxes. Their work includes:

1. competing with other state institutions for money,
2. defending proposed increases in higher-education budgets and protecting against cuts,
3. establishing an institution's identity in the minds of legislators, and
4. responding to lawmakers' requests for favors.

Said Robert Dickens, coordinator of government relations for the University of Nevada at Reno: "When I say I'm a lobbyist, some people look at me as if I need a shower. It's a new business with the universities, and some people think it's a dirty business. But nothing's dirtier than not having resources."

The declining federal support for higher education also has led to an increase in the number of government relations experts representing universities in Washington, D.C. Their work complements that of the American Council on Education, the National Association of Land-Grant Universities, and the Association of American Universities. They not only lobby members of Congress regarding legislation that might have an adverse or favorable effect on their clients but also seek information from federal agencies about new programs and uncommitted funds.

The Community   As in the case of industry, a college or university must maintain a good relationship with the members of the community in which it is situated. The greatest supporters that an institution may have are the people within its immediate sphere of influence, many of whom mingle with its faculty, staff members, and students. Tax dollars also are an immense benefit, although the fact that university property is tax exempt may impose a strain unless the institution voluntarily agrees to some form of compensation for services such as fire and police protection.

In order to bridge the town–gown gap, faculty and staff members are encouraged to achieve community visibility through work with civic and other organizations. Business groups often take the lead. The Chamber of Commerce in Lawrence, Kansas, for example, for many years sponsored an annual barbecue, including various other activities, to give faculty and townspeople an opportunity to get to know each other better. Community relations, however, can be severely tested when there is campus scandal and controversy. See the PR Casebook about Duke University's lacrosse scandal on page 562.

Prospective Students   Suffering from declining revenues, increased costs of operation, and a dwindling pool of prospective students occasioned by lower birthrates, many colleges have turned to highly competitive recruiting methods. Some, in the "hard-sell" classification, use extensive advertising in print and broadcast media and on

PRCASEBOOK

Duke University Defends Reputation in Lacrosse Scandal

Scandal and controversy seem to gravitate to powerful and visible institutions. Despite public relations efforts to maintain a long-standing reputation, it may be tarnished in an instant by a single incident. Restoring the image requires tenacity, delicacy, and grace.

In April 2006, two Duke University lacrosse players were indicted for allegedly raping an African American exotic dancer that they had hired for a party. The ensuing scandal seriously tarnished the North Carolina school's reputation. Salacious details about the players' alleged behavior, the school's tolerance of rowdy conduct, and public perception of the university as a bastion of white elitism presented challenges to Duke's public relations division.

The scandal led to intense media scrutiny and a barrage of telephone calls, letters, and e-mails from both detractors and defenders. According to David Jarmul, Duke VP for news and communications, "The challenge here is that the central facts of the story have been so much in dispute." He added that the university wanted to "make it clear to the news media that we're not going to engage in the daily ins and outs of the legal case."

This approach, however, didn't please everyone. Critics accused the university of taking a position of "tepid and pious legalism" after Duke president Richard H. Brodhead said, "The issues at root are very serious and are a source of outrage, and yet we know we need to balance that against waiting until the facts are established, and each day brings fresh surprises." Many parents and alumni, however, criticized the media coverage and a cadre of Duke professors that seemed to presume that the indicted students were guilty. The community was also split because the incident underscored issues of class and race. The population of Durham, home of Duke, is 45 percent black—but only 10 percent of its freshman class in 2005 was black.

As the controversy heated up, the university hired Burson-Marsteller to coach administrators, faculty, staff, and students on how to speak to the media. Later in the year, Duke also retained Edelman Worldwide for ongoing counseling work. According to *New York Times* writer Duff Wilson, a group of Duke supporters also hired Robert Bennett, a former lawyer for Bill Clinton, to "help mount a public-relations campaign counteracting the negative attention on the university." Alumni and trustee resources with legal, journalistic, and public relations backgrounds have also pitched in.

Demonstrators listen to Duke president Richard Brodhead, right, at a news conference about the men's lacrosse team on March 28, 2006; AP Photo by sara D. Davis.

As the case moved forward, critical attention shifted from Duke and its student-athletes to the growing sense that the district attorney, Mike Nifong, was ignoring and even suppressing exculpatory evidence, such as DNA tests that might have cleared the accused. Media coverage began to question the merits of the charges as well as the politically ambitious motives of Nifong. In 2007, a book entitled *Until Proven Innocent: Political Correctness and the Shameful Injustices of the Duke Lacrosse Rape Case* (see suggested readings) found that the academic community at Duke tended to impugn the three accused or remain silent throughout the ordeal.

The concern about Nifong's prosecution of the alleged rape case reached the point that the State Attorney General's office took over the case. It found no credible evidence against the three Duke lacrosse students and dropped all charges against them. In other proceedings, Nifong was disbarred and resigned from the post of Durham District Attorney. In July 2007, Nifong issued an apology to the students and admitted there was "no credible evidence" against them.

Despite the damage to Duke's reputation as an elite university, as well as the criticism of its academic community for making ideological gains at the expense of three students, a record number of more than 19,000 high school seniors vied for 3,800 spots in the next class. The improvement of town–gown relationships, however, will take some time as Duke continues to work on improving the diversity of its students and fostering multicultural understanding among the faculty and students.

on the job ETHICS

Doctoring Photos to Show Diversity

It was a great photo for the cover of the new University of Wisconsin admissions brochure. It showed a group of happy and cheering students at a football game. The photo, however, was not exactly accurate; it had been doctored.

The original picture contained no black faces, but university officials desperately wanted their admissions materials to reflect a diverse student body. So, using photo-design software, the director of university publications and the director of undergraduate admissions simply asked their staff to add one.

Meanwhile, at the University of Idaho, the school's Web site showed another group of smiling students with two faces—one black and one Asian—that had been digitally pasted onto white bodies.

The digital manipulation of photographs to show diversity raises some ethical questions. The implicit message of a photograph is that it shows something that actually occurred. So, in the interest of political correctness and diversity, should photos be changed?

One defense is that the photograph isn't really a fake; it's entirely

reasonable that a crowd at a football game would include blacks and Asians. Another argument is that doctoring a photo is artistic license. If a technician airbrushes a student picking his nose out of a photo, no one seems to mind. Others, however, say it's wrong to lie about who was in a particular photograph.

What do you think? If you were the director of publications for a university, would you use digital techniques to alter a photo for the purpose of showing diversity in the student body?

---

billboards. Other colleges and universities have replaced their catalogues and brochures with four-color, slick materials that use bright graphics and catchy headlines to lure students. Most, if not all, now use the Web. On occasion, recruiting materials can raise ethical questions. Such a situation is outlined in the Ethics box on this page.

Various other recruiting devices are used. Vanderbilt University sent personalized videotapes to about 40 highly coveted high school seniors. The College of the Atlantic took prospective students on a 90-foot sailing yacht party. Stanford University was host to 750 high school students who stayed overnight in dormitory rooms, visited classes, attended a musical program, and participated in a campus scavenger hunt. Brown University each spring sponsors a party for up to 250 prospects on an Amtrak train traveling between Washington and Providence, Rhode Island.

As competition for students has increased, so have the costs of recruiting them. Expenditures on admissions and recruitment have run about $2 million or more for private universities and in excess of $1.5 million for public universities. This high level of activity creates many opportunities for employment in public relations and development.

The purchase of mailing lists is a common tool of student recruitment. Each of approximately 900 colleges annually buys from 10,000 to 15,000 names and addresses of high school students who have taken College Board Examinations. The most sought-after prospects are National Merit Scholarship winners, and it is not uncommon for competing universities to shower a prospect with such lures as free tuition for four years, a private dorm room, guarantees of priority registration, and so on.

Support for Advancement Officers

Most public relations, alumni, and development leaders—known as *advancement officers*—enjoy the many services of the Council for Advancement and Support of Education (CASE), with headquarters in Washington, D.C. The aims of CASE are described as building public understanding, stepping up the level of alumni involvement and support, strengthening communication with internal and external audiences, improving government relations, and increasing private financial support. Among CASE's current objectives are: (1) helping leaders at historically black institutions advance in their careers, (2) publicizing a code of ethics, (3) developing gift and expenditure reporting standards, (4) improving the communication of university research to the public, and (5) studying the impact of new technologies.

Representing more than 2,400 institutional members, CASE serves nationally as a principal public affairs arm for education, monitoring federal rights legislation and regulations and working with the American Council on Education and other associations on education-related issues. The organization provides district conferences and institutes, evaluation and critique services, a certification program, awards, reference materials, and placement opportunities. Thousands each summer attend its four-day assembly, replete with workshops.

Elementary and Secondary Schools

The strategic planning and skillful execution of public relations programs have materially strengthened many of the nation's elementary and secondary school systems during recent decades.

Response to Contemporary Issues

On the surface, the opportunities for public relations professionals in primary and secondary schools may seem limited. Most schools are public, supported by taxpayer dollars, and thus, there appears to be little necessity for public relations competing with other schools or handling conflict.

In fact, however, the strategic planning and skillful execution of public relations programs have materially strengthened many of the nation's elementary and secondary school systems during recent decades. Public relations has greatly affected the outcome of issues ranging from parental support for learning initiatives to voting for property tax increases to support schools. The 2002 No Child Left Behind Act, billed as the most sweeping educational reform since the Higher Education Act of 1965, places great emphasis on test scores, improving student performance, and accountability.

Thus, to compete for resources, funding, and, in effect, clients, it has become incumbent for schools to skillfully promote their successes or explain their failures. The hot-button issue of school choice has further introduced the concept of marketplace competition between public and private schools, among school districts, and between individual schools as well. Likewise, recent tragedies such as shooting sprees have unfortunately drawn attention to the need for skilled crises communication specialists in many communities.

Another controversial issue in the schools is the availability of so-called junk food from various vendors such as Coca-Cola and Pepsi. Public demand for more healthy snacks and less sugar-flavored drinks was fueled by national media attention to obesity in children, and various vendors have responded by offering greater choice in school vending machines. A related controversy is whether schools should give exclusive contracts to vendors. The critics say this limits choice; the schools, always seeking additional resources, say such contracts pay for activities not funded by the community or state. Pepsi, for example, paid $2.1 million to the Jefferson County school district in Colorado for an exclusive contract to provide all the vending machines on campus and to serve Pepsi in school cafeterias.

Reaching the Publics

The primary publics of a school system are teachers, children, parents, staff, and the community. As in all public relations, research, planning, action, and evaluation comprise the essential steps with which to reach these publics. On the desks of information directors, communication coordinators, and school–community relations specialists (or whatever the title may be, and it varies widely) are booklets prepared by national and state offices detailing hundreds of ways in which they may carry out their mission. Perhaps the best way to describe school public relations in its major aspects is to examine some of the outstanding communication programs in elementary and secondary school public relations.

Building Community Support   When almost one-third of the elementary schools in the Fort Worth Independent School District tested low in pupils' reading skills, the superintendent asked the public for help. Business leaders, librarians, and teachers, coordinated by the schools' community relations division, developed a yearlong awareness campaign with the theme, "Reading Takes You Places."

Communication plans included news releases, bilingual fliers to parents and community leaders, and television and cable messages, with personal contacts before each activity. Newspapers, the city transportation authority, and advertising companies provided free advertising.

Business firms supported such activities as book donations to libraries and a Reading Rodeo attended by more than 700 children in 69 schools. Community groups such as the Dallas Mavericks and museums also participated. The Reading Summit involving sponsorship by the Governor's Business Council drew broad media coverage. By year's end, only three schools failed to meet state expectations, and a 91 percent improvement rate was recorded in the number of low-performance schools.

Beating the Odds at the Polls   Supporters of the Everett (Washington) School District faced a difficult problem: winning a tax levy election that required turning out 40 percent of the voters who voted in the last major election and getting 60 percent of them to vote "yes." The almost 50 percent of voters receiving a permanent absentee ballot were traditionally very negative toward tax measures, and 70 percent of households in the district had no school-age children.

Discarding traditional communication methods, the citizens' committee planned a highly focused campaign. It sought to identify likely "yes" voters and to aim all signs, mailings, brochures, and personal contact at them.

Two campaigns were waged: one for absentee voters and one for election-day voters. About 20 people devoted 25 evenings to phoning targeted voters, getting out mailings, and writing personal messages. On election day, poll watchers looked for "yes" walk-ins; those who had not voted by 4 P.M. were called and reminded to vote.

The levy passed with an almost 64 percent "yes" vote. All project goals were met or exceeded. The committee analyzed every aspect of the election, including the database

on the job
A MULTICULTURAL WORLD

Australian School Rebuilds Its Tarnished Reputation

The Anglican Church Grammar School in Brisbane, Australia, faced with a series of sexual abuse claims, had a major public relations problem on its hands. Extensive media coverage had caused considerable anxiety among past and current parents, as well as the entire community.

The school, known as "Churchie," engaged Rowland Communications Group to work with the school's board of directors and headmaster on communication strategies that would reassure the community that the school was taking the charges seriously and was putting strict policies in effect to prevent future cases. They developed a policy of "victim-first" communication and put a priority on first informing the imme-

diate school community of parents, students, and alumni.

To assess the situation, Rowland first audited every Australian media story about sexual abuse claims by past and current students in other schools. The firm also identified key opinion leaders in Brisbane who could be effective spokespersons for the school.

Communication tools to key audiences included (1) regular staff updates, (2) letters to parents, (3) student briefings via assemblies, (4) teachers, (5) newsletter articles and a Web site, and (6) media advisories. Meetings also were held with the editors of the daily newspaper, the *Courier Journal*, which had prominently displayed sexual abuse allegations against current and for-

mer staff for several months. After the headmaster met with the editor and explained the proactive steps "Churchie" was taking, fairer and more supportive stories appeared.

All media coverage, once the communications program started, portrayed key messages about the school's efforts to deal with the alleged victims and the new policies in place. The headmaster received hundreds of supportive calls, e-mails, and letters. No students on "Churchie's" waiting list withdrew, and the school reclaimed much of its traditional reputation as an outstanding institution.

As a result, the IPRA gave the school and Rowland a Golden Globe award for conducting an outstanding crisis recovery program.

---

of 12,000 district supporters, and began a continuing campaign aimed at turning "maybe" voters to "yes" voters in the next election.

Crisis Communication   For emergencies such as earthquakes, sudden loss of utilities, severe storms, hazardous material spills, explosions, fires, tornadoes, school shootings, plane crashes, bomb threats—for all such crises, a communication plan should be in readiness. See also the Multicultural World box on this page about how a school handled sexual abuse allegations.

Such plan components were dwarfed by the tragic shooting of 12 students and a teacher at Columbine High School in Colorado. Winner of a Silver Anvil Award from the Public Relations Society of America, the school system's public relations professionals were thrust into the spotlight as the voice of the community as well as the organization. The team managed speculation and rumor flamed by 750 media outlets worldwide; helped the community deal with the unforgettable experience and the heartrending images; and restored calm and confidence to the school system and thereby to the community.

The public relations executive for the school district, Rick Kaufman, drew on his emergency medical technician experience to help victims at the site, then organized a crisis communication team to handle the onslaught of media coverage and inquiries. Symbolic of the eloquence of the communication efforts and the perspective provided by the communication team is this quote by Marilyn Saltzman, manager of communication services: ". . . Columbine is a beautiful flower that blooms in the mountains of Colorado . . . I would hate for it to be a synonym for 'massacre.'" While effectively managing the immediate crisis, the communication department has helped to heal a community and move forward.

Marketing of Public Schools   A pioneer in public opinion surveying in education, William J. Banach, administrative director at the Macomb Intermediate School District in Mount Clemens, Michigan, developed a two-year plan designed to discover what the public wants in its schools. The plan also sought ways to respond to those desires and to educate citizens about actions the school could and could not take. Banach based the campaign on what he termed "the 90-7-3 concept of school communication":

> Ninety percent of the school's image is who we are and what we do 24 hours a day. How school people think, act, and appear and what they say are key factors in marketing. This is why staff training is an integral part of a marketing program—to help people understand their communication roles and how important they are.
>
> Seven percent of the marketing effort is listening—tuning in to find out what people like, don't like, want, don't want. Anything we do to know more about our "customers" is worth doing.
>
> Three percent of marketing is outbound communication—publications, posters, news releases, and other visible and tangible items.

In successive phases, the marketing plan at Mount Clemens was targeted at (1) elementary parents, with a focus on reading, writing, and arithmetic; (2) secondary students and their parents, emphasizing "the basics and beyond" and beginning with specific objectives based on survey results and meetings with student leaders; and (3) citizens without children in school.

Arrangements were made for teachers to apply "No. 1" apple stickers to outstanding student papers, and all classroom papers were sent home each Friday. Posters welcoming visitors were placed at each school. The slogan "Your public schools . . . There's no better place to learn" was displayed on billboards, calendars, bookmarks, bumper stickers, T-shirt transfers, and thank-you cards.

A survey made a year after the campaign began revealed enhanced public confidence in the schools. The Macomb Plan, as it is called, has attracted national attention.

Other Educational Initiatives

A wide range of other nonprofit organizations involved in education, such as foundations, nontraditional schools, communities, and membership organizations, have public relations concerns as well. Some provide funds to existing schools, colleges and universities, or support scholarship through grants to students or programs. Examples operating on a large scale include Ewing Marion Kauffman Foundation. Others sponsor broadly defined educational programs such as PBS documentaries or fund art exhibitions, concerts, and theatrical productions. The Pew Charitable Trust and the Annenberg Foundation are two of the largest organizations in the United States devoted to educational initiatives. Other organizations operate schools or training programs directly.

Many opportunities exist for public relations specialists in educational forums outside of colleges, universities, and schools. Before embarking on a career, however, there are two considerations. First, much of the work is related to fund-raising. With few exceptions, nonprofits in the educational sector constantly struggle to meet operating expenses. Second, the pay scales for employees of nonprofit organizations devoted to education is significantly lower than for public relations professionals in the corporate world.

Many corporations create nonprofit divisions with educational missions or enter into partnership with nonprofit organizations. For example, MetLife established a foundation to help disseminate information about Alzheimer's disease. They also provide awards for medical research and services, support cultural institutions, and publicize the concerns of American teachers. Ford Motor Company sponsors a Youth & Adult Automotive Training Center through its North American Educational Initiatives program, a nonprofit division of the company.

Having a nonprofit foundation devoted to education serves the public relations purpose of showing that corporations are good citizens, particularly in the post-Enron/Tyco/WorldCom climate. In the same spirit, companies such as Procter & Gamble, Toyota Motors, and Starbucks recently have initiated programs to send executives on "externships" to work with students and schools.

SUMMARY

Colleges and Universities

Public relations at colleges and universities involves both development, or fund-raising, and enhancing the prestige of the institution. The office of development and public relations may conduct meetings, publish newsletters, and arrange tours. The audiences for communications will include alumni, students, prospective students, faculty and staff, government, and the general public.

Elementary and Secondary Schools

Public education has received increasing attention in recent years from the media, especially during political campaigns. Issues include school vouchers, curriculum standards, bilingual education, integration, book censorship, sex education, and school violence. Public relations practitioners working with the schools must address all these areas, reaching such publics as teachers, children, parents, staff, and the community. Goals will include building community support for programs and encouraging financial support through taxes. Schools also must have communications plans in readiness for crisis situations, whether these involve earthquakes, power loss, severe weather, fires, bomb threats, or school violence.

Other Educational Initiatives

Foundations, nontraditional schools, communities, and membership organizations frequently support existing educational institutions or initiate their own programs. Like colleges and schools, these initiatives often depend on public relations professionals for their success.

CASE ACTIVITY What Would You Do?

The tragedy of Virginia Tech, where a disaffected student killed 33 individuals and wounded many others (see the box on page 558), has forced all colleges and universities to rethink their crisis plans and how to best communicate with students in an emergency.

You're the director of university relations for Southern State University, a campus of 20,000 students located just outside the state capital. The campus police call you at 10:30 P.M. to tell you that two students have been shot and wounded, one seriously, after an argument that had begun in a university cafeteria resumed on the street. Police arrested one suspect, a student, at the scene, but a second student suspect was at large on the campus and presumed to be carrying the gun used to shoot the two students during the argument.

Given this information, what would you do? The memory of Virginia Tech is still fresh in your mind and you're aware that university officials were later criticized in an official state report for not having locked down the campus and alerting students more quickly. At the same time, you're concerned about unnecessarily causing panic among the students in the residence halls and others who may be returning to campus later in the evening. You also know that the media monitors the police band and reporters soon will be starting to call you and arriving on campus. The university president, no doubt, will be concerned about the image of the university and how this "incident" will affect student recruitment.

You have to make some quick decisions. Should you just tell the police to keep you informed on finding the second suspect, or would you immediately implement a plan to inform all the students about the situation? Would you call the university president and recommend a lockdown of the entire campus? Do you need to call others on your staff to brief them and set up a communications center as soon as possible?

QUESTIONS for Review and Discussion

1. Who is the chief public relations officer on a college or university campus? Why?
2. A college news bureau is involved in a vast array of day-to-day public relations operations. Name five or six of these functions.
3. With what primary public does a sound university public relations program begin? Why? List eight other constituencies that must be addressed in such a program.
4. In what ways may powerful alumni and other friends provide support for an institution of higher learning? What is the role of the development office in gaining this support? What is CASE, and what support does it provide for public relations and alumni officers?
5. What strategic plan did a citizens committee of the Everett (Washington) School District employ to win its bond-issue election?
6. Do you agree with the marketing concept used by public relations people in the Macomb Intermediate School District in Mount Clemens, Michigan? Describe the key points of this plan in explaining your answer.
7. What public relations problems may be evident when a community turns down a bond issue to improve school financing? What public relations actions do you consider important in building and maintaining strong support of schools?

SUGGESTED READINGS

Arenson, Karen. "Duke Grappling With Impact of Scandal on Its Reputation." *New York Times,* April 7, 2006, p. A14.

Brainard, Jeffrey. "Lobbying to Bring Home the Bacon: In Pursuit of Earmarks and to Influence Policy, Higher Education Has Become a Major Player on Capitol Hill." *Chronicle of Higher Education,* October 22, 2004, pp. A26–36.

Bush, Michael. "VA Tech Creates Comms Team in Wake of Tragedy." *PRWeek,* April 23, 2007, pp. 1, 24.

Dinmore, Guy. "Shootings Threaten University's Reputation." *Financial Times,* April 18, 2007. Virginia Tech University.

Drozdowski, Mark J. "The Fund Raiser: Certifiable." *Chronicle of Higher Education,* July 16, 2004, p. C3.

Kim, Sei-Hill, Carvalho, John P., and Cooksey, Christy E. "Exploring the Effects of Negative Publicity: News Coverage and Public Perceptions of a University." *Public Relations Review,* Vol. 33, No. 2, 2007, pp. 233–235.

McAllister, Sheila M., and Taylor, Maureen. "Community College Web Sites as Tools for Fostering Dialogue." *Public Relations Review,* Vol. 33, No. 2, 2007, pp. 230–232.

Taylor, Sturat, Jr., and Johnson, K. C. *Until Proven Innocent: Political Correctness and the Shameful Injustices of the Duke Lacrosse Rape Case.* New York: Thomas Dunne Books, 2007.

Tindall, Natalie T. J. "Fund-raising Models at Public Historically Black Colleges and Universities." *Public Relations Review,* Vol. 33, No. 2, 2007, pp. 201–205.

Trickett, Eleanor. "An Educational Story: University Communicators Find Themselves Juggling Multiple Stakeholders in Their Outreach Efforts." *PRWeek,* August 28, 2006, p. 19.

Walters, Anne K. "Soft Drinks, Hard Feelings: Widespread Student Protests About Alleged Practices of Coca-Cola Overseas Prompt Some Colleges to Rethink Deals." *Chronicle of Higher Education,* April 14, 2006, pp. A30–32.

CHAPTER 22

Entertainment, Sports, and Travel

Fascination with Celebrity

A dominant factor in today's mass media is the publicizing and glorifying of celebrities. Sports heroes and television personalities in particular, along with radio talk show hosts, members of the British royal family, movie stars, high-profile criminals, and some politicians, are written about, photographed, and discussed almost incessantly.

In some cases, such celebrity results from natural public curiosity about an individual's achievements or position in life. Frequently, however, it is carefully nurtured by publicists for the client's ego satisfaction or commercial gain.

The publicity buildup of individuals is outside the mainstream of public relations work, and some professional practitioners are embarrassed by the exaggerations and tactics used by promoters of so-called beautiful people. Nevertheless, all students of public relations should know how the personal publicity trade operates. At some point, knowledge of personal publicity techniques may be useful.

Enduring Celebrity: When the Good and Beautiful Die Young

Diana, Princess of Wales, was a worldwide celebrity as the divorced wife of Prince Charles, heir to the British throne. Her svelte, gracious manner and high-fashion clothing, plus public interest in the collapse of her once-romantic marriage, created huge media attention. She appeared on the cover of *People Weekly* 41 times in a 16-year period and became known to headline writers as "Princess Di."

Princess Diana's death in a dramatic, high-speed race to elude press photographers captured world attention. Diana joined a tragic list of celebrities taken all too young from their lives of fame and adulation, including people such as James Dean, Elvis, John Lennon, and John F. Kennedy as well as his brother Robert. According to Irving Rein, author of *High Visibility*, celebrities exist in one-sided, idealized relationships in which the celebrity demands nothing of us. And, unlike our family and workmates, we get to pick our celebrity idols.

In death, this ideal, though distant, relationship is severed, and the youthful image is frozen in time. The tragedy and the timeless glamor galvanize us into a mass audience. Princess Diana's funeral was viewed by an estimated 2.5 billion people around the world. An estimated 152,000 visitors to her burial shrine on the family estate paid $24 each to see her childhood home, view family movies in a remodeled stable, and gaze at her island mausoleum. Even in death, both adulation and revenue can follow from celebrity.

The Mystique of Personality

Why is the public so eager to read about and watch personalities it regards as celebrities? What drives individuals to seek such attention?

The abundance of mass media outlets today and their intense competition for audiences draws on the natural instinct of humans to know about each other's lives. Appearances on talk shows, fawning Television interviews, sympathetic magazine articles, online chat sessions, and ghostwritten books contribute to the buildup.

Christine Kelly of *Sassy* magazine writes bluntly, "No-talents become celebrities all the time," a fact that she attributes largely to television. "Once TV started, the whole celeb-creation and worship careened out of control . . . TV gives the false impression that celebrities are talking right to you, and you feel like they're your friends."

Here are some of the motivating factors in the cult of personality.

Fame

Some individuals draw public attention due to their accomplishments or positions. The president of the United States is automatically a celebrity. So is the pope.

Notoriety

Even people who commit major crimes or are involved unfavorably in spectacular trials are treated as celebrities. Barbara Goldsmith commented on this phenomenon in the *New York Times:*

> The line between fame and notoriety has been erased. Today we are faced with a vast confusing jumble of celebrities: the talented and the untalented, heroes and villains, people of accomplishment and those who have accomplished nothing at all, the criteria of their celebrity being that their images encapsulate some form of the American dream, that they give enough of an appearance of leadership, heroism, wealth, success, danger, glamour and excitement to feed our fantasies. We no longer demand reality, only that which is real-seeming.

> Goldsmith adds, "The public appetite for celebrity and pseudo-event has grown to Pantagruelian proportions, and for the first time in history, the machinery of communications is able to keep up with these demands, even to outrun them, creating new needs we never knew existed. To one extent or another, all the branches of the media have become complicitous to this pursuit. . . ."

Self-Glorification

Donald Trump, a New York real-estate high roller with an insatiable desire for publicity, is a striking example of the urge for self-glorification. He put his name on the buildings and casinos he bought and has a personal press agent in addition to the Trump Organization's aggressive public relations department. He has even telephoned reporters with stories about himself. Most recently, Trump is the star of the television show *The Apprentice*, whose TV ratings benefited in 2007 from his inflammatory war of words with Rosie O'Donnell, cohost at the time of a talk show called *The View*. Love him or loathe him, "The Donald," as he is sometimes called, is the consummate newsmaker and celebrity. He is also a remarkable survivor of personal and business crises and scandals.

Repair of a Bad Image

Public relations counselors who specialize in handling individuals sometimes work to create a positive image for a prominent person who has been cast in an unfavorable light by news stories by using variations on the following techniques:

◆ proclaim dismay and lack of knowledge when the facts support innocence

◆ make reparations when a celebrity punches a journalist or breaks a paparazi's camera

◆ reverse the role from offender to crusader for the new cause

◆ arrange an event or conference to make the new commitment real

◆ proclaim the new role through media relations efforts

on the job
INSIGHTS

Celebrity Publicists Have It Easy—Not!

Many aspiring public relations students believe that it would be fun and glamorous to work in entertainment public relations. And, in fact, the glamor and glitz, as well as the fascination of the personalities, do exist. But being a publicist to the stars can have its drawbacks, a truism that dates back to the ancient Mayan civilization. Mayan rulers of independent municipalities vied for loyalty primarily through events and publicity to achieve celebrity status for themselves. According to an article in *Antiquity,* scribes who failed to raise the celebrity status of their rulers could have fingernails removed and fingers broken.

Nothing quite so dire takes place in modern celebrity public relations. The challenges have more to do with a hectic pace, late hours, and the demands of magazines such as *People* and *GQ* for exclusive interviews. The paparazzi with their invasive cameras and tabloids with their scurrilous headlines both seek to do damage to your celebrity client—simply to sell newspapers and tabloids. Your job as a celebrity publicist is to manage these forces effectively for your client.

Perhaps the biggest challenge, though, is to deal with wrongdoing on the part of a celebrity. Whether this behavior is Paris Hilton going to jail for DUI or Britney Spears's somewhat chaotic lifestyle, the publicist will face some hectic days. Anita Chabria of *PRWeek* offers the following dos and don'ts of litigation Public Relation for celebs:

Elliott Mintz is shown here with two of his famous clients, Paris (right) and Nicky (left) Hilton. Mintz has worked as a celebrity publicist since his days with John Lennon in the 1980s.

DOS	DON'TS
Do make sure that your statements are accurate. The press will pick up on even innocent mistakes as potential lies.	Don't keep quiet. Give an attorney respect, but don't fear giving an opinion if he or she is hamming it up too much in court or in front of the cameras.
Do get written approval of all statements before releasing them.	Don't avoid giving details. If it's in the public record, it's fair game.
Do ask the attorney to speak directly to media. It ensures that statements are worded correctly.	Don't talk too much. Keep it brief and to the point, without adding details of your own.

According to celebrity Public Relation counselor Howard Rubenstein, who has worked in the field more than 50 years, the combination of constructive actions and celebrity publicity has a compelling effect on audiences who want to believe in redemption for superstars. See the Insights box on this page that describes the work of a celebrity publicist.

Desire for Money

Personal publicity can build on itself. A publicist may arrange for an obscure film actress to attend a party as the guest of a well-known performer and then issue a news release about the couple. Another party and another news release follow. Soon, the news releases refer to the actress as a celebrity. Presto, she is one. No one officially proclaims who has celebrity status, but once a critical mass of coverage occurs, that celebrity's value in the marketplace rises. Contracts and sales of everything from books to movies to television series, as well as endorsements and appearance fees, are suddenly under negotiation by members of the celebrity's entourage.

Once established as a star, companies such as Celebrity Connection provide unique services. Celebrity Connection's Web site, www.celebconn.com, describes the company as "a unique global firm dedicated to creating relationships between you, your clients, and the celebrity community and finding you the right celebrity for your cause. We provide services ranging from celebrity acquisition and coordination to total event management."

Indicative of the commercialization of personality is the success of companies that keep databases on well-known persons and offer daily bulletins on their comings and goings. The databases also have the names of managers, lawyers, and publicists who represent celebrities. The daily bulletins tip off the media about availability of prominent people for a television talk show or a feature interview. These services help business, industry, and charities locate celebrities who might serve as a spokesperson or a charity chairperson or add glamor to a major event.

Psychological Explanations

Psychologists offer varied explanations of why the public becomes impressed—fascinated might be the more accurate word—by highly publicized individuals. In pretelevision days, the publicity departments of the motion picture studios promoted their male and female stars as glamorous figures who lived in a special world of privilege and wealth. Dreaming of achieving such glory for themselves, young people with and without talent came to Hollywood to crash the magical gates, almost always in vain.

Many ordinary people leading routine lives yearn for heroes. Professional and big-time college sports provide personalities for hero worship. Publicists emphasize the performances of certain players, and television game announcers often build up the stars' roles out of proportion to their achievements; this emphasis creates hero figures for youthful sports enthusiasts to emulate. Similar exaggerated treatment is applied to entertainers and politicians. Syndicated gossip columnist Liz Smith once tried to explain the American cult of personality by saying, "Maybe it's because we all want someone to look up to or spit on, and we don't have royalty."

In addition to admiration for individual performers, members of the public develop a vicarious sense of belonging that creates support for athletic teams. Sports publicists exploit this feeling in numerous ways. A winning baseball team becomes "our" team in conversations among patrons of a bar. To signify their loyalty, children and adults alike wear baseball caps bearing the insignia of their favorite major league teams. It isn't surprising that alumni of a university gnaw their fingernails while watching their school basketball team in a tight game, but the same intensity of support is found among fans who have no direct tie to the school.

Still another factor is the desire for entertainment. Reading fan magazines, watching a favorite star being interviewed, or lining up in front of a box office hours before it opens to be sure of getting a ticket—these are ways to bring variety and a little excitement into the daily routine of life.

A public relations practitioner assigned to build up the public image of an individual should analyze the ways in which these psychological factors can be applied. Because the client's cooperation is vital in promotional work, a wise publicist explains this background and tells the client why various actions are planned.

The Practitioner's Responsibility

Handling publicity for an individual carries special responsibilities. Often the client turns to the publicist for personal advice, especially when trouble arises.

Damage Control

A practitioner handling an individual client is responsible for protecting the client from bad publicity as well as generating positive news. When the client appears in a bad light because of misbehavior or an irresponsible public statement, the publicist must try to minimize the harm done to the client's public image. The objective is damage control.

Politicians who say something controversial in public, and then later wish they hadn't, try to squirm out of the predicament by claiming they were misquoted. This is a foolish defense unless the politician can prove conclusively that he or she was indeed quoted incorrectly. Reporters resent accusations of inaccuracy and may hold a grudge against the accuser. If the accused reporter has the politician's statement on tape, the politician appears even worse. A better defense is for the politician to explain what he or she intended and to express regret for the slip of the tongue.

A similar approach is recommended for Hollywood celebrities who are caught in scandalous acts or unfounded rumor mills. Experts suggest immediate response so that the momentum of subsequent stories is minimized. A brief, honest statement of regret for bad behavior or denial of rumors works well. Television's mass audience enjoys celebrity news. Television lends itself to a short statement that makes a perfect 20-second sound bite to fit in a brief story. Then the celebrity needs to disappear from sight and take care of personal matters. See the PR Casebook on page 576 about Mel Gibson's work on damage control.

Ethical Problems for Publicists

Personal misconduct by a client, or the appearance of misconduct, strains a practitioner's ingenuity and at times his or her ethical principles. Some practitioners will lie outright to protect a client, a dishonest practice that looks even worse if the media shows the statement to be a lie. On occasion, a practitioner acting in good faith may be victimized because the client has lied.

Issuing a prepared statement to explain the client's conduct, while leaving reporters and their editors dissatisfied, is regarded as safer than having the client call a news conference, unless the client is a victim of circumstances and is best served by talking fully and openly. A middle ground that NFL star Michael Vick used was to make a statement to the media apologizing for his active role in a dogfighting operation that exposed dogs to cruelty and death. See also Chapter 12 and the use of litigation public relations in the Vick case.

Although Vick did not take questions, he was given credit for speaking without notes in his own words. Some critics, however, thought his statement about finding religion in his hour of shame was a bit overdone. The decision about holding a news

PRCASEBOOK

Mel Gibson's Greatest Role: Restoring Reputation

When actor Mel Gibson was picked up on charges of drunken driving in the summer of 2006, he was accused of making anti-Semitic comments to the arresting officers. While that offense alone would make a celebrity publicist cringe, it was intensified by the fact that Gibson, a devout Christian, had previously been accused of being anti-Semitic and had made apologies to members of the Jewish community and faith. It might have seemed like déjà vu for Gibson's publicist.

Gibson had come under fire by members of the Jewish community when he directed and produced *The Passion of the Christ*. Many believed the film portrayed Jews in a way that incited racism and hatred against them. In contrast, Christians made up the core of the film's audience, with some Christian ministers urging their church members to

Mel Gibson in new role as apologist.

attend the movie. At the time of this conflict, in 2004, Gibson made the talk show rounds and denied all accusations that he was an anti-Semite. *The Passion of the Christ* was a wild success, grossing more than $600 million worldwide.

Following his 2006 arrest on drunken driving charges and his reported tirade against Jews, Gibson made a somewhat convoluted apology, saying the statements he made he did not "believe to be true" and calling his remarks "despicable." This first apology was rejected by many Jewish leaders, including the leadership of the Anti-Defamation League (ADL), as "insufficient" and "unremorseful."

Gibson made a more complete statement two days later. He said,

> I want to apologize specifically to everyone in the Jewish community for the vitriolic and harmful words that I said to a law enforcement officer the night I was arrested on a DUI charge. . . . I am not an anti-Semite. I am not a bigo . . . Hatred of any kind goes against my faith. I'm not just asking for forgiveness. I would like to take it one step further, and meet with leaders in the Jewish community, with whom I can have a one-on-one discussion to discern the appropriate path for healing.

ADL national director Abraham H. Foxman said, "We are glad that Mel Gibson has finally owned up to the fact that he made anti-Semitic remarks and his apology sounds sincere. Once he completes his rehabilitation for alcohol abuse, we will be ready and willing to help him with his second rehabilitation to combat this disease of prejudice."

Public Relation experts at the time suggested that Gibson's fuller apology may have come too late to save him. Celebrity crisis expert Richard Levick told the Associated Press, "In the first 24 hours, people start forming opinions. He has constantly been behind the story and needs to get out front. What he's done through actions has turned perception into reality. People presume he is anti-Semitic." But celebrity publicist Michael Levine told the AP, "The best defense is a good offense and the only offense is a relentless one." Levine said that Gibson's public relations team followed the four principles of celebrity crisis management—speed, humility, contrition, and personal responsibility. "If you go with those four things, you generally do pretty well in America," Levine said.

While the conventional wisdom suggests the stance Levine outlines and the one Gibson took, Public Relation researchers Lisa Lyon and Glen T. Cameron found that preexisting reputation affects response strategy. They found that if you have a bad reputation, apology can actually backfire or boomerang. Because of Gibson's preexisting reputation within the Jewish community, time will tell whether the court of public opinion will reward Gibson's conventional strategy or whether he would have

been better served by a more defensive or even a stonewalling strategy. Questions to consider:

- Do you think that a bad track record is a factor canceling out the four principles of celebrity crisis management?
- Do you think that being defensive or stonewalling by stalling or ignoring critics and media inquiries can work?
- Do you think that it is ethical to avoid an apology to prevent backlash from occurring?

conference also is influenced by how poised and self-controlled the client is. Under questioning—or even grilling—a person may say something that compounds the problem. (Defensive news conferences are discussed further in Chapter 16.) Also, see the Case Activity box on page 590 about Michael Vick.

Conducting a Personality Campaign

A campaign to generate public awareness of an individual should be planned just as meticulously as any other public relations project. Practitioners conducting such campaigns follow a standard step-by-step process.

Interview the Client

The client should answer a detailed personal questionnaire. The practitioner should be a dogged, probing interviewer, digging for interesting and possibly newsworthy facts about the person's life, activities, and beliefs. When talking about themselves, individuals frequently fail to realize that certain elements of their experiences have publicity value under the right circumstances.

Perhaps, for example, the client is a little-known actress who has won a role as a Midwestern farmer's young wife in a motion picture. During her get-acquainted talks with the publicist, she happens to mention in passing that while growing up in a small town she belonged to the 4-H Club. Not only must practitioners draw out such details from their clients, they must also have the ingenuity to develop these facts as story angles. When the actress is placed as a guest on a television talk show, the publicist should prompt her in advance to recall incidents from her 4-H experience. Two or three humorous anecdotes about mishaps with pigs and chickens, tossed into the interview, give it verve.

Prepare a Biography of the Client

The basic biography should be limited to four typed pages, perhaps fewer. News and feature angles should be placed high in the "bio," as it is termed, so an editor or producer can find them quickly. The biography, a portrait and other photographs of the client, and, if possible, additional personal background items should be assembled in a media kit.

Plan a Marketing Strategy

The practitioner should determine precisely what is to be sold. Is the purpose only to increase public awareness of the individual, or is it to publicize the client's product, such as a new television series, motion picture, or book? Next, the practitioner should decide which audiences are the most important to reach. For instance, an interview with a romantic operatic tenor on a rock 'n' roll radio station would be inadvisable. But an appearance by the singer on a public television station's talk show would be right on target. A politician trying to project herself as a representative of minority groups should be scheduled to speak before audiences in minority neighborhoods and placed on radio stations whose demographic reports show that they attract minority listeners.

Conduct the Campaign

In most cases, the best course is to project the client on multiple media simultaneously. Radio and television appearances create public awareness and often make newspaper feature stories easier to obtain. The process works in reverse as well. Using telephone calls and "pitch" letters to editors and program directors, the publicist should propose print and on-air interviews with the client. Always include a news or feature angle for the interviewer to develop. Because magazine articles require longer to reach print, the publicist should begin efforts to obtain them as early as feasible.

An interview in an important magazine—a rising female movie star in *Cosmopolitan* or *People*, for example—has major impact among women readers. Backstage maneuvering often takes place before such an interview appears. Agents for entertainers on their way up eagerly seek to obtain such an interview. When a personality is "hot" or at the top of the ladder, however, magazine editors compete for the privilege of publishing the interview. The star's agent plays them off against each other, perhaps offering exclusivity but demanding such rewards as a cover picture of the star, the right to choose the interviewer (friendly, of course), and even approval of the article. Editors of some magazines yield to publicists' demands. Other publications refuse to do so.

News Releases　　News releases are an important publicity tool, but the practitioner should avoid too much puffery.

Photographs　　Photographs of the client should be submitted to the print media as often as justifiable. Media kits usually include the standard head-and-shoulders portrait, often called a "mug shot." Photographs of the client doing something interesting or appearing in a newsworthy group may be published merely with a caption, without an accompanying story. The practitioner and the photographer should be inventive, putting the client into unusual situations. The justification for a successful submission may be thin if the picture is not colorful and/or timely. If the client seeks national attention, such pictures should be submitted to the news services so that, if newsworthy, they will be distributed to hundreds of newspapers. (Requirements for photographs are discussed in Chapter 15.)

Sharply increased awareness of sexual exploitation has largely eliminated "cheesecake" pictures—photographs of nubile young women in which the news angle often is as skimpy as their attire. Cheesecake photographs still are printed in the trade press, even though they are seldom seen in daily newspapers in America. Certain British and Australian newspapers, however, continue to publish large photos of skimpily clad young women, who are often topless.

Public Appearances   Another way to intensify awareness of individual clients is to arrange for them to appear frequently in public places. Commercial organizations at times invite celebrities of various types or pay them fees to dress up dinner meetings, conventions, and even store openings.

Awards   A much-used device, and a successful one, is to have a client receive an award. The practitioner should be alert for news of awards to be given and nominate the client for appropriate ones. Follow-up communications with persuasive material from the practitioner may convince the sponsor to make the award to the client. In some instances, the idea of an award is proposed to an organization by a practitioner, whose client then conveniently is declared the first recipient. The entertainment business generates immense amounts of publicity for individuals and shows with its Oscar and Emmy awards. Winning an Academy Award greatly strengthens a performer's career.

Psychologists believe that televised awards ceremonies give viewers a sense of structure in life. This return to normalcy partly explains why the Emmy awards ceremony was rescheduled twice after the September 11 attack on the World Trade Center and Pentagon so that "the show could go on."

Nicknames and Labels   Creating catchy nicknames for clients, especially sports and entertainment figures, helps the practitioner get their names into print. Celebrity worshipers like to call their heroes and heroines by nicknames, as though they have personal relationships with them. Thus, we see and hear familiarities for celebrities such as those listed by PR.com in Table 22.1.

A questionable variation of the nickname consists of adding a descriptive word to the name of the person being publicized to create a desirable image or career association. Sometimes this is done to provide a respectable veneer for a person of dubious background. In the Palm Springs resort area, to cite one instance, a socially active figure named Ray Ryan hired a practitioner whose task was to build up the image of Ryan as a well-to-do oilman. In every news release about Ryan and every telegram inviting social, business, and media individuals to Ryan's elaborate parties, the practitioner referred to his client as "oilman Ray Ryan." Publications in the area consistently printed "oilman Ray Ryan," generating the effect the publicist desired. Actually, Ryan also was involved in big-time professional gambling—an involvement apparently responsible for the fact that when he turned the ignition key of his automobile one day, a bomb planted in the car killed him.

Record the Results

Those who employ practitioners want tangible results in return for their fees. The practitioner also needs to compile and analyze the results of a personality campaign to determine the effectiveness of the various methods used. Tearsheets, photographs, copies of news releases, and video clips of the public appearances should be given to the client. Clipping services help the practitioner assemble this material. At the end of the campaign, or at intervals in a long-term program, summaries of what has been accomplished should be submitted to the client.

Table 22.1

Top 25 Celebrity Nicknames

PR.com chose these nicknames as the best celebrity nicknames in 2005. What do you think are the most memorable celebrity nicknames right now? How would you use the nickname to build brand identity for the celebrity?

1.	Regis Philbin	**Big Daddy**
2.	Arnold Schwarzenegger	**The Governator**
3.	Sean Combs	**Puff Daddy**, Puffy, P. Diddy
4.	Madonna	**The Material Girl**, Madge
5.	Dwayne Johnson	**The Rock**, The Great One
6.	Britney Spears	**Pinkey**
7.	Jennifer Lopez	**J.Lo**, La Lopez
8.	Michael Jackson	**Wacko Jacko**, King Of Pop
9.	Donald Trump	**The Donald**, The Don
10.	Kelly Ripa	**Brown Sugar**, Pipa
11.	Howard Stern	**King of All Media**
12.	Oprah Winfrey	**Deepak Oprah**, O
13.	Randy Jackson	**The Dawg**, The Emperor
14.	Charles Barkley	**Sir Charles**
15.	Steven Tyler	**Demon Of Screamin**
16.	Mark Wahlberg	**Marky Mark**
17.	Bette Midler	**The Divine Miss M**
18.	Sylvester Stallone	**Italian Stallion**, Sly
19.	Mariah Carey	**Mimi**
20.	Simon Cowell	**Judge Dread**
21.	George W. Bush	**Dubya**, Junior
22.	Marshall Mathers	**Eminem**, Slim Shady
23.	Bill Clinton	**Bubba**
24.	Will Smith	**Fresh Prince**
25.	Shaquille O'Neal	**Superman**, The Big Aristotle

Promoting an Entertainment Event

Attracting attendance at an event—anything from a theatrical performance to a fund-raising fashion show or a street carnival—requires a well-planned publicity campaign.

Publicity to Stimulate Ticket Sales

The primary goal of any campaign for an entertainment event is to sell tickets. An advance publicity buildup informs listeners, readers, and viewers that an event will occur and stimulates their desire to attend. Rarely, except for community events publicized in smaller cities, do newspaper stories and broadcasts about an entertainment event include detailed information on ticket prices and availability. Those facts usually are deemed too commercial by editors and should be announced in paid advertising.

However, some newspapers may include prices, times, and so on in tabular listings of scheduled entertainments. Performance dates usually are included in publicity stories.

Stories about a forthcoming theatrical event, motion picture, rock concert, book, or similar event should concentrate on the personalities, style, and popularity of the activity or product. Every time the product or show is mentioned, public awareness grows. Thus, astute practitioners search for fresh news angles to produce as many stories as possible. The promotion of Harry Potter is a good example.

An Example: Publicizing a Play

The methods for publicizing a new play are the same whether the work will be performed on Broadway by professionals or in the local municipal auditorium by an amateur community theater group.

Stories include an announcement that the play will be presented, followed by releases reporting the casting of lead characters, the beginning of rehearsals, and the opening date. Feature stories, or "readers," discuss the play's theme and background, with quotations from the playwright and director inserted to emphasize an important point. In interviews, the play's star can tell why he or she finds the role significant or amusing.

Photographs of show scenes, taken in costume during rehearsal, should be distributed to the media to give potential customers a preview. As a reminder, a brief "opening tonight" story may be distributed. If a newspaper lists theatrical events in tabular form, the practitioner should submit an entry about the show. In some instances, publicity also can be generated through use of e-mail and the World Wide Web.

The "Drip-Drip-Drip" Technique

Motion picture studios, television production firms, and networks apply the principle of "drip-drip-drip" publicity when a show is being shot. In other words, there is a steady output of information about the production. A public relations specialist, called a unit man or woman, is assigned to a film during production and turns out a flow of stories for the general and trade press and plays host to media visitors to the set. The television networks mail out daily news bulletins about their shows to media television editors. They assemble the editors annually to preview new programs and interview their stars. The heaviest barrage of publicity is released shortly before the show openings.

A much-publicized device is to have a star unveil his or her star in the cement of the Hollywood Walk of Fame, just before the star's new film appears. Videotaped recordings of the event turn up on Television stations across the country.

One danger of excessive promotion of an event, however, is that audience expectation may become too high, so that the performance proves to be a disappointment. A skilled practitioner will stay away from "hype" that can lead to a sense of anticlimax.

A Look at the Movie Industry

Movie and DVD public relations departments use market research, demographics, and psychographics to define the target audiences they seek to reach. Most motion picture publicity is aimed at 18- to 24-year-olds, where the largest audience lies. Seventy-five percent of the film audience is under age 39, although increased attendance by older moviegoers has become evident recently.

Professional entertainment publicity work is concentrated in New York and Los Angeles, the former as the nation's theatrical center and the latter as the motion picture

on the job
INSIGHTS

Public Relations Magic for Harry Potter

The lines formed early. Parties were held. People of all ages, many in costume, patiently waited until the midnight countdown. New Year's Eve in July? No, it was the arrival of J. K. Rowling's seventh and final book about a young wizard. In the first 24 hours, U.S. sales of the long-awaited *Harry Potter and the Deathly Hallows* totaled 8.3 million copies. All this without a single piece of paid advertising.

The sale of the previous six books, totaling 325 million worldwide, guaranteed a ready market of *Potter* fans for the final installment, but Scholastic Publishers also used a public relations and marketing strategy to fuel interest in the book. One tactic was the sending of a purple three-decker Knight Bus across the United States. The bus, used in the *Potter* books to transport witches and wizards, began its tour on June 1, 2007, in New York and returned to the city for the July 21 launch. The bus was a traveling video studio where fans could record tributes to Harry Potter.

These tributes were then placed on the Scholastic Web site for the book, which fueled fan interest in the approaching launch date. The Web site also posted the Seven

Questions of Harry Potter, aimed at stimulating discussion and debate about what happens to Harry and his friends in the final book. The debates and arguments were also picked up by other bloggers and even the mainstream press.

Another integral part of the campaign was the involvement of major book chains such as Borders and independent booksellers. They promoted the book within their stores and encouraged *Potter* fans to reserve a copy in advance. Book stores also organized publication parties and costume contests on Friday night in preparation for the midnight launch. Borders, for example, sold 1.2 million books by organizing various events at its 1,200 stores worldwide (including its Waldenbooks stores). The book chain also estimated that 800,000 people attended these events worldwide. Media coverage of the midnight parties was also an extra boost for generating publicity for the book.

Harry Potter is now part of the global vocabulary, but it wasn't always so. Kris Moran, director of publicity for Scholastic, remembers that she took J. K. Rowling on a publicity tour of several U.S. cities in 1998, a year after the first book was published in England. The book signings were not arduous; in Seattle, only five people came. "No one knew who she was back then," Moran told *Public Relations Tactics*.

The lines formed early. Parties were held. People of all ages patiently waited for the midnight countdown. New Year's in July? No, it was the arrival of J. K. Rowling's seventh and final book, "Harry Potter and the Deathly Hallows." Here, fans scramble for the book at midnight in a Berlin book store.

center. (American television production is divided primarily between these two cities, with the larger portion in Los Angeles.)

A typical Los Angeles–area public relations firm specializing in personalities and entertainment has two staffs: one staff of "planters," who deliver to media offices publicity stories about individual clients and the projects in which they are engaged, and another staff of "bookers," whose job is to place clients on talk shows and in other public appearances. Some publicity stories are for general release; others are prepared especially for a single media outlet such as a syndicated Hollywood columnist or a major newspaper. The latter type is marked "exclusive," permitting the publication or station that uses it to claim credit for "breaking" the story.

Entertainment firms may specialize in arranging product placement in movies and television programs. Usually the movie or television producers trade visible placement of a product in the show in exchange for free use of the item in the film. The fast-food industry also provides excellent opportunities for market-based public relations involving giveaways of film characters with meals. Movies such as *Shrek* received huge boosts in visibility and ticket sales. Characters from a film can provide a key incentive to young customers in the highly competitive takeout business, providing a large but transitory advantage in the so-called burger wars.

Sports Publicity

The sports mania flourishing in the United States and in various forms around the world is stimulated by intense public relations efforts. Programs at both the big-time college and professional levels seek to arouse public interest in teams and players, sell tickets to games, and publicize the corporate sponsors who subsidize many events. Increasingly, too, sports publicists work with marketing specialists to promote the sale of booster souvenirs and clothing, a lucrative sideline for teams.

Sports publicists use the normal tools of public relations—media kits, statistics, interviews, television appearances, and the like. But dealing with facts is only part of their role. They also try to stir emotions. For college publicists, this means creating enthusiasm among alumni and making the school glamorous and exciting in order to recruit high school students. Publicists for professional teams work to make them appear to be hometown representatives of civic pride, not merely athletes playing for high salaries.

Sometimes these efforts succeed spectacularly, if the team is a winner. When a team is an inept loser, however, the sports publicist's life turns grim. He or she must find ways to soothe the public's displeasure and, through methods such as having players conduct clinics at playgrounds and make sympathetic visits to hospitals, create a mood of patient hopefulness: "Wait 'til next year!"

Emerging sports increasingly compete for prominence and fan loyalty against more established sports. Soccer is widely popular among youth in America, leading to hopes among its promoters that the professional game will make inroads in the U.S. sports market. NASCAR auto racing has steadily increased media market share in the new century. Ironically, a sport with early-20th-century roots in Southern bootlegging and local races among good ol' boys now commands huge television and radio audiences, with significant market share among middle-class women. The traditional, loyal fan base at events attracting over 100,000 spectators is now joined by a much wider fan profile drawn to national race coverage.

on the job ETHICS

A Difficult Sports Secret

You are a sports information officer for a university whose high-scoring basketball team hopes to win the national championship. One evening in the locker room you overhear two top players talking about how they shaved points in two recent games by intentionally missing free throws. Your team won the games, but by a smaller margin than the Las Vegas oddsmakers had predicted. Gamblers rewarded them with gifts of expensive sports cars, kept hidden at an off-campus location. You hear that the players are planning to shave points again in the early rounds of the upcoming national tournament for hefty cash payments.

If you keep the cheating secret, the university might win the national title and obtain generous contributions from enthusiastic alumni. If you report your information to an academic or police authority and a public gambling scandal occurs, the school will suffer disqualification, shame, and financial loss. You will be vilified by many in the university community for "blowing the whistle" when the outcome of games was never put in jeopardy by these players. You consider a constructive approach, because your team did win the previous games. You could tell the players that you know about their scheme and demand that they play competitively from now on or you will report them to the NCAA.

If you don't report the circumstantial evidence you have, will you be guilty of unethical behavior? What about criminal charges against you for aiding and abetting a criminal act? If you do report the previous incident, what sort of crisis management approach would you develop?

Because sports in America is big business, with $150 billion in gross annual revenues, an unseemly side frequently crops up in sports coverage. The impasse between players and owners in the National Hockey League (NHL) caused fans to lose patience with both the wealthy owners and the highly paid players. Intractable positions by both sides threatened the future of the professional league and continue to dampen its success. On other occasions, ethical questions arise about how, or even when, to protect players who get themselves in trouble. See the Ethics box on this page.

Public relations plays a critical role in sports, far beyond the promotion of celebrities. Two important areas are sports crisis management and sponsorship management. According to John Eckel of Hill and Knowlton Sports, professional communicators must deal with the media focus on issues ranging from player strikes to high ticket and concession costs to boorish athletes who deny that they are role models, even while they benefit from their visibility as role models. Jay Rosenstein of Cohn & Wolfe attributes much of sports crisis public relations to the "human factor in the sports world, where egos are otherworldly, behavior is reminiscent of the entertainment world, and media focus is unrelenting."

Sponsorship of Sporting Events

Corporate sponsorship of sporting events has also become big business. In 2006, for example, almost $9 billion was spent in the U.S. on sports sponsorships. IEG, Inc.,

on the job
A MULTICULTURAL WORLD

Major League Baseball Reaching Out to Diverse Stakeholders

More than any other professional sport, Major League Baseball (MLB) has, historically, reflected America's diverse demographics. As the nation's ethnic composition continues to change, however, engaging the diverse fans has become even more of a priority for baseball. The league has concerns about its market position with a number of key stakeholders:

- Latin American fans
- Asian audiences in the United States and increasingly across the Pacific Rim
- predominantly African American youth missing opportunities to play baseball due to conditions in inner-city neighborhoods
- youth and young adults

Strategic communication programs are underway by MLB, as well as by particular teams with special connections to local communities, that can make a huge difference in grassroots support for the MLB franchise while also making turnstiles clank at the ballpark entrances.

A remarkable complement of innovative public relations strategies are underway to build relationships between "America's Pastime" and the changing face of America. Consider this sampling:

Los Angeles Dodgers

- engaging the 40% Latin American portion of home game attendees with Spanish-language broadcasts
- Spanish-language Web site
- In-language blog, LosDodgers.com
- Viva Los Dodgers fan appreciation day
- Carne Asada Sunday with Nomar Garciaparra

San Francisco Giants

- trademarked name "Gigantes"
- more about relationship-building than getting bodies in seats

NY Yankees

- positive relationships with "different ethnic racial (sic) communities"
- construction worker training to assure hiring for new Yankee Stadium
- million-dollar giveaways of products, uniforms, and equipment to youth recreation and education programs

MLB

- multicultural outreach integrated into games, broadcasts, and promotional themes
- Asian heritage nights
- Japanese-language commercials on general market broadcasts
- Asian-language Web sites and online fan communities
- overseas licensing, branding and sponsorship deals

Probably the most newsworthy effort has been the MLB program to rebuild the African American player base in baseball. In 1974, 27 percent of players were African American; 2006 saw that number plummet to 8.4 percent. The league attributes the

> " When we started this program, we agreed that you just don't reach out to a community. You must invite them to be a part of the family before saying, 'Here's how you buy tickets.' "
>
> ———*Jason Pearl*, VP of the San Francisco Giants

(CONTINUED)

drop to lack of inner-city playing fields as well as increased money and prestige in competing professional sports such as the NBA and NFL. Teams are hosting community leaders and churches as well as joining forces to build baseball fields. Scholarships, summer jobs, and support of the RBI (Reviving Baseball in Inner Cities) program help underserved teens become MLB draft prospects. And the $10 million Urban Youth Academy in California hosts a World Series of RBI teams.

Notable throughout the league is the melding of public relations strategies and tactics with more traditional marketing/sales efforts to build lasting relationships with diverse fans from many ethnic backgrounds.

Source: Schmelzer, Randi, and Bush, Michael. "Multicultural Hits the Big Leagues." *PRWeek,* August, 20, 2007, pp. 14–15.

The publicity machine. Public relations personnel work hard to get clients on television talk shows. Here, injured Rugby player Mark Zupan chats with video journalist Damien Fahey on MTV's Total Request Live in New York City.

(www.sponsorship.com) that tracks such data, also estimates that the sports sponsorship market will increase to more than $13 billion by 2011.

The Olympics is the most expensive form of sports sponsorship. Companies are sponsoring the 2008 games in Beijing paid about $100 million each for the privilege, and an estimated total $1.5 billion in sponsorship fees was generated. The advertising agency DDB Needham studied the effectiveness of Olympic sponsorship and found that corporations had to do more, however, than just sponsor the games to make their investment pay off in terms of increased sales or visibility. Corporations also had to make major investments in marketing and publicizing their sponsorship and integrating other public relations and marketing activities around the games. See Chapter 17 for more information on corporate sponsorships.

In general, a corporation's association with the Olympics is considered a positive strategy to boost its visibility and reputation, but the Beijing Olympics posed some public relations challenges. Activist organizations concerned about human rights in China and a host of other concerns such as environmental pollution pressured corporations to show that they were part of the solution and not part of the problem. Consequently, several Olympic sponsors also spent considerable sums on "green" projects in China. Coke, for example, touted its water conservation projects on the Yantze River, and Volkswagen planted thousands of trees in Inner Mongolia.

Travel Promotion

With money in their pockets, people want to go places and see things. Stimulating that desire and then turning it into the purchase of tickets and reservations is the goal of the travel industry. Public relations has an essential role in the process, not only in attracting visitors to destinations but in keeping them happy once they arrive.

Like entertainment and sports, travel draws from the public's recreation dollars. Often its promoters intertwine their projects with those of entertainment and sports entrepreneurs.

Phases of Travel Promotion

Traditionally, the practice of travel public relations has involved three steps:

1. Stimulating the public's desire to visit a place
2. Arranging for the travelers to reach it
3. Making certain that visitors are comfortable, well treated, and entertained when they get there

Recently, terrorism has focused travel public relations specialists on a crucial new element—protecting the travelers' safety and sense of security.

There's always something new in the travel industry. Here, skiers enjoy an indoor slope in the United Arab Emirate regardless of how sweltering the weather may be outside. The recreational venue adds to the over-the-top exuberance that Dubai cultivates as it grows into a major destination for well-heeled tourists worldwide.

Stimulation is accomplished through travel articles in magazines and newspapers, alluring brochures distributed by travel agents and by direct mail, travel films, and videos, and presentations on the Web. Solicitation of associations and companies to hold conventions in a given place encourages travel by groups.

Some publications have their own travel writers; others purchase freelance articles and pictures. Well-done articles by public relations practitioners about travel destinations often are published, too, if written in an informational manner without resorting to blatant salesmanship and purple prose. Aware of public resistance to such exaggeration, *Condé Nast Traveler* magazine carries the slogan "Truth in Travel" on its cover. In fact, *O'Dwyer's PR Services Report* warns that "PR overkill" results from indiscriminate distribution of news releases, nagging follow-up calls to editors about releases, ignorance about the publication being pitched with a story, and excessive handling of writers on arranged trips so that the writer finds it difficult to get a complete picture of the travel destination.

U.S. travel agencies distribute literature, sponsor travel fairs, and encourage group travel by showing destination films at invitational meetings. Cities and states operate convention and travel departments to encourage tourism. A widely used method of promoting travel is the familiarization trip, commonly called a "fam trip," in which travel writers and/or travel salespeople are invited to a resort, theme park, or other destination for an inspection visit. In the past, fam trips often were loosely structured mass junkets. Today they are smaller and more focused.

Good treatment of travelers is a critical phase of travel promotion. If a couple spends a large sum on a trip, then encounters poor accommodations, rude hotel clerks, misplaced luggage, and inferior sightseeing arrangements, they come home angry. And they will tell their friends vehemently how bad the trip was.

Even the best arrangements go awry at times. Planes are late, tour members miss the bus, and bad weather riles tempers. This is where the personal touch means so much. An attentive, cheerful tour director or hotel manager can soothe guests, and a "make-good" gesture such as a free drink or meal does wonders. Careful training of travel personnel is essential. Many travelers, especially in foreign countries, are uneasy in strange surroundings and depend more on others than they would at home.

Fear of Terrorism

The tragic events of September 11 in New York, Washington, D.C., and Pennsylvania created an upsurge of fear and uncertainty about traveling. The Travel Industry Association of America estimates that the impact two months after the terrorist attacks was $43 billion in lost revenue and the disappearance of 527,000 tourism-related jobs. President George W. Bush taped two public service announcements to encourage travel on behalf of the industry. Nevertheless, Americans were shocked to realize how vulnerable their country was to terrorism.

Security measures were strengthened at airports and aboard airplanes, causing travelers inconvenience and delay. Even so, security experts emphasize the impossibility of a 100 percent guarantee against terrorist attacks.

Travel Business Booms on the Internet

Airline tickets, hotel accommodations, and travel packages can be readily shopped for and then booked on the Web. Consumers have found the convenience and the discounted Internet specials to be highly attractive, resulting in a major increase in online travel transactions. Web sites such as Travelocity.com not only offer complete airline booking services but also provide e-mail notification to members of fare changes for itineraries selected by the online user. Airlines and hotels find that last-minute inventory of seats or rooms can be sold effectively online. Because of such online commerce, hotels, resorts, and cruise lines can afford to mount extensive Web sites that provide outstanding information to consumers and journalists alike.

Appeals to Target Audiences

Travel promoters identify target audiences, creating special appeals and trips for them. Great Britain's skillfully designed publicity in the United States is a successful example. Its basic appeal is an invitation to visit the country's historic places and pageants. It also offers London theatrical tours, golf expeditions to famous courses in Scotland, genealogical research parties for those seeking family roots, and tours of the cathedrals. Special tours can be arranged for other purposes as well.

Packaging   Packaging is a key word in travel public relations. Cruises for family reunions or school groups, family skiing vacations, university alumni study groups, archaeological expeditions, even trips to remote Tibet are just a few of the so-called niche travel packages that are offered. A package usually consists of a prepaid arrangement for transportation, housing, most meals, and entertainment, with a professional escort to handle the details. Supplementary side trips often are offered for extra fees.

Appeals to Seniors   The largest special travel audience of all is older citizens. Retired persons have time to travel, and many have ample money to do so. Hotels, motels, and airlines frequently offer discounts to attract them. As a means of keeping old-school loyalties alive, many colleges conduct alumni tours, heavily attended by senior citizens.

A large percentage of cruise passengers, especially on longer voyages, are retirees. Alert travel promoters design trips with them in mind, including such niceties as pairing compatible widows to share cabins and arranging trips ashore that require little walking. Shipboard entertainment and recreational activities with appeal to older persons—nostalgic music for dancing rather than current hits, for example—are important, too.

Times of Crisis

Public relations in travel requires crisis management, just as in corporate work. Crises come in many forms, from those of life and death to the quality of customer service.

The Caribbean island of Aruba, for example, is a popular destination for U.S. tourists (about one million annually) but its exotic image of clear water, beautiful beaches, and swaying palm trees was considerably shaken in May of 2005. That was the month that Natalee Holloway, a 18-year-old from Alabama on a class graduation trip, disappeared from one of Aruba's resorts. The disappearance—and the strong inference of foul play—became a major story in the print and broadcast media. At one point, 60 foreign reporters were on the Dutch island covering the case. Howard Kutz, media critic for the *Washington Post*, said, "Cable TV is treating this as the crime of the century, or at least, the obsession of the moment." He told the *Christian Science Monitor* that Aruba had garnered more media coverage over Holloway than it has had in the last 20 years.

The Holloway story was a major crisis for the Aruba tourism industry, and other Caribbean islands were also concerned that tourism would decline because of the negative coverage. The story continued to garner headlines as Holloway's mother gave extensive interviews and loudly complained about the lack of progress the Aruba police were making in finding her daughter. The Alabama legislature even got into the act and threatened a boycott of the island until the case was solved.

Aruba's public relations firm, Quinn & Co. in New York, originally retained to promote the island's beaches and resorts, had to immediately switch gears and do crisis management. One tactic was to centralize information about the police investigation and to give regular updates on progress in the case. The firm also worked with cruise lines, travel agents, and airlines to assure them that Aruba was safe and still an attractive destination. The government also issued a statement saying, "This comes as a shock to Aruba where crime against tourists is almost non-existent," noting the island's repeat visitor rate of 40 percent, the highest in the Caribbean.

A year later, in 2006, no trace of Natalee Holloway had been found and no one had been charged with her presumed murder. The story, however, faded from the headlines and the media moved on. In Aruba, tourism is about back to normal.

On a different level, the luxurious ocean liner *Queen Elizabeth II* departed on a high-priced cruise before refurbishing was completed. Many passengers had unpleasant trips because some facilities were in disrepair, leading to one news report describing the ship as a floating construction project. Others had their reservations cancelled because their cabins had not been completed. After bad international publicity and a class-action suit by some passengers, the Cunard cruise line offered a settlement. It gave full refunds of cruise fares plus a travel credit for a future cruise.

SUMMARY

Fascination with Celebrity

Today's mass media focus on the publicizing and glorification of celebrities in the fields of sports and entertainment and even high-profile criminals, some politicians, and members of the British royal family. Although the publicity buildup of individuals is not in the mainstream of public relations work, students in the field should learn how the personal publicity trade operates.

Enduring Celebrity: When the Good and Beautiful Die Young
Lady Diana Spencer achieved celebrity status through her marriage to Charles, Prince of Wales and heir to the British

throne. The public was obsessed with her clothing, her public appearances, her eating disorder, and the failure of her marriage. Her early death has frozen her youthful image in time, and visitors to her family estate have paid to view the site of her burial.

The Mystique of Personality

Celebrities are motivated by fame (or notoriety), self-glorification, the attempt at positive image creation, and the desire for monetary gain. The public is impressed because of wish fulfillment, hero worship, a vicarious sense of belonging, and a desire for entertainment.

The Practitioner's Responsibility

A big factor for the public relations practitioner handling a personality will be damage control from misbehavior or an irresponsible public statement. This may strain the practitioner's ethical principles; it is never wise to lie to protect a client.

Conducting a Personality Campaign

A practitioner planning a campaign to generate public awareness of an individual must interview the client, prepare a biography, plan a marketing strategy, and conduct the campaign through news releases, photographs, and public appearances.

Promoting an Entertainment Event

Publicity campaigns to promote events may include publicity to stimulate ticket sales. The "drip-drip-drip" technique involves a steady output of information as the event is being planned. The motion picture industry defines target audiences.

Sports Publicity

Sports publicists promote both big-time college and professional teams. This effort becomes more difficult when the team isn't winning. Emerging sports must compete for prominence and fan loyalty with more established sports. Some publicity focuses on building images of star players. Publicity efforts will also include both sports crisis and sponsorship management. A major aspect of sports is corporate sponsorships, which generates billions of dollars.

Travel Promotion

Travel promotion will involve encouraging the public's desire to visit a place, arranging for them to reach it, making sure they enjoy their trip, and protecting their safety. Campaigns may include a familiarization trip to increase travel agents' awareness. Retirees are a major audience for the tourism business.

CASE ACTIVITY What Would You Do?

Michael Vick, star quarterback for the Atlanta Falcons, pled guilty in August 2007 to federal dogfighting charges, admitting he took part in an illegal, interstate enterprise known as Bad Newz Kennels and helped kill underperforming dogs. After a heartfelt apology at a news conference, Vick was given 23 months in early December. His future NFL salary, his endorsements, and his prospects for someday returning to professional football with strong fan and player support hung in the balance.

Now, your celebrity public relations firm has been hired to develop a strategic communication plan for his comeback. Michael Vick hopes to recapture the limelight and public support that he needs at least as much as his passing ability and foot speed. The overall goal should be to focus attention on his many talents and his redemption as a young man who made terrible and cruel decisions

that are his responsibility. The focus of your firm's retainer to work for Vick is to counsel the athlete about constructive investments and personal actions that can become the basis for a publicity program to shape a new reputation and a new life for Vick after his legal penalties are paid.

The firm is instructed to use traditional celebrity promotion tactics but also to capitalize on new technologies. You have suggested that a crisis communication plan also be implemented in the event of any further, although unforeseen, developments on the legal front or any further erosion of the financial picture for Vick. What would be your three main objectives, and what strategies would you showcase to achieve them? For your crisis communication plan, how would you handle further charges against Vick, whether misdemeanors or serious charges?

QUESTIONS for Review and Discussion

1. Why do public relations students need to understand how the personal publicity trade functions, even if they do not plan to handle theatrical or sports clients?

2. Which of the five motivating factors in the cult of personality (fame, notoriety, self-glorification, repair of bad image, desire for money) make the most sense to you and why?

3. Name two psychological factors underlying the American obsession with celebrities.

4. When politicians say something they wish they hadn't and it is published, they often claim that they were misquoted. Why is this poor policy?

5. What is the first step in preparing a campaign to increase the public's awareness of an individual client?

6. What is a "bio"? What should it contain?

7. "Cheesecake" photographs once were commonplace in American newspapers, but few are published now. Why is this so?

8. Why do practitioners put emphasis on certain players on sports teams?

9. How much do corporations spend on sports sponsorships? In what ways do you think a corporation benefits from paying $100 million to be a sponsor of the Olympics?

10. What are the basic phases of travel promotion?

SUGGESTED READINGS

Anderson, William B. "Crafting the National Pastime's Image: The History of Major-League, Baseball Public Relations." *Journalism and Communication Monographs,* Vol. 5, No. 1, 2003, pp. 1–43.

Cobb, Chris. "Harry Potter's PR Magic: A Look Inside the PR Plan That Fuels Pottermania." *Public Relations Tactics,* August 2007, pp. 1, 9, 11.

Gingerich, Jon. "Celebrities Use Gossip as Form of PR." *O'Dwyer's PR Report,* April 2006, pp. 1, 14.

Hardin, Robin, and McClung, Steven. "Collegiate Sports Information: A Profile of the Profession." *Public Relations Quarterly,* Summer 2002, pp. 35–39.

Hindman, Elizabeth B. "The Princess and the Paparazzi: Blame, Responsibility, and the Media's Role in the Death of Diana." *Journalism and Mass Communication Quarterly,* Vol. 80, Autumn 2003, pp. 666–668.

Landler, Mark. "The Hard Sell in Germany: Marketing Is Just as Intense as World Cup's Zealous Fans." *New York Times,* June 7, 2006, pp. C1, C4.

Miller, Amanda Christine. "Resort Builds Buzz with Books." *PRWeek,* May 29, 2006, p. 19.

Noyes, Jesse. "NFL Tackles the China Trade; Pats in PR Blitz for Game, Team, Merchandise." *Boston Herald,* June 25, 2007, Finance Section, p. 22.

Pope, Kyle. "Walking Miss Hilton: Once a Lennon Pal, He Now Works the Heiress Night Shift." *New York Times,* August 27, 2006, pp. ST1, 13.

Quinn, Florence. "Resort Push Proves Fertile." *PRWeek,* January 15, 2007, p. 27.

Schmelzer, Randi, and Bush, Michael. "Multicultural Hits the Big Leagues." *PRWeek,* August, 20, 2007, pp. 14–15.

Schmetzer, Randi. "Full Steam Ahead: The Cruise Industry is Growing Its Business With PR." *PRWeek,* October 16, 2006, p. 21.

DIRECTORY OF USEFUL WEB SITES

Public relations requires research and facts. Here's a sampling of sites on the Internet where you can find information.

General Information

www.highbeam.com: Provides full-text articles from multiple sources, including newspapers, newswires, magazines, etc.

www.newsindex.com: Offers access to hundreds of articles.

www.writersdigest.com/101sites/: "Best Web Sites for Writers," from dictionaries to general reference tools and writer's organizations.

www.bartleby.com/people/Strunk-W.html: Strunk & White's The Elements of Style online.

www.pollingreport.com: Compilation of findings from surveys regarding trends in public opinion.

thomas.loc.gov: Site of the Library of Congress and the starting point for legislative and Congressional information.

www.infoplease.com: Online almanacs on various topics from business to history and sports.

www.biography.com: Backgrounds on current and historical figures.

www.acronymfinder.com: Definitions of acronyms, abbreviations, and initialisms.

www.howstuffworks.com: Descriptions, diagrams, and photos that show how devices work.

www.statistics.com: Statistics from government agencies and other sources on a range of subjects.

www.ipl.org: The Internet Public Library; a University of Michigan site that gives links to all kinds of sources, from dictionaries to writing guides to newspapers.

resourceshelf.freepint.com: A favorite among reference librarians.

www.salary.com: Salaries in all fields, including public relations.

Public Relations

www.about.com: Provides multiple guide sites. Public relations site offers articles, directories, forums, etc.

www.pr-education.org: An aggregation of PR-related sites and services.

www.prplace.com: Lists Internet addresses and hot links to PR organizations and how-to information in the public relations field.

www.prcentral.com: Good source of case studies, also offers a news release library.

www.businesswire.com: News releases by company and industry.

www.prnewswire.com: News releases by company and industry.

www.workinpr.com: Job announcements, trends in employment, etc.

www.tsnn.com: The Trade Show News Network.

Organizations

www.prfirms.org: Council of Public Relations Firms

www.iabc.com: International Associa-tion of Business Communicators (IABC)

www.prsa.org: Public Relations Society of America (PRSA)

www.ipra.org: International Public Relations Association (IPRA)

www.pac.org: Public Affairs Council

www.niri.org: National Investor Relations Institute (NIRI)

www.instituteforpr.com: Institute of Public Relations (IPR)

www.ifea.com: International Festivals and Events Association (IFEA)

Publications

www.odwyerpr.com: O'Dwyer's PR/Marketing Communications Web site

www.prandmarketing.com: PR News

www.prexec.com: Ragan's newsletters and public relations resources

www.prsa.org/: Public Relations Tactics and Strategist Online

www.prweekus.com: PRWeek

www.iabc.com/cw: Communication World

www.briefings.com: Communication Briefings

BIBLIOGRAPHY OF SELECTED BOOKS, DIRECTORIES, AND PERIODICALS

General Books

Belasen, Alan. The Theory and Practice of Corporate Communication: A Competing Values Perspective. Thousand Oaks, CA: Sage Publications, 2007.

Bobbitt, Randy, and Sullivan, Ruth. Developing the Public Relations Campaign: A Team-Based Approach. Boston: Allyn and Bacon, 2005.

Botan, Carl, and Hazelton, Vincent. Public Relations Theory II. Mahwah, NJ: Lawrence Erlbaum Associates, 2006.

Cameron, Glen T., Wilcox, Dennis L., Reber, Bryan H., and Shin, J. Public Relations Today: Managing Competition and Conflict. Boston: Allyn & Bacon, 2008.

Caywood, Clarke, editor. The Handbook of Strategic Public Relations and Integrated Communications. New York: McGraw-Hill, 1997.

Cottle, Simon. News, Public Relations, and Power. Thousand Oaks, CA: Sage Publications, 2003.

Cutlip, Scott M., Center, Allen H., and Broom, Glen M. Effective Public Relations, 9th ed. Upper Saddle River, NJ: Prentice Hall, 2005.

Grunig, James E., editor. Excellence in Public Relations and Communication Management. Hillsdale, NJ: Lawrence Erlbaum, 1992.

Grunig, Larissa A., Grunig, James E., and Dozier, David M. Excellent Public Relations and Effective Organizations. Mahwah, NJ: Lawrence Erlbaum, 2002.

Guth, David W., and Marsh, Charles. Public Relations: A Values-Driven Approach. Boston, 3rd ed. Allyn and Bacon, 2005.

Hansen-Horn, Tricia, and Neff, Bonita D. Public Relations: From Theory to Practice. Boston: Allyn & Bacon, 2008.

Harris, Thomas L. Value-Added Public Relations : The secret weapon of integrated marketing. Lincolnwood, IL: NTC Contemporary Books, 1998.

Heath, Robert L., and Coombs, W. Timothy. Today's Public Relations: An Introduction. Thousand Oaks, CA: Sage Publications, 2006.

Heath, Robert L., editor. Encyclopedia of Pubic Relations. Thousand Oaks, CA: Sage Publications, 2004.

Heath, Robert L., editor. Handbook of Public Relations. Thousand Oaks, CA: Sage Publications, 2001.

L'Etang, Jacquie, and Pieczka, Magda. Public Relations: Critical Debates andContemporary Practices. Mahwah, NJ: Lawrence Erlbaum Associates, 2006.

Lattimore, Dan, Baskin, Otis, Heiman, Suzette T., Toth, Elizabeth, and VanLeuven, James K. Public Relations: The Profession and the Practice, 2d ed. New York: McGraw-Hill, 2007.

Matera, Fran R., and Artique, Ray J. Public Relations Campaigns and Techniques: Building Bridges to the 21st Century. Boston: Allyn and Bacon, 2000.

McElreath, Mark. Managing Systematic and Ethical Public Relations Campaigns, 2d ed. Madison, WI: Brown & Benchmark, 1997.

Mickey, Thomas J. Deconstructing Public Relations: Public Relations Criticism. Mahwah, NJ: Lawrence Erlbaum, 2003.

Newsom, Doug, Turk, Judy Vanslyke, and Kruckeberg, Dean. This Is PR: The Realities of Public Relations, 9th ed. Belmont, CA: Thomson/Wadsworth, 2007.

Seitel, Fraser P. The Practice of Public Relations, 10th ed. Upper Saddle River, NJ: Prentice Hall, 2006.

Shankman, Peter. Can we do that?! : Outrageous PR stunts that work?! New York: John Wiley & Sons, 2007.

Smith, Ronald D. Strategic Planning for Public Relations, 2d ed. Mahwah, NJ: Lawrence Erlbaum, 2005.

Toth, Elizabeth L., editor. The Future of Excellence in Public Relations and Communication Management: Challenges for the Next Generation. Routledge, 2006.

Toth, Elizabeth L., and Heath, Robert L., editors. Rhetorical and Critical Approaches to Public Relations. Hillsdale, NJ: Lawrence Erlbaum, 1992.

Wilcox, Dennis L., and Cameron, Glen T. Public Relations: Strategies and Tactics, 9th ed. Boston: Allyn and Bacon, 2009.

Wilson, Laurie J. Strategic Program Planning for Effective Public Relations Campaigns. Dubuque, 4th ed. IA: Kendall-Hunt, 2004.

Special Interest Books

Business/Management

Austin, Erica W., and Pinkleton, Bruce E. Strategic Public Relations Management, 2d ed. Mahwah, NJ: Lawrence Erlbaum, 2006.

Belasen, Alan T. The Theory and Practice of Corporate Communication: A Competing Values Perspective. Thousands Oaks, CA: 2007.

Berger, Bruce, K., and Reber, Bryan H. Gaining influence in public relations: The role of resistance in practice, Mahwah, NJ: Lawrence Erlbaum Associates. 2006.

Ferguson, Sherry D. Communication Planning: An Integrated Approach.

Thousand Oaks, CA: Sage
Publications, 1999.

Ledingham, John A., and Bruning,
Stephen D. Public Relations as
Relationship Management.
Mahwah: Lawrence Erlbaum, 2001.

Careers

Helitzer, Melvin. The Dream Job:
Sports Publicity, Promotion, and
Public Relations, 3d ed. Athens,
OH: University Sports Press, 1999.

Mogel, Leonard. Making It in Public
Relations: An Insider's Guide to
Career Opportunities, 2d ed.
Mahwah, NJ: Lawrence Erlbaum,
2002.

Ross, Billy I., and Johnson, Keith F.,
editors. Where Shall I Go to
Study Advertising and Public
Relations? Lubbock, TX:
Advertising Education
Publications, 2004. (Pamphlet
listing college and university
programs.)

Sequin, James, editor. Business
Communications: The Real
World and Your Career. Belmont,
CA: Southwestern College
Publishing, 2000.

Case Studies

Center, Allen, Jackson, Patrick,
Smith, Stacey, and Stansberry,
Frank. Public Relations Practices:
Managerial Case Studies and
Problems, 7th ed. Upper Saddle
River, NJ: Prentice Hall, 2007.

Guth, David W., and Marsh, Charles.
Adventures in Public Relations:
Case Studies and Critical
Thinking. Boston: Allyn & Bacon,
2005.

Hagley, Tom. Writing Winning
Proposals—Cases, Boston:
Allyn & Bacon, 2005.

Hendrix, Jerry A., and Hayes, Darrell
C. Public Relations Cases, 7th ed.
Belmont, CA: Thomson/
Wadsworth, 2007.

Lamb, Lawrence F., and McKee,
Kathy Brittain. Applied Public
Relations: Cases in Stakeholder
Management. Mahwah, NJ:
Lawrence Erlbaum, 2004.

Moss, Danny, and DeSanto, Barbara.
Public Relations Cases: Inter-
national Perspectives. New York:
Routledge, 2001.

Peterson, Gary L. Communicating
in Organizations: A Casebook.
Needham Heights, MA: Allyn and
Bacon, 2000.

Communication/
Persuasion

Bryant, Jennings, and Zillmann, Dolf.
Media Effects: Advances in
Theory and Research, 2d ed.
Hillsdale, NJ: Lawrence Erlbaum,
2002.

DeFleur, Melvin L., and Dennis,
Everette E. Understanding Mass
Communication. Boston:
Houghton Mifflin, 2001.

Jowett, Garth S., and O'Donnell,
Victoria. Propaganda and
Persuasion. 4th ed. Thousand
Oaks, CA: Sage Publications, 2005.

Larson, Charles U. Persuasion:
Reception and Responsibility, 11th
ed. Belmont, CA: Thomson/
Wadsworth, 2006.

Moloney, K. Rethinking Public
Relations: PR Propaganda and
Democracy, 2d ed. London:
Routledge. 2006.

Perloff, Richard M. The Dynamics
of Persuasion: Communication
and Attitudes in the 21st Century.
Routledge, 2007.

Samovar, Larry, Porter, Richard, and
McDaniel, Edwin, R. Intercultural
Communication: A Reader, 11th ed.
Belmont, CA: Wadsworth, 2005.

Severin, Werner, and Tankard, James.
Communication Theories: Origins,
Methods, Uses, 5th ed. New York:
Longman, 2000.

Simons, Herbert W., Morreale,
Joanne, and Gronbeck, Bruce.
Persuasion in Society. Thousand
Oaks, CA: Sage Publications, 2000.

Crisis Communications

Adamson, Jim. The Denny's Story:
How a Company in Crisis
Resurrected Its Good Name. New
York: John Wiley & Sons, 2001.

Coombs, W. Timothy. Ongoing
Crisis Communication: Planning,
Managing, and Responding, 2d ed.
Thousand Oaks, CA: Sage
Publications, 2007.

Fearn-Banks, Kathleen. Crisis
Communications: A Casebook
Approach, 3d ed. Mahwah, NJ:
Lawrence Erlbaum, 2007.

Hearit, Keith M. Crisis Management
By Apology: Corporate Response
to Allegations of Wrongdoing.
Routledge, 2005.

Lerbinger, Otto. The Crisis
Manager: Facing Risk and
Responsibility. Mahwah, NJ:
Lawrence Erlbaum, 1997.

Millar, Dan P., and Heath, Robert L.,
editors. Responding to Crisis: A
Rhetorical Approach to Crisis
Communications. Mahwah, NJ:
Lawrence Erlbaum, 2004.

Seeger, Matthew W, Sellnow,
Timothy L., and Ulmer, Robert R.
Communication and Organiza-
tional Crisis. Westport, CN:
Praeger Publishers, 2004.

Cultural
Diversity/Gender

Alexander, A., and Hanson, J., editors.
Taking Sides: Clashing Views on
Controversial Issues in Mass
Media and Society, 8th ed. New
York: McGraw-Hill. 2005.

Banks, Stephen P. Multicultural
Public Relations: A Social
Interpretive Approach, 2d ed.
Thousand Oaks, CA: Sage
Publications, 2000.

Biagi, Shirley, and Kern-Foxworth,
Marilyn. Facing Differences:
Race, Gender, and Mass Media.
Thousand Oaks, CA: Pine Forge
Press, 1997.

Grunig, Larissa A., Toth, Elizabeth
L., and Hon, Linda C. Women in
Public Relations: How Gender
Influences Practice. New York:
Guilford Publications, 2001.

Education

Bagin, Don, Gallagher, Donald, and
Moore, Edward, H. The School
and Community Relations, 9th ed.
Boston: Allyn and Bacon, 2007.

Kowalski, Theodore J. Public Relations in Schools, 4th ed. Upper Saddle River, NJ: Prentice Hall, 2007.

Employee Relations

D'Aprix, Roger. Communicating for Change: Connecting the Workplace with the Market-place. San Francisco: Jossey-Bass, 1996.

Holtz, Shel. Corporate Conversations: A Guide to Crafting Effective and Appropriate Internal Communications. AMACOM/ American Management Association, 2003.

Jablin, Fred M., and Putnam, Linda, editors. The New Handbook of Organizational Communication: Advances in Theory, Research, and Methods. Thousand Oaks, CA: Sage Publications, 2004.

Peterson, Gary L. Communicating in Organizations, 2d ed. Boston: Allyn and Bacon, 2000.

Spicer, Christopher. Organizational Public Relations: A Political Perspective. Mahwah, NJ: Lawrence Erlbaum, 1997.

Ethics

Day, Louis A. Ethics in Media Communica-tions: Cases and Controversies, 5th ed. Belmont, CA: Wadsworth, 2005.

McElreath, Mark P. Managing Systematic and Ethical Public Relations. Dubuque, IA: Brown and Benchmark, 1997.

Seib, Philip, and Fitzpatrick, Kathy. Public Relations Ethics. Belmont, CA: Thomson/Wadsworth, 1995.

Stauber, John, and Rampton, Sheldon. Toxic Sludge Is Good for You: Damn Lies and the Public Relations Industry. Monroe, ME: Common Courage Press, 1995. (Critical analysis of public relations.)

Fitzpatrick, Kathy, R., and Bronstein, Carolyn. Ethics in Public Relations: Responsible Advocacy. Thousand Oaks, CA: Sage Publications, 2006.

Financial/Investor Relations

Higgins, Richard B. Best Practices in Global Investor Relations. Westport, CT: Green-wood, 2000.

Marcus, Bruce W. Competing for Capital: Investor Relations in a Dynamic World. New York: John Wiley & Sons, 2005.

Fund-Raising/ Development

Weinstein, Stanley. The Complete Guide to Fund-Raising Management, 2d ed. New York: John Wiley & Sons, 2002.

Ciconte, Barbara K., and Jacob, Jeanne G. Fund Raising Basics: A Complete Guide. Gaithersburg, MD: Aspen Publications, 1997.

Kelly, Kathleen S. Effective Fund-Raising Management. Mahwah, NJ: Lawrence Erlbaum, 1996.

Rosso, Henry. Achieving Excellence in Fund-Raising. San Francisco: Jossey-Bass, 1991.

Government/Public Affairs

Fitzwater, Marlin. Call the Briefing! Reagan & Bush, Sam & Helen; a Decade with Presidents and the Press. New York: New York Times Books, 1995.

Lee, Mordecai. Government Public Relations: A Reader. Routledge. 2007.

Lerbinger, Otto. Corporate Public Affairs: Interacting With Interest Groups, Media, and Government. Routledge. 2005.

Walsh, Kenneth T. Feeding the Beast: The White House Versus the Press. Xlibris Corporation, 2002.

History

Cutlip, Scott M. Public Relations History: From the Seventeenth to the Twentieth Century. Hillsdale, NJ: Lawrence Erlbaum, 1995.

Cutlip, Scott M. The Unseen Power: Public Relations: A History. Hillsdale, NJ: Lawrence Erlbaum, 1994.

Ewen, Stuart. PR! A Social History of Spin. New York: Basic Books, 1998.

Griese, Noel. Arthur W. Page: Publisher, Public Relations Pioneer, Patriot. Atlanta: Anvil Publishers, 2001.

Lee, Mordecai. The First Presidential Communications Agency: FDR's Office of Government Reports. Albany, NY: State University of New York Press, 2005.

Miller, Karen S. The Voice of Business: Hill & Knowlton and Post-War Public Relations. Chapel Hill: University of North Carolina Press, 1999.

Tye, Larry. The Father of Spin: Edward L. Bernays and the Birth of Public Relations. Holt Paperbacks, 2002.

International

Curtin, Patricia A. International Public Relations: Negotiating Culture, Identity, and Power, Thousand Oaks, CA: Sage Publications, 2007.

Grunig, Larissa A., and Grunig, James E. Excellent Public Relations and Effective Organizations: A Study of Communication Management in Three Countries. Mahwah, NJ: Lawrence Erlbaum, 2002.

Hall, Bradford J. Among Cultures: The Challenge of Communica-tion, 2d ed. Belmont, CA: Thomson/Wadsworth, 2005.

Jandt, Fred E. Intercultural Communication: An Introduction, 3rd. Thousand Oaks, CA: Sage Publications, 2001.

Newsom, Doug. Bridging the Gaps in Global Communication, Malden, MA: Blackwell Publishing, 2007.

Parkinson, Michael, and Ekachai, Daradirek Gee. International and Intercultural Public Relations: A Campaign Case Approach. Boston: Allyn & Bacon, 2006.

Rudd, Jill E. Communicating in Global Business Negotiations: A Geocentric Approach. Thousand Oaks, CA: Sage, 2007

Samovar, Larry A., Porter, Richard E, and McDaniel, Edwin R. Intercultural Communication: A Reader, 11th ed. Belmont, CA: Thomson/Wadsworth, 2006.

Schmidt, Wallace V., Conaway, Roger N., Easton, Susan S., and Wardrope, William J. Communicating Globally: Intercultural Communication and International Business. Thousand Oaks, CA: Sage, 2007.

Sriramesh, Krishnamurthy, and Vercic, Dejan. The Global Public Relations Handbook: Theory Research, and Practice. Mahwah, NJ: Lawrence Erlbaum Associates, 2003.

Internet/World Wide Web

Albarran, Alan B., and Goff, David H. Understanding the Web: Social, Political, and Economic Dimensions of the Internet. Ames, IA: Iowa State University Press, 2000.

Kelleher, Tom. Public Relations Online: Lasting Concepts for Changing Media. Thousand Oaks, CA: Sage Publications, 2006.

McGuire, Mary, Stilborne, Linda, McAdams, Melinda, and Hyatt, Laurel. The Internet Handbook for Writers, Researchers, and Journalists. New York: Guilford Publications, 2000.

Middleburg, Don. Winning PR in the Wired World. New York: McGraw-Hill, 2001.

Sterne, Jim, and Priore, Anthony. E-Mail Marketing: Using E-Mail to Reach Your Target Audience and Build Customer Relationships. New York: John Wiley & Sons, 2001.

Witmer, Diane F. Spinning the Web: A Handbook for Public Relations on the Internet. Boston: Allyn and Bacon: 2000.

Issues Management

Heath, Robert L. Strategic Issues Management: Organizations and Public Policy Challenges, 2d ed. Thousand Oaks, CA: Sage Publications, 1997.

Mitroff, Ian I. Managing Crises Before They Happen. New York: AMACOM, 2001.

Law

Gower, Karla K. Legal and Ethical Restraints on Public Relations. Prospect Heights, IL: Waveland Press, 2003.

Haggerty, James F. Winning Your Case with Public Relations. New York: John Wiley & Sons, 2003.

Middleton, Kent, and Lee, William E. Law of Public Communication, 7th ed. Boston: Allyn and Bacon, 2008.

Parkinson, Michael, and Parkinson, Marie L. Public Relations Law. Routledge. 2007.

Pember, Don, R., and Calvert, C. Mass Media Law. New York: McGraw-Hill. 2006.

Roschwalb, Susanne A., and Stack, Richard A. Litigation Public Relations: Courting Public Opinion. Washington, D.C.: Fred B. Rothman, 1995.

Marketing

Duncan, Tom. Principles of Advertising and IMC, 2nd ed. New York: McGraw-Hill, 2004.

Gillis, Tamara. The IABC Handbook of Organizational Communication: A Guide to Internal Communication, Public Relations, Marketing and Leadership. New York: John Wiley & Sons, 2006.

Gronstedt, Anders. The Customer Century: Lessons from World Class Companies in Integrated Marketing and Communications. New York: Routlege, 2000.

Levine, Michael. A Branded World: Adventures in Public Relations and the Creation of Superbrands.

New York: John Wiley & Sons, 2003.

Henry, Rene A. Marketing Public Relations: The HOWS That Make It Work. Ames, IA: Iowa State University Press, 2000.

Schreiber, Alfred L., and Lenson Barry. Multicultural Marketing. Chicago, IL: NTC Contemporary Publishing, 2001.

Schultz, Don E., and Barnes, Beth E. Strategic Brand Communications Campaigns. Lincolnwood, IL: NTC Contemporary Books, 1999.

Media/Press Relations

Hart, Hal. Successful Spokespersons Are Made, Not Born. Bloomington, IN: First Books Library, 2001.

Howard, Carole M., and Mathews, Wilima K. On Deadline: Managing Media Relations, 4th ed. Prospect Heights, IL: Waveland Press, 2006.

Mindich, David T.Z. Tuned Out: Why Americans Under 40 Don't Follow the News, New York: Oxford University Press, 2005.

Strick, Michael, and Mayer, Allan. Spin: How to Turn the Power of the Press to Your Advantage. Washington, D.C.: Regnery Publishing, 1998.

Wallack, Lawrence, Woodruff, Katie, Dorfman, Lori Elizabeth, Diaz, Iris, and Dorman Lori. News for a Change: An Advocate's Guide to Working with the Media. Thousand Oaks, CA: Sage Publications, 1999.

Nonprofit Groups/Health Agencies

Andreasen, A.R. Social marketing in the 21st Century, Thousand Oaks, CA: Sage Publications Inc. 2006.

Berkowitz, Eric N., Pol, Louis G., and Thomas, Richard K. Healthcare Marketing Research: Tools and Techniques for Analyzing and Understanding Today's Healthcare Environment. New York: McGraw-Hill, 1997.

Feinglass, Art. The Public Relations Handbook for Nonprofits: A Comprehensive and Practical Guide. New York: John Wiley & Sons, 2005.

Matthew Kreuter, David Farrell, Laura Brennan, Barbara K. Rimer. Tailoring Health Messages: Customizing Communication with Computer Technology, Mahwah, NJ: Lawrence Erlbaum Associates, 2000.

Rice, Ronald E., and Atkin, Charles K. Public Communication Campaigns, 3d ed. Thousand Oaks, CA: Sage Publications, 2001.

Rungard, Sue, and French, Ylca. Marketing and Public Relations Handbook for Museums, Galleries, and Heritage Attractions. Walnut Creek, CA : Altamira Press, 2000.

Publicity

See Special Events or Writing in Public Relations sections

Reputation

Doorley, John, and Garcia, Helio F. Reputation Management: The Key to Successful Public Relations and Corporate Communication. Routledge, 2006.

Gaines-Ross, Leslie. Corporate Reputation: 12 Steps to Safeguarding and Recovering Reputation. New York: John Wiley & Sons, 2008.

Roger, Haywood. Manage your reputation: how to plan public relations to build & protect the organization's most powerful asset, 2d ed. New York: McGraw-Hill, 2004.

Research Methods

Berger, Arthur Asa. Media and Communication Research Methods: An Introduction to Qualitative and Quantitative Research Approaches. Thousand Oaks, CA: Sage Publications, 2000.

Demers, David, P. Dictionary of Mass Communication and Media Research: A Guide for Students, Scholars and Professionals. Spokane, WA: Marquette Books. 2005.

Ferguson, Sherry D. Researching the Public Opinion Environment: Theories and Methods. Thousand Oaks, CA: Sage Publications, 2000.

Fern, Edward F. Advanced Focus Group Research. Thousand Oaks, CA: Sage Publications, 2001.

Frey, Lawrence R., Botan, Carl H., and Kreps, Gary L. Investigating Communication: An Introduction to Research Methods, 3d ed. Boston: Allyn and Bacon, 2005.

Gubrium, Jaber E., and Holstein, James A. Handbook of Interview Research: Context & Method. Thousand Oaks, CA: Sage Publications, 2001.

Gunter, Barrie. Media Research Methods: Measuring Audiences, Reactions, Impact. Thousand Oaks, CA: Sage Publications, 2000.

Stacks, Don W. Primer of Public Relations Research. New York: The Guilford Press, 2002.

Special Events

Allen, Judy. The Executive's Guide to Corporate Events and Business Entertaining: How to Choose and Use Corporate Functions to Increase Brand Awareness, Develop New Business, Nurture Customer Loyalty and Drive Growth. New York: John Wiley & Sons, 2007.

Allen, Judy. Marketing Your Event Planning Business: A Creative Approach to Gaining the Competitive Edge. New York: John Wiley & Sons, 2004.

Allen, Judy. Event Planning Ethics and Etiquette: A Principled Approach to the Business of Special Event Management. New York: John Wiley & Sons, 2003.

Allen, Judy. The Business of Event Planning: Behind-the-Scenes Secrets of Successful Special Events. Etobicoke, Ontario: John Wiley & Sons, 2002.

Allen, Judy. Event Planning: The Ultimate Guide to Successful Meetings, Corporate Events, Fundraising Galas, Conferences, Conventions, Incentives and Other Special Events. New York: John Wiley & Sons, 2000.

Goldblatt, Joe Jeff. Special events: best practices in modern event management. New York: John Wiley & Sons, 1997.

Jasso, Gayle. Special Events from A to Z. Thousand Oaks, CA: Sage Publications, 1996.

Wendroff, Alan L. Special Events: Proven Strategies for Nonprofit Fundraising, 2d ed. New York: John Wiley & Sons, 2003.

Speeches/Presentations

Beebe, Steven A., and Beebe, Susan. Public Speaking: An Audience-Centered Approach, 6th ed. Boston: Allyn and Bacon, 2006.

Brody, Marjorie. Speaking Your Way to the Top: Making Powerful Business Presentations. Boston: Allyn and Bacon, 1998.

Daly, John A., and Engleberg, Isa. Presentations in Everyday Life: Strategies for Effective Speaking with Practical Public Speaking: A Guide to Moving from Theory to Practice. Boston: Houghton Mifflin, 2001.

DiSanza, James R., and Legge, Nancy, J. Business and Professional Communication: Plans, Processes, and Performance, 3d ed. Boston: Allyn and Bacon, 2005.

Fujishin, Randy. The Natural Speaker, 5th ed. Boston: Allyn and Bacon, 2005.

Writing in Public Relations

Aronson, Merry, Spetner, Don, and Ames, Carol. The Public Relations Writer's Handbook: The Digital Age, 2d ed. New York: John Wiley & Sons, 2007.

Bivins, Thomas H. Public Relations Writing: The Essentials of Style and Format, 6th ed. Boston, MA: McGraw-Hill, 2007.

Carstarphen, Meta G., and Wells, Richard A. *Writing PR: A Multimedia Approach.* Boston: Allyn and Bacon, 2004.

Diggs-Brown, Barbara. *The PR Style Guide: Formats for Public Relations Practice.* Belmont, CA: Thomson/Wadsworth, 2007.

Morton, Linda P. *Strategic Publications: Designing for Target Publics.* Best Books Plus, 2006.

Newsom, Doug, and Haynes, Jim. *Public Relations Writing: Form and Style,* 8th ed. Belmont, CA: Thomson/Wadsworth, 2007.

Smith, Ronald D. *Becoming a Public Relations Writer: A Writing Process Workbook for the Profession.* Routledge, 2007.

Treadwell, Donald, and Treadwell, Jill B. *Public Relations Writing: Principles in Practice,* 2d ed. Thousand Oaks, CA: Sage Publications, 2005.

Whitaker, W. Richard, Ramsey, Janet E., and Smith, Ronald D. *Media Writing: Print, Broadcast, and Public Relations,* 2d ed. Mahwah, NJ: Lawrence Erlbaum, 2005.

Wilcox, Dennis L. *Public Relations Writing and Media Techniques,* 6th edition. Boston: Allyn and Bacon, 2009.

Zappala, Joseph M., and Carden, Ann R. *Public Relations Worktext: A Writing and Planning Resource.* Mahwah, NJ: Lawrence Erlbaum, 2004.

Directories

Directories are valuable tools for public relations personnel who need to communicate with a variety of specialized audiences. The following is a selected list of the leading national and international directories.

Media Directories

All-In-One Media Directory. Gebbie Press, Box 1000, New Paltz, NY 12561.

American College Media Directory. Vineberg Communications, 6120 Grand Central Parkway, Forest Hills, NY 11375.

Bacon's Media Directories: Newspaper/ Magazines, Radio/TV/ Cable, Media Calendar, Business Media, International Media Directory, New York Publicity Outlets, Metro California Outlets, Computer & High-Tech Media, and Medical & Health Media. Bacon Information, Inc., 332 S. Michigan Avenue, Chicago, IL 60604.

Broadcasting Cable Yearbook. Broadcasting & Cable Magazine, PO Box 7820, Torrance, CA 90504.

Burrelle's Media Directories: Newspapers and Related Media, Magazines and Newsletters, Radio, Television, and Cable. Burrelle's Media Directory, 75 E. Northfield Rd., Livingston, NJ 07039.

Cable & Station Coverage Atlas. Warren Publications, 2115 Ward Court NW, Washington, D.C. 20037.

College Media Directory. Oxbridge Communications, 150 Fifth Avenue, Suite 302, New York, NY 10011.

Editor & Publisher International Yearbook. Editor & Publisher, 11 W. 19th St., New York, NY 10011-4234.

Gale's Directory of Publications Broadcast Media. Gale Group, PO Box 9187, Farmington Hills, MI 48333.

Hispanic Americans Information Directory. Gale Group, 27500 Drake Road, Farmington Hills, MI 48331-335.

Hudson's Washington News Media Contacts Directory. Hudson Associates, PO Box 311, Rhine-beck, NY 12572.

Literary Marketplace. R. R. Bowker Company, 245 W. 17th St., New York, NY 10011.

National Directory of Community Newspapers. American Newspaper Representatives, 1700 W. Beaver Road, Suite 340, Troy, MI 48084.

National Directory of Magazines. Oxbridge Communications, 150 Fifth Avenue, Suite 302, New York, NY 10011.

North American Senior Media Directory. Gem Publishing Group, 250 E. Riverview Circle, Reno, NV 89509.

Publicists Guide to Senior Media. Promo Works, 4165 E. Thousand Oaks Blvd., Suite 335, Westlake Village, CA 91362.

Standard Rate and Data Services: Business Publications, Community Publications, Newspapers, and Spot Radio. SRDS, 3004 Glenview Rd., Wilmette, IL 60091.

The Top 200+ TV New Talk and Magazine Shows. Bradley Communications, PO Box 1206, Lansdowne, PA 19050.

The U.S. All Media E-mail Directory. Direct Contact Media Services, PO Box 6726, Kennewick, WA 99336.

International Media Directories

Asia Pacific Media Guide. Asian News Service, 633 West 5th Street, Suite 2020, Los Angeles, CA 90071.

Benn's Media. Benn's Business Information Services, Riverbank House, Angelhare, Tonbridge, Kent TN9 1SE, United Kingdom.

Central American Media Directory. Florida International University School of Journalism, North Miami Campus, 3000 N.E. 151st Street, Miami, FL 33181.

Dun's Europe. Dun & Bradstreet Information Services, 3 Sylvan Way, Persipanny, NJ 07054.

European Media Yearbook: Western and Eastern Europe. CIT Publications, 3 Colleton Crescent, Exeter/Devon EX2 4DG, England.

Hollis PR Annual and Hollis Europe. Harlequin House, 7 High Street, Teddington, England TW11 8EL.

Urlichs International Periodicals Directory. Reed Elsevier, 121 Chanlon Road, New Providence, NJ 07974.

Willing's Press Guide. Harlequin House, 7 High Street, Teddington, England TW11 8EL.

World Radio/TV Handbook. BPI Communications, 1695 Oak Street, Lakewood, NJ 08701.

Other Selected Directories

Awards, Honors, and Prizes. Gale Research, PO Box 9187, Farmington Hills, MI 48333.

Broadcast Interview Source. BIS, Inc., 2233 Wisconsin Avenue, Washington, D.C. 20007.

Business Organizations, Agencies, and Publications Directory. Gale Research, PO Box 9187, Farmington Hills, MI 48333.

The Celebrity Source. The Celebrity Source, 8033 Sunset Blvd., Suite 1108, Los Angeles, CA 90046.

Congressional Yellow Book. Leadership Directories, 1301 Pennsylvania Avenue NW, Suite 925, Washington, D.C. 20004.

CorpTech® Directory of Technology Companies. CorpTech, 12 Alfred Street, Suite 200, Woburn, MA 01801–9998.

Directory of Online Databases. Online Information Services, 152 Main Road, Long Hanborough, Oxford OX7 2JY, England.

Hudson's Subscription Newsletter Directory. Hudson Associates, PO Box 311, Rhinebeck, NY 12572.

The National Directory of Mailing Lists. Oxbridge Communications, 150 Fifth Avenue, New York, NY 10011.

Bulldog Reporter's National PR Pitch Book. Infocom Group, 5900 Hollis Street, Suite R2, Emeryville, CA 94608-2008.

O'Dwyer's Directory of Corporate Communications; Directory of PR Executives; Directory of PR Firms. O'Dwyer's 271 Madison Avenue, New York, NY 10016.

Professional Freelance Writer's Directory. National Writer's Association, 1450 South Havana Street, Suite 424, Aurora, CO 80012.

The Society of American Travel Writer's Directory. Society of American Travel, 4101 Lake Boone Trail, Suite 201, Raleigh, NC 27607.

The Sourcebook of Multicultural Experts. Multicultural Marketing Resources, 332 Bleeker Street, Suite G41, New York, NY 10014.

Yearbook of Experts, Authorities, and Spokes-persons. Broadcast Interview Source, 2233 Wisconsin Avenue NW, Suite 301, Washington, D.C. 20007.

Periodicals

CASE Currents. Council for the Advancement and Support of Education, 11 Dupont Circle, Washington, DC. 20036. Monthly.

Communication Briefings. 700 Black Horse Pike, Suite 110, Blackwood, NJ 08012. Monthly.

Communication World. International Association of Business Communicators (IABC), One Hallidie Plaza, Suite 600, San Francisco, CA 94102. Bi-monthly.

International Public Relations Review. International Public Relations Association (IPRA). Cardinal House, 7 Woseley Road, East Molesey, Surrey KT8 9EL, United Kingdom. Quarterly.

Investor Relations Update. National Investor Relations Institute (NIRI), 8045 Leesburg Pike, Suite 600, Vienna, VA 22182. Monthly.

Jack O'Dwyer's PR Newsletter. O'Dwyer's, 271 Madison Ave., New York, NY 10016. Weekly.

Journal of Public Relations Research. Lawrence Erlbaum, 10 Industrial Ave., Mahwah, NJ 07430. Quarterly.

O'Dwyer's PR Services Report. O'Dwyer's, 271 Madison Ave., New York, NY 10016. Monthly.

pr reporter. Box 600, Exeter, NH 03833. Weekly.

PRWeek. 220 Fifth Avenue, New York, NY 10001. Weekly.

Public Relations News. 1201 Seven Locks Road, Potomac, MD 20854-3394. Weekly.

Public Relations Quarterly. 44 W. Market St., Rhinebeck, NY 12572. Quarterly.

Public Relations Review. JAI Press, 100 Prospect St., PO Box 811, Stamford, CT 06904-0811. Quarterly.

Public Relations Strategist. Public Relations Society of America (PRSA), 33 Maiden Lane, New York, NY 10038-5150. Quarterly.

Public Relations Tactics. Public Relations Society of America (PRSA), 33 Maiden Lane, New York, NY 10038-5150. Monthly.

Ragan Report. 212 West Superior St., Suite 200, Chicago, IL 60605. Weekly.

Special Events Report. International Events Group, 213 W. Institute Pl., Chicago, IL 60605. Biweekly.

Chapter 1

p. 1: James Woodson/Digital Vision/ Getty Images Royalty Free; p. 3: Courtesy of Cheryl Georgas, the Hershey Company, and Whitney Miller, JSH&A Public Relations; p. 8: Courtesy of Diane Wagner, Bank of America; p. 14: ©HBO/ Courtesy Everett Collection; p. 15: ©The New Yorker Collection 2004/Mick Stevens from cartoonbank.com. All rights reserved. p. 26: Courtesy of Wal-Mart; p. 34, 35: Courtesy of The Forest Alliance and Jodi Moss, Porter Novelli public relations.

Chapter 2

p. 39: LOU DEMATTEIS/Reuters/ Corbis; p. 40: Burke/Triolo Productions/Newscom; p. 41: Library of Congress #LC-USZC4-3170; p. 42: Bettmann/Corbis; p. 46: Library of Congress; p. 49: Bettmann/Corbis; p. 51: ©2004 Metropolitan Transit Authority; p. 52: Courtesy of Edward Bernays; p. 60: AP Images.

Chapter 3

p. 72: Jon Feingersh/Blend Images/ Getty Images Royalty Free; p. 74: ©The New Yorker Collection 2007/Mick Stevens from cartoon-bank.com. All rights reserved. p. 75, 76, 86: Public Relations Society of America; p. 80: Courtesy of J.D. O'Dwyer Company and artist Bill Kreese; p. Courtesy of Frank Ovaitt, Institute for Public Relations; p. 92: Courtesy of Judith T. Phair.

Chapter 4

p. 97: Jon Feingersh/Iconica/Getty Images Rights Ready; p. 100: Courtesy of Amazon.com; p. 111: Courtesy of Derek Creevey, Edelman Worldwide; p. 113: AP Images/Pablo Martinez Monsivais; p. 114: Courtesy

of Rachel Foltz, Ogilvy Public Relations Worldwide; p. 119: Courtesy of Stacy Nobles, Wolters Kluwer Corporate Legal Services; p. 124: Courtesy of Brian Cox, Fleishman-Hillard.

Chapter 5

p. 127: Tim Hall/Digital Vision/ Getty Images Royalty Free; p. 131: Courtesy of Philips Norelco/Norelco Bodygroom/www.shaveeverywhere. com and Allison Ross, Manning, Selvage & Lee public relations; p. 136: Jeff Greenberg/PhotoEdit, Inc.

Chapter 6

p. 150: Getty Images for Reebok/Getty Images; p. 151: LWA/Stone/Getty Images; p. 156: Reprinted with Permission of Sunkist Growers, Inc. All rights reserved.

Chapter 7

p. 170: Neville Elder/Corbis; p. 177: Courtesy of Gillette Company and Jodi Moss, Porter Novelli public relations; p. 188: Boston Globe/ Bill Greene /Landov.

Chapter 8

p. 193: Michael Newman/PhotoEdit, Inc.; p. 199: Courtesy of Muppets Holding Company and Jodi Moss, Porter Novelli public relations.

Chapter 9

p. 213: Dennis MacDonald/ PhotoEdit, Inc.; p. 216: Bob Daemmrich/The Image Works; p. 230: Kevin Winter/Getty Images; p. 233: Courtesy of Kansas City Health Department and Brian Cox, Fleishman-Hillard; p. 236: Courtesy of Defenders of Wildlife:

Photo Credit: ©1998 Tom Soucek/ AlaskaStock.

Chapter 10

p. 244: Digital Vision/Getty Images Royalty Free; p. 245: Michael O'Neill/Sports Illustrated; p. 258: J. Emilio Flores/The New York Times; p. 270: Ryan Pyle/The New York Times.

Chapter 11

p. 275: AP Images/Nam Y. Huh; p. 284: Courtesy of Royal Caribbean International and Brian Cox, Fleishman-Hillard; p. 285: Courtesy of Brian Cox, Fleishman-Hillard; p. 286: Paramount Pictues/The Kobal Collection; p. 288: REUTERS/Chip East/Newscom; p. 290: Courtesy of Disney Corporation; p. 296: Courtesy of Glen Cameron.

Chapter 12

p. 299: Jason Merritt/FilmMagic/ Getty Images; p. 302: AP Images/ Mark Lennihan; p. 307: Ryan Pyle/The New York Times; p. 313: Courtesy of Matthew Ceniceros, FedEx Corporation; p. 316: Li Linlin/ JHSB/ChinaFotoPress/Getty Images; p. 320: AP Images/Bebeto Matthews; p. 326: AP Images/ Susan Walsh; p. 331: REUTERS/ Jason Reed/Landov.

Chapter 13

p. 335: AP Images/Joerg Sarbach; p. 338: AP Images/Edward Parsons/ UNHCR; p. 339: Courtesy of Derek Creevey, Edelman Worldwide; p. 341: Courtesy of Philips Norelco/ Norelco Bodygroom/www.shaveeverywhere. com and Allison Ross, Manning, Selvage & Lee public relations; p. 343: Courtesy of Purina/Arc

Worldwide; p. 344: ©Morgan/ Greenpeace; p. 345: United Nations High Commission for Refugees; p. 359: YOSHIKAZU TSUNO/AFP/ Getty Images/ Newscom; p. 361: Courtesy of Radley Moss, Text100.

Chapter 14

p. 366: MANPREET ROMANA/ AFP/Getty Images; p. 370: Reprinted with Permission of Sunkist Growers, Inc. All rights reserved; p. 373: Courtesy of Boggiato Produce Company and Cindy Railing, Railing & Associates; p. 375: Courtesy of Nestle Purina PetCare Company and Brian Agnes, Family Features; p. 376: Courtesy of Royal Caribbean International and Brian Cox, Fleishman-Hillard; p. 378: Courtesy of Philips Norelco/Norelco Bodygroom/www.shaveeverywhere. com and Allison Ross, Manning, Selvage & Lee public relations; p. 379, 384: Courtesy of Tracey Parsons, HJ Heinz Company, and Stephanie Ackerman, Jack Horner Communications.

Chapter 15

p. 389: AP Images/Cameron Bloch; p. 397: Courtesy Pepsi-Cola Company; p. 400: Courtesy of March of Dimes/D S Simon Productions Inc.; p. 403: Courtesy of Rotary International; p. 407: Dave Bjerke/ WireImage/Getty Images; p. 410: AP Images/Paul Sakuma.

Chapter 16

p. 418: Gaye Gerard/Getty Images; p. 421: Dennis Van Tine/Landov; p. 426: John Sciully/WireImage. com; p. 428: Courtesy of Saudi Aramco; p. 435: Matthew Cavanaugh/epa/ Corbis.

Chapter 17

p. 444: Richard Levine/Alamy; p. 452: AP Images/Anat Givon; p. 457: AP Images/Jerry Laizure; p. 459: Courtesy of Kimberly-Clark Corporation; p. 465: Adrian Bradshaw/epa/Corbis; p. 469: Business Wire/Getty Images.

Chapter 18

p. 473: Joe Raedle/Getty Images/ Newscom; p. 477: AP Images/ Paul Sakuma; p. 480: Carlos Barria/Reuters/Corbis; p. 489: AP Images/Laurent Rebours; p. 492, 496: Courtesy of Centers for Disease Control and Prevention; p. 494: Jason Reed/Reuters/Landov.

Chapter 19

p. 503: Toshifumi Kitamura/AFP/ Getty Images; p. 508: Federal Express Corporation; p. 510: AP Images/Ralph Radford; p. 514: Reuters/Corbis; p. 521: IPA Frontline; p. 522: Courtesy of Galjina Ognjanov and Belgrade Cultural Network; p. 524: Cathay Pacific Airlines.

Chapter 20

p. 528: AP Images/Teh Eng Koon; p. 530: Bill Pugliano/Getty Images; p. 533: Bryan Smith/ Zuma Press/ Newscom; p. 534: ©2005 Men Can Stop Rape, Inc. Photo by Lotte Hansen. For more information about the MyStrength Campaign, visit www.MyStrength.org; p. 537: Courtesy of Kathy Valentine, CFA Institute; p. 549: Courtesy of Rachel Foltz, Ogilvy Public Relations Worldwide; p. 551: AP Images/M. Spencer Green.

Chapter 21

p. 555: Rick Wilking/Reuters; p. 558: Jason Hornick/Potomac News/ WpN; p. 559: Reprinted with permission of the Iowa State University Alumni Association and Visions magazine. Photo by Jim Heemstra; p. 562: AP Images/Sara D. Davis.

Chapter 22

p. 570: Marc Serota/Getty Images; p. 573: Jeff Vespa/WireImage for The Weinstein Company/Getty Images; p. 576: Russel Wong/Corbis; p. 582: Johannes Eisele/ dpa/Corbis; p. 586: Evan Agostini/ Getty Images; p. 587: Stephanie Kuykendal/Corbis.

PRACTICE TESTS MULTIPLE CHOICE

CHAPTER 1   WHAT IS PUBLIC RELATIONS?

1. Stakeholders in public relations are primarily referred to as
   a. stockholders.
   b. customers.
   c. publics.
   d. influentials.

2. The first step in any successful public relations campaign is
   a. an action plan.
   b. research.
   c. situation analysis.
   d. communication.

3. Which of the following is not a common term or reference found in definitions of public relations?
   a. deliberate
   b. serving public interest
   c. objective
   d. management function

4. Public relations practitioners write primarily for _____ audiences.
   a. segmented, targeted
   b. general-interest
   c. active (uses and gratification type)
   d. multicultural

5. Which of the following institutions is not usually associated with public information?
   a. social service agencies
   b. universities
   c. corporations
   d. government agencies

6. Which body established seven key courses for a typical college public relations curriculum?
   a. Public Relations Task Force
   b. Public Relations Society of America
   c. Integrated Communications Council
   d. Commission on Public Relations Education

7. *Publicist* would be most likely considered an "honorable" term in the
   a. entertainment business.
   b. corporate world.
   c. nonprofit sector.
   d. agency business.

8. FedEx's "Flight of the Penguins" and Virginia's "Smart Beginnings" are examples of public relations
   a. crises.
   b. advertisements.
   c. campaigns.
   d. fundraisers.

9. Which area contains the highest number of employed public relations professionals?
   a. nonprofit organizations/foundations
   b. public relations firms
   c. government (all levels)
   d. corporations (private and public)

10. The term *spin* was coined by
    a. Edward Bernays.
    b. William Safire.
    c. Ivy Lee.
    d. George Creel.

11. Which is not a correct "matching pair"?
    a. public relations/objective
    b. journalism/one-channel focus
    c. advertising/paid media
    d. marketing/consumers and sales

12. _____ is considered the highest job level in public relations.
    a. Supervisor
    b. Manager
    c. Director
    d. Executive

13. Which of the following is not a typical role/task for a public relations technician?
    a. organizing events
    b. strategic counseling
    c. writing brochures
    d. writing news releases

14. Which factor does not explain the salary gap between genders?
    a. number of years in the field
    b. technician duties versus managerial responsibilities
    c. lack of licensing measures
    d. women attempting to balance work and family

15. In economic terms, the public relations field is most extensively developed in
    a. Canada.
    b. Hong Kong.
    c. United States.
    d. Australia.

16. _____ is generally the lowest-paying salaried job sector in communications?
    a. Public relations
    b. World Wide Web
    c. Advertising
    d. Broadcasting

17. The dialogue among apparel and footwear manufacturers (e.g., Nike, Tommy Hilfiger) in the wake of negative publicity around sweatshop conditions resulted in the creation of the
    a. Ethics in Apparel Act.
    b. Fair Labor Association.
    c. Human Welfare Coalition.
    d. McCain-Feingold Act.

18. Which phase of the RACE acronym revolves around "execution"?
    a. communication
    b. evaluation
    c. action
    d. research

19. Public relations elements such as feedback, research, and communication are part of a cyclical process that eventually leads into
    a. program assessment and adjustment.
    b. symmetrical communication.
    c. issues management.
    d. image adjustment.

20. Which is not part of the public relations cycle?
    a. policy formation
    b. programming
    c. research and analysis
    d. networking

21. Generally, the public relations cycle notes that public relations is essentially a(n)
    a. middle ground or linking agent.
    b. input.
    c. end product.
    d. one-way facilitator.

22. The changing focus of public relations includes the long-standing (and increasingly outdated) notion that practitioners should primarily be trained as
    a. event planners.
    b. boundary spanners.
    c. journalists.
    d. marketing specialists.

23. Which is not considered an essential ability for a public relations practitioner?
    a. networking
    b. writing skill
    c. problem-solving
    d. business competence

24. According to the Commission on Public Relations Education, any PR curriculum should have five basic courses, one of which is
    a. issues and crisis management.
    b. campaigns.
    c. media and society.
    d. human resource management.

25. Cultural literacy implies many traits. _____ is not one of them.
    a. Shared frame of reference
    b. Being well educated in arts and humanities
    c. Well roundedness
    d. Linguistic/language knowledge

26. Which of the following is an accurate statement regarding the relationship between public relations and advertising?
    a. Advertising material is often dictated by media gatekeepers.
    b. Advertising is primarily addressed to broadcast audiences.
    c. Public relations is wider in scope.
    d. Advertising is usually less costly.

27. Which statement is not true with regard to internships?
    a. An internship is one of seven recommended college public relations courses.
    b. There is a strong correlation between paid internships and starting salaries in the field.
    c. Recent graduates are often hired full-time by their internship employers.
    d. Primarily, they provide managerial experience for undergraduates.

28. Since opening its economy to market capitalism, _____ is considered "the new frontier."
    a. the Soviet Union
    b. China
    c. Mexico
    d. Canada

29. According to a 2006 report, the median annual salary for recent graduates in public relations was
    a. $30,000.
    b. $25,000.
    c. $22,000.
    d. $35,000.

30. Which of the following is not one of the "four Ps" of marketing strategy?
    a. philanthropy
    b. promotion
    c. place
    d. product

CHAPTER 2   THE EVOLUTION OF PUBLIC RELATIONS

1. Who was the first person to coin the term *public relations counsel*?
   a. Edward Bernays
   b. Ivy Lee
   c. George Creel
   d. Amos Kendall

2. In 1900, Henry Ford obtained coverage of the Model T automobile by demonstrating it to a reporter from which newspaper?
   a. *Chicago Tribune*
   b. *Washington Post*
   c. *New York Times*
   d. *Detroit Tribune*

3. In reputation management, public relations personnel do not use research for
   a. environmental monitoring.
   b. networking and corporate ladder-enhancing.
   c. communication audits.
   d. social audits.

4. Which of the following is not an ancient instance of public relations?
   a. Julius Caesar publishing a book to further his ambitions
   b. Apostles spreading Christianity throughout the world
   c. Thomas Paine's star-making stunts
   d. the Rosetta Stone touting the pharaoh's accomplishments

5. The Boston Tea Party is an example of a
   a. publicity stunt.
   b. campaign.
   c. fundraiser.
   d. crisis management tactic.

6. This publicist/press agent introduced Tom Thumb and many other famed entertainment ventures.
   a. Thomas Paine
   b. Amos Kendall
   c. P.T. Barnum
   d. Edward Bernays

7. The Colorado Fuel & Iron Company strike, stemming from the Ludlow Massacre, resulted in which person hiring outside public relations counsel to help resolve the issue?
   a. John Rockefeller
   b. William Vanderbilt
   c. Andrew Carnegie
   d. George Creel

8. Which of the following is not an innovative, successful campaign launched by Edward Bernays?
   a. sculpture contests for Ivory Soap
   b. President Franklin Delano Roosevelt's fireside chats
   c. building a following for Ballet Russe during World War I
   d. Light's Golden Jubilee, a celebration of the 50th anniversary of the electric light bulb

9. This pioneering woman was considered the grande dame of fashion public relations.
   a. Leone Baxter
   b. Eleanor Lambert
   c. Doris Fleischman
   d. Jenny Lind

10. Relationship management builds specifically on which Grunig model of public relations?
    a. two-way symmetrical communication
    b. two-way asymmetrical communication
    c. public information
    d. press agentry and publicity

11. _____ was/were essentially a publicity release touting the Pharaoh's accomplishments, which provided the key to modern understanding of ancient Egyptian hieroglyphics.
    a. The Crusades
    b. The Rosetta Stone
    c. Stories of the Acropolis
    d. Stone tablets

12. The word *propaganda* dates back to
    a. the Civil War.
    b. the American Revolution.
    c. Pope Gregory XV in the seventeenth century.
    d. the Lutheran Reformation.

13. Which of the following is an incorrect observation with regard to public relations in the specified time period?
    a. The 1800s were marked by the press agentry model.
    b. The 1940s were an era of reform in the stock market and investor relations.
    c. The 1960s were marked by protests and rights issues.
    d. The 1920s featured a shift to the psychological and sociological effects of persuasion.

14. This country is considered the "Pacific birthplace" of public relations.
    a. the Philippines
    b. Thailand
    c. Hong Kong
    d. Japan

15. _____ authored the influential pamphlet *Common Sense*.
    a. Benjamin Franklin
    b. Amos Kendall
    c. Thomas Paine
    d. Edward Bernays

16. President Andrew Jackson greatly benefited from the counsel of
    a. George Creel.
    b. Theodore Roosevelt.
    c. Amos Kendall.
    d. Ivy Lee.

17. Which of the following is a reason for the influx of women working in public relations?
    a. Women find public relations a more challenging environment than a field such as newspaper work.
    b. A woman can start a public relations firm with relatively little capital.
    c. Women are more savvy than men in persuasion techniques.
    d. Women are harder to convince than men.

18. Which of the following is one of Ivy Lee's important contributions to public relations?
    a. product positioning
    b. discouraging top executives from public comment
    c. maintaining cautious communication with news media
    d. emphasizing the necessity of humanizing business

19. Before the collapse of the Soviet Union in 1991, most public relations was conducted by
    a. corporations.
    b. the government.
    c. PR and advertising agencies.
    d. journalists.

20. The promotion of such figures as Tom Thumb and Jenny Lind was based, in large part, on first inviting key opinion leaders to their performances. In public relations, this technique is called
    a. card stacking.
    b. two-step flow.
    c. third-party endorsement.
    d. positioning.

21. _____ advocated that public relations was a management function, and that a company's performance should dictate public approval.
    a. Arthur W. Page
    b. Elmer Davis
    c. George Creel
    d. James Grunig

22. _____ assembled a group of premier communicators that provided a profound public relations boost to American efforts in World War I.
    a. Edward Bernays
    b. George Creel
    c. Elmer Davis
    d. Burson Marsteller

23. Sites such as YouTube and MySpace are often referred to as
    a. wikis.
    b. social media.
    c. search engines.
    d. mediated channels.

24. _____, organized in Boston with Harvard College as its most prestigious client, was the first publicity firm.
    a. Hill & Knowlton
    b. Parker & Lee
    c. Ketchum
    d. The Publicity Bureau

25. The term _____ describes the way an organizational environment affects a female's rise to top management.
    a. compensatory symmetry
    b. gender deconstruction
    c. structionalist perspective
    d. gendering

26. Which statement is not indicative of the Westinghouse corporation in the 1880s?
    a. launched a campaign against Thomas Edison's notion of direct current
    b. avoided advocacy strategies in lieu of symmetrical dialogue
    c. created the first known in-house publicity department in the U.S.
    d. worked to make alternating current the standard in the U.S.

27. Theodore Roosevelt was the first president to make extensive use of what communication device?
    a. propaganda
    b. fireside chats
    c. sound bites
    d. press conferences

28. _____ is considered the father of public relations research.
    a. Rex Harlow
    b. Arthur W. Page
    c. Ivy Lee
    d. Edward Bernays

29. Which item is not associated with the two-way asymmetric model of public relations?
a. balanced effects
b. persuasion
c. marketing and advertising departments in competitive businesses
d. Edward Bernays

30. Which of the following does not describe the Ludlow Massacre?
a. happened during a strike of Colorado fuel and iron plant workers
b. involved Ivy Lee counseling John Rockefeller, Sr.
c. situation was partially resolved through issue of bulletins to key opinion leaders
d. resulted in a famous book titled *The Engineering of Consent*

CHAPTER 3   ETHICS AND PROFESSIONALISM

1. _____ is a core value stipulated by PRSA.
   a. Advocacy
   b. Collaboration
   c. Objectivity
   d. Philanthropy

2. Which of the following is not part of PRSA's accreditation process?
   a. designation of "APR" for those who succeed
   b. at least five years' experience in public relations
   c. passing a rigorous written exam, among other steps
   d. being licensed in public relations.

3. Celebrities appearing on talk shows raise an issue of
   a. absolutism.
   b. transparency.
   c. propaganda.
   d. symbolism.

4. Which of the following is not a guideline established by IPRA and other global organizations to reduce "pay for play" in the world's media?
   a. News material should appear as a result of the news judgment of journalists and editors, not as a result of payment or other inducements.
   b. Paid material should be clearly identified as advertising, sponsorship, or promotion.
   c. No journalist or media representative should ever suggest that news coverage will appear for any reason other than its merit.
   d. Media should refrain from instituting stifling written policies regarding receipts of gifts or discounted products/services.

5. _____ best describes the situation with commentator Armstrong Williams and the No Child Left Behind Act.
   a. Press agentry
   b. Structionalist perspective
   c. Pay for play
   d. Transparency

6. The Golden Rule says
   a. to love your neighbor as yourself.
   b. right is always right.
   c. to trust your first instincts.
   d. the customer is always right.

7. Special/corporate interest groups are most likely to fund
   a. ethical councils.
   b. grassroots lobbyists.
   c. front groups.
   d. nonprofit initiatives.

8. Nearly half of Arabic-language journalists are more likely to use a news release if it is accompanied by a(n)
   a. English version.
   b. gift.
   c. front group.
   d. video.

9. Which is not a quality exhibited by a professional?
   a. a sense of independence
   b. manifest concern for the competence and honor of the profession as a whole
   c. consistently outperforming competitors within an ethical construct
   d. a higher loyalty to the standards of the profession than to their employer

10. _____ is the Kantian virtue in which every decision is either "right" or "wrong."
   a. Existentialism
   b. Absolutism
   c. Situationalism
   d. Post-constructivism

11. The willingness to represent issues or products that go against your own beliefs and moral code would suggest a(n) _____ mentality.
   a. management
   b. absolutist
   c. technician
   d. situationalist

12. Decisions based on what would cause the least harm or the most good are considered
   a. situationalist.
   b. Marxist.
   c. absolutist.
   d. unilateral.

13. Most professional membership groups believe that the primary purpose of establishing codes of ethics is
   a. enforcement.
   b. punitive.
   c. education and information.
   d. for public relations purposes.

14. Which of the following is a code of good practice regarding video releases?
    a. Intentionally false and misleading information is acceptable in dire circumstances.
    b. The sponsor of the VNR should not be identified because of conflict of interest issues.
    c. The sponsor must specifically state why the VNR is a proper fit for the targeted media outlet.
    d. Persons interviewed in the VNR must be accurately identified by name, title and affiliation.

15. The best known think tank for public relations research is
    a. the Public Relations Society of America.
    b. the International Association of Business Communicators.
    c. the Institute for Public Relations.
    d. the Strategic Communications Commission.

16. The major goal for public relations accreditation is to
    a. license potential practitioners.
    b. increase membership into the PR field.
    c. improve standards and professionalism.
    d. eliminate the need for punitive measures for code violators.

17. "Grassroots" campaigns to achieve public relations goals (e.g., a counter group to a "save the environment" organization) are often undertaken by
    a. government operatives.
    b. front groups.
    c. socially aware media outlets.
    d. clandestine advocacy groups.

18. Which of the following is not a requirement for accreditation by the PRSA?
    a. at least five years of professional experience in public relations or teaching
    b. completion of a preview course
    c. completion of a "readiness" questionnaire
    d. portfolio submission to a panel of professional peers

19. The 2006 report by the Commission on Public Relations Education recommended which of the following for public relations majors?
    a. a strong background in marketing
    b. that coursework in public relations should comprise 25–40 percent of all undergraduate hours
    c. at least one-third of public relations coursework should focus on topics specified by the Commission
    d. experience in student or local mass media outlets

20. Whether a bribe is intended or not, the sending of gifts to media representatives is almost always considered
    a. unavoidable.
    b. a conflict of interest.
    c. a last-ditch measure.
    d. an expectation of the media.

21. _____ is particularly ambiguous with regard to ethics.
    a. Nonprofit public relations
    b. Automotive enthusiast journalism
    c. The PRSA accreditation program
    d. Sponsorship of the codes

22. Magazines serving a particular industry or a specific area such as home decorating or bridal fashions are increasingly blurring the line between
    a. objectivity and persuasion.
    b. news features and advertisements.
    c. ethics and legal matters.
    d. journalists and bloggers.

23. Which tactic did Coca-Cola Company employ in 2006 to engage employees about its values and culture?
    a. hold a National Taste Challenge
    b. increase stock options and ownership plans
    c. support multilingual gatekeeper campaigns
    d. Blog Fest

24. Which is a hallmark of a public relations professional?
    a. a sense of dependence
    b. a sense of responsibility to stockholders
    c. a concern for integrity of the profession
    d. a high loyalty to the employer of the moment

25. Which of the following is a "careerist" value?
    a. job security
    b. intrinsic satisfaction
    c. serving the public interest
    d. ethical values

26. The largest national public relations organization in the world is the
    a. Public Relations Society of America.
    b. International Association of Business Communicators.
    c. American Marketing Association.
    d. Institute for Public Relations.

27. _____ were the device used to communicate false notions of happy customers during a staged RV trip to Wal-Mart stores across the United States.
    a. Blogs
    b. News releases
    c. Videos
    d. Public service announcements

28. Which value is the least important to public relations practitioners, according to Grunig and Hunt?
    a. job security
    b. prestige in the organization
    c. the public interest
    d. salary level

29. The social justice approach posits that everyone should be treated
    a. based on their social standing.
    b. equally.
    c. in a utilitarian fashion.
    d. well, without government interference.

30. What is the most practical consideration facing a public relations specialist?
    a. fundraising
    b. dealings with the news media
    c. hierarchical and organizational issues
    d. internal communications

CHAPTER 4   PUBLIC RELATIONS DEPARTMENTS AND FIRMS

1. Which figure most closely resembles a typical return on investment (ROI) for public relations work?
   a. 82 percent
   b. 120 percent
   c. 184 percent
   d. 235 percent

2. The dominant coalition perspective of public relations gives credence to the practitioner's
   a. personal interests.
   b. autonomy and authority.
   c. need to collaborate and bond.
   d. prioritizing techniques.

3. The most admired *Fortune* 500 companies think of public relations as more of a(n)
   a. subservient entity to marketing divisions.
   b. external function, primarily for media relations.
   c. potential revenue source.
   d. strategic management tool.

4. Public relations is primarily considered which type of function in a typical organization?
   a. line
   b. concurring authority
   c. staff
   d. measurement

5. Which case study would PR practitioners most likely describe as compulsory-advisory?
   a. Tylenol/Johnson & Johnson
   b. Exxon Valdez
   c. Enron
   d. Norfolk Southern Railroad

6. Which public is primarily targeted by marketing and advertising professionals?
   a. legislators
   b. customers
   c. media
   d. actives/influentials

7. Which knowledge set is not required for a manager of a public relations department?
   a. strategic and operational knowledge
   b. human resource management
   c. negotiation knowledge
   d. persuasion knowledge

8. Which public relations activity is most frequently outsourced?
   a. writing and communications
   b. publicity
   c. strategy and planning
   d. event planning

9. Which department/group is likely to experience friction with public relations?
   a. accounting
   b. issues management team
   c. human resources
   d. line managers

10. Who should be responsible for employee communications?
    a. human resources
    b. administrative assistants for CEOs/VPs
    c. public relations
    d. legal staff with requisite outsourcing to specialized firms

11. A company chairman or CEO would usually be considered part of the
    a. C-Suite.
    b. technical leadership.
    c. editorial process.
    d. media/speechwriting team.

12. Which of the following is not a reason why large holding companies find the acquisition of public relations firms so attractive?
    a. to integrate various communication disciplines into "total communication networks"
    b. nonprofit tax write-offs and other money shelters
    c. It's an attractive business investment.
    d. to increase the value of the company portfolio

13. Which method is one of the most common used by public relations firms to charge for their services?
    a. per diem
    b. weekly plus overhead/rights fees
    c. retainer fee
    d. licensing fee

14. Fleishman-Hillard resigned from this account after deciding that the firm could not ethically defend the client's position.
    a. Ford
    b. Firestone
    c. Enron
    d. Johnson & Johnson

15. A(n) _____ level of influence would best describe a partnership (or potential conflict) with the legal department.
    a. advisory
    b. compulsory-advisory
    c. concurring authority
    d. command authority

16. Grunig's IABC Foundation research study *Excellence in Public Relations and Communication Management* notes that
    a. public relations only increases costs for litigation regulation and legislation.
    b. public relations helps the organization make money by cultivating relationships.
    c. persuasive communication is the utopian model.
    d. public relations should replace marketing and advertising as financial liaisons for the company.

17. Which component was not part of Fleishman-Hillard's outreach program to inner-city children afflicted with asthma?
    a. building support and cooperation with school principals and parent coordinators
    b. developing educational brochures and posters
    c. lobbying Congress for legislation for asthma research
    d. having medical specialists visit schools to diagnose and counsel

18. According to a recent study, the average budget for corporate communications/public relations in *Fortune* 500 was
    a. $2.2 million.
    b. $5 million.
    c. $8.5 million.
    d. $15.5 million.

19. In _____ organizations, the public relations department has high authority and power and is part of the "dominant coalition."
    a. compulsory-advisory
    b. streamlined
    c. mixed motives
    d. mixed organic/mechanical

20. Which of the following is not a key element of research knowledge?
    a. performing environmental scanning
    b. determining public reactions to your organization
    c. conducting evaluation
    d. using attitude theory

21. Many practitioners self-select technician roles because they
    a. lack knowledge in research, environmental scanning, problem-solving, and management.
    b. already have a working relationship with media.
    c. lack ability to forge relationships.
    d. wish to avoid office politics.

22. Which of the following is not a core area of specialized expertise noted by the *Excellence in Public Relations and Communication Management* study?
    a. strategic and operational management knowledge
    b. negotiation knowledge
    c. media relations knowledge
    d. persuasion knowledge

23. When organizational policy requires that line managers must act on the advice of appropriate staff experts before deciding on a strategy, it is referred to as a(n)
    a. compulsory-advisory concept.
    b. concurring authority concept.
    c. command authority concept.
    d. autonomous concept.

24. The standard industry practice is to bill clients
    a. at least triple a person's salary.
    b. a going industry rate mandated by IABC.
    c. at least double a person's salary.
    d. commensurate with account managers in the current local marketplace.

25. A common approach to engage the services of a public relations firm is to issue a
    a. request for proposal.
    b. position paper.
    c. press release.
    d. concurring authority.

26. The practice of purchasing expert communication services from outside the organization is referred to as
    a. boundary spanning.
    b. outsourcing.
    c. encroachment.
    d. environmental scanning.

27. Until the 1970s, the largest public relations firms were independently owned by
    a. founders.
    b. families.
    c. government contractors.
    d. marketing companies.

28. The person in charge of one major account or several smaller ones is an
    a. account executive.
    b. account manager.
    c. account supervisor.
    d. account liaison.

29. The average billable rate (per hour) across all public relations firm sizes and billable titles is
    a. $100.
    b. $153.
    c. $213.
    d. $307.

30. _____ is the specialty area that is performed by in-house departments more than any other.
    a. Media relations
    b. Employee communications
    c. Special events
    d. Brand communication

CHAPTER 5 RESEARCH

1. In basic terms, research is a form of
   a. listening.
   b. networking.
   c. planning.
   d. trial and error.

2. An estimated 90 percent of organizational crises are caused by
   a. unexpected "natural disasters."
   b. internal operational problems.
   c. significant economic and/or social fluctuations among key publics.
   d. a lack of an adequate crisis plan.

3. The content analysis research technique essentially revolves around
   a. counting and categorizing.
   b. copy testing.
   c. piggybacking.
   d. database management.

4. A focus group should be led by a
   a. CEO or other lead administrator.
   b. public relations representative from the company wanting research.
   c. trained moderator.
   d. group consensus.

5. What type of survey questions are best for examining respondents' perceptions and attitudes?
   a. yes-no
   b. open-ended
   c. Likert
   d. true-false

6. Which technique best describes a piggyback survey, i.e., buying questions in a national survey?
   a. sample
   b. omnibus
   c. quota
   d. benchmarking

7. This research technique stems from observation.
   a. sampling
   b. piggybacking
   c. ethnography
   d. content analysis

8. Which of the following does not indicate a nonprobability survey?
   a. not random
   b. mall intercept survey
   c. survey of those outside a record store
   d. phone book or other "list" survey

9. A sample of 1,500 people will have approximately a _____ margin for error.
   a. 3 percent
   b. 6 percent
   c. 1 percent
   d. 10 percent

10. Which of the following is not a guideline for questionnaire construction?
    a. State the objectives of the survey.
    b. Use closed-ended answers.
    c. Edit out leading questions.
    d. Avoid using/allowing space for open-ended comments.

11. Which of the following is not a perceived advantage of using a piggyback survey?
    a. It's cheaper than sending out your own survey.
    b. A credible firm will offer expertise in conducting surveys.
    c. It provides a wide snapshot or breadth of public opinion.
    d. It allows potential affiliations with national organizations such as Gallup and Roper.

12. Which of the following is not indicative of quantitative research?
    a. a focus group
    b. often expensive and complicated
    c. gives a greater ability to generalize to large populations
    d. a survey

13. _____ was not a reinforcement strategy utilized by the New Hampshire paper industry in the aftermath of some bad press.
    a. Worker safety
    b. Employment issues
    c. Environmental responsibility
    d. Overhauling their current industry efforts

14. Archival research can explain the following, except
    a. the success of the product or service in the past.
    b. the analysis of what geographical areas provide the most sales.
    c. the profile of the typical customer who buys the product or uses the service.
    d. the "static" inventories of organizational materials.

15. Highly charged words that elicit an emotional reaction from the survey respondent are often part of _____ research.
    a. advocacy
    b. objective
    c. government
    d. quota sampling

16. Content analysis refers to which technique?
    a. concept testing
    b. benchmarking
    c. searching/counting key words or concepts
    d. readability formulas

17. Another term for an intercept interview is
    a. piggyback interview.
    b. probability sample.
    c. convenience poll.
    d. stealth lobbying.

18. In _____, people are carefully selected for their expertise or influence.
    a. benchmarking
    b. copy testing
    c. probability sampling
    d. purposive interviewing

19. Which of the following is not an advantage of a telephone survey?
    a. immediate feedback
    b. more personal form of communication
    c. access to phone numbers
    d. high response rate

20. Copy testing involves asking representatives of the target audience to
    a. read or view materials in draft form.
    b. review materials after production.
    c. assist in editing existing materials.
    d. take surveys in an informal setting.

21. In a probability sample, members of the targeted audience have
    a. a say in survey administration.
    b. an equal chance of being selected for the survey.
    c. been chosen in a quota system.
    d. proven more likely to participate in the research.

22. The most precise random sampling is usually done from
    a. lists that give the names of everyone in the targeted audience.
    b. urban areas.
    c. Fortune 500 companies.
    d. telephone books.

23. Advocacy research is sometimes problematic because of
    a. biased wording on questionnaires.
    b. economic considerations.
    c. a lack of objectivity and symmetry.
    d. the political affiliations of agencies administering surveys.

24. This technique generally provides the least amount of information regarding respondents' perceptions and attitudes.
    a. Likert scale
    b. yes-no survey questions
    c. focus group
    d. interview

25. Courtesy bias usually accompanies a _____.
    a. propaganda position
    b. politically correct response
    c. euphemistic tendency
    d. knee-jerk reaction

26. _____ is not a major source for conducting a strong academic literature review.
    a. Lexis-Nexis
    b. InfoTrac
    c. Factiva
    d. Google

27. If one wanted to find census information about people living in Boston, which of the following would be the best source?
    a. the *Statistical Abstract of the United States*
    b. a Boston telephone book
    c. Standard & Poor's Index
    d. the Boston Chamber of Commerce

28. Drawing a random sample to match the characteristics of the audience is known as
    a. benchmarking.
    b. copy testing.
    c. quota sampling.
    d. demographic testing.

29. In a recent survey of PR practitioners, _____ were cited as the most utilized research technique.
    a. surveys
    b. focus groups
    c. interviews
    d. literature/database reviews

30. Which of the following is not a biased question?
    a. Do you believe that college bookstores should stop charging excessive prices for textbooks?
    b. Do you believe that college bookstores should charge needy students on financial aid less money for texts?
    c. Do you believe college bookstores should sell text to students at cost?
    d. Do you believe college bookstores gouge students for textbooks?

CHAPTER 6   PROGRAM PLANNING

1. Objectives are usually stated in terms of
   a. program outcomes.
   b. inputs.
   c. tactics.
   d. motivation.

2. The lion's share of any public relations budget is earmarked for what particular area?
   a. special events
   b. media relations
   c. internal and retention incentives/issues
   d. staff and administrative time

3. Which characteristic is not indicative of a Gantt chart?
   a. a two-sided matrix
   b. a scheduling chart
   c. used often in budgeting situations
   d. can be formatted through Excel and other programs

4. Which of the following situations rarely requires a public relations campaign?
   a. a remedial program
   b. a cyclical project
   c. a one-time project
   d. a reinforcement program

5. _____ objectives are bottom-line oriented and based on clearly measurable results that can be quantified.
   a. Motivational
   b. Informational
   c. Strategic
   d. Tactical

6. Which of the following publics would not be a traditional target for the Tyson Foods "Fight Against Hunger" campaign?
   a. grocery retailers
   b. key business and civic leaders
   c. company team members throughout the country
   d. media outlets

7. The best approach to public relations planning is
   a. strategic and systematic.
   b. cost-effective and participatory.
   c. straightforward and tactical.
   d. asymmetrical and persuasive.

8. Which of the following was not one of the reasons for aiming the Sunkist "Take a Stand" program primarily at women?
   a. because of family ties/considerations
   b. because women are a keen public with regard to business media
   c. because women make most purchasing decisions
   d. because women look at charitable activities of organizations during decision-making process

9. Which of the following is generally not a major component of the public relations planning process?
   a. calendar/timetable
   b. development of strategies and tactics
   c. situation analysis
   d. development of media kits

10. According to the Amazon.com Thought-Process Model, which element emphasizes the idea that you want the audience to remember, e.g., the brand or action?
    a. media vehicle
    b. execution
    c. headline/thought bubble
    d. audience/objectives/strategies

11. Counting media impressions is one way to quantify which type of objective?
    a. informational
    b. motivational
    c. one-time
    d. strategic

12. An organization uses a reinforcement public relations program
    a. to clarify its expectations and ideals.
    b. to reaffirm its problems.
    c. to remind media of its honors.
    d. in an ongoing effort to preserve its reputation.

13. A strategy statement
    a. describes a tactical response.
    b. measures objectives.
    c. describes how an objective will be achieved.
    d. is a prerequisite for a Gantt chart.

14. The specific, sequential activities that put strategies into operation and help achieve stated objectives are known as
    a. audits.
    b. tactics.
    c. content analyses.
    d. strategies.

15. Which of the following is not a factor in establishing a calendar and timetable for a program?
    a. the timing of a campaign
    b. the scheduling of tactics
    c. calendar compilation
    d. financial considerations

16. Which aspect below was not part of India's PR campaign to increase condom use?
    a. partnerships and endorsements
    b. meetings with editorial boards of major publications
    c. use of new media
    d. abstinence appeals

17. A budget usually is divided into two categories: _____ and _____ .
    a. media, non-media
    b. staff time, out-of-pocket expenses
    c. debits, expenses
    d. pre-campaign, post-campaign

18. To make sure they accomplish their purpose, objectives must be all of the following, EXCEPT
    a. addressed in the planning stage.
    b. measurable.
    c. evaluated after the campaign.
    d. motivational in nature.

19. Loss of market share and declining sales would usually require a
    a. reinforcement campaign.
    b. one-time project.
    c. remedial campaign.
    d. justification strategy.

20. A stated objective should be evaluated using which of the following questions?
    a. Does it alleviate the situation?
    b. Is it far-reaching?
    c. Can success be measured in meaningful terms?
    d. Is it profitable or bottom-line oriented?

21. Campaigns for crops or for tax software programs likely utilize a
    a. remedial approach.
    b. reinforcement approach.
    c. psychographic approach.
    d. seasonal approach.

22. Which of the following was not a stated objective of the Pokemon campaign?
    a. Secure at least 500 stories in key media outlets.
    b. Saturate the fast-food and cable cartoon markets.
    c. Engage core customers and drive them to the Web site.
    d. Reinforce brand through trade media.

23. What is the first step in formulating a public relations program?
    a. Research the facts.
    b. Understand the situation.
    c. Set objectives.
    d. Define the audience.

24. Which of the following is a good example of an informational objective?
    a. Increase attendance at this year's concert by 50 percent.
    b. Increase public awareness of this year's concert series.
    c. Increase Web site hits.
    d. Increase volume of toll-free phone calls.

25. Which of the following is not one of Judith Rich's recommendations for achieving creativity?
    a. Encourage spontaneity and playfulness.
    b. Let people dream big.
    c. Creativity should be a challenge not a chore.
    d. Product launches are generally overrated and not well received.

26. According to the management by objective perspective, photographs, graphs, films and artwork are
    a. qualitative communication.
    b. reinforcement campaigns.
    c. nonverbal support.
    d. a Gantt chart.

27. A(n) _____ is a somewhat broad statement describing how an objective is to be achieved.
    a. demographic
    b. evaluation
    c. strategy
    d. situation

28. Which of the following is not usually considered an "out-of-pocket" budget expense?
    a. salaries
    b. video news releases
    c. media kits
    d. transportation

29. For campaigns of at least $100,000, _____ percent is typically reserved for salaries and administrative fees.
    a. 30
    b. 50
    c. 70
    d. 90

30. It is good practice to allocate about 10 percent of a public relations budget to
    a. program inputs.
    b. contingencies or unexpected costs.
    c. interns.
    d. media relations initiatives.

CHAPTER 7   COMMUNICATION

1. Changing someone's overt behavior
   a. is the first objective of a communicator.
   b. depends primarily on message exposure.
   c. is the most difficult and final objective of a communicator.
   d. is less important than message acceptance.

2. Which of the following is not a correct pairing of media category and example?
   a. direct mail/public media
   b. World Wide Web/interactive media
   c. brochure/controlled media
   d. media/public media

3. In the symmetrical model, what is the principal objective of public relations?
   a. persuasion
   b. bottom line
   c. publicity and exposure
   d. mutual understanding

4. Which of the following is not one of the basic elements of Schram's communication model?
   a. encoder
   b. channel
   c. feedback
   d. salience/meaning

5. Which of the following would not be considered a triggering event?
   a. a natural disaster
   b. the purchase of an automobile
   c. launching a new product
   d. the announcement of a book by a popular author

6. When corporations invest considerable time and money to make their names and logos a symbol for quality and service, it is called
   a. copyright.
   b. recall.
   c. branding.
   d. networking.

7. Who is the famed author of *Diffusions of Innovation*?
   a. Sigmund Freud
   b. James Grunig
   c. Everett Rogers
   d. Philip Kotler

8. Which of the following is a goal of the communication process?
   a. transfer of power
   b. nurturing
   c. persuasion
   d. setting objectives

9. _____ is a technique in which one begins a message with a statement that reflects audience values and dispositions.
   a. Triggering
   b. Channeling
   c. Uses and gratification
   d. Sleeper effect

10. Which of the following is one of the outside variables that helps to determine Grunig's objectives for communicators?
    a. predispositions to the message
    b. feasibility of objectives
    c. perceptions of the message
    d. educational context

11. The most effective two-way communication is
    a. email.
    b. teacher–student interaction.
    c. two people talking to each other.
    d. parent–child interaction.

12. The basic premise for the uses and gratification perspective is that the communication process is
    a. passive.
    b. not need-based.
    c. interactive.
    d. one-way.

13. Style and creativity are most necessary for _____ audiences.
    a. active
    b. dissonant
    c. younger
    d. passive

14. Audience attention is generally lower at the
    a. middle of the message.
    b. crux of the message.
    c. beginning of the message.
    d. start of the program.

15. Readability formulas are generally measured by
    a. average sentence length and number of one-syllable words per 100 words.
    b. outside firms.
    c. test groups of randomly selected students.
    d. audience makeup.

16. An "AREMO-4196 with a 4U industrial rack-mount chassis" means little or nothing to the average reader, and is considered
    a. euphemistic.
    b. politically correct.
    c. jargon.
    d. clichés.

17. The sleeper effect refers to
    a. a decreased tendency over time to reject material presented by an untrustworthy source.
    b. a spiral of silence.
    c. remnants of a poor campaign.
    d. a lack of fresh objectives.

18. A term less offensive than the one that represents reality is a
    a. jargon.
    b. cliche.
    c. salvo.
    d. euphemism.

19. Cognitive dissonance theory suggests that a person will not believe a message that is
    a. incongruent with others on the bandwagon.
    b. politically motivated.
    c. contrary to their dispositions.
    d. not easily understood.

20. A low-involvement audience will not respond to
    a. details and logical argument.
    b. attractive spokespersons.
    c. humor.
    d. a multiplicity of arguments.

21. According to Everett Rogers, author of *Diffusion of Innovation*, _____ is the degree to which an innovation is perceived as being consistent with existing values of potential adopters.
    a. relative advantage
    b. uses and gratification
    c. compatibility
    d. trialability

22. According to Rogers, those most likely to be last in adopting ideas are known as
    a. laggards.
    b. early majority.
    c. innovators.
    d. compatibles.

23. _____ is the least effective form of communication for generating audience feedback.
    a. A focus group
    b. A small group
    c. Mass media
    d. A symposium

24. Print media relies predominantly on
    a. sight.
    b. feedback.
    c. touch.
    d. emotion.

25. Word of mouth campaigns are often controversial for their
    a. lack of research.
    b. reliance on new media techniques.
    c. political overtones.
    d. stealth nature.

26. _____ are an essential tool to reach active information-seeking individuals.
    a. Reality programs
    b. Catchy slogans and posters
    c. Design programs
    d. Booths at trade shows

27. The natural tendency for a message to dissipate (lose information) is called
    a. transfer.
    b. disassociation.
    c. message entropy.
    d. sleeper effect.

28. _____ are the first to buy new products, most notably first-generation electronic devices such as the new iPhone.
    a. Laggards
    b. Influentials
    c. Early adopters
    d. Opinion leaders

29. Which of the following is not a common cliché?
    a. unique
    b. objective
    c. integrated
    d. sophisticated

30. Which of the following is not a characteristic of the Decision-Making Unit?
    a. competitive advantage
    b. socioeconomic characteristics
    c. personality variables
    d. communication behavior

CHAPTER 8   EVALUATION

1. Which method below is not a widely used for evaluating public relations efforts?
   a. measurement of production
   b. strategies and tactics
   c. message exposure
   d. audience attitudes

2. Which of the following is the most advanced level of evaluation?
   a. audience awareness, comprehension, and retention of the message
   b. compilations of message distribution and media placement
   c. measurement of changes in attitudes, opinions, and behavior
   d. measuring value of secondary and ancillary research materials

3. An assessment of an organization's entire communication program is called a
   a. communication audit.
   b. message audit.
   c. benchmark.
   d. systematic tracker.

4. _____ is a measurement of audience attitudes before, during and after a public relations campaign.
   a. Copy testing
   b. A baseline study
   c. Channeling
   d. A media impression

5. Which of the following is not indicative of advertising equivalency?
   a. It is somewhat suspect, and there's a rapid decline in the practice.
   b. The technique reinforces the opinion of many media gatekeepers that all news releases are just attempts to get free advertising.
   c. It is a longstanding barometer used by many organizations to measure media success.
   d. It is a more important and viable practice for nonprofit organizations than for corporations.

6. Which of the following is not an advantage of systematic tracking and content analysis of news clippings?
   a. The continuing, regular feedback helps determine whether an organization's publicity efforts are paying off in terms of placements and mention of key messages.
   b. It allows for categorization so that practitioners and/or editors can shift focus depending on the respective media coverage of said categories.
   c. It enables benchmarking before and after a campaign.
   d. It provides a viable alternative to primary research.

7. The second level of public relations evaluation determines
   a. the number of attendees at an event.
   b. advertising equivalency.
   c. the cost of reaching each audience member.
   d. audience awareness and understanding of the message.

8. A(n) _____ is an approach to pretesting commonly used in product marketing.
   a. pilot test
   b. organizational audit
   c. intercept survey
   d. split-messaging

9. Day-after recall measures
   a. Web site hits.
   b. purchasing intent.
   c. audience awareness and comprehension.
   d. semantic issues/barriers.

10. Which of the following methods is not used to evaluate a company newsletter or magazine?
    a. content analysis
    b. readership interest surveys
    c. application of readability formulas
    d. use of ethics councils

11. _____ is the measurement of results against established objectives set during the planning process.
    a. Evaluation
    b. Channeling
    c. Situation analysis
    d. Copy testing

12. Motivational objectives are more difficult to accomplish because
    a. it is difficult to calculate attendance figures.
    b. other variables may intervene.
    c. they lack the clarity of informational objectives.
    d. there is high competition for available dollars.

13. Of the four major components of a public relations campaign, which usually receives about 5 percent of the overall budget?
    a. research
    b. action plan
    c. communication
    d. evaluation

14. By being involved in an organization's strategic plan, public relations can have a broader role and can set objectives that are clearly linked to
    a. sales.
    b. demographics.
    c. communication audits.
    d. media inquiries/needs.

15. The most widely practiced (and often least reliable) form of evaluating public relations programs is
    a. the longitudinal study.
    b. the compilation of press clippings and radio-television mentions.
    c. attendance figures.
    d. the benchmarking study.

16. A 16-inch article in a trade magazine that charges $300 per column inch in advertising would be worth $4,800 in which particular evaluation approach?
    a. media impressions
    b. advertising equivalency
    c. cost-per-person
    d. content analysis

17. Computer software and databases make it possible for _____ to evaluate media placements using several variables.
    a. advertising equivalency
    b. systematic tracking
    c. media impressions
    d. split-messaging

18. Benchmarking is a measurement of
    a. audience attitudes and opinions.
    b. media impressions.
    c. advertising equivalency.
    d. communication devices.

19. _____ measure(s) the number of people who have been exposed to a message.
    a. Advertising equivalency
    b. Media impressions
    c. Systematic tracking
    d. Benchmarking

20. What two variables are used to calculate cost-per-thousand?
    a. total media impressions and potential readership
    b. media outlets and advertising equivalency
    c. audience attendance and overall event costs
    d. total media impressions and cost of the publicity of the program

21. Pilot testing is a variation of
    a. perception analysis.
    b. copy testing.
    c. pretesting.
    d. split-messaging.

22. The most common method for evaluating a meeting is
    a. benchmarking.
    b. day-after recall.
    c. an evaluation form.
    d. brainstorming.

23. Which of the following is used to evaluate newsletters and brochures?
    a. sales
    b. readership recall of articles
    c. Web compatibility
    d. internal reward structures

24. A readership interest survey becomes more valuable when it is compared with the
    a. audience audit.
    b. characteristics of target audience.
    c. content analysis of a publication.
    d. circulation figures of a publication.

25. This measurement technique tests multiple appeals among different audiences and is especially effective in direct mail campaigns.
    a. pilot testing
    b. split-messaging
    c. day-after recall
    d. benchmarking

26. Before any public relations program can be properly evaluated, it must have a clearly established set of
    a. media guidelines.
    b. measurable objectives.
    c. investment priorities.
    d. ethical/professional standards.

27. Which of the following has been credited for the progress in systematic evaluation of public relations campaigns?
    a. more communication expertise by public relations personnel
    b. more sophisticated computer programs
    c. larger budgets for research
    d. higher management taking more burden for meaningful results

28. Systematic tracking results in
    a. immediate media acceptance of audience behavior.
    b. market penetration of information.
    c. instant analysis of a speech.
    d. real-time audience acceptance of the message.

29. Generally, the first survey in a baseline study (the pre-test) measures the
    a. status quo.
    b. motivational objectives.
    c. market penetration of an audience.
    d. more general audience.

30. According to the Ketchum Public Relations Effectiveness Yardstick, _____ is not an advanced form of measurement.
    a. behavior change
    b. attitude change
    c. message comprehension
    d. opinion change

CHAPTER 9   PUBLIC OPINION AND PERSUASION

1. Products and services benefit from favorable statements by experts; this is known as
   a. propaganda.
   b. transfer.
   c. third-party endorsement.
   d. two-step flow.

2. Aristotle's notion of *pathos* equates to
   a. source credibility.
   b. an emotional appeal.
   c. a logical argument.
   d. feedback.

3. The attempt to classify people according to their lifestyle, attitudes, and beliefs is known as
   a. demographics.
   b. positioning.
   c. psychographics.
   d. framing.

4. The propaganda technique that implies or directly states that everyone wants a product or that an idea has overwhelming support is the _____ technique.
   a. testimonial
   b. card stacking
   c. bandwagon
   d. transfer

5. The context through which messages are interpreted is known as
   a. self-perception.
   b. self-selection.
   c. propaganda.
   d. channeling.

6. Which of the following is not a perceived advantage of using celebrity endorsers?
   a. saturation
   b. charisma
   c. awareness
   d. transfer

7. Maslow's hierarchy of needs explains why some public information campaigns have difficulty getting the message across to _____ , the people classified at the lower end of the VALS lifestyle categories.
   a. belongers
   b. self-actualizers
   c. early adopters
   d. survivors/sustainers

8. Based on the ideas of _____ , public relations practitioners sometimes use escalation strategies—promoting and generating controversy to gain positive attention in the marketplace of ideas.
   a. cultivation analysis
   b. conflict theory
   c. chaos theory
   d. agenda setting

9. The persuasion technique that sets a positive tone at the start of a conversation or speech is known as
   a. yes-yes.
   b. structured choice.
   c. response or mobilization.
   d. asking for more/settling for less.

10. Opinion is not easily changed when _____ is involved.
    a. propaganda
    b. the government
    c. the presence of opinion leaders
    d. self-interest

11. What are the two reasons for the profound influence of public-opinion momentum?
    a. increased media scrutiny; increasingly active audience
    b. accuracy of polling procedures; more value placed on audience ideas
    c. public's tendency to be passive; varying levels of audience engagement
    d. increased media channels; people caring about a multitude of issues

12. The Million Man March is an example of
    a. grassroots participation.
    b. corporate citizenship.
    c. populist propaganda.
    d. crisis management.

13. Katz and Lazarsfeld's two-step flow theory stemmed from a study on
    a. television viewing habits.
    b. electoral choices.
    c. media convergence.
    d. framing analysis.

14. This stage in the life cycle of public opinion includes behaviors such as drafting legislation or compromising with other publics.
    a. resolution
    b. government regulation/involvement
    c. issue definition
    d. public awareness

15. Which of the following is not a trait of an opinion leader?
    a. avid user of the mass media
    b. early adopter of new ideas
    c. seeks out good organizers and "mobilizers"
    d. highly interested in subject matter

16. An *application story* is primarily utilized by
    a. upper-level management.
    b. the trade press.
    c. propagandists.
    d. print journalism columnists.

17. Mass media effects increase when
    a. they come from a print source.
    b. a specific medium has a greater reputation.
    c. parental guidance is apparent.
    d. people cannot verify information through personal experience and knowledge.

18. Selecting certain facts, themes, and treatments to shape a story is known as
    a. cultivation.
    b. public journalism.
    c. agenda setting.
    d. framing.

19. Persuasive communication on behalf of clients is the _____ view of public relations.
    a. eroding
    b. dominant public
    c. most expensive
    d. most sincere

20. The most difficult persuasive task is to
    a. crystallize latent opinions.
    b. conserve favorable opinions.
    c. change or neutralize hostile opinions.
    d. enlighten constituents.

21. Which of these source credibility factors is a major reason why celebrities (or politicians) are chosen as spokespersons?
    a. expertise
    b. sincerity
    c. transfer
    d. charisma

22. Newsrooms refer to story ideas such as "old man starving because of welfare red tape" as
    a. passé.
    b. humanizing an issue.
    c. headliners.
    d. testimonials.

23. Bill Clinton playing up his Arkansas roots would be an example of this propaganda technique.
    a. testimonial
    b. plain folks
    c. bandwagon
    d. glittering generalities

24. Selecting facts and data to build an overwhelming case on one side of an issue while concealing the other side is known as
    a. glittering generalities.
    b. card stacking.
    c. bandwagon.
    d. propaganda.

25. The value of information and its newsworthiness are based on
    a. timing and context.
    b. bottom-line potential.
    c. gatekeeper preferences.
    d. geography and psychographics.

26. Typically, an audience member would be more likely to oppose a message if the speaker
    a. gives only one side of the argument.
    b. gives all sides of the argument.
    c. appeals to target audience.
    d. sticks to one major theme.

27. The mass media influences a person's opinion most when the information provided
    a. comes from multiple sources.
    b. has high emotional appeal.
    c. is at the top of a page or a broadcast.
    d. doesn't conflict with any of the individual's existing attitudes or opinions.

28. Journalists rely on these people to give statements when a specific issue relates to their areas of responsibility/concern.
    a. formal opinion leaders
    b. informal opinion leaders
    c. survivors and sustainers
    d. public relations liaisons

29. If a utility wants people to conserve energy, it must distribute a message that contains
    a. strong fear arousal.
    b. convincing statistics.
    c. suggestions for action.
    d. media accounts.

30. _____ and _____ pioneered agenda setting theory.
    a. Elihu Katz/Paul Lazarsfeld
    b. George Creel/Ivy Lee
    c. Max McCombs/Don Shaw
    d. Morton Deutsch/Peter Colman

CHAPTER 10   CONFLICT MANAGEMENT: DEALING WITH ISSUES, RISKS, AND CRISES

1. Which of the following is not a likely source for competition in the nonprofit sector?
   a. market share
   b. volunteers
   c. political influence
   d. grants

2. This method of managing conflict requires an assessment of the demands that a threat makes on an organization and its available resources.
   a. conflict resolution
   b. muscular public relations
   c. threat appraisal model
   d. crisis management

3. Perception of risk increases when the messages of experts
   a. conflict.
   b. concur.
   c. are published.
   d. differ from those of competitors.

4. Which term describes constantly reading/listening to/watching current affairs with an eye to an organization's interests?
   a. issues tracking
   b. environmental scanning
   c. conflict positioning
   d. litigation

5. Pepsi used a _____ strategy to avoid a massive recall in light of a hoax involving a syringe in a can?
   a. ingratiating
   b. apologetic
   c. denial
   d. corrective action

6. Which phase of the contingency continuum involves strategies that bolster or repair an organization's reputation?
   a. recovery
   b. strategic
   c. reactive
   d. issues management

7. One major difference between the handling of the Exxon and Pepsi crises was the
   a. use of an administrative face immediately after the incident was made public.
   b. use of defensive strategies and tactics.
   c. decision not to pull products to protect customer safety or company image.
   d. intense media scrutiny in the immediate aftermath of the incident.

8. Offering coupons or charitable donations are typical in which type of crisis strategy?
   a. justification
   b. mortification
   c. ingratiation
   d. corrective action

9. Referring to an organization's clean record and good reputation is known as a _____ strategy.
   a. bolstering
   b. defeasibility
   c. transcendence
   d. justification

10. Which of the following is not a foundation of reputation?
    a. economic performance
    b. social responsiveness
    c. brand equity
    d. delivering valuable outcomes to stakeholders

11. The majority of organizational crises are
    a. self-inflicted because management minimizes or denies them.
    b. unavoidable even with strong crisis management initiatives.
    c. covered by regional or national media.
    d. external.

12. Often, an apology in the aftermath of a crisis isn't effective because of the
    a. damage already done.
    b. media frenzy involved.
    c. hypocrisy factor.
    d. defensive, unforgiving nature of most Americans.

13. The basic concept of crisis management is
    a. reactive communication.
    b. constituent support.
    c. proactive planning.
    d. negotiation.

14. Which of the following is a strategy of the issues management approach?
    a. analyze bottom-line ramifications
    b. react to surprises
    c. anticipate threats
    d. dissect crises

15. A _____ strategy takes steps to repair damage from the crisis and to prevent it from happening again.
    a. mortification
    b. ingratiation
    c. justification
    d. corrective action

16. In a recent hoax, a woman claimed to find a human finger in a bowl of Wendy's chili. Which strategy did Wendy's first employ in the aftermath of the resulting crisis?
    a. Build a post-incident strategy to enhance the brand.
    b. Brief and mobilize employees.
    c. Conduct due diligence to make sure the brand wasn't at fault.
    d. Ensure that Wendy's core values drove all decisions and response.

17. On the contingency/crisis continuum, risk communication takes place during the _____ phase.
    a. strategic
    b. reactive
    c. recovery
    d. economic

18. Which of the following is not a rule of thumb during a crisis situation?
    a. Designate a single spokesperson.
    b. Never say "no comment."
    c. Provide a constant flow of information.
    d. Put company needs and ideals at the forefront of your actions.

19. Image restoration can alleviate problems that pertain specifically to
    a. reputation management.
    b. contingency theory.
    c. muscular PR.
    d. environmental scanning.

20. Which of the following is not an example of risk communication?
    a. congressional hearings
    b. radioactive waste disposal
    c. placement of drug-abuse centers in neighborhoods
    d. food products

21. Which of the following is not one of the external variables identified in contingency theory?
    a. external threats
    b. characteristics of those fomenting the conflict
    c. industry environment
    d. risk/reward

22. Fair play, strength in competition, and advocacy are all ideals of
    a. muscular PR.
    b. issue identification.
    c. crisis communication.
    d. benchmarking.

23. According to a recent study, which of the following is not one of the top-three triggers for a crisis?
    a. financial irregularities
    b. unethical behavior
    c. media overzealousness
    d. executive misconduct

24. Which of these actions was not taken by the Chinese government to restore its reputation after a number of product recalls and safety issues?
    a. improve food safety standards
    b. ask other advanced nations for advice on punitive measures
    c. tighten controls on chemicals used by seafood and meat producers
    d. making producers more accountable for selling unsafe goods

25. Which of the following does not apply to the Abu Ghraib case?
    a. It involved a prison scandal in Iraq.
    b. Osama bin Laden launched a campaign on the television network Al Jazeera.
    c. The Pentagon ignored early evidence about humiliation of prisoners.
    d. It is an example of a conflict that was allowed to smolder.

26. Which of the following is a phase of the conflict management life cycle?
    a. monitoring media for emerging issues
    b. taking reactive steps
    c. benchmarking
    d. avoiding volatile issues

27. Which of the following is not a component of strategic conflict management?
    a. competition
    b. conflict
    c. management
    d. justification

28. Nearly 9 out of 10 business crises are
    a. unexpected.
    b. preventable.
    c. the result of poor public relations.
    d. external.

29. This image restoration strategy distinguishes an act from other similar but more offensive acts.
    a. justification
    b. transcendence
    c. differentiation
    d. minimization

30. Taking preventive actions that forestall conflict occurs in the
    a. proactive phase.
    b. strategic phase.
    c. reactive phase.
    d. recovery phase.

CHAPTER 11   REACHING A MULTICULTURAL AND DIVERSE AUDIENCE

1. The medium in which a communicator likely has the most influence is
   a. newspapers.
   b. the Internet.
   c. magazines.
   d. television.

2. Which of the following is the most offensive term for persons with disability?
   a. deaf
   b. mobility impaired
   c. crippled
   d. physically disabled

3. This demographic makes more than 80 percent of household purchase decisions.
   a. women
   b. men
   c. Generation X
   d. the middle-class

4. Who coined the phrase "fifteen minutes of fame"?
   a. Edward Bernays
   b. Simon Cowell
   c. Andy Warhol
   d. Marshal McLuhan

5. Which of the following is not a way that technology has changed the practice of public relations?
   a. It has made it more difficult to access an international audience.
   b. It has made it easier to segment the mass audience.
   c. It has led to a shorter attention span among the public.
   d. It allows the audience to control when and where they consume media content.

6. Which of the following generalizations does not reflect current audience trends?
   a. fervent support for multiple issues
   b. heavy emphasis on celebrity and personality
   c. strong distrust of authority
   d. expanding international audience for public relations

7. This major American city has an Asian-American population approaching 20 percent.
   a. Miami
   b. San Francisco
   c. Atlanta
   d. Boston

8. According to a recent survey on media usage, _____ is the most heavily used media?
   a. major network news
   b. local TV news
   c. cable TV news
   d. local newspapers

9. Which statement about online media is incorrect?
   a. Online media have expanded drastically from their original, supplemental role.
   b. About three-quarters of Americans have Internet access.
   c. Online media are primarily the domain of affluent, well educated people.
   d. Electronic media delivery systems will eventually take over print media.

10. Celebrity endorsements generally have _____ credibility among consumers.
    a. moderate
    b. more media
    c. an almost cult-like
    d. low

11. The Pakistan breast cancer campaign/case study faced stiff initial challenges because of
    a. Pakistan's sensitivity to public discussion of women's breasts.
    b. Pakistan's problem with terrorism.
    c. liberal Muslim societal values.
    d. a lack of funding and resources.

12. According to a recent study by Jeff Garber, which of the following is not characteristic of the gay community?
    a. high brand loyalty
    b. well educated
    c. median income of $65,000 per year
    d. does not respond well to ads that specifically target a gay/lesbian audience

13. The most significant feature of the mass audience in the United States is
    a. diversity.
    b. economic power.
    c. literacy issues.
    d. passivity.

14. Which of the following is not a primary characteristic of the senior audience?
    a. excellent source of volunteers
    b. vote consistently
    c. easily convinced by fads
    d. more avid consumers of mass media

15. According to a recent article in *The Strategist*, which characteristic is not shared by Hispanics, African Americans, and Asian Americans?
    a. a deep family network with a strong mother or father figure
    b. weak bonds between friends and family
    c. importance of music, food and religion
    d. strong loyalty to brands that try to reach them in culturally relevant ways

16. Which medium below is most effective for delivering messages that require the receiver to contemplate and absorb details?
    a. television
    b. the Internet
    c. print media
    d. radio

17. This president resigned in the wake of the Watergate scandal.
    a. Richard Nixon
    b. Lyndon Johnson
    c. Jimmy Carter
    d. F.D. Roosevelt

18. Which of the following does not apply to Hispanic audiences?
    a. They listen to radio more than most other audiences.
    b. Television programs do especially well in the 18–34 demographic.
    c. Movies such as *Nacho Libre* are made with them in mind.
    d. They are more likely to read traditional American print press than Spanish-only publications.

19. Which tactic successfully built brand affinity with potential African-American cruise goers?
    a. a free, live art auction
    b. specialized cuisine options
    c. educational programs
    d. pursuing more persons of color to work in higher levels of cruise management

20. How much time per day, on average, do Americans spend watching television?
    a. 4.5 hours
    b. 2 hours
    c. 1 hour
    d. 7 hours

21. Which of the following is not an advantage of using radio?
    a. flexibility
    b. ability to reach target audiences
    c. fewer stations than television
    d. less expensive than some other media alternatives

22. Members of Generation Y usually gain their trust from
    a. media sources.
    b. parents/guardians.
    c. targeted/advertised products that gain brand loyalty.
    d. relationships.

23. Which of the following is most likely to interest baby boomers?
    a. self-actualization needs
    b. health issues
    c. social networking
    d. interactive media

24. In 2007, Disney took the unconventional step of promoting packages
    a. for children-only cruises.
    b. for superhero/fantasy cruises.
    c. allowing gay couples to exchange wedding vows.
    d. for homeless persons.

25. In the foreseeable future, it is likely that electronic media delivery systems will
    a. fall out of use.
    b. become the primary source of information.
    c. slow their growth.
    d. be less customizable.

26. This famed radio/television personality was fired after his insensitive comments about members of the Rutgers University women's basketball team.
    a. Rush Limbaugh
    b. Howard Stern
    c. Don Imus
    d. Reverend Al Sharpton

27. Which of the following is not a reason women need sensitivity and diversity training in the workplace?
    a. differing work ethic
    b. dress code considerations
    c. up to four generations with different communication styles
    d. concerns about male smokers

28. Communication channels that reach directly to the audience are
    a. controlled media.
    b. symmetry.
    c. gatekeeping.
    d. injection techniques.

29. By the year 2010, 50 million Americans will be
    a. 65 or older.
    b. Hispanic.
    c. functionally illiterate.
    d. some sort of media gatekeeper.

30. Which of the following is not characteristic of the "supermom" market segment?
    a. They make up about five percent of all mothers.
    b. They have at least 75 friends with whom they try to keep in touch.
    c. They spend at least nine hours per week on the Internet.
    d. They seek out expert advice about purchasing and restaurant decisions.

CHAPTER 12   PUBLIC RELATIONS AND THE LAW

1. Public relations personnel can be held legally liable if they provide advice or tacitly support an illegal activity of a client or employer. This area of liability is called
   a. fair comment.
   b. conspiracy.
   c. obstruction of justice.
   d. stonewalling.

2. Which of the following materials are in the public domain and cannot be copyrighted?
   a. corporate slogans
   b. individual inventions
   c. government documents
   d. music or lyrics from non-licensed artists

3. Which of the following statements is not accurate in regard to the length of copyright protection?
   a. Current length of a U.S. copyright is the life of creator plus 70 years for individual works.
   b. Previously, U.S. copyright protection lasted 50 years, but it was changed with the "Mickey Mouse" law.
   c. In Europe, copyright protection lasts 50 years.
   d. For copyrights held by corporations, protection lasts 75 years from the time of publication.

4. Which type of person/entity would have the least protection from, or the least likelihood of winning, defamation suits?
   a. a private citizens
   b. a police officer or firefighter
   c. a lawyer
   d. a corporation

5. The Sarbanes-Oxley Act relates to
   a. corporate transparency.
   b. political copyright.
   c. political fundraising.
   d. advertising practices.

6. Which of the following guidelines does not have to be followed when writing product publicity materials?
   a. Information should be accurate and substantiated.
   b. Celebrities/spokespersons should actually use the products they endorse.
   c. Avoid terms such as "independent research study" without proof.
   d. "Green" or healthy marketing tools should be a foremost pitching tool.

7. What is the source of most cases of plagiarism by college students?
   a. "straight copies" from the Internet
   b. students from within the university
   c. sources of authority inside the university
   d. underground databases

8. Which of the following is not a way in which a public relations practitioner can be named a co-conspirator in an illegal activity?
   a. participates in an illegal action (e.g., bribing a government official)
   b. purchases time/space in underground media
   c. counsels/guides the policy behind an illegal action
   d. helps establish a "front group" which conceals information

9. Any false statement about a person (or organization) that creates public hatred, contempt or ridicule, or inflicts injury on reputation is
   a. trespass.
   b. infringement.
   c. conspiracy.
   d. defamation.

10. Which of the following is not a FDA guideline for video, audio and print news releases on health care topics?
    a. "fair balance" in disclosing the risks and benefits of the drug or treatment
    b. clear statement of the drug or treatment's limitations
    c. supplementary documentation that gives full prescribing information
    d. emphasis on trained health care professionals as spokespersons rather than celebrity endorsements

11. Which of the following devices is not used by public relations practitioners to help an organization protect its trademarks?
    a. always capitalize uses of a trademark
    b. prohibit use by other organizations, even nonprofit agencies
    c. never use a trademark as a noun
    d. use a trademark as an adjective modifying a noun

12. Corporate speech was the primary theme in this Supreme Court case.
    a. *Roe v. Wade*
    b. *Nike v. Kasky*
    c. *Cytryn v. Cook*
    d. *Food Lion v. ABC/Capital Cities*

13. Which of the following is unrelated to the enforcement of regulations against indecency on broadcast outlets?
    a. Janet Jackson's "wardrobe malfunction" during the halftime show at the 2004 Super Bowl
    b. complaints against Howard Stern and other Clear Channel radio personalities.
    c. discussion of sexual and reproductive health on talk shows
    d. lawsuits against Larry Flynt

14. Which factor is not usually considered when an organization is giving plant tours?
    a. media coverage/exposure
    b. logistics
    c. work interruptions
    d. amount of staffing required

15. Photo releases, employee newsletters, and media inquiries about employees are all sensitive subjects when it comes to _____ in the workplace.
    a. product publicity
    b. copyright
    c. invasion of privacy
    d. fair comment

16. To use a likeness/photo of celebrities such as Elvis, one must pay a
    a. freelance photographer or artist.
    b. licensing fee.
    c. trademark company.
    d. specialized lawyer or firm.

17. _____ public relations extends beyond legal counsel, especially with regard to high-profile cases such as those of Michael Vick and Martha Stewart.
    a. Conspiracy
    b. Litigation
    c. Corporate
    d. Damage control

18. Which of the following is one of the reasons why corporations are considered public figures?
    a. They engage in advertising and promotion, offering products/services to the public.
    b. They are rarely involved in matters of public controversy and public policy.
    c. They employ line managers in many marketing and advertising ventures.
    d. They have profound access to the government.

19. The landmark *Reid* Case, decided by the Supreme Court in 1989, revolved around
    a. fair comment by newspaper critics.
    b. misappropriation of personality.
    c. the rights of freelance writers.
    d. invasion of privacy.

20. Which of the following cases is not about public disclosure and insider trading?
    a. Food Lion/ABC
    b. Texas Gulf Sulphur
    c. Martha Stewart
    d. Enron

21. Misappropriation of personality usually involves
    a. public figures.
    b. government officials.
    c. fair use.
    d. the Securities and Exchange Commission.

22. The concept of *fair use* allows the use of copyrighted material for
    a. fair comment.
    b. free speech.
    c. freelancing.
    d. educational purposes.

23. The Federal Trade Commission oversees
    a. truth in advertising.
    b. stockholder rights.
    c. international trade agreements.
    d. issues in corporate transparency.

24. An idea for promoting a product cannot be
    a. copyrighted.
    b. trademarked.
    c. held accountable by the government.
    d. accessed by corporate entities.

25. Under copyright law, freelance and commercial photographers
    a. must turn over negatives/originals to clients.
    b. retain ownership of their work.
    c. are free from regulations.
    d. are under state laws.

26. Which of the following is an SEC regulation that is pertinent to public relations personnel?
    a. Meetings with ad agency reps must be fully disclosed to government officials.
    b. Information should be withheld.
    c. Timely disclosure is laudable but not always feasible.
    d. Insider trading is illegal.

27. Organizations hosting open houses should prepare in the following ways, EXCEPT
    a. training volunteers for emergency medical assistance.
    b. arranging for extra liability insurance.
    c. hiring off-duty police for security and traffic control.
    d. contracting with food and souvenir vendors.

28. The FTC's guidelines for green marketing also apply to
   a. the use of "low-carb" in promoting food products.
   b. bottom-line objectives.
   c. lowering gasoline prices.
   d. philanthropy.

29. The courts are increasingly applying the _____ to financial information to determine whether it creates a misleading representation of the organization or its products.
   a. Supreme Court litmus tests
   b. Federal Trade Commission standards
   c. copyright laws
   d. mosaic doctrine

30. Most lawsuits and complaints involving employee newsletters are usually the result of
   a. "personals" columns.
   b. feature articles about employees.
   c. use of employee pictures.
   d. misappropriation of personality.

CHAPTER 13   NEW TECHNOLOGIES IN PUBLIC RELATIONS

1. What is the leading trend in public relations?
   a. hiring men to bridge the gender gap
   b. the use of technology
   c. cutting back on outsourcing
   d. movement toward licensing in the profession

2. Editors pay the closest attention to releases sent via which mode of transmission?
   a. fax
   b. hand delivery
   c. express mail
   d. electronically through satellites and similar measures

3. The CD/DVD version of a media kit is known as a(n)
   a. press disc.
   b. video news release.
   c. moblog.
   d. e-kit.

4. Software such as Dragon Naturally Speaking that helps with recognizing human speech falls under which category?
   a. artificial intelligence
   b. experts system programming
   c. digital transparency
   d. dictation/voice generation

5. Which of the following statements about broadband is false?
   a. Cell and dish satellite companies have now broken the broadband barrier.
   b. Broadband enables PR professionals to meet the 15-second rule for loading time.
   c. Broadband enables the Internet to offer Voice over Internet Protocol (VoIP) telephone service.
   d. Better broadband will help increase a company's virtual presence.

6. The significant gap between Western countries, who have made most of the gains in Internet technology, and the rest of the world is referred to as the
   a. information superhighway.
   b. computerized chasm.
   c. global village.
   d. digital divide.

7. The term _____ refers to cable and other high-capacity services, like satellite and DSL, that enable practitioners to meet acceptable guidelines for loading time while offering broadcast-quality video and unlimited information to media, investors, and other publics.
   a. mainstreaming
   b. virtual presence
   c. broadband
   d. blogging

8. Which of the following is not a brand of personal digital assistant?
   a. Palm Pilot
   b. Treo
   c. iMac
   d. BlackBerry

9. _____ is the natural spread of ideas over the Internet that helps spur social movements and trends.
   a. Mobbing
   b. Viral marketing
   c. E-fluentialism
   d. Webconferencing

10. Which of the following is not a major difference between a news release delivery system and a news service?
    a. Media outlets pay large fees to receive reports from news services.
    b. News release delivery companies are paid by creators of news releases to distribute those releases to the media, who pay nothing to receive them.
    c. Issue tracking through online news release delivery systems can be more thorough.
    d. Media-related services such as the Associated Press are more credible.

11. Which essential public relations skill is not greatly enhanced by the use of computers?
    a. interpersonal relations
    b. project management
    c. time billing
    d. digital presentation

12. Essentially, YouTube is a(n) _____ device.
    a. instant messaging
    b. social networking
    c. media-controlled
    d. video sharing

13. Which statement about the creation of the Internet is correct?
    a. Researchers could immediately link computers in Third World countries.
    b. Microsoft and America Online partnered for national distribution.
    c. The creation of the Internet began in the 1950s.
    d. The Internet originally worked as a government–academic tool.

14. Which of the following is not an RSS reader or feeder?
    a. Google
    b. NewsDesk
    c. Dogpile Search
    d. NewsGator

15. These special Web sites are used as collaborative spaces where ideas/guidelines can be shared with and developed by multiple audiences.
    a. wikis
    b. moblogs
    c. RSS sites
    d. astroturfs

16. Which of the following is not cited as a primary example of online, two-way communication?
    a. Google and other Internet search engines
    b. personalized satellite radio
    c. viral marketing
    d. Amazon.com and similar companies personalizing customer greetings

17. Which characteristic of the Internet is particularly important to public relations professionals?
    a. It is the most cost-effective medium.
    b. It is the best medium to counter terrorism.
    c. Content is becoming much more closely controlled.
    d. Issue tracking is more thorough and far more immediate.

18. Moblogging is possible because of
    a. an emotional, group mentality in cyberspace.
    b. music devices such as iPhone.
    c. cell phones with cameras.
    d. special interest groups.

19. Manipulating copy and graphics on a computer screen to design and format reports, newsletters, brochures and presentations is known as
    a. cyberscanning.
    b. desktop publishing.
    c. importing.
    d. content repurposing.

20. A single document can be sent simultaneously to hundreds of recipients through a
    a. listserv.
    b. desktop.
    c. broadcast fax.
    d. laser loop.

21. An audio or video broadcast posted to a Web site for download is a(n)
    a. podcasts.
    b. moblogs.
    c. e-kits.
    d. wikis.

22. Which Internet characteristic is not particularly important to public relations professionals?
    a. It is dependent on key gatekeepers.
    b. Its reach is worldwide.
    c. Its content is virtually uncontrolled.
    d. It enables more thorough issue tracking.

23. Who would a public relations practitioner contact to get quotes for the costs of teleconferencing?
    a. the person(s) at the other end of the conference
    b. the telephone company
    c. vendors
    d. the local cable provider

24. Most Web site planning is done by
    a. CEOs or upper-level managers.
    b. public relations experts.
    c. trial and error.
    d. those with computer or industrial technology backgrounds.

25. Christopher Reeve was able to do 45 consecutive interviews through the help of a
    a. satellite media tour.
    b. cellular phone.
    c. personal digital assistant.
    d. moderator.

26. Using a phone to drive people to Web-based survey instruments is known as a(n)
    a. broadband technique.
    b. hybrid survey.
    c. online focus group.
    d. cybertracking tactic.

27. Who would be the typical audience for the promotion of research software like SPSS?
    a. media outlets
    b. employees
    c. outside clients
    d. viewers and listeners

28. The Clinton/Lewinsky scandal really gained traction and public scrutiny through the Starr Report, first released via
    a. *The Washington Post.*
    b. leaks from the White House.
    c. the Internet.
    d. a media briefing from the President's press secretary.

29. Using _____, PR professionals can have audiences view a speech or video over the Internet and provide their opinion of the message in real time.
    a. online theater research
    b. hybrid surveys
    c. copy testing
    d. 3-Dimensional Text Mapping

30. The term _____ describes the efforts of supposed grassroots organizations that turn out to be sponsored organizations.
    a. cyberheckling
    b. astroturfing
    c. pseudomarketing
    d. moblogging

1. The first news release was issued by
   a. Edward Bernays.
   b. Ivy Lee.
   c. James Grunig.
   d. George Creel.

2. Which of the following is not a traditional news value?
   a. global focus
   b. newsworthiness
   c. timeliness
   d. reader interest

3. Journalists first consult _____ in the aftermath of an organizational crisis?
   a. the company CEO
   b. company brochures
   c. the company Web site
   d. their editors

4. A media advisory usually describes
   a. long-term media objectives.
   b. media surveillance issues.
   c. interview, photo, and video prospects.
   d. framing/bias language and ground rules.

5. Which of the following was not part of the Heinz smart release?
   a. embedded links to photos and videos
   b. a 100th anniversary celebration
   c. hyperlinks to charts and related information
   d. tags for key search terms linked to more than 300 social networks

6. The _____ is not normally part of a dateline in a news release.
   a. city
   b. state
   c. release date
   d. headline

7. Which of the following is not a critical consideration for global news releases?
   a. Internet access
   b. cultural differences
   c. political issues
   d. language

8. The following are formatting guidelines for a print news release, EXCEPT
   a. Use 8-1/2 x 11-inch white paper.
   b. Include a bold-faced headline and a dateline.
   c. Never split a paragraph from one page to the next.
   d. Avoid letterhead because it looks too eager and self-important.

9. The following are formatting guidelines for an e-mail/Internet news release, EXCEPT
   a. Insert a boilerplate paragraph.
   b. Limit the release to 200 words in five short paragraphs or less.
   c. Use bulleted points.
   d. Paste the text into the email, rather than sending it as an attachment.

10. Media cover trends because
   a. consumers have an increased sense of creativity and style.
   b. their editors/reporters are more fad-conscious.
   c. "style over substance" is the trendy rule of thumb.
   d. there is a relative dearth of hard news.

11. Which of the following is not a critical element of photo composition?
   a. tight shot within minimal background
   b. emphasis on detail and not on whole scenes
   c. reducing gaps between individuals and objects
   d. including many key individuals to enhance publishing chances

12. Approximately how much does it cost to distribute a 400-word smart news release throughout the U.S.?
   a. $200
   b. $650
   c. $900
   d. $1,250

13. Which of the following is not characteristic of mat releases?
   a. They are ready for print ("camera-ready").
   b. They often take a feature angle.
   c. They are used primarily in trade publications.
   d. Sophisticated versions consist of an entire page layout that a newspaper can use at no cost.

14. Which of these features is not typical of a media kit folder?
   a. It is usually 9 x 12 inches with four surfaces.
   b. Back cover shows name and address of the organization.
   c. A common feature is a slot on the inside page for the business card of the public relations contact person.
   d. Folders usually include the specific logo of the media (coverage) being sought.

15. Which statement about media advisories is incorrect?
    a. They are usually lists of short, bulleted items.
    b. They are typically created months or even a year before a major event.
    c. They let the media know about an interview opportunity with a visiting expert.
    d. They are also known as media alerts.

16. Which of the following is commonly included in a media kit?
    a. a background piece
    b. e-zine/webzine links and printouts
    c. an advertisement
    d. annual reports

17. Which item is not essential to a good online newsroom?
    a. current and archived news releases
    b. product information
    c. exact replicas of the print or broadcast stories
    d. photographs

18. Which statement about the inverted pyramid structure is incorrect?
    a. The first 3-4 lines are critical.
    b. Editors cut stories from the bottom.
    c. Readers are engrossed by the full story.
    d. Headlines are a key focal point.

19. The greatest downside to issuing an e-kit is the
    a. storage considerations.
    b. overall costs.
    c. media adaptability.
    d. time it takes journalists and gatekeepers to review one.

20. The opening paragraph of a news release should
    a. be a minimum of 6 lines in length.
    b. mirror the headline.
    c. answer the "five Ws" with a tight summary lead.
    d. be triple-spaced for easier editing.

21. The key to a successful e-mail news release is
    a. sending accompanying artwork.
    b. using Word attachments.
    c. including more information than the print version.
    d. a good subject line.

22. A typical newsletter is best described as
    a. formal.
    b. timely.
    c. informal.
    d. internal.

23. _____ is not a problem when emailing news releases.
    a. The lack of credibility associated with newer technologies
    b. Antispam software
    c. An attachment
    d. Excessive copy/text

24. _____ is a good technique for writing media alerts and leads to stories in inverted-pyramid format.
    a. Answering the "5 Ws"
    b. Telling a good story
    c. Leaving the headlines to the gatekeepers
    d. Using transitions and quotes

25. *Business Wire* and *PR Newswire* are
    a. media databases.
    b. electronic news services.
    c. advocacy outlets.
    d. broadcast bureaus.

26. The typical resolution for a Web site is _____; it is _____ for a print publication.
    a. 72 dpi; 300 dpi
    b. 300 dpi; 72 dpi
    c. 200 dpi; 600 dpi
    d. 600 dpi; 200 dpi

27. Which of the following is not important to be aware of when pitching a story?
    a. the kinds of stories that a publication usually runs or a broadcast outlet usually airs
    b. upcoming deadlines
    c. the type of coverage that has been given to competing organizations
    d. a journalist's beat and the stories (s)he written in the past

28. When describing a product, editors will almost always find the word _____ meaningless.
    a. source.
    b. unique.
    c. survey.
    d. embargo.

29. Which item is least likely to arrive in publishable form?
    a. a VNR
    b. a PSA
    c. a news release
    d. a pitch letter

30. The preeminent style guide for public relations practitioners is
    a. the *Associated Press Stylebook*.
    b. the *Fiske Guide*.
    c. *O'Dwyer's Handbook*.
    d. *Roget's Thesaurus*.

CHAPTER 15 RADIO, TELEVISION, AND THE WEB

1. Video news releases are usually
   a. made in-house.
   b. outsourced to an agency or firm.
   c. produced by television network affiliates.
   d. about 12–15 minutes in length.

2. A(n) _____ is least likely to be a "talking head" in a public service announcement.
   a. actor
   b. politician
   c. popular local news anchor
   d. college student

3. Which item is not typically included in an audio news release?
   a. a suggested anchor lead and tag
   b. a script for a field reporter
   c. teleprompter information
   d. a cut (quote) to an expert being interviewed

4. Which guideline for radio PSAs and news releases is incorrect?
   a. type in uppercase
   b. double-space
   c. prepare various lengths
   d. submit a single PSA on a subject

5. The following are differences between an audio news release and a print media release, EXCEPT
   a. An ANR is more concerned with spelling, especially with proper names.
   b. A radio release is written for the ear.
   c. An ANR is more concise than a print release.
   d. The writing style for an ANR is more informal and conversational.

6. CBS's *60 Minutes* is an example of a
   a. documentary.
   b. magazine program.
   c. docudrama.
   d. "dramareality."

7. Which of the following is not one of Medialink's tips for the production of video news releases?
   a. Always use a stand-up reporter.
   b. Keep soundbites short.
   c. Give television news directors maximum flexibility.
   d. Provide good graphics and animation.

8. Which approach will not get an organization's news and viewpoints on local television?
   a. sending a media alert/advisory to the assignment editor
   b. sending a different release than the local print media receive
   c. making a phone or e-mail pitch to the assignment editor to emphasize the visual aspects of the story
   d. producing a video news release

9. A typical video news release lasts about
   a. 30 seconds.
   b. 90 seconds.
   c. three minutes.
   d. five minutes.

10. Which of the following is not a guideline for formatting and producing radio public service announcements?
    a. Avoid exact timing of segments to allow for gatekeeper/anchor flexibility.
    b. Use uppercase.
    c. Use double-spaced type.
    d. Submit multiple PSAs on the same subject in various lengths.

11. Because it is fee-based, product placement in a television show falls into the category of _____ rather than public relations.
    a. corporate sponsorship
    b. pay for play
    c. journalism
    d. advertising/marketing

12. The best way to communicate with the Hispanic audience is
    a. print media.
    b. Web channels.
    c. radio and television.
    d. simple English-Spanish translations.

13. When distributing a video news release (or before), one should always send this accompanying document.
    a. an advisory
    b. an actuality
    c. a media kit
    d. a pitch letter

14. VNRs have a better chance of garnering airtime if they
    a. are sponsored by corporations.
    b. include inflection patterns of potential reporters.
    c. are submitted by national firms.
    d. have a local angle.

15. Which of the following is not characteristic of B-roll footage?
    a. It helps to "visualize" op-ed pieces.
    b. It contains video without narration.
    c. It accompanies video news releases.
    d. It supplements local news stories.

16. What is the length of the typical soundbite in a news program?
    a. 10 seconds or less
    b. 20 seconds or less
    c. 30 seconds or less
    d. 45 seconds or less

17. In general, guests on talk shows should do which of the following?
    a. Be cautious.
    b. Give strong opinions.
    c. Debate in a demonstrative manner.
    d. Grab audience attention through shocks and stunts.

18. Arranging for selected items to appear on a television show is a practice known as
    a. viral marketing.
    b. planting.
    c. booking.
    d. product placement.

19. A well prepared video news release usually gets about _____ station airings.
    a. 15
    b. 45
    c. 60
    d. 85

20. A booker would deal with a talk show's
    a. executive producer.
    b. host.
    c. talent coordinator.
    d. community relations director.

21. Satellite is the most cost-effective way of distributing
    a. email.
    b. VNRs.
    c. speech text.
    d. actualities.

22. Which celebrity was not cited as having been paid to appear on a national talk show on which she promoted a product?
    a. Martha Stewart
    b. Kathleen Turner
    c. Peggy Fleming
    d. Lauren Bacall

23. In general, a Webcast of a news conference or an earnings report, including the question-and-answer session, lasts about
    a. 30 minutes.
    b. two hours.
    c. four hours.
    d. one hour.

24. Issues placement on popular TV programs usually involves
    a. scenery.
    b. plotlines.
    c. use of rolling credits.
    d. ratings points.

25. A regularly updated online personal journal is commonly referred to as a
    a. blog.
    b. listserv.
    c. Webcast.
    d. wiki.

26. Which is a guideline for a successful satellite media tour?
    a. Localize the SMT.
    b. Use a monochromatic background.
    c. Be liberal with the available talent pool.
    d. Make follow-up calls to producers.

27. Most radio news directors prefer to receive their actualities via
    a. the Web.
    b. satellite.
    c. wire services.
    d. telephone.

28. A major selling point for a radio media tour is the
    a. low cost and convenience.
    b. remote capability.
    c. universality.
    d. actuality/sound bite presence.

29. The preferred length for an audio news release is
    a. 30 seconds.
    b. 45 seconds.
    c. one minute.
    d. two minutes.

30. This group organized volunteer efforts and a bilingual public relations effort to help pregnant women and sick/premature babies during the Hurricane Katrina crisis.
    a. Johnson & Johnson
    b. FEMA
    c. Nestlé
    d. March of Dimes

CHAPTER 16   MEDIA INTERVIEWS, NEWS CONFERENCES, AND SPEECHES

1. The first step in speechwriting is determining the
   a. potential outcomes of the speech.
   b. behavioral tendencies of the audience.
   c. composition of the audience.
   d. message.

2. A civic club, like the Rotary Club or the Lions, would require a speechwriting tone that is more
   a. persuasive.
   b. propagandist.
   c. confrontational.
   d. objective.

3. *Oprah* is best classified as a
   a. nationally syndicated talk show.
   b. network talk show.
   c. national syndication company.
   d. public broadcasting program.

4. An audience's typical attention span for a speech is about
   a. 5 minutes.
   b. 15–20 minutes.
   c. 30–40 minutes.
   d. one hour.

5. Which element is not critical to a good PowerPoint slide?
   a. descriptive text
   b. the 4 by 4 rule
   c. 24- to 28-point type
   d. 2-inch margins

6. At a press party, the standard practice is to make your pitch to media members
   a. at the beginning of the socializing period.
   b. at the end of the socializing period.
   c. after distributing fact sheets.
   d. only to those unfamiliar with your organization or issue.

7. The worst time for a press conference is
   a. late morning.
   b. early afternoon.
   c. Monday afternoon.
   d. Friday afternoon.

8. Which variable is not important when making a presentation with visual aids?
   a. information retention
   b. meeting lengths
   c. reaching group consensus
   d. making the speaker/organization appear more cutting-edge

9. When sending advance text of a speech to journalists, always include a(n)
   a. soundbite suggestion.
   b. news release.
   c. element of presentation software.
   d. embargo date.

10. This person's job is to teach executives how to be concise and stay on message during a speech or interview.
    a. media trainer
    b. human resource manager
    c. director of communications
    d. chosen head of media pool

11. Which of the following is not a type of media tour?
    a. a junket, during which editors and reporters are invited to activities like inspecting a company's manufacturing facilities or watching previews of network TV programs in New York or Hollywood
    b. a familiarization (fam) trip, offered to travel writers and editors by the tourism industry
    c. an organization's executives travel to key cities to talk with selected editors, used primarily in high-tech industries
    d. media invite key public relations practitioners for a summit on best practices and ethics

12. Speechwriters should avoid using all of these, EXCEPT
    a. contractions.
    b. modifiers.
    c. complicated words/phrases.
    d. long sentences.

13. Speaking "off-the-record" means that
    a. you're speaking glibly and not formally.
    b. you're asking the reporter not to publish your answers.
    c. you're proposing something that is outside your normal viewpoint.
    d. reporters shouldn't share this information with other reporters.

14. Kinetics refers to
    a. posture.
    b. bonding.
    c. motion/gestures.
    d. friction.

15. The best approach when dealing with a hostile audience is to
    a. engage in the battle and search for answers.
    b. avoid topics that will upset them.
    c. enlist the advice of confrontational front groups geared in handling such situations.
    d. find some common ground with the audience.

16. In a news conference, admitting that a situation is bad and asserting that the organization plans to correct it is a strategy known as
    a. justification.
    b. mortification.
    c. pressing.
    d. transfer.

17. A regularly scheduled news conference is known as a
    a. press party.
    b. fam trip.
    c. briefing.
    d. junket.

18. A good rule-of-thumb is to invite media to a news conference at least _____ in advance.
    a. three days
    b. two weeks
    c. one month
    d. three months

19. A press party is a(n) _____ process.
    a. softening-up.
    b. formal.
    c. fluid.
    d. integrated.

20. Which of the following is not characteristic of a print interview?
    a. The interview is generally short, no longer than 10 minutes.
    b. The interviewer weaves bits from conversation together in direct and indirect quotation form.
    c. The interviewee has no control over what is published.
    d. Requests to "approve" an interview story before it is published are often considered censorship.

21. Some travel organizations lavish free trips on journalists in the hopes of positive coverage. The practice of accepting these trips is often disparagingly referred to as
    a. jazz journalism.
    b. junket journalism.
    c. swag.
    d. paparazzi.

22. Which of the following is not a valid guideline for word choice in speeches?
    a. Use personal pronouns.
    b. Make comparisons and contrasts.
    c. Vary sentence length.
    d. Use passive verbs.

23. Which of the following is not a principal requirement for a successful radio or television broadcast?
    a. interviewer's charisma/appearance
    b. preparation
    c. concise speech
    d. relaxation

24. A major speech for a large convention should include
    a. a teleprompter.
    b. 35mm slides and video clips.
    c. anecdotes/humor.
    d. handouts.

25. Most news conferences have a(n) _____ intent.
    a. defensive
    b. advocating
    c. positive
    d. entertaining

26. A key element in training executives to deal with the media is
    a. the mock interview.
    b. channeling.
    c. damage control.
    d. role reversal.

27. Travel and tourism practitioners often employ the media relations practice of
    a. symbolism.
    b. parsimony.
    c. shared governance.
    d. "fam" trips.

28. A visual aid that usually consists of information on poster boards or a large-page tablet mounted on an easel is a(n)
    a. actuality.
    b. Gantt chart.
    c. flip chart.
    d. LCD.

29. In general, an answer to a question during a radio or television interview should be no longer than
    a. 20 seconds.
    b. 30 seconds.
    c. 45 seconds.
    d. one minute.

30. The first words of a speech are often devoted to
    a. a human-interest story.
    b. the needs of the sponsoring organization.
    c. statistics.
    d. setting the stage.

CHAPTER 17   CORPORATIONS

1. The most effective conduit for a corporation to get its message across and to achieve business goals is probably
   a. legislators.
   b. media.
   c. special-interest groups.
   d. chambers of commerce and/or convention and visitors' bureaus.

2. Nike began to work in earnest on its sweatshop crisis after _____ became involved.
   a. striking garment workers
   b. media gatekeepers
   c. activist groups
   d. its closest industry partners

3. Which of the following is not one of the three actions American businesses were asked to undertake in the white paper *Restoring Trust in Business*?
   a. Adopt ethical principles.
   b. Pursue philanthropic ventures and publicize them to key publics.
   c. Pursue transparency and disclosure.
   d. Make trust a fundamental precept of corporate governance.

4. Approximately one-quarter of Americans believe that U.S. corporations are
   a. trustworthy.
   b. profitable.
   c. partnering with nonprofit organizations.
   d. neglecting the public interest.

5. Corporate sponsorship is a form of
   a. benchmarking.
   b. research.
   c. cause-related marketing.
   d. media partnership.

6. Which of the following is not a key factor in Americans' distrust of corporations?
   a. greed
   b. corporate misdeeds
   c. "pseudo-philanthropy"
   d. remoteness

7. Which of the following is not a reason why corporations seek better reputations?
   a. Responsible business practices ward off increased government regulation.
   b. Companies with good policies/reputations have less employee turnover.
   c. Corporate reputation affects the bottom line.
   d. A good reputation curries favor with longtime stockholders.

8. Which factor is not inherent to an effective boycott?
   a. good organization
   b. media attention
   c. damage to the bottom line of the offending organization
   d. inclusion of high-profile boycotters

9. Employees are considered the organization's
   a. ambassadors.
   b. latent publics.
   c. windows to management.
   d. most volatile link.

10. The large number of FedEx script references and signage in the movie *Cast Away* is one example of
    a. product placement.
    b. issues placement.
    c. corporate social responsibility.
    d. corporate transparency.

11. Which of the following questions is not central to a company's decision to sponsor an event?
    a. Is the event/organization compatible with company values?
    b. Will the event be televised?
    c. Is there an opportunity for employee involvement?
    d. Does the event include local celebrities?

12. The front line of public relations is
    a. strong media relations.
    b. corporate involvement.
    c. customer service.
    d. fundraising or profits.

13. Which corporate sponsorship pairing is incorrect?
    a. Lexus/polo
    b. Minute Maid/Wrigley Field
    c. Lincoln Financial Group/Philadelphia Eagles
    d. Volvo/tennis

14. Which of the following is not one of the steps McDonald's took in reaction to the documentary *Super Size Me*?
    a. It made its global nutritionist available to media outlets.
    b. It distributed ANRs and VNRs about diet and exercise.
    c. It discouraged top-level employees from talking about the "misrepresentation" of the film.
    d. It sent briefing materials to its 2,700 franchises so that employees could be informed during media inquiries.

15. The refusal to buy the products or services of an offending company is a
    a. boycott.
    b. recall.
    c. consumer coup.
    d. standoff.

16. Publicity hype and verbal sleight-of-hand is especially discouraged in
    a. investor relations.
    b. entertainment public relations.
    c. product launches.
    d. western Europe.

17. This corporation was damaged by a recent racial discrimination scandal involving recorded tapes of company executives.
    a. Texaco
    b. Enron
    c. Johnson & Johnson
    d. Wendy's

18. This 1986 Supreme Court case revolved around sexual harassment issues.
    a. *Monitor Savings Bank v. Vinson*
    b. *Nike v. Kasky*
    c. *Food Lion v. ABC*
    d. *Cytryn v. Cook*

19. Major problems with toys manufactured by Chinese subcontractors resulted in this a(n) _____, often used in the automobile industry.
    a. defensive strategy
    b. hard sell
    c. ingratiation
    d. product recall

20. The definite benchmark of how buyers feel about products is
    a. the Dow Jones Index.
    b. *Consumer Reports*.
    c. Craig's List.
    d. the American Customer Satisfaction Index.

21. In the Dell/Sony laptop crisis, Dell resisted the inclination to
    a. avoid recalling the products.
    b. ignore the problem or shift blame to Sony.
    c. involve the media.
    d. take a positive approach.

22. The primary PR function of human resources is
    a. employee communications.
    b. legal ramifications.
    c. external publics.
    d. labor relations/union issues.

23. Corporate-sponsored events are popular because they
    a. generate internal goodwill.
    b. give product brands high visibility.
    c. create company image through transfer.
    d. are associated with more activist consumers.

24. According to *PR Week*, which of the following is a proactive step for an organization trying to manage its reputation?
    a. Work with groups that want solutions, not publicity.
    b. Prevent transparency.
    c. Use emotion when dealing with advocacy groups.
    d. Give up if results aren't immediate.

25. The highest-paid professionals in the public relations field are
    a. agency supervisors.
    b. entertainment practitioners/press agents.
    c. Web designers or managers.
    d. investor relations personnel.

26. The outsourcing of white-collar jobs to other countries is known as
    a. cultural imperialism.
    b. channeling.
    c. offshoring.
    d. boycotting.

27. Dannon's partnership with the National Wildlife Federation is an example of
    a. product publicity.
    b. cause-related marketing.
    c. issues management.
    d. corporate sponsorship.

28. Which of the following is a potential downside to corporate philanthropy?
    a. financial ambiguity
    b. backlash from special-interest groups against the sponsored cause
    c. misappropriation of personality
    d. a class-action suit

29. Making a claim to an environmental conscience without the actions to back it up is derisively called
    a. cause-related marketing.
    b. offshoring.
    c. enviro-posing.
    d. greenwashing.

30. Which policy is not typical among the best companies for working mothers?
    a. flex time
    b. compressed workweeks
    c. job-sharing
    d. stock options geared solely to those with families

CHAPTER 18 POLITICS AND GOVERNMENT

1. After being chastised for its business dealings in China, Google decided to embark on a(n)
   a. boycott of Eastern nations.
   b. lobbying effort based in Washington, D.C.
   c. influence-peddling campaign.
   d. trip to China to denounce their tactics.

2. Advocacy ads and bulk faxing are most prevalent in
   a. grassroots lobbying.
   b. stealth lobbying.
   c. influence peddling.
   d. 527s.

3. The use of front groups is often referred to as
   a. grassroots lobbying.
   b. backdoor gifting.
   c. stealth lobbying.
   d. transparent.

4. Michael Moore's recent film *Sicko* was an attack on
   a. the military leadership problems in the Republican party.
   b. the health care and pharmaceutical industry in the United States.
   c. the health of America's automotive industry.
   d. President Clinton's private life.

5. _____, described by *Time* magazine as "the man who bought Washington," was the motivation for new lobbying legislation.
   a. Jeffrey Skilling
   b. Joseph Feingold
   c. Jack Abramoff
   d. Jody Powell

6. According to Michael Crowley of the *New York Times*, BlackBerries and oxfords symbolize the new culture of war opposition, as opposed to the 1960s
   a. collaboration.
   b. "street-protest ethos."
   c. drugs and destruction.
   d. disintermediation.

7. The lobbying reform act does not
   a. define the term *lobbyist*.
   b. require that lobbyists register with Congress.
   c. impose tougher restrictions on eating and drinking.
   d. address political action committees.

8. Presidential campaign fundraising figures are filed with the
   a. Federal Communications Commission.
   b. Federal Election Commission.
   c. Federal Trade Commission.
   d. Internal Revenue Service.

9. This presidential candidate co-sponsored a major congressional bill regarding campaign finance reform.
   a. John McCain
   b. Hillary Clinton
   c. Barack Obama
   d. Mitt Romney

10. Of the $4 billion spent in the 2004 election, the presidential candidates spent $600 million on
    a. grassroots lobbying.
    b. staffing/workers.
    c. paid advertising.
    d. travel.

11. Which commentator received $240,000 to promote the No Child Left Behind Act?
    a. Dan Rather
    b. Armstrong Williams
    c. Rush Limbaugh
    d. Sean Hannity

12. Which of the following does not usually fall under the auspices of a city information service?
    a. an airport
    b. transit services
    c. campaign finance reform
    d. a convention and visitors bureau

13. Which of the following is a function of government relations specialists?
    a. "massaging" management's views
    b. acting in a compulsory-advisory function for future legislation
    c. cooperating with media on projects of mutual benefit
    d. motivating employees to participate in the lobbying process

14. Which of the following is not a euphemism for someone in government public relations?
    a. administrative aide.
    b. public information officer.
    c. director of public affairs.
    d. director of development.

15. The Federal Emergency Management Agency (FEMA), already infamous for its mishandling of Hurricane Katrina, suffered further damage to its reputation in 2007 when it hosted a
    a. staged/fake news conference.
    b. rally for the war effort.
    c. concert for politicians.
    d. party for large insurance companies/adjusters.

16. _____ is not a major lobbying group in Washington, D.C.
    a. American Association for Retired Persons.
    b. National Rifle Association.
    c. Swift Boat Veterans for Truth.
    d. American Israel Public Affairs Committee.

17. Influence peddlers primarily capitalize on
    a. grassroots lobbyists.
    b. connections.
    c. soft money.
    d. issue advertising.

18. "Franking" privileges are usually the privy of
    a. administrative aides.
    b. corporate heads.
    c. lobbyists.
    d. incumbents.

19. The presidential stagecraft that has received the most press and criticism is
    a. George H.W. Bush's "1000 Points of Light."
    b. Reagan's "cupped ear" technique.
    c. Clinton's appearance on *Arsenio* playing the saxophone.
    d. George W. Bush's appearance on an aircraft carrier with the banner "Mission Accomplished."

20. Which issue would least likely be addressed in a state information campaign?
    a. litter/recycling
    b. tourism
    c. parking revenues
    d. economic development

21. Reporters' heavy dependence on handouts is
    a. considered necessary to ensure press accuracy.
    b. a major source of press hostility.
    c. the direct result of excellent public relations.
    d. the aftermath of poor teaching by journalism professors/mentors.

22. Public affairs roots can be traced back to this discovery by Napoleon's troops.
    a. the Rosetta Stone
    b. the Magna Carta
    c. landowners bartering with farmers
    d. the Gillett Amendment

23. Which statement is not characteristic of MoveOn.org?
    a. formed during the Clinton administration
    b. uses low-key/underscored tactics because media respond better to reason than to stunts and rallies
    c. is a 527-type organization
    d. usually supports liberal causes

24. More than 20 public/government information specialists, whose primary duty is to work with moviemakers and TV producers, are employed by
    a. the Pentagon.
    b. Hollywood.
    c. the American Screen Actors Guild.
    d. the House Public Affairs Committee.

25. Early in the 20th century, Congress passed a law limiting the authority of the executive branch to spend taxpayer money on public relations efforts to
    a. gain support for the president's pet projects.
    b. influence "swing" voters.
    c. legislate election reforms.
    d. advocate for party colleagues.

26. This public relations office was established in World War II and sent news releases on behalf of the military.
    a. Fleet Home Town News Center
    b. Voice of America
    c. U.S. Information Agency
    d. Sons of America

27. Ronald Reagan was considered the
    a. master communicator.
    b. high priest of the consumer movement.
    c. Prince of Peace.
    d. Capitol Hill thespian.

28. The White House director of communications supervises the
    a. chief of staff.
    b. press secretary.
    c. speaker of the House.
    d. White House counsel.

29. The White House _____ handles the task of briefing reporters.
    a. director of communications
    b. House speaker
    c. chief of staff
    d. press secretary

30. John Kerry's bid for the presidency was derailed by
    a. Howard Dean.
    b. The Swift Boat Veterans for Truth.
    c. deciding to launch his campaign on an aircraft carrier.
    d. campaign finance reform.

CHAPTER 19 GLOBAL PUBLIC RELATIONS

1. The most critical and underutilized tool in international public relations is probably the understanding of foreign
   a. language.
   b. exchange rates.
   c. culture.
   d. correspondents.

2. PR firms representing other nations are usually hired by an embassy
   a. after an edict from Congress.
   b. after an open bidding process for the account.
   c. after a complete media analysis.
   d. every four years.

3. This cultural dimension measures how well a society tolerates ambiguity.
   a. power distance
   b. collectivism
   c. uncertainty avoidance
   d. long-term orientation

4. A(n) _____ situation derives most of its meaning from written or verbalized statements.
   a. low-context
   b. high-context
   c. mixed-motives
   d. Eastern

5. Which of the following is not one of the main difficulties a corporation encounters when it conducts business in another country?
   a. language differences
   b. differences in laws and cultural mores
   c. employee training
   d. perception in home country

6. Which contrast is not illustrated in the Guth-Marsh summary of cultural dimensions?
   a. individualism–collectivism
   b. competitiveness–compassion
   c. past traditions–future orientations
   d. profiteering–philanthropy

7. All legal, political, fund-raising, public relations and lobbying consultants hired by foreign governments to work in the United States must register with the
   a. Department of Justice.
   b. White House.
   c. Congress.
   d. Better Business Bureau.

8. Which of the following is not an ethical dilemma faced by public relations firms hired by foreign governments?
   a. deciding whether to represent a country whose human rights violations may reflect adversely on the agency itself
   b. discouraging heads of nations that have violated human rights from altering practices that conflict with their desired public image
   c. convincing officials of a client country that the American press is independent from government control and that coverage may not be 100 percent favorable
   d. deciding whether to represent a nation whose autocratic heads of state have drastically reduced civil liberties and crushed any opposition

9. _____ describes the American government's effort to be the major disseminator of information around the world.
   a. Propaganda
   b. Intervention tactic
   c. Public diplomacy
   d. Cultural imperialism

10. Starbucks has been cited as a Western company whose objectives and deeds contributed to a(n)
    a. worldwide boycott.
    b. political breakthrough.
    c. increased understanding of American virtues.
    d. erosion of Chinese culture.

11. Following World War II, the most immediate threat to American security was the
    a. Vietnam War.
    b. Bay of Pigs Invasion.
    c. Iran-Contra Affair.
    d. Cold War with Soviet and Eastern Bloc countries.

12. The United States Information Agency was created by
    a. George Creel.
    b. Harry Truman.
    c. Dwight Eisenhower.
    d. the McCain-Feingold Act.

13. One of the basic objectives of U.S. firms hired by foreign governments is to
    a. regulate.
    b. generate tourism.
    c. change attitudes and behaviors of dissident factions.
    d. break language barriers.

14. According to Ketchum's David Drobis, the benefits of globalization must be communicated to the following groups, EXCEPT
    a. the American trade press.
    b. companies.
    c. non-governmental organizations.
    d. international trade/banking institutions.

15. Which of the following is not an example of a foreign company that spends a large amount of money to lobby the U.S. government?
    a. BP (based in England)
    b. Sony (based in China)
    c. GlaxoSmithKline (based in England)
    d. Daimler Chrysler (based in Germany)

16. With regard to labor, health, and environmental issues, the public perceives nongovernmental organizations as
    a. less credible than news media.
    b. more credible than news media.
    c. underfunded and overzealous.
    d. bureaucratic.

17. The first requirement for anyone embarking on an international government career is
    a. a protocol job.
    b. the Civil Service Test.
    c. bilingual training.
    d. the U.S. Foreign Service Officers' exam.

18. International public relations growth has been primarily influenced by
    a. wars of aggression.
    b. social change.
    c. the engineering of consent.
    d. a rise in nationalism.

19. Which of the following is not a nongovernmental organization?
    a. Greenpeace
    b. Voice of America
    c. Oxfam
    d. Doctors Without Borders

20. Which of the following is not a reason why industries in other nations employ American public relations firms?
    a. to hold off protectionist moves threatening their company or industry
    b. to support expansion of the client's markets in the United States
    c. to defeat legislation affecting the sale of a client's product
    d. to establish "common-market" tactics that will act as cultural binders

21. Carl Levin, a Burson-Marsteller executive, says that foreign governments retain American public relations firms in order to
    a. advance their political objectives.
    b. encourage wider American acceptance of their language.
    c. discourage risky investments.
    d. provide caution and discretion on issues that affect their standing in the U.S. and world community.

22. The toughest part about winning the war on terrorism has been
    a. toppling the Taliban.
    b. removing Saddam Hussein's government in Baghdad.
    c. convincing Congress to buy into aggressive actions.
    d. generating long-term (positive) worldwide public opinion.

23. China's explosive growth can be traced to
    a. governmental interference with birth control.
    b. subsidies from Western nations.
    c. industrialization and adoption of a relatively free market economy.
    d. literacy demands.

24. Firms practicing international public relations encounter the following problems, EXCEPT
    a. deciding to represent a country, such as Uzbekistan or Zimbabwe, whose human rights violations may reflect adversely on the agency itself.
    b. persuading the heads of a nation that has violated human rights to alter some of their practices to better reflect the public image they desire.
    c. convincing officials of a client country, which may totally control the flow of news internally, that the American press is independent from government control.
    d. using intervention tactics like "warning flares" before potential conflicts.

25. Thought leaders trust non-governmental organizations more than government or corporations because they believe NGOs are motivated by
    a. morals.
    b. logic.
    c. feedback.
    d. research.

26. Non-Western styles of communication are often
    a. high-context.
    b. low-context.
    c. baseless according to foreign media.
    d. concrete and data/text driven.

27. Which of the following does not describe public relations in the Middle East?
    a. relatively immature
    b. unstructured
    c. lacking in trained personnel
    d. devoid of marketing notions

28. The U.S. Department of State took over most of the functions of the _____, which was disbanded in 1999?
    a. U.S. Information Agency
    b. U.S. Department of the Interior
    c. U.S. Department of Federal Affairs
    d. Voice of America

29. Which country/region engages in the practice of *zakazukhi*, paying to get a news release published or broadcast?
    a. Russia
    b. China
    c. the Middle East
    d. the United States

30. Which of the following is not one of the "World Citizens Guide" brochure tips to avoid looking like an "ugly American"?
    a. Read a map.
    b. Slow down.
    c. Be politically active.
    d. Speak lower and slower.

CHAPTER 20   NONPROFIT ORGANIZATIONS

1. When pitching stories to gatekeepers about nonprofit activities, it's best to tell stories in terms of
   a. individuals.
   b. abstractions.
   c. statistics.
   d. totality of achievements.

2. Approximately _____ percent of Americans volunteer time for charitable causes.
   a. 10
   b. 20
   c. 30
   d. 50

3. Which of the following is not a goal of a professional organization?
   a. to establish a code of ethics
   b. to engage in collective bargaining between employers and employees
   c. to set standards for professional performance
   d. to encourage continuing education

4. Serious, dramatic messages can be widely dispersed
   a. by sending genre-appropriate news releases.
   b. through targeted emails and Internet strategies.
   c. by staging an event made for television coverage.
   d. through word of mouth from high-profile stakeholders.

5. Terms like *patron* or *founder* often indicate
   a. historical significance.
   b. the size of a donor's gift.
   c. the level of command within the organization.
   d. those who establish charitable programs.

6. Which is not a typical function of staffers in a trade association?
   a. monitoring congressional activity
   b. lobbying for or against legislation
   c. communicating late-breaking developments to the membership
   d. shielding busy government officials from unnecessary information

7. Which tactic was not used by the Save Darfur Coalition?
   a. partnering with NAACP chapters to lobby
   b. taking out a series of one-page ads in *The Wall Street Journal* and the *New York Times*.
   c. pressuring American corporations to divest from Sudanese companies
   d. avoiding the use of celebrity spokespersons

8. The following are categories of social agencies, EXCEPT
   a. health agencies.
   b. religious organizations.
   c. advocacy organizations.
   d. foundations.

9. Which type of organization has lost the most political clout since the 1970s?
   a. labor unions
   b. social agencies
   c. government lobbyists
   d. educational foundations

10. Which famous fundraising tactic has entertainment icon Jerry Lewis used on behalf of the Muscular Dystrophy Association?
    a. concert
    b. circus
    c. telethon
    d. variety show

11. People who volunteer are usually not motivated by
    a. extrinsic rewards.
    b. a sense of making a personal contribution to society.
    c. social contacts.
    d. social prestige.

12. Which of the following is not a primary function of a chamber of commerce?
    a. to produce the brochures and maps sent to individuals who seek information about visiting the city or who are considering moving to the area
    b. to promote health and wellness programs for concerned citizens of the city
    c. to conduct polls and compile statistics about the economic health of the city
    d. to attract conventions and new businesses to the city

13. A critical benefit for nonprofit groups is that they are
    a. relatively uninfluenced by media gatekeepers.
    b. tax-exempt.
    c. helped by government intervention.
    d. 529 organizations.

14. Which action is fundamental to the success of nonprofits?
    a. creating research campaigns that stimulate public interest and participation
    b. establishing lofty fund-raising goals
    c. developing a strong group of staffers/ volunteers
    d. assembling high-profile media to publicize achievements

15. Which of the following is not characteristic of a brochure?
    a. the quickest way to inform the public
    b. a good first-impression tool
    c. answers the reader's questions
    d. is written in detail for a well-educated audience

16. The American union with the largest membership is the
    a. Service Employees International Union.
    b. AFL-CIO.
    c. National Education Association.
    d. Teamsters.

17. Organizations use _____ to file lawsuits seeking court rulings favorable to their projects or attempting to block unfavorable projects.
    a. litigation
    b. lobbying
    c. reconciliation
    d. activism

18. A fund-raising campaign is usually organized along _____ lines.
    a. party
    b. quasi-military
    c. sponsorship
    d. social

19. PETA is a
    a. professional organization.
    b. trade association.
    c. grassroots political organization.
    d. social issue organization.

20. Which of the following is not a commercial method for raising money?
    a. licensing the use of an organization's name to endorse a product and receiving payment for each item sold
    b. sharing profits with a corporation to receive a share of its profits from sales of a special product
    c. operating a business that generates revenue for the organization
    d. "exchanging" employees with partnering corporations for camaraderie purposes

21. Individuals provide _____ of total charitable giving in the United States.
    a. three-quarters
    b. one-half
    c. one-fourth
    d. two-thirds

22. The Red Dress campaign, featuring Laura Bush, focuses on _____, the number-one killer of women.
    a. heart disease
    b. breast cancer
    c. AIDS
    d. cervical cancer

23. _____ is a key motivation for charitable giving.
    a. Parental proclivity
    b. Tax shelter
    c. Peer pressure
    d. Family concern

24. The largest chunk of all corporate donations is earmarked for
    a. local charities.
    b. major projects.
    c. health measures.
    d. Third World nations.

25. In a capital campaign, fund-raising emphasis is placed on
    a. grant opportunities.
    b. small to moderate donations from individuals.
    c. substantial gifts from corporations and individuals.
    d. local governmental officials.

26. McDonald's partnership with the Environmental Defense Fund to help solve pollution problems is an example of
    a. lobbying.
    b. chambering.
    c. reconciliation.
    d. fund-raising.

27. The largest and most publicized donations are made by
    a. corporations and foundations.
    b. the federal government.
    c. individuals.
    d. anonymous donors.

28. In general, the goals of professional associations include
    a. promoting standards of sales performance.
    b. determining requirements for entrance to the field.
    c. negotiating with employers for higher wages.
    d. monitoring litigation.

29. The NAACP would be best described as a _____ agency.
    a. service
    b. religious
    c. cause
    d. political

30. According to a recent survey, the majority of lawyers promote their services
    a. by entertaining current and prospective clients.
    b. through advertising in the Yellow Pages.
    c. in blogs.
    d. in cable TV ads.

CHAPTER 21 EDUCATION

1. A subject of recent controversy has been the decisions of some high schools to sign exclusive vending contracts with
   a. soft drink companies.
   b. building inspectors.
   c. utility companies.
   d. school uniform manufacturers.

2. Which function does not usually fall under the auspices of a university public relations director?
   a. publications
   b. fund-raising efforts
   c. special events
   d. news service

3. Which public relations lesson did not emerge from the Virginia Tech tragedy?
   a. the need for a more caring and vigilant campus culture
   b. the need for a distinction between the proactive and reactive performance of public relations staff
   c. the need to make the university relations department an integral part of crisis management
   d. the need for greater precautions in notifying the administration about people entering and leaving campus

4. Which of the following is not an objective of the Council for Advancement and Support of Education (CASE) at this time?
   a. increasing the fund-raising capacity of schools in order to create sufficient endowments
   b. studying the impact of new technologies
   c. developing gift and expenditure reporting standards
   d. helping leaders at historically black institutions advance in their careers

5. The chief public relations officer of a college or university is the
   a. communications director.
   b. dean.
   c. alumni director.
   d. president.

6. The development office is responsible for the _____ of an educational institution.
   a. prestige and financial support
   b. curriculum
   c. faculty hiring
   d. publicity

7. The most visible aspect of a university public relations program is its
   a. athletic office.
   b. development office.
   c. news bureau.
   d. registrar's office.

8. The greatest determinant of a student's allegiance to the institution is
   a. the success of its athletic teams.
   b. its social/Greek organizations.
   c. parental influence.
   d. the quality of the teaching.

9. Fund-raising phonathons are usually staffed by
   a. current college students.
   b. key university administrators.
   c. high profile athletic or academic personnel.
   d. outside/outsourced companies with no affiliation to the university.

10. Good morale among faculty and staff happens in large measure through
    a. better technology and infrastructure.
    b. communication.
    c. financial incentives.
    d. actions of principal and superintendent.

11. _____ was cited for its caring, visionary handling of a tragic shooting in which 12 students were killed.
    a. Columbine High School
    b. Virginia Tech
    c. Everett High School
    d. Anglican Church Grammar School.

12. "Town-gown" refers to the relationship between
    a. students and alumni.
    b. city officials and religious leaders.
    c. faculty and alumni.
    d. universities and their surrounding communities.

13. Which statement does not apply to the Duke University lacrosse scandal?
    a. District Attorney Mike Nifong brought the case forward with little evidence.
    b. The scandal caused a sharp decline in student applications the following year.
    c. Burson-Marsteller was hired to coach administrators in how to deal with media inquiries.
    d. Class and race were major factors in public opinion.

14. Which tactic was not used by the Fort Worth (Texas) School District to help rectify low reading scores?
    a. a Reading Rodeo
    b. participation from the NBA's Dallas Mavericks
    c. the "90-7-3" concept
    d. sponsorship from Governor's Business Council

15. The University of Maryland's $1 billion fund-raising goal for 2011 is an example of a _____ campaign.
    a. stealth
    b. land-grant
    c. capital
    d. benchmark

16. Which population segment was not targeted in the marketing plan employed by the Macomb Intermediate School District in Mount Clemens, Michigan?
    a. parents of elementary students
    b. secondary students and parents
    c. politicians and school board members
    d. citizens without children in school

17. What public relations purpose does it serve for a corporation to create a nonprofit division?
    a. They receive recognition for the work the nonprofit does.
    b. It shows that the corporations are good citizens.
    c. Executives get real-world experience through "externships."
    d. They get exclusive access to the resulting medical research and services.

18. Which statement about digital manipulation of photos is incorrect?
    a. It is used increasingly.
    b. It can be used to imply diversity.
    c. It is often considered unethical.
    d. It is primarily practiced in substandard institutions.

19. Based on the Stanford University organizational chart, to whom does the Vice President for Public Affairs report?
    a. the university president
    b. the university communications leaders
    c. the community relations officials
    d. the Director of Development

20. One of the functions of a university's government relations specialist is
    a. responding to lawmakers' requests for favors.
    b. counseling in a compulsory-advisory fashion before legislation is introduced.
    c. competing with other federal institutions for money.
    d. lobbying against proposed increases in higher-education budgets and encouraging cuts.

21. Capital campaigns for universities are generally
    a. quick-hitting.
    b. precursors to annual operating fund campaigns.
    c. long-range.
    d. unsuccessful without government assistance.

22. The median salary for the top public relations officer is highest at
    a. private universities.
    b. universities in the urban Northeast.
    c. universities with doctoral programs.
    d. universities with *Fortune* 500-sponsored business schools.

23. A public relations campaign in the Everett (Washington) School District centered on a
    a. school security/endangerment issue.
    b. tax levy election.
    c. bilingual reading initiative.
    d. controversy involving soda/junk food vendors.

24. The No Child Left Behind Act of 2002 greatly emphasized the following, EXCEPT
    a. test scores.
    b. improving student performance.
    c. keeping students engaged in the schools they were "zoned" in.
    d. accountability.

25. In universities, the office of alumni relations usually falls under the jurisdiction of the
    a. development office.
    b. public relations office.
    c. provost's office.
    d. news bureau.

26. Those wishing to embark on careers as public relations practitioners in the education field must think about two major considerations:
    a. counseling skills and teaching skills.
    b. much of the work is in fund-raising and the pay for corporate public relations is much higher.
    c. the cost of union membership and dealing with problem children/parents.
    d. harsher standards and the need for advanced degree(s).

27. The "3" in the "90-7-3" concept of school communication represents the percentage that focuses on
    a. the school's image.
    b. outbound communication.
    c. listening effort.
    d. media relations.

28. When another person/organization agrees to give the same amount as an already enlisted donor, this is known as a(n)
    a. matching grant.
    b. town-gown grant.
    c. co-op.
    d. "educause."

29. Recently, Vanderbilt University sent which promotional tool to 40 coveted high-school seniors?
    a. personalized blogs
    b. figurines of the Commodore mascot
    c. a signed letter from the university president
    d. personalized videotapes

30. Which contemporary issue does not currently pose a challenge to public relations practitioners in elementary and secondary schools?
    a. school choice
    b. competing for resources/funding
    c. a downward spiral in counseling by teachers and parents
    d. tragedies like school shootings

CHAPTER 22 ENTERTAINMENT, SPORTS, AND TRAVEL

1. Which statement about celebrity is false?
   a. Celebrities exist in one-sided, idealized relationships with fans.
   b. Publicizing and glorifying celebrities is a dominant factor in today's mass media.
   c. Building up publicity around individuals is a key function of mainstream public relations.
   d. The sudden death of a celebrity freezes his/her youthful image in time.

2. The best course in conducting a personality campaign is to
   a. focus on individual media types one-by-one.
   b. start with broadcast media.
   c. project the client on multiple media simultaneously.
   d. take advantage of cutting-edge interactive/Internet strategies.

3. _____ is not one of the four principles of celebrity crisis management.
   a. Recovery
   b. Speed
   c. Humility
   d. Contrition

4. A steady output of information about a movie or television production is known as
   a. the "drip-drip-drip" technique.
   b. mainstreaming.
   c. extended piloting.
   d. the MUSTS technique.

5. The largest percentage of cruise passengers, especially on longer voyages, are
   a. foreign tourists.
   b. retirees.
   c. high-income socialites.
   d. referred by hotel concierges and/or CVB/chamber personnel.

6. Ancient Mayan rulers vied for loyalty through
   a. barbaric rituals.
   b. crude media outlets.
   c. events and publicity to achieve celebrity status.
   d. outreach programs with Incas and Aztecs.

7. Which of the following is not a motivating factor in the cult of personality?
   a. notoriety.
   b. self-satisfaction.
   c. repair of bad image.
   d. desire for money.

8. Which of the following is a supplemental component of a "bio," rather than a required element?
   a. news and feature angles about the client
   b. a detailed history of the client's background and achievements in easy-to-read form
   c. a photo of the client
   d. multimedia component (e.g., slides, DVD, etc.)

9. When client's public image is being harmed, the PR practitioner's basic objective is
   a. recovery of assets.
   b. damage control.
   c. ingratiation to harmed publics.
   d. stonewalling pushy media until fact-finding is complete.

10. Which aspect of travel promotion is a recent development?
    a. calming perceived safety fears through persuasion techniques
    b. stimulating the public's desire to visit a place
    c. arranging for the travelers to reach it
    d. making certain that visitors are comfortable, are treated well, and are entertained when they get there

11. The Natalee Holloway disappearance/case was a major public relations crisis for
    a. the Aruba tourism industry.
    b. media in search of answers.
    c. school groups who plan on taking getaways/excursions.
    d. medical examiners and police investigators.

12. Psychologists believe that major televised awards shows give viewers a sense of
    a. vicarious belonging.
    b. structure in life.
    c. self-indulgence.
    d. false hope.

13. Having a donor's name placed on a building would be an example of fulfilling that person's need for
    a. notoriety.
    b. fame.
    c. self-glorification.
    d. media coverage.

14. _____ is the celebrity publicist for the Hilton sisters.
    a. Ken Sunshine
    b. Harvey Levin
    c. Donald Trump
    d. Elliott Mintz

15. Photos, copies of news releases, video clips of public appearances can all be assembled with
    a. satellite technology.
    b. clipping services.
    c. bookers and planters.
    d. personality campaigns.

16. Sports publicists exploit _____ , a feeling that prompts fans wear jerseys and caps, and refer to a team as "their" team.
    a. hero worship
    b. a vicarious sense of belonging
    c. self-selection
    d. ego satisfaction

17. According Jay Rosenstein of Cohn & Wolfe, the following attributes create the need for sports crisis public relations, EXCEPT
    a. cheating and point-shaving scandals
    b. otherwordly egos
    c. behavior reminiscent of those in the entertainment world
    d. unrelenting media focus

18. The primary goal of any campaign for an entertainment event is
    a. positive media coverage.
    b. raising awareness of a performer.
    c. to generate market buzz, especially through viral means.
    d. to sell tickets.

19. The target audience for a familiarization (fam) trip is
    a. families.
    b. concert/music media.
    c. travel writers.
    d. socialites and entertainment media.

20. The type of photograph most commonly submitted in entertainment media press kits is the
    a. head and shoulders (mug) shot.
    b. action shot.
    c. group shot of actors/singers.
    d. frontal shot of the event venue/building.

21. Which of the following is not characteristic of a feature story or "reader" about a play?
    a. It discusses the play's theme and background.
    b. It includes quotes from the playwright and director.
    c. It aims to quell critics' remarks.
    d. It can generate interviews with play's star.

22. Persons who schedule (movie) clients on talk shows and in other public appearances are known as
    a. bookers.
    b. planters.
    c. influentials.
    d. producers.

23. *Harry Potter and the Deathly Hallows* sold 8.3 million copies without a single piece of
    a. media coverage.
    b. publisher input.
    c. market surveying.
    d. advertising.

24. _____ is the star of *The Apprentice* and a master of the art of self-glorification.
    a. Danny Bonaduce
    b. Donald Trump
    c. Rosie O'Donnell
    d. Jeff Probst

25. Which of the following was not a source of controversy for Mel Gibson?
    a. directing and producing *The Passion of the Christ*
    b. drunk driving charges
    c. anti-Semitic remarks
    d. taking top billing over co-star Danny Glover

26. Which statement about Major League Baseball fans is false?
    a. The Asian-American and Pacific Rim audience is increasing.
    b. Baseball was one of the last professional sports to embrace a diverse audience.
    c. Potential African-American fans are missing the opportunity to play baseball because of the conditions in inner-city neighborhoods.
    d. Latin-American fans form a strong allegiance.

27. When conducting a personality campaign, practitioners should avoid _____ on behalf of their clients.
    a. puffery
    b. interviews
    c. photographs
    d. overexposure

28. The most expensive form of sports sponsorship is the
    a. Super Bowl.
    b. Olympics.
    c. World Cup.
    d. NCAA Final Four.

29. Most movie promotion is aimed at the _____ year-old audience.
    a. 18- to 24-
    b. 25- to 34-
    c. 35- to 44-
    d. 45- to 54-

30. In essence, sports publicists try to
    a. stir emotions.
    b. promote individuals over team success.
    c. use strategies that have worked well in the entertainment industry.
    d. rely on statistics to sell/tell a story.